ECONOMETRICS
VOLUME 2
Topics for Time Series and Large Panel Data

ECONOMETRICS
VOLUME 2
Topics for Time Series and Large Panel Data

Pierre Perron
Boston University, USA

World Scientific

NEW JERSEY • LONDON • SINGAPORE • BEIJING • SHANGHAI • HONG KONG • TAIPEI • CHENNAI • TOKYO

Published by

World Scientific Publishing Co. Pte. Ltd.

5 Toh Tuck Link, Singapore 596224

USA office: 27 Warren Street, Suite 401-402, Hackensack, NJ 07601

UK office: 57 Shelton Street, Covent Garden, London WC2H 9HE

Library of Congress Cataloging-in-Publication Data
Names: Perron, Pierre, 1959– author
Title: Econometrics / Pierre Perron, Boston University, USA.
Other titles: Topics for time series and large panel data
Description: New Jersey : World Scientific, [2026] | Includes bibliographical references and index. |
Contents: Volume 1. Basic theory and topics for cross-section data --
Volume 2. Topics for time series and large panel data.
Identifiers: LCCN 2025001969 | ISBN 9789819810871 hardcover vol. 1 |
ISBN 9789819810901 hardcover vol. 2 | ISBN 9789819810888 ebook vol. 1 |
ISBN 9789819810918 ebook vol. 2 | ISBN 9789819810895 ebook for individuals vol. 1 |
ISBN 9789819810925 ebook for individuals vol. 2
Subjects: LCSH: Econometrics
Classification: LCC HB139 .P457 2025 | DDC 330.01/5195--dc23/eng/20250613
LC record available at https://lccn.loc.gov/2025001969

British Library Cataloguing-in-Publication Data
A catalogue record for this book is available from the British Library.

For any available supplementary material, please visit
https://www.worldscientific.com/worldscibooks/10.1142/14247#t=suppl

Desk Editors: Murali Appadurai/Pui Yee Lum

Typeset by Stallion Press
Email: enquiries@stallionpress.com

Printed in Singapore

I wish to dedicate this book to my wife Regina Celia Cati who has for a long time been the most loving, trusted, and helpful life companion.

Preface

This textbook is intended for graduate instructions in econometrics at the MA, MSc, or PhD levels. It covers a wide range of topics related to econometric tools used with cross-sectional, time series, and panel data. There are several aspects in which this book departs from traditional textbooks. First, the emphasis is on having the readers understand the main issues, concepts, and methods. The mathematical aspects are kept to a minimum and the emphasis is on providing an intuitive understanding. Many examples and discussions are provided. There is no attempt at providing the most sophisticated results holding under some minimal assumptions. Our approach is rather to impose some mild conditions (most often satisfied in applied work) and discuss the tools, how to implement them, and how to interpret the results. Hence, minimal mathematical prerequisites are needed. Some knowledge of matrix algebra and basic probability theory is useful, but Chapters 34–35 cover a review of whatever is needed. Since the goal is to provide as much as possible an intuitive understanding of econometrics in general and how various parts fit together, very few proofs are provided, especially for the more advanced material. Extensive references are provided for those who wish to dig deeper in the mathematical aspects of the theories.

The core methods are provided in Chapters 1–26. With respect to this material, a second point of departure from the usual treatment is that all chapters apply equally to cross-section and time series data. Many textbooks first deal with the core methods in the context of cross-section data, most often a random sample and then relegate issues related to time series to later chapters. In our opinion, this is counterproductive. The methods are the same. What is different are the conditions under which the methods are suitable and how to implement them. Hence, a great deal of effort is devoted to highlight under which contexts the methods are valid for both cases. Special attention is put on the issue of exogeneity or lack thereof of time series variables in the model. In this aspect, Chapters 11–13 offer a very substantial different treatment.

Chapters 27–33 deal with topics applicable to cross-section data and a panel data with a small time series dimension. Then, Chapters 36–52 deal mostly with methods for time series data and panel data models with a large time dimension, though Chapter 52 is applicable to both. The intent was to provide up-to-date methods. Hence, several new developments are covered.

Given the length of the book, it is divided in two volumes. The first is from Chapters 1 to 35, which cover the main methods applicable to both cross-sections and time series data, as well as those applicable only with cross-section data and panels with a small time dimension. Then, Volume 2 pertains to time series topics. In case an instructor wants to use this volume solely for a time series course, Chapters 8 and 21 are reprinted at the beginning, though various parts still make references to many results and methods discussed elsewhere in Volume 1.

Most chapters include many exercises. These span the range from easy to difficult. These come from problem sets and exams administered over many years (with some provided by colleagues). I may have taken a few of them from other textbooks in the early stages of my career. I can't remember which. I apologize for what could be viewed as "stealing some". A complete set of solutions (not borrowed in all cases) is available. It is a 500-page document with detailed solutions.

The material in this two-volume book could easily cover about four semester courses. The core methods in Chapters 1–26 could be the material for a two-course sequence, then Chapters 27–33 could be used in a one-semester course on topics related to cross-sections and panels with a small time dimension. Volume 2 could be used for a course in time series. For the latter, the extent of the topics covered are too large for a single course, so the instructors would have to choose which topics to omit or spread them over more than one course.

About the Author

Professor Pierre Perron received his B.A. in Economics from McGill University, Montreal, Canada, MA in Economics from Queens University, Kingston, Canada, and PhD in Economics from Yale University, Connecticut, USA. He has been a Professor at the Department of Economics at Boston University since 1997, prior to which he was a full Professor at the University of Montreal and an Assistant Professor at Princeton University. He was a Visiting Professor at Pontificia Universidade Catolica, Brazil, Université de Bourgogne, France, and Universidade de Sao Paolo, Brazil, as well as a Visiting Scholar at Centre de Recherche en Économie et Statistique, Institut Nationale de la Statistique et des Études Économiques, Paris, France, and Département de Statistiques, Université Libre de Bruxelles, Belgium. Professor Perron was a co-editor for the *Econometrics Journal* and was on the editorial board of numerous journals, such as *Econometrica*, the *Journal of Econometrics*, *Econometrics Reviews*, *Econometric Theory*, *Economics Letters*, *Review of Economics and Statistics*. He was a referee for numerous other journals and grant agencies.

He is an elected fellow of the Econometric Society and the International Association for Applied Econometrics as well as a fellow of the *Journal of Econometrics* and a distinguished author of the *Journal of Time Series Analysis*. He was selected as a 2020 Clarivate Citation Laureate *for the statistical analysis of non-stationary time series*, which is intended for researchers whose work is deemed to be 'of Nobel class', as demonstrated by analysis carried out by the Institute for Scientific Information^{TM} (ISI). A special issue was published in his honor by the *Journal of Econometrics* for his contributions to research and graduate student mentoring in 2021. He is listed in ScholarGPS as a Lifetime Highly Ranked Researcher (top 0.05%). He also has two papers in the category "Top 100 All-Time Highly Cited Papers in Economics". He also received the distinction of "Doctor Honoris Causa" from the Pontificia Universidad Católica del Perú (Lima, Perú) in 2023.

Professor Perron has published over 100 papers in many refereed journals, such as *Econometrica*, the *Journal of Econometrics*, *the Journal of Business and Economic Statistics*, the *Journal of the American Statistical Association*, *Econometric Theory*, *Biometrika*, *Nature Geoscience*, to name a few. He has also contributed many book chapters and is the recipient of various grants from the National Science Foundation, the Fonds pour la Formation de Chercheurs et l'Aide à la Recherche du Québec, the Social Sciences and Humanities Research Council of Canada, and the Natural Sciences and Engineering Council of Canada. Professor Perron has presented his work at numerous conferences, both national and international. He also acted as the main Ph.D. supervisor for over 25 students and numerous others as secondary or external advisors. His work is very highly cited in economics as well as in a variety of other fields.

Acknowledgments

The starting point of this book was a set of class notes written in the Fall of 1988 for two PhD courses at Princeton University. These got revised and updated throughout some 30 years when teaching at Boston University (and a little at the Université de Montréal since they did not allow me to teach much econometrics). I am grateful to all the generations of students who made comments that gradually helped improve the notes and the problem sets.

I started the book project in 2020 during the COVID pandemic. Initially, it was supposed to be a joint venture with my colleague Zhongjun Qu. Unfortunately, he decided to opt out. Still, I owe him the most gratitude and heartfelt thanks. He shared many of his class notes on GMM, simulated method of moments, DGSE, VAR, quantile regressions, volatility models, and non-parametric methods. I heavily built upon them to write the chapters related to these topics. We also had extensive discussions and he provided various useful comments. Hiroaiki Kaido shared his lecture notes and some exercises on limited variables (mostly binary) and large N–small T panel models.

Of course, I had the help of many others. Various PhD students helped me in writing preliminary drafts for some chapters. These include Emilio González-Coya (Lasso, large N and T panel data model, and principal components), Marco Olivari (forecasting and numerical methods), Pablo Guzman Pinto (diff in diff and RD), and Chen Gao (limited dependent variable and demand system estimation). Some helped me with short sections: Alessandro Casini (DK-HAC), Anlong Qin (Markov switching), Guang Zhang (nonlinear state space), and Yan Liu (limited depend variables). Various useful comments were provided by Adam McCloskey, Zhongjun Qu, Jean-Jacques Forneron, Kevin Lang, Yan Liu, Marc Rysman, Regina Cati, Chen Gao, and students when teaching the classes. Several students helped with the solutions for the exercises following various drafts from generations of prior students. These include Guang Zhang, Anlong Qin, Alejandro Cichevski, Emilio González-Coya, Marco Olivari, and especially Yan Liu, who did truly remarkable work. Also, Zhongjun Qu, Hiroaiki Kaido, and Guido Kuersteiner allowed me to use some of their problem sets and exams.

For proof-reading various chapters, I am grateful to Alessandro Casini, Aruzhan Nurlankul, Samuel Messer, Haoran Pan, Anlong Qin, Seungyoo Shin, Chengyang Zhu, and especially Adam McCloskey. Alejandro Cichevski and Marco Olivari helped cleaning up the references. For help with the figures, I thank Guang Zhang, Alejandro Cichevski, Emilio González-Coya, Marco Olivari, Regina Cati, and Francisco Estrada.

Of course, I remain responsible for any errors or inaccurate descriptions.

Contents

Prologue: Reprint of Chapters 8 and 21 from Volume 1

Chapter 8

Introduction to Time Series

We now consider a brief introduction to time series processes. This is of general interest in its own right. Also, we introduce possible dynamics in the error process in the following chapters. The types of models covered here will give an idea of what the structure of this dynamic can be. More generally, in later chapters, we cover more specific types of time-series models.

Time-series theory is a mixture of probabilistic and statistical concepts. The probabilistic part is to study and characterize the probability distribution of sets of variables $\{x_t\}$ that will typically be dependent through time. The statistical problem is to characterize the probability distribution of the time series given observations $x_1, \ldots, x_T$. The resulting stochastic model can be used in at least two ways: (a) understanding the stochastic process and (b) prediction of future observations.

When x_t is a discrete time parameter process, the index set for t can be defined more precisely as $t = 0, 1, \ldots, T = N/h$, where N is the span of the data, h is the sampling interval, and T is the number of observations. In this book, we shall not need to specify h explicitly, as we consider it fixed. Without loss of generality, we set $h \equiv 1$ and so $T = N$. When considering the asymptotic analysis in this framework, $T \to \infty$ implies $N \to \infty$ at the same rate. In several applications (e.g., high-frequency financial data), it is more useful to let $T \to \infty$ allowing h to change as T increases, in particular keeping N fixed. This is often referred to as a "continuous record asymptotic" framework.

8.1 Stationarity and lack thereof

The standard time-series literature often assumes the process to be stationary. There are two types of stationarity criterion used:

Definition 8.1 (Strict Stationarity). x_t is strictly stationary if the finite-dimensional distributions are translation invariant, i.e.,

$$(x_{t_1}, \ldots, x_{t_n}) \overset{d}{=} (x_{t_1+h}, \ldots, x_{t_n+h}) \quad \forall h, n.$$

The concept of strict stationarity is often too strong. It is therefore useful to introduce an alternative concept of stationarity which only involves the first two moments of the process.

Definition 8.2 (Weak Stationarity, Covariance Stationarity, or Second-order Stationarity). The time series x_t is said to be weakly stationary (or covariance stationary or second-order stationary) if

(1) $E(x_t) = c$ for all t, where $c \in \mathbb{R}$,
(2) $E(x_t^2) = \sigma^2 < \infty$, for all t,
(3) $\text{Cov}(x_t, x_s) = \text{Cov}(x_{t+r}, x_{s+r})$ for all r, t, and s.

If x_t is such that $E(x_t^2) < \infty$ for all t, then strict stationarity implies covariance stationarity. But weak stationarity implies strict stationarity only if the data are normally distributed (since the Gaussian or normal distribution is completely characterized by its first two moments).

Weak stationarity implies that the mean and variance is the same for all observations and that the autocovariance function depends only on the distance between the observations, not where in time they are located.

The concepts of stationarity typically do not directly apply to many data series observed in (macro)economic contexts, namely those that are trending. Economic data usually have trends. Examples are US GDP and money stock. A quick examination of their plots will show that the series display trends and have sudden rises and drops. Those features are also to some extent shared by US short term interest rates and inflation rates, although those processes do not grow over time (in other words, they do not have a linear trend, but may have a stochastic trend). It is therefore important to at least get rid of the trend. This can be done in several ways, but the most common are the following: (a) using growth rates; since we most often deal with the logarithmic transformation of the series, this amounts to taking first-differences; (b) detrend the series using some pre-specified trend function; examples include a linear trend, a quadratic one, a linear trend with changes in slope and/or intercept, etc. In economics, a big debate concerns how to remove the trend component. See the works of Brockwell and Davis (1991, Chapter 1.4) and Anderson (1971) for a discussion of trend removal; also the work of Priestley (1981, Chapter 7.7), which is, however, more technical. Other methods based on state-space models are possible.

Is it reasonable to assume any time series to be weakly stationary? Well, it depends on the series, of course. One has to adopt a pragmatic stance. Even a weakly stationary process without other restrictions already has $T+1$ parameters (one mean, one variance, and $T-1$ autocovariances). Allowing the mean to change over time without restrictions would further add $T-1$ parameters and so on for the variances and the autocovariances if these are allowed to change. With so many parameters, inference becomes impossible. We can only estimate a number of parameters that is relatively small compared to the available sample size T. So, even with weakly stationary processes, we will need to impose addition structures, i.e., some parametric model with a small number of parameters.

The bottom line is that we should view the weakly stationary assumption as adequate "until proven guilty". The most important case in which the assumptions are violated concerns changes in the parameters, e.g., the mean or the variance. These changes can be abrupt (i.e., a structural change) or smooth. In such cases, we need (a) methods to detect departures from weak stationarity and (b) models to capture the changes. These are covered later. If the changes are appropriately accounted for, the remaining noise component is often close to being weakly stationary, close enough to be able to apply the models described in this chapter.

8.2 The autocovariance and autocorrelation functions

We start with a definition of the autocovariance and autocorrelation functions when the time-series process x_t has finite mean μ and variance σ^2. When x_t is second-order stationary, the following properties hold.

Definition 8.3 (Autocovariance Function). Let x_t be such that $E(x_t^2) < \infty$ for all t; the autocovariance function is given by $R(\tau) = E(x_t - \mu)(x_{t-\tau} - \mu)$.

Definition 8.4 (Autocorrelation Function). The autocorrelation function at lag τ is given by

$$\rho(\tau) = \frac{R(\tau)}{\mathrm{Var}(x_t)} = \frac{R(\tau)}{\sigma^2} = \frac{R(\tau)}{R(0)}.$$

Remark 8.1. A weakly stationary process is completely characterized by its mean and autocovariance function, or its mean, autocorrelation function, and variance. The autocovariances depend on the units of the data, while the autocorrelations are unit-free.

Definition 8.5 (White Noise). A stochastic process x_t satisfying the following three conditions is called a white noise process:

(1) $E(x_t) = 0$ for all t;
(2) $E(x_t^2) = \sigma^2$, the same for all t;
(3) $E(x_t x_s) = 0$ for all $t \neq s$.

The white noise process is the building block for more complex weakly stationary processes.

Properties of $R(\tau)$ and $\rho(\tau)$. For the autocovariance function, we have the following:

(1) $R(0) = \sigma^2$.
(2) $|R(\tau)| \leq R(0)$ for all τ.
(3) If x_t is real valued, then $R(\tau)$ is an even function, i.e., $R(\tau) = R(-\tau)$.

Similarly for the autocorrelation function, we have the following:

(1) $\rho(0) = 1$.
(2) $|\rho(\tau)| \leq 1$ for all τ.
(3) If x_t is real valued, then $\rho(\tau)$ is an even function, i.e., $\rho(\tau) = \rho(-\tau)$.

Note that, henceforth, we shall simply use the label "stationary process" understanding that what is meant is "weakly stationary" or "second-order stationary". Another interesting property is the following:

Lemma 8.1. *$R(\tau)$ is positive definite in the sense that for any set of time points $t_1, t_2, \ldots, t_n$ and all real $z_1, z_2, \ldots, z_n$:*

$$\sum_{r=1}^{n} \sum_{s=1}^{n} R(t_r - t_s) z_r z_s \geq 0.$$

Proof. Let $w = \sum_{r=1}^{n} z_r x_{t_r}$, then

$$0 \leq \text{Var}(w) = \sum_{r=1}^{n} \sum_{s=1}^{n} z_r z_s \text{Cov}\{x_{t_r}, x_{t_s}\}$$

$$= \sum_{r=1}^{n} \sum_{s=1}^{n} z_r z_s R(t_r - t_s).$$

One can also prove the following more general theorem (see the work of Brockwell and Davis, 1991, p. 27).

Proposition 8.1. *A real-valued even function defined on the set $\mathbb{Z}$ of all integers is non-negative definite if and only if it is the autocovariance function of a stationary time series.*

8.3 Wold's decomposition theorem

We now discuss a fundamental result in the theory of stationary stochastic processes known as Wold's decomposition theorem. It states that **any** stationary process can be represented as the sum of two components: The first is a deterministic component and the second is a linear combination of uncorrelated random variables with mean zero. This is stated more precisely in the following:

Theorem 8.1 (Wold's Theorem). *Any stationary stochastic process x_t can be expressed in the form*

$$x_t = d_t + v_t,$$

where we have the following:

(1) d_t *and* v_t *are uncorrelated processes, i.e.,* $E(d_t v_s) = 0$ *for all* t, s.
(2) v_t *is regular with one sided linear representation*:

$$v_t = \sum_{i=0}^{\infty} g_i e_{t-i}, \tag{8.1}$$

with $g_0 = 1$,

$$\sum_{i=0}^{\infty} g_i^2 < \infty,$$

and e_t *is a white noise process given by*

$$e_t = x_t - E(x_t | x_{t-1}, x_{t-2}, \ldots),$$

with $E(x_t|x_{t-1}, x_{t-2}, \ldots)$ *being the best linear prediction of* x_t *based on* $\{x_{t-1}, x_{t-2}, \ldots\}$*, the past observations.*
(3) *The sequence* g_i *and process* e_t *are uniquely determined.*
(4) d_t *is singular, i.e., it can be predicted from its own past with zero prediction variance.*

An outline of the proof is presented in Section 8.8.

Remark 8.2. Even though the process may be nonlinear, the decomposition is linear and is determined by the second moments of the process. Thus, we can hope to approximate any process by a linear one. This does not mean a nonlinear process will not give a better approximation but gives some hope that a parsimonious linear model that can be written as a function of past *i.i.d.* random variables can be a useful approximation.

This proposition was first proved by Wold (1938). See the work of Sargent (1987, pp. 286–290) for a sketch of the intuition behind this result. Useful references are the works of Priestley (1981, pp. 755–758) and Brockwell and Davis (1991, Chapter 5.7). Note that the Wold decomposition is unique. In other words, if two stationary processes have the same Wold decomposition, they are the same process. In practice, we ignore the component d_t or simply replace it by the mean of the process, which is independent of time. We shall do so throughout. For examples of stationary processes involving a component d_t, see the work of Brockwell and Davis (1991, p. 183 and Exercise 5.20).

Remark 8.3. To give an idea of what is involved with such a process, consider the simple example

$$x_t = Y + e_t, \tag{8.2}$$

where $Y \sim N(0, \sigma_Y^2)$ and $e_t \sim i.i.d.\ N(0, \sigma_e^2)$. Think about Y as being the random mean value draw at the date when the process started. Then, x_t are random fluctuations around Y. However, a curious feature emerges. We learn from basic probability theory that a law of large numbers specifies that

$$T^{-1}\sum_{t=1}^{T} x_t \xrightarrow{p} \lim_{T\to\infty} T^{-1}\sum_{t=1}^{T} E(x_t). \tag{8.3}$$

However, this relationship does not hold when the data are generated by (8.2). To see this, note that

$$plim_{T\to\infty}T^{-1}\sum_{t=1}^{T} x_t = plim_{T\to\infty}T^{-1}\sum_{t=1}^{T}(Y + e_t) = Y$$

since $plim_{T\to\infty}T^{-1}\sum_{t=1}^{T} e_t = 0$ using a standard law of large numbers. On the other hand,

$$\lim_{T\to\infty} T^{-1}\sum_{t=1}^{T} E(x_t) = 0$$

since

$$E(x_t) = 0.$$

Hence, (8.3) fails to hold. The way we go about this problem in practice is to assume that the mean of the process is some **fixed unknown constant**, say μ, so that

$$x_t = \mu + e_t.$$

Then, (8.3) holds since

$$plim_{T\to\infty}T^{-1}\sum_{t=1}^{T}x_t = plim_{T\to\infty}T^{-1}\sum_{t=1}^{T}(\mu + e_t) = \mu$$

and

$$\lim_{T\to\infty} T^{-1}\sum_{t=1}^{T}E(x_t) = \mu.$$

Finding the Wold decomposition in principle requires fitting an infinite number of parameters $(g_1, g_2, \ldots)$ to the data. With a finite number of observations on $(x_1, x_2, \ldots, x_T)$, this is not possible. However, with

$$x_t = G(L)e_t,$$

we can think of $(g_1, g_2, \ldots)$ as coefficients in an infinite order polynomial function:

$$G(L) = 1 + g_1L + g_2L^2 + \cdots,$$

and approximate the function using a ratio of two finite-order polynomials

$$G(L) \approx \frac{B(L)}{A(L)} \equiv \frac{1 + b_1L + b_2L^2 + \cdots + b_qL^q}{1 + a_1L + a_2L^2 + \cdots + a_pL^p}.$$

Indeed, the ratio of two finite polynomials in L can provide a good approximation to any infinite moving-average polynomial. This motivates the study of Autoregressive Moving Average (ARMA) process.

8.4 The autoregressive moving average models

The class of autoregressive moving-average (ARMA) processes is the most popular special case of discrete time parameter models. It was popularized via the important book by Box and Jenkins (1970). It provides a parsimonious way to represent stationary processes as a linear combination of uncorrelated random variables with a special class of weights. The Wold decomposition theorem implies that

ARMA models serve as a good approximation to a wide class of stationary processes. Ignoring the mean, the basic ARMA models include, with $\{e_t\}$ denoting a white noise process,

$$\begin{aligned} \mathrm{AR}(1) &: x_t = ax_{t-1} + e_t, \\ \mathrm{MA}(1) &: x_t = e_t + be_{t-1}, \\ \mathrm{AR}(p) &: x_t = a_1 x_{t-1} + a_2 x_{t-2} + \cdots + a_p x_{t-p} + e_t, \\ \mathrm{MA}(q) &: x_t = e_t + b_1 e_{t-1} + \cdots + b_q e_{t-q}, \\ \mathrm{ARMA}(p,q) &: x_t - a_1 x_{t-1} - \cdots - a_p x_{t-p} = e_t + b_1 e_{t-1} + \cdots + b_q e_{t-q}. \end{aligned}$$

Remark 8.4. In this chapter, we assume that the ARMA(p,q) process has mean zero. This is done without loss of generality since our goal is to find conditions on the coefficients which ensure that $\{x_t\}$ is a stationary process and to highlight the properties of the autocovariance function in some special cases. Alternatively, assume that the mean has been subtracted.

To better represent and manipulate ARMA models, it is useful to work with lag operators. The lag operator, represented by the symbol L, moves the index back one time unit, i.e., $Lx_t \equiv x_{t-1}$. A double application of the lag operator, indicated by L^2, moves the index back two time units, i.e., $L^2 x_t \equiv x_{t-2}$. In general, for any integer j, $L^j x_t \equiv x_{t-j}$. Similarly, for a negative number, $-j$, we define $L^{-j} x_t \equiv x_{t+j}$. In the notation of lag operator, the above ARMA models can be represented as

$$\begin{aligned} \mathrm{AR}(1) &: (1 - aL)x_t = e_t, \\ \mathrm{MA}(1) &: x_t = (1 + bL)e_t, \\ \mathrm{AR}(p) &: (1 - a_1 L - \cdots - a_p L^p)x_t = e_t, \\ \mathrm{MA}(q) &: x_t = (1 + b_1 L + \cdots + b_q L^q)e_t, \\ \mathrm{ARMA}(p,q) &: (1 - a_1 L - a_2 L^2 - \cdots - a_p L^p)x_t \\ &= (1 + b_1 L + \cdots + b_q L^q)e_t. \end{aligned}$$

Or simply defining

$$\begin{aligned} A(L) &= (1 - a_1 L - \cdots - a_p L^p), \\ B(L) &= (1 + b_1 L + \cdots + b_q L^q), \end{aligned}$$

we have

$$\text{AR}(p) : A(L)x_t = e_t,$$

$$\text{MA}(q) : x_t = B(L)e_t,$$

$$\text{ARMA}(p, q) : A(L)x_t = B(L)e_t.$$

This notation is used throughout. The usefulness of the lag operator lies in the fact that it follows exactly the same algebraic rules as the multiplication operator. For this reason, it is tempting to use the expression "multiply x_t by L" rather than "operate on x_t by L". Although the latter expression is technically more correct, the use of the former shorthand expression to facilitate the exposition is universally accepted and we use it as well. When applying the lag operator, we are free to use the standard commutative, associative, and distributive algebraic laws, for example,

- $(a + bL)L = aL + bL^2$,
- $(1 - a_1L)(1 - a_2L) = 1 - a_1L - a_2L + a_1a_2L^2$.

We can also use the inversion formula when the resulting series converges, for example,

$$(1 - aL)^{-1} = 1 + aL + a^2L^2 + \cdots + a^nL^n + \cdots \quad \text{if } |a| < 1.$$

The above result is very useful because it offers a way to convert AR processes to MA processes and vice versa.

8.4.1 AR(1) model

We first give a precise definition for the AR(1) model:

Definition 8.6 (Autoregressive of Order One). The process x_t is called autoregressive of order one or AR(1) if x_t satisfies the following equation:

$$x_t = ax_{t-1} + e_t, \quad t = \ldots, -1, 0, 1, \ldots, \tag{8.4}$$

where e_t is white noise. The process x_t is called a stationary AR(1) process if it is stationary and satisfies equation (8.4).

An AR(1) model is a special case of a Markov process:

Definition 8.7 (Markov Process). x_t is said to be a Markov process if

$$p(x_t|x_{t-s}; s \geq 1) = p(x_t|x_{t-1}),$$

where $p(x_t|\mathcal{F})$ is the distribution of x_t conditional on $\mathcal{F}$. In other words, a Markov process depends only on the value in the previous period.

AR(1) to MA(∞): We can find the equivalent MA representation of an AR(1) process via recursive substitutions or by using the lag operator. Using the first approach,

$$\begin{aligned} x_t &= ax_{t-1} + e_t \\ &= a(ax_{t-2} + e_{t-1}) + e_t \\ &\dots \\ &= a^k x_{t-k} + \sum_{j=0}^{k-1} a^j e_{t-j}. \end{aligned}$$

Hence, if $|a| < 1$, then

$$plim_{k\to\infty} a^k x_{t-k} = 0$$

and

$$x_t = \sum_{j=0}^{\infty} a^j e_{t-j}. \tag{8.5}$$

The same result can be reached using lag operator. Recall the Taylor expansion,

$$(1 - z)^{-1} = 1 + z + z^2 + \cdots \quad \text{for } |z| < 1.$$

Hence,

$$(1 - aL)x_t = e_t$$

implies

$$\begin{aligned} x_t &= (1 - aL)^{-1} e_t \\ &= (1 + aL + a^2L^2 + \cdots) e_t \\ &= \sum_{j=0}^{\infty} a^j e_{t-j}, \end{aligned}$$

for $|a| < 1$. If $a = 1$, $x_t = \sum_{j=0}^{t} e_j$ for some initial time period labeled 0 (when $a = -1$, $x_t = \sum_{j=0}^{t} (-1)^j e_j$). The latter case is non-stationary.

8.4.2 Stationarity of AR(1) processes

Proposition 8.2. *The process x_t defined in* (8.4) *is stationary if $|a| < 1$ and* $\text{Var}(e_t) = \sigma^2 < \infty$. *In other words, x_t is stationary if it has finite second moment and the root of $A(z) = 0$, with $A(z) = 1 - az$, is greater than unity.*

Proof. From (8.5), (i) $E(x_t) = 0$, independent of t, (ii)

$$\text{Var}(x_t) = \sum_{j=0}^{\infty} a^{2j} \text{Var}(e_{t-j}) = \sigma^2 \sum_{j=0}^{\infty} a^{2j} = \sigma^2/(1 - a^2),$$

which is finite if $|a| < 1$, and (iii)

$$\begin{aligned} E(x_t x_{t+\tau}) &= E\left(\sum_{j=0}^{\infty} a^j e_{t-j}\right)\left(\sum_{j=0}^{\infty} a^j e_{t+\tau-j}\right) \\ &= \sum_{j=0}^{\infty} a^{j+\tau} a^j E(e_{t-j}^2) = \sigma^2 \frac{a^\tau}{1 - a^2} \quad \text{if } \tau \geq 0 \\ &= \sum_{j=0}^{\infty} a^{j+|\tau|} E(e_{t+|\tau|-j}) \\ &= \sigma^2 \frac{a^{|\tau|}}{1 - a^2} \quad \text{if } \tau < 0. \end{aligned}$$

Hence,

$$E(x_t x_{t+\tau}) = \sigma^2 \frac{a^{|\tau|}}{1 - a^2} \quad \text{for any } t \text{ and } \tau.$$

Consider the equation $A(z) = 1 - az = 0$. The solution or root of this polynomial is $(1/a)$. Hence, the requirement that $|a| < 1$ is equivalent to the requirement that the root of the equation $A(z) = 0$ be greater the unity.

Remark 8.5. To summarize, for a stationary AR(1) process, the autocovariance and autocorrelation functions are

$$R(\tau) = \sigma^2 a^{|\tau|}/(1 - a^2)$$

and

$$\rho(\tau) = a^{|\tau|},$$

respectively.

8.4.3 The AR(2) model

We now consider a stationary AR(2) process, i.e., a stationary process generated by

$$(1 - a_1 L - a_2 L^2)x_t = e_t \quad \text{with } t = \ldots, -1, 0, 1, \ldots, \tag{8.6}$$

where again e_t is a white noise process. To obtain the MA(∞) representation, start with

$$(1 - a_1 L - a_2 L^2)x_t = e_t.$$

The polynomial $A(z) = 1 - a_1 z - a_2 z^2$ has two roots, denoted by λ_1 and λ_2. They satisfy

$$\lambda_1 \lambda_2 = -1/a_2,$$
$$\lambda_1 + \lambda_2 = -a_1/a_2.$$

Note that λ_1 and λ_2 may be equal or they may also be complex, in which case they are complex conjugates. The lag polynomial can be factored as

$$A(L) = (1 - (1/\lambda_1)L)(1 - (1/\lambda_2)L).$$

If $|\lambda_1| > 1$ and $|\lambda_2| > 1$, the lag polynomial can be inverted so that

$$x_t = \frac{1}{(1-(1/\lambda_1)L)(1-(1/\lambda_2)L)} e_t.$$

If $\lambda_1 \neq \lambda_2$, we have

$$\begin{aligned} x_t &= \frac{1}{(1-(1/\lambda_1)L)(1-(1/\lambda_2)L)} e_t \\ &= \left(\frac{\lambda_2}{\lambda_2 - \lambda_1} \frac{1}{(1-(1/\lambda_1)L)} - \frac{\lambda_1}{\lambda_2 - \lambda_1} \frac{1}{(1-(1/\lambda_2)L)} \right) e_t \\ &= \sum_{j=0}^{\infty} \left(\frac{\lambda_2}{\lambda_2 - \lambda_1} \lambda_1^{-j} - \frac{\lambda_1}{\lambda_2 - \lambda_1} \lambda_2^{-j} \right) e_{t-j}. \end{aligned}$$

If $\lambda_1 = \lambda_2 = \lambda$, we have

$$x_t = \frac{1}{(1-\lambda^{-1}L)^2} e_t = \sum_{j=0}^{\infty} (j+1)\lambda^{-j} e_{t-j}.$$

Proposition 8.3. *The* AR(2) *process* x_t *is stationary if* $\mathrm{Var}(e_t) = \sigma^2 < \infty$ *and the roots of the lag polynomial* $A(z) = 1 - a_1 z - a_2 z^2$ *are outside of the unit circle.*

The proof is left as an exercise. The above result can be generalized to AR(p) models. Care, however, should be taken since the roots can be real or complex valued. The requirement $|\lambda| > 1$ should be understood as the modulus of a complex number or the absolute value of a real number. In general, if $\lambda = \alpha + \beta i$, then the modulus is $|\lambda| = \sqrt{\alpha^2 + \beta^2}$.

8.4.4 Additional discussions of the AR(2) model

We now provide a more extensive treatment of the AR(2) model:

$$x_t = a_1 x_{t-1} + a_2 x_{t-2} + e_t, \tag{8.7}$$

where $e_t \sim i.i.d.\left(0, \sigma_e^2\right)$ and the initial conditions x_0 and x_1 are independent of e_t for all t and have a distribution with finite mean and variance for all T. As discussed above, the process (8.7) can be written as

$$(1 - a_1 L - a_2 L^2) x_t = e_t,$$

or, equivalently, as

$$(1 - (1/\lambda_1)L)\,(1 - (1/\lambda_2)L)\, x_t = e_t, \tag{8.8}$$

where λ_1 and λ_2 are the roots of the quadratic equation

$$f(z) = 1 - a_1 z - a_2 z^2 = 0.$$

Equivalently, we can write

$$(1 - \mu_1 L)\,(1 - \mu_2 L)\, x_t = e_t, \tag{8.9}$$

where μ_1, μ_2 are the roots of the quadratic equation

$$g(z) = z^2 - a_1 z - a_2 = 0.$$

For the following derivations, it will be easier to work with the representation (8.9), in which case what is required is that the roots μ_1, μ_2 be inside the unit circle. Processes of the form (8.7) are an extension to a stochastic context of standard non-homogeneous difference equations. As is well known, the solution to such difference equations is the sum of an homogeneous and a particular solution. In our case, we have that the homogeneous solution is the solution of the homogeneous equation

$$x_t + a_1 x_{t-1} + a_2 x_{t-2} = 0,$$

with a solution of the form

$$x_t^h = A_1(\mu_1)^t + A_2(\mu_2)^t,$$

where A_1 and A_2 depend upon the initial conditions. The particular solution is given by

$$x_t^p = \left[\frac{1}{(1-\mu_1 L)(1-\mu_2 L)}\right] e_t \tag{8.10}$$

$$\begin{aligned}
&= \frac{1}{(\mu_1-\mu_2)}\left(\frac{\mu_1}{(1-\mu_1 L)} - \frac{\mu_2}{(1-\mu_2 L)}\right) e_t \\
&= \frac{1}{(\mu_1-\mu_2)}\left(\sum_{s=0}^{\infty}\left((\mu_1)^{s+1} - (\mu_2)^{s+1}\right) L^s\right) e_t \\
&= \sum_{s=0}^{\infty}\left(\frac{(\mu_1)^{s+1} - (\mu_2)^{s+1}}{\mu_1-\mu_2}\right) e_{t-s} \qquad \text{if } \mu_1 \neq \mu_2.
\end{aligned} \tag{8.11}$$

Remark 8.6. To justify the equality from the second to the third line, define

$$z_t = (1-\mu_1 L)^{-1}(\mu_1)e_t$$

or

$$(1-\mu_1 L)\, z_t = (\mu_1)e_t$$

so that

$$\begin{aligned}
z_t &= \mu_1 L z_t + \mu_1 e_t \\
&= \mu_1 L(\mu_1 L z_t + \mu_1 e_t) + \mu_1 e_t \\
&= (\mu_1)^2 L^2 z_t + (\mu_1)^2 L e_t + \mu_1 e_t \\
&\;\vdots \\
&= \sum_{s=0}^{\infty}(\mu_1)^{s+1} L^s e_t \\
&= \sum_{s=0}^{\infty}(\mu_1)^{s+1} e_{t-s}.
\end{aligned}$$

Hence, the overall solution for the process x_t is given by

$$x_t = x_t^h + x_t^p.$$

From both solutions x_t^h and x_t^p, x_t will be weakly stationary if $|\mu_1| < 1$ and $|\mu_2| < 1$. If these conditions hold, then x_t^p will have finite variance.

Conditions on a_1 and a_2 for stationarity. We now search for conditions on a_1 and a_2 for the process x_t to be stationary. We assume, with no loss of generality, that the roots μ_1 and μ_2 are distinct. As discussed above, the process will be stationary if these roots are "smaller than one". Care, however, must be taken since these roots can be real or complex valued. Now for the roots of

$$f(z) = 1 - a_1 z - a_2 z^2 = 0$$

to be outside the unit circle, we require that the roots of

$$g(z) = z^2 - a_1 z - a_2 = 0$$

be inside the unit circle. These roots are

$$\mu_1, \mu_2 = \frac{a_1 \pm \sqrt{a_1^2 + 4a_2}}{2}.$$

Complex roots. We start with the case where the roots are complex. Then,

$$a_1^2 + 4a_2 < 0$$

and

$$\mu_1, \mu_2 = \frac{a_1}{2} \pm i\frac{\left(-4a_2 - a_1^2\right)^{1/2}}{2},$$

where i is the imaginary number $i = \sqrt{-1}$. When the roots are complex, we cannot refer to $|\mu_1|$ and $|\mu_2| < 1$ as absolute values. Instead of absolute value, we interpret $|\cdot|$ as the length in geometrical terms. Recall the representation of a complex number in Polar coordinates: $a + bi$; see Figure 8.1.

We let r be the radius $r = \left(a^2 + b^2\right)^{1/2}$. We have $r < 1$ if $\left(a^2 + b^2\right)^{1/2} < 1$. Note that μ_1 and μ_2 are complex conjugates and, hence, have the same radius given by

$$|\mu_1| = |\mu_2| = \left(\frac{a_1^2}{4} - a_2 - \frac{a_1^2}{4}\right)^{1/2} = (-a_2)^{1/2}$$

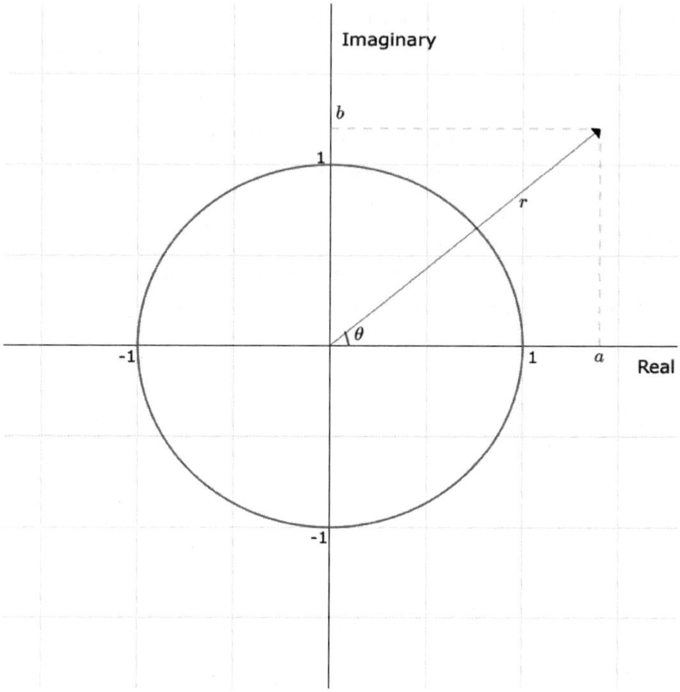

Figure 8.1. Complex roots.

and the stationarity condition is

$$a_2 > -1.$$

Remark 8.7. We can express the roots in polar form as

$$\mu_1 = |r| \exp(i\theta),$$
$$\mu_2 = |r| \exp(-i\theta),$$

where r is the radius and θ the angle. Here, $|r| = (-a_2)^{1/2}$ and $\cos(\theta) = a_1/[2\,(-a_2)^{1/2}]$. Using the fact that

$$\exp(i\theta) - \exp(-i\theta) = 2i\sin(\theta),$$

we can write the particular solution (8.11) as

$$x_t^p = \frac{1}{\sin(\theta)} \sum_{s=0}^{\infty} |r|^s \sin(\theta(s+1))e_{t-s}.$$

Hence, the solution to x_t^p can be viewed as a contaminated or randomized periodic function. In such cases, we label the solution as "pseudo-periodic" or "pseudo-cyclical".

Unequal real roots. We now consider the case where the roots are real valued and distinct. Consider a graph of the function $g(z)$ as depicted in Figure 8.2. It is easy to show that $g(z)$ has a minimum at $a_1/2$.

We want the roots of $g(z)$ to lie inside the interval $(-1, 1)$ so we need $g(1)$ and $g(-1)$, the function $g(z)$ evaluated at $z = 1$ and $z = -1$, to be greater than 0 and that the minimum be also inside the interval $(-1, 1)$. This gives the following conditions:

- $g(1) > 0 \Rightarrow (1 - a_1 - a_2) > 0 \Rightarrow a_1 + a_2 < 1$;
- $g(-1) > 0 \Rightarrow (1 + a_1 - a_2) > 0 \Rightarrow a_2 - a_1 < 1$;
- $|a_1/2| < 1 \Rightarrow a_1^2 < 4$ or $|a_1| < 2$.

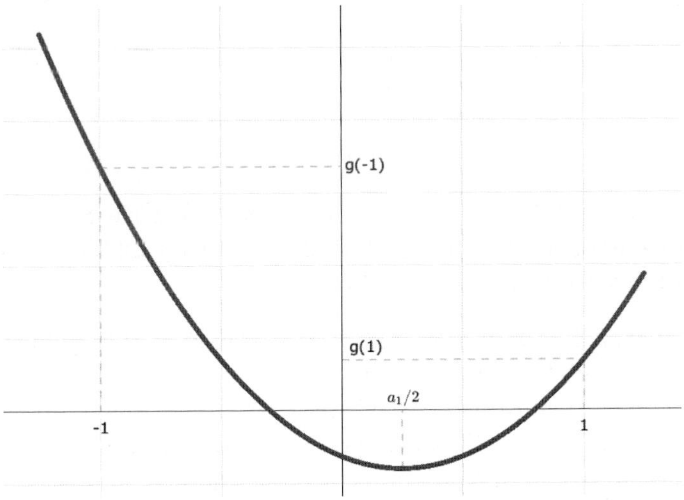

Figure 8.2. Unequal real roots.

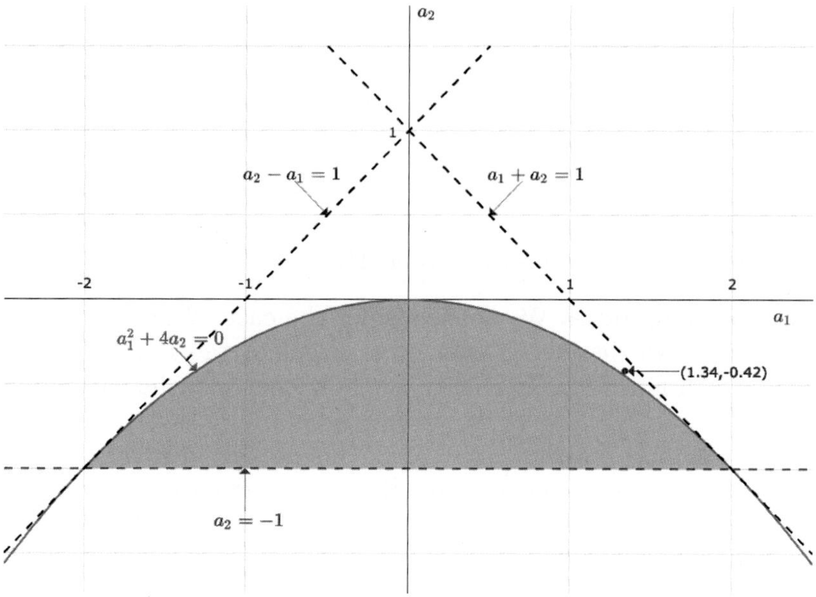

Figure 8.3. Stability triangle.

Combining these three conditions with the one pertaining to the case of complex roots $a_2 > -1$, we have that x_t is stationary if

$$a_2 > -1,$$
$$a_1 + a_2 < 1,$$
$$a_2 - a_1 < 1.$$

This defines a stability triangle depicted in Figure 8.3. Stationary processes correspond to the value of a_1 and a_2 inside the triangle, with complex roots in the shaded region.

Example 8.1 (Samuelson (1939)). Consider the following simple a Keynesian-type model where y_t is the (log) real GNP, c_t is the (log) real consumption, I_t is the (log) investment, and g_t is the (log) government expenditure. With α the marginal propensity to consume, the consumption equation is defined as (omitting all error terms for simplicity)

$$c_t = \alpha y_{t-1}.$$

The investment equation is given by

$$I_t = \beta(c_t - c_{t-1}),$$

and we have the accounting identity

$$y_t = c_t + I_t + g_t.$$

Since consumption depends on the lagged level of income, the consumption equation implies a multiplier effect of changes in income. On the other hand, since the investment equation depends on the growth of consumption, it describes an accelerator effect. Setting $g_t = 0$ for simplicity, this system implies an AR(2) for (log) real GNP given by

$$y_t = \alpha(1+\beta)y_{t-1} - \alpha\beta y_{t-2}.$$

Hence,

$$\begin{aligned} a_1 &= \alpha(1+\beta), \\ a_2 &= -\alpha\beta. \end{aligned}$$

The theory imposes the marginal propensity to consume to be positive and less than one, i.e., $0 < \alpha < 1$ and the accelerator coefficient $\beta > 0$. These restrictions imply the following restrictions on the autoregressive coefficients:

$$\begin{aligned} &a_2 < 0, \\ &0 < (a_1 + a_2) < 1. \end{aligned}$$

Hence, the model implies a stationary solution for GNP and permits "pseudo-cycles".

Example 8.2 (Blanchard (1981)). Using quarterly US data on detrended log GNP, y_t^d, for the period 47:3–78:4, an AR(2) was found to fit the data reasonably well and the estimates are

$$y_t^d = 1.34y_{t-1}^d - .42y_{t-2}^d + e_t.$$

Note that a similar result holds with other sample periods. These point estimates imply the following: (a) The process for detrended log real GNP is stationary ($0 < a_1 + a_2 = .92 < 1$); (b) the restrictions imposed by Samuelson's multiplier-accelerator model are satisfied ($a_2 = -.42 < 0$) but the estimates do not imply a cyclical pattern ($a_1^2 + 4a_2 = .1156 > 0$); (c) there is a "hump-shaped" behavior for the effect of a unit shock on the level of detrended log real GNP. The effects of these shocks are given by the coefficients of the moving average representation. Simple calculations reveal these to be (from lag 0 to lag 8) as follows: 1.00, 1.34, 1.38, 1.28, 1.14, 0.99, 0.84, 0.72, 0.61. But these conclusions are based on point estimates and do not take into account sampling variability. In particular, an important issue is as follows:

- Is the point estimate for the sum of the autoregressive coefficients significantly different from 1?

It turns out that with a sample of size near $T = 100$, the median of the estimate of the sum of the autoregressive coefficients is near 0.92. The estimate is very downward-biased; see the discussion in Section 21.3. Hence, it is difficult to judge whether the true process is stationary or not, i.e., inside the triangle or on the line of non-stationarity. This is the problem of testing for a unit root to which we shall return in later chapters. To see the importance of the conclusion, let us consider the arguments put forward by Blanchard (1981). He considered a decomposition of aggregate output as the sum of the contributions from consumption and investment. He first argued that given the results stated above, the output is stationary. On the other hand, the influential paper by Hall (1978) argued that (with quadratic marginal utility) consumption should be integrated, i.e., have a unit root or random walk component. On the other hand, all the theoretical arguments pointed to the fact that investment should be mean-reverting, mostly due to adjustment costs. In standard Keynesian models, the effect of consumption on output is labeled the multiplier effect, while for investment it is labeled the accelerator effect. If (detrended) aggregate output is indeed stationary, then the effect of consumption must be small relative to those of investment (since a non-stationary component would then dominate). Hence, his conclusion is that the multiplier is dead and the accelerator is alive. But he paid very little attention to the actual stochastic properties of aggregate output. He took at face value the fact that an estimate of 0.92 for the sum of the autoregressive coefficients is solid evidence in favor of stationarity. It turns out that this evidence is at best tenuous. If detrended aggregate output is indeed non-stationary (true value of the sum of the autoregressive coefficients being one), then his conclusions are overturned. The accelerator is dead and the multiplier is alive.

While the previous example is quite simplistic, it gives the flavor for the importance of deciding whether the statistical evidence favors a unit root or stationary process.

8.4.5 AR(p) processes

Consider now the general AR(p) process of the form

$$A(L)x_t = e_t,$$

with $A(L) = 1 - a_1L - a_2L^2 - \cdots - a_pL^p$. We can show the following:

(1) The process x_t is stationary if $\text{Var}(e_t) = \sigma^2 < \infty$ and the roots of the lag polynomial are outside the unit circle.
(2) If the process is stationary, then it is invertible so that

$$x_t = A(L)^{-1}e_t - \sum_{j=0}^{\infty} g_j c_{t-j}.$$

(3) The variance and autocorrelation function can be computed by solving the Yule–Walker equations, as discussed in the following.

8.4.6 Economic interpretation of AR processes

Models of the autoregressive type often occur in economics. The main mechanism behind it is often ascribed to cost of adjustment, inertia, habit formation, etc. It is fairly intuitive that if a shock occurs, its impact will take a while to be felt through the economy. A simple AR process captures this feature well. Indeed, for most aggregate time-series variables, fitting a simple AR(1) captures most of the correlation and quite often an AR(2) is sufficient, e.g., for the growth rate of real U.S. GDP.

8.4.7 Yule–Walker equations for AR(p) processes

The variance and autocorrelation function of AR(p) process can be found by solving the Yule–Walker equations (Walker, 1931; Yule, 1927). As an example, consider the AR(2) process:

$$x_t - a_1 x_{t-1} - a_2 x_{t-2} = e_t.$$

Multiplying both sides by $x_t, x_{t-1}, x_{t-2}, \ldots$, taking expectations, and dividing by $R(0)$, we obtain

$$1 - a_1\rho(1) - a_2\rho(2) = \sigma^2/R(0), \tag{8.12}$$

$$\rho(1) - a_1\rho(0) - a_2\rho(1) = 0, \tag{8.13}$$

$$\rho(2) - a_1\rho(1) - a_2\rho(0) = 0, \tag{8.14}$$

and

$$\rho(\tau) - a_1\rho(\tau-1) - a_2\rho(\tau-2) = 0 \quad \text{for } \tau \geq 3. \tag{8.15}$$

Solving (8.13) and (8.14),

$$\rho(1) = \frac{a_1}{1-a_2}; \quad \rho(2) = \frac{a_1^2}{1-a_2} + a_2.$$

Substituting in (8.12), we obtain the variance

$$R(0) = \frac{(1-a_2)\sigma^2}{(1+a_2)(1+a_1-a_2)(1-a_1-a_2)}.$$

Now, (8.15) can be solved recursively to obtain $\rho(\tau)$ with $\tau \geq 3$. The Yule–Walker equations using an estimated general AR(p) process are given by $\hat{a}_p = (\hat{a}_{1,T}, \ldots, \hat{a}_{p,T})'$ such that

$$\hat{\Gamma}_p \hat{a}_p = \hat{\rho}_p,$$

where

$$\hat{\Gamma}_p = [\hat{\rho}(i-j)]_{i,j=1}^p,$$

$$\hat{\rho}_p = (\hat{\rho}(1), \ldots, \hat{\rho}(p))',$$

$$\hat{\rho}(s) = T^{-1} \sum_{t=1}^{T-|s|} (x_t - \bar{x})(x_{t+|s|} - \bar{x}),$$

with the sample mean $\bar{x} = T^{-1}\sum_{t=1}^{T} x_t$. While they do not lend themselves easily to obtain a closed form expression, they can easily be programmed.

8.4.8 MA(q) processes

Consider now a general MA(q) process of the form

$$x_t = B(L)e_t,$$

with

$$B(L) = 1 + b_1 L + b_2 L^2 + \cdots + b_q L^q.$$

An important thing to note is that an MA(q) process is always stationary, provided $\mathrm{Var}(e_t) = \sigma^2 < \infty$. To see this, consider the first and the second moments:

$$\begin{aligned} E(x_t) &= 0, \\ \mathrm{Var}(x_t) &= \sigma^2(1 + b_1^2 + \cdots + b_q^2), \\ E(x_t x_{t-\tau}) &= \sigma^2(b_{|\tau|} + b_{|\tau|+1}b_1 + \cdots + b_q b_{q-|\tau|}) \quad \text{if } |\tau| \leq q \\ &= 0 \text{ if } |\tau| > q. \end{aligned}$$

The autocorrelation function is given by

$$\begin{aligned} \rho(\tau) &= \sum_{s=|\tau|}^{q} b_s b_{s-|\tau|} / \sum_{s=0}^{q} b_s^2 \text{ if } |\tau| \leq q \\ &= 0 \text{ if } |\tau| > q. \end{aligned}$$

Note the difference between AR(p) and MA(q) process. Autoregressive processes in general have autocorrelations which decays gradually (exponentially); moving-average processes have autocorrelations which "cut off" after lag q.

8.4.9 Economic interpretation of MA processes

To illustrate the role of MA processes, it is best to take a simple example. Suppose that the aim of the central bank (e.g., the Federal

Reserve or any monetary authority in the country of interest) is to stabilize the rate of growth of the (log of the) price level. This amounts to target a given level for inflation since inflation is well approximated by the change in the log of the price level for small to moderate values. So, let x_t be the inflation rate sampled quarterly, say. If a shock to inflation occurs at quarter t, it is too late for the monetary authorities to react. However, if their goal is price stability and they actually have the power to act, then they will take measures to counteract the shock. This leads to an MA(1) of the form

$$x_t = e_t + \theta e_{t-1},$$

with $\theta < 0$. No action means $\theta = 0$, and perfect price stability means $\theta = -1$, which is a non-invertible process so that the (log of the) price level has stationary deviations around a fixed trend. It is indeed the case that inflation is well described by a moving-average process (along with an autoregressive part). Perron (1994a) analyzed the time-series properties of inflation for Canada during the period 1947–1992. For the full sample, the MA parameter is around -0.6. For the period 1973–1981, it is basically zero, while for the period 1982–1992 it is very near -1. What does this imply? First, a value of θ near 0 during the 1970s means that the central bank was either unwilling or unable to achieve price stability. Informal talks with some officers working during this period confirmed that "they were lost about what to do". This was a time of high uncertainty created by an unprecedented supply shock. Then, in 1982, the Bank of Canada appointed a new governor whose mandate was to restore price stability over anything else. A value θ near -1 indicates that he was successful.

A related argument has been put forward by Stock and Watson (2007) who argued that inflation has become harder to forecast because the MA component has become closer to -1. This is due to the fact that autoregressions are often used to make forecasts. When the process is nearly invertible, even a rather long autoregression provides a poor approximation. See the following section.

Another example where MA processes occur frequently is for models with rational expectations. As a concrete example, consider a simple forward looking monetary policy reaction function with only a forward component for future inflation four quarters ahead:

$$r_t = x_t'\beta + \alpha E(y_{t+4}|\Phi_t) \quad (t = 1, \ldots, T-4),$$

where r_t is the Federal Funds rate (nominal interest rate), y_t is inflation this quarter, $E(y_{t+4}|\Phi_t)$ is the expected value one year ahead, and x_t are some covariates, such as the marginal cost of labor or the output gap. Here, Φ_t is the information set available at time t, assumed to be the same for economic agents and the econometricians. For analyses related to the issues discussed here, see the work of Clarida *et al.* (2000). Four quarters ahead for the expected inflation is often used to account for the lagged effect of monetary policy. Note that we have not introduced an error term yet on purpose. We do not observe $E(y_{t+4}|\Phi_t)$ (i.e., no survey data is used). Hence, we re-write the model as

$$r_t = x_t'\beta + \alpha y_{t+4} + u_t,$$

where

$$u_t = \alpha(E(y_{t+4}|\Phi_t) - y_{t+4})$$

is the forecast error assuming rational expectations, i.e, the efficient use of all information. Clearly, y_{t+4} is correlated with u_t so that an IV procedure is needed to consistently estimate the parameters. It can be shown that u_t is an MA(3) process. To see this, assuming that y_t is stationary, it has the following Wold decomposition:

$$y_t = \Theta(L)v_t = \sum_{j=0}^{\infty} \phi_j v_{t-j},$$

where $\Theta(L) = \sum_{j=0}^{\infty} \phi_j L^j$ with $\phi_0 = 1$, and

$$v_t = y_t - E(y_t|y_{t-1}, y_{t-2}, \ldots),$$

see Section 8.3. Then,

$$\begin{aligned} E(y_{t+4}|\Phi_t) &= E\left(\sum_{j=0}^{\infty} \phi_j v_{t+4-j}|\Phi_t\right) \\ &= \sum_{j=4}^{\infty} \phi_j v_{t+4-j} \end{aligned}$$

and

$$\begin{aligned}u_t &= \alpha(E(y_{t+4}|\Phi_t) - y_{t+4})\\&= \alpha\left(\sum_{j=4}^{\infty}\phi_j v_{t+4-j} - \sum_{j=0}^{\infty}\phi_j v_{t+4-j}\right)\\&= -\alpha(v_{t+4} + \phi_1 v_{t+3} + \phi_2 v_{t+2} + \phi_3 v_{t+1}).\end{aligned}$$

Hence, u_t is an MA(3) process, with expectation 0 conditional on information at time t. In general, if you have expectation of some variable k periods ahead, the errors will be an MA$(k-1)$. See Section 13.5 for methods to estimate such models.

8.4.10 Invertibility of MA(q) processes

Of interest is whether there exists an AR representation for an MA(q) process. This is important partly because we can then approximate an MA(q) model by some finite AR model, which can be estimated using OLS. This is simpler than estimating directly an MA(q) model, which involves nonlinear optimizations. The conditions for the existence of an AR representation are made precise in the following definition.

Definition 8.8 (Invertibility of an MA(q) Process). The MA(q) process is said to be invertible if there exists a sequence $\{a_j\}_{j=0}^{\infty}$ such that $e_t = \sum_{j=0}^{\infty} a_j x_{t-j}$ with $\sum_{j=0}^{\infty} |a_j| < \infty$.

Stationarity itself is not sufficient for invertibility. To see this, consider the simple example

$$x_t = e_t - e_{t-1}.$$

The process x_t is obviously stationary but not invertible. The MA(q) process is invertible if and only if all the roots of the lag polynomial $B(L) = 1 + b_1 L + \cdots + b_q L^q$ are outside of unit circle. This invertibility condition is the same as required to identify an MA(q) process. For any non-invertible MA(1) process (more generally for MA(q) processes), there always exists an invertible MA(1) process with the same first and second moment properties. Hence, they are observationally equivalent using moments up to second order. For example, consider the non-invertible MA(1) process

$$x_t = (1 - cL)e_t,$$

where $c > 1$ and e_t is *i.i.d.* $(0, \sigma_\varepsilon^2)$. The same second moments are obtained for the process

$$x_t = (1 - \tilde{c}L)\tilde{e}_t,$$

where

$$\tilde{c} = c^{-1}$$

and

$$\tilde{e}_t \sim i.i.d.\ (0, c^2\sigma_\varepsilon^2).$$

This generalizes to an MA(q) process. Hence, imposing that the roots of the moving-average polynomial are outside the unit circle acts as an identification condition, not only one that ensures invertibility.

This does not mean that non-invertible models are of no concern in economics. Hansen and Sargent (1991) provide a specific economic model in which a non-invertible structural moving average process arises. In the model, a set of economic variables, say X_t, are generated by an invertible moving average process. Another set of economic variables, say Y_t, are expectation variables, generated as discounted sums of the expected future of X_t. They then consider what would happen if only the data Y_t were available to the econometrician. They show that the implied moving average process of Y_t, written in terms of the structural shocks driving X_t, is not invertible. A simple version of the model is as follows: Suppose Y_t and X_t are two scalar time series, with X_t generated by the MA(1) process

$$X_t = e_t - \theta e_{t-1}.$$

Suppose Y_t is related to X_t by the expectation equation, where E_t denotes the expectation conditional on information available at time t:

$$Y_t = E_t \sum_{i=0}^{\infty} \beta^i X_{t+i} = X_t + \beta E_t X_{t+1} = (1 - \beta\theta)\, e_t - \theta e_{t-1} = C(L)e_t.$$

The root of $C(z)$ is $(1 - \beta\theta)/\theta$, which may be less than 1 even when the root of $(1 - \theta z)$ is greater than 1. For example, if $\theta = \beta = 0.8$.

8.4.11 ARMA(p, q) processes

Consider now the general ARMA(p, q) process of the form

$$A(L)x_t = B(L)e_t, \tag{8.16}$$

with

$$\begin{aligned} A(L) &= 1 - a_1 L - a_2 L^2 - \cdots - a_p L^p, \\ B(L) &= 1 + b_1 L + b_2 L^2 + \cdots + b_q L^q. \end{aligned}$$

The treatment of this more general case is simply a combination of the conditions for the pure AR(p) and MA(q) processes. The issues that need some attention are as follows:

- **Identification:** We require the lag polynomials $A(L)$ and $B(L)$ to have no common factors. Otherwise, the system is not identified. To see this, suppose that

$$\begin{aligned} A(L) &= C(L)D(L), \\ B(L) &= C(L)E(L), \end{aligned}$$

then the ARMA(p, q) process

$$\begin{aligned} A(L)x_t &= B(L)e_t, \\ C(L)D(L)x_t &= C(L)E(L)e_t \end{aligned} \tag{8.17}$$

is equivalent to the process

$$D(L)x_t = E(L)e_t$$

since the polynomial $C(L)$ cancels from both sides of (8.17). Hence, the coefficients of the polynomial $C(L)$ cannot be identified.

- **Stationarity:** The process x_t is stationary if and only if all the roots of $A(L)$ are outside of the unit circle and e_t have finite variance.

• **Invertibility and Identification:** The ARMA(p, q) process is said to be invertible if there exists a sequence $\{\pi_j\}_{j=0}^{\infty}$ such that

$$e_t = \sum_{j=0}^{\infty} \pi_j x_{t-j},$$

with $\sum_{j=0}^{\infty} |\pi_j| < \infty$. Invertibility means the process can be represented as an infinite order AR process. As discussed above, it also acts as an identification condition. An ARMA(p, q) process is invertible if and only if the lag polynomial $B(L)$ has all roots outside the unit circle. The requirement for invertibility lies in the interest of having a unified theory for stationary ARMA(p, q) processes, which is intuitively desirable since they then all have an (infinite) autoregressive representation. Many aspects of time-series econometrics are concerned with the study of non-stationary or non-invertible processes. It still remains that the class of stationary and invertible ARMA(p, q) processes is the building block for more complex non-stationary or non-invertible processes.

8.4.12 The partial autocorrelation function

In general, a partial correlation is a conditional correlation. It is the correlation between two variables under the assumption that we know and take into account the values of some other set of variables. For a time series, the partial autocorrelation between x_t and x_{t-k} is defined as the conditional correlation between x_t and x_{t-k}, conditional on $x_{t-k+1}, \ldots, x_{t-1}$, the set of observations that come between the time points t and $t - k$.

The first-order partial autocorrelation is the same as the first-order autocorrelation. For higher order lags, it is defined by

$$\text{PAC}(k) = \frac{\text{Cov}(x_t, x_{t-k} | x_{t-k+1}, \ldots, x_{t-1})}{\text{Var}(x_t | x_{t-k+1}, \ldots, x_{t-1}) \text{Var}(x_{t-k} | x_{t-k+1}, \ldots, x_{t-1})}.$$

There are algorithms for estimating the partial autocorrelations based on the sample autocorrelations; see the works of Box *et al.* (2015) and Brockwell (2009). Let $\hat{x}_t$ be the fitted value from the following OLS regression:

$$x_t = \beta_1 x_{t+1} + \beta_2 x_{t+2} + \cdots + \beta_{k-1} x_{t+k-1} + e_t.$$

Then, the partial autocorrelation function can be computed as

$$\text{PAC}(k) = \text{Corr}(x_t - \hat{x}_t, x_{t+k} - \hat{x}_{t+k}),$$

where Corr is the sample correlation. The usefulness of the partial autocorrelation function is the following. As discussed above, the autocorrelations are 0 after lag q for an MA(q), while they decay exponentially to zero for AR(p) processes. The inverse holds for the partial autocorrelation function. Their values are 0 after lag p for an AR(p) process, while they decay smoothly for MA(q) processes. Hence, in the spirit of the analysis advocated by Box and Jenkins (1970), one can use them to get a sense of whether the process is a pure MA(q) or an AR(p). However, care must be exercised as the limit distribution and corresponding confidence intervals are complex functions of the true values of the autocorrelations at all lags. Now, it is more common to identify the nature of the models using information criteria. These are discussed in Chapter 36.

8.4.13 The effect of additive noise

Often, a series is contaminated by noise or measurement errors. This affects the properties of the series. It induces a moving average component, which as the variance of noise increases is such that the AR and MA roots cancel and we get closer to a random process. To illustrate this feature, consider a scalar observable random variable y_t generated by an AR(1) contaminated with *i.i.d.* measurement errors, i.e.,

$$y_t = x_t + u_t, \tag{8.18}$$

where

$$x_t = \alpha x_{t-1} + e_t,$$

with $0 < \alpha \leq 1$, $u_t \sim i.i.d.\ (0, \sigma_u^2)$, $e_t \sim i.i.d.\ (0, \sigma_e^2)$, and u_t and e_t are independent. We first show that y_t also has an equivalent representation in terms of a constrained ARMA(1, 1) process

$$y_t = \alpha y_{t-1} + v_t + \theta v_{t-1},$$

where $v_t \sim i.i.d(0, \sigma_v^2)$. In particular, the implied sign of the moving average coefficient is the negative of the sign of α. Since

$$\begin{aligned} y_t &= x_t + u_t, \\ \alpha y_{t-1} &= \alpha x_{t-1} + \alpha u_{t-1}, \end{aligned}$$

we have

$$y_t - \alpha y_{t-1} = x_t - \alpha x_{t-1} + u_t - \alpha u_{t-1} = e_t + u_t - \alpha u_{t-1}.$$

Let $z_t = y_t - \alpha y_{t-1}$, we want to show z_t has an MA(1) representation. It is easy to see that z_t is stationary with mean $E(z_t) = 0$. Since a stationary stochastic process can be completely characterized by its autocovariance function, next we calculate the autocovariance function of z_t:

$$\begin{aligned} R(0) &= E(z_t^2) = \sigma_e^2 + (1+\alpha^2)\sigma_u^2, \\ R(1) &= E(z_t z_{t-1}) = -\alpha\sigma_u^2, \\ R(\tau) &= E(z_t z_{t-\tau}) = 0, \quad \text{for } |\tau| > 1. \end{aligned}$$

Hence, z_t has an MA(1) representation given by

$$z_t = y_t - \alpha y_{t-1} = v_t + \theta v_{t-1}.$$

Thus,

$$\begin{aligned} R(0) &= \sigma_e^2 + (1+\alpha^2)\sigma_u^2 = (1+\theta^2)\sigma_v^2, \\ R(1) &= -\alpha\sigma_u^2 = \theta\sigma_v^2. \end{aligned}$$

The two equations implicitly define θ and σ_v^2. Also, from the second equation, we have $\theta < 0$ if $\alpha > 0$. Substituting the expression for $R(0)$ into that for $R(1)$, we have the following equation for θ:

$$\alpha\sigma_u^2\theta^2 + [\sigma_u^2 + (1+\alpha^2)\sigma_u^2]\theta + \alpha\sigma_u^2 = 0.$$

This is a second-order polynomial equation and the condition for the roots to be real is

$$\Delta = [\sigma_e^2 + (1+\alpha^2)\sigma_u^2]^2 - 4(\alpha\sigma_u^2)^2 > 0.$$

To ensure that z_t is invertible, we choose the root such that $|\theta| < 1$. Thus,

$$\theta = \frac{-[\sigma_e^2 + (1+\alpha^2)\sigma_u^2] + \sqrt{\Delta}}{2\alpha\sigma_u^2}.$$

It is easy to show as σ_u^2 gets large, θ approaches $-\alpha$; hence, the roots cancel and y_t becomes uncorrelated. Accordingly, an increase in σ_u^2 imparts a downward bias on the first-order correlation coefficient. Similar arguments generalize to more complex ARMA processes for x_t. Hence, the presence of additive noise makes it more difficult to extract the underlying signal generating x_t, which is often the object of interest. Methods to estimate all the parameters of the model (8.18), accounting for the effect of the noise, are discussed in Chapter 39.

8.5 Causality and time reversibility

Allowing the possibility of solutions to ARMA processes in terms of an infinite sum of *i.i.d.* random variables raises interesting issues about what is meant by the definition of a stationary solution. Consider the AR(1) process

$$x_t = \alpha x_{t-1} + e_t, \tag{8.19}$$

where e_t is *i.i.d.* $(0, \sigma_e^2)$ but now $|\alpha| > 1$. It is easily seen that a solution of the form

$$x_t = \sum_{j=1}^{\infty} \alpha^j e_{t-j} \tag{8.20}$$

is not mean square convergent. Consider, however, rewriting (8.19) as

$$x_{t+1} = \alpha x_t + e_{t+1}, \tag{8.21}$$

and, upon re-arrangement,

$$x_t = \alpha^{-1} x_{t+1} - \alpha^{-1} e_{t+1}.$$

Upon recursive substitution, we obtain a solution of the form

$$x_t = -\sum_{j=1}^{\infty} \alpha^{-j} e_{t+j}, \tag{8.22}$$

which is mean-squared convergent since $|\alpha^{-j}| < 1$ and, hence, is a valid solution. Such a solution, though mathematically valid, is not appealing at least with economic data since it specifies that the current value of the variable at time t depends on *future* innovations. For that reason, we usually restrict the class of possible solutions to be of the form (8.20), i.e., independent of the future. Such solutions are often called *causal.* A causal process is essentially what we have been labeling as a stationary process throughout. Similar considerations hold with more general ARMA(p, q) processes. The only ones without a stationary solution are those with a root exactly on the unit circle (e.g., a unit root). All others have two stationary solutions: one that is causal, i.e., which can be expressed as a function of past innovations, and one that is non-causal and expressed as a solution of future innovations. The latter is of no interest in economic applications (indeed almost all applications); hence, when we refer to a stationary process, it shall be understood that it is causal.

8.6 Short versus long memory

We need to make a distinction between short- and long-memory processes. The reason is that limit results pertaining to stationary processes can be different according to the rate of decay of the weights of the moving-average representation. The relevant technical condition in the Wold representation theorem is that

$$\sum_{i=0}^{\infty} g_i^2 < \infty. \tag{8.23}$$

Now, this requirement encompasses a wide class of processes; for example, processes with weights that decay exponentially or at some polynomial rate. We call short-memory processes stationary processes such that

$$\sum_{i=0}^{\infty} i^2 g_i^2 < \infty \tag{8.24}$$

or

$$\sum_{i=0}^{\infty} i|g_i| < \infty. \tag{8.25}$$

The condition (8.24) is weaker than the condition (8.25), but the latter is often easier to use in deriving results. Hence, we most often use (8.25). In practice, it makes virtually no difference which condition is adopted. Both are much stronger than (8.23). Processes which satisfy (8.25) include all processes with moving-average weights that decay geometrically. This is the case for all stationary and invertible ARMA(p, q) processes. For example, consider the AR(1) process

$$x_t = ax_{t-1} + e_t,$$

with $|a| < 1$. The moving-average representation is given by

$$x_t = \sum_{i=0}^{\infty} g^i e_{t-i}$$

so that $g_i = a^i$. Hence,

$$\sum_{i=0}^{\infty} i|g_i| = \sum_{i=0}^{\infty} ia^i = \frac{a}{(1-a)^2} < \infty.$$

A more common definition of a short-memory process is one for which

$$\sum_{i=0}^{\infty} |\rho(i)| < \infty, \tag{8.26}$$

where $\rho(i)$ is the autocorrelation at delay i. Since for an AR(1), $\rho(i) = |a|^i/(1-a^2)$, condition (8.26) is satisfied. There is, however, a wide class of stationary processes which satisfy (8.23) but not (8.25). A popular class of such models is the fractionally integrated process. An example is the process defined by

$$(1-L)^d x_t = e_t,$$

where $e_t \sim i.i.d.\ (0, \sigma^2)$ and d is a real-valued parameter in the interval $(0, 0.5)$. The weights in the moving-average representation are given by, using the binomial expansion,

$$g_k = \frac{d(d+1)\cdots(d+k-1)}{k!} = \frac{(k+d-1)!}{k!(d-1)!},$$

for $k \geq 1$. It can be shown that for large values of k, the autocorrelation function is approximately

$$\rho(k) \approx ck^{2d-1},$$

for some constant c. Hence, the rate of decay of the autocorrelations is of an hyperbolic rate, much slower than that for a short-memory stationary process which is of a geometric rate, i.e., $\rho(k) \approx ca^k$. Hence,

$$\sum_{i=0}^{\infty} |\rho(i)| \approx c \sum_{i=0}^{\infty} i^{2d-1},$$

which is infinite if $0 < d < 0.5$. Yet, the coefficients g_k satisfy (8.23) so that the process is stationary. Figure 8.4 presents a graph of the weights of the moving average representation for an AR(1) process

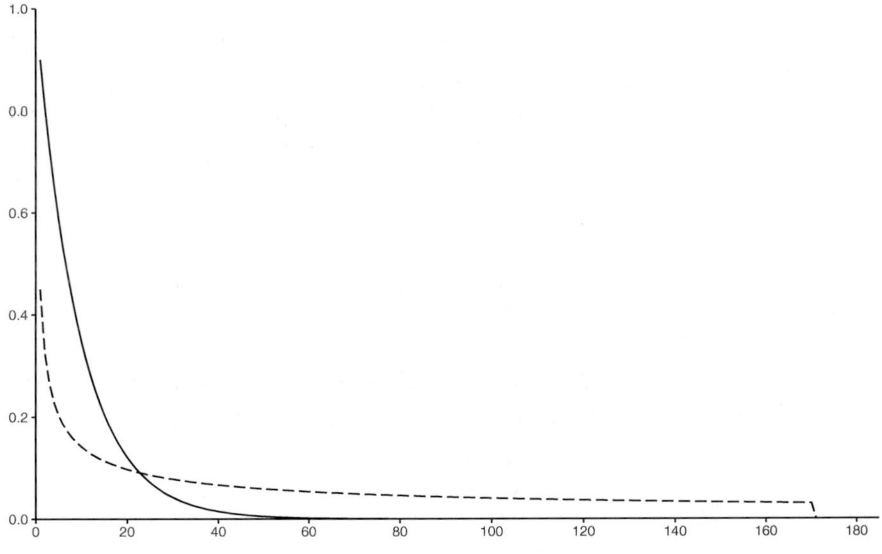

Figure 8.4. Weights of the moving average representation: AR(1) process with $a = 0.9$ (solid line) and fractionally integrated process with parameter $d = 0.45$ (dashed line).

with parameter $a = 0.9$ and for a fractionally integrated process with parameter $d = 0.45$. For the former, the decay to zero is quite rapid but for the latter the weights are non-negligible even at lag 150. Hence, the terminology "long-memory" for the latter.

With short-memory processes, the standard central limit theorems with a normal asymptotic distribution hold. Such is not the case with long-memory processes. Hence, the need to make the distinction.

8.7 Central limit theorem

We assume that x_t is a discrete parameter stationary process with

$$\begin{aligned} E(x_t) &= \mu, \\ \text{Var}\,(x_t) &= \sigma^2, \\ \text{Cov}\,(x_t, x_{t+\tau}) &= R\,(\tau) = \sigma^2 \rho\,(\tau). \end{aligned}$$

From Wold's decomposition theorem, we have that

$$x_t = \mu + C(L)e_t = \mu + \sum_{i=0}^{\infty} c_i e_{t-i}, \tag{8.27}$$

where

$$C(L) = \sum_{i=0}^{\infty} c_i L^i, \tag{8.28}$$

with $c_0 = 1$,

$$\sum_{i=0}^{\infty} c_i^2 < \infty,$$

and $e_t \sim i.i.d.\ (0, \sigma_e^2)$. To derive the limiting distribution, we assume a stronger condition on the moving-average coefficients, namely that

$$\sum_{i=0}^{\infty} i|c_i| < \infty, \tag{8.29}$$

so that it is a short-memory process, a condition satisfied by all stationary ARMA processes. To derive a central limit theorem for the sample mean, we use the fact that x_t has the representation (8.1) with the restriction (8.29). The treatment given here is due to Phillips and Solo (1992). The method of derivation uses what is often referred to as the Beveridge and Nelson (1981) decomposition. It is simply a decomposition of the moving average polynomial $C(L)$ given by

$$C(L) = C(1) - (1 - L)\tilde{C}(L), \tag{8.30}$$

where

$$\tilde{C}(L) = \sum_{i=0}^{\infty} \tilde{c}_i L^i,$$

with

$$\tilde{c}_i = \sum_{k=i+1}^{\infty} c_k.$$

We first state a preliminary result that will be used in subsequent developments.

Lemma 8.2. $\sum_{i=0}^{\infty} i|c_i| < \infty$ *implies* $\sum_{i=0}^{\infty} \tilde{c}_i^2 < \infty$.

Proof. We prove a stronger result, namely that

$$\sum_{i=0}^{\infty} |c_i| < \infty \quad \text{implies} \sum_{i=0}^{\infty} \tilde{c}_i^2 < \infty.$$

We have

$$\left(\sum_{i=0}^{\infty} |\tilde{c}_i|\right)^2 = \sum_{i=0}^{\infty} \tilde{c}_i^2 + 2\sum_{i=0}^{\infty} \sum_{j=i+1}^{\infty} |\tilde{c}_i||\tilde{c}_j|.$$

Since the second term is non-negative, we have

$$\left(\sum_{i=0}^{\infty} |\tilde{c}_i|\right)^2 \geq \sum_{i=0}^{\infty} \tilde{c}_i^2,$$

which implies

$$\sum_{i=0}^{\infty} \tilde{c}_i^2 < \infty \quad \text{if} \sum_{i=0}^{\infty} |c_i| < \infty.$$

The result follows because

$$\sum_{i=0}^{\infty} i|c_i| < \infty \quad \text{implies} \sum_{i=0}^{\infty} |\tilde{c}_i| < \infty$$

since for $i \geq 1$, $i|c_i| \geq |c_i|$.

Using the decomposition (8.30), we can write

$$\begin{aligned} x_t - \mu &= [C(1) - (1 - L)\tilde{C}(L)]e_t \\ &= C(1)e_t - (1 - L)\tilde{e}_t, \end{aligned}$$

where

$$\tilde{e}_t = \tilde{C}(L)e_t = \sum_{i=0}^{\infty} \tilde{c}_i e_{t-i}.$$

Hence,

$$T^{-1/2} \sum_{t=1}^{T} (x_t - \mu) = C(1)T^{-1/2} \sum_{t=1}^{T} e_t - T^{-1/2}(\tilde{e}_T - \tilde{e}_0). \qquad (8.31)$$

Remark 8.8. The conditions of the lemma show the need for the assumption of a short-memory process. Otherwise, the results to be stated below do not hold.

We now consider the second term.

Lemma 8.3. $T^{-1/2}(\tilde{e}_T - \tilde{e}_0) \xrightarrow{p} 0$.

Proof. We only consider the term $T^{-1/2}\tilde{e}_T$; the proof is exactly the same for the other term. We show the stronger result of convergence in mean square. We have

$$\begin{aligned} E(T^{-1/2}\tilde{e}_T)^2 &= T^{-1}E(\tilde{e}_T^2) = T^{-1}E\left(\sum_{i=0}^{\infty}\tilde{c}_i e_{T-i}\right)^2 \\ &= T^{-1}\sum_{i=0}^{\infty}\tilde{c}_i^2 E(e_{T-i}^2) = \sigma_e^2 T^{-1}\sum_{i=0}^{\infty}\tilde{c}_i^2 \\ &\to 0, \end{aligned}$$

since $\sum_{i=0}^{\infty}\tilde{c}_i^2$ is finite. Hence,

$$T^{-1/2}\sum_{t=1}^{T}(x_t - \mu) = C(1)T^{-1/2}\sum_{t=1}^{T}e_t + o_p(1),$$

and, using a CLT for *i.i.d.* random variables, we have

$$T^{-1/2}\sum_{t=1}^{T}(x_t - \mu) = T^{1/2}(\bar{X} - \mu) \xrightarrow{d} N(0, \sigma_e^2 C(1)^2). \tag{8.32}$$

The CLT for the sample average of time series data given by (8.32) is quite different from that obtained using a random sample of *i.i.d.* data. The main difference is the presence of the term $C(1)^2$ in the variance. It is useful to try to understand why the difference occurs and why multiplying σ_e^2 by $C(1)^2$ is the appropriate modification. The sampling variability of an estimate is essentially determined by the effect of a shock e_t. With a random sample, this shock has variance, say, σ_e^2 and affects only individual or unit t. The effect is the same for all and σ_e^2 is the sole measure of the variability in the estimate. However, with time series data, a shock e_t has an impact not only at period t but also, in principle, for all subsequent periods. To see this, consider the moving-average representation of x_t given by (8.27) reproduced here for convenience:

$$x_t = \mu + \sum_{i=0}^{\infty} c_i e_{t-i}.$$

A unit shock $e_t = 1$ at time t has an impact on the variability of the series at time t given by $c_0 = 1$. Next period, e_t becomes e_{t-1} in the representation for x_{t+1} and the effect of the same shock becomes c_1. Again, for two periods ahead, the effect of the shock is c_2, and so on. Hence, the cumulative effect of a unit shock on the total change in the series through time is given by $C(1) = \sum_{i=0}^{\infty} c_i$. This translates into an impact on the total variability of the series through time induced by a single shock with variance σ_e^2 at time t given by $\sigma_e^2 C(1)^2$. For the readers with some advanced knowledge of time series, the quantity $\sigma_e^2 C(1)^2$ is equivalent to (2π) times the spectral density function at frequency 0 of the process x_t.

8.8 Proof of Wold's decomposition theorem

This proof is taken from the work of Priestley (1981). We first define the following notation:

Definition 8.9. Let $\tilde{x}_{t+m}$ be the projection of x_{t+m} on H_t, the space spanned by $\{x_t, x_{t-1}, \dots\}$, *i.e.*,

$$\tilde{x}_{t+m} = E\left[x_{t+m} \mid x_t, x_{t-1}, \dots\right].$$

Note that $\tilde{x}_{t+m}$ is a best predictor in the sense that it minimizes the mean-squared error $E[\{x_{t+m} - \tilde{x}_{t+m}\}^2]$; see the work of Priestley (1981), Section 10.1. We define this quantity as

$$\sigma_m^2 = E[\{x_{t+m} - \tilde{x}_{t+m}\}^2], \quad m = 1, 2, 3, \dots.$$

Note that since x_t is stationary, σ_m^2 does not depend upon t. The process is called "**regular**" or non-deterministic if $\sigma_1^2 > 0$ (which implies $\sigma_m^2 > 0$ for all m). A process is called "**singular**" or deterministic if $\sigma_1^2 = 0$ (which implies $\sigma_m^2 = 0$ for all m).

Define $e_t = x_t - \tilde{x}_t$ with $\tilde{x}_t$ the projection of x_t on H_{t-1}, the space spanned by $\{x_{t-1}, x_{t-2}, \dots\}$. Since

$$E\left[e_t | x_{t-1}, x_{t-2}, \dots\right] = E\left[x_t - \tilde{x}_t | x_{t-1}, x_{t-2}, \dots\right] = 0,$$

we have $e_t \perp H_{t-1}$ (i.e., e_t is orthogonal to the space spanned by H_{t-1}). Similarly, we have $e_t \perp H_s$ for any $s \leq t-1$. Consider any pair $\{e_s, e_t\}$ with $s < t$. We have $e_t \perp H_s \subseteq H_{t-1}$ and $e_s \in H_s$. Hence, $e_t \perp e_s$, i.e., $E\left[e_t e_s\right] = 0$, for all $s \neq t$. Now, let (a) $H_t(e)$ be the subspace spanned by $\{e_t, e_{t-1}, \dots\}$ and (b) v_t be the projection of x_t

on $H_t(e)$. Note that v_t must be a linear combination of $\{e_t, e_{t-1}, \dots\}$. Hence,

$$v_t = \sum_{i=0}^{\infty} g_i e_{t-i}.$$

What are the g_i's?
Since the e_t's are uncorrelated, we have

$$g_i = E\left[v_t e_{t-i}\right] / \sigma_e^2.$$

But

$$v_t = x_t - (x_t - v_t)$$

and

$$E\left[v_t e_{t-i}\right] = E\left[x_t e_{t-i}\right] - E\left[(x_t - v_t) e_{t-i}\right] = E\left[x_t e_{t-i}\right] \qquad (8.33)$$

since $(x_t - v_t)$ is in the space orthogonal to that in which $\{e_{t-i}\}$ lies. Hence, $g_i = E\left[x_t e_{t-i}\right] / \sigma_e^2$, where $\sigma_e^2 = E\left[e_t^2\right]$. It follows that

$$g_0 = E\left[x_t e_t\right] / \sigma_e^2 = E\left[(\tilde{x}_t + e_t) e_t\right] / \sigma_e^2$$

since $E\left[\tilde{x}_t e_t\right] = 0$ given that e_t is orthogonal to $\tilde{x}_t$. Consider now the singular part d_t. Write $d_t = x_t - v_t$. Then, (i) for $s \leq t$, from (8.33),

$$E\left[d_t e_s\right] = E\left[\left(x_t - v_t\right) e_s\right] = E\left[x_t e_s\right] - E\left[v_t e_s\right] = 0$$

and (ii) for $s > t$, $d_t \in H_t$ since it is known at time t and $e_s \perp H_t$ since the future e_t's are independent of past x's. Hence, $e_s \perp H_t$ and $E\left[e_s d_t\right] = 0$ for all s, t. Therefore, $v_s \perp d_t$, for all s, t. Since v_t and d_t are orthogonal,

$$\text{Var}\left(x_t\right) = \text{Var}\left(d_t\right) + \text{Var}\left(v_t\right)$$

and

$$\sigma_e^2 \left(\sum_{i=0}^{\infty} g_i^2 \right) = \text{Var}\left(v_t\right) \leq \text{Var}\left(x_t\right) < \infty,$$

where the last inequality follows because x_t is stationary. What remains to be proved is that d_t is singular. We have

$$d_t \in H_t \equiv H_{t-1} \oplus \{e_t\},$$

where $\{e_t\}$ is the one-dimensional space spanned by e_t. Now, $e_t \perp d_t$ and, hence, $d_t \in H_{t-1}$. Similarly, $H_{t-1} \equiv H_{t-2} \oplus \{e_{t-1}\}$ and $e_{t-1} \perp d_t$. Hence, $d_t \in H_{t-2}$. By iterations, $d_t \in H_{t-s}$ for all $s \geq 0$. Hence,

$$d_t \in H_{-\infty} = \bigcap_{j=-\infty}^{t} H_j,$$

and d_t is determined by the remote past of x_t. We finally have to show that the projection of d_t on H_{t-1}, the space spanned by $\{x_{t-1}, x_{t-2}, \ldots\}$, is the same as the projection of d_t on $H_{t-1}(d)$ the space spanned by $\{d_t, d_{t-1}, \ldots\}$. Write

$$H_{t-1} = H_{t-1}(d) \oplus H_{t-1}(e).$$

Since d_t is orthogonal to e_s for all s, $d_t \in H_{t-1}(d)$ and, hence, $H_t(d) \equiv H_{t-1}(d)$ for all t and $d_t \in H_{t-s}(d)$ for all $s \geq 0$. Hence,

$$d_t \in H_{-\infty}(d) = \bigcap_{j=-\infty}^{t} H_j(d)$$

so that d_t is determined by its own remote past and can be predicted with zero variance.

8.9 Exercises

Exercise 8.1. Prove Properties 2 and 3 of the autocovariance function

Hint: For Property 2, use Cauchy–Schwarz inequality.

Exercise 8.2. Prove Proposition 8.3 (you may assumes the two roots are distinct).

Exercise 8.3. Give an example of a stationary AR(2) process with complex roots.

Exercise 8.4. Verify that the MA(q) process is invertible if and only if all the roots of the lag polynomial $B(L) = 1 + b_1L + \cdots + b_qL^q$ are outside the unit circle.

Exercise 8.5. Derive the autocovariance and autocorrelation functions for the following stochastic processes: (a) $u_t = e_t + \alpha e_{t-1} + \beta e_{t-2}$; (b) $u_t = e_t$; (c) $u_t = \theta u_{t-1} + e_t + \alpha e_{t-1}$, where e_t is *i.i.d.* $(0, \sigma_e^2)$.

Exercise 8.6. Let $X_t = a + bt + Y_t$, where $\{Y_t,\ t = 0, \pm 1, \pm 2, \ldots\}$ is *i.i.d.* $(0, \sigma^2)$ and a, b are constants. Define $W_t = (2q+1)^{-1} \sum_{j=-q}^{q} X_{t-j}$. Compute the mean and autocovariance function of $\{W_t\}$. Note that although $\{W_t\}$ is not stationary, its autocovariance function $R(t+h, t) = \mathrm{Cov}(W_{t+h}, W_t)$ does not depend upon t. Discuss your results in relation to the smoothing of a time series.

Exercise 8.7. If $X_t = a + bt$ $(t = 1, \ldots, T)$, show that the sample autocorrelations have the property $\hat{\rho}(k) \to 1$ as $T \to \infty$ for each fixed k.

Exercise 8.8. Suppose that $X_t = \sum_{j=0}^{\infty} \psi_j e_{t-j}$; $e_t \sim$ *i.i.d.* $(0, \sigma^2)$, where $\sum_{j=0}^{\infty} |\psi_j| < \infty$. Show that $\sum_{h=-\infty}^{\infty} |R(h)| < \infty$, where $R(h)$ is the autocovariance function of $\{X_t\}$.

Exercise 8.9. Let $\{X_t\}$ be an ARMA(1, 1) process given by $X_t - \phi X_{t-1} = e_t + \theta e_{t-1}$, $e_t \sim$ *i.i.d.* $(0, \sigma^2)$, where $|\phi| < 1$ and $|\theta| < 1$. Determine the coefficients of the Wold representation of $\{X_t\}$. Show that the autocorrelation function of $\{X_t\}$ is given by

$$\rho(1) = \frac{(1 + \phi\theta)(\phi + \theta)}{(1 + \theta^2 + 2\phi\theta)},$$

$$\rho(h) = \phi^{h-1}\rho(1) \quad h \geq 1.$$

Exercise 8.10. Suppose you have a time series described by the following ARMA process:

$$y_t = 1.2y_{t-1} - 0.2y_{t-2} + u_t - 0.6u_{t-1}.$$

What is the long run effect of a unit shock in u_t on the level of y_t?

Exercise 8.11. Show that if u_t is MA(1) and w_t is white noise,

$$y_t = u_t + w_t$$

is MA(1) and calculate the corresponding parameters.

Hint: A stationary stochastic process can be completely characterized by its autocovariance function.

Exercise 8.12. Derive a bound for the autocorrelation at lag 1 of an invertible MA(1) process.

Exercise 8.13. Consider the MA(2) process given by $x_t = b_2e_{t-2} + b_1e_{t-1} + e_t$, $e_t \sim i.i.d.\ (0, \sigma_e^2)$. (a) Find a finite order mixed ARMA process that is observationally equivalent. (b) Find a non-invertible moving average process that is observationally equivalent.

Exercise 8.14. Consider the following MA(2) process

$$x_t = (1 + 2.4L + 0.8L^2)e_t,$$

where $E(e_te_s) = 1$ if $t = s$ and 0 otherwise. (a) Is this process stationary? If so, calculate its autocovariance function. (b) Show that it is not invertible and find the invertible representation for the process. Calculate the autocovariances of the invertible representation and verify that they are the same as those obtained in part (a).

Exercise 8.15. Consider the following ARMA(2, 2) model:

$$x_t = 1.3x_{t-1} - 0.4x_{t-2} + \epsilon_t - 1.2\epsilon_{t-1} + 0.2\epsilon_{t-2}, \quad \epsilon_t \sim \text{i.i.d } (0, 1).$$

(a) Is x_t weakly stationary? If so, compute the autocovariance function. (b) Is x_t a causal ARMA process? Is it invertible? (c) If x_t is causal, find the infinite order MA representation. (d) Using your favorite programming language, generate the previous process, and compute the sample autocorrelations and the sample partial autocorrelations.

Exercise 8.16. Many economists who work with asset market data use time-averaged data. This is unavoidable in working with consumption data. In order to evaluate the effects of time averaging, consider the following: (a) Suppose that the variable X_t evolves according to a random walk. That is, $X_t = X_{t-1} + u_t$, where u_t is *i.i.d.* Consider the sequence Z_t, where $Z_t = X_{2t-1} + X_{2t}$. That is, $Z_1 = X_1 + X_2$, $Z_2 = X_3 + X_4$, etc. Will Z_t be a random walk? Calculate the correlation coefficient of $(Z_t - Z_{t-1})$ and $(Z_{t-1} - Z_{t-2})$. (b) Many series are thought to evolve as continuous time random walks. To examine the effects of time averaging in this case, let X_t follow a random walk. Let $Z_t = X_{nt-n+1} + X_{nt-n+2} + \cdots + X_{nt}$. Calculate

$$\lim_{n\to\infty} \frac{E(Z_t - Z_{t-1})(Z_{t-1} - Z_{t-2})}{E(Z_t - Z_{t-1})^2}.$$

Exercise 8.17. Suppose y_t is an AR(1) process: $y_t = \rho y_{t-1} + e_t$, where $y_0 = 0$ and $e_t \sim i.i.d.\ N(0, \sigma^2)$ for $t = 1, \ldots, T$. Define $y_t^* = y_t - y_{t-1}$. Derive

$$plim_{T\to\infty} \frac{\sum_{t=2}^{T} y_{t-1}^* y_t^*}{\sum_{t=2}^{T} y_{t-1}^{*2}},$$

for the following two cases: $\rho = 1$ and $|\rho| < 1$.

Exercise 8.18. Assume that ε_t is $i.i.d.$ with $E\left(\varepsilon_t^4\right) < \infty$, $E\left(\varepsilon_t\right) = 0$, and $E\left(\varepsilon_t^2\right) = 1$. Let ϕ_1 and ϕ_2 be such that $\phi(L) = 1 - \phi_1 L - \phi_2 L^2$ has all its roots outside the unit circle. Assume that x_t is the stationary solution to

$$\phi(L) x_t = \varepsilon_t.$$

(a) You are given a sample $x_1, \ldots, x_T$ of observations. Find the best linear predictor in the mean square sense of x_{T+1} and x_{T+2}. (b) Calculate the MSE of your forecast conditional on $x_1, \ldots, x_T$, i.e., calculate $E((x_{T+h} - \hat{x}_{T+h})^2 | x_T, x_{T-1}, \ldots)$, where $\hat{x}_{T+h}$ is the h-step ahead forecast. (c) Find the unconditional MSE of the forecast.

Exercise 8.19 (Computer). Download the daily data for SP 500 stock returns starting from 1925 to the latest available. This can be done using the CRSP dataset via the WRDS interface: https://wrds-www.wharton.upenn.edu/. Plot the autocorrelation function of stock returns. Does it suggest a short or long memory process? Consider the absolute value of returns as a proxy for the variance. Plot the autocorrelation function of absolute return. Does it suggest a short or long memory process?

Chapter 21

Unit Roots and Cointegration

We now consider important topics that apply to time-series data, namely unit root process, cointegration, and spurious regression. Here, we only provide the main arguments with as little complications as possible. A more complete treatment of the various issues (and more) is given in Chapters 44–46. Useful surveys are Campbell and Perron (1991), Stock (1994), Watson (1994), Haldrup and Jansson (2006), Johansen (2006), and Perron (2006). We start with an example due to Hendry (1980). He investigated the relation between money (M3), M_t, and prices (CPI), P_t, using quarterly U.K. data from 1964(II) to 1975(II). A simple structural regression (with standard error in parentheses) gives

$$\begin{aligned} P_t &= \underset{(0.003)}{-0.02} + \underset{(0.016)}{0.73}\, M_t + \hat{u}_t, \\ R^2 &= 0.984 \quad \text{S.E.} = 1.7 \quad \text{DW} = 0.3. \end{aligned} \tag{21.1}$$

The fit is excellent and the coefficient on M_t is highly significant, but the Durbin–Watson (DW) statistic is small indicating the presence of serial correlation in the errors; S.E. = 1.7 is the standard error of the regression, which is of no importance here. So, he considers a dynamic equation introducing a lagged value of P_t and M_t:

$$\begin{aligned} P_t &= \underset{(0.003)}{0.02} + \underset{(0.057)}{0.995} P_{t-1} - \underset{(0.097)}{0.00}\, M_t + \underset{(0.094)}{0.02}\, M_{t-1} + \hat{e}_t, \\ R^2 &= 0.999 \quad \text{S.E.} = 0.5 \quad \text{DW} = 1.6. \end{aligned}$$

The R^2 is even higher, but M_t is now insignificant and a prediction test rejects the constancy of the parameters of the equation. It seems that we can make money matter or not by choosing an appropriate specification. He then entertained the idea that a given variable C_t causes prices. The structural equation is

$$P_t = \underset{(0.55)}{10.9} - \underset{(0.23)}{3.2C_t} + \underset{(0.02)}{0.39\,C_t^2} + \hat{u}_t,$$

$$R^2 = 0.982 \quad S = 3.6 \quad \text{DW} = 0.1. \tag{21.2}$$

Again, the R^2 is high and C is significant, but the DW is very small indicating very strongly correlated errors. He then tries a dynamic specification with a Cochrane–Orcutt procedure, which corrects for first-order serial correlation (see Section 13.2.2):

$$P_t = \underset{(3.6)}{21.1} - \underset{(1.4)}{7.2\,C_t} + \underset{(0.13)}{0.78\,C_t^2} + \hat{e}_t + \underset{(0.02)}{0.94}\,\hat{e}_{t-1},$$

$$R^2 = 0.998 \quad \text{S.E.} = 1.2.$$

The fit is good and the parameters are highly significant. There is no autocorrelation left in the residuals and the equation passes a number of tests for misspecification. Hence, one should conclude that the money supply has no impact on aggregate prices but that whatever C_t is does. The problem is that C_t is cumulative rainfall in the U.K. What is going on? The second example is certainly one of *spurious* regression. These examples are some of the problems we encounter when dealing with processes or variables that contain a unit root (or a random walk) component.

The issues we need to deal with are as follows: (1) How can we decide whether a regression is spurious or not? (2) Certainly, money affects prices in the long run, but how can we establish that? Is regression (21.1) reliable?

Remark 21.1. This example points to the importance of residual analysis by tests, such as that of DW, when checking for misspecification.

21.1 Unit roots

The choice of the cumulative rainfall variable was not made at random. There is a clear reason behind this choice. Let

r_j $(j = 1, \ldots, T)$ be the amount of rain at date j. Then, $C_t = \sum_{j=1}^{t} r_j$ for $t = 1, \ldots, T$, or

$$C_t = C_{t-1} + r_t \tag{21.3}$$

for $t = 2, \ldots, T$. If $r_t = r^* + e_t$ with $e_t \sim i.i.d.$ with mean 0 and finite variance, say, as might be the case in the U.K., then cumulative rainfall (21.3) is an example of a random walk with drift process, i.e.,

$$C_t = C_0 + r^*t + \sum_{j=1}^{t} e_j,$$

with $\sum_{j=1}^{t} e_j$ being a random walk. A similar feature holds for log prices P_t, which is the accumulation of past inflation rates, i.e., $P_t = \sum_{j=1}^{t} \pi_j$, with π_j the inflation rate at time j. Let $\pi_t = \pi + v_t$. In general, v_t will be serially correlated. In this case, P_t is said to be a unit root process with drift given by

$$P_t = P_0 + \pi t + \sum_{j=1}^{t} v_j.$$

Here, $\sum_{j=1}^{t} v_j$ is a unit root process, though not necessarily a random walk since v_t can be serially correlated.

In what follows, we start our discussion ignoring a drift or trend. We come back later to the more general case. Recall the first-order autoregressive model

$$y_t = \alpha y_{t-1} + e_t, \quad e_t \sim i.i.d.\ (0, \sigma^2). \tag{21.4}$$

We call such a process with $\alpha = 1$ a random walk. We then have

$$\Delta y_t = y_t - y_{t-1} = e_t.$$

The first difference of the process is $i.i.d.$ $(0, \sigma^2)$. The following are some implications:

(1) Each shock e_t has a long-term effect on the *level* of y_t.

To see this, write (21.4) (by recursive substitution) and with $\alpha = 1$ as

$$y_t = y_0 + \sum_{j=1}^{t} e_j. \tag{21.5}$$

Since each shock has a permanent effect on future levels of y_t, a 1% unexpected increase in y_t *today* should increase our predicted value of future y_t's by 1% for all future periods. In this simple example, with $e_t \sim i.i.d.\ (0, \sigma^2)$, the best predictor of y_t tomorrow is the actual value of y_t today, i.e.,

$$E[y_{t+1}|\Phi_t] = E[y_t|\Phi_t] + E[e_{t+1}|\Phi_t] = y_t, \tag{21.6}$$

where Φ_t is all information known at time t. Such processes are often called "martingales". The relation (21.6) holds because $y_t \in \Phi_t$ and $E[e_{t+1}|\Phi_t] = 0$ since $e_t \sim i.i.d.\ (0, \sigma^2)$ and, hence, unpredictable. The most important implication of the unit root is the permanent effects of shocks. This is what causes all the trouble in estimation and inference.

The root of the terminology "random walk" is loosely related to the pattern of a very drunk person, who can take a step backward, then two steps forward, and so on in a random fashion. Hence, the best predictor of the drunk's position in the future is simply its current position. The term random walk was first introduced by Pearson (1905), although it was used before by Louis Bachelier in his Ph.D. dissertation titled "The Theory of Speculation" (Bachelier, 1900) to describe efficient financial markets.

(2) The variance of y_t increases with t. From (21.5), assuming y_0 is fixed for simplicity,

$$\mathrm{Var}(y_t) = \mathrm{Var}\left(\sum_{j=1}^{t} e_j\right) = t\sigma^2.$$

Hence, this is a non-stationary process because its second moment depends upon t.

(3) The Mann–Wald theorem breaks down. Consider estimating α by OLS in the regression

$$y_t = \alpha y_{t-1} + e_t.$$

We saw that if $|\alpha| < 1$, the asymptotic normality still holds. However, things are different if $\alpha = 1$; we no longer have asymptotic normality. This is the case because the requirement

$$T^{-1} \sum_{t=1}^{T} y_{t-1}^2 \xrightarrow{p} Q$$

with Q a fixed positive definite matrix, does not hold. Instead, we have

$$T^{-2}\sum_{t=1}^{T} y_{t-1}^2 \xrightarrow{d} G$$

with G some random variable (as opposed to a constant). Note that the scaling factor is T^{-2} instead of T^{-1}. But what is important is the fact that G is now random. This is what complicates inference.

Example 21.1. Let

$$\hat{\alpha} = \sum_{t=1}^{T} y_t y_{t-1} / \sum_{t=1}^{T} y_{t-1}^2$$

be the OLS of α. It can be shown that

$$T(\hat{\alpha} - 1) \xrightarrow{d} \frac{(1/2)(W(1)^2 - 1)}{\int_0^1 W(t)^2 dt},$$

where $W(t)$ is called a Wiener process such that $W(t) \sim N(0, t)$. This is explained in detail in Chapter 44. For now, the details are not important. What is to be noted is that we have a non-normal asymptotic distribution and the rate of convergence of $\hat{\alpha}$ to its true value is fast, T instead of the usual $\sqrt{T}$.

21.2 Differenced versus trend-stationary models

The random walk model is quite restrictive. Think about the log of the aggregate price level in the above example. It is then the cumulative sum of the inflation rate, which is often correlated. Most of the time, we want to allow for additional short-run correlation in the series; i.e., a process such as

$$\Delta y_t = v_t, \tag{21.7}$$

where v_t is a stationary process exhibiting some correlation (but not having a unit root itself). Note that (21.7) implies that

$$y_t = y_0 + \sum_{j=1}^{t} v_j.$$

We can specify v_t as a stationary and invertible ARMA model of the form

$$A(L)v_t = B(L)e_t, \quad e_t \sim i.i.d.\ (0, \sigma^2).$$

Since v_t is a stationary and invertible process, it can be represented as an MA(∞), i.e.,

$$v_t = A(L)^{-1}B(L)e_t \equiv \psi(L)e_t \equiv \left(\sum_{i=0}^{\infty} \psi_i L^i\right) e_t.$$

Then, y_t is stationary when considering its first differences so that the model is often called "differenced-stationary". As discussed in Chapter 8, the long-run effect of a unit shock e_t on the level of y_t is given by the sum of the MA coefficients, i.e., $\sum_{i=0}^{\infty} \psi_i = \psi(1)$. Many macroeconomic time series have a tendency to increase over time. In such cases, we need to include a deterministic trend component called a drift, e.g.,

$$\Delta y_t = \mu + v_t, \quad A(L)v_t = B(L)e_t. \tag{21.8}$$

Then,

$$y_t = y_0 + \mu t + \sum_{j=1}^{t} v_j. \tag{21.9}$$

The trend function of y_t is then composed of two parts: (i) a deterministic part given by the drift term and (ii) a stochastic part that is a function of the permanent effect of each shock e_t on the level of y_t; see below for more details. Since shocks have a permanent effect, they change our long-term forecast of the level of the series which is a plausible definition of the trend of a series. So, in this case, the trend function shifts every period and is, hence, stochastic. For this reason, such models are called stochastic trend models (also called difference stationary models); see, e.g., Stock and Watson (1988).

The trend function can be obtained using the so-called Beveridge–Nelson decomposition; see Beveridge and Nelson (1981). Consider the moving-average representation of Δy_t given by

$$\Delta y_t = \mu + \psi(L)e_t.$$

Now, decompose $\psi(L)$ as

$$\psi(L) = \psi(1) + (1 - L)\psi^*(L),$$

where

$$\psi^*(L) = -\sum_{i=1}^{\infty} \psi_i^* L^i$$

with

$$\psi_i^* = \sum_{j=i+1}^{\infty} \psi_j.$$

Then, we can write

$$\Delta y_j = \mu + [\psi(1) + (1 - L)\psi^*(L)]e_j,$$

or

$$y_t = y_0 + \mu t + \psi(1)\sum_{j=1}^{t} e_j + w_t, \tag{21.10}$$

where $w_t = \psi^*(L)e_t$ is a stationary random variable. Now, a plausible definition of a trend function is the long-term conditional forecast. That is, $E(y_{t+k}|y_s; s \leq t)$ for k large. Using (21.10) and the fact that $E[e_{t+j}|\Phi_t] = 0$, where Φ_t is the information set at time t, $E\left(\sum_{j=t+1}^{t+k} e_j|\Phi_t\right) = 0$, and we have

$$E(y_{t+k}|\Phi_t) = y_0 + \mu(t + k) + \psi(1)\sum_{j=1}^{t} e_j + E(w_{t+k}|\Phi_t).$$

Since w_t is short-memory stationary and, hence, any event separated by a long time span will be independent, then

$$\lim_{k\to\infty} E(w_{t+k}|\Phi_t) = 0.$$

Therefore, we can view the component

$$y_0 + \mu t + \psi(1) \sum_{j=1}^{t} e_j \tag{21.11}$$

as the trend with

$$y_0 + \mu t,$$

the deterministic component, and

$$\psi(1) \sum_{j=1}^{t} e_j,$$

a scaled random walk, the stochastic component. Note that since the stochastic component has variance given by $\sigma_e^2 \psi(1)^2 t$, which increases without bound as t increases, the deterministic part $y_0 + \mu t$ does not act as an attractor, i.e., something to which the series tends to revert to. Indeed, a unit root process has no attractor. Note also that given the trend specification given by (21.11), the trend is changing every period. See Figure 21.1.

An alternative in modeling stochastic variables that increase over time is to make the trend function purely deterministic, i.e.,

$$\begin{aligned} y_t &= c + \beta t + w_t, \\ C(L) w_t &= D(L) e_t \end{aligned} \tag{21.12}$$

with again $e_t \sim i.i.d.\ (0, \sigma^2)$ assuming that the roots of both $C(L)$ and $D(L)$ are outside the unit circle. This is called the Trend Stationary (TS) model because the deviations from the trend function are transitory, i.e., the shocks e_t have no permanent long-run effects. In fact, here the trend $c + \beta t$ acts as an attractor to which the series tend to revert to; see Figure 21.2 for typical DS and TS processes obtained via simulations.

An important issue is how to make a distinction between (21.8) and (21.12). This is the issue of unit root testing.

Remark 21.2. Trend-stationary processes are often referred to as $I(0)$ processes, while those with a unit root as $I(1)$. This is because for unit root or DS processes, the stochastic term is the summation

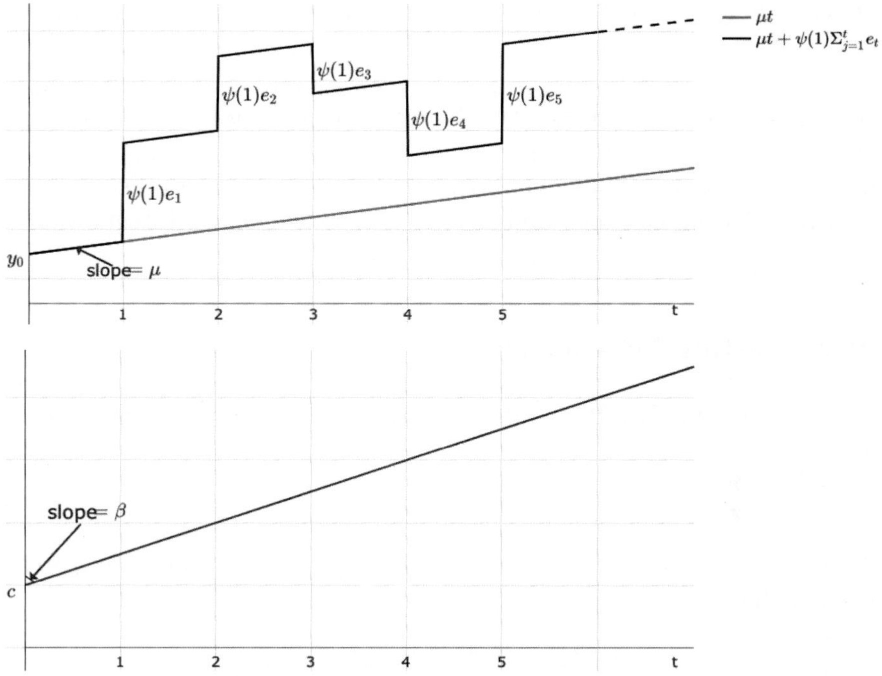

Figure 21.1. Stochastic versus deterministic trend.

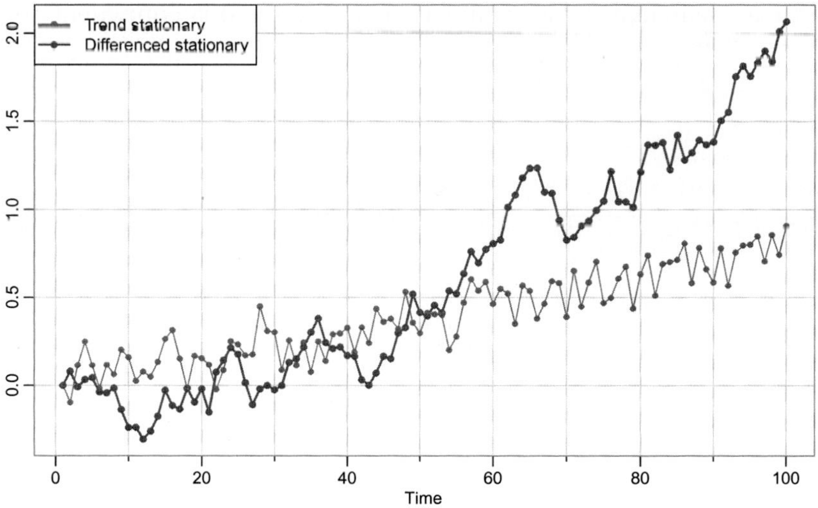

Figure 21.2. Differenced versus trend-stationary processes.

of past shocks as in (21.9). Hence, the global stochastic component is the one-time integration of the past errors. So, we label them as integrated of order 1. For TS process, the global error term is simply the current shock as in (21.12), hence no integration is involved and we label them as $I(0)$. It is possible to have processes that are $I(d)$ for $d > 1$, but we do not cover them in this chapter. As discussed in Section 8.6, one can also define $I(d)$ processes for non-integer values of d.

21.3 Testing for a unit root

Consider a general AR(p) model (without deterministic components for now):

$$A(L)y_t = e_t.$$

If there is a single unit root in y_t, the autoregressive polynomial $A(L)$ is such that

$$(1 - L)A^*(L) = A(L),$$

where $A^*(L)$ is polynomial of order $p - 1$ with all roots outside the unit circle. Hence, $A(1) = 0$. This implies that the sum of the autoregressive coefficients must equal 1 since $A(L) = 0$ is equivalent to

$$(1 - a_1 - \cdots - a_p) = 0,$$

or

$$1 - \sum_{j=1}^{p} a_j = 0,$$

or

$$\sum_{j=1}^{p} a_j = 1.$$

Let

$$\alpha = \sum_{j=1}^{p} a_j,$$

and $d_i = -\sum_{j=i}^{p} a_j$. The alternative of interest is most often that the process is stationary (possibly around a deterministic trend function), in which case

$$\alpha = \sum_{j=1}^{p} a_j < 1,$$

think about the case with $p = 1$. Then, y_t can be written as (try to show it as an exercise)

$$y_t = \alpha y_{t-1} + \sum_{j=2}^{p} d_j \Delta y_{t-j+1} + e_t,$$

and we want to test H_0: $\alpha = 1$ versus H_1: $\alpha < 1$. In a more general model with a trend component, we consider the regression (called Dickey–Fuller procedure)

$$y_t = \mu + \beta t + \alpha y_{t-1} + \sum_{j=2}^{p} d_j \Delta y_{t-j+1} + e_t. \tag{21.13}$$

Equation (21.13) is estimated by OLS and the t-statistic on $\hat{\alpha}$ is used to test for a unit root ($H_0 : \alpha = 1$). Note that one can also use the regression

$$\Delta y_t = \mu + \beta t + \theta y_{t-1} + \sum_{j=2}^{p} d_j \Delta y_{t-j+1} + e_t,$$

where $\theta = \alpha - 1$. Hence, testing for $\alpha = 1$ is equivalent to testing for $\theta = 0$, whose t-statistic is printed by all software packages. This is the so-called (Augmented) Dickey–Fuller (ADF) test for a unit root; see Dickey and Fuller (1979).

Remark 21.3. If y_t is an ARMA(p, q) process, we approximate it by a long AR(k); say

$$y_t = \mu + \beta t + \alpha y_{t-1} + \sum_{j=1}^{k_T} d_j \Delta y_{t-j} + e_{kt},$$

where e_{kt} is approximately *i.i.d.* and becomes so as k increases. If k_T increases at a suitable rate with T (the sample size), the test will have the same asymptotic distribution under the null hypothesis; see Said and Dickey (1984), Ng and Perron (1995), and Chang and Park (2002). The technical requirements are that

$$k_T \to \infty,$$
$$k_T^2/T \to 0,$$

as $T \to \infty$. To select the lag order one can use some information criterion or some general to specific testing procedure; see Ng and Perron (1995) and Ng and Perron (2001). The most popular methods are discussed in the following and a more comprehensive treatment is contained in Chapter 45.

The asymptotic distribution of the t-statistic is not $N(0, 1)$. Also, it depends on the nature of the deterministic components included. Tabulated critical values are given in Fuller (1996). They are reproduced in Table 21.1 at the end of Section 21.3.3. For example, with a linear trend, the 5% left-tail critical value is -3.41; quite different from the usual -1.645 from the normal distribution. Indeed, the distribution is very skewed with a long tail on the left of $\alpha = 1$ and basically no mass above $\alpha > 1$.

It is of interest to try to understand why the distribution is very skewed to the left with basically no mass above 1. For concreteness, consider the case with a fitted linear time trend. Hence, the DGP is $y_t = c + \delta t + v_t$ and $v_t = \alpha v_{t-1} + e_t$. The regression is

$$y_t = \mu + \beta t + \alpha y_{t-1} + e_t. \tag{21.14}$$

We set $c = \delta = 0$ without loss of generality since the t-statistic obtained from applying OLS to (21.14) is invariant to the value of the trend component in the DGP. It is, however, not invariant to the initial condition v_0, unless $\alpha = 1$. We set $v_0 = 1$ and $T = 100$. The probability density function of the t-statistic for testing $\alpha = 1$ is plotted in Figure 21.3 under the null hypothesis, while Figure 21.4 presents a plot of the probability density function of the normalized bias $T(\hat{\alpha} - 1)$. Figure 21.5 plots the a typical realization of three processes: (a) $\alpha = 1$, (b) $\alpha = 0.95$, and (c) $\alpha = 1.05$. A look at the graphs shows that it is very easy to distinguish a process with $\alpha > 1$ from one with $\alpha \leq 1$. The distribution of the t-statistic under the null hypothesis tells us something about the likelihood of having a true

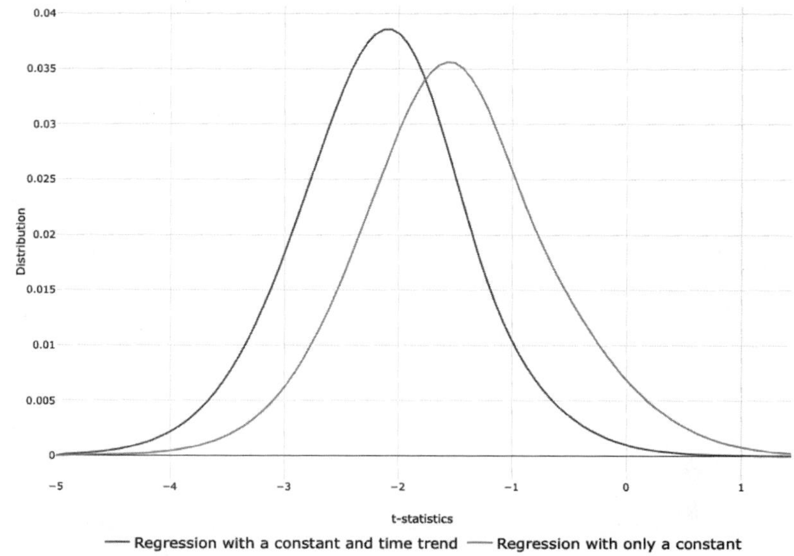

Figure 21.3. The pdf of the t-statistic for testing $\alpha = 1$.

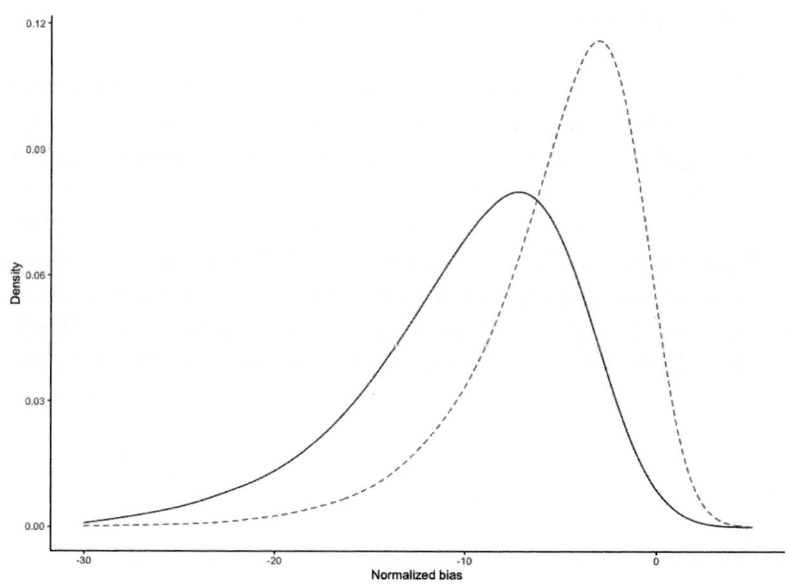

Figure 21.4. Probability density function of $T(\hat{\alpha} - 1)$ when the DGP is a random walk. The dashed line is for the case with only a constant in the regression, while the solid line is for the case with both a constant and a time trend.

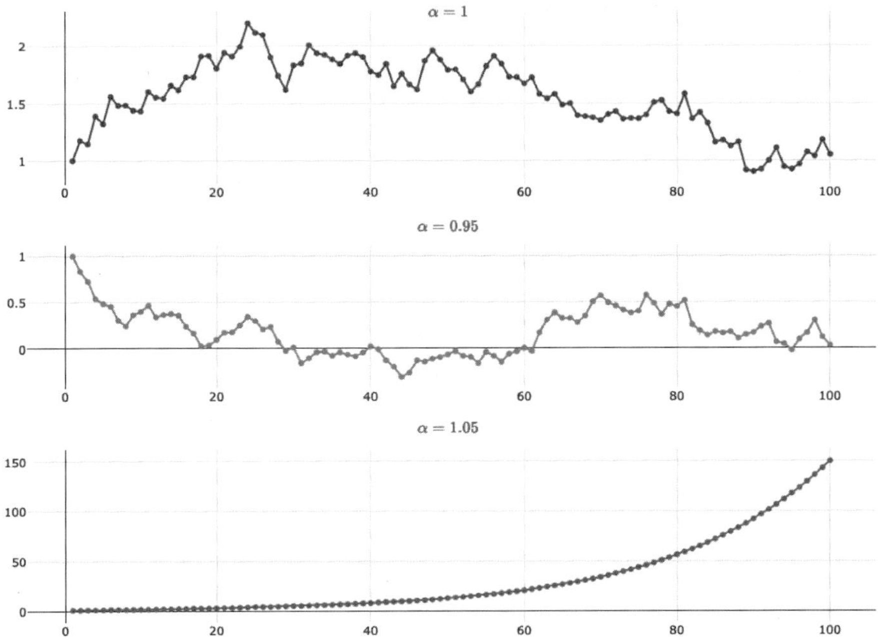

Figure 21.5. Realizations of three AR(1) processes: $\alpha = 1$; $\alpha = 0.95$; $\alpha = 1.05$.

process with various values of α when $\alpha = 1$. Since a process with $\alpha > 1$ is so different from one with $\alpha = 1$, the likelihood of observing a process with $\alpha > 1$ when $\alpha = 1$ is very small. Hence, there is no (or little) mass above one. So, where does the mass of the distribution function go? There is no other choice than to go to the left. Indeed, processes with $\alpha = 1$ and $\alpha = 0.95$ are quite similar, i.e., more difficult to distinguish. Hence, the very left skewed distribution. This is especially evident when looking at the normalized bias $T(\hat{\alpha} - 1)$ whose pdf is generated from a random walk and depicted in Figure 21.4 for the cases with a constant only and a constant and a time trend.

For a more detailed analysis, see Evans and Savin (1981b, 1984), Nankervis and Savin (1985), and Andrews (1993a).

Remark 21.4. If there is no trend component (no drift), we can use a regression without a trend term; the critical values are different and may yield more powerful procedures. But it is good to start with a trend in the regression; see the discussion in Perron (1988); for a similar treatment that is more recent, see Harvey *et al.* (2009b).

21.3.1 Near-observational issue

Given the large critical values, the test may have quite low power against the TS alternative with an autoregressive component showing substantial persistence, e.g., $y_t = \alpha y_{t-1} + e_t$; α above 0.85 or so. This has been shown to be the case. Even as T increases, you can always make α even closer to 1 so that any test will have no power. So, we can't really distinguish a DS process from one that has a root near 1. For instance, you may have an AR(1) process of the form $y_t = 0.99y_{t-1} + e_t$ with $e_t \sim i.i.d.\ (0, \sigma_e^2)$. Strictly, then y_t is $I(0)$. It is, however, so close to an $I(1)$ process given by the random walk $y_t = y_{t-1} + e_t$ that we may for all practical purposes label it as an $I(1)$ process. The same near-observational equivalence holds when considering an $MA(1)$ in first differences, say

$$y_t = y_{t-1} + e_t + \theta e_{t-1}.$$

If $-1 < \theta < 1$, the process is $I(1)$. If $\theta = -1$, it is $I(0)$. But for values of θ very close to -1, say -0.99, the process, while strictly $I(1)$, is nearly observationally equivalent to an $I(0)$ process, in this case a simple $i.i.d.$ process $y_t = e_t$. Here, the $I(1)$ process is nearly observationally equivalent to an $I(0) i.i.d.$ process.

Hence, since we usually do not restrict the range of the parameters (here α and θ), strictly speaking, it is impossible to know the truth. If your aim is to obtain the truth, simply forget it. This belongs to a class of testing problems that are usually referred to as ill-posed or ill-defined; see Pötscher (2002) or Dufour (1997). References directly dealing with the unit root versus stationarity issue include Cochrane (1991), Blough (1992), Pantula (1991), and DeJong *et al.* (1992). But it is still useful to perform unit root test as the outcome will often be a useful guide for subsequent steps to take; e.g., forecasting, which asymptotic distribution provides a better approximation, should we consider cointegrated systems and the associated methods of inference, etc. See Campbell and Perron (1991).

21.3.2 Other "old-generation" procedures

The other class of "old-generation" tests that are popular are those of Phillips and Perron (1988) (see also Phillips, 1987). They are fully non-parametric in the sense that they are not based on any autoregressive approximation. They start with the following regression estimated by OLS:

$$y_t = \hat{\alpha} y_{t-1} + \hat{\beta} z_t + \hat{u}_t, \tag{21.15}$$

where z_t is a vector of deterministic components; e.g., a constant or a constant and a time trend. Two tests were proposed given by

$$Z_\alpha = T(\hat{\alpha} - 1) - \frac{\hat{\sigma}^2 - \hat{\sigma}_u^2}{2T^{-2}\sum_{t=1}^{T}(y_{t-1}^*)^2}$$

and

$$Z_t = \left(\frac{\hat{\sigma}_u}{\hat{\sigma}}\right) t_{\hat{\alpha}} - \frac{\hat{\sigma}^2 - \hat{\sigma}_u^2}{2\hat{\sigma}(T^{-2}\sum_{t=1}^{T}(y_{t-1}^*)^2)^{1/2}},$$

where $\hat{\sigma}_u^2 = T^{-1}\sum_{t=1}^{T}\hat{u}_t^2$, with $\hat{u}_t$ the residual from (21.15) estimated by OLS; y_{t-1}^* are the residuals from a regression of y_{t-1} on z_t. Also, $\hat{\sigma}^2$ is an estimate of the long-run variance of u_t, given by

$$\hat{\sigma}^2 = T^{-1}\sum_{t=1}^{T}\hat{u}_t^2 + T^{-1}\sum_{j=1}^{T-1}\lambda(j,m)\sum_{t=j+1}^{T}\hat{u}_t\hat{u}_{t-j}$$

for some weight function $\lambda(j,m)$ and bandwidth m, though other estimators are possible. See Chapter 11 for the basics or Chapter 38 for a more detailed and extensive treatment. Under $H_0 : \alpha = 1$, the limit distribution of Z_t is the same as that of the ADF, while the limit distribution of the test Z_α is different. See Table 21.1 for the critical values. Dickey and Fuller (1981) also proposed joint tests, for instance, testing the null $H_0 : \beta = 0$, $\alpha = 1$ in (21.14) since when $\alpha = 1$, we should have $\beta = 0$ when only a linear trend is present. Perron (1990b) proposed joint tests similar to those of Dickey and Fuller (1981).

21.3.3 "New-generation" procedures

Two important papers produced a new generation of unit root tests that have better size and power: Elliott *et al.* (1996) and Ng and Perron (2001). The details are presented in Chapter 45.

Elliott *et al.* (1996) showed that much improved power can be obtained using so-called GLS-detrended data. Let $\bar{\alpha} = 1 + \bar{c}/T$ and define

$$y_t^{\bar{\alpha}} = y_t - \bar{\alpha} y_{t-1},$$
$$z_t^{\bar{\alpha}} = z_t - \bar{\alpha} z_{t-1}$$

for $t = 2, \ldots, T$ and $y_1^{\bar{\alpha}} = y_1$, $z_1^{\bar{\alpha}} = z_1$. These are usually called quasi-differenced data. The estimate $\hat{\gamma}^{\text{GLS}}$ is the GLS estimate of γ from the model

$$y_t = \gamma z_t + v_t$$

assuming that v_t is an AR(1) with parameter $\bar{\alpha}$; see Section 13.2. They recommend $\bar{c} = -7.0$ when $z_t = 1$ and $\bar{c} = -13.5$ when $z_t = (1, t)$. They proposed a feasible point optimal test P_T (see Section 45.7). But the more commonly used proposed test is the ADF^{GLS}. Denote the GLS detrended data by

$$\tilde{y}_t = y_t - \hat{\gamma}^{\text{GLS}} z_t.$$

Consider the ADF test constructed with GLS detrended data, labeled ADF^{GLS}, i.e., the t-statistic for testing that $\alpha = 1$ in the OLS regression

$$\tilde{y}_t = \alpha \tilde{y}_{t-1} + \sum_{i=1}^{k} b_i \Delta \tilde{y}_{t-i} + e_{tk}. \tag{21.16}$$

Elliott *et al.* (1996) found that it has an asymptotic power function very close to the Gaussian local asymptotic power envelop. They also found the ADF^{GLS} and P_T tests to have local asymptotic power quite superior to the standard ADF, Z_t and MZ$_t$ (which share a common local asymptotic power function). The issue that remains to have good exact size in finite samples is to use a good method to select the truncation lag order k. We return to this in the following, after describing the class of M tests proposed by Ng and Perron (2001). More details are in Sections 45.8 and 45.9. Ng and Perron (2001) proposed the following test with GLS-detrended data:

$$\text{MZ}_\alpha^{\text{GLS}} = \frac{T^{-1}\tilde{y}_T^2 - s_{\text{AR}}^2}{2T^{-2}\sum_{t=1}^{T}\tilde{y}_{t-1}^2},$$

where

$$s_{\mathrm{AR}}^2 = \frac{\hat{\sigma}_{ek}^2}{\left(1 - \sum_{i=1}^k \hat{b}_i\right)^2},$$

with

$$\hat{\sigma}_{ek}^2 = T^{-1} \sum_{t=k+1}^{T} \hat{e}_{tk}^2,$$

and $\hat{b}_i$ and $\hat{e}_{tk}$ obtained from the following OLS regression:

$$\Delta\hat{y}_t = \hat{b}_0 \hat{y}_{t-1} + \sum_{i=1}^{k} \hat{b}_i \Delta\hat{y}_{t-i} + \hat{e}_{tk}. \tag{21.17}$$

Note that this last equation is simply the ADF regression. They also considered the following alternative tests:

$$\mathrm{MSB}^{\mathrm{GLS}} = \left(T^{-2} \sum_{t=1}^{T} \tilde{y}_{t-1}^2 / s_{\mathrm{AR}}^2\right)^{1/2}$$

and

$$\mathrm{MZ}_t^{\mathrm{GLS}} = \mathrm{MSB}^{\mathrm{GLS}} * \mathrm{MZ}_\alpha^{\mathrm{GLS}}.$$

These tests are collectively referred to as the M^{GLS} tests. The asymptotic critical values of the tests are presented in Table 21.1. Ng and Perron (2001) also considered a modified point-optimal test. It is given by

$$\mathrm{MP}_T^{\mathrm{GLS}} = \left[\bar{c}T^{-2} \sum_{t=1}^{T} \tilde{y}_{t-1}^2 - \bar{c}T^{-1} \tilde{y}_T^2\right] \Big/ \, s_{\mathrm{AR}}^2$$

if only a constant is included as deterministic regressor, while if a constant and a time trend are included, it is given by

$$\mathrm{MP}_T^{\mathrm{GLS}} = \left[\bar{c}T^{-2} \sum_{t=1}^{T} \tilde{y}_{t-1}^2 - (1 - \bar{c})T^{-1} \tilde{y}_T^2\right] \Big/ \, s_{\mathrm{AR}}^2.$$

The main issue for a good performance of the ADF^{GLS} and the class of M tests is a good choice of k in either regression (21.16) or (21.17), which are the same. Ng and Perron (2001) proposed a modified information criterion given by

$$\mathrm{MIC}(k) = \ln(\hat{\sigma}_{ek}^2) + C_T(\tau_T(k) + k)/(T - k_{\max}),$$

where

$$\tau_T(k) = (\hat{\sigma}_{ek}^2)^{-1}\hat{b}_0^2 \sum_{t=k_{\max}+1}^{T} \tilde{y}_{t-1}^2$$

and

$$\hat{\sigma}_{ek}^2 = (T - k_{\max})^{-1} \sum_{t=k_{\max}+1}^{T} \hat{e}_{tk}^2.$$

The minimization is taken over the range $k \in [0, k_{\max}]$. This is a modification of the usual information criteria, such as AIC and BIC; see Section 36.4. We have the MAIC when $C_T = 2$ and the MBIC when $C_T = \ln(T)$. Ng and Perron (2001) recommend using the MAIC. They show that the "new-generation" tests then have good size and power in finite samples. Perron and Qu (2007) suggested an important modification to have tests with good power "globally" (i.e., not only good local asymptotic power). The $\mathrm{ADF}^{\mathrm{GLS}}$ test and s_{AR}^2 are still constructed using GLS detrended data as specified above, but the selection of the autoregressive order k uses the MAIC constructed with OLS detrended data, i.e., replacing $\tilde{y}_t$ by $\hat{y}_t$, the residuals from a regression of y_t on z_t and using the autoregression

$$\Delta\hat{y}_t = \check{b}_0\hat{y}_{t-1} + \sum_{i=1}^{k} \check{b}_i\Delta\hat{y}_{t-i} + \check{e}_{tk}. \qquad (21.18)$$

One can also use a regression in levels with the deterministic components added as regressors, i.e.,

$$\Delta y_t = c + \delta t + \hat{b}_0 y_{t-1} + \sum_{i=1}^{k} \hat{b}_i\Delta y_{t-i} + \hat{e}_{tk}.$$

The results are virtually the same by the Frish–Waugh–Lowell Theorem 2.1.3. So the modification involves a two step procedure. First,

Table 21.1. Left-tailed critical values of the unit root tests.

	Constant only			Constant + time trend		
	10%	5%	1%	10%	5%	1%
ADF, Z_t	−2.57	−2.86	−3.43	−3.12	−3.41	−3.96
Z_α	−11.3	−14.1	−20.7	−18.3	−21.8	−29.5
ADF^{GLS}, MZ_t^{GLS}	−1.62	−1.98	−2.58	−2.62	−2.91	−3.42
$\text{MZ}_\alpha^{\text{GLS}}$	−5.7	−8.1	−13.8	−14.2	−17.3	−23.8
MSB^{GLS}	0.275	0.233	0.174	0.185	0.168	0.143

Source: Reprinted with permission from Dickey and Fuller (1979) and Ng and Perron (2001).

use (21.18) to construct

$$\text{MAIC}(k) = \ln(\breve{\sigma}_k^2) + 2(\tau_T(k) + k)/(T - k_{\max})$$

with

$$\tau_T(k) = (\breve{\sigma}_k^2)^{-1}\breve{b}_0^2 \sum_{t=k_{\max}+1}^{T} \hat{y}_{t-1}^2$$

and

$$\breve{\sigma}_k^2 = (T - k_{\max})^{-1} \sum_{t=k_{\max}+1}^{T} \breve{e}_{tk}^2.$$

Once the order is selected as the minimizer of $\text{MAIC}(k)$, say k_{MAIC}, estimate (21.16) or (21.17) with k_{MAIC} lags to construct s_{AR}^2 or the ADF^{GLS} test. See Section 45.11 for more details.

Table 21.1 presents the critical values of the unit root tests discussed so far, obtained from the references cited.

21.4 Span versus frequency of observations

It is important to note that the power of unit root tests (any of them) depends much more on the total span of the observations, say N, rather than the number of observations T. The longer the span, the higher the power. This was first highlighted in Shiller and Perron (1985) with more details in Perron (1989c) and a theoretical analysis in Perron (1991c).

The idea is fairly intuitive. The alternative of stationarity implies reversions of the process toward some attractor (e.g., a constant or a linear trend). The more such reversions available in a given sample, the higher the evidence in favor of stationarity, hence the higher the power of the tests. Such reversions occur over a given time span. The larger the span of the data, the more reversions occur. The number of observations available is basically irrelevant. Since $N = Th$ where h is the sampling interval, this means that having a sample of data with a long span but fewer observations is preferable to having a shorter span with many more observations sampled at a higher frequency. For instance, indices of real economic activity (e.g., industrial production) are available at an annual frequency since 1860 (e.g., Nelson and Plosser, 1982) so that, roughly, $T = 160$ (in 2020). One could alternatively use quarterly data for the post World War II period (1945–2020, say) so that $T = 300$, or monthly data stating in 1960, say, so that $T = 720$. It turns out that unit root tests have much higher power with yearly data and lowest with monthly data (in the cases described) even though the number of observations is much smaller.

If the span of the data N is fixed, more observations (sampled at higher frequency) are only marginally better and the power does not converge to one even if the sample size T increases to infinity; see Perron (1991c). This is one case of interesting features that can occur with time series data. Here, the message is as follows: don't necessarily go for a larger sample. A long span of data is preferable, which brings another problem, namely the fact that some important events may have occurred that altered the shape of the trend; e.g., the Great Crash of 1929 (change in level), World War II (change in level and slope for some European countries), and the oil price shock of 1973, which was the onset of a much discussed productivity slowdown (change in slope). The effect of such events are discussed in the following section.

21.5 Unit roots and trend breaks

A seminal study is Nelson and Plosser (1982). They applied the Dickey–Fuller procedure to a wide variety of time series and they could not reject the unit root. Other studies have found the same result, e.g., Campbell and Mankiw (1987), Perron (1988), among many others. It was the current wisdom that most aggregate economic time series are characterized by the presence of a unit root (usually with drift).

In an important paper, Perron (1989b) challenged this view. His argument was that the deterministic part of the trend function of many macroeconomic time series, e.g., real GDP, has changed in 1929 and 1973. In 1929, it was a change in the intercept (the crash) and in 1973, a change in the slope of the trend function (the productivity slowdown). The presence of infrequent shifts in the trend function biases the unit root tests toward a non-rejection of the null hypothesis of a unit root even if it is false. If allowance is made for the presence of such shifts, the unit root is rejected for most series.

As discussed in Section 21.2, a popular trend-cycle decomposition is that suggested by Beveridge and Nelson (1981). The trend is specified as the long-run forecast of the series conditional on current information, which results in the following trend:

$$\tau_t = \mu + \beta t + \psi(1)\sum_{j=1}^{t} e_j$$

while the cycle is given by

$$c_t = \tilde{\psi}(L)e_t$$

with

$$\tilde{\psi}(L) = \sum_{j=0}^{\infty} \tilde{\psi}_j L^j,$$

where $\tilde{\psi}_j = \sum_{i=j+1}^{\infty} \psi_i$. Here, the trend has two components: a deterministic one (a linear trend given by $\mu+\beta t$) and a stochastic one specified by a random walk weighted by $\psi(1)$. Hence, the trend exhibits changes every period in the form of level shifts. Note that if one considered a process which is potentially integrated of order 2, the trend would exhibit changes in both level and slope every period. When the process has no unit root, $\psi(1) = 0$ and the trend is a linear deterministic function of time.

Within this framework, one can view the unit root versus trend-stationary problem as addressing the following question: do the data support the view that the trend is changing every period or never? The empirical analysis of Nelson and Plosser (1982) provided strong evidence that, if the comparison is restricted to these polar cases, the data support the view that a trend which 'always' changes is a better description than a trend that 'never' changes (using a variety of US macroeconomic variables, furthermore many other studies have reached similar conclusions for other series and other countries).

The question is then as follows: why restrict the comparison to 'never' or 'always'? Would it not be preferable to make a comparison between 'always' and 'sometimes'? Ideally, then, the proper question to ask would be as follows: 'what is the frequency of permanent shocks?'. This is a question for which no satisfactory framework has been provided and, as such, it still remains a very important item for further research.

The basic motivation for the work initiated by Perron (1989b, 1990a) is to take a stand on what is 'sometimes'. The specific number chosen then becomes case-specific. His argument was that in many cases of interest, especially with historical macroeconomic time series including those analyzed by Nelson and Plosser (1982), the relevant number of changes is relatively small, in many cases only one. These changes are then associated with important historical events: the Great Crash (US and Canada, 1929, change in level), the oil price shock (G7 countries, 1973, change in slope), World War II (European countries, change in level and slope), World War I (United Kingdom, 1917, change in level), and so on. As far as statistical modeling is concerned, the main conceptual issue is to view such changes as possibly stochastic but of a different nature than shocks that occur every period, i.e., drawn from a different distribution. However, the argument that such large changes are infrequent makes it difficult to specify and estimate a probability distribution for them. The approach is then to model these infrequent large changes in the trend as structural changes. The question asked by unit root tests is then as follows: 'do the data favor a view that the trend is 'always' changing or is changing at most occasionally?' or 'if allowance is made for the possibility of some few large permanent changes in the trend function, is a unit root present in the structure of the stochastic component?' Note that two important qualifications need to be made. First, the setup allows but does not impose such large changes. Second, by "permanent" what should be understood is not that it will last forever but that, given a sample of data, the change is still in effect. For instance, the decrease in the slope of the trend function after 1973 for US real GDP is still in effect, though the recession of 2007–2008 seems to have induced a further decrease in the trend (see Perron and Wada, 2009; Perron *et al.*, 2020). The results of Perron (1989b) were extended to non-trending data in Perron (1990a).

An important result in Perron (1989b, 1990a) is that if there is a change in slope, standard tests (i.e., these which do not allow such changes) will have zero asymptotic power even if the null hypothesis of stationarity is true. If the changes are of the "level shifts" type, the power will be substantially decreased in finite samples and go to zero as the magnitudes of the shifts increase. Perron (1994b) shows that this bias is more pronounced as the order of the autoregression k increases. This can explain the widespread non-rejection when using standard tests as done in, e.g., Nelson and Plosser (1982) and many others. See Section 50.2 for more details.

Perron (1989b, 1990a) proposed various tests assuming a known break date, which has been extended by several authors; see Section 50.3. The methodology adopted by Perron (1989b, 1990a) was criticized by, among others, Christiano (1992), on the ground that using a framework whereby the break is treated as fixed is inappropriate. The argument is that the choice of the break date is inevitably linked to the historical record and, hence, involves an element of data mining. He showed that if one did a systematic search for a break when the series is actually a unit root process without break, using fixed break critical value would entail a test with substantial size distortions. While the argument is correct, it is difficult to quantify the extent of the 'data-mining' problem in Perron (1989b) study. Indeed, no systematic search was done, the break dates were selected as obvious candidates (the Crash of 1929 and the productivity slowdown after 1973), and the same break date was used for all series. Given the intractability of correctly assessing the right p-values for the tests reported, the ensuing literature addressed the problem by adopting a completely agnostic approach where a complete and systematic search was done. While this leads to tests with the correct asymptotic size (under some conditions to be discussed), it obviously implies a reduction in power.

Tests for a unit root with unknown break dates in trends are discussed more extensively in Section 50.4. One test that has become very popular is the Zivot and Andrews (1992) test. It takes the minimum value of the ADF-type unit root tests allowing for a break over all possible break dates, imposing a trimming at the end-points (the need for a trimming was relaxed in Perron, 1997a). There is, however, a fundamental problem with this test. It allows the break to occur only under the alternative hypothesis. It cannot occur under the null hypothesis. Hence, there is an asymmetric treatment of the specification of the trend under the null and alternative hypotheses. In particular, the stated limit result is not valid if a break is present under the null hypothesis. Vogelsang and Perron (1998) show that, in this case, the test diverges to $-\infty$ when a shift in slope is present. This implies that a rejection can be due to the presence of a unit root process with a breaking trend. So, irrespective of how popular these tests have become, they should not be applied.

It took a while to devise tests that are valid with breaks in trends under both the null and alternative hypotheses. These were proposed by Kim and Perron (2009b) for the single break case and extended to the multiple break case by Carrion-i Silvestre *et al.* (2009). These and other tests are discussed in Section 50.4.

21.6 Spurious regression and cointegration

The concept of cointegration was laid out in Engle and Granger (1987) following work by Granger (1986). Here, we only provide the basic ideas and some main results. A more complete and detailed treatment is contained in Chapter 46. Denote by $I(1)$ a variable that is integrated of order one, i.e., which has a unit root, and by $I(0)$ a variable which is (trend) stationary.

Definition 21.1. Let x_t and y_t be $I(1)$. Then, x_t and y_t are said to be *cointegrated* if there exists a scalar b (say) such that

$$x_t - by_t \sim I(0),$$

i.e., if there exists a linear combination that eliminates the unit root non-stationary component.

$I(1)$ series have a stochastic trend component which defines the long-term behavior of the series. If two series are correlated with each other in the *long run*, then their stochastic trend component must be in some proportion to each other so that some linear combinations should annihilate them. Hence, even though each series when viewed in isolation has no attractor, a pair may be attracted to each other in the long run. So, cointegrated series are related in the long run but may have short-term (temporary) divergences. This short-term behavior is modeled by the following "error-correction" model.

The error-correction representation follows from the so-called Granger representation theorem. If $x_t,\ y_t \sim I(1)$ and are cointegrated, then there exists a generating mechanism of the form

$$\Delta x_t = \mu_1 + \rho_1 z_{t-1} + \text{ lags of } (\Delta x_t,\ \Delta y_t) + e_{1t},$$
$$\Delta y_t = \mu_2 + \rho_2 z_{t-1} + \text{ lags of } (\Delta x_t,\ \Delta y_t) + e_{2t}, \qquad (21.19)$$

where

$$z_t = x_t - by_t \sim I(0).$$

These are sets of dynamic equations. In a sense, since x_t and y_t are related in the long run, z_t measures the extent to which the system (x_t, y_t) is out of equilibrium; it is often called the "equilibrium error". The coefficients ρ_1 and ρ_2 are non-zero (jointly) when there is cointegration. They dictate how fast the system reverts back to the long-run target equilibrium level. For example, suppose x_t is consumption and y_t is income. If $z_t > 0$, then we currently consume to much in relation to the long-run target level. Hence, we need to either (a) reduce consumption or (b) increase income by working more. Accordingly, we expect $\rho_1 < 0$ and $\rho_2 > 0$, for the system to be stable in the long-run.

The Error Correction Model (ECM) representation is also useful since it predicts that if two variables are cointegrated, then they must be forecastable, at least to some extent. To see the implications, consider the prices of two assets (say two stocks traded on the same market). Can they be cointegrated? If they were, then according to the ECM representation, we could forecast them. If you believe in some form of market efficiency, this should not be the case. Hence, they should not be cointegrated. Consider now the prices of the same asset but traded on two different exchanges, say Tokyo and New York. Should they be cointegrated? Yes, otherwise there would be obvious arbitrage opportunities. Not only that but the coefficients ρ_1 and ρ_2 will be very large to reflect very rapid adjustments so that the prices are back in line when the second market opens. So, cointegration, along with the ECM, is a rich and useful framework. For an early review, see Hendry (1986). For early influential treatments, see Davidson *et al.* (1978), Salmon (1982), Hendry and Richard (1982), and Hendry *et al.* (1984).

21.6.1 Estimation of cointegrated systems

The simplest procedure to estimate cointegrated models is as follows:

1. Run a preliminary cointegrating regression

$$x_t = c + by_t + e_t$$

   by OLS. Under the null of cointegration, $\hat{b}$ converges to b at rate T; i.e., it is super-consistent; $T(\hat{b} - b) = O_p(1)$ (see Stock, 1987).
2. Construct $z_t = x_t - \hat{c} - \hat{b}y_t = \hat{e}_t$ and substitute it in (21.19).
3. Estimate (21.19) by OLS.

This two-step procedure gives consistent estimates given the "super-consistency" rate of $\hat{b}$, the estimate of the cointegrating parameter. While this OLS estimate is consistent, its limit distribution depends on nuisance parameters due to (a) the endogeneity issue (the correlation between the errors and the regressors) and (b) serial correlation in the errors (of in the "disequilibrium error").

Note that with integrated or unit root regressors, things are very different from the cases studied before; e.g., weakly stationary short-memory processes. Then correlation between the errors and regressors caused outright inconsistent estimates; see Chapter 10. Here, there is no such inconsistency and, furthermore, the estimates are consistent at an even faster rate (T instead of $T^{1/2}$). The endogeneity effect is, however, still present, though only in affecting the limit distribution, which is non-normal.

There has been a plethora of proposals to have single-equation estimates of the cointegrating vector. We cannot review them all in this book. We only state our favorite method. It is simple and works relatively well in finite samples. It is usually called the "Dynamic OLS" regression and is due to Saikkonen (1991) (see also Stock and Watson, 1993). It gets rid of the endogeneity problem by adding leads and lags (and current value) of the first differences of the regressors.

Hence, in the simple bivariate setting considered here, the regression takes the form

$$y_t = c + ax_t + \sum_{j=-m_1}^{m_2} d_j \Delta x_{t-j} + \eta_t. \tag{21.20}$$

In practice, more lags are added than leads. Methods to select the number of leads and lags are discussed in Kejriwal and Perron (2008a) who recommend the use of Information Criteria such as the AIC or BIC; see Section 36.4. It still remains that the errors in regression (21.20) are, in general, serially correlated. Hence, we need to construct standard errors that are robust to autocorrelation (and heteroskedasticity) in the errors. But this has already been covered; see Section 11.6. Note that the method extends trivially to the case with an arbitrary number of variables in x_t (assuming that y_t is part of the cointegrating relation). We simply need to interpret it as a vector. The resulting limit distributing of the t-test on a (or one of its component if a vector) is standard normal. Similarly, the F-test for general test on a have a limiting chi-square distribution.

In the context of a multivariate model, the single-equation method described above may not be the most efficient, though it may be more robust. Under correct specification of the multivariate model, a system approach to estimation has been suggested by Johansen (1988, 1991). While it is very popular, a detailed treatment is postponed to Chapter 46, given that it requires some knowledge of Vector Autoregressive (VAR) models, covered in Chapter 41.

21.6.2 Spurious regression

If x_t and y_t are not cointegrated, then there exist no linear combination of x_t and y_t such that

$$x_t - by_t \sim I(0).$$

Instead, for any linear combination of x_t and y_t, we have

$$x_t - dy_t \sim I(1).$$

So, if we run a regression by OLS of the form

$$x_t = \hat{c} + \hat{d}y_t + \hat{e}_t, \tag{21.21}$$

the residuals will be $I(1)$ and hence have a unit root. This shows up as a very low Durbin–Watson statistic. Recall the example with P and C (cumulative rainfall) given earlier. When x_t and y_t are not cointegrated and we run a regression of the form (21.21), this leads to the so-called spurious regression problem; see Granger and Newbold (1974). For example, suppose that x_t and y_t are independent random walks. Then, from regression (21.21), we would have, as $T \to \infty$ (see Phillips, 1986): (1) DW $\xrightarrow{p} 0$; R^2 converges to some random variable with support close to 1; $t_{\hat{d}} \xrightarrow{p} \infty$. Therefore, the fit and the significance of the regressors seem good, but it is all spurious.

To go back to the example at the beginning of this chapter, the implications are follows. For the Money and Prices example, regression (21.1) is a valid long-term relation. There is substantial correlation in the errors (here labeled as the equilibrium error) but not enough to rule out a cointegrating relation. On the other hand, when considering Cumulative rainfall and Prices, regression (21.2) is a spurious one. The DW statistic was close enough to zero to indicate integrated errors.

21.6.3 Testing for cointegration

The basic idea is to test whether the residuals in (21.21) have a unit root or not. Preliminary evidence can be obtained from the DW statistic, but this is not a formal test. It depends on nuisance parameters, the correlation structure of the variables, etc. One procedure is to apply the ADF unit root test discussed earlier to the estimated least-squares residuals $\hat{e}_t$ from the regression (21.21). This is fine and is called a residuals-based test for cointegration. But the asymptotic distribution is not the same as in testing for a unit root on some original series. The critical values depend on (a) the number of regressors included, (b) whether a constant or a constant and a time trend are included as regressors, and (c) whether the true data-generating process contains a deterministic trend (Hansen, 1992a). The limit distributions of this and other residuals-based tests were derived by Phillips and Ouliaris (1990). Note that here the null hypothesis is no-cointegration, while the alternative hypothesis is the presence of cointegration. One could think of deriving the test with the highest local asymptotic power function as was done when testing for a unit root. It turns out that, at least to this day, this is an unsolved problem because the parameters of the cointegrating vector are not identified under the null hypothesis of no-cointegration. Nevertheless, it may be useful to consider unit root tests that have optimal properties in the unit root case and apply them to the residuals of the cointegrating regression. This was done by Perron and Rodríguez (2016) who showed that important power gains can be obtained over applying standard "old-generation" unit root tests as in Phillips and Ouliaris (1990). See Section 46.2.2 for details.

Again, a plethora of tests have been proposed. It is not the scope of this book to review them. We simply discuss the most relevant ones. Of course, testing can also be done within a full system of equations as done in Johansen (1991); see also Johansen and Juselius (1990). This is covered in Chapter 46.

21.6.4 ARDL regressions

For the more general case, consider a set of n variables $z_t = (y_t, x_t)$ with x_t a $n-1$ vector. We have the following more general definition.

Definition 21.2 (Cointegration). A vector of variables z_t is said to be cointegrated if there exists at least one n-element vector β_i such that $\beta_i' z_t$ is trend-stationary, with β_i labeled as a cointegrating vector. If there exist r such linearly independent vectors β_i $(i = 1, \ldots, r)$, we say that y_t is cointegrated with cointegrating rank r. The $n \times r$ matrix $\beta = (\beta_1, \ldots, \beta_r)$ is called the matrix of cointegrating vectors or the cointegrating matrix. The r elements of the vector $\beta' y_t$ are trend-stationary.

If the data are trending so that

$$y_t = \kappa + \delta t + v_t,$$

where $v_t = (v_1, \ldots, v_n)'$ is an n vector of variables that are either $I(1)$ or $I(0)$, $\kappa = (\kappa_1, \ldots, \kappa_n)'$ and $\delta = (\delta_1, \ldots, \delta_n)'$. Then we usually also require that

$$\beta' \delta = 0$$

so that the same cointegrating vectors eliminate both sources of non-stationarity due to the potential $I(1)$ stochastic components and the deterministic trends. See Chapter 46. Note, however, that this is not necessary. There are cases for which the cointegrating vectors only eliminates the stochastic non-stationarity.

If all elements of z_t are $I(0)$, the system is trivially cointegrated with n cointegrating vectors, those that simply pick each variable individually. Then, the methods covered previously apply. If all elements are $I(1)$ and $r = 0$, there is no cointegrated vector and one simply carry estimation and inference using the first difference of the variables. Things are more complex when $0 < r < n$ which implies the presence of at least two $I(1)$ variables. Then, one needs to use methods developed for cointegrated systems; see Chapter 46.

Often, the outcome of unit root tests may be ambiguous, or one may want a method robust without prior knowledge about the $I(0)$ and $I(1)$ nature of the variables and what the cointegrating rank is. Pesaran *et al.* (2001) provide such a method in a context that resemble the popular AutoRegressive Distributed Lags (ARDL) model, i.e., a model involving lags of both the dependent variables and the regressors. The aim is to assess whether there is a level relationship from x_t to y_t, assuming no level relationship from y_t to x_t, i.e., no feedback. This amounts to having the vector x_t being weakly exogenous for y_t and we say that x_t are the long-run forcing for y_t.

They show that standard Wald tests of interest, in some restricted error correction model, have distributions that are bounded above by the case with all variables x_t being $I(1)$ and bounded below by the case with all variables x_t being $I(0)$. The cointegrating rank of x_t can be arbitrary. So, if the outcome of the Wald test is below the lower bounds, the conclusion is a non-rejection of the null hypothesis. If it is above the upper bound, we conclude in favor of a rejection. If the outcome is between the bounds, then the procedure is inconclusive and one needs to carry a proper cointegration analysis to obtain reliable inference.

The nature of the model is the following. We consider a conditional error correction model, conditional on $\{y_{t-1}, x_{t-1}, \Delta x_t, \Delta x_{t-1}, \ldots, \Delta y_{t-1}, \Delta y_{t-2}, \ldots\}$ and the no feedback assumption (see Section 46.1.3 for details). Assuming trending regressors, it is given by the following, labeled Case 5 (following the notation in Pesaran *et al.*, 2001):

$$\Delta y_t = a + bt + \delta y_{t-1} + \gamma x_{t-1} + \sum_{i=1}^{k} \phi_i' \Delta z_{t-i} + \omega \Delta x_t + u_t, \quad (21.22)$$

where $z_t = (y_t, x_t)$. Note that this can be interpreted as an ARDL model since the regressors involve the current values of x_t and lagged values of both x_t and y_t. The number of lags can be different for Δy_t and Δx_t. Note also that the conditional ECM or ARDL allows for short-run feedbacks from the lagged values of Δy_t.

Under the assumption that $\delta \neq 0$, then there exists a conditional level relationship of the form

$$y_t = c + gt + \theta x_t + v_t,$$

where c, g, and θ are functions of the original parameters of the model. If $\delta = 0$ and $\gamma' = 0$, there exists no such level relationship and y_t is $I(1)$ irrespective of the nature of x_t. These can be verified from (21.22) since then none of the right-hand side variables can be $I(1)$ (and therefore cointegrated with y_t) so that Δy_t is $I(0)$ which implies that y_t is $I(1)$. Hence, a test for a level relationship from x_t to y_t would be a Wald test for testing

$$H_0 : \delta = \gamma' = 0 \tag{21.23}$$

versus the alternative that both are non-zero. One could also do a simple test that $\delta = 0$, which also implies no level relationship. However, if $\delta \neq 0$ and $\gamma' = 0$, we have a degenerate case in the sense that y_t is $I(0)$ and depends only on its own lags. On the other hand, if $\delta = 0$ and $\gamma' \neq 0$, then y_t is $I(1)$. Since, in general, we wish not to assume anything about the nature of the integration of all the variables, it makes sense to test the joint null hypothesis (21.23).

There are other cases of interest depending on the assumptions about the trend components. As such with the coefficient b unrestricted in (21.22), the model can imply a quadratic trend for y_t (since y_t is the partial sums of the variables on the right-hand side). A more efficient procedure would imposes restrictions that forbids this case. This lead to the constrained model, labeled Case 4:

$$\Delta y_t = a + \delta(y_{t-1} - \beta^* t) + \gamma' x_{t-1} + \sum_{i=1}^{k} \phi_i' \Delta z_{t-i} + \omega \Delta x_t + u_t.$$

This can be estimated using the regression (21.22) imposing the constraint that $b = \delta\beta^*$. If the data are non-trending, including only a constant is sufficient. Again one can consider the unconstrained case, labeled Case 3:

$$\Delta y_t = a + \delta y_{t-1} + \gamma' x_{t-1} + \sum_{i=1}^{k} \phi_i' \Delta z_{t-i} + \omega \Delta x_t + u_t. \qquad (21.24)$$

This can imply a trend in y_t, so again the following restricted case might be useful, labeled Case 2:

$$\Delta y_t = \delta(y_{t-1} - a^*) + \gamma' x_{t-1} + \sum_{i=1}^{k} \phi_i' \Delta z_{t-i} + \omega \Delta x_t + u_t.$$

This can be estimated using regression (21.24) using the restriction $a = \delta a^*$. Finally, in some less common cases, the data may have mean zero. Then no deterministic components are included so that the estimated model, labeled Case 1, is given by

$$\Delta y_t = \delta y_{t-1} + \gamma' x_{t-1} + \sum_{i=1}^{k} \phi_i' \Delta z_{t-i} + \omega \Delta x_t + u_t.$$

Pesaran *et al.* (2001) provide critical values at various significance levels and for up to 10 regressors in the vector x_t for Cases 1–5. As stated above, these consist of upper and lower bounds.

21.7 Exercises

Exercise 21.1. The following model was estimated for y_t, here 100 times the log of quarterly U.S. real GNP (t =1952:II to 1984:IV):

$$\begin{aligned}\Delta y_t &= 0.555 + 0.312\Delta y_{t-1} + 0.122\Delta y_{t-2} - 0.116\Delta y_{t-3} \\ &\quad - 0.081\Delta y_{t-4} + u_t. \qquad (21.25)\end{aligned}$$

(a) What is the permanent (long-run) effect of a unit change in u_t on the level of real GNP? (b) Assume the log of private consumption c_t is cointegrated with y_t so that

$$c_t - \alpha y_t \sim I(0). \qquad (21.26)$$

Is the information provided by (21.25) and (21.26) sufficient to determine the permanent effect of a one-unit change in u_t on c_t? If yes, give the answer; if no, explain why.

Exercise 21.2. Consider the following time series model:

$$x_t = \beta_0 + \beta_1 t + \varepsilon_t, \varepsilon_t \sim i.i.d.\ (0, \sigma^2).$$

(a) Use least squares to detrend x_t. What is the autocovariance function for the cyclical component? (b) Use first differences to detrend x_t. What is the autocovariance function for the cyclical component? (c) Use first differences to detrend x_t assuming that $\varepsilon_t = \rho\varepsilon_{t-1} + u_t$. What is the autocovariance function for the cyclical component? Now assume that the true model is given by a random walk with drift:

$$x_t = \mu + x_{t-1} + \varepsilon_t.$$

(d) Use first differences to detrend x_t. What is the autocovariance function of the cyclical component? (e) Use a fitted linear trend by least squares to detrend x_t. What is the autocovariance function of the cyclical component? (f) Simulate the results obtained for $T = 100$ and $\sigma^2 = 1$, and plot the autocorrelation function for the two models considered using the two detrending methods. Comment on the results.

Exercise 21.3 (Review). Suppose that the first difference of some variable y_t is generated by the following stationary and invertible ARMA(p, q) process:

$$A(L)(\Delta y_t - \mu) = B(L)e_t,$$

where

$$A(L) = 1 - a_1 L - \cdots - a_p L^p,$$
$$B(L) = 1 + b_1 L + \cdots + b_q L^q$$

and $e_t \sim i.i.d.\ (0, \sigma^2)$. (a) What are the restrictions on the polynomials $A(L)$ and $B(L)$? (b) What is the trend function of the series y_t? (Be sure to define your concept of trend.) (c) What is the effect of a unit shock on the level of y_t in the long run?

Exercise 21.4 (Computer). The data generating process is given by

$$y_t = \alpha_0 y_{t-1} + e_t,$$

where $e_t \sim i.i.d.\ N(0,1)$. Consider first estimating by OLS an autoregression without a constant or time trend, i.e.,

$$y_t = \alpha y_{t-1} + e_t. \tag{21.27}$$

Let $\hat{\alpha}$ be the OLS estimate and t_{α_0} the t-statistic for testing the null hypothesis that $\alpha = \alpha_0$. Do the following simulation exercises with $N = 10{,}000$ replications. (a) Simulate the bias of $\hat{\alpha}$ and the finite sample distribution of t_{α_0} for $\alpha_0 = 0, 0.5, 0.75, 0.9, 0.95,$ and 0.99. Plot the cumulative distribution function (cdf) and probability density function (pdf) for these six cases as well as the cdf and pdf of the asymptotic distribution of t_{α_0}. Do this exercise for $T = 25$, 100, and 500. Discuss and interpret your results. (b) Repeat the exercise, for the same data-generating process, when the estimated regression (21.27) includes (i) a constant and (ii) a constant and a time trend. Is the bias increasing as the number of deterministic components increases? Does the quality of the asymptotic approximation deteriorate? (c) Repeat the same for the case with a unit root $\alpha_0 = 1$, this time with $T(\hat{\alpha} - 1)$ instead of t_{α_0}. For the bias, discuss your results. For this unit root case, do the cdf and pdf for $T = 10$, 25, 50, and 100. (Note: To compute the pdf, use a normal kernel and the bandwidth set to $h = 1.06\sigma n^{-1/5}$, where σ is the standard deviation of the simulated values and n is the number of simulations. For more information, refer to Silverman (1986) or Chapter 26.)

Chapter 36

Estimation of Time Series Models

In this chapter, we discuss several issues related to estimation in time series models. We start with a brief discussion of the estimation of the autocovariance function. We then mention a few things about estimating autoregressive models. The bulk of this chapter is devoted to (a) approximate MLE methods for $ARMA$ model involving the so-called back-forecasting approach and (b) methods to estimate the order of autoregressive processes using information criteria.

36.1 Estimation of the autocovariance function

Usually two kinds of estimators are proposed that differ only by some scaling. These are, in the case of a zero mean process,

$$\hat{R}^*(\tau) = \frac{1}{T-|\tau|}\sum_{t=1}^{T-|\tau|} x_t x_{t+|\tau|}$$

and

$$\hat{R}(\tau) = T^{-1}\sum_{t=1}^{T-|\tau|} x_t x_{t+|\tau|}.$$

It is straightforward to show that $\hat{R}^*(\tau)$ is an unbiased estimate of $R(\tau)$ while $\hat{R}(\tau)$ is a biased estimate. Hence, one may think that the former would be the preferred estimate. There is, however, some evidence that $\hat{R}(\tau)$ has smaller variance and mean-squared error in finite samples. This is especially true for long lags. As an extreme, consider the autocovariance at lag $T-1$, then $\hat{R}^*(T-1) = x_T x_1$, which can be whatever the first and last data points happen to be, while in theory it should be nearly zero, which is the case using $\hat{R}(T-1)$ since it takes value $x_T x_1/T$. Furthermore, as a function of τ, $\hat{R}(\tau)$ is positive semi-definite, a property shared by the autocovariance function $R(\tau)$, which can be useful in some contexts. In the case of an unknown mean, the estimates are

$$\hat{R}^*(\tau) = \frac{1}{T-|\tau|} \sum_{t=1}^{T-|\tau|} (x_t - \bar{X})(x_{t+|\tau|} - \bar{X})$$

and

$$\hat{R}(\tau) = T^{-1} \sum_{t=1}^{T-|\tau|} (x_t - \bar{X})(x_{t+|\tau|} - \bar{X}).$$

With an estimated mean, neither estimate is unbiased and $\hat{R}(\tau)$ is still a positive semi-definite function while $\hat{R}^*(\tau)$ is not. For these reasons, we use $\hat{R}(\tau)$ as the estimate in what follows. The asymptotic properties are, nevertheless, the same.

Remark 36.1. In Exercise 36.2, you are asked to show that $\sum_{|\tau|<T} \hat{R}(\tau) = 0$, which implies that $\sum_{|\tau|<T} \hat{\rho}(\tau) = 0$, where $\hat{\rho}(\tau) = \hat{R}(\tau)/\hat{R}(0)$ are the autocorrelations; see the work of Percival (1993). This is a simple but important result. It basically implies that the estimates at long lags are meaningless. Take for instance a simple $AR(1)$ model $x_t = ax_{t-1} + e_t$ with e_t having mean 0 and variance σ^2, the population autocovariance function is $\sigma^2 a^{|\tau|}/(1-a^2)$ and the autocorrelation function is $a^{|\tau|}$, both of which are positive for all delays τ when $a > 0$. The sample autocorrelations will be good estimates for small lags. However, given the stated properties, they will by construction be negative for some large delays to ensure that $\sum_{|\tau|<T} \hat{R}(\tau) = 0$. Accordingly, one should not try to infer some patterns from the estimates of the autocorrelation function using the

full set of delays or lags. Meaningful conclusions can be obtained from the first few lagged values, which depend of course on the sample size T.

36.1.1 Properties of $\hat{R}(\tau)$ and $\hat{\rho}(\tau)$

We first show that $\hat{R}(\tau)$ is asymptotically unbiased. First, note that

$$\begin{aligned}
&\sum_{t=1}^{T-|\tau|} (x_t-\mu)(x_{t+|\tau|}-\mu) \\
&\quad = \sum_{t=1}^{T-|\tau|} [(x_t-\bar{X})+(\bar{X}-\mu)][(x_{t+|\tau|}-\bar{X})+(\bar{X}-\mu)] \\
&\quad \approx \sum_{t=1}^{T-|\tau|} \left[(x_t-\bar{X})(x_{t+|\tau|}-\bar{X})\right] + (T-|\tau|)\left(\bar{X}-\mu\right)^2,
\end{aligned}$$

where the approximation arises from

$$\sum_{t=1}^{T-|\tau|} (x_t-\bar{X}) \approx \sum_{t=1}^{T} (x_t-\bar{X}) = 0.$$

Hence,

$$\begin{aligned}
E[\hat{R}(\tau)] &= E\left[T^{-1}\sum_{t=1}^{T-|\tau|} \left[(x_t-\bar{X})\left(x_{t+|\tau|}-\bar{X}\right)\right]\right] \\
&\approx T^{-1}\sum_{t=1}^{T-|\tau|} E\left\{(x_t-\mu)\left(x_{t+|\tau|}-\mu\right)\right\} \\
&\quad - [(T-|\tau|)/T]E\left[\bar{X}-\mu\right]^2 \\
&\approx [(T-|\tau|)/T]R(\tau) - [(T-|\tau|)/T]\left[T^{-1}2\pi h(0)\right] \\
&= R(\tau) - (|\tau|/T)R(\tau) - [(T-|\tau|)/T^2]2\pi h(0) \to R(\tau) \\
&\quad \text{as } T\to\infty,
\end{aligned}$$

where $h(0)$ is the spectral density function of x_t at frequency zero, to be introduced and discussed in Chapter 37. We now discuss the variance and covariances of the sample autocovariances. We simply summarize some main results without proof. For a derivation, see the work of Priestley (1981, pp. 324–327). Suppose μ is known and is set to 0 without loss of generality and we have normality. Consider

$$\hat{R}(\tau) = T^{-1} \sum_{t=1}^{T-|\tau|} x_t x_{t+|\tau|}.$$

The results are stated in the following propositions.

Proposition 36.1. *As $T \to \infty$, we have*

$$T\text{Var}(\hat{R}(\tau)) \to \sum_{m=-\infty}^{\infty} \left\{R(m)^2 + R(m+\tau) R(m-\tau)\right\}$$

and

$$\begin{aligned} &T\text{Cov}(\hat{R}(\tau), \hat{R}(\tau+v)) \\ &\quad \to \sum_{m=-\infty}^{\infty} \{R(m) R(m+v) + R(m+\tau+v) R(m-\tau)\}. \quad (36.1) \end{aligned}$$

Consider now the same features for the sample autocorrelation function defined by

$$\hat{\rho}(\tau) = \hat{R}(\tau) / \hat{R}(0), \quad \tau = 0, \ldots, (T-1).$$

We first note that we have the approximation:

$$E[\hat{\rho}(\tau)] \sim (1 - |\tau| / T) \rho(\tau)$$

so that $\hat{\rho}(\tau)$ is asymptotically unbiased. The covariances are stated as follows; see the work of Priestley (1981).

Proposition 36.2. *As $T \to \infty$, we have*

$$
\begin{aligned}
&T\mathrm{Cov}\left\{\hat{\rho}(\tau), \hat{\rho}(\tau+v)\right\} \\
&\quad \to \sum_{m=-\infty}^{\infty} \big[\rho(m)\rho(m+v) + \rho(m+\tau+v)\rho(m-\tau) \\
&\qquad + 2\rho(\tau)\rho(\tau+v)\rho^2(m) - 2\rho(\tau)\rho(m)\rho(m-\tau-v) \\
&\qquad - 2\rho(\tau+v)\rho(m)\rho(m-\tau)\big].
\end{aligned}
\tag{36.2}
$$

Let us now consider the asymptotic distributions. Under the additional assumption that $E(e_t^4) < \infty$, we have asymptotic normality. For a formal derivation of the asymptotic distribution, see the work of Brockwell and Davis (1991, Chapter 7.3).

Proposition 36.3. *If the process is Gaussian, then jointly for $j = 0, \ldots, n$:*

$$\sqrt{T}\left\{\hat{R}(0) - R(0)\right\}, \ldots, \sqrt{T}\left\{\hat{R}(n) - R(n)\right\} \xrightarrow{d} N(0, v_1),$$

where v_1 is given by (36.1). *Also, without the need for the assumption that the process is Gaussian,*

$$\sqrt{T}\left\{\hat{\rho}(1) - \rho(1)\right\}, \ldots, \sqrt{T}\left\{\hat{\rho}(n) - \rho(n)\right\} \xrightarrow{d} N(0, v_2),$$

where v_2 is given by (36.2).

The important thing to get from these results is that, even in the case of making inference about a single autocorrelation at lag τ, its asymptotic distribution depends in a complex way on the true autocorrelation function at ALL lags; see equation (36.2). Hence, in practice, it would be very difficult to ascertain whether some autocorrelations at some lags are significant.

36.1.2 The white noise case and related issues

Things simplify greatly if x_t is a white noise process, i.e., $\rho(0) = 1$, and $\rho(\tau) = 0$ for $\tau \neq 0$. Then, for $v \neq 0$,

$$
\begin{aligned}
T\mathrm{Cov}\left(\hat{\rho}(\tau), \hat{\rho}(\tau+v)\right) &\to 0 \\
\mathrm{Var}\left(\hat{\rho}(\tau)\right) &\sim T^{-1}
\end{aligned}
$$

and

$$T\text{Var}\left(\hat{\rho}\left(\tau\right)\right) \to 1.$$

Hence,

$$T\hat{\rho}\left(\tau\right) \sim N\left(0,1\right).$$

This is a widely used result in the Box and Jenkins (1970) analysis to assess the significance of the autocorrelations. This suggests a 95% confidence interval for the autocorrelation function given

$$\hat{\rho}\left(\tau\right) \pm 1.96/T^{1/2}.$$

Most software packages will plot the sample autocorrelation function in a graph that contains two horizontal lines corresponding to $\hat{\rho}\left(\tau\right) \pm 1.96/T^{1/2}$ (most often 1.96 is replaced by 2). Hence, one is supposed to use these lines to judge whether sample autocorrelations at various lags are significantly different from 0. While this may be a useful device for experienced practitioners (see the work of Granger and Newbold, 1986), it is not proper statistical inference. To illustrate this, consider the following graph depicted in Figure 36.1.

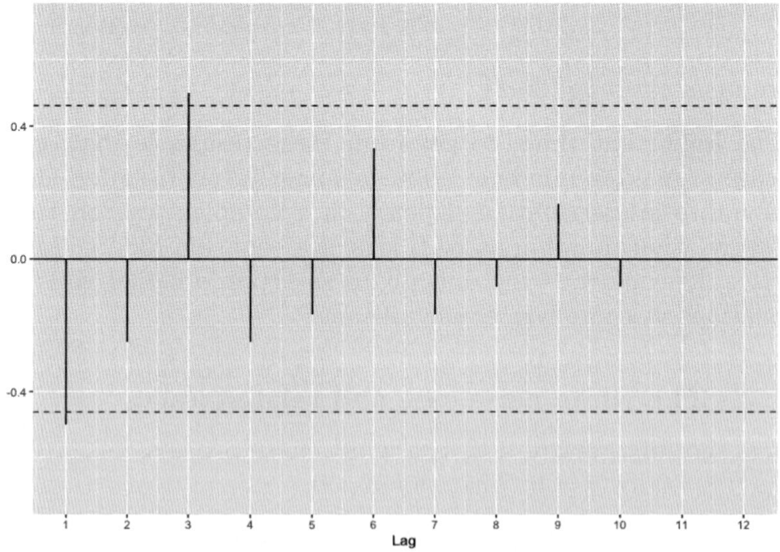

Figure 36.1. Sample autocorrelations.

Here, the sample autocorrelations at lags 1 and 3 are above the line but that of lag 2 is slightly below the line. From the above asymptotic distribution results, making inference about whether the autocorrelation at lag 1 is significant requires us to know whether the values at lags 2 and 3 are significant. But to ascertain this fact, we need to know whether the value at lag one is significant. Hence, we are led to a circular problem. There is no way around it.

The problem lies in how the null and alternative hypotheses are specified. Here, $H_0 : \rho(\tau) = 0$ versus $H_1 : \rho(\tau) \neq 0$, with the values of $\rho(j)$ for $j \neq \tau$ unspecified under both H_0 and H_1. This is complicated in view of the limit variance (36.2).

A more feasible testing problem is the following: $H_0 : \rho(\tau) = 0$ for all τ versus $H_1 : \rho(\tau) \neq 0$ for some τ. This can be achieved via a Box and Pierce (1970)-type statistic:

$$Q = T\sum_{j=1}^{m} \hat{\rho}(j)^2,$$

for some pre-selected m, whose value usually depends on the sample size. A close variant is the Ljung and Box (1978) test, which incorporates some finite sample corrections and has better finite sample properties. It is given by

$$Q^* = T(T+2)\sum_{j=1}^{m} \hat{\rho}(j)^2 /(T-j).$$

The limit distribution of both Q and Q^* is chi-square with m degrees of freedom. However, its main use is to verify if any serial correlation is left in the residuals after fitting a model, either a linear regression model or some ARMA models, whose method of estimation is discussed in the following. In both cases, m needs to be changed to $m-k$, where k is the number of parameters when the autocorrelations are constructed from an estimated model with k parameters.

Another tool often encountered for the specification of time series models is the partial autocorrelation function; see, e.g., Brockwell and Davis (1991) and Section 8.4.12. Unlike the standard autocorrelation function, it takes value 0 for lags greater than p when the process is an $AR(p)$. The autocorrelation function takes value 0 for lags greater than q when the process is an $MA(q)$. But both the partial and standard autocorrelation functions suffer from the same drawback as discussed above. They are also difficult to interpret when dealing with $ARMA$ processes; see the discussion in the work of Granger and Newbold (1986).

Nowadays, the preferred method to estimate the order of $ARMA$ models is to use information criterion. These are discussed in Section 36.4.

36.2 Estimation of autoregressive models

The model of interest is

$$\begin{aligned} x_t &= c + a_1 x_{t-1} + a_2 x_{t-2} + \cdots + a_p x_{t-p} + e_t, \\ t &= p+1, \ldots, T; \quad e_t \sim i.i.d.\ \left(0, \sigma_e^2\right). \end{aligned}$$

The usual method of estimation is OLS. This is maximum likelihood conditional on the initial observation $x_1, \ldots, x_p$ if the errors are normally distributed. This is easiest seen by noting that

$$e_1 = x_1 - c - a_1 x_0 - a_2 x_{-1} \cdots - a_p x_{1-p},$$

which cannot be computed because $x_0, \ldots, x_{1-p}$ are not observed. If we want to assume normality, we can estimate by exact unconditional MLE. It is however quite complex relative to OLS; see Section 15.10.4.

Given stationarity, i.e., the roots of $A(L) = 0$ lie outside the unit circle, the asymptotic distributions of the t-statistics are all standard normal; the parameter estimates are also asymptotically normally distributed. There is, however, a problem concerning the adequacy of the normal approximation. The normal approximation to the exact distribution becomes less adequate as the roots get closer to 1. The discrepancies can indeed be large. We postpone to later a fuller examination of the distributional properties of OLS in AR models.

If one wants to impose the stationarity assumption, a popular alternative is to use the Yule–Walker equations, see Section 8.4.7. This is not often applied in economics as we care about nonstationary processes. Hence, the method of estimation adopted is almost always OLS.

36.3 Estimation of models with a moving-average component

The model is

$$\begin{aligned} x_t &= \mu + B(L)\, e_t \\ &= \mu + e_t + b_1 e_{t-1} + \cdots + b_q e_{t-q}, \end{aligned} \tag{36.3}$$

for $t = 1, \ldots, T$. The roots of $B(z)$ are outside the unit circle and $e_t \sim i.i.d.\ N\left(0, \sigma_e^2\right)$. Here, we cannot use OLS since

$$A(L)\, x_t = B(L)^{-1}\, x_t = e_t$$

involves an infinite number of parameters. We assume normality for the errors and work with an approximate maximum likelihood technique. The difference in the techniques to be discussed involves the assumption made about the set of "initial" errors $\{e_{-(q-1)}, \ldots, e_0\}$. In the first method, we set them equal to their unconditional expectation, that is, 0. In the second, we use their expectation conditional on the data and the structure of the process. We discuss how to construct the (approximate) likelihood function for a given set of parameter values $\theta = (b_1, \ldots, b_q, \sigma_e^2)$. Then, standard numerical optimization techniques can be used to maximize the function and get parameter estimates.

Remark 36.2. It is very easy to allow for an autoregressive component. For instance, if the model is an $ARMA(p, q)$, then in (36.3) one simply replaces x_t by $x_t - a_1 x_{t-1} - \cdots - a_p x_{t-p}$. Everything else remains the same, hence we do not delve more on this extension so as not to overburden the notation.

Remark 36.3. What we discuss are approximate MLE methods. For a method to obtain the exact MLE, see Chapter 39. It is, however, much more involved. Most softwares rely on the approximate MLE discussed in Section 36.3.2.

36.3.1 Using the unconditional expectation

It is useful, for the sake of a better understanding, to start with the case for which the value of the initial errors is set to their unconditional expectation, i.e.,

$$e_0 = e_{-1} = \cdots = e_{-(q-1)} = 0.$$

Then, with given parameter values, we can compute $(e_1, \ldots, e_T)$ via the following recursion starting from $t = 1$ to $t = T$:

$$
\begin{aligned}
e_1 &= x_1 - \mu, \\
e_2 &= x_2 - \mu - b_1 e_1, \\
e_3 &= x_3 - \mu - b_1 e_2 - b_2 e_1, \\
&\vdots \\
e_q &= x_q - \mu - b_1 e_{q-1} - b_2 e_{q-2} - \cdots - b_{q-1} e_1, \\
e_t &= x_t - \mu - b_1 e_{t-1} - b_2 e_{t-2} - \cdots - b_q e_{t-q}, \qquad q < t \leq T.
\end{aligned}
$$

The conditional log-likelihood function is then

$$
L(\theta) = \text{const} - (2\sigma_e^2)^{-1} \sum_{t=1}^{T} e_t^2,
$$

which can be maximized using numerical optimization techniques.

36.3.2 Using the conditional expectation

Setting the values of the initial errors to zero (their unconditional expectation) involves making use of less information than possible. We can instead use the structure of the model to start with their conditional values, i.e., $E[e_t|\theta, X]$ for $t = -(q-1), \ldots, 0$. Then, one could minimize

$$
Q(\theta) = \sum_{t=-(q-1)}^{T} \tilde{e}_t^2, \tag{36.4}
$$

where

$$
\tilde{e}_t = E[e_t|X, \theta].
$$

It is shown in the appendix that this amounts to approximate MLE where a determinant is set to one. An ingenious method to obtain these conditional expectations is to use a forward non-causal model, which is observationally equivalent to the backward causal model of interest (see Section 8.5). To get the main idea of this method, let us first consider a simple MA(1) model given by

$$x_t = e_t + be_{t-1}. \tag{36.5}$$

Let a_t $(t = 1, \ldots, T + 1)$ be a sequence of *i.i.d.* random variables (uncorrelated with e_t). The forward non-causal model is

$$x_t = (1 + bF)\, a_t = a_t + ba_{t+1} \quad (t = 1, \ldots, T), \tag{36.6}$$

where F is the forward operator, i.e., $Fa_t = a_{t+1}$. The backward (36.5) and forward (36.6) models are observationally equivalent and, hence, can equally well represent the correlation structure in the data. Taking conditional expectations of the forward model (36.6), we have

$$E\,[x_t|\theta, X] = E\,[a_t|\theta, X] + bE\,[a_{t+1}|\theta, X],$$

for $t = 1, \ldots, T$. Now, set

$$E\,[a_{T+1}|\theta, X] = 0. \tag{36.7}$$

We see in the following why imposing any sensible value makes no difference in practice. Then,

$$x_T = E\,[a_T|\theta, X].$$

We can use the following recursion backward in time from $t = T$ to $t = 1$:

$$E\,[a_t|\theta, X] = x_t - bE\,[a_{t+1}|\theta, X].$$

Hence, we obtain $E\,[a_t|\theta, X]$ for $t = T, \ldots, 1$. Now, using the forward model (36.6), x_t is correlated with a_t $(t = 1, \ldots, T+1)$ but not with a_0. Hence, $E\,[a_0|\theta, X] = 0$, and

$$E\,[x_0|\theta, X] = bE\,[a_1|\theta, X].$$

Note that the condition (36.7) is inconsequential since via the recursion, whatever value is used is geometrically discounted. For instance, if $T = 100$ and $b = -0.90$, even if we set $E\,[a_{T+1}|\theta, X] = 100$, its effect at the end of the loop will be $100 \times (0.90\hat{\ }100)$, less than 0.003.

Now, use the backward equation (36.5). Taking expectations

$$E\left[x_t|\theta, X\right] = E\left[e_t|\theta, X\right] + bE\left[e_{t-1}|\theta, X\right]. \tag{36.8}$$

Start with

$$E\left[e_0|\theta, X\right] = E\left[x_0|\theta, X\right] = bE\left[a_1|\theta, X\right]$$

because $E[e_{-1}|\theta, X] = 0$ since an MA(1) process depends only on the current and previous value of the errors. Use $E\left[x_t|\theta, X\right] = x_t$ and the recursion (36.8) for $t = 1, \ldots, T$, to get a series of conditional expectations

$$E\left[e_t|\theta, X\right],$$

for $t = 0, \ldots, T$. This allows computing the function (36.4), which can then be minimized numerically. This is called the "back-forecasting" method because we use the forward model to construct a "back-forecast" of x_0.

36.3.3 The case with an $MA(q)$ model

We now generalize the above discussion to the case of an $MA(q)$ model. Nothing of substance is new. We only present it for the sake of completeness. The backward model is

$$x_t = B\left(L\right)e_t. \tag{36.9}$$

There exists an equivalent non-causal solution given by the following "forward" model:

$$x_t = B\left(F\right)a_t, \tag{36.10}$$

where $Fa_t = a_{t+1}$ and $a_t \sim i.i.d.\ N\left(0, \sigma_a^2\right)$. Taking expectation conditional on θ, the model and $X = (x_T, \ldots, x_1)$, on both sides of (36.10):

$$E\left[x_t|\theta, X\right] = B\left(F\right)E\left[a_t|\theta, X\right], \tag{36.11}$$

for $t = 1, \ldots, T$, where we have $E\left[x_t|\theta, X\right] = x_t$ $(t = 1, \ldots, T)$ and $E\left[a_{-j}|\theta, X\right] = 0$ for $j \geq 0$. Start with $E\left[a_{T+i}|\theta, X\right] = 0$, for $i > 0$.

Then, compute $E[a_{T-j}|\theta, X]$ for $j = 0, \ldots, T-1$ using (36.11) to obtain $E[x_t|\theta, X]$ for $t = 0, -1, \ldots, -(q-1)$. Now, take conditional expectations on both sides of (36.9):

$$E[x_t|\theta, X] = B(L)\, E[e_t|\theta, X],$$

and use $E[x_t|\theta, X]$, $t = 0, -1, \ldots, -(q-1)$, to get an estimate of $E[e_t|\theta, X]$ for $t = -(q-1), \ldots, T$. Then, construct the function (36.4) and minimize it using numerical optimization techniques. Here, the number of back-forecasts is q, namely for $E[x_t|\theta, X]$, $t = 0, \ldots, (q-1)$.

36.3.4 Estimation of parameters in *ARMA* models

In the general case, the model is

$$\begin{aligned} A(L)\, x_t &= \mu + B(L)\, e_t, \\ A(L) &= 1 + a_1 L + a_2 L + \cdots + a_p L^p, \\ B(L) &= 1 + b_1 L + b_2 L^2 + \cdots + b_q L^q. \end{aligned}$$

The method of estimation is basically the same as in the pure MA case, as discussed in Remark 36.2. We use normality of the errors e_t and approximate the likelihood function of $(x_1, \ldots, x_T)$ to obtain estimates of a's and b's and σ_e^2 using numerical optimization. We can again use back-forecasting. The conditions for identification are as follows: (1) $A(z)$ and $B(z)$ have no common factors; (2) all roots of $A(z)$ and $B(z)$ lie outside the unit circle; (3) a_p and b_q are not both zero. Several extensions and variants of MLE have been proposed (see, e.g., Priestley, 1981, Chapter 5.4)

Standard Errors and Confidence Intervals

Given the stationarity and short-memory assumptions, the inference in ARMA models follows the general principle of inference using maximum likelihood. In particular, asymptotic normality is still in effect and the standard errors of the parameters can be obtained from an estimate of the Hessian matrix of the likelihood. Again, the adequacy of the normality assumption will depend upon the closeness of the roots of $A(L)$ and $B(L)$ to unity.

36.4 Determining the order of the model

A popular method to estimate the order of an $ARMA(p, q)$ model is to use information criteria. As more parameters are introduced, the maximized log likelihood function will necessarily be greater. But for each increase in the number of parameters, the increase in L will be less and less important. The idea is then to choose a model which has the greatest likelihood value after some correction for a penalty on the number of parameters. A vast number of penalty terms have been suggested in the statistics literature. By far, the most commonly used are the Akaike (1974) (AIC) and Schwarz (1978) Bayesian Information Criterion (BIC). We cover the theory for the AIC. We then generalize it to a class of information criteria and discuss their properties.

36.4.1 The Akaike criterion

It is instructive to study the main arguments leading to the information criterion suggested by Akaike (1974). The treatment follows the works of Ng and Perron (2005) and Gouriéroux and Monfort (1997). A similar treatment is provided for the BIC proposed by Schwarz (1978) in the work of Ng and Perron (2005). We suppose that the data generating process is an $AR(p)$ model:

$$x_t = c + \sum_{i=1}^{p} \beta_i x_{t-i} + e_t, \quad (t = p+1, \ldots, T), \tag{36.12}$$

with p fixed but unknown. The estimated candidate models to approximate the process are $AR(k)$ regressions of the form:

$$x_t = c + \sum_{i=1}^{k} \beta_i x_{t-i} + e_{tk}, \quad (t = k+1, \ldots, T), \tag{36.13}$$

for $k = 0, \ldots, k_{\max}$, with $k_{\max}$ some pre-specified value. Let β^0 be the true value of β under the true model (36.12). Let $\hat{\beta}(k)$ be the MLE (or OLS, since they are asymptotically equivalent) and $N = T - n$, with n the number of observations we condition upon. We return to that later, here simply note that n must be at least k. The Kullback–Leibler distance (see also Chapter 19) between the true model and the estimated one is

$$Q = E_0(\ln[f(x|\beta^0)] - \ln[f(x|\hat{\beta}(k))]), \tag{36.14}$$

where E_0 denotes expectation taken with respect to the true model (36.12). Let

$$\beta(k) = plim_{T\to\infty}\hat{\beta}(k).$$

For instance, if $k \geq p$,

$$\beta(k) = (\beta_1, \ldots, \beta_p, 0, \ldots, 0),$$

and, if $k < p$, $\beta(k)$ depends on k and the true parameters $(\beta_1, \ldots, \beta_p)$. Note that Q is non-negative. We want to find the value of k that minimizes this distance. Now, the sample counterpart is

$$\tilde{Q} = N^{-1} \sum_{t=n+1}^{T} \ln[f(x_t|\beta^0)] - N^{-1} \sum_{t=n+1}^{T} \ln[f(x_t|\hat{\beta}(k))]. \tag{36.15}$$

Note that $\tilde{Q} \xrightarrow{p} Q$ using a law of large numbers, so $\tilde{Q}$ is effectively an estimate of the Kullback–Leibler distance Q. Note that minimizing $\tilde{Q}$ with respect to k is equivalent to

$$\max_k N^{-1} \sum_{t=n+1}^{T} \ln[f(x_t|\hat{\beta}(k))],$$

provided the first term does not depend on k, which requires N and n not to depend on k. But,

$$N^{-1} \sum_{t=n+1}^{T} \ln[f(x_t|\hat{\beta}(k))]$$

is increasing in k since more regressors can only (weakly) increase the value of the likelihood function, so there is no inner solution.

Akaike's idea was to work instead with an estimate of the distance Q that is unbiased to order T, i.e., with an estimate Q^* such that

$$\lim_{T\to\infty} E_0(N(Q - Q^*)) = 0. \tag{36.16}$$

To find such an estimate, first take a Taylor series expansion on the second term of (36.14) around $\beta(k)$ and then

$$NQ = (2\sigma^2)^{-1}(\hat{\beta}(k) - \beta\,(k))' \sum_{t=n+1}^{T} x_t' x_t(\hat{\beta}(k) - \beta(k)) + o_p(1).$$

Also, take a Taylor series expansion on the first term of (36.15) around $\hat{\beta}(k)$; then,

$$N\tilde{Q} = -(2\sigma^2)^{-1}(\hat{\beta}(k) - \beta\,(k))' \sum_{t=n+1}^{T} x_t' x_t(\hat{\beta}(k) - \beta(k)) + o_p(1).$$

Define

$$\Phi_T(k) = \sigma^{-2}(\hat{\beta}(k) - \beta\,(k))' \sum_{t=n+1}^{T} x_t' x_t(\hat{\beta}(k) - \beta(k)).$$

An estimate of Q that is unbiased to order T is

$$Q^* = \tilde{Q} + \Phi(k)/N.$$

This follows since

$$\begin{aligned} N(Q - Q^*) &= N(Q - \tilde{Q} - \Phi(k)/N) \\ &= \frac{\Phi(k)}{2} + \frac{\Phi(k)}{2} - \Phi(k) + o_p(1) \\ &= o_p(1). \end{aligned}$$

So, (36.16) is satisfied. Hence,

$$Q^* = N^{-1} \sum_{t=n+1}^{T} \ln[f(x_t|\beta^0)] - N^{-1} \sum_{t=n+1}^{T} \ln[f(x_t|\hat{\beta}(k))] + N^{-1}\Phi(k)$$

and minimizing Q^* with respect to k is equivalent to maximizing

$$N^{-1}\sum_{t=n+1}^{T}\ln[f(x_t|\hat{\beta}(k))] - N^{-1}\Phi(k).$$

This expression involves unknown elements, via $\Phi(k)$ which depends on β and cannot be used in practice. However, since the main requirement is that we obtain a Q^* that satisfies (36.16), we can replace $\Phi(k)$ by its expected value in large samples. Now, $\Phi(k)$ is the F test for testing the hypothesis that the coefficient are $\beta(k)$ so that

$$\Phi(k) \xrightarrow{d} \chi_k^2$$

and

$$\lim_{T\to\infty} E_0(\Phi(k)) = k.$$

Hence, a Q^* that is unbiased to order T for Q and involves no unknown elements is given by

$$Q^* = N^{-1}\sum_{t=n+1}^{T}\ln[f(x_t|\hat{\beta}(k))]) - N^{-1}k. \tag{36.17}$$

Assuming that the errors are *i.i.d.* normally distributed, maximizing this last expression is equivalent to (see Example 15.6 and Exercise 36.1)

$$\min_k \left\{\ln(\hat{\sigma}_{ek}^2) + 2k/N\right\}, \tag{36.18}$$

where

$$\hat{\sigma}_{ek}^2 = N^{-1}\sum_{t=n+1}^{T}\hat{e}_{tk}^2,$$

with $\hat{e}_{tk}$ the estimated residuals from a kth-order autoregression estimated using data from date n to date T.

The derivations above are valid provided N is invariant to k across models being compared, otherwise the first component of (36.15) depends on k and all the arguments break down. Hence, N cannot depend on k. This means that n, the number of observations we condition upon must be fixed across models. This can be achieved by setting $n = k_{\max}$, i.e., using the same number of effective observations when estimating the various autoregressions of different orders.

This makes intuitive sense since the goal is to compare how well models with different values of k fit the data. This comparison should be done on an equal footing, that is, using the same number of observations for all candidate models. Otherwise, if one uses all the possible data for all k (i.e., set $n = k$), candidates with lower values of k will be estimated with more observations, hence a better fit. Ng and Perron (2005) provided extensive simulation evidence that setting $n = k_{\max}$ and, hence, $N = T - k_{\max}$ was the appropriate thing to do. Setting $n = k$ leads to the worst outcome. Unfortunately, this fact is not well understood in most textbook treatments. Also, Ng and Perron (2005) reported that, at the time, popular software such as Eviews used $n = k$.

36.4.2 A class of information criteria

We can extend this idea of imposing a penalty factor of order k by considering a class of information criteria defined by

$$IC(k) = \ln(\hat{\sigma}_{ek}^2) + (C_N/N)k,$$

where

$$\hat{\sigma}_{ek}^2 = N^{-1} \sum_{t=k_{\max}+1}^{T} \hat{e}_{tk}^2$$

and again $N = T - k_{\max}$. The various criteria differ according to the weight C_N assigned to the penalty factor k. The following conditions are imposed on the weight C_N.

Assumption 36.1. $C_N > 0$ and $C_N/N \to 0$ as $N \to \infty$.

The information criterion of Akaike corresponds to the case with $C_N = 2$. Another popular criterion is the so-called Bayesian or Schwarz (1978) criterion in which case $C_N = \ln(N)$. Many other penalty factors have been proposed in the literature; see the work of Ng and Perron (2005) and the references therein.

36.4.3 Asymptotic properties with $ARMA$ models

The method can easily be extended to select the order of an $ARMA(p, q)$ model. The model is estimated with values of p and q for p ranging from 0 to $p_{\max}$ and q ranging from 0 to $q_{\max}$. Also, $N = T - p_{\max}$ so that $p_{\max}$ initial values are used and all models are estimated with $T - p_{\max}$ effective observations.

Let $\hat{e}^2_{t,p,q}$ be the estimated residuals when estimating an $ARMA(p, q)$ model using, e.g., the back-forecasting method discussed in Section 36.3.2. Then, the estimates of p and q are chosen as the minimizers of

$$\min_{p,q} \left\{ \ln(\hat{\sigma}^2_{e,p,q}) + 2(p+q)/N \right\},$$

where

$$\hat{\sigma}^2_{e,p,q} = N^{-1} \sum_{t=p_{\max}+1}^{T} \hat{e}^2_{t,p,q}.$$

Suppose the data-generating process is an $ARMA(p^*, q^*)$. The true orders p^* and q^* are unknown but known to be smaller than some upper bound $p_{\max}$ and $q_{\max}$. It was shown that the estimates so obtained are consistent provided $C_N \to \infty$ and $C_N/N \to 0$, as $N \to \infty$; see the work of Hannan and Deistler (2012). Hence, the Bayesian information criterion with $C_N = \ln(N)$ yields consistent estimates. The Akaike information criterion which corresponds to the case $C_N = 2$ does not yield consistent estimates, but it was shown that the estimated orders have a probability limit that is no lower than the true values. Furthermore, as shown by Shibata (1980), the order selected by AIC (for an $AR(p)$) is, nevertheless, asymptotically optimal under normal errors for infinite AR processes.

These asymptotic results should be taken with a grain of salt. Anytime you see asymptotic results being compared via some logarithmic rate of increase, one should be suspicious as $\log(T)$ increases very slowly with T, so slow that it should make no difference in finite sample. For instance, $\ln(100) = 4.6$ and $\ln(1{,}000{,}000) = 13.8$, hardly a big difference. What transpires from finite sample simulations is that the AIC tends to over-estimate the orders of the model, whether pure AR or mixed $ARMA$, while the BIC tends to under-select the orders.

Hence, as always, it is good to perform robustness checks. A good strategy is to estimate the orders using both the AIC and BIC. If they give the same answer, fine. If not, go back to the model and see which specification is more appropriate; e.g., are the last coefficients significant. Most importantly, always check whether any correlation is left in the estimated residuals. This can be done using the Box–Pierce of Ljung–Box statistics described in Section 36.1.2.

36.4.4 Asymptotic properties with linear processes

Suppose the data satisfies a linear short-memory process given by

$$x_t = \mu + C(L)e_t = \mu + \sum_{i=0}^{\infty} c_i e_{t-i},$$

where

$$C(L) = \sum_{i=0}^{\infty} c_i L^i,$$

with $c_0 = 1$, $\sum_{i=0}^{\infty} i|c_i| < \infty$ and $e_t \sim i.i.d.(0, \sigma_e^2)$. An information criterion is used to select the order of an approximate autoregressive model, the order of which is supposed to be in the range from 0 to $k_{\max}$. For technical reasons, we suppose that $k_{\max} = o_p(T^{1/3})$. Denote the selected order by k_{ic}, then under assumption 36.1, it is shown in the work of Hannan and Deistler (2012) that

$$k_{ic} = O_p(\ln(T))$$

so that the selected order increases at rate $\ln(T)$. This rate is very slow, indeed slower than any polynomial rate, T^a, for any a arbitrarily small. This will play an important role later. The slow rate is due to the fact that we are dealing with short-memory processes, which typically involve a geometric rate of decay of the autoregressive parameters in the representation

$$A(L)(x_t - \mu) = e_t,$$

with $A(L) = C(L)^{-1}$. Hence, typically a short-order autoregression is sufficient to approximate the process. The exception is when there is a strong negative moving-average component, in which case the information criteria typically perform badly.

36.5 Appendix: Back-forecasting as approximate MLE

The material in this appendix is mostly from the work of Priestley (1981). The basis of the method is to derive the joint distribution of $(x_1 \ldots x_T)$ by starting from the joint distribution of

$$\left(e_{-(q-1)}, \ldots, e_{-1}, e_0, e_1, \ldots, e_T\right).$$

For simplicity, let $\mu = 0$, then we have the set of equations:

$$\begin{aligned}
e_{-(q-1)} &= e_{-(q-1)}, \\
&\vdots \\
e_{-1} &= e_{-1}, \\
e_0 &= e_0, \\
e_1 &= x_1 - b_1 e_0 - b_2 e_{-1} - \cdots - b_q e_{-(q-1)}, \\
&\vdots \\
e_T &= x_T - b_1 e_{T-1} - b_2 e_{T-2} - \cdots - b_q e_{T-q}.
\end{aligned}$$

This can be written (in vector form) as

$$e = LX + Me_*,$$

where

$$\begin{aligned}
e &= \left(e_{-(q-1)}, \ldots, e_0, \ldots, e_T\right)', \\
e_* &= \left(e_{-(q-1)}, \ldots, e_0\right)',
\end{aligned}$$

L is a $(T+q) \times T$ matrix of coefficients, and M is a $(T+q) \times q$ matrix of coefficients. Both L and M depend on $(b_1, \ldots, b_q)$ and can be obtained through the above set of equations. The joint probability density function of e is

$$f(e) = \left(\frac{1}{2\pi\sigma_e^2}\right)^{(T+q)/2} \exp\left[-\left(e'e/2\sigma_e^2\right)\right].$$

The Jacobian of the transformation from $(e_1, \ldots, e_T)$ to $(x_1, \ldots, x_T)$ is unity, hence the joint probability density function of (X, e_*) is

$$f(X, e_*) = \left(\frac{1}{2\pi\sigma_e^2}\right)^{(T+q)/2} \exp\left[-\tilde{Q}(\theta, e_*)/2\sigma_e^2\right],$$

where

$$\tilde{Q}(\theta, e_*) = (LX + Me_*)'(LX + Me_*).$$

Let $\tilde{e}_*$ be the value of e_* which minimizes $\tilde{Q}(\theta, e_*)$ for fixed X. By standard projection arguments,

$$\tilde{e}_* = -\left(M'M\right)^{-1} M'LX.$$

That is, $\tilde{e}_*$ is the least square coefficient of e_* in the regression

$$LX = -Me_* + u.$$

By definition, we have

$$\begin{aligned}\tilde{Q}(\theta, e_*) &= (LX + Me_*)'(LX + Me_*) \\ &= (LX + M\tilde{e}_*)'(LX + M\tilde{e}_*) \\ &\quad + (e_* - \tilde{e}_*)' M'M (e_* - \tilde{e}_*) \\ &\quad + 2(LX + M\tilde{e}_*)' M (e_* - \tilde{e}).\end{aligned}$$

The last term is 0 since $(LX + M\tilde{e}_*)$ and $M(e_* - \tilde{e})$ are orthogonal. Hence,

$$\tilde{Q}(\theta, e_*) = Q(\theta) + (e_* - \tilde{e}_*)' M'M (e_* - \tilde{e}_*),$$

where

$$Q(\theta) = (LX + M\tilde{e}_*)'(LX + M\tilde{e}_*).$$

The joint probability density function of $(X, \tilde{e}_*)$ is then

$$\begin{aligned}&f(X, e_*|\theta) \\ &= \left(\frac{1}{2\pi\sigma_e^2}\right)^{(T+q)/2} \exp\left(-\frac{1}{2\sigma_e^2}[Q(\theta) + (e_* - \tilde{e}_*)' M'M (e_* - \tilde{e}_*)]\right).\end{aligned} \tag{36.19}$$

Now, decompose this joint probability density function as follows:

$$f(X, e_*|\theta) = f(X|\theta) f(e_*|X, \theta).$$

Here, $f(X|\theta)$ is the marginal density function of the data and $f(e_*|X,\theta)$ the marginal density function of the initial errors e_* conditional on the X's. We have

$$f(X|\theta) = \left(\frac{1}{2\pi\sigma_e^2}\right)^{T/2} |M'M|^{-1/2} \exp\left(-\frac{Q(\theta)}{2\sigma_e^2}\right) \tag{36.20}$$

and

$$f(e_*|X,\theta) = \left(\frac{1}{2\pi\sigma_e^2}\right)^{q/2} |M'M|^{1/2} \exp\left\{-\frac{(e_* - \tilde{e}_*)' M'M (e_* - \tilde{e}_*)}{2\sigma_e^2}\right\}. \tag{36.21}$$

The MLE of θ can be obtained by maximizing $f(X|\theta)$. The unconditional (on e_*) likelihood of θ, given X, is the same as $f(X|\theta)$, treating X as fixed now and θ as the variables, so that

$$f(\theta|X) = (2\pi\sigma_e^2)^{-T/2} |M'M|^{-1/2} \exp\left(-\frac{Q(\theta)}{2\sigma_e^2}\right).$$

Typically, for large T, $|M'M|^{-1/2}$ is close to 1, though this may not be a good approximation in some cases, e.g., for an MA(1), then $|M'M|^{-1/2} \approx (1-\theta^2)^{1/2}$, so the approximation may be bad if $|\theta|$ is close to 1. Hence, for large T, we may ignore $|M'M|^{-1/2}$ (the determinant) and maximum likelihood reduces to minimizing

$$Q(\theta) = (LX + M\tilde{e}_*)'(LX + M\tilde{e}_*).$$

From (36.21), $\tilde{e}_*$ is the expectation of e_* conditional on X and the parameters of the model. Using

$$e = LX + Me_*,$$

we have

$$\begin{aligned} E[e|X,\theta] &= LX + ME[e_*|X,\theta] \\ &= LX + M\tilde{e}_*. \end{aligned}$$

Hence, approximate maximum likelihood is equivalent to minimizing

$$Q(\theta) = \sum_{t=-(q-1)}^{T} \tilde{e}_t^2,$$

where $\tilde{e}_t$ is the conditional expectation of e_t, given by, in vector form:

$$\tilde{e} = E[e|X, \theta] = LX + M\tilde{\varepsilon}_*.$$

36.6 Exercises

Exercise 36.1. Show that maximizing (36.17) assuming a normal distribution is the same as minimizing (36.18).

Exercise 36.2. Show that for any series the sample autocovariances

$$\hat{R}(h) = T^{-1} \sum_{t=1}^{T-h} (X_t - \bar{X}_T)(X_{t+h} - \bar{X}_T)$$

with $\bar{X}_T = T^{-1} \sum_{t=1}^{T} X_t$ satisfy the relation $\sum_{|h|<T} \hat{R}(h) = 0$.

Exercise 36.3. For a stationary AR(1) process with autoregressive coefficient ϕ, show that

$$T^{1/2}(\hat{\rho}(1) - \phi)/(1 - \hat{\rho}(1)^2)^{1/2} \xrightarrow{d} N(0, 1).$$

Exercise 36.4. Find the asymptotic distribution of $\hat{\rho}(2)/\hat{\rho}(1)$ for the Gaussian $MA(1)$ process $X_t = e_t + \theta e_{t-1}$ with $e_t \sim i.i.d.(0, \upsilon)$ and $0 < |\theta| < 1$.

Exercise 36.5. Show that if $T > p$, the likelihood of the observations $\{x_1, \ldots, x_T\}$ of a stationary $AR(p)$ process

$$x_t - \phi_1 x_{t-1} - \cdots - \phi_p x_{t-p} = e_t,$$

with $e_t \sim i.i.d.N(0, \sigma^2)$, is

$$L(\phi, \sigma^2) = (2\pi\sigma^2)^{-T/2}[\det(G_p)]^{-1/2} \exp\left\{ -(2\sigma^2)^{-1} \left[X_p' G_p^{-1} X_p + \sum_{t=p+1}^{T} (x_t - \phi_1 x_{t-1} - \cdots - \phi_p x_{t-p})^2 \right] \right\},$$

where $X_p = (x_1, \ldots, x_p)'$ and $G_p = \sigma^{-2}\Gamma_p = \sigma^{-2}E(X_p X_p')$.

Exercise 36.6 (Computer). The exercise involves analyzing inflation rate series for the G-7 countries (US, Canada, Japan, Germany, United Kingdom, France, and Italy). From the OECD International Sector Database (https://data.oecd.org/), download the quarterly GDP deflators from 1960:1 to the last available observation. From these, you first construct inflation series as 400 times the first differences of the natural logarithm of the GDP deflator. For each country, perform the following analysis. (a) Plot the series and the autocorrelation function (the 7 series on one page and the 7 autocorrelation functions on another). (b) Estimate an $ARMA(1,1)$ and interpret the results. (c) Find the best $ARMA(p,q)$ model for p and q ranging from 0 to 2 (9 possible models) using the AIC and the BIC. Compute the autoregressive and moving average roots. (d) Repeat (c) for the first-difference of each series. For questions (e)–(g), consider only the case of the USA, Japan, and France. (e) Estimate the mean of the series by the sample average and construct a 95% confidence interval using the following four procedures to construct the spectral density function at frequency 0: (i) a parametric method using the $ARMA(1,1)$ model for y_t obtained in item (b); (ii) an autoregressive-based estimate of the spectral density function at frequency 0 (using the BIC to select the number of lags with $k_{\max} = int(12(T/100)^{1/4})$); (iii) a non-parametric method based on weighted sums of autocovariances using the quadratic spectral window and Andrews' (1991) method to select the bandwidth with an $AR(1)$ approximation for the true DGP; (iv) the same as in (iii) but with an $ARMA(1,1)$ approximation for the DGP. Comment on any substantial differences in the estimates obtained using the four methods. Which measure obtained would you think as most appropriate? In all cases, state the values of m or k selected. (f) Do the results in (e) change if you use the Parzen window (instead of the quadratic spectral)? Do they change if you use pre-whitening with an AR(1)? If so, explain. (g) A measure of importance in macroeconomic analysis is the so-called persistence measure or long-run effect of a unit shock on the level of the series. Assuming that Δy_t is stationary (it could be overdifferenced), by Wold's theorem, it can be represented as $\Delta y_t = \mu + C(L)e_t$. Then, the long run effect of a shock is given by $C(1)$. A closely related statistic is $V = 2\pi f_{\Delta y}(0)$, where $f_{\Delta y}(0)$ is the normalized spectral density function of Δy_t at frequency 0. What is the relation between $C(1)$ and V? When are they equivalent? Compute an estimate of V using the four methods discussed in part (e) now applied to the first differences of the series. Comment on any substantial differences in the estimates obtained using the four methods. Which measure obtained would you think as most appropriate?

Chapter 37

Spectral Analysis: Theory

In this chapter, our aim is to derive a mathematical expression that can help us quantify the following:

- How much of the total variability of a series can be attributed to movements of different periods or lengths? Are movements of short or long duration responsible for most of the variability of a given economic time series?

37.1 Motivation and main issues

The main goal of spectral analysis, at least in economics, is to obtain a straightforward theoretical expression and estimates of it that can answer the following question: What is the relative importance of movements of various frequencies in explaining the total variation in a given series? By total variation, it is often useful to think in terms of the "total bouncing up and down" that occurs in a series. Of course, we will need to make these concepts more precise. Take the example depicted in Figure 37.1. Here, one can see two types of approximately cyclical movements: one with a short-period (high frequency) and the other with a long-period (low frequency). Which one contributes more to the total variation in the series? Recall that period is 2π/frequency.

The way the graph is constructed, the answer is that a low-frequency component makes the series vary by a substantially larger amount (think about the range between the cycles) than the

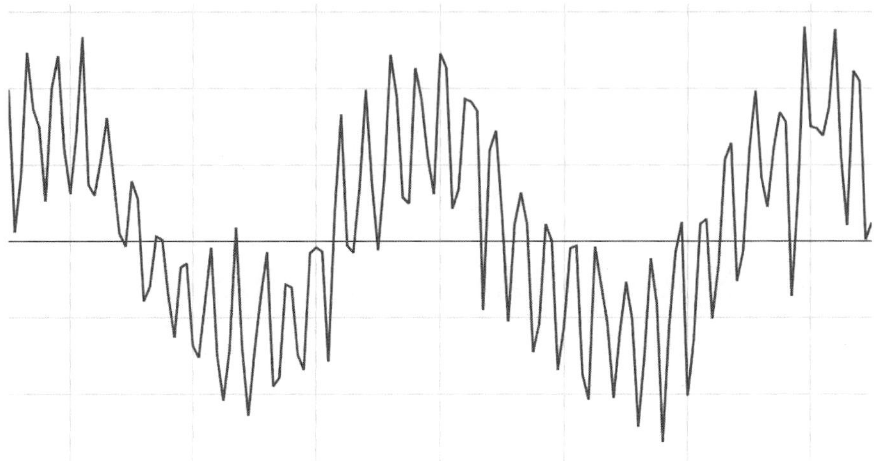

Figure 37.1. A series with two approximate cyclical components.

high-frequency one, even though the latter appears to have more "action", which is simply a reflection of the fact that it is a movement of higher frequency.

It is useful to think about the axis of a graph that would depict the function of interest. Obviously, the horizontal axis should be frequency. But with what range? Of course, it should start at 0. This may sound strange at first since it seems to indicate a movement of infinite duration and you may wonder, rightly so, what is this in the real world. In economic jargon, think about this as the "long-run". But this still begs the question about what the "long-run" is. Recall from Chapter 8 that the long-run cumulative impact of a series is a central ingredient to perform inference in time-series models as it dictates the variance of the limit distribution of the sample average (among other quantities). It is this quantity that we want to capture when we refer to the zero frequency. As we see later, the value of the function we seek at the zero frequency is indeed the equivalent (up to some scaling) as this limit variance that we need to deal with.

What about the right-end point of the horizontal axis? Think about making inference about the position of the series at some point in a cycle and then fitting a line across the cycles. We obviously need at least two periods to have two observations in each cycle. Having two such points is the minimal requirement to at least draw some kind of connection. Hence, the maximal frequency will be π since two periods are equivalent to $(2\pi/\pi)$. It does not mean that cycles of higher frequency than π or duration smaller than two units (e.g., two quarters with quarterly data or two months with monthly data) do not exist. It is simply that we cannot say anything about them given the limitations imposed by the sampling nature of our data.

What about the vertical axis? Here, and basically everywhere with this topic, the terminology comes from physics. But it is easy to get an intuition for stationary data. What is the energy to sustain a stationary series over an infinite period of time? Think about energy as some kind of force that makes the series moves (labor input, capital, technology, and so on). It should be intuitive that it must be infinite since the variance of a stationary process is constant and, hence, underlying forces are constantly being required to sustain its variations. Now, consider power, which is energy per unit of time. This is much more likely to be a finite and well-defined quantity. It is indeed the case as we see more precisely in the following. Hence, the vertical axis will be "power spectral density function". The graph for the example above then looks something like Figure 37.2.

This would be the power spectral density function of a series with a strong seasonal movement (the right peak) and a strong "business cycle" component (the left peak). Hence, this allows us to define precisely what characterizes a "business cycle". It occurs when there is a peak in the power spectral density function at some frequency

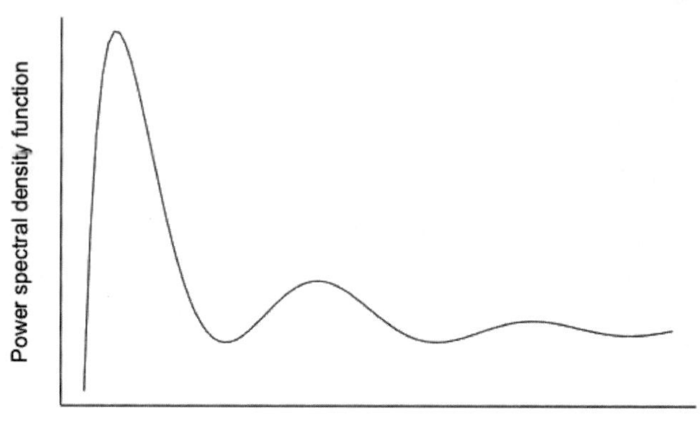

Figure 37.2. Power spectral density function for the series depicted in Figure 37.1.

within a range that we can classify as pertaining to a macroeconomic cycle; a common range is 1.5–8 years (e.g., Baxter and King, 1999), though longer durations have also been considered; see Section 37.5.2.

The perceptive reader might wonder why the graph does not simply have two spikes corresponding to the two cyclical movements. The answer is that in Figure 37.1 the cyclical movements are not perfect periodic functions; they are contaminated by errors (drawn on purpose). This noisy cyclical nature gives rise to "leakages" around the main frequency; i.e., it makes a discrete spectrum become a smoother version with non-zero values at most frequencies. We return to that in Section 37.2.3.

What is the typical spectral density function of most economic time series? An early investigation, which became a classic, is the work of Granger (1966). He documented the following feature that applies for most series; see Figure 37.3. Things have not changed since then, and it is still a good characterization even with the advent of more sophisticated techniques.

It shows that the main contributions to total variation are the low frequencies, i.e., the long-run-type movements. The other important

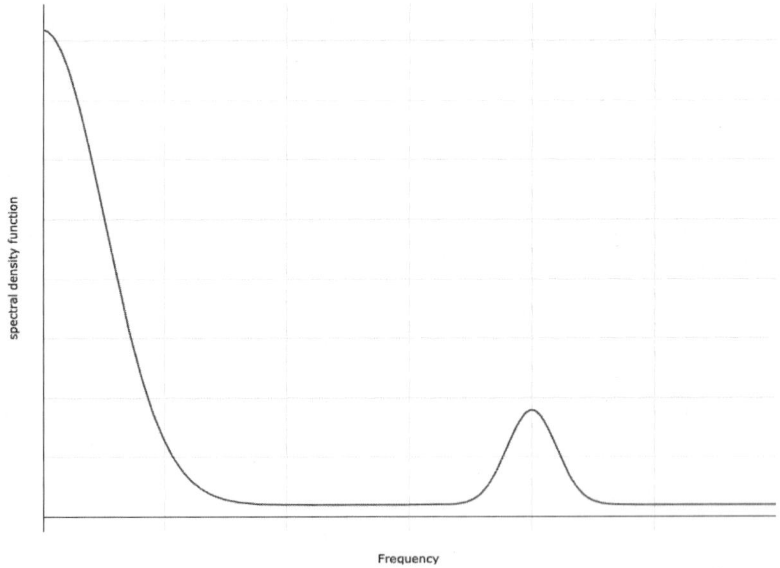

Figure 37.3. Typical spectral density function of most economic time series.

source is seasonality associated with a movement of period one-year. There is no evidence of business cycles. Granger (1966) recognized that such a "typical spectral density function" may be due to the presence of trends. He nevertheless argues that the same pattern remains even with properly detrended economic data. The main message is that most of the action is at the low frequencies, except for seasonal movements.

For a review of applications of spectral analysis in econometrics, see the work of Engle and Granger (1984). For a treatment of band spectral regressions, see the works of Engle (1974) and Engle (1980) (see also Section 49.8.2).

37.2 Theoretical results

This issue of movements of different lengths takes us to the concept of periodic functions. We therefore start with deterministic functions of this type. We take a rather long route to finally arrive at an easy expression. The detour will, however, help us better understand the practical interpretation of the mathematical expression. The successive topics to be covered are as follows:

1. Fourier series for deterministic functions with periodicity 2π,
2. Fourier series for deterministic functions with general periodicity,
3. spectral analysis of deterministic periodic functions with general periodicity,
4. Fourier integrals for non-periodic deterministic functions,
5. energy density function for non-periodic deterministic functions,
6. spectral analysis of stationary continuous time stochastic processes, and finally,
7. spectral density function for discrete time stationary stochastic processes.

Readers not interested in a full treatment of the theory can skip to Section 37.3. There might be a minor lack of understanding about where the exact form for the function comes from but not at the expense of being able to apply the results. The treatment in the following sections follows closely the work of Priestley (1981). Our treatment avoids excessive technical details. Some readers may be offended by the lack of rigor. Our intention is not to provide rigorous proofs but rather to provide enough details so that an understanding of the main issues is obtained.

37.2.1 Fourier series for functions with periodicity 2π

We start with the concept of a Fourier series given by

$$x(t) = \sum_{n=1}^{\infty} (a_n \cos(nt) + b_n \sin(nt)) + 1/2\, a_0, \tag{37.1}$$

where $\{a_n\}$ and $\{b_n\}$ are arbitrary sequences of constants (subject to convergence of the infinite summation). These are called Fourier coefficients. We state, without proof, the following important result.

Proposition 37.1. *Any periodic deterministic function (of periodicity 2π) can be represented by a Fourier series.*

This is a strong result and points to the fact that sine and cosine functions are the building blocks from which we can construct periodic functions.

Lemma 37.1. *We can express the Fourier coefficients as (provided some regularity conditions hold)*

$$a_m = \frac{1}{\pi}\int_{-\pi}^{\pi} x(t)\cos(mt)\,dt, \quad m = 0, 1, 2, \ldots,$$

$$b_m = \frac{1}{\pi}\int_{-\pi}^{\pi} x(t)\sin(mt)\,dt.$$

These are called Euler–Fourier formulae.

Remark 37.1. One of the regularity conditions is that $x(t)$ must be absolutely integrable, i.e., $\int_{-\pi}^{\pi} |x(t)|dt < \infty$. This will become important later.

Proof. We consider deriving the representation of the coefficients a_m. The steps for deriving the coefficients b_m are basically identical.

Multiply each sides of (37.1) by $\cos(mt)$ and integrate from $-\pi$ to π:

$$\begin{aligned}\int_{-\pi}^{\pi} x(t)\cos(mt)dt &= (1/2)a_0 \int_{-\pi}^{\pi} \cos(mt)dt \\ &\quad + \sum_{n=1}^{\infty} \left\{ a_n \int_{-\pi}^{\pi} \cos(nt)\cos(mt)dt \right. \\ &\quad \left. + b_n \int_{-\pi}^{\pi} \sin(nt)\cos(mt)dt \right\}, \qquad (37.2)\end{aligned}$$

for $m = 0, 1, \ldots$. From the properties of sine and cosine functions, we have

$$\int_{-\pi}^{\pi} \cos(nt)\cos(mt)dt = 0, \quad m \neq n,$$

$$\int_{-\pi}^{\pi} \sin(nt)\cos(mt)dt = 0, \quad \text{all } m, n,$$

$$\int_{-\pi}^{\pi} \sin(nt)\sin(mt)dt = 0, \quad m \neq n.$$

So, all terms on the right-hand side of (37.2) vanish except one and we have

$$\int_{-\pi}^{\pi} x(t)\cos(mt)dt = a_m \int_{-\pi}^{\pi} \cos^2(mt)dt = a_m\pi$$

so that

$$a_m = \frac{1}{\pi}\int_{-\pi}^{\pi} x(t)\cos(mt)\,dt.$$

To derive the coefficients b_m, the steps are the same except that one multiplies (37.1) by $\sin(mt)$ instead of $\cos(mt)$.

37.2.2 Fourier series for functions of general periodicity

To analyze functions of general periodicity, we simply work with functions of periodicity 2π and replace the time scale, i.e., we define a new function $y(\pi t/T) = x(t)$ so that $x(t)$ has periodicity $2T$ and $y(t)$ has periodicity 2π so that

$$y(s) = (1/2)a_0 + \sum_{n=1}^{\infty} (a_n \cos(ns) + b_n \sin(ns)).$$

Let $s = \pi t/T$. Then,

$$x(t) \equiv y(\pi t/T) = (1/2)a_0 + \sum_{n=1}^{\infty} [a_n \cos(\pi nt/T) + b_n \sin(\pi nt/T)].$$

The Fourier coefficients are

$$a_n = (1/\pi) \int_{-\pi}^{\pi} y(s) \cos(ns)\, ds \equiv T^{-1} \int_{-T}^{T} x(t) \cos(\pi nt/T)\, dt,$$

$$b_n = (1/\pi) \int_{-\pi}^{\pi} y(s) \sin(ns)\, ds \equiv T^{-1} \int_{-T}^{T} x(t) \sin(\pi nt/T)\, dt.$$

Remark 37.2. A regularity condition here is that $\int_{-T}^{T} |x(t)|dt < \infty$.

37.2.3 Spectral analysis of periodic functions with general periodicity

Define the total energy over an interval $(-T, T)$ as

$$\int_{-T}^{T} x(t)^2\, dt.$$

Think of this as the variance of a zero mean process. It is not difficult to show that (see Exercise 37.1):

$$\int_{-T}^{T} x(t)^2\, dt = T\left[(1/2)a_0^2 + \sum_{n=1}^{\infty} \left(a_n^2 + b_n^2\right)\right]. \tag{37.3}$$

Now, let

$$c_0 = a_0/2$$

and

$$c_n = \left[(1/2)\left(a_n^2 + b_n^2\right)\right]^{1/2}.$$

Then,

$$\int_{-T}^{T} x(t)^2\, dt = 2T\left\{\sum_{n=0}^{\infty} c_n^2\right\}. \tag{37.4}$$

We have the following representation for total power over the interval $(-T, T)$:

$$\begin{aligned}\text{Total power over } (-T,T) &= \text{Total energy over } (-T,T)/2T \\ &= \sum_{n=0}^{\infty} c_n^2.\end{aligned}$$

So, we interpret the coefficients c_n^2 as the contribution to the total power from the term in the Fourier series of $x(t)$ with frequency $(n/2T)$ units. A plot of c_n^2 against $n/2T$ gives a discrete power spectrum. It is discrete because we are still dealing with deterministic periodic processes. See Figure 37.4 for an example.

Think of this graph as the power spectrum of radio station waves in your city, assuming you listen to radio via the old non-internet way with a receptor that captures signals sent electromagnetically,

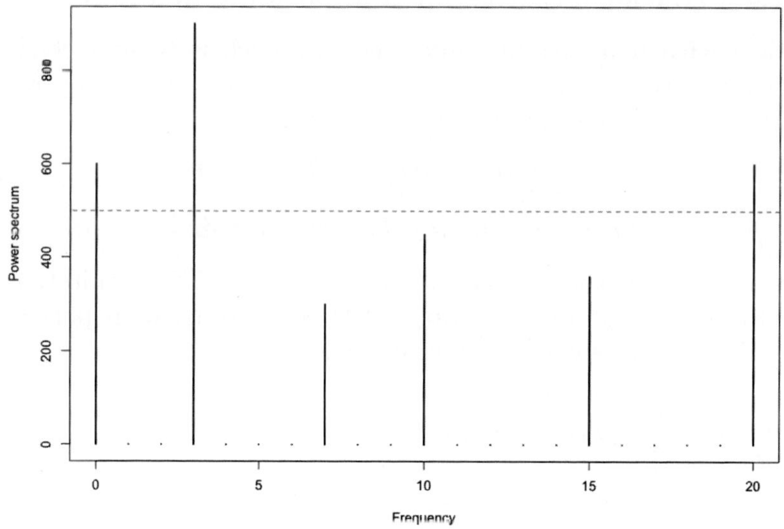

Figure 37.4. Discrete power spectrum.

e.g., what is still being used in a car (without WIFI). The different radio stations send signals at pre-determined specific frequencies. Some may be close by, hence high power, while some may be further away, hence lower power. If you have listened to radio in, say, a car, there is usually a scan button. This is simply a power spectral density finder that stops when the signal reaches a particular threshold (the horizontal dashed line in the graph). If the signal is weaker than the pre-specified threshold, you can use a dial button to reach the particular frequency you want. Now, while the radio signals are sent at fixed frequencies, things like pollution, buildings, clouds, etc. might distort the signals sent. They then become random. This has the effect of making the discrete power spectrum into a continuous one, i.e., a bell shape around the correct frequency. Hence, randomness induces a continuum of relevant frequencies. In the radio example, this shows up as a weak but still detectable signal near the frequency of interest. In the old days (for some of us), the trick was to have a "good enough" receiver to be able to focus on the relevant frequencies. The cool kids on the block would have a receiver with two dials, the secondary one being used to fine-tune the receiver around the strongest signal.

37.2.4 Fourier integrals for non-periodic functions

To deal with non-periodic functions, the trick is to first construct a Fourier series which will represent the actual series $x(t)$ over an interval $(-T, T)$ and define the new function

$$x_T^*(t) = x(t), \quad -T \leq t \leq T,$$
$$x_T^*(t + 2pT) = x_T^*(t), \quad p = 1, 2, 3, \ldots.$$

That is, we repeat the function defined over $(-T, T)$ infinitely many times outside that interval. So, $x_T^*(t)$ is periodic, with period $2T$, and may be expressed as a Fourier series, i.e.,

$$x_T^*(t) = \sum_{n=1}^{\infty} [a_n \cos(2\pi f_n t) + b_n \sin(2\pi f_n t)] + (1/2)a_0, \qquad (37.5)$$

where

$$f_n = n/(2T)$$

and $b_0 = 0$. Using the relations

$$\cos x = (1/2)\left[\exp(ix) + \exp(-ix)\right]$$

and

$$\sin x = (1/2i)\left[\exp(ix) - \exp(-ix)\right],$$

we can rewrite (37.5) as

$$x_T^*(t) = \sum_{n=-\infty}^{\infty} A_n \exp(2\pi i f_n t), \tag{37.6}$$

where

$$A_n = \begin{cases} (1/2)\left(a_n - ib_n\right), & n \geq 1, \\ (1/2)a_0, & n = 0, \\ (1/2)\left(a_{|n|} + ib_{|n|}\right), & n \leq -1. \end{cases}$$

Recall that the Fourier coefficients are

$$a_n = T^{-1}\int_{-T}^{T} x_T^*(t)\cos(\pi nt/T)\,dt,$$

$$b_n = T^{-1}\int_{-T}^{T} x_T^*(t)\sin(\pi nt/T)\,dt.$$

Hence,

$$\begin{aligned} A_n &= (1/2)T^{-1}\int_{-T}^{T} x_T^*(t)\exp(-2\pi i f_n t)dt \\ &= (1/2)T^{-1}\int_{-T}^{T} x(t)\exp(-2\pi i f_n t)dt, \end{aligned}$$

where the last equality follows since $x(t)$ and $x_T^*(t)$ are identical over $(-T, T)$. Therefore,

$$x(t) = x_T^*(t) = \sum_{n=-\infty}^{\infty}\left(\int_{-T}^{T} x(t)\exp(-2\pi i f_n t)dt\right)\exp(2\pi i f_n t)\Delta f_n \tag{37.7}$$

over the interval $-T \leq t \leq T$, where, recalling that $f_n = n/(2T)$,

$$\Delta f_n = f_n - f_{n-1} = 1/(2T).$$

Now, let T increase to ∞. Then, $\Delta f_n \to 0$, and we have a continuous set of frequency points f_n, and (37.7) becomes (given some regularity conditions)

$$x(t) = \int_{-\infty}^{\infty} p(f) \exp(2\pi i f t) df,$$

which is the Fourier integral representation of $x(t)$, where

$$p(f) = \int_{-\infty}^{\infty} x(t) \exp(-2\pi i f t) dt$$

is the Fourier transform of $x(t)$.

Remark 37.3. The important point here is that we have a continuous range of frequency points contrary to general periodic functions.

Alternative representation in terms of angular frequencies. It is often common to express $x(t)$ and $p(f)$ in terms of angular frequencies. Transform f to $w = 2\pi f$, then $dw = 2\pi df$ and

$$x(t) = \frac{1}{\sqrt{2\pi}} \int_{-\infty}^{\infty} G(w) \exp(iwt) dw, \tag{37.8}$$

$$G(w) = \frac{1}{\sqrt{2\pi}} \int_{-\infty}^{\infty} x(t) \exp(-iwt) dt. \tag{37.9}$$

Finally, we can express the total energy of the process as follows, where as a matter of notation $|z|^2$ represents the complex conjugate product of the complex number z:

Proposition 37.2. *A representation for the "total energy" of $x(t)$ is*

$$\int_{-\infty}^{\infty} x^2(t) \, dt = \int_{-\infty}^{\infty} |G(w)|^2 \, dw.$$

Therefore, $\{ |G(w)|^2 \, dw \}$ represents the contribution to total energy from those components of $x(t)$ whose frequencies are between w and

$w + dw$. $|G(w)|^2$ is something like an energy density function and a plot of $G(w)^2$ against w gives an energy spectral density function.

Proof. From (37.8) and (37.9), we have

$$\begin{aligned}\int_{-\infty}^{\infty} x^2(t)\,dt &= \int_{-\infty}^{\infty} x(t)\left\{\frac{1}{\sqrt{2\pi}}\int_{-\infty}^{\infty} G(w)\exp(iwt)dw\right\}dt\\ &= \int_{-\infty}^{\infty} G(w)\left\{\frac{1}{\sqrt{2\pi}}\int_{-\infty}^{\infty} x(t)\exp(iwt)dt\right\}dw\end{aligned}$$

upon some regularity conditions. Since

$$\left\{\frac{1}{\sqrt{2\pi}}\int_{-\infty}^{\infty} x(t)\exp(iwt)dt\right\}$$

is the complex conjugate of $G(w)$, we have

$$\int_{-\infty}^{\infty} x^2(t)\,dt = \int_{-\infty}^{\infty} |G(w)|^2\,dw.$$

37.2.5 Spectral analysis of stationary continuous time stochastic processes

We now start adapting these results to the case of continuous time stochastic processes. In deriving the Fourier integrals for non-periodic deterministic functions, a regularity condition stated was the integrability of $x(t)$, *i.e.*,

$$\int_{-\infty}^{\infty} |x(t)|\,dt < \infty. \tag{37.10}$$

This almost certainly implies that $x(t) \to 0$ as $T \to \pm\infty$. If $x(t)$ is a stationary process, it certainly cannot behave in the same manner; indeed, we do not have $x(t) \to 0$ as $T \to \pm\infty$. So, we start using a truncation technique. Define

$$x_T(t) = \begin{cases} x(t), & -T \le t \le T,\\ 0, & \text{otherwise.}\end{cases}$$

Then, $x_T(t)$ satisfies (37.10), i.e., it is absolutely integrable since it is 0 outside the range $(-T, T)$. But $x_T(t)$ is not periodic. Assuming continuity, we may express $x_T(t)$ as a Fourier integral in the form (37.8) and (37.9), i.e.,

$$x_T(t) = \frac{1}{\sqrt{2\pi}} \int_{-\infty}^{\infty} G_T(w) \exp(iwt) dw,$$

where

$$\begin{aligned} G_T(w) &= \frac{1}{\sqrt{2\pi}} \int_{-\infty}^{\infty} x_T(t) \exp(-iwt) dt \\ &= \frac{1}{\sqrt{2\pi}} \int_{-T}^{T} x(t) \exp(-iwt) dt \, . \end{aligned}$$

The interpretation of $|G_T(w)|^2 dw$ is the contribution to the total energy of $x_T(t)$ contributed by those components with frequencies in a neighborhood of w. The problem is that we cannot let T increase to infinity since $\lim_{T\to\infty} |G_T(w)|^2$ will not exist. The intuition is that the energy to sustain a stationary process must be infinite since there is non-zero variability at all time points. So, instead of working with the energy concept, we work with "power"; i.e., energy per unit of time. In this case,

$$\lim_{T\to\infty} \frac{|G_T(w)|^2}{2T} \tag{37.11}$$

will be finite under suitable regularity conditions. So, we have the following interpretation: (37.11) is the proportion of the total power of $x(t)$ contributed by components with frequencies in a neighborhood of w. Since we are concerned with the whole stochastic process as opposed to a particular realization, we average over all realizations and consider the quantity

$$h(w) = \lim_{T\to\infty} \left[E\left\{ \frac{|G_T(w)|^2}{2T} \right\} \right],$$

which we interpret as follows: $h(w)\, dw$ is the average (over all realizations) of the contribution to the total power from components in

$x(t)$ with frequencies in a neighborhood of w. We have the following definition.

Definition 37.1. The (non-normalized) power spectral density function of $x(t)$ is

$$h(w) = \lim_{T\to\infty} [E\{|G_T(w)|^2 /(2T)\}].$$

An important result is that $h(w)$ is simply the Fourier transform of the autocovariance function $R(\tau)$.

Theorem 37.1. *If $x(t)$ is a mean zero continuous time stationary process with spectral density function $h(w)$ and autocovariance function $R(\tau)$,*

$$h(w) = \frac{1}{2\pi}\int_{-\infty}^{\infty} \exp(-iw\tau)R(\tau)\,d\tau.$$

Similarly, $R(\tau)$ is the inverse Fourier transform of $h(w)$, i.e.,

$$R(\tau) = \int_{-\infty}^{\infty} \exp(iw\tau)h(w)\,dw.$$

Proof. We give some heuristic proof that is intended to convey the intuition behind the developments but skips many technical steps (we also assume all the regularity conditions for the interchange of integrals and expectation operators). We have

$$\begin{aligned} E\left\{\frac{|G_T(w)|^2}{2T}\right\} &= E\left\{\frac{1}{2\pi}\frac{1}{2T}\int_{-T}^{T} x(t)\exp(-iwt)dt \right. \\ &\qquad \left. \times \int_{-T}^{T} x(s)\exp(iws)ds\right\} \\ &= \frac{1}{2\pi}\frac{1}{2T}\int_{-T}^{T}\int_{-T}^{T} \exp(iw(s-t))E[x(t)\,x(s)]dtds \\ &= \frac{1}{2\pi}\frac{1}{2T}\int_{-T}^{T}\int_{-T}^{T} \exp(iw(s-t))R(t-s)dtds. \end{aligned}$$

Now, let $\tau = t - s$,

$$E\left\{\frac{|G_T(w)|^2}{2T}\right\} = \frac{1}{2\pi}\frac{1}{2T}\int_{-T}^{T}\int_{-T}^{T}\exp(-iw\tau)R(\tau)dsd\tau$$

$$= \frac{1}{2\pi}\frac{1}{2T}\int_{-T}^{T}ds\int_{-T}^{T}\exp(-iw\tau)R(\tau)d\tau$$

$$= \frac{1}{2\pi}\int_{-T}^{T}\exp(-iw\tau)R(\tau)d\tau,$$

and, taking limits,

$$h(w) = \lim_{T\to\infty}\left[E\left\{\frac{|G_T(w)|^2}{2T}\right\}\right] = \frac{1}{2\pi}\int_{-\infty}^{\infty}\exp(-iw\tau)R(\tau)d\tau.$$

Definition 37.2 (Normalized Power Spectral Density Function). Let $\sigma_x^2 = R(0)$. Then, the normalized power spectral density function of x is $f(w) = h(w)/\sigma_x^2$.

This quantity has the following interpretation: $f(w)\,dw$ is the average (over all realizations) of the proportion of the total power contributed by components with frequencies in a neighborhood of w. It is a proportion because

$$\sigma_x^2 = R(0) = \int_{-\infty}^{\infty} h(w)\,dw$$

is the total power. Since $\rho(\tau) = R(\tau)/\sigma_x^2$, we have

$$f(w) = \frac{1}{2\pi}\int_{-\infty}^{\infty}\exp(-iw\tau)\rho(\tau)\,d\tau$$

and

$$\rho(\tau) = \int_{-\infty}^{\infty}\exp(iw\tau)f(w)\,dw,$$

i.e., $f(w)$ is the Fourier transform of the autocorrelation function $\rho(\tau)$.

37.3 Discrete-parameter processes

All that we have done so far is valid for continuous time processes only; i.e., as if $x(t)$ was observed continuously. For a discrete time process, denoted x_t, we need some modifications. We recall the Fourier transform of the autocovariance function

$$R(\tau) = \int_{-\infty}^{\infty} \exp(iw\tau) h(w)\, dw$$

and note that for discrete processes τ is integer-valued. We can write (De Moivre's theorem):

$$\exp(iw\tau) = \cos(\tau w) + i \sin(\tau w),$$

and we have

$$\cos(\tau(w + 2s\pi)) = \cos(\tau w),$$
$$\sin(\tau(w + 2s\pi)) = \sin(\tau w),$$

for any integer s. Hence,

$$\exp(iw\tau) = \mathrm{cxp}(i\tau(w + 2s\pi)).$$

Therefore, the components in x_t with frequencies $w \pm s(2\pi)$ will appear to have frequency w. This is referred to as the aliasing effect, i.e., w is the "alias" of all the frequencies $w \pm s(2\pi)$ (s an integer). See Figure 37.5 for an example.

The implication is that there is no point in defining a spectral quantity outside the range $(-\pi, \pi)$. Hence, we cannot say anything about movements with periods lower than two units of time (recall period=2π/frequency).

This feature is fairly intuitive. Suppose that we have quarterly data, then it is obvious that we cannot infer anything about "high frequency" movements, such as daily variations. These daily movements will appear with quarterly data as being described by some "lower-frequency" movements (their alias). Another way to understand this is that if we want to fit some kind of correspondence

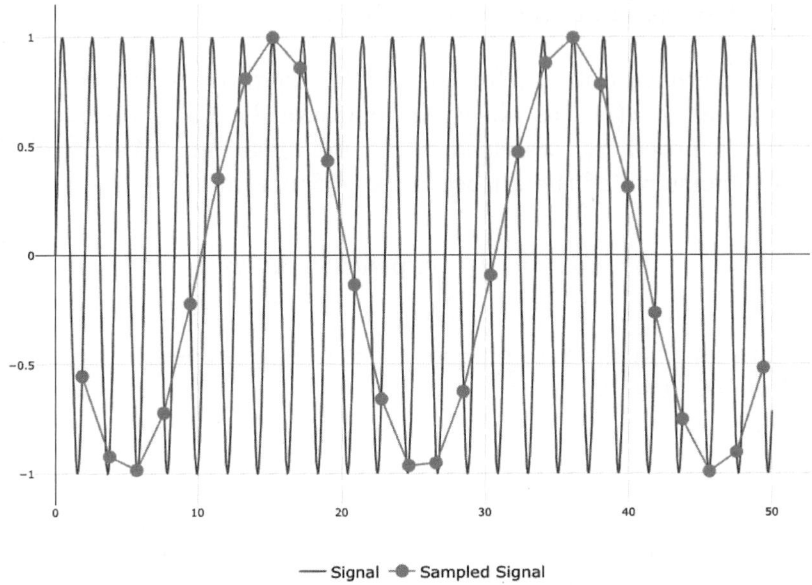

Figure 37.5. Aliasing effect.

between points across different portions of a cyclical component, we need at least two data points, otherwise no fit is even possible.

Therefore, in discrete time, we have

$$\rho(\tau) = \int_{-\pi}^{\pi} \exp(iw\tau) f(w)\, dw, \quad \tau = 0, \pm 1, \pm 2, \ldots,$$

and

$$f(w) = \frac{1}{2\pi} \sum_{\tau=-\infty}^{\infty} \rho(\tau) \exp(-iw\tau), \quad -\pi \leq w \leq \pi.$$

Note that we now have a summation instead of an integral. Similarly, the non-normalized quantities are

$$R(\tau) = \int_{-\pi}^{\pi} \exp(iw\tau) h(w)\, dw, \quad \tau = 0, \pm 1, \pm 2, \ldots,$$

and

$$h(w) = \frac{1}{2\pi} \sum_{\tau=-\infty}^{\infty} R(\tau) \exp(-iw\tau), \quad -\pi \leq w \leq \pi,$$

so that $h(w)$ is the discrete Fourier transform of the autocovariance function. When the process is real-valued, as we assume, $R(\tau)$ is even, i.e., $R(\tau) = R(-\tau)$, and so

$$h(w) = \frac{1}{2\pi} R(0) + \frac{1}{\pi} \sum_{\tau=1}^{\infty} R(\tau) \cos(\tau w)$$

since

$$2\cos(\tau w) = \exp(-iw\tau) + \exp(iw\tau),$$

or we can also write (since $\cos(-\tau w) = \cos(\tau w)$),

$$h(w) = \frac{1}{2\pi} \sum_{\tau=-\infty}^{\infty} R(\tau) \cos(\tau w), \quad -\pi \leq w \leq \pi. \tag{37.12}$$

Furthermore, it is easy to show that $h(w)$ is even, i.e., $h(w) = h(-w)$, since $\cos(\tau w) = \cos(-\tau w)$; hence, we can restrict the range of $h(w)$ under study to $(0, \pi)$.

37.4 Results for linear processes

We start with a result that is of independent interest and also useful in other contexts.

37.4.1 The autocovariance generating function

The autocovariance generating function is very useful in subsequent discussions. There is nothing magic behind it. It is simply a device that we invent to make our derivations easier later on, nothing more. It comes from nowhere. It is simply a definition given by

$$G(z) = \sum_{k=-\infty}^{\infty} R(k) z^k.$$

All that it says is that the function $G(z)$ is a two-sided infinite polynomial in z with the autocovariance at delay k as the weight on the kth power of z. Since, for real-valued processes, the autocovariance function is such that $R(k) = R(-k)$, the weights on the terms z^k and z^{-k} are the same. Such a constructed device will be useful because for linear processes an easy expression can be found.

Recall that from the Wold decomposition theorem of Chapter 8, of which *ARMA* processes are a special case, any stationary process has a linear representation in terms of *i.i.d.* random variables. To that effect, suppose that x_t is generated by the linear process

$$x_t = \sum_{j=0}^{\infty} c_j e_{t-j}, \quad e_t \sim i.i.d.\left(0, \sigma_e^2\right),$$

with $c_0 = 1$, or

$$x_t = C\left(L\right) e_t,$$

where

$$C\left(L\right) = \sum_{j=0}^{\infty} c_j L^j.$$

Then, the autocovariance function is given by

$$\begin{aligned} R\left(k\right) &= E\left[x_t x_{t+|k|}\right] \\ &= E\left[\sum_{j=0}^{\infty}\sum_{i=0}^{\infty} c_j c_i e_{t-j} e_{t+|k|-i}\right] \\ &= \sum_{j=0}^{\infty}\sum_{i=0}^{\infty} c_j c_i E\left[e_{t-j} e_{t+|k|-i}\right] \\ &= \sigma_e^2 \sum_{j=0}^{\infty} c_j c_{j+|k|}. \end{aligned}$$

The last equality follows since $E[e_{t-j}e_{t+|k|-i}]$ is non-zero only when $i = j + |k|$. Hence,

$$\begin{aligned} G(z) &= \sigma_e^2 \sum_{k=-\infty}^{\infty} \sum_{j=0}^{\infty} c_j c_{j+|k|} z^k \\ &= \sigma_e^2 \left[\sum_{j=0}^{\infty} c_j^2 + \sum_{k=1}^{\infty} \sum_{j=0}^{\infty} c_j c_{j+k} (z^k + z^{-k}) \right] \\ &= \sigma_e^2 \left(\sum_{j=0}^{\infty} c_j z^j \right) \left(\sum_{k=0}^{\infty} c_k z^{-k} \right) \\ &= \sigma_e^2 C(z) C(z^{-1}). \end{aligned}$$

This expression can be very helpful in finding autocovariances, but we mainly use it to obtain easy expressions when dealing with the spectral density function and related quantities for linear processes.

Example 37.1. Consider the MA(1) process where $C(z) = 1 + b_1 z$. We have

$$\begin{aligned} G(z) &= \sigma_e^2 (1 + b_1 z)(1 + b_1 z^{-1}) \\ &= \sigma_e^2 \left(1 + b_1 z + b_1 z^{-1} + b_1^2\right). \end{aligned}$$

Hence,

$$\begin{aligned} R(0) &= \left(1 + b_1^2\right) \sigma_e^2, \\ R(1) &= b_1 \sigma_e^2, \end{aligned}$$

and $R(k) = 0$ for $k > 1$, a result we derived earlier using "brute force" derivations in Chapter 8.

37.4.2 Spectral density function for linear processes

Using the autocovariance generating function, we have that

$$h(w) = (2\pi)^{-1} G\left(e^{-iw}\right),$$

i.e., the autocovariance generating function evaluated at $z = e^{-iw}$. This is very helpful since we have an easy expression for the autocovariance generating function in terms of the linear representation of a stationary process of the form

$$x_t = C(L)e_t,$$
$$e_t \sim i.i.d.(0, \sigma_e^2)$$

(valid for all stationary $ARMA$ models). So,

$$h(w) = \frac{\sigma_e^2}{2\pi} C\left(e^{-iw}\right) C\left(e^{iw}\right) = \frac{\sigma_e^2}{2\pi} \left|C\left(e^{-iw}\right)\right|^2.$$

For stationary $ARMA$ processes of the form

$$A(L)\, x_t = B(L)\, e_t,$$

we have

$$x_t = A(L)^{-1} B(L)\, e_t \equiv C(L)\, e_t$$

and

$$h(w) = \frac{\sigma_e^2}{2\pi} \frac{B\left(e^{-iw}\right) B\left(e^{iw}\right)}{A\left(e^{-iw}\right) A\left(e^{iw}\right)}.$$

Example 37.2 (White noise process). $B(z) = A(z) = 1$ and $h(w) = \sigma_e^2/(2\pi)$. Hence, the spectral density function is constant and the total power is uniformly distributed over all frequencies, just as the color white is light composed of all colors (frequencies) in equal amounts. Hence, the terminology "white noise".

Example 37.3 (Spectral Density at Frequency 0).

$$h(0) = (\sigma_e^2/(2\pi)) C(1)^2, \tag{37.13}$$

with $C(1) = \sum_{i=0}^{\infty} c_i$, the sum of the moving average coefficients. Recall from Chapter 8 that the cumulative long-run effect of a shock on the level of the series is given by $C(1)$; hence, there is a direct link between that quantity and the spectral density function at frequency zero. More importantly, recall the Central Limit Theorem (CLT) for the sample average of a stationary (linear) process given by

$$T^{-1/2}\sum_{t=1}^{T}(x_t - \mu) = T^{-1/2}(\bar{X} - \mu) \xrightarrow{d} N(0, \sigma_e^2 C(1)^2), \tag{37.14}$$

which, using (37.13), can be expressed as

$$T^{-1/2}\sum_{t=1}^{T}(x_t - \mu) = T^{-1/2}(\bar{X} - \mu) \xrightarrow{d} N(0, 2\pi h(0)). \tag{37.15}$$

This is the main reason why the spectral density function at frequency zero plays such an important role when making inference with time-series data. Indeed, we see in the following chapter how all the material discussed in Chapter 11 about HAC (Heteroskedasticity and Autocorrelation Consistent) estimation is simply an application of methods to estimate $2\pi h(0)$.

37.5 Filtered series

We now look at the effect of linear filters on the spectral density function of some series. The results to be presented are deceptively simple but at the same time impressively powerful with a wide range of applications. We first cover the theory and then use the results to discuss three applications related to (a) business cycles, (b) seasonal adjustment, and (c) band-pass filters to extract the "cyclical" component of a time series.

37.5.1 Theory

Suppose that the original data are x_t and that y_t is some filtered version (i.e., a linear combination of past, present, and future values) of x_t given by

$$y_t = \psi(L)\, x_t,$$

with

$$\psi(L) = \sum_{j=-m_1}^{m_2} \psi_j L^j.$$

We have the following result.

Proposition 37.3. *The spectral density function of the filtered series y_t in terms of the spectral density function of the original stationary series x_t is given by*

$$h_y(w) = \left|\psi\left(e^{-iw}\right)\right|^2 h_x(w).$$

$\left|\psi\left(e^{-iw}\right)\right|^2$ *is called either the transfer function or filter function or squared gain function.*

Proof. We have

$$h_x(w) = (2\pi)^{-1} G_x\left(e^{-iw}\right),$$

where $G_x(\cdot)$ is the autocovariance generating function of x_t. Now, since x_t is stationary, it can be represented by the linear process

$$x_t = C(L)\,\varepsilon_t$$

and

$$y_t = \psi(L)\,x_t = \psi(L)\,C(L)\,\varepsilon_t.$$

Hence,

$$\begin{aligned} G_y(L) &= \sigma_e^2 \psi(L)\,C(L)\,\psi\left(L^{-1}\right) C\left(L^{-1}\right) \\ &= \psi(L)\,\psi\left(L^{-1}\right) G_x(L). \end{aligned}$$

Finally,

$$\begin{aligned} h_y(w) &= (2\pi)^{-1} G_y\left(e^{-iw}\right) \\ &= (2\pi)^{-1}\psi\left(e^{-iw}\right)\psi\left(e^{iw}\right) G_x\left(e^{-iw}\right) \\ &= \left|\psi\left(e^{-iw}\right)\right|^2 h_x(w). \end{aligned}$$

Of course, if we take $x_t = e_t$, an *i.i.d.* series, we have $h_x(w) = \sigma_e^2/(2\pi)$ and

$$h_y(w) = \frac{\sigma_e^2}{2\pi}\left|\psi\left(e^{-iw}\right)\right|^2.$$

We, therefore, recover our earlier result.

The theory of linear filters has many applications. A prominent one is in the analysis of seasonality where the goal is to apply some filter to remove the seasonal components without affecting, as much as possible, the spectral density function at other frequencies. A graph of the squared gain function can also be useful to see if a particular filter has desirable properties. It can also be used to purge the series from movements of particular frequencies (or durations). For instance, it can get rid of the very low and high-frequency components to obtain what could be viewed as a cyclical component being affected only by movements of "medium" durations. Another application is to see the effect of various transformations and their induced effect on the statistical properties of the series. We first discuss one such application related to business cycles.

37.5.2 Application: Kuznet's business cycles

Much of the material discussed here follows the work of Sargent (1979). It has long been popular in macroeconomics to analyze and document business cycles. We can say that there is a business cycle if the spectral density function contains a peak strictly in the interval $(0, \pi)$ not related to seasonal fluctuations. With such a peak, we can say that most of the variability of a given series is accounted for by movements of some periodicity or frequency which accords with the common notion of a business cycle. Famous presumed documentation of business cycles include the following: (a) Kitchin (1923) inventory cycle of 3–5 years, (b) Juglar (1889) fixed-investment cycle of 7–11 years, and (c) Kondratieff (1935) wave or long technological cycle of 45–60 years. The most famous one was that of Kuznets (1958) (see also Kuznets (1946) and Kuznets (1930)) who claimed that real economic activity was characterized by cycles of approximate period 20 years. It is instructive to see the details of the transformations of the data applied by Kuznet and their effect on his conclusion.

Denote by x_t the logarithm of the original annual real GNP series. Since such series are likely to be measured with errors (especially in the pre-World War II period used), Kuznet applied a 5-year moving average in an attempt to remove this idiosyncratic noise. Hence, we have the first transformation given by

$$z_t = A(L)x_t = (1/5)[L^{-2} + L^{-1} + 1 + L + L^2]x_t.$$

A second source of concern was that the data were trending and that one should allow for some changes over time in this trend function. In an attempt to remove this influence (and make the series stationary), Kuznet analyzed centered 10-year differences, that is, he considered the following filtered version:

$$y_t = z_{t+5} - z_{t-5} = B(L)z_t = [L^{-5} - L^5]z_t.$$

Hence, the series analyzed by Kuznet was the filtered version of the original data given by

$$y_t = A(L)B(L)x_t.$$

The effect of the linear filter on the statistical properties can be analyzed by the squared gain function given by

$$|A(e^{-iw})B(e^{-iw})|^2.$$

A graph of this squared gain function is given in Figure 37.6 along with that of the components $A(L)$ and $B(L)$ to get a better understanding of where the source of the problem lies. It is clear that it has a strong peak at the frequency $\pi/10$ which, with annual data, corresponds to a period of 20 years. Hence, irrespective of the nature of the original series, the application of the two linear transformations implies that a strong peak in the spectral density function will be found at a frequency corresponding to a period of 20 years. But this can hardly be conceived as evidence for the presence of a business cycle since it is simply an artifact of the transformations. We should stress that the transformations were, indeed, quite sensible. Their effect on the transformed series could hardly have been anticipated *ex ante* (at the time, no filtering theory of the type covered here was available). What Figure 37.6 reveals is that $B(L)$ is periodic with high peaks, including at $\pi/10$. The transfer function of $A(L)$ starts at one and declines rapidly to zero. Hence, the combination of the two makes the first peak at $\pi/10$ dominant. This points to the usefulness of the filtering theory in uncovering hidden features of particular transformations.

37.5.3 Application: Seasonal adjustment

Seasonal adjustment filters are usually analyzed as linear filters. The U.S. Census X-11 and Statistics Canada X-11 *ARIMA* methods,

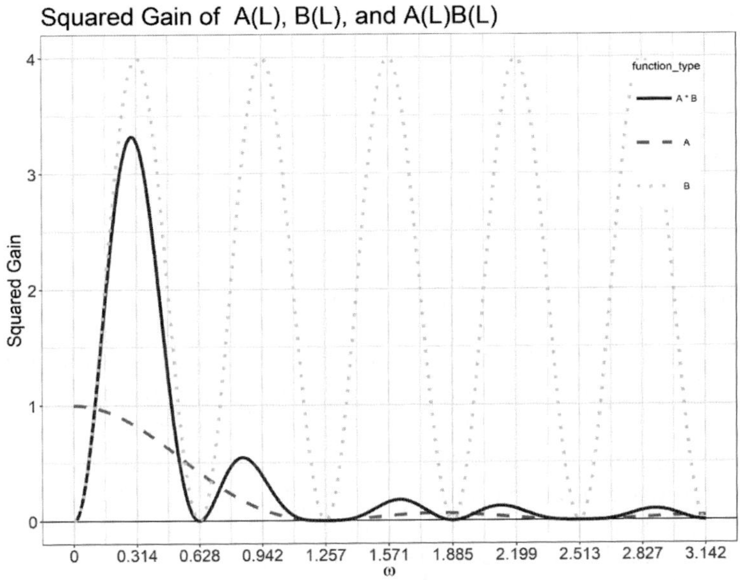

Figure 37.6. Transfer function of Kuznet's filter $A(L)B(L)$ and the components $A(L)$ and $B(L)$.

which are widely applied in Canada, the U.S., and several other countries, use a set of moving averages to produce seasonally adjusted data. Likewise, the so-called "model-based" seasonal adjustment filters, which are designed on the principle of optimal linear signal extraction theory, are also linear filters. In practice, however, seasonal adjustment methods such as the X-11 produce seasonally adjusted series which are not the output of a linear filter. Although the basic idea of moving averages is simple, the sets of filters used with X-11 change through time and hence imply a time-varying filtering of the original data. Nevertheless, we focus our attention on the linear approximation. Note that the U.S. Census Bureau has produced further upgrades, such as the X-13ARIMA-SEATS and the X-12-ARIMA. Still the X-11 remains the default in many softwares and the basis of the more recent methods. Since our aim is simply to provide insights into the method used, we focus on the linear filter of the X-11 method.

We first need to define what is meant by a seasonal component and then discuss which ones are present with either quarterly or monthly data.

Definition 37.3. A seasonal component is one with a period such that the event occurs at the same date or more precisely unit of measurement (e.g., quarters or months) each year.

Harmonics for Quarterly and Monthly Data

For quarterly data, we have periods of

1. one year or 4 quarters or frequency $\pi/2$,
2. 6 months or 2 quarters or frequency π.

These are the only ones. One could think of movements of period, say, one quarter or one month. While these may be present, we are constrained by the fact that we cannot say anything about them since we cannot infer anything with a frequency above π.

For monthly data, we have periods of

1. one year or 12 months or frequency $\pi/6$,
2. 6 months or frequency $\pi/3$,
3. 4 months or frequency $\pi/2$,
4. 3 months or frequency $2\pi/3$,
5. 12/5 months or frequency $5\pi/6$,
6. 2 months or frequency π.

Again, we cannot say anything about movements of shorter durations. These seasonal movements are usually called the "harmonics" (from some analogy with music and tonality). If we want to extract the seasonal component, then the ideal filter would look something like Figure 37.7. The filter would be one at all frequencies between 0 and π, except at the "harmonics" in which case the filter would suddenly dip to zero. Of course, in practice, one cannot have a sudden dip to zero; some kind of gradual dip is inevitable, creating "valleys", but a good filter would have these valleys as narrow as possible. We next present a brief description of the most commonly used seasonal adjustment filter. As we see, it comes quite close to reproducing the ideal filter.

The Linear Version of the Census X-11 Method

Much of the following material is from the work of Ghysels and Perron (1993). The Census X-11 program is the most widely

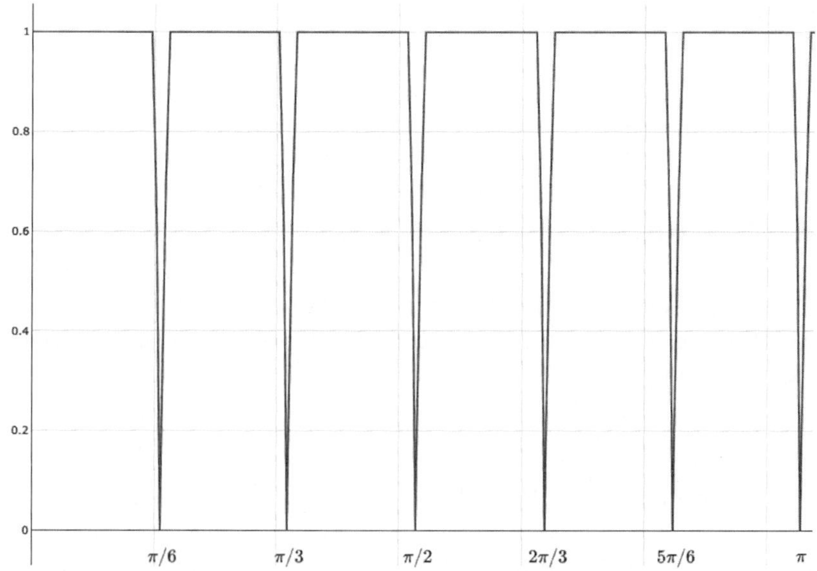

Figure 37.7. Ideal filter; monthly case.

applied adjustment procedure. It was the product of several decades of research. Its development started in the early 1930s by researchers at the N.B.E.R. (see, e.g., Macaulay, 1931) and it emerged as a fully operational procedure in the mid-1960s due to work by Julius Shiskin and his collaborators at the U.S. Bureau of the Census (see the work of Shiskin *et al.*, 1967). The program consists of a set of moving average filters which are applied to the data sequentially. It was noted that the program does not amount to a linear data transformation in almost all practical circumstances. The X-11 program can be represented by a linear filter when the default option is considered. Several authors, including Wallis (1974), Laroque (1977), Dagum (1983), Burridge and Wallis (1984), Ghysels (1984), and Ghysels and Perron (1993), have studied the quarterly and/or monthly linear X-11 filters. The exact structure of the linear approximation for the quarterly filter is presented in the work of Laroque (1977). We discuss in more details the filter weights of the linear approximation to the monthly filter.

The different steps of the X-11 monthly filter are as follows. A centered 13-term moving average is initially subtracted from the original series using the filter

$$\begin{aligned}SM(L) &= 1 - (1/24)(1 + L)(1 + L + \cdots + L^{11})L^{-6} \\ &\approx -0.042L^6 - 0.083L^5 - 0.083L^4 - 0.083L^3 \\ &\quad - 0.083L^2 - 0.083L + 0.917 - 0.083L^{-1} \\ &\quad - 0.083L^{-2} - 0.083L^{-3} - 0.083L^{-4} - 0.083L^{-5} - 0.042L^{-6}.\end{aligned}$$

The filtered series obtained is a first estimate of the seasonal plus noise part of the series. A first estimate of the seasonal part is obtained by applying the filter

$$\begin{aligned}M_1(L) &= (1/9)(L^s + 1 + L^{-s}) \\ &\approx 0.111L^{2s} + 0.222L^s + 0.333 + 0.222L^{-s} + 0.111L^{-2s},\end{aligned}$$

with $s = 12$. In order to have the seasonal components sum to unity over one year, the filter $SM(L)$ is applied once more. The whole process yields a first estimate of the seasonal component. This estimate is subtracted from the original series after which a Henderson moving average given by

$$\begin{aligned}HM(L) &= -0.019L^6 - 0.028L^5 + 0.066L^3 + 0.147L^2 \\ &\quad + 0.214L + 0.240 + 0.214L^{-1} + 0.147L^{-2} \\ &\quad + 0.066L^{-3} - 0.028L^{-5} - 0.019L^{-6} \qquad (37.16)\end{aligned}$$

is applied to obtain a second estimate of the trend–cycle component. The latter is subtracted from the original series to obtain a second estimate of the seasonal plus noise from which a final estimate of the seasonal component is obtained via the application of the filter

$$\begin{aligned}M_2(L) &= (1/15)(L^s + 1 + L^{-s})(L^{2s} + L^s + 1 + L^{-s} + L^{-2s}) \\ &\approx 0.067L^{3s} + 0.133L^{2s} + 0.200L^s + 0.200 + 0.200L^{-s} \\ &\quad + 0.133L^{-2s} + 0.067L^{-3s},\end{aligned}$$

again with $s = 12$. Finally, in order to have the seasonal components sum to unity, the filter $SM(L)$ is applied again. Consequently, adding up these steps and denoting $V^M_{X-11}(L)$ as the linear approximation, we have

$$\begin{aligned} V^M_{X-11}(L) &= 1 - SM(L) \times \{M_2(L)(1 - HM(L) \\ &\quad [1 - SM(L)M_1(L)SM(L)])\} \\ &= 1 - SM(L)M_2(L) + SM(L)M_2(L)HM(L) \\ &\quad - SM^3(L)M_1(L)M_2(L)HM(L). \end{aligned} \tag{37.17}$$

Summary

The coefficients of this filter are presented in Table 37.1. Each coefficient is applied twice: once for the lag and once for the lead terms.

Table 37.1. Filter weights of the linear monthly X-11 filter.

Lags					
0	0.819	23	0.011	46	−0.003
1	0.019	24	−0.121	47	−0.005
2	0.018	25	0.013	48	−0.005
3	0.017	26	0.013	49	−0.003
4	0.016	27	0.013	50	−0.001
5	0.015	28	0.013	51	0.002
6	0.014	29	0.012	52	0.003
7	0.013	30	0.008	53	0.003
8	0.014	31	0.005	54	0.002
9	0.015	32	0.004	55	0.001
10	0.018	33	0.003	56	0.000
11	0.020	34	0.003	57	−0.001
12	−0.179	35	0.004	58	−0.001
13	0.021	36	−0.063	59	−0.001
14	0.020	37	0.005	60	−0.001
15	0.018	38	0.007	61	−0.001
16	0.016	39	0.008	62	−0.001
17	0.015	40	0.008	63	0.001
18	0.012	41	0.008	64	0.001
19	0.009	42	0.005	65	0.001
20	0.009	43	0.002	66	0.000
21	0.009	44	0.001	67	0.000
22	0.010	45	−0.001	68	0.000

Source: Ghysels and Perron (1993), Table A.1. Reproduced with permission from Elsevier.

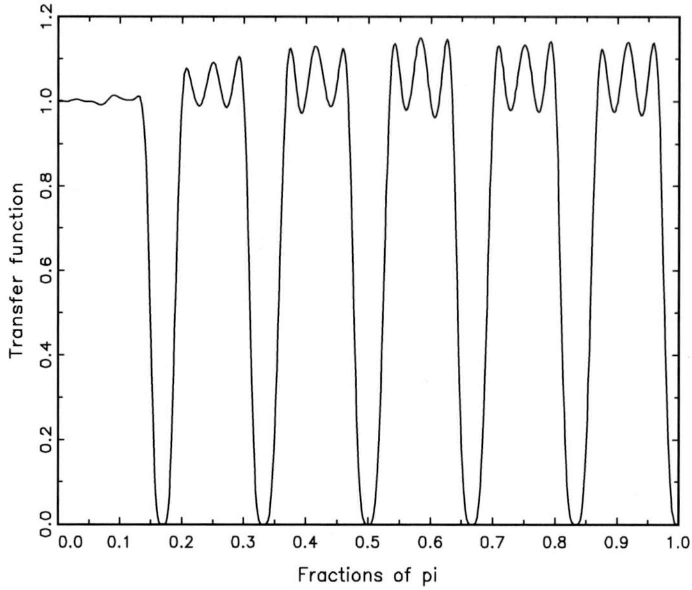

Figure 37.8. Transfer function of the linear monthly X-11 filter.
Source: Ghysels and Perron (1993), Figure A.1. Reproduced with permission from Elsevier.

The transfer function is reported in Figure 37.8. As desired, the transfer function of the final X-11 monthly filter has a large dip at the seasonal frequencies and wiggles around one at all other frequencies.

The quarterly X-11 filter, analyzed by Laroque (1977), is constructed in a similar fashion. The final filter denoted by $V^Q_{X-11}(L)$ is composed of

$$\begin{aligned} SQ(L) &= 1 - (1/8)(1+L)(1+L+L^2+L^3)L^{-2} \\ &= 0.125L^2 - 0.250L + 0.750 - 0.250L^{-1} - 0.125L^{-2} \\ HQ(L) &= -0.073L^2 + 0.294L + 0.558 + 0.294L^{-1} - 0.073L^{-2} \end{aligned}$$

along with $M_1(L)$ and $M_2(L)$, evaluated at $s = 4$. Again using (37.17) one can calculate the implied weights for the filter. They appear in Table 37.2. The transfer function of the final quarterly filter is reported in Figure 37.9 and exhibits features similar to the monthly filter.

Overall, these monthly and quarterly versions of the linear filter work quite well. The important things are first that the filter is

Table 37.2. Filter weight of the linear quarterly X-11 filter.

Lags			
0	0.858	14	0.016
1	0.051	15	−0.005
2	0.041	16	−0.010
3	0.050	17	0.000
4	−0.140	18	0.008
5	0.055	19	−0.002
6	0.034	20	−0.003
7	0.029	21	0.000
8	−0.097	22	0.002
9	0.038	23	0.000
10	0.025	24	0.000
11	0.012	25	0.000
12	−0.053	26	0.000
13	0.021	27	0.000

Source: Ghysels and Perron (1993), Table A.2. Reproduced with permission from Elsevier.

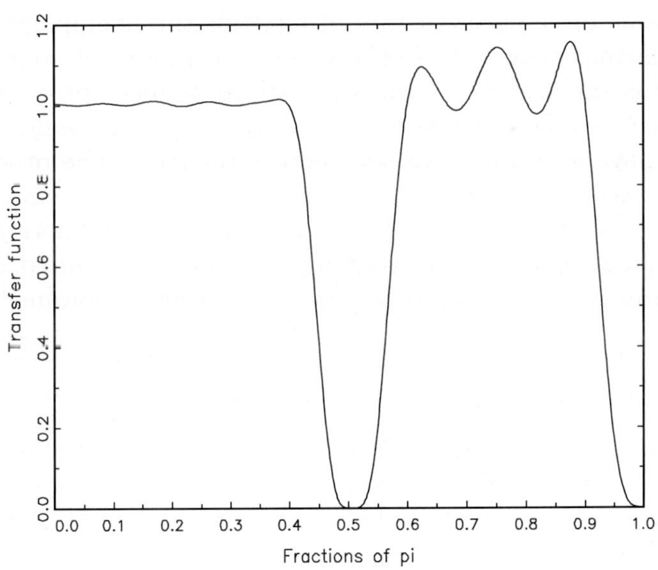

Figure 37.9. Transfer function of the linear quarterly X-11 filter.
Source: Ghysels and Perron (1993), Figure A.2. Reproduced with permission from Elsevier.

flat at one at low frequencies (before the first harmonic) so that the movements of main interest in economics are unchanged. The second important feature is that the valleys near the harmonics are quite narrow. The wiggles around one in between the harmonics are of no consequence in economics. Movements associated with such frequencies are of little to no importance in the vast majority of cases.

An important feature of the seasonal adjustment filters is that they are two-sided. Hence, if a seasonally adjusted figure is needed this month or quarter, one needs future values. The way to proceed is to forecast such values. The most popular method is to use an $ARIMA$ model. The forecasted values are then treated as the future observations to apply the filter. Hence, the method is commonly referred to as the Census X-11 $ARIMA$ seasonal adjustment procedure.

This implies that as time goes by, previous seasonally adjusted figures are revised since values that were used as forecasts at the time are now available as actual data. In practice, such revisions can be important up to a year or so as the weights of the filter become small quite rapidly. One often reads in the press (or the internet) that a value of the growth rate of GNP or the unemployment rate a few quarters prior has been revised. An important source of the revisions is this feature of the seasonal adjustment procedure since most macroeconomic figures are reported on a seasonally adjusted basis to have useful comparisons across the year. The other source for revisions is obviously the improvement in the data themselves. For instance, sampling is sparse on a monthly basis but more complete on an annual scale. Hence, past figures based on limited sampling are constantly being revised as new information is obtained.

37.5.4 Application: Band-pass filter

We now discuss an application of filtering theory used to extract the cyclical component of a time series. The material follows the works of Baxter and King (1999) and Christiano and Fitzgerald (2003). For this, we need to define a range of frequencies that we wish to associate with a "business cycle range". Baxter and King (1999) define this range as $w^a = 2\pi/32$ to $w^b = 2\pi/6$, i.e., 1.5–8 years with quarterly data.

Remark 37.4. Beaudry *et al.* (2020) argued that a more representative range for business cycle analysis is from 2 to 50 quarters. The argument is that the length between recessions has become longer on average. They argue that many economic time series display a peak in the spectral density function at frequencies corresponding to movements between 32 and 50 quarters.

Let $\beta(w)$ be a spectral density function (or squared gain function) of the desired filter. Define the filter as

$$b(L) = \sum_{h=-\infty}^{\infty} b_h L^h,$$

$$b_h = \int_{-\pi}^{\pi} \beta(w) e^{iwh} dw.$$

Definition 37.4 (Low-Pass Filter). A low-pass filter keeps only components with frequencies $-\bar{w} \leq w \leq \bar{w}$; see Figure 37.10. That is,

$$\beta(w) = \begin{cases} 1, & |w| \leq \bar{w}, \\ 0, & \text{otherwise.} \end{cases}$$

It follows that

$$b_h = \frac{1}{2\pi} \int_{-\bar{w}}^{\bar{w}} e^{iwh} dw = \begin{cases} \bar{w}/\pi, & h = 0, \\ \sin(\bar{w}h)/(\pi h), & \text{otherwise.} \end{cases}$$

Remark 37.5. Symmetric filters whose coefficients sum to zero eliminate deterministic trends (up to a second-order polynomial in time). See Exercise 37.3.

Definition 37.5 (Band-Pass Filter). Consider two low-pass filters with cutoffs $\bar{w} = w^a$ and $\bar{w} = w^b$, where $w^a < w^b$. Then, a band-pass filter is the difference between two low-pass filters, with resulting squared gain function $\beta(w) = \beta^b(w) - \beta^a(w)$. See Figure 37.11.

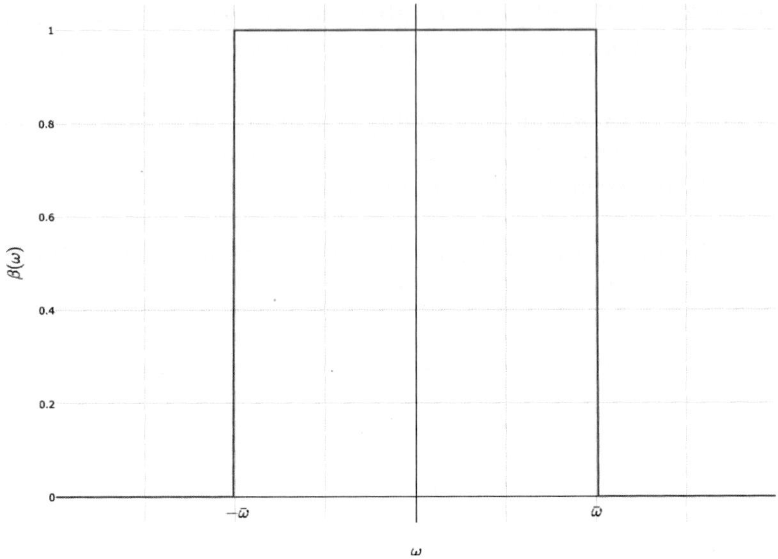

Figure 37.10. Low-pass filter.

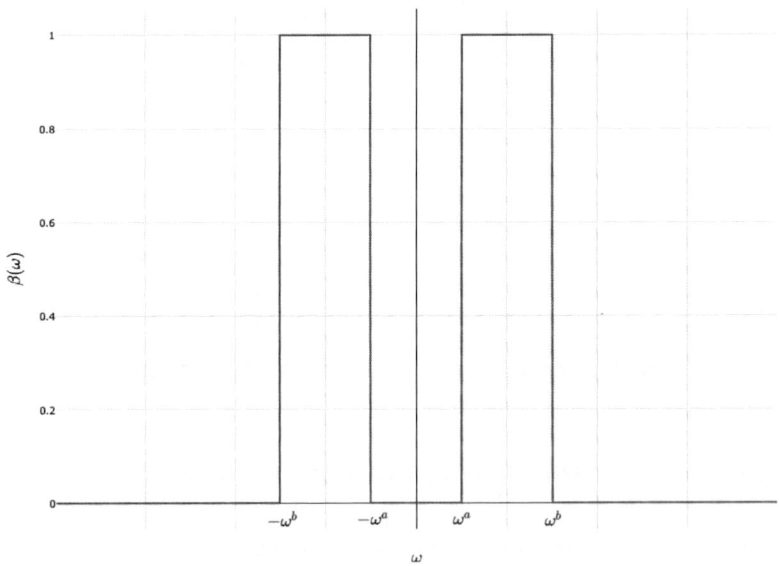

Figure 37.11. Band-pass filter.

The solutions for the weights are

$$b_h = b_h^b - b_h^a = \begin{cases} (w^b - w^a)/\pi, & h = 0, \\ [\sin(w^b h) - \sin(w^a h)]/(\pi h), & \text{otherwise.} \end{cases}$$

Hence, the ideal filter is a symmetric infinite two-sided sum. In finite samples, one needs to truncate this sum at some value K, i.e., apply the filter

$$\alpha_k(L) = \sum_{h=-K}^{K} b_h L^h.$$

But this causes a problem in that the truncation may imply a squared gain function not equal to zero outside (w_a, w_b). More importantly, it may imply that the trend and the zero frequency movements are not eliminated. To ensure the elimination of these features, we need to ensure that the squared gain function at $w = 0$ is 0. Recall that the squared gain function of a low-pass filter is $|\sum_{h=-k}^{k} b_h e^{-iwh}|$ so that at frequency zero it is given by $(\sum_{h=-k}^{k} b_h)^2$. Accordingly, we need to make a correction to the low-pass filter coefficients as follows:

$$a_h = b_h + \theta,$$

where

$$\theta = \left(1 - \sum_{h=-K}^{K} b_h\right) \Big/ (2K + 1).$$

This then implies that $\sum_{h=-K}^{K} a_h = 1$, as desired. The band-pass coefficients are then

$$b_h = (b_h^b - b_h^a) + (\theta^b - \theta^a),$$

and $\sum_{h=-K}^{K} a_h = 0$, as desired. The filter is usually applied with $w^a = 2\pi/32$ and $w^b = 2\pi/6$. Graphs of the resulting filter for various values of K (against the ideal filter) are presented in Figure 37.12.

Here, the issue is a trade-off between (a) how well the truncated filter fits the ideal one and (b) the value of K, since a larger value entails a loss of information given the fact that a filtered cycle cannot be obtained for the last K observations. Baxter and King (1999)

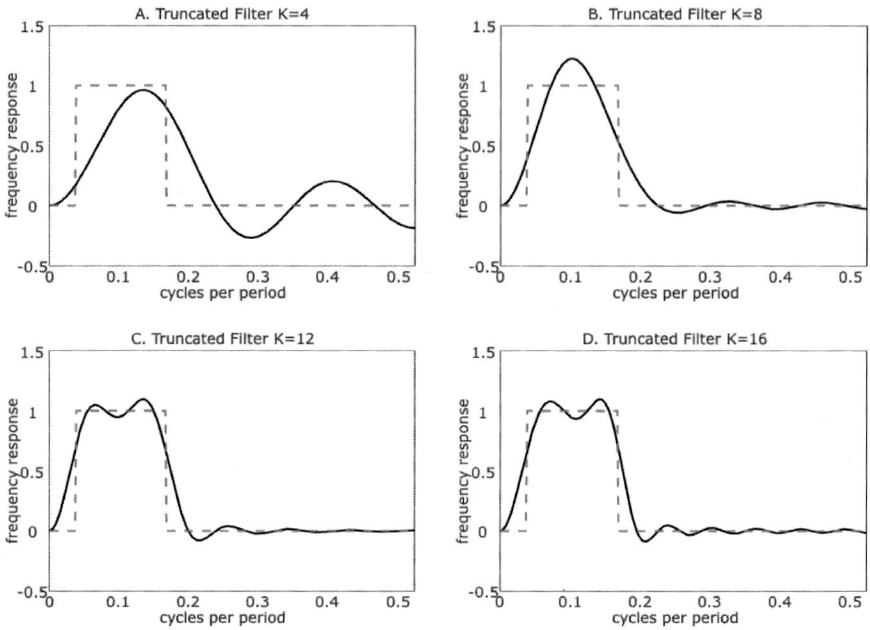

Figure 37.12. Constrained approximate band-pass filters.
Source: Baxter and King (1999). Reproduced with permission from MIT Press.

decided that the best trade-off was obtained setting $K = 8$. We compare this band-pass filter with other methods to extract the cyclical component of a time series in Section 39.4.2.

Christiano and Fitzgerald (2003) took a similar route but with the end result being a filter applicable to all data points (including the first and last) though it is neither time-invariant nor symmetric. It also includes a one-sided version which can be used to construct filtered-type estimates. The starting point is the same, with a band-pass filter

$$y_t = B(L)x_t,$$

where x_t is the original data and y_t is the filtered version using the ideal band-pass filter given by

$$B(L) = \sum_{j=-\infty}^{\infty} B_j L^j,$$

with

$$B(e^{-iw}) = 1, \quad \text{for } w \in (a,b) \cup (-b,-a)$$
$$= 0, \quad \text{otherwise.}$$

Instead of truncating the infinite sum, they consider the following set of projection problems:

$$\hat{y}_t = P(y_t|X), \quad \text{for } t = 1, \ldots, T,$$

where $X = (x_1, \ldots, x_T)$ and $\hat{y}_t$ is the best approximation (estimate) of y_t given the data X. The solution is the following linear function of the data:

$$\hat{y}_t = \sum_{j=-f}^{p} \hat{B}_j^{p,f} x_{t-j},$$

where $f = T - t$ and $p = t - 1$, and the coefficients $\hat{B}_j^{p,f}$ solve

$$\min_{\hat{B}_j^{p,f}, j=-f,\ldots,p} E[(y_t - \hat{y}_t)^2|X].$$

Let the spectral density function of x_t be $f_x(w)$, the solution is then given by

$$\min_{\hat{B}_j^{p,f}, j=-f,\ldots,p} \int_{-\pi}^{\pi} |B(e^{-iw}) - \hat{B}^{p,f}(e^{-iw})| f_x(w) dw,$$

where

$$\hat{B}^{p,f}(L) = \sum_{j=-f}^{p} \hat{B}_j^{p,f} L^j.$$

There are several features that are worth noting: (1) the solution depends on $f_x(w)$ and, hence, the true structure of the data, which is unknown, and (2) the minimization problem depends on the time index t, hence T different filters are used, one for each date. In particular, this implies different weights on past and future observations so that the filter is neither stationary nor symmetric (recall that to eliminate trends, one needs a symmetric filter).

The suggestion is to use as a pseudo-DGP, a random walk for x_t, i.e.,

$$x_t = x_{t-1} + e_t,$$

where e_t is an *i.i.d.* process with mean zero. Then,

$$f_x(w) = \frac{1}{(1 - e^{-iw})(1 - e^{iw})}.$$

The filtered series is then given by

$$\begin{aligned}\hat{y}_t = B_0 x_t + B_1 x_{t+1} + \cdots + B_{T-1-t} x_{T-1} + \tilde{B}_{T-t} x_T \\ + B_1 x_{t-1} + \cdots + B_{t-2} x_2 + \tilde{B}_{t-1} x_1,\end{aligned}$$

for $t = 3, \ldots, T-2$, where

$$\begin{aligned}B_j &= [\sin(jb) - \sin(ja)] / (\pi j), \quad j \geq 1, \\ B_0 &= [b - a]/\pi,\end{aligned}$$

where $a = (2\pi)/p_u$ and $b = (2\pi)/p_l$ with p_u and p_l the upper and lower bounds, respectively, of the periods considered of interest; as before, the range is 1.5–8 years so that $a = 2\pi/32$ and $b = 2\pi/6$, for quarterly data. Also,

$$\tilde{B}_{T-t} = -(1/2)B_0 - \sum_{j=1}^{T-t-1} B_j,$$

and $\tilde{B}_{t-1}$ solves

$$0 = B_0 + B_1 + \cdots + B_{T-1-t} + \tilde{B}_{T-t} + B_1 + \cdots + B_{t-2} + \tilde{B}_{t-1}.$$

Christiano and Fitzgerald (2003) argued that the lack of time-invariance and asymmetry of the filter do not cause any notable problems; e.g., the asymmetry is small. Also, using a random walk as the approximating DGP leads, in practice, to results (nearly) as good as if the true DGP were used. Also, the filtered version appears stationary, which is desirable.

But the bottom line is that when considering the traditional business cycle band (1.5–8 years), the proposed filter is, for all practical purposes, equivalent to the filters proposed by Baxter and King (1999) and Hodrick and Prescott (1997), the latter being discussed in detail in Section 39.4.1. They argue, however, that gains can be obtained when considering a band-pass filter applied to low-frequency components, e.g., with periods between 8 and 20 years.

37.6 Exercises

Exercise 37.1. Prove Equation (37.3).

Exercise 37.2. Prove Equation (37.6).

Exercise 37.3. Suppose y_t is generated by

$$y_t = \mu + \beta t + z_t$$

where z_t is a stationary process. Let $y_t^f = \varphi(L)y_t$ be a filtered version of y_t with $\varphi(L) = \sum_{i=-m}^{m} \varphi_i L^i$. (a) What conditions on the filter would ensure that the trend function of y_t^f is the same as that of y_t? Show that these conditions also imply that z_t and $\varphi(L)z_t$ have the same power spectral density function at frequency zero. (b) What condition on the filter is needed to eliminate the trend and the zero frequency component?

Exercise 37.4. Determine the autocovariance function of the process with spectral density $h(\omega) = (\pi - |\omega|)/\pi^2$ $(-\pi \leq \omega \leq \pi)$.

Exercise 37.5. Compute the spectral density $h(\omega), 0 \leq \omega \leq \pi$, of the stationary process $X_t - 0.99X_{t-3} = e_t$, $e_t \sim i.i.d.\ (0, \sigma^2)$. Does the spectral density suggest that the sample paths of $\{X_t\}$ will exhibit oscillatory behavior? If so, what is the approximate period of the oscillation? Compute the spectral density of the filtered process $Y_t - (1/3)(X_{t+1} + X_t + X_{t-1})$ and compare the numerical values of the spectral densities of $\{X_t\}$ and $\{Y_t\}$ at frequency $2\pi/3$ radian per unit of time. What effect would you expect the filter to have on the oscillations of $\{X_t\}$?

Exercise 37.6. The spectral density of $\{X_t\}$ on $[0, \pi]$ is

$$h(\omega) = \begin{cases} 100, & \pi/6 - 0.01 < \omega < \pi/6 + 0.01 \\ 0, & \text{otherwise} \end{cases}$$

and $h(\omega) = h(-\omega)$ on $[-\pi, 0]$. (a) Evaluate the covariance function of $\{X_t\}$ at lags 0 and 1. (b) Find the spectral density of the process

$\{Y_t\}$, where $Y_t = \Delta_{12}X_t = X_t - X_{t-12}$. (c) What is the variance of Y_t? (d) Obtain the squared gain function of the filter Δ_{12} and explain its effect on sinusoids with frequencies near 0 and near $\pi/6$.

Exercise 37.7. Suppose that you have quarterly data for a process x_t generated by the following $ARMA(1,1)$ process $x_t = \alpha x_{t-1} + e_t + \theta e_{t-1}$, where $e_t \sim i.i.d.(0, \sigma_e^2)$. In order to alleviate short-run fluctuations, we consider the following centered moving-average:

$$x_t^* = (x_{t-2} + x_{t-1} + x_t + x_{t+1} + x_{t+2})/5.$$

(a) What is the spectral density function of x_t^*? (b) Are the spectral densities at frequency zero the same for x_t^* and x_t?

Exercise 37.8. Suppose that the log of real GDP y_t is modeled via

$$y_t = \tau_t + c_t,$$

$$\tau_t = \tau_{t-1} + e_t,$$

where c_t is a stationary stochastic process and $e_t \sim i.i.d.(0, \sigma_e^2)$ independent of c_t. Here, τ_t is the trend and c_t the cyclical component. Consider the properties of the rate of growth of real GDP $\Delta y_t = y_t - y_{t-1}$. Show that (2π) times the **normalized** spectral density function (i.e., the spectral density function divided by the variance) at frequency zero of Δy_t is bounded above by 1. Use this result to show that this structural model implies that the reduced form of Δy_t cannot be an AR(1) with positive coefficient.

Exercise 37.9. You have a sample of quarterly data on a given macroeconomic time series. You want to analyze the nature of its business cycle component, which we can define as movements with periods between 2 quarters and 8 years, say. Your series is trending and may contain both stochastic and deterministic trends. Hence, you analyze the series in first-differences. (a) What is the transfer function, or squared gain function of your filter? (b) Figure 37.13 shows a plot of this function (assuming you gave the correct answer). From this graph, what can you say about the effect of the filter on the nature of the business cycle component? Is first-differencing a good idea? What could be done instead?

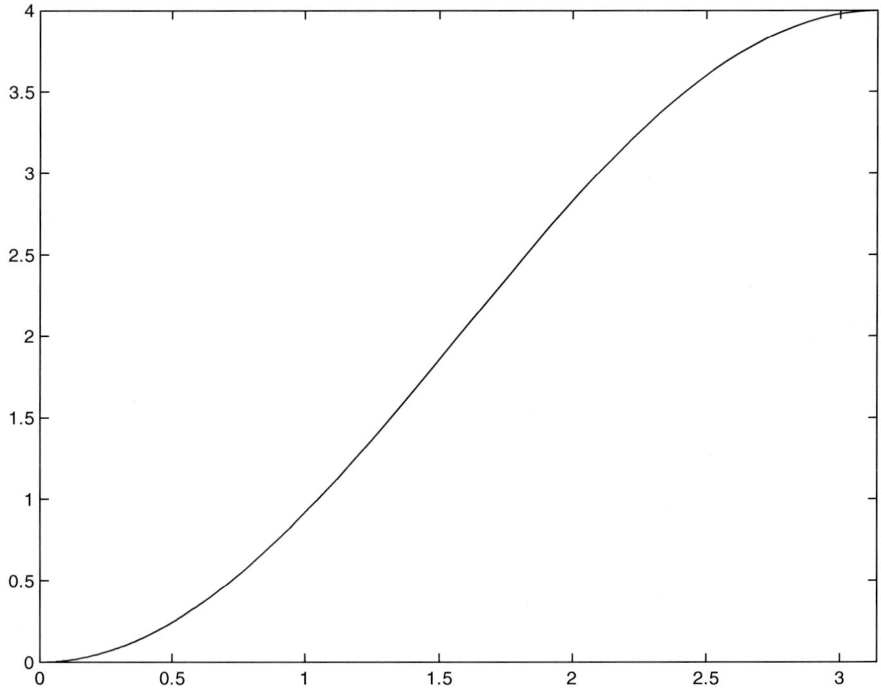

Figure 37.13. Squared gain function of the filter $(1 - L)$.

Exercise 37.10. Assume that ε_t and v_t are *i.i.d.* sequences of random variables, independent of one another, with $E(\varepsilon_t^4) < \infty$, $E(v_t^4) < \infty$, $E(\varepsilon_t) = E(v_t) = 0$, and $E(\varepsilon_t^2) = E(v_t^2) = 1$. Let x_t be the stationary solution to the stochastic difference equation for all t

$$x_t = \phi x_{t-1} + v_t \quad \text{for } |\phi| < 1, \tag{37.18}$$

and let y_t be given as

$$y_t = x_t + \varepsilon_t. \tag{37.19}$$

(a) Show that y_t is a stationary process. What is the univariate representation of y_t in terms of v_t and ε_t ? (b) Find the spectral density of y_t. (c) Suppose you observe a sample of $\{x_t, y_t\}_{t=1}^T$ generated by

(37.18) and (37.19). Consider the OLS estimator

$$\hat{\beta} = \frac{\sum_{t=2}^{T} y_t x_t}{\sum_{t=2}^{T} x_t^2}.$$

Find the probability limit of $\hat{\beta}$. Make suitable assumptions about initial conditions of (37.18) if necessary. Find the limit distribution of $\hat{\beta}$ after appropriate centering and rescaling. Is the OLS estimator efficient? (d) Now, assume that ε_t and v_t are correlated. Find a consistent estimator of β and determine the limit distribution of your estimator.

Chapter 38

Spectral Analysis: Estimation

We are interested in estimating

$$h(w) = (2\pi)^{-1} \sum_{s=-\infty}^{\infty} R(s) \exp(-iws), \quad -\pi \leq w \leq \pi,$$

or, given that $R(s)$ is even with real-valued variables,

$$h(w) = (2\pi)^{-1} \sum_{s=-\infty}^{\infty} R(s) \cos(sw), \quad -\pi \leq w \leq \pi,$$

where

$$R(s) = E[(x_t - \mu)(x_{t+s} - \mu)].$$

For simplicity, we assume that $\mu = 0$ in what follows. The results remain the same if the mean is estimated by the sample average of the data and subtracted from the observations. Also, we consider estimates of $h(w)$ and not of

$$f(w) = (2\pi)^{-1} \sum_{s=-\infty}^{\infty} \rho(s) \exp(-iws).$$

The derivations involving the former are simpler and the distributional properties remain qualitatively the same. An estimate of $f(w)$

can be obtained as

$$\hat{f}(w) = \hat{h}(w)/\hat{R}(0),$$

where

$$\hat{R}(0) = T^{-1}\sum_{t=1}^{T}(x_t - \bar{X})^2,$$

the sample variance of the observations, with $\bar{X} = T^{-1}\sum_{t=1}^{T} x_t$. A natural estimator of $h(w)$ consists in replacing $R(s)$ by its sample value $\hat{R}(s)$ and truncating, i.e.,

$$\hat{h}_0(w) = (2\pi)^{-1}\sum_{s=-(T-1)}^{T-1}\hat{R}(s)\cos(sw),$$

where

$$\hat{R}(s) = T^{-1}\sum_{t=1}^{T-|s|} x_t x_{t+s},$$

or more usually

$$\hat{R}(s) = T^{-1}\sum_{t=1}^{T-|s|}(x_t - \bar{X})(x_{t+s} - \bar{X}).$$

We analyze the properties of this estimator.

38.1 Properties of the periodogram

We start with the definition of the finite Fourier transform of x_t.

Definition 38.1. The **finite Fourier transform** of the observations is defined by

$$v_x(w) = (2\pi T)^{-1/2}\sum_{t=1}^{T} x_t \exp(-iwt), \quad -\pi \le w \le \pi.$$

We recall that we defined the Fourier transform of $x\,(t)$ by

$$\int_{-\infty}^{\infty} x\,(t)\exp(-2\pi i f t)dt,$$

for some frequency f when $x\,(t)$ was a continuous time process. The finite Fourier transform is defined analogously.

Note that $\upsilon_x\,(w)$ is defined for all w in $(-\pi, \pi)$ but is usually evaluated numerically only at a discrete set of frequencies: $0, 2\pi/T, 4\pi/T, 6\pi/T, \ldots$, i.e.,

$$\upsilon_x\,(w_p), \quad \text{for } w_p = 2\pi p/T \quad \text{and} \quad p = 0, 1, \ldots, [T/2].$$

These are called the Fourier frequencies. To compute the finite Fourier transform, one can use the "fast Fourier transform" algorithm, which is highly efficient and computationally reduces the number of operation from an order of $O(T^2)$ to an order $O(T\log(T))$. The modern version of this algorithm is attributed to Cooley and Tukey (1965), though it can be traced to Carl Friedrich Gauss's unpublished work in 1805; see the work of Heideman *et al.* (1985). This algorithm was included in "Top 10 Algorithms of 20th Century" by the IEEE magazine Computing in Science & Engineering, given its importance in various fields.

We then have the following definition of the periodogram of x_t.

Definition 38.2. Let $I_T\,(w)$ be the periodogram of x_t based on a sample of size T. Then,

$$\begin{aligned} I_T\,(w) &= (2\pi T)^{-1}\left|\sum_{t=1}^{T} x_t \exp(-iwt)\right|^2 \\ &= (2\pi T)^{-1}\left(\sum_{t=1}^{T} x_t \exp(-iwt)\right)\left(\sum_{t=1}^{T} x_t \exp(iwt)\right). \end{aligned}$$

Hence, the periodogram is expressed in terms of the finite Fourier transform as

$$I_T\,(w) = |\xi_x\,(w)|^2 = \xi_x\,(w)\,\xi_x^*\,(w),$$

where $*$ denotes the complex conjugate.

We have the following relation between the periodogram of x_t and the estimate $\hat{h}_0(w)$.

Lemma 38.1. *$\hat{h}_0(w)$ is the* ***periodogram*** *of x_t.*

Proof.

$$
\begin{aligned}
I_T(w) &= (2\pi T)^{-1} \left| \sum_{t=1}^{T} x_t \exp(-iwt) \right|^2 \\
&= (2\pi T)^{-1} \left[\sum_{t=1}^{T} x_t \exp(-iwt) \right] \left[\sum_{r=1}^{T} x_r \exp(iwr) \right] \\
&= (2\pi T)^{-1} \left[\sum_{t=1}^{T} \sum_{r=1}^{T} x_t x_r \cos((t-r)w) \right]. \qquad (38.1)
\end{aligned}
$$

In going from the second to the third line, we note that the *sin* terms vanish due to the symmetry of $x_t x_r$. We now apply an argument using this symmetry. The double summation in (38.1) effectively makes a sum over rows and then adds all rows. Using the symmetry of the terms $x_t x_r \cos((t-r)w)$, we can, instead, sum over diagonals. Transform the indices from $t \Rightarrow t, r \Rightarrow s = (t-r)$. There are $2T-1$ diagonals with s going from $-(T-1)$ to $(T-1)$. On each diagonal, there are $T-|s|$ terms. Hence,

$$
\begin{aligned}
I_T(w) &= (2\pi)^{-1} \sum_{s=-(T-1)}^{(T-1)} \left\{ T^{-1} \sum_{t=1}^{T-|s|} x_t x_{t+|s|} \right\} \cos(sw) \\
&= (2\pi)^{-1} \sum_{s=-(T-1)}^{(T-1)} \hat{R}(s) \cos(sw) = \hat{h}_0(w).
\end{aligned}
$$

The main theoretical results about the properties of $I_T(w)$ or $\hat{h}_0(w)$ are summarized as follows (the proofs of 1–2 are in the appendix):

1. $I_T(w)$ is an asymptotically unbiased estimate of $h(w)$.
2. $I_T(w)$ is not a consistent estimate of $h(w)$.

3. $I_T(w)$ is the maximum likelihood estimate of $h(w)$ if the observations are normally distributed. This implies a breakdown of the asymptotic optimality properties of MLE.
4. The periodogram ordinates are "sufficient statistics" for $h(w)$, i.e., they contain all the necessary information. So, when devising an appropriate estimate, one needs only consider the class of estimates constructed using the periodogram ordinates.

38.1.1 Intuitive reason for the inconsistency of the periodogram

We recall that

$$\hat{h}_0(w) = (2\pi)^{-1} \sum_{s=-(T-1)}^{(T-1)} \hat{R}(s)\cos(sw)$$

$$= (2\pi)^{-1} R(0) + (1/\pi) \sum_{s=1}^{(T-1)} \hat{R}(s)\cos(sw).$$

The estimate $\hat{h}_0(w)$ involves T sample autocovariances, the variance of each being of order T^{-1}. The cumulative effect of the T terms produces a variance which is non-zero even as T increases. There are "too many" sample autocovariances or things to estimate for the estimator to be consistent. One way to reduce the number of autocovariances is simply to omit some terms, i.e.,

$$\hat{h}_*(w) = (2\pi)^{-1} \sum_{s=-m_T}^{m_T} \hat{R}(s)\cos(sw),$$

for $m_T < (T-1)$, where m_T is a truncation point or truncation lag parameter. Now,

$$E[\hat{h}_*(w)] = (2\pi)^{-1} \sum_{s=-m_T}^{m_T} (1 - |s|/T)\, R(s)\cos(sw) \to h(w),$$

as $m_T \to \infty$.

So, if

$$m_T \to \infty,$$

as $T \to \infty$, the estimate will be asymptotically unbiased. Furthermore, if $m_T \to \infty$ as $T \to \infty$ but slowly relative to T so that

$$m_T/T \to 0,$$

as $T \to \infty$, then $\hat{h}_*(w)$ will be a consistent estimate of $h(w)$. This indeed turns out to be the case. Intuitively, the fact that $m_T/T \to 0$ as $T \to \infty$ implies that we are trying to estimate a negligible number of things relative to the total sample size. Hence, as T increases, there is an infinite amount of information per things we are trying to estimate so that $\hat{h}_0(w)$ is consistent.

38.2 A more general class of estimates

The estimate $\hat{h}_*(w)$ still does not take into account the fact that the autocovariances at lags close to m_T are not as precisely estimated as the autocovariances at lags close to 0. One way to take into account this feature is to put linearly declining weights on the lagged autocovariances. This leads to the estimate

$$\hat{h}_{*,2}(w) = (2\pi)^{-1}\hat{R}(0) + (1/\pi)\sum_{s=1}^{m_T}(1 - s/(m_T+1))\hat{R}(s)\cos(sw).$$

This particular weighting scheme was proposed by Bartlett (1950). A feature of importance is that, unlike $\hat{h}_*(w)$, $\hat{h}_{*,2}(w)$ ensures a non-negative estimate as we see later. In general, the use of some truncation or linearly declining weights is quite arbitrary (though sensible). More generally, what is required is that we give less weight to higher lagged autocovariances. Hence, we can think of a general class of estimators given by

$$\hat{h}_\lambda(w) = (2\pi)^{-1}\hat{R}(0) + (1/\pi)\sum_{s=1}^{T-1}\lambda(s, m_T)\hat{R}(s)\cos(sw)$$

$$= (2\pi)^{-1}\sum_{s=-(T-1)}^{T-1}\lambda(s, m_T)\hat{R}(s)\cos(sw),$$

where $\lambda(j, m_T)$ is some weighting function. The parameter m_T is called a bandwidth. If the weight function is such that

$$\lambda(s, m_T) = 0 \quad \text{if } s > m_T,$$

then m_T acts as a truncation lag parameter. Otherwise, it dictates the general shape of the weight function. Here, we want $\lambda(s, m_T)$ to decrease gradually so as to make the contribution of the tail of the sample autocovariance function smaller.

38.3 Alternative representation

We recall that

$$I_T(w) = (2\pi)^{-1} \sum_{s=-(T-1)}^{(T-1)} \hat{R}(s) \exp(-isw).$$

Inverting, then, for $|s| \leq (T-1)$,

$$\hat{R}(s) = \int_{-\pi}^{\pi} I_T(\theta) \exp(is\theta) d\theta.$$

Substituting, we have

$$\hat{h}_\lambda(w) = \int_{-\pi}^{\pi} I_T(\theta) \left\{ (2\pi)^{-1} \sum_{s=-(T-1)}^{(T-1)} \lambda(s, m_T) \exp(-is(w-\theta)) \right\} d\theta$$

or

$$\hat{h}_\lambda(w) = \int_{-\pi}^{\pi} I_T(\theta) W(m_T, w-\theta) d\theta, \tag{38.2}$$

where

$$W(m_T, \theta) = (2\pi)^{-1} \sum_{s=-(T-1)}^{(T-1)} \lambda(s, m_T) \exp(-is\theta).$$

Hence, $\hat{h}_\lambda(w)$ can be expressed as a weighted integral of the periodogram (recall the sufficiency argument). Here, the weight function $W(m_T, \theta)$ is the discrete Fourier transform of the sequence of weights

$\lambda(s, m_T)$. Typically, $W(m_T, x)$ is concentrated around $x = 0$. Hence, the largest weight is given to frequencies around $\theta = w$; so, $\hat{h}_\lambda(w)$ is a locally weighted average of the periodogram ordinates in the neighborhood of the frequency w.

Remark 38.1. If the weight function $W(\cdot)$ is non-negative everywhere, then by (38.2), the estimate $\hat{h}_\lambda(w)$ will be non-negative. This is a useful property because $h(w)$ is non-negative for all w.

Remark 38.2. We recall the periodogram ordinates, which are asymptotically unbiased but inconsistent. Note that when estimating a power spectral density function, our aim is not to estimate a collection of point-valued quantities but rather to estimate a whole function. Think about estimating non-parametrically a curve; see Chapter 26. Then, what is usually done is to take a weighted average of the observations in a neighborhood of the point to be estimated. The same idea applies here and translates into taking a weighted average of the periodogram ordinates around the desired frequency w. This is exactly what is achieved when considering the general class of weighted estimates as demonstrated by the representation (38.2).

38.4 Examples of weight functions

Example 38.1. The **"truncated periodogram"** window is given by

$$\lambda(s, m_T) = \begin{cases} 1 & \text{if } |s| \leq m_T, \\ 0, & \text{otherwise.} \end{cases}$$

Then,

$$W(m_T, \theta) = (2\pi)^{-1} \sum_{s=-m_T}^{m_T} \cos(s\theta) = (2\pi)^{-1} \left[\frac{\sin[(m_T + 1/2)\theta]}{\sin(\theta/2)} \right].$$

The function $W(\theta)$ is not non-negative everywhere so this weight function will not yield a non-negative estimate by construction. The function is presented in Figure 38.1.

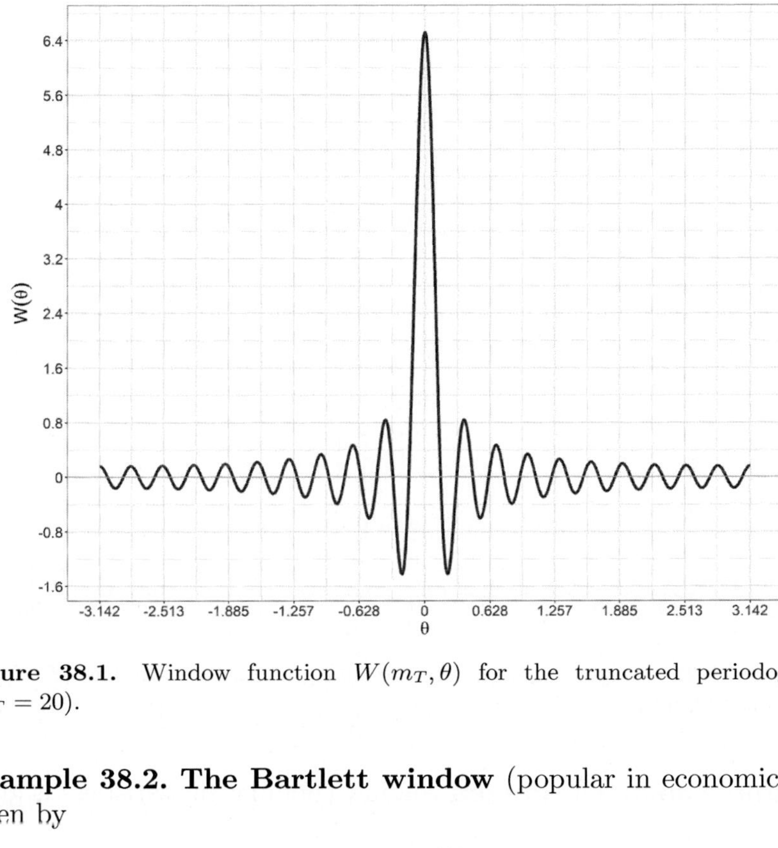

Figure 38.1. Window function $W(m_T, \theta)$ for the truncated periodogram $(m_T = 20)$.

Example 38.2. The Bartlett window (popular in economics) is given by

$$\lambda(s, m_T) = \begin{cases} 1 - |s|/m_T, & |s| \leq m_T, \\ 0, & |s| > m_T. \end{cases}$$

Then,

$$\begin{aligned} W(m_T, \theta) &= (2\pi)^{-1} \sum_{s=-m_T}^{m_T} (1 - |s|/m_T) \cos(s\theta) \\ &= (2\pi m_T)^{-1} \left\{ \frac{\sin(m_T\theta/2)}{\sin(\theta/2)} \right\}^2, \end{aligned}$$

which is positive for all θ. So, by construction, the estimate will be non-negative. The weight function $\lambda(s, m_T)$ is presented in Figure 38.2 for $T = 200$ and $m_T = 10$, 40, 80.

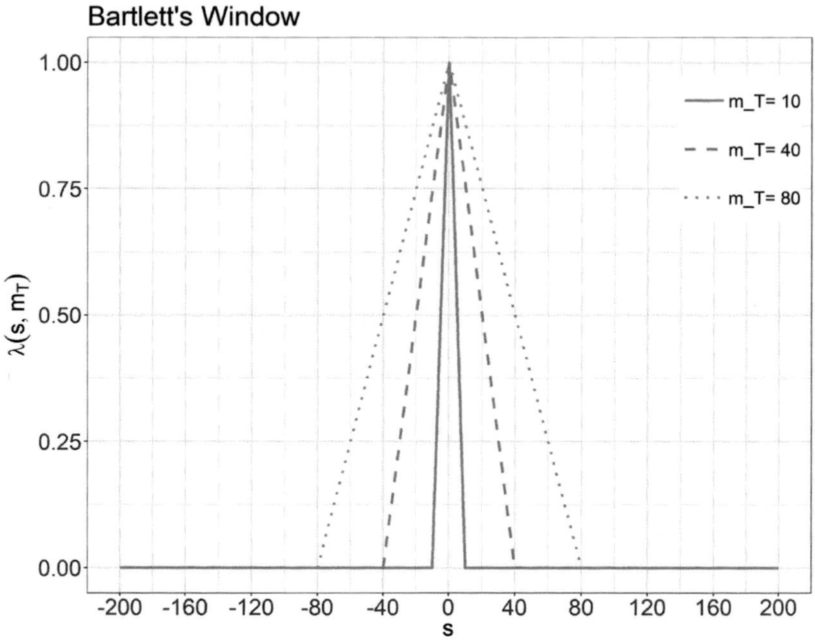

Figure 38.2. Weight function $\lambda(s, m_T)$ for the Bartlett window ($T = 200$, $m_T = 10$, 40, 80).

Example 38.3. The **Parzen** window (popular in statistics) is given by

$$\lambda(s, m_T) = \begin{cases} 1 - 6(|s|/m_T)^2 + 6(|s|/m_T)^3, & |s| \leq m_T/2, \\ 2(1 - |s|/m_T)^3, & m_T/2 \leq |s| \leq m_T, \\ 0, & |s| > m_T. \end{cases}$$

The weight function $\lambda(s, m_T)$ is presented in Figure 38.3 for $T = 200$ and $m_T = 10$, 40, 80. We can also show that $W(m_T, \theta) \geq 0$ for all θ, hence this weight function also yields a non-negative estimate.

Example 38.4. The **Tukey–Hanning** window is given by

$$\lambda(s, m_T) = \begin{cases} (1 + \cos(\pi s/m_T))/2, & \text{if } |s| \leq m_T, \\ 0, & \text{otherwise.} \end{cases}$$

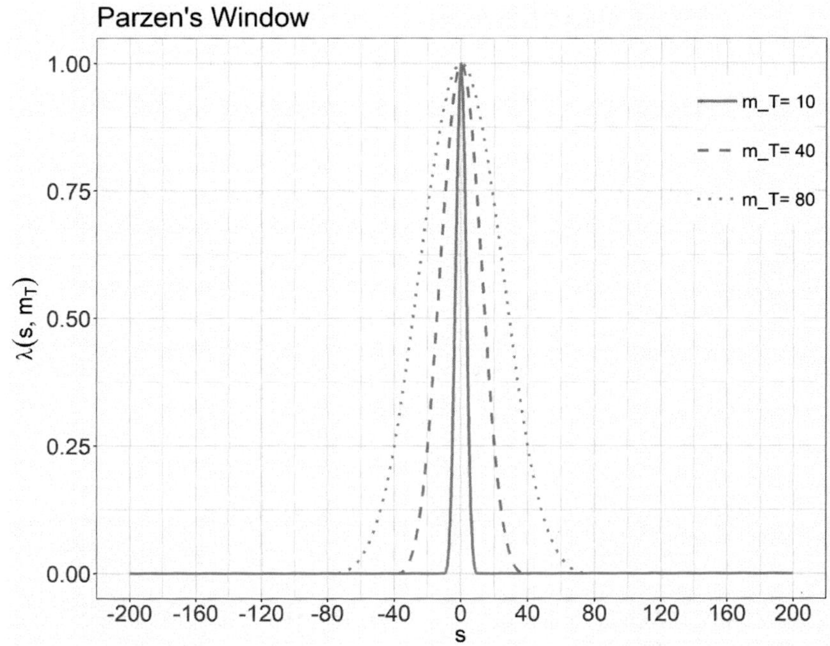

Figure 38.3. Weight function $\lambda(s, m_T)$ for the Parzen window ($T = 200$, $m_T = 10, 40, 80$).

This weight function also yields a non-negative estimate by construction. The weight function $\lambda(s, m_T)$ is presented in Figure 38.4 for $T = 200$ and $m_T = 10, 40, 80$.

Example 38.5. The **quadratic spectral** window, Andrews (1991b), is

$$\lambda(s, m_T) = 3(\sin(\delta)/\delta - \cos(\delta))/\delta^2,$$

where $\delta = 6\pi s/(5m_T)$. The weight function is presented in Figure 38.5 for $T = 200$ and $m_T = 10, 40, 80$. Note the negative weights in the tails. Intuitively, this occurs so as to cancel the noise in the tail, which involves very noisy (imprecise) estimates of the autocovariances that are strongly correlated. Again, the associated weight function $W(m_T, \theta)$ is non-negative, hence the estimate will be non-negative by construction.

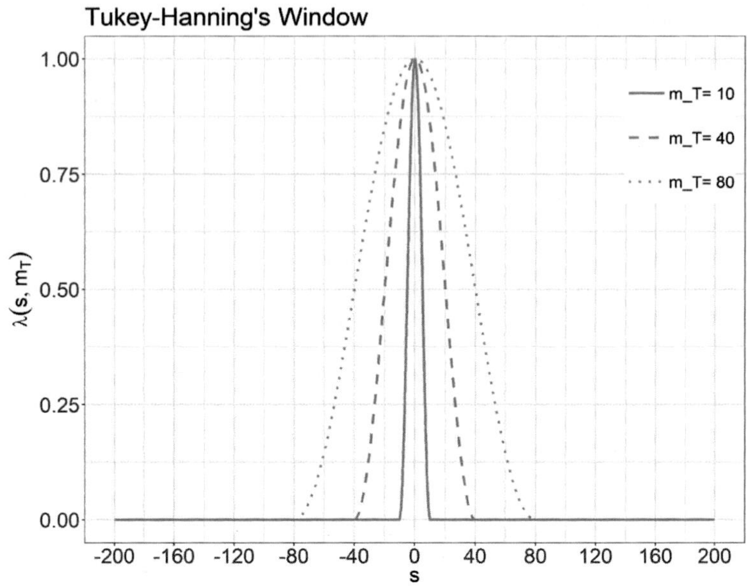

Figure 38.4. Weight function $\lambda(s, m_T)$ for the Tukey–Hanning window ($T = 200$, $m_T = 10$, 40, 80).

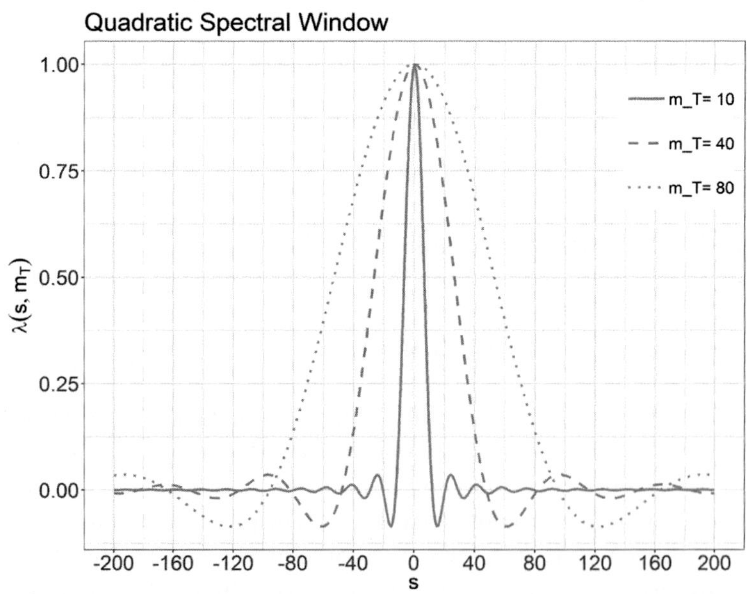

Figure 38.5. Weight function $\lambda(s, m_T)$ for the Quadratic Spectral window ($T = 200$, $m_T = 10, 40, 80$).

Remark 38.3. Except for the quadratic spectral window, the autocovariances at lags greater than m_T receive zero weight. Hence, the bandwidth acts as a truncation lag parameter. For the quadratic spectral window, all lags of the sample autocovariance function are considered and the bandwidth parameter m_T acts to change the shape of the weight function.

There are many other examples of windows; see the works of Priestley (1981) and Ng and Perron (1996). Which one we choose is relatively unimportant for the precision of the estimates compared to the choice of m_T, the bandwidth, or truncation lag parameter. However, substantial evidence showed that the Parzen, Tukey–Hanning, or quadratic spectral leads to estimates with better finite sample properties (lower bias and mean-square errors) compared to using the Bartlett.

38.5 Asymptotic properties

We now briefly summarize the asymptotic properties of the estimates obtained under some regularity conditions; see, e.g., the work of Priestley (1981). Denote the window kernel by

$$k\left(s/m_T\right) = \lambda\left(s, m_T\right).$$

Example 38.6. For the Bartlett window, we have

$$k\left(u\right) = \begin{cases} 1 - |u|, & |u| \leq 1, \\ 0, & |u| > 1. \end{cases}$$

First, the estimates are asymptotically unbiased, that is,

$$\lim_{T \to \infty} E[\hat{h}_\lambda\left(w\right)] = h\left(w\right).$$

They are also consistent since

$$\operatorname{Var}(\hat{h}_\lambda\left(w\right)) \sim \left(1 + \delta_{w,0,\pi}\right) h^2\left(w\right) T^{-1} \left\{ \sum_{s=-(T-1)}^{(T-1)} \lambda_T^2\left(s, m_T\right) \right\}$$

or

$$\lim_{T\to\infty}\left[(T/m_T)\text{Var}(\hat{h}_\lambda(w))\right] = (1+\delta_{w,0,\pi})\, h^2(w)\int_{-\infty}^{\infty} k^2(u)\, du, \tag{38.3}$$

where $\delta_{w,0,\pi} = 1$ if $w = 0, \pi$; 0 otherwise. Hence, if $m_T/T \to 0$, we have consistency. The limit distribution depends on the weight function via the kernel function $k(u)$ and the square of the true spectral density function. Note also that the stated value is doubled at the boundary points $w = 0, \pi$. As discussed in Section 37.3, the spectral density function over frequencies $[-\pi, 0]$ is a mirror image of those in the range $[0, \pi]$ and the function repeats itself for $w \pm s(2\pi)$ (s an integer). Hence, the observations in a neighborhood of $w = 0$ or π are the same on both sides. This double-counting must be taken into account, which leads to the doubling in variance.

Example 38.7. For the Bartlett window,

$$\int_{-\infty}^{\infty} k^2(u)\, du = 2\int_0^1 (1-u)^2\, du = 2/3,$$

hence,

$$\lim_{T\to\infty}\left[(T/m_T)\text{Var}(\hat{h}_\lambda(w))\right] = (1+\delta_{w,0,\pi})\, h^2(w)\,(2/3).$$

We also have asymptotic normality, i.e.,

$$\sqrt{T/m_T}\left[\hat{h}_\lambda(w) - h(w)\right] \xrightarrow{d} N(0, V),$$

where V is given by (38.3). We can therefore construct asymptotic confidence intervals.

Remark 38.4. For us, in the following treatment and in empirical work, the exact form of the asymptotic variance is not that important as it is not common to make inference about given values of the spectral density function. Rather, what will interest us mostly is the value at the zero frequency and its estimate as an input to construct confidence intervals for various quantities; see, e.g., Section 37.4.2. But since we desire precise estimates, what will be of more concern to us is the rate of convergence, $\sqrt{T/m_T}$, which is influenced by the rate of increase of the bandwidth m_T as T increases. The faster the rate of increase of m_T, the slower the rate of convergence. This will enable us to compare the benefits and drawbacks of using various weight functions (e.g., the Bartlett versus the others discussed in this chapter) and also to compare this class of estimates versus another one discussed later.

38.6 Pre-whitening

Simulations and analytical evidence have shown that the class of estimates considered above have poor properties in the presence of strong serial correlation in the data; see, e.g., the work of Andrews and Monahan (1992) on which this section is based. Since this is a feature of importance with economic data, it would be desirable to have methods to alleviate this problem. One that has been suggested is the so-called pre-whitening procedure. The basic method starts by filtering the data using an $AR(1)$ model. The reason for using an $AR(1)$ model is that with economic data at least, oftentimes (though there are important exceptions) what accounts for most of the correlation structure is strong positive serial correlation at lag one, which is captured by the $AR(1)$. We start by estimating a first-order autoregression by OLS:

$$x_t = c + \hat{a}x_{t-1} + \hat{v}_t.$$

The pre-whitened process is then defined by the following filtered version of $\tilde{x}_t = x_t - \bar{X}$, the demeaned version of x_t with $\bar{X} = T^{-1}\sum_{t=1}^{T} x_t$:

$$\hat{v}_t = (1 - \hat{a}L)\tilde{x}_t.$$

It is called pre-whitening the data since this filter removes a part of the correlation (substantially if there is strong first-order correlation). Hence, it makes the filtered process closer to that of an *i.i.d.* series, i.e., a white noise process.

One can estimate the spectral density function of $\hat{v}_t$ using the methods described in the previous sections. Call such an estimate $\hat{h}_v(w)$. Then, one can recover an estimate of the spectral density function of the original data using the relation (recall the filtering theorem of Section 37.5.1):

$$\hat{h}_x(w) = \frac{1}{|1 - \hat{a}e^{iw}|^2}\hat{h}_v(w).$$

This last step is sometimes called "re-coloring" since it transforms the function to one that corresponds to something that is further away from a white noise process. It adds back the correlation and hence, in a sense, puts back color in the process.

Instead of using an $AR(1)$, one could also use an $AR(p)$ to get rid of the strong correlation in x_t. The pre-whitened quantities are the OLS residuals from the regression

$$\tilde{x}_t = \sum_{j=1}^{p} \hat{a}_j \tilde{x}_{t-j} + \hat{v}_t,$$

and the "re-coloring" step is

$$\hat{h}_x(w) = \frac{1}{|1 - \sum_{j=1}^{p} \hat{a}_j e^{ijw}|^2}\hat{h}_v(w).$$

38.7 Autoregressive spectral density estimates

A natural extension of the pre-whitening procedure stems from the following idea. If one considers an autoregressive process of a high enough order, it may be the case that the residuals are close enough to being white noise so that the kernel-based step can altogether be avoided. This is indeed the case for a large class of short-memory stationary processes, as shown by Berk (1974). This gives a very simple procedure. First, estimate an autoregression of order, say, k_T:

$$x_t = \hat{c} + \sum_{j=1}^{k_T} \hat{a}_j x_{t-j} + \hat{e}_{tk}. \tag{38.4}$$

Let

$$\hat{\sigma}_{ek}^2 = T^{-1} \sum_{t=k_T+1}^{T} \hat{e}_{tk}^2,$$

then the estimate of $h_x(w)$ is given by

$$\hat{h}_x(w) = \frac{1}{2\pi} \frac{\hat{\sigma}^2_{ek}}{|1 - \sum_{j=1}^{k_T} \hat{a}_j e^{ijw}|^2}.$$

Berk (1974) showed this estimate to be consistent provided the following set of sufficient conditions hold:

1. x_t is a linear process, $x_t = \mu + C(L)e_t$ with $C(L) = 1 + \sum_{i=1}^{\infty} c_i L^i$ having all roots outside the unit circle, $e_t \sim i.i.d.(0, \sigma^2)$ with $E(e_t^4) < \infty$.
2. The spectral density $h_x(w) = (\sigma^2/(2\pi))|C(e^{iw})|^2$ is finite.
3. k_T is chosen such that $k_T \to \infty$ and $k_T^3/T \to 0$ as $T \to \infty$.
4. Let $A(L) = 1 + \sum_{i=1}^{\infty} a_i L^i = 1/C(L)$; k_T is chosen such that

$$k_T^{1/2} \sum_{j=1}^{\infty} |a_{k_T+j}| \to 0 \tag{38.5}$$

as $T \to \infty$.

Note that (38.5) involves a trade-off between the allowed rate of increase of k_T and the rate of decay of the autoregressive coefficients. The other conditions are quite standard: (1) restricts the analysis to linear processes that are invertible, (2) ensures that the limiting value is well defined and finite, and (3) ensures that the regressors are not asymptotically collinear.

These conditions are satisfied for all $ARMA(p, q)$ processes for any rate of increase of k_T (subject to condition (3)). This is because, for large k_T, $|a_{k_T}| \propto \lambda^{k_T}$ for some $0 < \lambda < 1$. Hence,

$$k_T^{1/2} \sum_{j=1}^{\infty} |a_{k_T+j}| \propto k_T^{1/2} \lambda^{k_T}.$$

Taking logs

$$\ln(k_T^{1/2} \lambda^{k_T}) = (1/2)\ln(k_T) + k_T \ln(\lambda),$$

which converges to ∞ as long as $k_T \to \infty$.

To obtain the limit distribution of the estimates, the same conditions are used, except that (2) and (4) are strengthened as follows:

2*. $h_x(w) > 0$.
4*. k_T is chosen such that

$$T^{1/2}\sum_{j=1}^{\infty}|a_{k_T+j}| \to 0. \tag{38.6}$$

Then,

$$\sqrt{T/k_T}(\hat{h}_x(w) - h_x(w)) \xrightarrow{d} N(0, 2(1+\delta_{w,0,\pi})h_x^2(w)).$$

Condition (2*) is needed since the limit distribution is degenerate when $h_x(w) = 0$. Condition (4*) is rather important. For example, if the process is a stationary and invertible $ARMA(p,q)$, a sufficient condition for (38.6) to hold is that $k_T \propto T^a$ for any $a > 0$, i.e., k_T grows at any polynomial rate. If k_T increases at a logarithmic rate, (38.6) is not guaranteed to hold for all permissible values of the parameters. This is of practical importance since the autoregressive order is often selected using an information criterion, which implies a logarithmic rate of increase for k_T (this is discussed later). Autoregressive spectral density estimators were advocated by Perron and Ng (1998) in the context of tests for unit roots; see Section 45.6.

38.8 Fully parametric estimates

The class of estimates considered so far are non-parametric in the sense that they do not impose a particular parametric structure for the data generating process. In some cases, one may have enough confidence in a particular specified structure so that a parametric estimate can be constructed. Consider, for example, the case where the data are generated by an $ARMA(p,q)$ process of the form

$$A(L)x_t = c + B(L)e_t,$$

with $e_t \sim i.i.d.(0, \sigma_e^2)$,

$$A(L) = 1 + \sum_{j=1}^{p} a_j L^j$$

and

$$B(L) = 1 + \sum_{j=1}^{q} b_j L^j.$$

Denote consistent estimates of the parameters by $\{\hat{a}_j, \hat{b}_i; j = 1, \ldots, p; i = 1, \ldots, q\}$ and $\hat{\sigma}_e^2$. Then, an estimate of $h_x(w)$ is given by

$$\hat{h}_x(w) = \frac{\hat{\sigma}_{ek}^2}{2\pi} \frac{|1 - \sum_{j=1}^{q} \hat{b}_j e^{ijw}|^2}{|1 - \sum_{j=1}^{p} \hat{a}_j e^{ijw}|^2}.$$

38.9 Zero-frequency estimates

The reader may have detected a strong similarity in the material of this chapter with that of Section 11.5 where we discussed Heteroskedasticity and Autocorrelation Consistent (HAC) covariance estimates in the linear model. This is indeed the case since

$$\begin{aligned}
\lim_{T\to\infty} T^{-1} E(x'\Omega x) &= R_v(0) + 2\sum_{j=1}^{\infty} R_v(j) \\
&= \sum_{j=-\infty}^{\infty} R_v(j) \\
&= 2\pi h_v(0),
\end{aligned}$$

where $h_v(0)$ is the spectral density function of $v_t = x_t u_t$ at frequency zero. See also the special case of the distribution of the sample average discussed in Section 8.7. The treatment of HAC estimation in econometrics came substantially after the development of methods related to spectral density estimation, some 30 or so years later. It took a while for econometricians to make the link between the two!

Hence, what is of most interest in econometrics is to have methods to estimate the spectral density function at frequency zero. We consider two main non-parametric methods: (1) the kernel-based method and (2) the autoregressive spectral density estimator. For the former, a parameter of importance is m_T, the bandwidth or truncation lag. For the latter, the parameter of importance is k_T, the order of the autoregression. We discuss how to select these in what follows.

38.9.1 Selecting m_T for the kernel-based methods

Since estimating $2\pi h_v(0)$ for a linear process is a special case of what is involved in a linear regression model (i.e., with only a constant included), the method to select m_T is the same as discussed in Section 11.8. Hence, here we only present a brief summary of the discussion in that section with some added results.

As shown in the work of Andrews (1991b), the asymptotic mean-squared error is a rather complicated function of (1) the weight function $\lambda(\cdot)$, (2) the bandwidth m_T, and (3) the true data generating process of x_t through some summary measure which we shall call α, say. So, we have

$$MSE = f(\lambda(\cdot), m_T, \alpha). \tag{38.7}$$

For a given data generating process and window, a value m_T^* can be evaluated which minimizes the asymptotic mean-squared error. Then, an estimate $\hat{m}_T$ can be obtained using the so-called "plug-in" method. This method works as follows. Take a data-generating process which you believe is a good approximation to the true data-generating process of x_t. Then, one can construct an estimate of the summary measure α as $\hat{\alpha}$ (this is discussed in the following). One can then solve for the value $\hat{m}_T$ which minimizes the function (38.7) to get

$$\hat{m}_T = g(\hat{\alpha}, \lambda(\cdot)).$$

The resulting functions are the following for some popular windows:

1. Bartlett: $\hat{m}_T = 1.1447(\hat{\alpha}(1)T)^{1/3}$;
2. Parzen: $\hat{m}_T = 2.6614(\hat{\alpha}(2)T)^{1/5}$;
3. Tukey–Hanning: $\hat{m}_T = 1.7462(\hat{\alpha}(2)T)^{1/5}$;
4. Quadratic Spectral: $\hat{m}_T = 1.3221(\hat{\alpha}(2)T)^{1/5}$.

Consider approximating x_t by an autoregression of order 1. That is, we consider the following regression:

$$x_t = c + \rho x_{t-1} + e_t.$$

Denote the estimate of ρ by $\hat{\rho}$. Then,

$$\hat{\alpha}(1) = 4\hat{\rho}^2/[(1-\hat{\rho})^2(1+\hat{\rho})^2],$$
$$\hat{\alpha}(2) = 4\hat{\rho}^2/(1-\hat{\rho})^4.$$

The reason for the difference in the parameter $\hat{\alpha}$ for the Bartlett and the other weight function is the same as that for the different rates of convergence of $\hat{m}_T$, namely the fact that the Bartlett window is non-differentiable at $m = 0$, while the others are.

Note that in most cases using an $AR(1)$ approximation will deliver a useful approximation. However, there are cases for which it will yield very poor estimates. This occurs, for instance, when dealing with processes having a strong negative MA component. Recall the discussion about inflation in Section 8.4.9. In this case, using an $ARMA(1,1)$ approximation will deliver much better results. Hence, it is advisable in practice to do some robustness check (as it always is). When using an $ARMA(1,1)$ approximation given by

$$x_t = c + \rho x_{t-1} + e_t + \psi e_{t-1},$$

with estimates denoted by $\hat{\rho}$, $\hat{\psi}$. The expression for $\hat{\alpha}$ is then

$$\hat{\alpha}(1) = \frac{4(1+\hat{\rho}\hat{\psi})^2(\hat{\rho}+\hat{\psi})^2}{(1-\hat{\rho})^4(1+\hat{\psi})^4},$$

$$\hat{\alpha}(2) = \frac{4(1+\hat{\rho}\hat{\psi})^2(\hat{\rho}+\hat{\psi})^2}{(1-\hat{\rho})^2(1+\hat{\rho})^2(1+\hat{\psi})^4}.$$

Again, as discussed in Section 11.8, it is not essential that we specify the true data-generating process, a good enough approximation is sufficient. The reason is that it will not change the consistency or rate of convergence of the estimate, as long as $\hat{m}_T \to \infty$ and $\hat{m}_T/T \to 0$, which is guaranteed via the specified formulae listed above for $\hat{m}_T$ when using different weight functions. What we seek to achieve is a finite sample adjustment that is as good as possible.

Remark 38.5. Note that here we need the weaker requirement $\hat{m}_T/T \to 0$ compared to that in Section 11.8, which was $\hat{m}_T^2/T \to 0$. This is because we are dealing with observed data and not the estimated residuals from an OLS regression. Hence, $\hat{m}_T$ can grow to infinity faster. This is, however, simply of theoretical interest as all the rules to select $\hat{m}_T$ satisfy both conditions.

Given the theoretical results discussed in the previous section, we are now in a position to make precise the statement in Remark 11.9. As discussed in Section 38.5, the rate of convergence of $\hat{h}_\lambda(w)$

is $(T/m_T)^{1/2}$. Hence, using the Bartlett weight function, it is $(T/T^{1/3})^{1/2} = T^{1/3}$. On the other hand, using any of the other weight functions listed above, the implied rate of convergence is $(T/T^{1/5})^{1/2} = T^{2/5}$, which is faster. Hence, the estimate using the Bartlett weight function has zero asymptotic relative efficiency compared to using the Parzen, Tukey–Hanning, or quadratic spectral. This is a strong theoretical argument for using one of the latter. Yet, despite only requiring a change to a simple line of code, the Bartlett (known as the Newey–West in econometrics) remains the most popular default value in most softwares. Maybe economists like triangles!

38.9.2 Selecting k_T for autoregressive-based estimates

For the autoregressive-based spectral density estimate, the main parameter of interest is the lag order k_T in the following regression:

$$x_t = \hat{c} + \sum_{j=1}^{k_T} \hat{a}_j x_{t-j} + \hat{e}_{tk}.$$

This is usually done via what is called an Information Criterion (IC). This was covered in Section 36.4. As discussed in Section 36.4.4, suppose the data follow a linear short-memory process and an information criterion is used to select the order of an approximate autoregressive model, the order of which is supposed to be in the range from 0 to $k_{\max}$. For technical reasons, we suppose that $k_{\max} = o_p(T^{1/3})$. Denote the selected order by k_{ic}, then under regularity assumptions stated in 36.4, we have

$$k_{ic} = O_p(\ln(T))$$

so that the selected order increases at rate $\ln(T)$; see the work of Shibata (1980) for the case with normally distributed series and the work of Hannan and Deistler (2012) for the more general case with stationary and invertible linear processes. This rate is very slow, indeed slower than any polynomial rate, T^a, for any a arbitrarily small. This result has the following implication. The rate of convergence of the resulting estimate is $\sqrt{T/\ln(T)}$. For kernel-based methods, the best optimal rate that can be obtained is of the order $T^{2/5}$. Hence, the former are asymptotically more efficient. Not only is this class of estimates asymptotically more efficient, but they are also far easier to compute. Only a least squares regression is required along with the simple equation

$$\hat{h}_x(0) = \frac{1}{2\pi} \frac{\hat{\sigma}^2_{ek}}{|1 - \sum_{j=1}^{k_{ic}} \hat{a}_j|^2},$$

where

$$\hat{\sigma}^2_{ek} = (T - k_{ic})^{-1} \sum_{t=k_{ic}+1}^{T} \hat{e}^2_{tk}.$$

Remark 38.6. For the important case of the zero frequency, the estimate reduces to

$$2\pi \hat{h}_x(0) = \frac{\hat{\sigma}^2_{k_{ic}}}{(1 - \sum_{j=1}^{k_{ic}} \hat{a}_j)^2}.$$

This corresponds to the estimate of the variance of the mean μ in a regression of the form

$$x_t = \mu + u_t$$

when applying a GLS estimation procedure based on an $AR(k_{ic})$ approximation. See Section 13.2.3. Here, since only a constant is involved as a regressor, GLS is asymptotically equivalent to OLS. Hence, no first-order efficiency gains can be expected. However, along with the theoretical results stated above, there is some evidence that this GLS-autoregressive-based approach yields better estimates in finite samples.

38.10 Appendix: Proofs of results in Section 38.1

The proofs follow closely those in the work of Priestley (1981).

(1) $I_T(w)$ is an asymptotically unbiased estimate of $h(w)$.

We give a heuristic argument that $I_T(w)$ is an asymptotically unbiased estimate of $h(w)$. For a more rigorous proof, see the work of Priestley (1981) (pp. 417–418). We have

$$E\left[I_T(w)\right] = (2\pi)^{-1} \sum_{s=-(T-1)}^{(T-1)} E[\hat{R}(s)] \cos(sw)$$

$$= (2\pi)^{-1} \sum_{s=-(T-1)}^{(T-1)} (1 - |s|/T)\, R(s) \cos(sw).$$

Since $(1 - |s|/T) \to 1$ as $T \to \infty$, and using the fact that

$$\sum_{s=-\infty}^{\infty} R(s) \cos(sw) < \infty,$$

we have

$$E\left[I_T(w)\right] \to (2\pi)^{-1} \sum_{s=-\infty}^{\infty} R(s) \cos(sw) = h(w).$$

(2) $I_T(w)$ is not a consistent estimate of $h(w)$.

Even if $I_T(w)$ is an asymptotically unbiased estimate of $h(w)$, its variance does not go to zero as the sample size increases and is therefore not a consistent estimate. As discussed in Section 37.5.1, we can view a stationary series $x_t = C(L)e_t$ as the filtered version of a white noise process, e_t, and the relation between the spectral density function of x_t and e_t is

$$h_x(w) = \left|C\left(e^{-iw}\right)\right|^2 h_e(w), \tag{38.8}$$

where $h_e(w) = (\sigma_e^2/(2\pi))$. As argued before, $I_T(w)$, the periodogram, is a finite sample version of $h(w)$; hence, a similar relation holds approximately, i.e.,

$$I_T(w) \approx \left|C\left(e^{-iw}\right)\right|^2 I_{T,e}(w), \tag{38.9}$$

where $I_{T,e}(w)$ denotes the periodogram of e_t, a white noise process. Combining (38.8) and (38.9) we have

$$I_T(w) \approx (2\pi/\sigma_e^2) h_x(w)\, I_{T,e}(w)$$

or

$$\frac{I_T(w)}{2\pi h_x(w)} \approx \frac{I_{T,e}(w)}{\sigma_e^2}.$$

So, we can deduce the properties of the term on the left-hand side by those on the right-hand side which are easier to obtain. Now, consider the periodogram of e evaluated at a particular frequency $w_p, w_p = 2\pi p/T$ $(p = 0, 1, \ldots, [T/2])$. We leave the proof of the following assertion as an exercise.

Proposition 38.1. *The periodogram of the white noise process e_t can be expressed as*

$$I_{T,e}(w) = (4\pi)^{-1}\{A(w)\}^2 + (4\pi)^{-1}\{B(w)\}^2,$$

where

$$A(w) = \sqrt{2/T}\sum_{t=1}^{T} e_t \cos(wt),$$

$$B(w) = \sqrt{2/T}\sum_{t=1}^{T} e_t \sin(wt).$$

Assuming normality, then $A(w)$ and $B(w)$ are independent normal random variables with mean 0 and variances

$$\operatorname{Var}(A(w_p)) = (2\sigma_e^2)T^{-1}\left(\sum_{t=1}^{T}\cos^2(w_p t)\right) = \begin{cases} \sigma_e^2 & \text{if } w_p \neq 0, \pi \\ 2\sigma_e^2 & \text{if } w_p = 0, \pi, \end{cases}$$

$$\operatorname{Var}(B(w_p)) = (2\sigma_e^2)T^{-1}\left(\sum_{t=1}^{T}\sin^2(w_p t)\right) = \begin{cases} \sigma_e^2 & \text{if } w_p \neq 0, \pi \\ 0 & \text{if } w_p = 0, \pi. \end{cases}$$

Hence, except at the boundaries $w_p = 0, \pi$, $I_{T,e}(w)$ is the sum of the square of two independent normal random variables and so is χ_2^2.

The covariance between the two random variables is

$$\operatorname{cov}\left(A\left(w_p\right), B\left(w_q\right)\right) = (2\sigma_e^2)T^{-1}\left(\sum_{t=1}^{T}\cos(w_p t)\sin(w_q t)\right) = 0,$$

$$\text{for all } p, q.$$

Therefore,

$$I_{T,e}\left(w_p\right) \approx \frac{\sigma_e^2}{4\pi}\chi_2^2, \quad \text{if } w_p \neq 0, \pi$$

and

$$\frac{I_T\left(w_p\right)}{2\pi h_x\left(w_p\right)} \approx \frac{1}{4\pi}\chi_2^2,$$

or

$$I_T\left(w_p\right) \approx \chi_2^2 h_x\left(w_p\right)/2.$$

Hence, since $E\left[\chi_\nu^2\right] = \nu$ and $\operatorname{Var}\left(\chi_\nu^2\right) = 2\nu$, we have

$$E\left[I_T\left(w_p\right)\right] \approx h_x\left(w_p\right),$$
$$\operatorname{Var}\left(I_T\left(w_p\right)\right) \approx h_x^2\left(w_p\right) = O_p\left(1\right).$$

So, $I_T\left(w_p\right)$ is not a consistent estimate of $h_x\left(w_p\right)$.

38.11 Exercises

Exercise 38.1. Prove Proposition 38.1.

Exercise 38.2 (Review). Consider a stationary stochastic process x_t. Let $h_x(0)$ be the non-normalized spectral density function at frequency zero of x_t. (a) Explain intuitively what the quantity $h_x(0)$ measures. (b) What is the mathematical definition of $h_x(0)$ in terms of the autocovariance function of x_t? (c) Discuss methods to consistently estimate $h_x(0)$, conditions on the truncation lag (or bandwidth) to ensure consistency, methods to select the truncation lag, or the bandwidth in practice. Suppose now that x_t is a stationary $ARMA$ process of the form $A(L)x_t = B(L)e_t$ with $e_t \sim i.i.d.\ (0, \sigma_e^2)$, $A(L) = 1 - a_1 L - \cdots - a_p L^p$, and $B(L) = 1 + b_1 L + \cdots + b_q L^q$. (d) Derive an expression for $h_x(0)$ in terms of the coefficient a_i, b_i, and σ_e^2. (e) Suppose also that x_t is the first-difference of some process y_t, i.e., $y_t = y_{t-1} + x_t$. What is the relationship between $h_x(0)$ and the long-run effect of a shock e_t on the level of y_t?

Chapter 39

State-Space Models

We now discuss the class of state-space models and how to obtain maximum likelihood estimates of the parameters based on the Kalman filter, originally developed by Kalman (1960), to construct the likelihood function; see also the works of Kalman and Bertram (1960) and Kalman (1963). Many of the developments in this chapter follow the treatment in the work of Harvey (1981, Chapters 4 and 1.2). A very detailed treatment is contained in the work of Harvey (1990); see also the works of Harvey (1987), Engle and Watson (1987), and Harvey and De Rossi (2006). State-space models and the Kalman filter to construct the required likelihood function are quite powerful techniques. They can be used to estimate a wide variety of models. The following types are a tiny subset of the possibilities: (1) models with missing observations, (2) models with time-varying parameters, (3) unobserved component models, (4) dynamic factor analysis, (5) continuous-time models with mixed stock and flow variables and possible aggregation, and (6) some nonlinear models.

39.1 Model and Motivation

We consider a general class of models described by the following two equations:

$$y_t = Z_t\alpha_t + S_t\varepsilon_t \tag{39.1}$$

and

$$\alpha_t = \mathcal{T}_t\alpha_{t-1} + R_t\eta_t, \tag{39.2}$$

for $t = 1, \ldots, T$, where

- y_t: $N \times 1$ vector of observed variables;
- α_t: $m \times 1$ vector of state variables;
- Z_t, S_t: fixed matrices of order $N \times m$ and $N \times n$;
- $\varepsilon_t \sim N(0, H_t)$: $n \times 1$ vector of *i.i.d.* errors with covariance matrix H_t $(n \times n)$;
- $\eta_t \sim N(0, Q_t)$: $g \times 1$ vector of *i.i.d.* errors with covariance matrix Q_t $(g \times g)$;
- ε_t, η_t: uncorrelated serially and with each other;
- $\mathcal{T}_t$ and R_t: fixed matrices of order $m \times m$ and $m \times g$, respectively;
- $E\left[\alpha_0 \eta_t'\right] = E\left[\alpha_0 \varepsilon_t'\right] = 0$.

Equation (39.1) is called the **measurement equation** and equation (39.2) the **transition equation**. Together they form what is called a state-space model. Many models may be represented in this form. The transition equation specifies the dynamics of an underlying unobserved process α_t called a state vector. Though it is in a Markovian form, it is possible, as we see, to have more complex lag structures such as $ARMA$ processes. Note that only the vector y_t is observed. The measurement equation specifies first how the actual observed variables are related to the elements of the state vector and second how measurement errors affect this relation via the random errors ε_t. Though the general model allows for time-varying parameters via the matrices Z_t, S_t, $\mathcal{T}_t$, R_t, H_t, and Q_t, in many cases, these are time-invariant and only involve a few unknown coefficients.

We give a few examples to illustrate how rich this class of model is and how useful it can be to get various types of estimates.

Example 39.1 (State-space representation of ARMA(2, 1) model). Consider a transition equation of the form

$$\begin{pmatrix} \alpha_t^{(1)} \\ \alpha_t^{(2)} \end{pmatrix} = \begin{bmatrix} \phi_1 & 1 \\ \phi_2 & 0 \end{bmatrix} \begin{pmatrix} \alpha_{t-1}^{(1)} \\ \alpha_{t-1}^{(2)} \end{pmatrix} + \begin{bmatrix} 1 \\ \theta \end{bmatrix} \eta_t,$$

where η_t is a scalar and $Q_t = \sigma_\eta^2$. Here, $\alpha_t^{(1)}$ is the first element of the state vector and $\alpha_t^{(2)}$ the second. Hence, $m = 2$. This system reduces to the following two equations:

$$\alpha_t^{(1)} = \phi_1 \alpha_{t-1}^{(1)} + \alpha_{t-1}^{(2)} + \eta_t \tag{39.3}$$

and

$$\alpha_t^{(2)} = \phi_2 \alpha_{t-1}^{(1)} + \theta \eta_t. \tag{39.4}$$

Lag equation (39.4) one period to obtain

$$\alpha_{t-1}^{(2)} = \phi_2 \alpha_{t-2}^{(1)} + \theta \eta_{t-1},$$

and substitute in equation (39.3). Then,

$$\alpha_t^{(1)} = \phi_1 \alpha_{t-1}^{(1)} + \phi_2 \alpha_{t-2}^{(1)} + \eta_t + \theta \eta_{t-1}.$$

So, the first element of the two-dimensional state vector α_t is effectively an $ARMA(2,1)$ process. It remains to specify that the actual data are these first (unobserved) elements and are measured without errors. Hence, the measurement equation for the scalar variable y_t is

$$y_t = \begin{bmatrix} 1 & 0 \end{bmatrix} \begin{pmatrix} \alpha_t^{(1)} \\ \alpha_t^{(2)} \end{pmatrix},$$

i.e., $Z_t = [1\ 0]$ and $S_t = 0$. Note that the actual structure of the second element of the state vector is of no consequence as we relate the observed variable to the first element only. Hence, the introduction of this second element can be viewed as an artificial device so that the first element has the desired structure. Here, the interest is in obtaining the MLE of the parameters $(\phi_1, \phi_2, \theta, \sigma_\eta^2)$.

Example 39.2 (State-space representation of an *ARMA* (p, q)). This example simply generalizes the previous one. Let

$$y_t = \phi_1 y_{t-1} + \cdots + \phi_m y_{t-m} + \eta_t + \theta_1 \eta_{t-1} + \cdots + \theta_{m-1} \eta_{t-m+1} \tag{39.5}$$

with $\eta_t \sim i.i.d.\, N\left(0, \sigma_\eta^2\right)$ represent the $ARMA\,(p, q)$ model with $m = \max\left(p, q+1\right)$. The Markovian representation of (39.5) is obtained by defining an $m \times 1$ vector α_t which obeys the following multivariate $AR(1)$ model:

$$\alpha_t = \underbrace{\begin{bmatrix} \phi_1 & \\ \phi_2 & I_{m-1} \\ \vdots & \vdots \\ \phi_m & 0' \end{bmatrix}}_{\mathcal{T}} \alpha_{t-1} + \underbrace{\begin{bmatrix} 1 \\ \theta_1 \\ \vdots \\ \theta_{m-1} \end{bmatrix}}_{R} \eta_t.$$

Note that if $p \neq q + 1$, we simply define some of the coefficients ϕ_i or θ_i to be 0. This is equation (39.2) with $\mathcal{T}$ and R constant and $Q_t = \sigma_\eta^2$. Again, the measurement equation (39.1) specifies that the observed data are the first element of the state vector and are measured without errors, i.e.,

$$y_t = (1, 0_{m-1})' \alpha_t$$

so that $Z_t = (1, 0_{m-1})'$ and $S_t = 0$.

Example 39.3 (Trend–cycle Decomposition). A typical decomposition of an economic time series is

$$y_t = \text{trend} + \text{cyclical}.$$

Here, the cyclical component is often interpreted as the output gap, the deviation from trend. The model is kept simple for the sake of exposition. More general specifications are possible but would not add to our understanding of the main issues involved. Consider the model

$$y_t = \mu_t + c_t, \tag{39.6}$$

where

$$\begin{aligned} \mu_t &= \mu_{t-1} + \beta_{t-1} + \tau_t, \\ \beta_t &= \beta_{t-1} + v_t, \\ c_t &= \phi_1 c_{t-1} + \phi_2 c_{t-2} + \omega_t, \end{aligned}$$

and $\tau_t \sim i.i.d.\ N\left(0, \sigma_\tau^2\right)$, $v_t \sim i.i.d.\ N\left(0, \sigma_v^2\right)$, $\omega_t \sim i.i.d.\ N\left(0, \sigma_\omega^2\right)$, τ_t and v_t are independent, though τ_t and ω_t can be correlated with

$E(\tau_t \omega_t) = \sigma_{\tau\omega}$. Note that one could add some irregular component to capture measurement errors. Here, μ_t is the trend, β_t the slope of the trend function, and τ_t and v_t allow the level and slope of the trend function to change slowly over time. Strictly speaking, this is a model that specifies the trend function to be an $I(2)$ process (one with two autoregressive unit roots). Typically, the estimate of σ_v^2 is quite small. If $\sigma_v^2 = 0$, then only the level of the trend is allowed to change and the process is $I(1)$. If $\sigma_v^2 = \sigma_\tau^2 = 0$, then the model reduces to

$$y_t = \alpha + \beta t + c_t,$$

a trend-stationary process. This model can be represented in state-space form with the state vector defined as

$$\alpha_t' = (\mu_t, \beta_t, c_t, c_{t-1})$$

and the transition equation as follows:

$$\alpha_t = \begin{bmatrix} \mu_t \\ \beta_t \\ c_t \\ c_{t-1} \end{bmatrix} = \underbrace{\begin{bmatrix} 1 & 1 & 0 & 0 \\ 0 & 1 & 0 & 0 \\ 0 & 0 & \phi_1 & \phi_2 \\ 0 & 0 & 1 & 0 \end{bmatrix}}_{\mathcal{T}} \underbrace{\begin{bmatrix} \mu_{t-1} \\ \beta_{t-1} \\ c_{t-1} \\ c_{t-2} \end{bmatrix}}_{\alpha_{t-1}} + \underbrace{\begin{bmatrix} \tau_t \\ v_t \\ \omega_t \\ 0 \end{bmatrix}}_{\eta_t}.$$

The covariance matrix of η_t is

$$Q = \begin{pmatrix} \sigma_\tau^2 & 0 & \sigma_{\tau\omega} & 0 \\ 0 & \sigma_v^2 & 0 & 0 \\ \sigma_{\tau\omega} & 0 & \sigma_\omega^2 & 0 \\ 0 & 0 & 0 & 0 \end{pmatrix}.$$

Note that it is singular. This is allowed. The measurement equation is

$$y_t = (1, 0, 1, 0)' \alpha_t, \tag{39.7}$$

i.e., $Z_t = (1, 0, 1, 0)'$, and $S_t = 0$. This model is identified as shown by Morley *et al.* (2003). Here, the model involves estimating the parameters $\sigma_\tau^2, \sigma_v^2, \sigma_\omega^2$ and $\sigma_{\tau\omega}$. These estimates are interesting *per se* because they can tell us something about the relative contribution of each component to the total variability of the series. For example, is the variability due to changes in the trend function more important than the variability due to the cyclical component? However, they are not the most interesting quantities. Most often one is interested in estimates of the trend and cycle. For example, most macroeconomic models have little or nothing to say about the trend as they pertain to stationary processes, i.e., the cyclical component. Hence, the need to extract a measure of the trend and cyclical components.

The trend–cycle decomposition using the state-space model can yield estimates of the trend and cycle. Here, obtaining one or the other is sufficient as they are related by (39.6). So, let us concentrate on obtaining an estimate of the cyclical component c_t. A first quantity of interest can be denoted by $c_{t|T}$, that is, the best estimate (in a sense to be made precise) of the cyclical component at time t using all information in the sample from $t = 1, \ldots, T$. These will be called "smoothed estimates". They are useful for a retrospective analysis; i.e., analyzing the properties of the cyclical component (variance, correlation structure, retrospective dating of business cycles, co-movements with other variables, etc.). This is what is required in most macroeconomic studies that want to see if a model fits the data well.

Another quantity of interest can be labeled as $c_{t|t}$, the best estimate of the cyclical component at time t given information available up to time t only (i.e., y_j for $j = 1, \ldots, t$). These will be called "filtered estimates". They are very useful to carry model evaluation in "real time". For instance, if you want to assess whether the central bank reacted according to this or that policy function. It is then unfair to use the smoothed estimates $c_{t|T}$ as these are based on information not available to the decision-makers at the time of the implementation of the policies. On the other hand, it is fair to use the filtered estimates $c_{t|t}$ since they are constructed using only information up to the time of the implementation. For an interesting application, see the work of Orphanides (2001).

Remark 39.1. It is useful to discuss what the measurement error term represents in the measurement equation (39.1). It is important to realize that it need not be due to standard issues of measurement errors only but rather to a broader concept of noise. To that effect, we consider the study of Estrada *et al.* (2024) who used a modified version of Example 39.3 with a noise component added in order to measure the autocorrelation of the climate signal in observed temperature data and investigate whether climate change had an effect on inducing increased persistence. So, the model is

$$y_t = \mu_t + c_t + e_t,$$

where μ_t is the trend, c_t is the cyclical component (a simple $AR(1)$), and e_t is the *i.i.d.* noise or measurement errors. The main analysis is based on the gridded ensemble median of monthly average near surface temperature anomalies from 1850:1 to 2021:12 from the HadCRUT.5.0.1.0 dataset36. The anomalies are relative to the monthly averages for the period 1961:1–1990:12. The spatial resolution is 5° longitude and 5° latitude. This is done for both land and oceans. The data are constructed as follows. For each day of the year, take the average of the temperatures over the period 1961:1–1990:12. Then, the "anomalies" used as data are the difference between the temperature at some date t minus the average over the base period. These are then averaged on a monthly basis. If one thinks in terms of pure measurement errors, then the data should be much more variable over the oceans compared to land. For land, we have precise instruments located at well-defined stations, which take temperature measurements at regular intervals. On the other hand, measurements over the surface of the oceans are less precise. They rely mostly on various devices installed on commercial vessels. However, recall that the data are constructed as so-called "anomalies", i.e., deviations from the current value with respect to some long-term average. Then, think about some summer date. For any given date, the temperature on land can vary widely, from frisky to oppressively hot. But this does not occur for ocean temperatures. They vary imperceptibly over a few days and very slowly over a month. It takes a long while to change the temperature of a large body of water, while on the contrary, simple changes in wind patterns can drastically affect land temperatures. This is why we go to the beach on hot land days (to refresh) and mostly avoid the water on cold summer days (except for some sports activity). So, here, what constitutes the "measurement error" e_t is by far dictated by random noise rather than measurement errors.

We develop in the following an estimation method to obtain the MLE. Of interest is that the method will deliver as a by-product filtered estimates of the state vector, $\alpha_{t|t}$ and, with a few more steps, it will be easy to obtain the smoothed estimates $\alpha_{t|T}$. In our example, since c_t and μ_t are elements of the state vector, one can obtain filtered and smoothed estimates for each.

39.2 The likelihood function

Recall from Chapter 15.9 that a likelihood function can be expressed via a prediction error decomposition given by

$$\log L\left(y\right) = c - (1/2)\sum_{t=1}^{T} \log f_t - (1/2)T \log \hat{\sigma}^2, \tag{39.8}$$

with c some constant,

$$v_t = y_t - \tilde{y}_{t|t-1} \sim N\left(0, \sigma^2 f_t\right),$$

where

$$\hat{\sigma}^2 = T^{-1} \sum_{t=1}^{T} v_t^2 / f_t \tag{39.9}$$

and

$$\tilde{y}_{t|t-1} = E\left[y_t | y_{t-1}, \ldots, y_1\right],$$

with $\tilde{y}_{t|t-1}$ the Minimum Mean Square Estimate ($MMSE$) of y_t given $y_{t-1}, \ldots, y_1$, $\tilde{y}_{1|0} = \mu_1$ and $\text{Var}(\tilde{y}_{1|0}) = \sigma^2 f_1$ (the exact treatment of the initial condition usually depends on the model; see Section 39.3.2) and

$$\sigma^2 f_t = \text{Var}\left(y_t | y_{t-1}, \ldots, y_1\right) = MSE\left[\tilde{y}_{t|t-1}\right].$$

So, to obtain the maximum likelihood estimates, we want to maximize (39.8) given (39.9). This framework makes clear what is needed to construct the likelihood function:

- the $MMSE$ of y_t given $\{y_{t-1}, \ldots, y_1\}$,
- the variance of the prediction errors f_t.

Once these quantities are obtained, one can evaluate the likelihood function for a given set of parameter values, say θ^* the vector of parameters in the state-space model, and use numerical optimization techniques to find the maximum likelihood estimates $\hat{\theta}$; see Chapter 16. The Kalman filter is simply a set of recursions to efficiently obtain the quantities of interest to construct the likelihood function. We discuss a special case in the following.

39.3 The Kalman filter

We consider the special case where $\mathcal{T}_t$, R_t, and Q_t are time invariant (common in economics). For a list of the relevant equations in the general case, see the work of Harvey (1981, p. 110). We also consider the case with y_t a scalar. This is not typical but will ease the presentation. Hence,

$$y_t = Z_t' \alpha_t + \varepsilon_t \tag{39.10}$$

and

$$\alpha_t = \mathcal{T} \alpha_{t-1} + R\eta_t, \tag{39.11}$$

where $\varepsilon_t \sim i.i.d.\ N\left(0, \sigma^2 h_t\right)$ and $\eta_t \sim i.i.d.\ N\left(0, \sigma^2 Q\right)$. We use the following notation:

- a_t: the $MMSE$ (minimum mean-square linear estimator) of α at time t;
- $a_{t|t-1}$: the $MMSE$ of α_t at time $t-1$.

We are first concerned about the optimal prediction of the state vector α_t; the optimal prediction of y_t is then easily obtained via the measurement equation (39.10). At time $t-1$, all information is incorporated in $a_{t-1} \equiv MMSE\left(\alpha_{t-1}\right)$. Let

$$\sigma^2 P_{t-1} = \mathrm{Cov}\left(a_{t-1}\right), \text{ a known matrix.}$$

Given (39.11) and $E\left[\eta_t | \Phi_{t-1}\right] = 0$, where Φ_{t-1} denotes the information available at time $t-1$, we have

$$a_{t|t-1} = \mathcal{T} a_{t-1}.$$

Subtract $\alpha_t = \mathcal{T}\alpha_{t-1} + R\eta_t$ from both sides so that

$$a_{t|t-1} - \alpha_t = \mathcal{T}\left(a_{t-1} - \alpha_{t-1}\right) - R\eta_t.$$

The $MMSE$ is unbiased, so the right-hand side has mean 0 and covariance matrix

$$\begin{aligned} E\left(a_{t|t-1} - \alpha_t\right)\left(a_{t|t-1} - \alpha_t\right)' &= \sigma^2 \mathcal{T} P_{t-1} \mathcal{T}' + \sigma^2 RQR' \\ &\equiv \sigma^2 P_{t|t-1} \end{aligned}$$

since η_t is uncorrelated with $\left(a_{t-1} - \alpha_{t-1}\right)$. Hence,

$$a_{t|t-1} - \alpha_t \sim N\left(0, \sigma^2 P_{t|t-1}\right).$$

The $MMSE$ of y_t at $t-1$ is, from (39.10) since $E(\varepsilon_t|\Phi_{t-1}) = 0$,

$$\tilde{y}_{t|t-1} = Z_t' a_{t|t-1},$$

and the prediction error is

$$v_t = y_t - \tilde{y}_{t|t-1} = Z_t'\left(\alpha_t - a_{t|t-1}\right) + \varepsilon_t.$$

The prediction errors have the following properties: (a) They are unbiased, $E\left[v_t\right] = 0$, and (b) their variance is given by

$$\begin{aligned} \operatorname{Var}\left(v_t\right) = E&\left[Z_t'\left(\alpha_t - a_{t|t-1}\right)\left(\alpha_t - a_{t|t-1}\right)' Z_t\right] \\ &+ E\left[\varepsilon_t^2\right] + 2E\left[Z_t'\left(\alpha_t - a_{t|t-1}\right)\varepsilon_t\right], \end{aligned}$$

and, since the last term is zero,

$$\operatorname{Var}\left(v_t\right) = \sigma^2 Z_t' P_{t|t-1} Z_t + \sigma^2 h_t \equiv \sigma^2 f_t. \tag{39.12}$$

39.3.1 Updating

As noted, all information at $t-1$ is contained in the optimal predictor $a_{t|t-1}$. The updating problem is to combine the new information at time t, namely the additional observation y_t, to produce the $MMSE$ of α_t: a_t. Consider the following two equations:

$$a_{t|t-1} = \alpha_t + \left(a_{t|t-1} - \alpha_t\right),$$
$$y_t = Z_t'\alpha_t + \varepsilon_t,$$

or, in matrix form,

$$\overset{x}{\begin{pmatrix} a_{t|t-1} \\ y_t \end{pmatrix}} = \overset{A}{\begin{pmatrix} I \\ Z_t' \end{pmatrix}} \alpha_t + \overset{U}{\begin{pmatrix} a_{t|t-1} - \alpha_t \\ \varepsilon_t \end{pmatrix}}. \tag{39.13}$$

The disturbances have mean 0 and covariance matrix

$$\sigma^2 V = \sigma^2 \begin{bmatrix} P_{t|t-1} & 0 \\ 0 & h_t \end{bmatrix}.$$

The $MMSE$ of α_t is the GLS estimator of α_t in (39.13); see the work of Harvey (1981, Chapter 4.2):

$$a_t = \left(A'V^{-1}A\right)^{-1} A'V^{-1}x$$

and

$$\mathrm{Var}(a_t) = \sigma^2 \left(A'V^{-1}A\right)^{-1}.$$

Note that this is a special case of a mixed estimation procedure, when combining sample and prior information. Hence, it can be given a Bayesian interpretation. Then,

$$\begin{aligned} a_t &= \left[\begin{pmatrix} I & Z_t \end{pmatrix} \begin{pmatrix} P_{t|t-1} & 0 \\ 0 & h_t \end{pmatrix}^{-1} \begin{pmatrix} I \\ Z_t' \end{pmatrix}\right]^{-1} \\ &\quad \times \left[\begin{pmatrix} I & Z_t \end{pmatrix} \begin{pmatrix} P_{t|t-1} & 0 \\ 0 & h_t \end{pmatrix}^{-1} \begin{pmatrix} a_{t|t-1} \\ y_t \end{pmatrix}\right] \\ &= \left(P_{t|t-1}^{-1} + Z_t Z_t'/h_t\right)^{-1} \left(P_{t|t-1}^{-1} a_{t|t-1} + Z_t y_t/h_t\right) \end{aligned}$$

or

$$a_t = P_t \left(P_{t|t-1}^{-1} a_{t|t-1} + Z_t y_t/h_t\right),$$

where

$$P_t = \left(P_{t|t-1}^{-1} + Z_t Z_t'/h_t\right)^{-1} = \left(A'V^{-1}A\right)^{-1}.$$

So,

$$a_t - \alpha_t \sim N\left(0, \sigma^2 P_t\right).$$

Remark 39.2. In the following, we use the matrix inversion formula:

$$\left[A + BCB'\right]^{-1} = A^{-1} - A^{-1}B\left(C^{-1} + B'A^{-1}B\right)^{-1}B'A^{-1}.$$

Let $P_{t|t-1}^{-1} = A,\ Z_t = B,\ 1/h_t = C$, then

$$P_t = P_{t|t-1} - P_{t|t-1}Z_t Z_t' P_{t|t-1}/f_t, \tag{39.14}$$

where, from (39.12),

$$f_t = Z_t' P_{t|t-1} Z_t + h_t. \tag{39.15}$$

Substituting for P_t in a_t gives (after rearrangements)

$$a_t = a_{t|t-1} + P_{t|t-1}Z_t\left(y_t - Z_t' a_{t|t-1}\right)/f_t. \tag{39.16}$$

The equations (39.14), (39.15), and (39.16) are the basic updating equations. Note that they do not require any matrix inversion.

Remark 39.3 (Interpretation of (39.16)). The prediction error is $\left(y_t - Z_t' a_{t|t-1}\right)$ and it contains all the new information in y_t and is used to update $a_{t|t-1}$ via the "Kalman Gain" $P_{t|t-1}Z_t/f_t$.

Remark 39.4. In the above derivations, we assumed that $h_t > 0$, but the updating equations can be shown to be still valid if $h_t = 0$. This is useful because this case is often encountered.

39.3.2 Issues with initial conditions

We now consider issues related to the specification of the initial values of P_0 to start the recursion. Two cases are of interest: one where stationarity is imposed and one where it is not. Imposing stationarity amounts to specifying $\sigma^2 P_0$ to be the unconditional variance of α_t. We have the following result.

Lemma 39.1. *Let P_0 be the unconditional variance of α_t. Then, P_0 must satisfy (given the transition equation)*

$$P_0 = \mathcal{T} P_0 \mathcal{T}' + RQR'.$$

Proof. The transition equation is

$$\alpha_t = \mathcal{T} \alpha_{t-1} + R\eta_t.$$

Post-multiply by α_t' and take expectations

$$E\left[\alpha_t \alpha_t'\right] = \mathcal{T} E\left[\alpha_{t-1}\alpha_t'\right] + RE\left[\eta_t \alpha_t'\right].$$

We have

- $E\left[\alpha_t \alpha_t'\right] = P_0$,
- $RE\left[\eta_t \alpha_t'\right] = RE\left[\eta_t\left(\alpha_{t-1}'\mathcal{T}' + \eta_t' R'\right)\right] = RQR'$,
- $\mathcal{T} E\left[\alpha_{t-1}\alpha_t'\right] = \mathcal{T} E\left[\alpha_{t-1}\left(\alpha_{t-1}'\mathcal{T}' + \eta_t' R'\right)\right] = \mathcal{T} P_0 \mathcal{T}'$.

Hence,

$$P_0 = \mathcal{T} P_0 \mathcal{T}' + RQR'.$$

This can be solved using the representation

$$\operatorname{vec}(P_0) = \left[I - \mathcal{T} \otimes \mathcal{T}\right]^{-1} \operatorname{vec}\left(RQR'\right).$$

In the non-stationary case, for instance, with unit root processes as in Example 39.3, we can construct the starting values from the observations themselves. This implies a loss of some degrees of freedom. A common practice is to set the initial value to some arbitrary number but specifying a very large variance. The idea is that, if the model is non-stationary, its unconditional distribution is unbounded. Hence, a large variance for the initial condition simply reflects our ignorance about its likely value.

39.3.3 Estimation of the parameters

The following is a summary of the steps needed to evaluate the likelihood function:

1. Start with some initial value for y_1 and its variance, i.e., $\tilde{y}_{1|0} = \mu_1$ and $\operatorname{Var}(\tilde{y}_{1|0}) = \sigma^2 f_1$.

2. Use the following steps to estimate the state vector at time t using information available at time $t-1$:

$$a_{t|t-1} = \mathcal{T} a_{t-1},$$
$$\sigma^2 P_{t|t-1} = \sigma^2 \mathcal{T} P_{t-1} \mathcal{T}' + \sigma^2 RQR'.$$

Then,

$$\tilde{y}_{t|t-1} = Z_t' a_{t|t-1},$$
$$\sigma^2 f_t = \sigma^2 Z_t' P_{t|t-1} Z_t + \sigma^2 h_t,$$

and

$$v_t = y_t - \tilde{y}_{t|t-1}.$$

3. Update P_t and a_t using the following formulae:

$$P_t = P_{t|t-1} - P_{t|t-1} Z_t Z_t' P_{t|t-1} / f_t,$$
$$a_t = a_{t|t-1} + P_{t|t-1} Z_t \left(y_t - Z_t' a_{t|t-1} \right) / f_t.$$

4. Repeat steps 2–3 for $t = 2, \ldots, T$.

Then, we simply use the form of the likelihood function derived before, that is, equation (39.8), to evaluate it at some given value of the parameters. The estimation is done using a numerical procedure to maximize the likelihood function to obtain the MLE.

39.3.4 Smoothing

We recall our model for the decomposition of an economic time series into a trend and a cyclical component. An issue of interest was to obtain smoothed estimate of the cyclical and trend components, i.e., $c_{t|T}$ and $\mu_{t|T}$. This involves estimating the state vector α_t using all observations in the sample. We already have estimates $a_{t|t-1}$ of α_t, but these are based only upon observations up to $t-1$ and so are not efficient (or not what is needed). We would like to have an estimate $a_{t|T}$ based upon the whole dataset. This is achieved using the smoothing equations. Let

$a_{t|T}$: smoothed estimate of α_t,

$P_{t|T}$: its covariance matrix.

Then, the smoothing equations are

$$a_{t|T} = a_t P_t^* \left(a_{t+1|T} - \mathcal{T}_{t+1} a_t\right)$$

and

$$P_{t|T} = P_t + P_t^* \left(P_{t+1|T} - P_{t+1|t}\right) P_t^{*\prime},$$

where

$$P_t^* = P_t \mathcal{T}_{t+1}^{\prime} P_{t+1|t}^{\prime},$$

for $t = T-1, \ldots, 1$, with initial values $a_{T|T} = a_T$ and $P_{T|T} = P_T$. So, the procedure is as follows:

1. Use the updating equations to construct $a_{t|t-1}$ recursively from $t = 1$ to $t = T$.
2. Then, use the smoothing equations to construct $a_{t|T}$ recursively from $t = T-1$ to $t = 1$.

39.4 Nonlinear and non-Gaussian state-space models

The Kalman filter is the optimal linear filter to minimize the mean square error of the estimates of the unobservable state variables. However, the basic Kalman filter is limited to linear and Gaussian models. Its implementation in nonlinear and non-Gaussian dynamic systems is more difficult. In this section, we review the basic class of models, provide examples, and review some estimation methods.

39.4.1 The class of nonlinear non-Gaussian models

We consider the following state-space model for a vector of observed variables y_t and some unobserved latent state vector α_t:

$$y_t = H_1(\alpha_t;\theta) + H_2(\alpha_t;\theta)\,\varepsilon_t, \tag{39.17}$$

$$\alpha_{t+1} = F(\alpha_t;\theta) + \eta_t. \tag{39.18}$$

Here, F, H_1, and H_2 are nonlinear functions of the state variable with parameter θ. We assume that ε_t and η_t are mutually independent random variables with ε_s and ε_t, $s \neq t$, serially independent. In addition, we assume that the initial state α_0 has a finite mean μ_0 and variance Σ_0. The errors can be non-Gaussian and have distributions given by $\eta_t \sim p_\eta(\cdot)$ and $\varepsilon_t \sim p_\varepsilon(\cdot)$, where $p_\eta(\cdot)$ and $p_\varepsilon(\cdot)$ are known parametric probability density functions with finite first two moments. Of course, the errors can be Gaussian, in which case the model is nonlinear with Gaussian errors; and vice versa, the model can be linear with non-Gaussian errors. Each of these two features requires a separate treatment from the standard linear and Gaussian state-space models analyzed earlier.

39.4.2 Examples

We start with two examples of nonlinear and Gaussian state-space models. The first is a quadratic term structure model and the second a stochastic volatility model.

Example 39.4 (Quadratic Term Structure Model). As an extension of the traditional affine term structure models, Monfort *et al.* (2015) considered the following state-space representation of the quadratic term structure model. Suppose α_t is an unobservable state vector of dimension n, and y_t is a vector of observable variables of dimension m. For example, y_t can be the nominal instantaneous interest rate. The quadratic term structure model is defined as

$$y_t = A + B\alpha_t + \sum_{k=1}^{m} e_k \alpha_t' C^{(k)} \alpha_t + \varepsilon_t,$$

$$\alpha_t = \phi + \varphi\alpha_{t-1} + \eta_t,$$

where ε_t and η_t are independent Gaussian white noises with identity variance matrices and e_k is the column selection vector of dimension m whose components are 0 except the kth one, which is equal to 1. The parameters of the model are ϕ, φ, A, B, and $C^{(k)}$. A quadratic term structure framework with a component-by-component version of the measurement equation was also explored by Ahn *et al.* (2002). The framework specifies the yield on a bond as a quadratic function of the underlying state variables. Ahn *et al.* (2002) showed that the quadratic term structure model can overcome some limitations inherent in affine term structure models. They also showed that it outperforms the affine term structure model in explaining historical bond price behavior in the United States.

Example 39.5 (Heston's Stochastic Volatility Model). Heston (1993) proposed a stochastic volatility model based on the Black and Scholes (1973) model for stock price dynamics and derived a closed-form solution for the price of a European call option on an asset with stochastic volatility. The following is a discrete-time version of Heston's model. We let S denote the stock price and s the returns, while Y_t denotes the log volatility of the stock price. The discrete-time model is

$$s_t = \ln \frac{S_t}{S_{t-1}} = \left(r - \frac{\exp(2Y_t)}{2}\right) + \exp(Y_t)\left[\sqrt{1-\rho^2}W_{1,t} + \rho W_{2,t}\right],$$

$$Y_{t+1} = \beta^* + e^{-\alpha}(Y_t - \beta^*) + \gamma\sqrt{\left(\frac{1-e^{-2\alpha}}{2\alpha}\right)}W_{2,t},$$

where W_1 and W_2 are two correlated Gaussian noises with correlation coefficient ρ, while r, β^*, γ, and α are parameters. This model and its continuous-time version allow for an arbitrary correlation between volatility and spot asset returns and they were applied in a number of studies; e.g., Bakshi *et al.* (1997) and Bates (1996). This model can be interpreted as a nonlinear and Gaussian state-space model by considering s as the observable variable or measurement and Y as the unobservable state variable entering the measurement equation through a nonlinear exponential transformation.

We next provide examples of linear non-Gaussian state-space models. The first is a regime switching model, the second a fat-tailed stochastic volatility model, and the third a shifting trend model for trend–cycle decomposition.

Example 39.6 (Regime Switching Model). This example is from the work of Hamilton (1994), which follows his earlier influential paper Hamilton (1989). Here, we consider an unobservable state variable s_t that can take a finite number of values $1, 2, \ldots, S$ corresponding to S different possible regimes. Also, we consider the following regression model:

$$y_t = x_t' \beta_{s_t} + \varepsilon_t,$$

where x_t is a $k \times 1$ vector of exogenous variables and $\varepsilon_t \sim i.i.d.$ $N\left(0, \sigma^2\right)$. The value of the coefficient β_{s_t} depends on the regime s_t. Denote

$$\zeta_t \equiv \left(y_t, y_{t-1}, \ldots, y_1, x_t', x_{t-1}', \ldots, x_1'\right)',$$

and assume

$$\begin{aligned}
&\text{Prob}\left(s_{t+1} = j | s_t = i, s_{t-1} = i_1, s_{t-2} = i_2, \ldots, \zeta_t\right) \\
&\quad = \text{Prob}\left(s_{t+1} = j | s_t = i\right)
\end{aligned}$$

so that the probabilities are Markovian. Let Π be an $S \times S$ matrix such that

$$\Pi_{ij} = \{\text{Prob}\left(s_{t+1} = j | s_t = i\right)\}.$$

Let ι_i denote the ith column of the identity matrix I_S, and construct ξ_t equal to ι_i when $s_t = i$. Then, the Markov chain of states implies

$$\xi_{t+1} = \Pi \xi_t + \eta_t \tag{39.19}$$

and

$$E\left(\xi_{t+j} | \xi_t, \xi_{t-1}, \ldots, \xi_1, \zeta_t\right) = \Pi^j \xi_t.$$

The regression model can be rewritten as

$$y_t = x_t' B \xi_t + \varepsilon_t, \tag{39.20}$$

where B is a $k \times S$ matrix whose ith column is given by β_i. The model in (39.19)–(39.20) is an example of a linear and non-Gaussian state-space model. The filter developed by Hamilton (1994) is a popular tool for this regime switching model. Other approaches are possible as discussed in the following.

Example 39.7 (Fat-tailed Stochastic Volatility Model). As an extension of the basic log-normal autoregressive stochastic volatility model of Taylor (1986), Kim *et al.* (1998) and Jacquier *et al.* (2004) considered the following fat-tailed stochastic volatility model:

$$\begin{aligned} y_t &= \sqrt{\alpha_t}\bar{\varepsilon}_t = \sqrt{\alpha_t}\sqrt{\lambda_t}\varepsilon_t, \\ \log \alpha_t &= \alpha + \beta \log \alpha_{t-1} + \sigma_\eta \eta_t, \quad t \geq 1, \\ \lambda_t &\sim p(\lambda_t|\nu), \end{aligned}$$

where y_t is the return from an asset and α_t is its volatility. The parameters of the model are α, β, σ_η, and ν. It is assumed that ε_t and η_t are independent random variables with $\varepsilon_t \sim i.i.d.\ N(0,1)$ and $\eta_t \sim i.i.d.\ N(0,1)$. The process λ_t is assumed to follow an $i.i.d$ inverse gamma distribution, or $\nu/\lambda_t \sim \chi^2_\nu$. This implies that the marginal distribution of $\sqrt{\lambda_t}\varepsilon_t$ is given by a Student's t_ν. The authors argued that the fat-tailed stochastic volatility model is more outlier-resistant than the basic stochastic volatility model. A likelihood-based inference method based on Markov Chain Monte Carlo (MCMC) for this model was discussed building on the work of Jacquier and Rossi (1994).

Example 39.8 (The Trend–Cycle Decomposition Model of Perron and Wada (2009)). To provide a flexible trend–cycle decomposition, Perron and Wada (2009) considered a generalized state-space model where some of the errors are non-normal. To understand the key ingredient, go back to the original model discussed in Example 39.3 with

$$y_t = \mu_t + c_t,$$

where

$$\begin{aligned} \mu_t &= \beta_t + \mu_{t-1} + \tau_t, \\ \beta_t &= \beta_{t-1} + v_t. \end{aligned}$$

The main difference from the previous model is the use of a non-normal distribution for the errors v_t. In order to allow infrequent changes in the slope of the trend function, they specify a mixture of normal distributions where a realization of v_t is a draw from one of two normal distributions, one with high and the other with small or zero variance. More specifically,

$$v_t = \lambda_t \gamma_{1t} + (1 - \lambda_t)\, \gamma_{2t},$$

where $\gamma_{it} \sim i.i.d.\ N(0, \sigma^2_{\gamma i})$ and λ_t is a Bernoulli random variable that takes value one with probability α_1, and value 0 with probability $1 - \alpha_1$. Here, we would expect α_1 to be close to one and $\sigma^2_{\gamma 1}$ to be zero so that most of the time, there is no change in the slope of the trend function. Furthermore, if $\sigma^2_{\gamma 2} > 0$, there will be occasional changes to the value of the slope. This implies a state-space model but with non-Gaussian errors. This model is discussed in more detail in Section 39.5.3.

39.4.3 An overview of some methods of estimation

The most common approach for nonlinear systems is the extended Kalman filter (EKF) developed by the NASA Ames project. Using a Taylor expansion of the nonlinear system around the current estimate of the state variables, the EKF is obtained based on a linear approximation of the original nonlinear system. A higher-order EKF was proposed by Jazwinski (1970) and Maybeck (1982). The EKF has proven to be a useful method for filtering with nonlinear systems. However, there is no guarantee of optimality in the mean-square error sense. In addition, the filter is unstable if the assumption of local linearity is violated.

A recent development related to the nonlinear filtering problem is the unscented Kalman filter (UKF) proposed by Julier and Uhlmann (1997); see also the works of Wan and Nelson (2000) and van der Merwe and Wan (2001). The UKF generates a discrete distribution with the same first and second moments as those of the nonlinear function, where each point in the discrete approximation can be directly transformed. We can then compute the mean and covariance of the transformed system as the estimate of the nonlinear transformation, without knowing its distribution precisely. The UKF is based on an unscented transformation that uses a set of appropriately chosen weighted points (called sigma points) to parameterize the means and covariances of probability distributions. The UKF is based on a small set of trial points; thus, it is not a truly global approximation of the nonlinear system. In addition, the application of the UKF is limited to models driven by Gaussian noise.

Particle filtering (Gordon *et al.* (1993), Del Moral (1996), Del Moral (1998)) is a simulation-based technique for filtering problems and has gained popularity in the last 30 years. The particle filter approximates the posterior distribution of the state variable using a set of particles; see Chapter 52. The state-space model can be nonlinear, and the distribution of the errors can take any form. Variants of the particle filter include the Bootstrap filter proposed by Gordon *et al.* (1993), the auxiliary particle filter proposed by Pitt and Shephard (1999), the unscented particle filter proposed by Van Der Merwe *et al.* (2000), and the Rao–Blackwellized particle filter proposed by Doucet *et al.* (2013). Del Moral (1996), Del Moral (1998), Del Moral and Guionnet (1999a), Del Moral and Guionnet (1999b) and Del Moral and Guionnet (2001) established its mathematical foundations. Applications of the particle filter in economics and econometrics can be found in the works of Kim *et al.* (1998), Flury and Shepard (2011), Creal *et al.* (2013), Fernández-Villaverde and Rubio-Ramìrez (2007), Fernández-Villaverde *et al.* (2011), and others. Lopes and Tsay (2011) provided a survey of applications of the particle filter in financial econometrics. A particle filter can be applied to a much wider range of dynamic systems than the Kalman filter and its variants. However, the particle filter suffers from two problems: sampling degeneracy and impoverishment. In the particle propagation process, the weight will concentrate on a few particles after only several iterations, and the weight of most particles will be close to zero. This is called sampling degeneracy. To address this problem, a resampling procedure was suggested by Kitagawa (1996). In resampling, a particle with a larger weight is more likely to be drawn, and particles with small weights are likely to be abandoned. This introduces the problem of sample impoverishment, which could negatively impact the quality of the particle filter, as we try to represent a distribution with very few distinct particles. The basics of some methods are discussed in Chapter 52.

For non-Gaussian models, the error distribution is approximated using Gaussian mixtures, a common approach in a wide variety of contexts. Then, for either linear or nonlinear models, the prediction and filtering distributions can be approximated by a mixture of Gaussian distributions. The means and variances of the Gaussian distributions are derived in a recursive two-step manner and can be computed in a closed-form manner for the linear model, or based on quasi-Monte Carlo simulations for nonlinear models. The merit of this approach for the general case is that it can transform the non-Gaussian model into several Gaussian models and one then solves each of them simultaneously. This approximation is performed by choosing values of the number m of normal components used, their variance P_i, and the weights associated with each component φ_i, for $i = -1, \ldots, m$. These parameters are chosen to minimize the relative entropy (measure of distance) between the true distribution $p_v(v)$ and its approximation $\tilde{p}_v(v)$. The approximation error is discussed in the works of Li and Barron (1999), Genovese and Wasserman (2000), Ghosal (2001) and Ghosal and van der Vaart (2007); the choice of m can be determined accordingly.

39.5 Applications: The problem of trend–cycle decomposition

As discussed in Example 39.3, state-space models can be used to obtain a trend–cycle decomposition. This is an important problem, especially in macroeconomics. We have already covered other methods based on the band-pass filter in Section 37.5.4. In this section, we review other procedures that have been proposed that can be cast into a linear or nonlinear state-space model and compare the resulting estimates using real GDP data for the United States. A discussion of the conflicting results is presented. For a selective review of business cycle fluctuations in U.S. macroeconomic time series, see the work of Stock and Watson (1999).

39.5.1 The Hodrick–Prescott filter

We already covered several methods to extract the cyclical component: the Beveridge and Nelson (1981) decomposition discussed in Section 37.5.4, the band-pass filter proposed by Baxter and King

(1999) and Christiano and Fitzgerald (2003) in Section 37.5.4, and various unobserved component models discussed in this chapter. The Hodrick and Prescott (1997) filter was originally proposed in the work of Hodrick and Prescott (1981); henceforth, the HP filter is by far the most popular in applied work, mostly due to its simplicity and, to some extent, some degree of inertia in the profession; i.e., if everyone uses it, I might as well use it, then nobody will complain. Hence, it is worth describing it in some detail and discussing its benefits and shortcomings. The discussion follows closely the work of Hamilton (2018), whose proposal we discuss further in the following.

The idea behind the HP filter is quite intuitive and appealing. Let y_t be the logarithmic transformation of a series of interest. We aim to extract a trend component labeled, say, y_t^* and accordingly a cyclical component defined by $c_t = y_t - y_t^*$. The idea is to minimize the deviations of y_t^* from y_t but imposing a penalty for the changes in the rate of growth in y_t^*. This leads to the following optimization problem:

$$\min_{\{y_t^*\}_{t=1}^T} \sum_{t=1}^T (y_t - y_t^*)^2 + \lambda \sum_{t=1}^T (\Delta y_t^* - \Delta y_{t-1}^*)^2.$$

Note that since the data are in logarithmic form, Δy_t^* is the growth rate of y_t^* and $\Delta y_t^* - \Delta y_{t-1}^*$ is the change in the growth rates. The parameter λ is of crucial importance and dictates the penalty imposed on having the fitted trend exhibit changes in growth rates. At the extremes, if $\lambda = 0$, $y_t^* = y_t$ and as $\lambda \to \infty$, y_t^* is a linear time trend. By far, the most popular choice is to use $\lambda = 1{,}600$ when using quarterly data.

This procedure is actually a linear filter, i.e., a linear combination of the data y_t $(t = 1, \ldots, T)$. To see this, let the $T \times 1$ vector y be

$$y = (y_T, \ldots, y_1)$$

and the $(T + 2) \times 1$ vector

$$y_t^* = (y_T^*, \ldots, y_0^*, y_{-1}^*).$$

Define the following matrices:

$$\underset{T\times(T+2)}{H} = \begin{bmatrix} I_T & \underset{T\times 2}{0} \end{bmatrix}$$

and

$$\underset{T\times(T+2)}{Q} = \begin{bmatrix} 1 & -2 & 1 & 0 & \cdots & 0 & 0 & 0 \\ 0 & 1 & -2 & 1 & \cdots & 0 & 0 & 0 \\ \vdots & \vdots & \vdots & \vdots & \cdots & \vdots & \vdots & \vdots \\ 0 & 0 & 0 & 0 & \cdots & -2 & 1 & 0 \\ 0 & 0 & 0 & 0 & \cdots & 1 & -2 & 1 \end{bmatrix}.$$

Then,

$$y^* = (H'H + \lambda Q'Q)^{-1} H'y \triangleq Ay. \tag{39.21}$$

See the works of Hamilton (2018) and Cornea-Madeira (2017) for computational details. It is also possible to view it as the solution to a state-space model to which the Kalman filter can be applied. The measurement equation is

$$y_t = y_t^* + c_t, \tag{39.22}$$

while the transition equation is

$$y_t^* = 2y_{t-1}^* - y_{t-2}^* + v_t, \tag{39.23}$$

where

$$v_t = \Delta^2 y_t^*,$$

the second difference of the trend component. Suppose that c_t and v_t are independent white noise processes (with variance σ_c^2 and σ_v^2, respectively) and also independent of the initial conditions (y_0^*, y_1^*). If we let the variance of the initial condition (y_0^*, y_1^*) be increasingly large, the solution to the state-space problem (39.22)–(39.23) becomes equivalent to (39.21) provided $\lambda = \sigma_c^2/\sigma_v^2$. This provides a way to efficiently compute the trend component using the Kalman filter algorithm. The conditions needed are, however, very strong, especially assuming c_t to be white noise, which makes no sense in virtually all applications.

So, what is the purpose of all that? It turns out that it provides a relatively intuitive way of deciding upon the value λ for the penalty factor. Hodrick and Prescott (1997) used a prior that large changes (in standard deviation terms) in the cyclical component within a quarter would be about 5%, while large changes in the trend would be near (1/8)%. This leads to $\lambda = \sigma_c^2/\sigma_v^2 = (5/(1/8))^2 = 1{,}600$. End of the story, that value has stuck unchallenged (at least in most practical applications) since they suggested that. The only minor exception was to adjust the value for other sampling intervals using the same principles; see the work of Ravn and Uhlig (2002). For annual data $\lambda = 1{,}600/4^4 = 6.25$, while for monthly data $\lambda = 1{,}600 \times 3^4 = 129{,}600$.

Why this value of $\lambda = 1{,}600$ has been almost universally accepted is probably best explained by the sociology of scientific publishing. Once the ball gets rolling and everybody uses the same value, then there is every incentive to continue using the same, even if you think it makes no sense. Some readers may be suspicious that you are trying to fudge the results if you adopt a different more reasonable value, unless you write a whole paper for why your value is better!

A striking feature of the HP filter is that it delivers a trend that follows closely the actual series, leaving very little in terms of variations to the cyclical component. This is in stark contrast to the unobserved component model when nonlinear features, such as a change in slope, are accounted for (e.g., when analyzing real GDP series). Whether this is good or bad depends on your prior view. I tend to favor having a large cycle which follows closely the NBER chronology. This can also be seen by looking at the squared gain function of the HP filter, plotted in Figure 39.1. We can see that the filter eliminates all movement of frequency lower than (roughly) $\pi/32$ (similar to the band-pass filter). The squared gain function then gradually increases and all movements of frequency higher than (roughly) $\pi/8$ are kept unchanged. Note that overall, the squared gain function of the HP filter is similar to that of the band-pass filter with $K = 8$ at low frequencies. Since this is the region of importance in economics, the two filters are expected to yield a similar cyclical component. This is indeed the case.

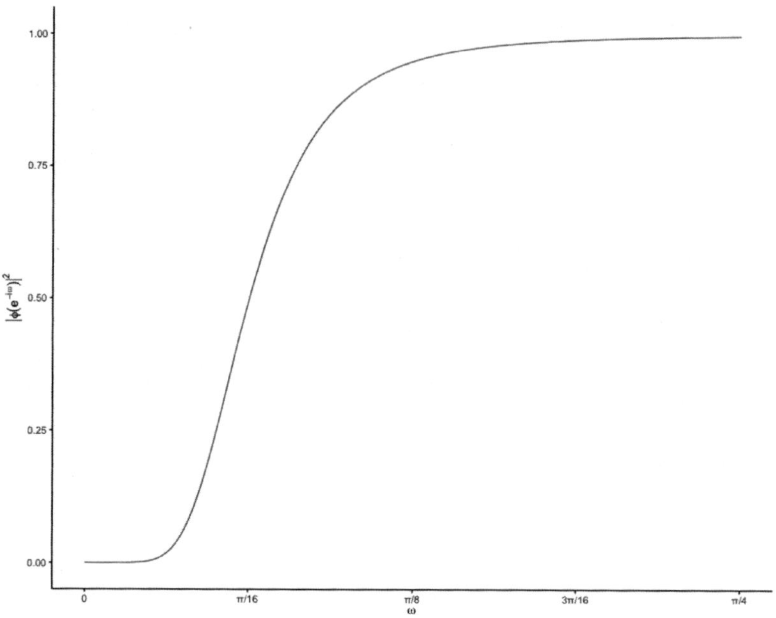

Figure 39.1. Squared gain function of the HP filter.

But besides this issue, which also plagues the Baxter and King (1999) band-pass filter methodology and the Beveridge and Nelson (1981) decomposition, there are many other reasons to be wary of the HP filter. These have been forcefully put forward by Hamilton (2018). We review some of his criticisms in the following:

1. The HP filter spuriously induces serial correlation. Consider y_t being a random walk, i.e., $y_t = y_{t-1} + e_t$ with e_t a martingale difference so that Δy_t cannot be predicted form past observations (e.g., y_t is the (log) price of some asset and Δy_t the return). If that is the true process, then one would hope that the estimated cyclical component (here the first difference Δy_t) would share the same properties. However, the HP filtered cyclical series exhibits serial correlation, especially near the middle of the sample; see the work of Cogley and Nason (1995). The extent of the correlation heavily depends on the penalty parameter λ.
2. The HP trend and cycle are based on the full set of data. Hence, at any point in time, future values influence the decompositions,

which in turn implies a spurious ability to predict future values of the cyclical component. A one-sided version can alleviate this problem but still induces side effects because it is not able to ascertain *ex post* genuine changes in trend from temporary deviations. Here, we agree with the fact that the HP filter leads to this problem but not solely because it uses the full sample. Indeed, the argument raised by Hamilton (2018) against the one-sided version points to the fact that using the full sample is indeed needed to have a good estimate of the cyclical or trend component. Also, as discussed above, unobserved component models use the full sample (provided the smoothed estimates are used) and do not suffer from the same problems.

3. The chosen value of λ makes no sense, i.e., it has no formal justification. We already discussed this issue before, but Hamilton (2018) makes a further, more damaging argument. Suppose that we take the state-space problem (39.22)–(39.23) seriously given that it is the basis for the choice of λ. Then, using common macroeconomic variables, estimates of the variances σ_c^2 and σ_v^2 are often similar or with the estimate of σ_c^2 smaller than that of σ_v^2. So, using $\lambda = \sigma_c^2/\sigma_v^2$, we should use values of λ near or below one, very far from the widely used value $\lambda = 1{,}600$.
4. The HP filter will remove a linear trend but not necessarily a unit root. It depends on the value of λ. If the original series is integrated (i.e., with a stochastic trend) and λ is large relative to the sample size T, the HP filter tends to simply detrend a random walk. Hence, the cyclical component will fail to be stationary and will inherit the stochastic trend of the original series. See the work of Phillips and Jin (2021).

Hamilton (2018) proposed an alternative method, which suffers from its own drawbacks. The main idea behind the method comes from asking the following question: "How different is the value at date $t + h$ from the value that we would have expected to see based on its behavior through date t?" (p. 836). This difference comes from the cyclical component. Hence, it is based on a forecasting principle.

The main justification is first that forecast errors from even nonstationary models are stationary, as we expect the cyclical component to be. Second, and more importantly, Hamilton (2018) argues that the primary reason we would make forecast errors, say 2 years ahead, is cyclical factors, e.g., whether a recession will occur. This last point is debatable. This argument is fine if the trend is stable, meaning a polynomial in time with invariant coefficients (i.e., no breaks) or some unit root type process, but not otherwise. Given this approach, the proposed method is akin to a filtered estimate as opposed to a smoothed one. To obtain the cyclical component at some date $t+h$, say, the information in the data beyond date $t+h$ is not used. Hence, the method is not suited to obtain a coherent picture of the trend *a posteriori* using the full sample.

The method entails choosing a forecast horizon h and a number of lags p to construct the following forecasting equation:

$$y_{t+h} = \beta_0 + \sum_{j=1}^{p} \beta_j y_{t-(j-1)} + v_{th}. \tag{39.24}$$

This regression is estimated by OLS and the estimate of the residuals, say $\hat{v}_{th}$, is the estimated cyclical component. The recommendation is to set h to 2 years, i.e., 8 for quarterly data. The suggested value for p is 4. The idea behind choosing $p = 4$ is that when estimating (39.24) by OLS, the residuals will, at least in large samples, be stationary provided the fourth difference of the series, $(1-L)^4 y_t$, is stationary. This should be enough for most series to account for up to 4 unit roots, or polynomial in time of order 4, and various forms of breaking trends. For instance, taking a second difference renders a linear trend with a change in slope stationary. The main ingredient making this suggestion feasible is that when estimating (39.24) by OLS, the parameter estimates will converge to values such that the fitted process is close to the required number of differences needed to render the series stationary. For instance, if $p = 1$, the regression is

$$y_{t+h} = \beta_0 + \beta_1 y_t + v_{th},$$

and the OLS estimate of β_1, say $\hat{\beta}_1$, will converge to one because y_t is either differenced-stationary (i.e., with a unit root) or trend-stationary with a non-zero trend. Then $\hat{v}_{th} \approx y_{t+h} - y_t$ (up to a constant) and, hence, stationary.

As mentioned above, the main drawback of the method suggested by Hamilton (2018) is that it is an online filtered procedure as opposed to being retrospective. Hence, it is not well suited to estimate trends that have discontinuities. Phillips and Shi (2021) tried to resurrect the HP filter so that it is better able to handle such features. The idea is very simple. Simply apply the HP filter in an iterative manner starting with the usual penalty $\lambda = 1{,}600$. That is, once the HP filter is applied, the cyclical component is again subject to a further application of the HP filter and so on subject to some stopping rule for the number of iterations. For the latter, they suggest using either a unit root test, i.e., stop if the unit root test rejects in favor of stationarity in which case the cyclical component is deemed stationary, or some information criterion of the BIC-type tailored to the specific problem being tackled.

The problem with the suggestion of Phillips and Shi (2021) is that, while the theory is fine, what happens in practice is rather different. We have already discussed how the HP filter ascribes a lot of the movements in a series to the trend, leaving little to be classified as the cyclical component. With further iterations, things are even worse and the fitted trend gets even closer to the actual series. This is basically the trick to get the procedure to fit some structural changes (e.g., a level shift) and make the fitted trend follow the series more closely. While they argue that their procedure is very robust to the initial penalty $\lambda = 1{,}600$, the end product is essentially an HP filter with a much lower penalty value.

39.5.2 The Gaussian state-space model

The following material is based mostly on the work of Perron and Wada (2009), which provides a framework useful to illustrate various issues and extensions. The dataset used is (log) quarterly US real GDP seasonally adjusted for the period 1947:1–1998:2. Consider the state-space or unobserved components model given by

$$y_t = \mu_t + c_t,$$

where

$$\begin{aligned}\mu_t &= \mu_{t-1} + \beta + \tau_t,\\ c_t &= \phi_1 c_{t-1} + \phi_2 c_{t-2} + \omega_t,\end{aligned}$$

and $\tau_t \sim i.i.d.\ N\left(0, \sigma_\tau^2\right)$, $\omega_t \sim i.i.d.\ N\left(0, \sigma_\omega^2\right)$, which can be correlated with $E(\tau_t \omega_t) = \sigma_{\tau\omega}$. This is the original model in Example 39.3

with $\sigma_v^2 = 0$ so that no change in slope is permitted. This is done with little or no loss of generality since with the real GDP series, the estimate of σ_v^2 is very small and this generalization leaves the trend–cycle decompositions virtually unchanged (see, e.g., Oh and Zivot, 2006).

A sufficient condition for identification is to specify a value for the covariance $\sigma_{T\omega}$. A popular choice is to set $\sigma_{T\omega} = 0$, that is, to specify that the shocks to the trend function are uncorrelated with the shocks to the cyclical component. This implies that the reduced form of the system is a constrained $ARMA(p, q^*)$ with $q^* = \max(p, q + 1)$. This specification will be denoted $UC0$. An alternative is to use an unconstrained $ARMA(p, q^*)$ process of the form

$$A(L)\Delta y_t = \mu_1 + B^*(L)u_t,$$

where $u_t \sim i.i.d.\ N(0, \sigma_u^2)$ with the value σ_u^2 depending on the parameters of the model. The trend function can then be obtained via the Beveridge and Nelson (1981) decomposition

$$BN_t = \mu_2 + BN_{t-1} + \varphi(1)u_t,$$

with $\varphi(1) = B^*(1)/A(1)$; see Chapter 21. An $AR(2)$ specification for the cyclical component was found to be adequate, and accordingly an $ARIMA(2, 1, 2)$ for the BN decomposition applies. Figure 39.2 presents the estimated trend and cycle for each method. As can be seen, the decompositions are very different. The BN decomposition ascribes most movements in the real GDP series to the trend function leaving a cyclical component that is very small and noisy and bears no resemblance to the NBER chronology, whose periods of recessions are indicated with a shaded area. On the other hand, the $UC0$ decomposition leaves more importance to the cyclical component whose peaks and troughs correspond somewhat more closely to the NBER chronology.

The great differences in the implied trend and cycle suggest that either or both of the crucial identifying assumptions are at odds with the data, i.e., the correlation between the shocks to the trend and the cycle may not be 0 or 1. Morley *et al.* (2003) recognized that it is possible to identify model (39.6) with $\sigma_{T\omega}$ unconstrained when an $AR(2)$ specification for the cycle is used. This decomposition is

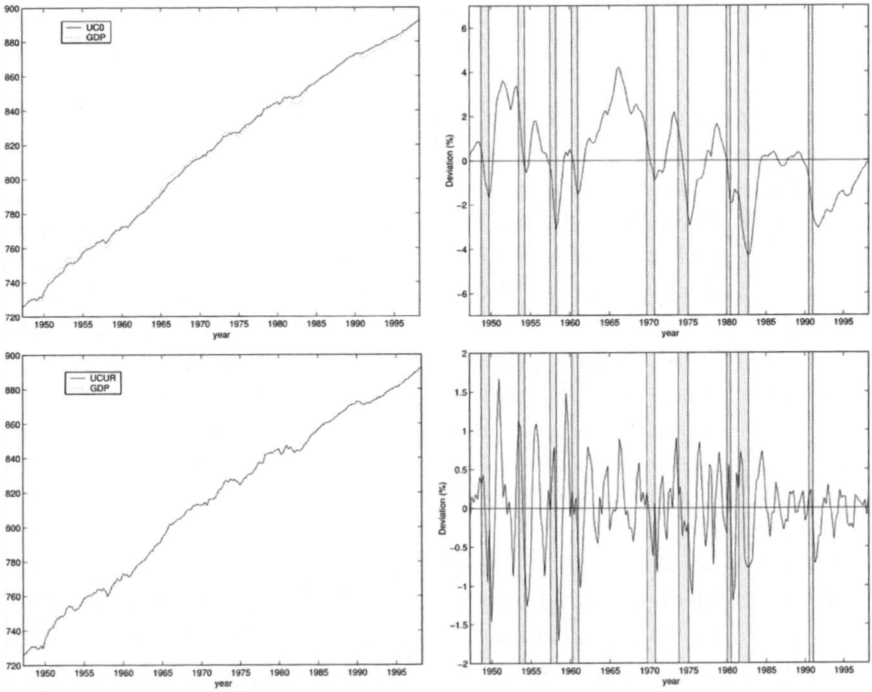

Figure 39.2. Trend and cycle decompositions of US log real GDP, 1947:1–1998:2. Top-left: Data and UC0 trend; top-right: UC0 cycle, i.e., unobserved component model assuming no correlation between the errors in the trend and the cycle; bottom-left: data and Beveridge–Nelson trend; bottom-right: BN cycle, equivalent to UCUR cycle, the unobserved component model allowing for correlation between the errors in the trend and the cycle; the shaded areas are the periods of recessions as defined by the NBER.

Source: Perron and Wada (2009), reproduced with permission from Elsevier.

labeled $UCUR$. The resulting trend–cycle decomposition is found to be indistinguishable from the BN decomposition in accordance with the results of the work of Morley *et al.* (2003). This suggests the following conclusions: (1) The data do not support the hypothesis that the correlation between the shocks to the trend and the cycle is 0 and (2) the results from the $UCUR$ model are compatible with the estimated unconstrained $ARIMA(2, 1, 2)$ model.

This analysis implies the following: (1) The trend dominates the series leaving only a small role to the cycle, (2) shocks to the trend are very negatively correlated with shocks to the cycle, and (3) the cycle bears no resemblance to the NBER chronology.

Various explanations have been advanced to explain these results. The argument put forward by Perron and Wada (2009) is that the basic models suffer from an important misspecification, which completely biases the results and their implications. A glimpse of the explanation can be gleaned from Figure 39.2, where it is seen that the cyclical component of the UC0 decomposition shows a marked decrease in mean from the pre to the post-1973 periods. The decrease in mean is such that the cyclical component completely misses the boom period of the late 1990s and classifies it as one of the following trend activities. A look at the numbers for the pre- and post-1973 period confirms this feature. Hence, if we take the results suggested by the UCUR or BN decompositions at face value, we are led to conclude that, on average, the post-1973 period has been subject to a sequence of negative shocks and the pre-1973 period enjoyed a sequence of positive shocks, a feature which is difficult to rationalize.

Perron and Wada (2009) showed that all these features are artifacts of a neglected change in the slope of the trend function in 1973 and that once this is accounted for, all methods agree on a single decomposition, which is albeit very different. Their initial approach is to allow for the possibility of a permanent change in the trend function of real GDP occurring in 1973:1, i.e., to specify

$$\mu_t = c + d1(t > T_b) + \mu_{t-1} + \eta_t, \tag{39.25}$$

where $1(A)$ is the indicator function for the event A and T_b is the observation corresponding to the time of break, 1973:1. The rest of the model stays the same. Note that this specification nests the previous ones. A change in the average rate of growth in 1973 is not imposed, simply allowed to happen.

As a matter of notation, the corresponding models are UC073, UCUR73, and BN73. The latter is estimated by an $ARIMA(2,1,2)$ model allowing for a change in the slope of the trend in 1973, which is referred to as $ARIMA73(2,1,2)$. The trend–cycle decompositions are presented in Figure 39.3. Despite the numerical differences in the point estimates, the trend–cycle decompositions for the three specifications, reported in Figure 39.3, are virtually identical. Hence, only one graph is reported. The results are now strikingly different. First, all three models agree on the point estimates of the rates of growth. It is 3.8% on an annual basis for the pre-1973 period and

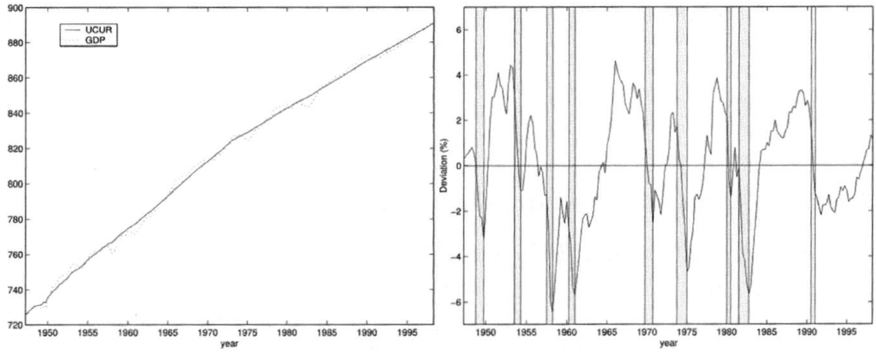

Figure 39.3. Trend and cycle decompositions allowing for a change in slope in 1973:1. Left panel: Data and trend; right panel: cycle with the shaded areas as the periods of recessions defined by the NBER.

Source: Perron and Wada (2009), reproduced with permission from Elsevier.

2.64% for the post-1973 period, thereby indicating a 31% decrease. The UC073 specification, which constrains the shocks to the trend and cycle to be uncorrelated, shows a point estimate of $\sigma_\tau = 0$, implying a deterministic trend function, i.e., all random variations are captured by the cyclical component. Basically the same results hold for the UCUR73 specification. The correlation of the shocks to the trend and the cycle is 1.0, perfectly positively correlated. This is expected if the true value of the variance of the noise to the trend function is zero since the covariance between the shocks to the trend and the shocks to the cycle is not identified. As discussed by Watson (1986), in such cases, the trend–cycle decomposition is well identified but the fact that the Kalman filter minimizes the mean-squared error of the estimates of the state vector implies that a perfect correlation will result since it allows a perfect fit to the state vector.

The implied cycle is very different from those without the change in trend. To summarize, the main qualitative features of the trend–cycle decompositions allowing for a change in the rate of growth in 1973:1 are as follows:

1. All three specifications lead to the same conclusions, and there are no conflicts anymore.
2. The average rate of growth has decreased 31% after 1973.
3. The trend function is piece-wise linear so that random variations are ascribed solely to the cyclical component.

4. The correlation of the shocks to the trend and cycle is trivially zero since the former is non-stochastic.
5. The cycle shows movements that follow closely the NBER chronology.

39.5.3 A non-Gaussian state-space model

In practice, one would like a method that does not pre-suppose a choice for such a break date but delivers it as an outcome of the trend–cycle decomposition procedure. To address this issue, Perron and Wada (2009) considered a generalized state-space model where some of the errors are non-normal. To understand the key ingredient, go back to the original model with

$$\begin{aligned} \mu_t &= \beta_t + \mu_{t-1} + \tau_t, \\ \beta_t &= \beta_{t-1} + v_t. \end{aligned} \tag{39.26}$$

The main difference is the use of a non-normal distribution for the errors v_t. The natural one to adopt in this context is a mixture of normal distributions where a realization of v_t is a draw from one of two normal distributions: one with high and the other with small or zero variance. More specifically,

$$v_t = \lambda_t \gamma_{1t} + (1 - \lambda_t)\, \gamma_{2t}, \tag{39.27}$$

where $\gamma_{it} \sim i.i.d.\ N(0, \sigma^2_{\gamma i})$ and λ_t is a Bernoulli random variable that takes value one with probability α_1 and value 0 with probability $1 - \alpha_1$. Here, we would expect α_1 to be close to one and $\sigma^2_{\gamma 1}$ to be zero so that most of the time, there is no change in the slope of the trend function. Furthermore, if $\sigma^2_{\gamma 2} > 0$, there will be occasional changes to the value of the slope. This implies a state-space model but with non-Gaussian errors.

The results are basically the same as with the exogenous-break specification. The estimate of the variance of the errors of the trend function σ^2_τ is nearly 0. Hence, except for changes in the slope β_t, the trend is deterministic. The innovations to the trend function are governed by a process that has standard deviation 0.0001 with probability 0.9 and one that has standard deviation 0.0633 with probability 0.10; i.e., most of the time, the slope does not vary. The changes occur smoothly around 1973:1.

The first panel in Figure 39.4 presents the cycle obtained from the HP filter with the usual value of the smoothing parameter $\lambda = 1{,}600$. The second panel presents the cycle obtained using the two-sided band-pass filter suggested by Baxter and King (1999) with 12 terms on each side. The cycles obtained are somewhat "in between" the Perron and Wada (2009) decomposition and the BN cycle. Both show much less variation than the Perron and Wada (2009) decomposition and slightly more than the BN cycle. Overall, they capture rather well the timing of the recessions but the depth of the recessions and the heights of the expansions are very different. For example, both the HP and BP cycles show the sixties as a period of average activities or very mild expansion following a mild recession in 1961, while the Perron and Wada (2009) method characterizes the sixties as a period of important and sustained expansion following a deep recession in 1961. The most striking feature is the magnitude of the cycle. The HP trend being stochastic, a lot of the movements in real GDP are due to movements in the trend and little is left for the cycle. While the BP filter does not estimate a trend directly, the overall picture is much the same.

Finally, the last panel in Figure 39.4 presents an interesting result about the HP filter. It gives the trend–cycle decomposition when the smoothing parameter is set to the very large number $\lambda = 800{,}000$. The results are then basically equivalent to those obtained with a trend that has a single shift in slope in 1973. So, we can, in a sense, reconcile the results. The HP filter depends crucially on the choice of the smoothing parameter λ and, as is well known, the best value depends on the underlying true structure of the process. The usual rule of thumb of setting $\lambda = 1{,}600$ is unlikely to be appropriate in most cases. Here, it seems that for the GDP series analyzed, $\lambda = 1{,}600$ is too small a value that has an effect of ascribing too much variation to the trend and too little to the cycle.

39.5.4 Summary and discussion

If one absolutely insists on labeling a cyclical component as pertaining to movements between a pre-determined set of frequencies, then a band-pass filter-type approach is dictated. But, as discussed, the HP filter or the Beveridge–Nelson decomposition, which does not aim in that direction, is essentially equivalent. In all cases, a lot of

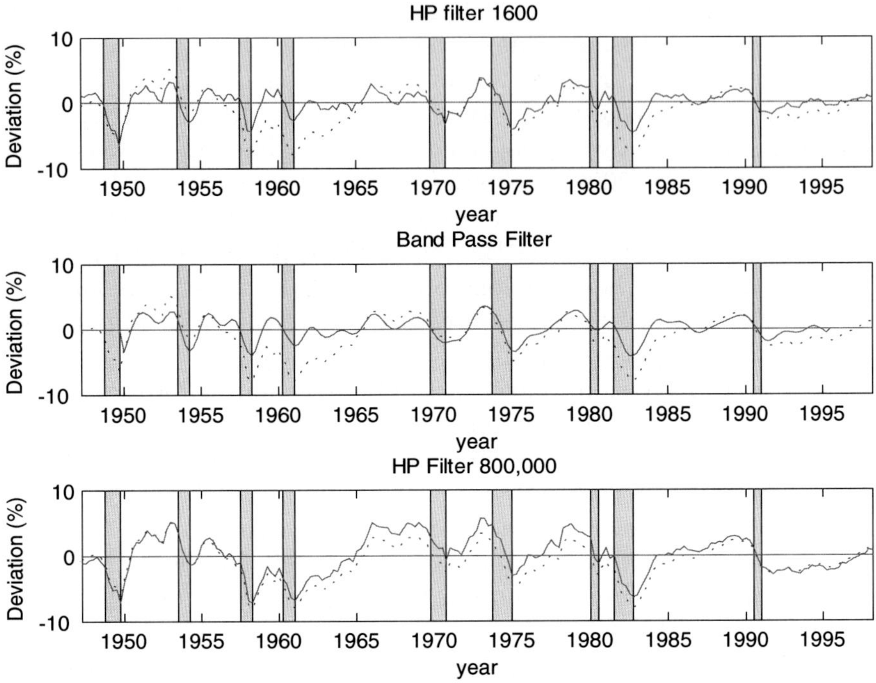

Figure 39.4. Comparisons of various cycles (solid lines) in relation to that obtained with the Gaussian mixture model (dashed lines). HP filter 1600 and HP filter 800,000 are the cycles obtained from the Hodrick–Prescott (1997) filter using $\lambda = 1{,}600$ (the usual default value) and $\lambda = 800{,}000$, respectively; band-pass filter is the filter proposed by Baxter and King (1999) which keeps movements having periods between 6 and 32 quarters; the shaded areas are the periods of recessions as defined by the NBER.

Source: Perron and Wada (2009), reproduced with permission from Elsevier.

the low-frequency movements that we would naturally ascribe to the cyclical component are erased. Think about a linear trend with an $AR(1)$ noise, i.e.,

$$y_t = c + \beta t + u_t,$$

$$u_t = \alpha u_{t-1} + e_t,$$

where $e_t \sim i.i.d.\ (0, 1)$. Then, we have a clear representation of what the trend is, i.e., $c + \beta t$, and the cyclical component is what remains, namely u_t. Band-pass and HP filters eliminate most of the movements induced by the cyclical $AR(1)$ component. This is illustrated in Figure 39.5, which plots on the left panel the spectral density

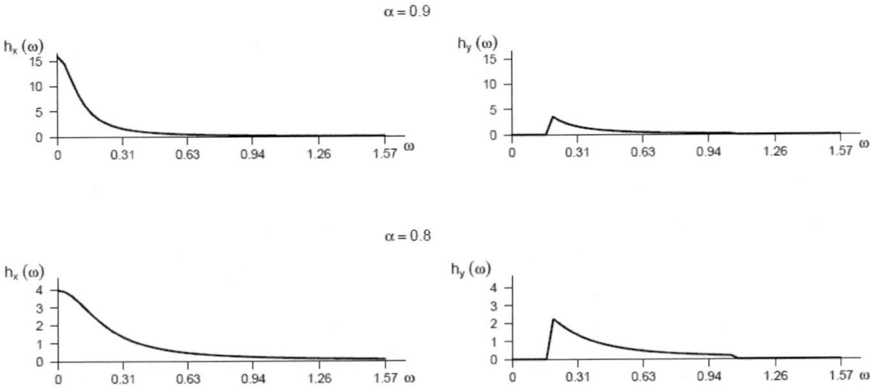

Figure 39.5. Left panel: Spectral density function of an $AR(1)$ process with parameter α; right panel: spectral density function of the same $AR(1)$ process after applying a band-pass filter. Top panels: $\alpha = 0.9$, bottom panels: $\alpha = 0.8$.

function of an $AR(1)$ process with autoregressive parameter 0.9 (top panels) or 0.8 (bottom panels), common values in applications. The noise is *i.i.d.* $(0, 1)$ so that the variance of the non-trending component is (approximately) $5.26 = 1/(1 - 0.9^2)$ when $\alpha = 0.9$ and $2.78 = 1/(1-0.8^2)$ when $\alpha = 0.8$. Then, we apply the ideal band-pass filter and eliminate all contributions outside the range $w^a = 2\pi/32$ to $w^b = 2\pi/6$. The variance of the resulting process is then 1.34 when $\alpha = 0.9$ and 1.16 when $\alpha = 0.8$ (see Exercise 39.2). These are major reductions: a 75% reduction in variance when $\alpha = 0.9$ and a 58% reduction when $\alpha = 0.8$.

This is the main reason why most methods end up with such a small cyclical component and the trend follows the series so closely. The need to estimate the trend in a non-parametric fashion, as done by all methods except those based on state-space models, forces eliminating all movements at the zero frequency and, most often, in a non-negligible neighborhood around zero. Short-run or cyclical components have important effects at low frequencies, even the zero frequency.

Of course, the same qualitative results hold for more general processes for the cyclical component than the simple one used for illustration. It is up to practitioners to decide whether eliminating the low-frequency component of a stationary process, which can be viewed as part of the cyclical component, is good or bad.

We discussed several methods for trend removal and the estimation of a cyclical component, here and in Section 37.5.4. Each method has its merits and drawbacks. In our opinion, the most reliable and flexible approach is the state-space modeling approach. It allows a clear separation between the trend and the cyclical component. It is very flexible and can account for various nonlinearities. It can deliver on-line (filtered) and off-line (smoothed) estimates. Of course, it is more difficult to implement as it requires substantial modeling expertise. It is not a black-box-type approach like all the others discussed. As always, there is no free lunch. No brain, no gain!

39.6 Markov-switching models

The regime-switching model introduced by Hamilton (1989) has found numerous applications in economics and finance. Surveys of this voluminous body of literature are available in the works of Hamilton (2010), Hamilton (2016), and Ang and Timmermann (2012).

In practice, the regime-switching model has mainly appeared in low-dimensional settings involving a single or a few time series as dependent variables. Hamilton (1989) examined the U.S. GNP series, Garcia and Perron (1996) used it to model the real U.S. interest rate, Masson (2000) considered exchange rates, Chauvet and Hamilton (2006) studied GDP growth, Hamilton (1988) and Hamilton (2005) examined interest rates, and Davig (2004) modeled the debt-output ratio. Diebold and Rudebusch (1996), Kim and Nelson (1998), Chauvet (1998), and Chauvet and Hamilton (2006) examined four time series (sales, income, employment, and industrial production) as a function of a latent factor exhibiting regime-switching.

To provide a concrete example, we consider the employment series (*Source*: Bureau of Labor Statistics; https://www.bls.gov/data/), whose growth rate is plotted in Figure 39.6. It is the quarterly growth rates of US total employees from 1972-II to 2019-IV. The shaded areas are the recession periods declared by the NBER. There are two interesting observations: (1) The growth rates during expansions are positive and much greater (in absolute value) than the declines during recessions and (2) the growth rates are more volatile during recessions. The motivation to use a Markov regime-switching model is to capture these nonlinear features. Consider an unobservable state

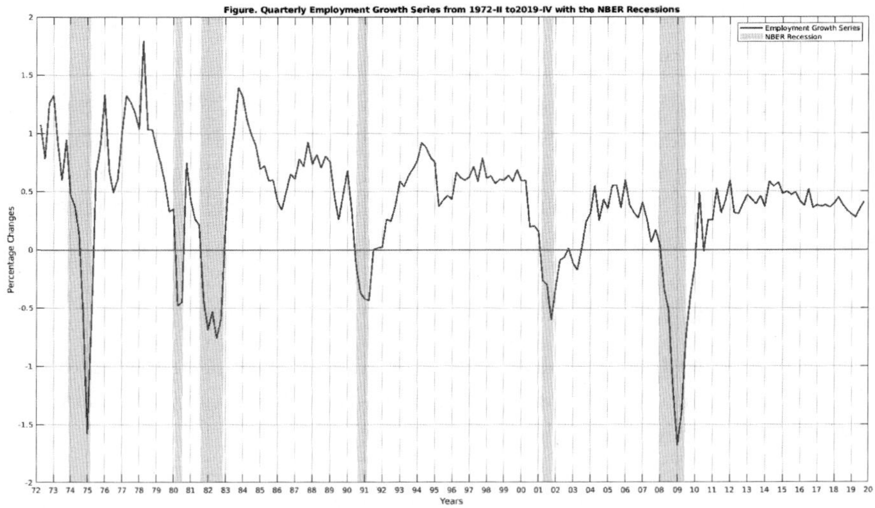

Figure 39.6. Quarterly employment growth rates from 1972-II to 2019-IV.

variable S_t following a two-state Markov chain with $S_t = 1$ denoting recessions and $S_t = 2$ expansions. The transition probabilities between states are given by the following matrix:

$$\begin{bmatrix} p_{11} & 1 - p_{22} \\ 1 - p_{11} & p_{22} \end{bmatrix},$$

where

$$\begin{aligned} &\text{prob}(S_t = 1|S_{t-1} = 1, S_{t-2} = i, \ldots, S_1 = j) \\ &\quad = \text{prob}(S_t = 1|S_{t-1} = 1) = p_{11}, \\ &\text{prob}(S_t = 2|S_{t-1} = 2, S_{t-2} = i', \ldots, S_1 = j') \\ &\quad = \text{prob}(S_t = 2|S_{t-1} = 2) = p_{22}, \end{aligned}$$

and $i, j, i', j' \in \{1, 2\}$. In the following subsection, we discuss two alternative specifications to model the growth rate of the employment series denoted by y_t $(t = 1, \ldots, T)$. There are two objectives: (1) forecast future observable variables y_{T+l} $(l = 1, \ldots, L)$ and (2) draw inference on the unobservable state variable S_t $(t = 1, \ldots, T + L)$, in particular about the probabilities of being in either a recession or expansionary period.

39.6.1 Two-state autoregressive Markov-switching models

The growth rate of the employment series y_t is modeled using a two-state autoregressive Markov-switching model. For simplicity, we assume the autoregressive order is $p = 1$. Based on the above two observations for the employment growth series, both the means and variances are state-dependent.

Specification I

The first specification assumes that the current observation y_t depends on the current and lagged states (S_t, S_{t-1}), with the following observation equation:

$$y_t = \mu_{S_t} + \phi_1 \left(y_{t-1} - \mu_{S_{t-1}}\right) + \epsilon_t, \tag{39.28}$$

where $\epsilon_t \sim N\left(0, \sigma^2_{S_t}\right)$ and

$$\begin{aligned} \mu_{S_t} &= \mu_1 \mathbf{1}_{\{S_t=1\}} + \mu_2 \mathbf{1}_{\{S_t=2\}}, \\ \sigma^2_{S_t} &= \sigma^2_1 \mathbf{1}_{\{S_t=1\}} + \sigma^2_2 \mathbf{1}_{\{S_t=2\}}, \end{aligned} \tag{39.29}$$

with $\mathbf{1}_{\{A\}}$ the indicator function for the event A.

Specification II

The second specification assumes that the current observation y_t depends only on the current state S_t, i.e.,

$$y_t = \mu_{S_t} + \phi_1 y_{t-1} + \epsilon_t, \tag{39.30}$$

and $\epsilon_t \sim N\left(0, \sigma^2_{S_t}\right)$. The two specifications are closely related. To see this, substitute the expression for μ_{S_t} in (39.29) into the measurement equation (39.28), we then have

$$\begin{aligned} y_t &= \mu_1 \mathbf{1}_{\{S_t=1\}} + \mu_2 \mathbf{1}_{\{S_t=2\}} - \phi_1 \mu_1 \mathbf{1}_{\{S_{t-1}=1\}} - \phi_1 \mu_2 \mathbf{1}_{\{S_{t-1}=2\}} \\ &\quad + \phi_1 y_{t-1} + \epsilon_t, \\ &\equiv \mu^*_1 \mathbf{1}_{\{S^*_t=1\}} + \mu^*_2 \mathbf{1}_{\{S^*_t=2\}} + \mu^*_3 \mathbf{1}_{\{S^*_t=3\}} + \mu^*_4 \mathbf{1}_{\{S^*_t=4\}} + \phi_1 y_{t-1} + \epsilon_t, \\ &\equiv \mu_{S^*_t} + \phi_1 y_{t-1} + \epsilon_t. \end{aligned} \tag{39.31}$$

Thus, specification I can be reformulated as specification II. Here, the new state variable S_t^* takes four discrete values defined as follows: $S_t^* = 1$ if $S_t = 1, S_{t-1} = 1$, $S_t^* = 2$ if $S_t = 1, S_{t-1} = 2$, $S_t^* = 3$ if $S_t = 2, S_{t-1} = 1$, and $S_t^* = 4$ if $S_t = 2, S_{t-1} = 2$. The switching means $\mu_i^*, i = 1, \ldots, 4$, are functions of the parameters μ_1, μ_2, and ϕ_1. From this, we can see that the second specification (39.30) is more general. However, as discussed in Section 39.6.3, the Hamilton filter for model specification (39.28) is more general. Since we focus on the Hamilton filter and related estimation and inference methods, we consider specification I throughout this section.

39.6.2 A state-space representation

Before deriving the Hamilton filter for model (39.28), we show how to reformulate it as a state-space model. Clearly, we already have a state variable S_t, then the measurement and transition equations are

$$y_t = \mu_{S_t} + \phi_1 \left(y_{t-1} - \mu_{S_{t-1}} \right) + \epsilon_t,$$

$$\text{prob}(S_t = 1 | S_{t-1} = 1) = p_{11},$$

$$\text{prob}(S_t = 2 | S_{t-1} = 2) = p_{22},$$

and $\epsilon_t \sim N\left(0, \sigma_{S_t}^2\right)$. The above state-space model is not standard. To derive the linear and non-Gaussian state-space model as in Example 39.6, we can define a new state variable ξ_t, where

$$\xi_t = \left(\mathbf{1}_{\{S_t^*=1\}}, \mathbf{1}_{\{S_t^*=2\}}, \mathbf{1}_{\{S_t^*=3\}}, \mathbf{1}_{\{S_t^*=4\}} \right)',$$

by using the specification in (39.31). Define

$$\mu^* = (\mu_1^*, \mu_2^*, \mu_3^*, \mu_4^*)',$$

$$V = (\sigma_1^2, \sigma_1^2, \sigma_2^2, \sigma_2^2)',$$

then the observation equation becomes

$$y_t = \mu^{*\prime} \xi_t + \phi_1 y_{t-1} + \epsilon_t, \tag{39.32}$$

with $\epsilon_t \sim N(0, V'\xi_t)$. The transition matrix for S_t^* is given by

$$\Pi = \begin{pmatrix} p_{11} & 0 & p_{12} & 0 \\ p_{11} & 0 & p_{12} & 0 \\ 0 & p_{21} & 0 & p_{22} \\ 0 & p_{21} & 0 & p_{22} \end{pmatrix}.$$

Then, it is trivial to show that $E(\xi_{t+1}|\xi_t, \ldots, \xi_1) = E(\xi_{t+1}|\xi_t) = \Pi\xi_t$, which implies that

$$\xi_{t+1} = \Pi\xi_t + \eta_{t+1}. \tag{39.33}$$

The measurement equation (39.32) and transition equation (39.33) form a linear and non-Gaussian state-space model for the autoregressive Markov regime-switching model (39.28). Note that the error term η_{t+1} takes a finite set of values, thus it is not suitable to approximate the distribution by Gaussian mixtures. Next, we discuss the widely used Hamilton filter to analyze regime-switching models, which take a different approach.

39.6.3 The Hamilton filter and estimation methods

Similar to the Kalman filter, when the model parameters are known, the Hamilton filter can be used to draw inference on the state variable S_t. When the model parameters are unknown, it is used to estimate the parameters and then draw inference about S_t using these parameter estimates. Assume that all the parameters in model (39.28) are known, we are interested in drawing inference about $S_t, t = 1, \ldots, T$ based on the observations $y_t, t = 1, \ldots, T$. Denote $\tilde{y}_t = \{y_t, \ldots, y_1\}$, $s_t \in \{1, 2\}$, and $S_{t|s} = E(\mathbf{1}_{\{S_t = s_t\}}|\tilde{y}_s)$, where $S_{t|s}$ is the estimate of S_t or the estimated probability of being in state s_t based on the information set $\tilde{y}_s$. Researchers are often interested in the three quantities: $S_{t|t-1}$, $S_{t|t}$, and $S_{t|T}$ which are called predicted, filtered, and smoothed estimates of S_t, respectively.

Using conditional probability, the Hamilton filter includes the following two steps:

(1) Predicting Step

$$f\left(y_t, S_t = s_t, S_{t-1} = s_{t-1}|\tilde{y}_{t-1}\right) \\ = f\left(y_t|S_t = s_t, S_{t-1} = s_{t-1}, \tilde{y}_{t-1}\right) \text{prob}\left(S_t = s_t, S_{t-1} = s_{t-1}|\tilde{y}_{t-1}\right), \tag{39.34}$$

where

$$f\left(y_t|S_t = s_t, S_{t-1} = s_{t-1}, \tilde{y}_{t-1}\right) \\ = \frac{1}{\sqrt{2\pi\sigma_{s_t}^2}} \exp\left(-\frac{\left(y_t - \mu_{s_t} - \phi_1\left(y_{t-1} - \mu_{s_{t-1}}\right)\right)^2}{2\sigma_{s_t}^2}\right)$$

and

$$\text{prob}\left(S_t = s_t, S_{t-1} = s_{t-1}|\tilde{y}_{t-1}\right) \\ = \text{prob}\left(S_t = s_t|S_{t-1} = s_{t-1}\right) \text{prob}\left(S_{t-1} = s_{t-1}|\tilde{y}_{t-1}\right). \tag{39.35}$$

Then, the predicted estimate of S_t is

$$S_{t|t-1} = \text{prob}\left(S_t = s_t|\tilde{y}_{t-1}\right) = \sum_{s_{t-1}=1}^{2} \text{prob}\left(S_t = s_t, S_{t-1} = s_{t-1}|\tilde{y}_{t-1}\right).$$

(2) Filtering Step. We start with the following result:

$$\text{prob}\left(S_t = s_t, S_{t-1} = s_{t-1}|\tilde{y}_t\right) \\ = \frac{f\left(y_t, S_t = s_t, S_{t-1} = s_{t-1}|\tilde{y}_{t-1}\right)}{\sum_{s_t=1}^{2}\sum_{s_{t-1}=1}^{2} f\left(y_t, S_t = s_t, S_{t-1} = s_{t-1}|\tilde{y}_{t-1}\right)}. \tag{39.36}$$

Then, the filtered estimate of S_t is

$$S_{t|t} = \text{prob}\left(S_t = s_t|\tilde{y}_t\right) = \sum_{s_{t-1}=1}^{2} \text{prob}\left(S_t = s_t, S_{t-1} = s_{t-1}|\tilde{y}_t\right).$$

Given the initial condition $\text{prob}\left(S_1 = s_1|y_1\right)$, we can iterate the two steps for $t = 2, \ldots, T$.

(3) The Likelihood Function. From (39.34), the sample likelihood function of y_t conditioning on $\tilde{y}_{t-1}$ is

$$f\left(y_t|\tilde{y}_{t-1}\right)=\sum_{s_t=1}^{2}\sum_{s_{t-1}=1}^{2} f\left(y_t, S_t=s_t, S_{t-1}=s_{t-1}|\tilde{y}_{t-1}\right). \quad (39.37)$$

(4) Smoothing Step. The smoothed estimate of S_t can be derived using the results in the predicting and filtering steps, see the work of Kim and Nelson (1999) for more details. For T, the smoothed estimate is the same as the filtered estimate. For $t=T-1,\ldots,1$, we have

$$S_{t|T}=\text{prob}(S_t=s_t|\tilde{y}_T)=\sum_{s_{t+1}=1}^{2}\text{prob}(S_t=s_t, S_{t+1}=s_{t+1}|\tilde{y}_T),$$

where

$$\begin{aligned}
&\text{prob}(S_t=s_t, S_{t+1}=s_{t+1}|\tilde{y}_T)\\
&\quad=\text{prob}(S_{t+1}=s_{t+1}|\tilde{y}_T)\text{prob}(S_t=s_t|S_{t+1}=s_{t+1},\tilde{y}_T)\\
&\quad=\text{prob}(S_{t+1}=s_{t+1}|\tilde{y}_T)\text{prob}(S_t=s_t|S_{t+1}=s_{t+1},\tilde{y}_t)\\
&\quad=\frac{\text{prob}(S_{t+1}=s_{t+1}|\tilde{y}_T)\text{prob}(S_t=s_t, S_{t+1}=s_{t+1}|\tilde{y}_t)}{\text{prob}(S_{t+1}=s_{t+1}|\tilde{y}_t)}\\
&\quad=\frac{\text{prob}(S_{t+1}=s_{t+1}|\tilde{y}_T)\text{prob}(S_t=s_t|\tilde{y}_t)\text{prob}(S_{t+1}=s_{t+1}|S_t=s_t)}{\text{prob}(S_{t+1}=s_{t+1}|\tilde{y}_t)}.
\end{aligned}$$

Thus, $S_{t|T}$ can be computed recursively.

When the model parameters are unknown, they can be estimated either via a maximum likelihood method or using a Gibbs sampling algorithm.

Maximum Likelihood Method

The maximum likelihood estimator for model (39.28) can be obtained numerically. Recall that the joint sample likelihood function is

$$f(y_1,\ldots,y_T)=f(y_T|\tilde{y}_{T-1})\cdots f(y_2|\tilde{y}_1)f(y_1)=f(y_1)\prod_{t=2}^{T}f(y_t|\tilde{y}_{t-1}).$$

Note that $f(y_t|\tilde{y}_{t-1})$ is a by-product of the Hamilton filter given in equation (39.37). Let the vector of the model parameters be $\theta = (\mu_1, \mu_2, \phi_1, \sigma_1^2, \sigma_2^2, p_{11}, p_{22})'$, then

$$\hat{\theta}_{MLE} = \arg_\theta \max\{\log(f(y_1, \ldots, y_T))\}.$$

Note that the regime-switching model has a "label-switching" problem; that is, without imposing ordering restrictions, the regimes are unidentified. One can use the restriction $\mu_1 < \mu_2$ for the maximization. Once the estimate $\hat{\theta}_{MLE}$ is obtained, inference about S_t can be obtained by the plug-in method via the Hamilton filter described above.

Gibbs Sampling Method

Unlike the maximum likelihood estimation, the Gibbs sampling method can tackle estimation, inference, and forecasting simultaneously. The quantities of interest are $\{\theta, \tilde{S}_T, S_{T+1}, y_{T+1}\}$, i.e., given the data $\tilde{y}_T$, we want to estimate θ, draw inference on $\tilde{S}_T$, as well as forecast S_{T+1} and y_{T+1}. Of course, one could forecast L steps ahead with minor modifications. All quantities are treated as random variables and can be drawn from some posterior distributions. We factor out the joint distribution given the data as follows:

$$\begin{aligned} &f\left(\tilde{S}_T; \mu_1, \mu_2, \sigma_1^2, \sigma_2^2, \phi_1; p_{11}, p_{22}; S_{T+1}; y_{T+1}|y_T\right) \\ &\quad = p(\tilde{S}_T|\tilde{y}_T, \theta) \times f(p_{11}, p_{22}|\tilde{S}_T) \times f(\mu_1, \mu_2, \sigma_1^2, \sigma_2^2, \phi_1|\tilde{S}_T, \tilde{y}_T) \\ &\qquad \times f(S_{T+1}|\tilde{S}_T; p_{11}, p_{22}) \times f(y_{T+1}|\tilde{y}_T, \tilde{S}_{T+1}, \theta). \end{aligned}$$

Consequently, the algorithm for model (39.28) includes the following five steps:

1. Given the parameters θ and the data $\tilde{y}_T$, generate $\tilde{S}_T$ from the conditional distribution $p(\tilde{S}_T|\theta, \tilde{y}_T)$.
2. Given $\tilde{S}_T$, generate (p_{11}, p_{22}) from the conditional distribution $f(p_{11}, p_{22}|\tilde{S}_T)$.
3. Given $\tilde{S}_T$ and the data $\tilde{y}_T$, generate $(\mu_1, \mu_2, \sigma_1^2, \sigma_2^2, \phi_1)$ from the conditional distribution $f(\mu_1, \mu_2, \sigma_1^2, \sigma_2^2, \phi_1|\tilde{S}_T, \tilde{y}_T)$.
4. Given $\tilde{S}_T$ and the parameters θ, generate S_{T+1} from the conditional distribution $f(S_{T+1}|\tilde{S}_T, p_{11}, p_{22})$.

5. Given $\tilde{S}_{T+1}$, the parameters θ, and the data $\tilde{y}_T$, generate y_{T+1} from the conditional distribution $f(y_{T+1}|\tilde{y}_T, \tilde{S}_{T+1}, \theta)$.

The first three steps are used to generate the parameters and state variables as discussed next in details. The last two steps trivially provide forecasts of future values.

Step 1. Generate the state variables $\tilde{S}_T = (S_1, \ldots, S_T)'$. Using the Markov property of S_t, the conditional distribution is

$$p(\tilde{S}_T|\theta, \tilde{y}_T) = p(S_T|\tilde{y}_T, \theta) \prod_{t=1}^{T-1} p(S_t|S_{t+1}, \tilde{y}_t, \theta),$$

where

$$p(S_t|S_{t+1}, \tilde{y}_t, \theta) = \frac{p(S_{t+1}|S_t)p(S_t|\tilde{y}_t, \theta)}{p(S_{t+1}|\tilde{y}_t, \theta)} \propto p(S_{t+1}|S_t)p(S_t|\tilde{y}_t, \theta).$$

Using the results from the Hamilton filter, draw S_T from $p(S_T|\tilde{y}_T; \theta)$ and S_t from $p(S_t|S_{t+1}, \tilde{y}_t; \theta)$ for $t = T-1, \ldots, 1$. Since $S_t \in \{1, 2\}$, draw S_t from a Bernoulli distribution. To draw S_T, first calculate the ratio

$$\frac{p(S_T = 1|\tilde{y}_T, \theta)}{p(S_T = 1|\tilde{y}_T, \theta) + p(S_T = 2|\tilde{y}_T, \theta)} \equiv R_T.$$

Then, randomly draw a number U_T from the uniform distribution $U(0, 1)$. If $U_T < R_T$, set $S_T = 1$, otherwise set $S_T = 2$. For $t = T-1, \ldots, 1$, follow the same steps with

$$\frac{p(S_{t+1}|S_t = 1)p(S_t = 1|\tilde{y}_t, \theta)}{p(S_{t+1}|S_t = 1)p(S_t = 1|\tilde{y}_t, \theta) + p(S_{t+1}|S_t = 2)p(S_t = 2|\tilde{y}_t, \theta)} \equiv R_t.$$

Step 2. Generate the transition probabilities (p_{11}, p_{22}). To generate (p_{11}, p_{22}), assume that the two parameters are independent and follow Beta distributions. The prior distributions are given by

$$p_{11} \sim \text{Beta}(\alpha_1, \beta_1),$$
$$p_{22} \sim \text{Beta}(\alpha_2, \beta_2).$$

Given $\tilde{S}_T$, the posterior distributions are

$$p_{11}|\tilde{S}_T \sim \text{Beta}(\alpha_1 + n_{11}, \beta_1 + n_{12}),$$
$$p_{22}|\tilde{S}_T \sim \text{Beta}(\alpha_2 + n_{22}, \beta_2 + n_{21}),$$

where n_{ij} refers to the number of transitions from state i to state j based on $\tilde{S}_T$.

Step 3(a). Generate the parameters ($\boldsymbol{\mu_1, \mu_2}$). Let $\mu = (\mu_1, \mu_2)'$, and assume its prior distribution is

$$\mu \sim N(\mu^*, V^*).$$

Given $(\sigma_1^2, \sigma_2^2, \phi_1)$, $\tilde{S}_T$, and $\tilde{y}_T$, the posterior distribution is

$$\mu|\tilde{y}_T, \tilde{S}_T, \sigma_1^2, \sigma_2^2, \phi_1 \sim N(\mu_*, V_*),$$

where

$$V_* = [V^{*-1} + X^{*'}X^*]^{-1},$$
$$\mu_* = V_*[V^{*-1}\mu^* + X^{*'}Y^*].$$

The quantities X^* and Y^* are transformations of the observation equation (39.28). Let

$$Y = \begin{pmatrix} y_2 - \phi_1 y_1 \\ \vdots \\ y_T - \phi_1 y_{T-1} \end{pmatrix},$$

$$X = \begin{pmatrix} \mathbf{1}_{\{S_2=1\}} - \phi_1 \mathbf{1}_{\{S_1=1\}} & \mathbf{1}_{\{S_2=2\}} - \phi_1 \mathbf{1}_{\{S_1=2\}} \\ \vdots & \vdots \\ \mathbf{1}_{\{S_T=1\}} - \phi_1 \mathbf{1}_{\{S_{T-1}=1\}} & \mathbf{1}_{\{S_T=2\}} - \phi_1 \mathbf{1}_{\{S_{T-1}=2\}} \end{pmatrix},$$

and $e = (\epsilon_2, \ldots, \epsilon_T)'$. Then,

$$E(ee') = \text{diag}\{\sigma_1^2 \mathbf{1}_{\{S_2=1\}} + \sigma_2^2 \mathbf{1}_{\{S_2=2\}}, \ldots, \sigma_1^2 \mathbf{1}_{\{S_T=1\}} + \sigma_2^2 \mathbf{1}_{\{S_T=2\}}\}$$
$$\equiv V,$$

and thus,

$$Y^* = V^{-1/2}Y, \quad X^* = V^{-1/2}X.$$

To identify the regimes, draw μ from the normal distribution with the restriction $\mu_1 < \mu_2$.

Step 3(b). Generate the parameters (σ_1^2, σ_2^2). Rewrite the switching variance as

$$\sigma_{S_t}^2 = \sigma_2^2 \left[1 + \left(\frac{\sigma_1^2}{\sigma_2^2} - 1\right) \mathbf{1}_{\{S_t=1\}}\right] = \sigma_2^2 \left[1 + h_2 \mathbf{1}_{\{S_t=1\}}\right],$$

where $h_2 = \sigma_1^2/\sigma_2^2 - 1$. Consider generating σ_1^2 first. Dividing both sides of the observation equation by σ_2, we have

$$y_t/\sigma_2 = \mu_{S_t}/\sigma_2 + \phi_1 \left(y_{t-1} - \mu_{S_{t-1}}\right)/\sigma_2 + \epsilon_t/\sigma_2, \tag{39.38}$$

with $\epsilon_t/\sigma_2 \sim N(0, 1 + h_2 \mathbf{1}_{\{S_t=1\}})$. Let $\bar{h}_2 = 1 + h_2$, and assume the following prior distribution for $\bar{h}_2$:

$$\bar{h}_2 \sim \text{Inverse Gamma}\left(\frac{d_{11}}{2}, \frac{v_{11}}{2}\right).$$

Then, the posterior distribution is

$$\bar{h}_2 | \sigma_2^2, \mu, \phi_1, \tilde{S}_T, \tilde{y}_T \sim \text{Inverse Gamma}\left(\frac{d_{12}}{2}, \frac{v_{12}}{2}\right),$$

where

$$d_{12} = d_{11} + T_1,$$
$$v_{12} = v_{11} + SSE_{\{S_t=1\}},$$

where $T_1 = \sum_{t=2}^{T} \mathbf{1}_{\{S_t=1\}}$ and $SSE_{\{S_t=1\}}$ is the sum of squared residuals for equation (39.38) at time periods $S_t = 1$. Then, we have $\sigma_1^2 = \bar{h}_2 \sigma_2^2$. To generate σ_2^2, first transform the observation equation as follows:

$$\frac{y_t}{\sqrt{1+h_2\mathbf{1}_{\{S_t=1\}}}} = \frac{\mu_{S_t} + \phi_1\left(y_{t-1} - \mu_{S_{t-1}}\right)}{\sqrt{1+h_2\mathbf{1}_{\{S_t=1\}}}} + \frac{\epsilon_t}{\sqrt{1+h_2\mathbf{1}_{\{S_t=1\}}}}. \tag{39.39}$$

Assume the following prior distribution for σ_2^2:

$$\sigma_2^2 \sim \text{Inverse Gamma}\left(\frac{d_{21}}{2}, \frac{v_{21}}{2}\right).$$

The posterior distribution is

$$\sigma_2^2|\bar{h}_2, \mu, \phi_1, \tilde{S}_T, \tilde{y}_T \sim \text{Inverse Gamma}\left(\frac{d_{22}}{2}, \frac{v_{22}}{2}\right),$$

where

$$\begin{aligned} d_{22} &= d_{21} + (T-1), \\ v_{22} &= v_{21} + SSE, \end{aligned}$$

with $T-1$ the sample size and SSE the sum of squared residuals for equation (39.39) over the full sample.

Step 3(c). Generate the parameter ϕ_1. The coefficient ϕ_1 can be simulated as in step 3(a), thus we omit the details.

Given reasonable initial values, the three steps can be iterated $M = 10{,}000$ times, say, discarding the first $B = 2{,}000$ draws to ensure a stationary outcome. Then, the quantities of interest can be computed based on the remaining draws.

39.6.4 An empirical application

In this application, we use the employment series discussed at the beginning of this section. The goal is to use various regime-switching models to identify US business cycles. We consider the following four models:

1. AR0.SM: $y_t = \mu_{S_t} + \epsilon_t, \epsilon_t \sim N(0, \sigma^2)$;
2. AR0.SMSV: $y_t = \mu_{S_t} + \epsilon_t, \epsilon_t \sim N(0, \sigma_{S_t}^2)$;

3. AR1.SM: $y_t = \mu_{S_t} + \phi_1 \left(y_{t-1} - \mu_{S_{t-1}} \right) + \epsilon_t, \epsilon_t \sim N(0, \sigma^2)$;
4. AR1.SMSV: $y_t = \mu_{S_t} + \phi_1 \left(y_{t-1} - \mu_{S_{t-1}} \right) + \epsilon_t, \epsilon_t \sim N(0, \sigma_{S_t}^2)$,

where

$$\begin{aligned} \mu_{S_t} &= \mu_1 \mathbf{1}_{\{S_t=1\}} + \mu_2 \mathbf{1}_{\{S_t=2\}}, \\ \sigma_{S_t}^2 &= \sigma_1^2 \mathbf{1}_{\{S_t=1\}} + \sigma_2^2 \mathbf{1}_{\{S_t=2\}}. \end{aligned}$$

The models are estimated by maximum likelihood since there are only a few parameters to be estimated. For high-dimensional models, the Gibbs sampling method should be used. The estimated parameters are reported in Table 39.1 and the standard errors are in parentheses.

For AR0.SM and AR0.SMSV, the estimated transition probabilities and switching means have similar values. They are not affected much by including switching variances. However, with transitory dynamics as in AR1.SM and AR1.SMSV, the AR coefficients are relatively large and AR1.SMSV produces quite different estimates for p_{11} and μ_1. Figures 39.7–39.10 plot the smoothed probabilities of recessions based on those estimates. The solid lines are recession probabilities using the four models and the shaded areas are the recession periods identified by the NBER.

From Figures 39.7 and 39.8, we find that the smoothed recession probabilities are close to the NBER's classification. However, the probabilities in Figure 39.9 miss the recession periods in the 1990s and early 2000s. The probabilities in Figure 39.10 misidentify the periods in the 1970s.

Table 39.1. Maximum likelihood estimates for the four models.

	$\hat{p}_{11}$	$\hat{p}_{22}$	$\hat{\mu}_1$	$\hat{\mu}_2$	$\hat{\sigma}^2$	$\hat{\sigma}_1^2$	$\hat{\sigma}_2^2$	$\hat{\phi}_1$
AR0.SM	0.83	0.96	−0.44	0.58	0.11	—	—	—
	(0.08)	(0.02)	(0.05)	(0.03)	(0.01)	—	—	—
AR0.SMSV	0.86	0.96	−0.31	0.60	—	0.23	0.09	—
	(0.08)	(0.02)	(0.11)	(0.03)	—	(0.06)	(0.01)	—
AR1.SM	0.68	0.98	−0.46	0.42	0.05	—	—	0.83
	(0.18)	(0.01)	(0.13)	(0.10)	(0.004)	—	—	(0.03)
AR1.SMSV	0.93	0.96	0.30	0.47	—	0.20	0.01	0.79
	(0.04)	(0.02)	(0.15)	(0.05)	—	(0.04)	(0.001)	(0.04)

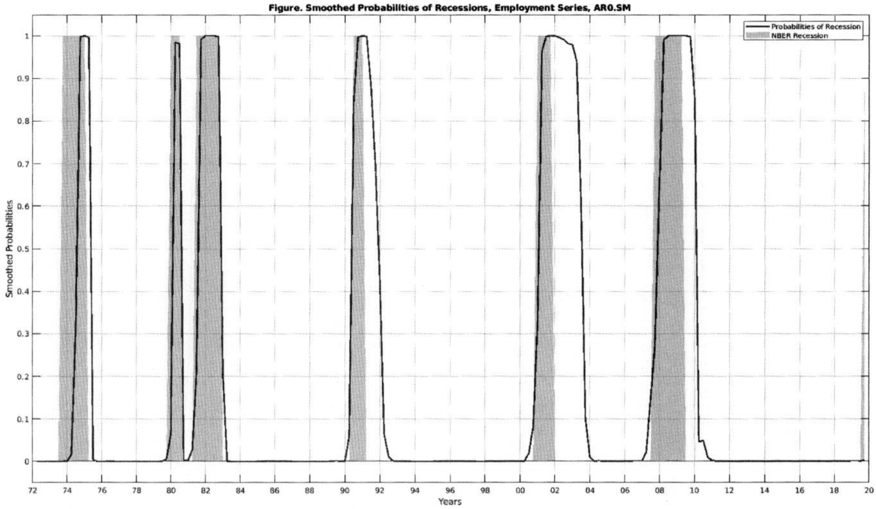

Figure 39.7. Smoothed probabilities of recessions: AR(0), switching in means.

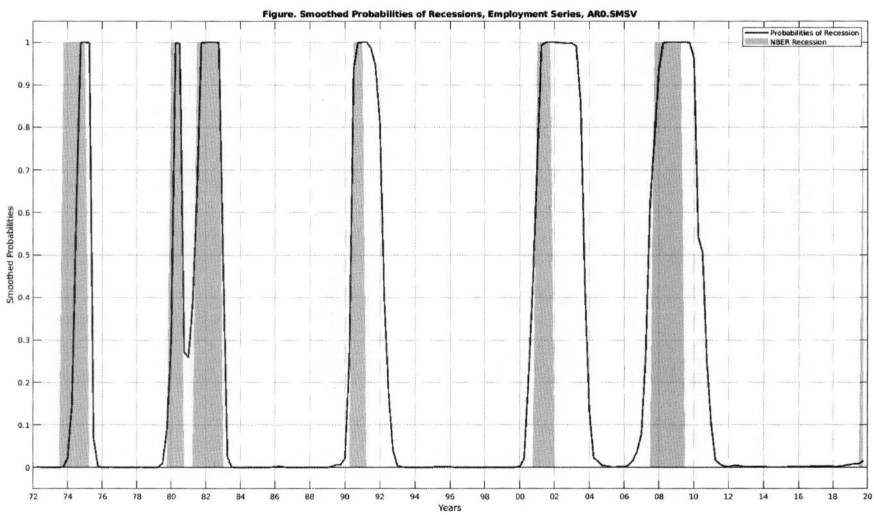

Figure 39.8. Smoothed probabilities of recessions: AR(0), switching in means and variances.

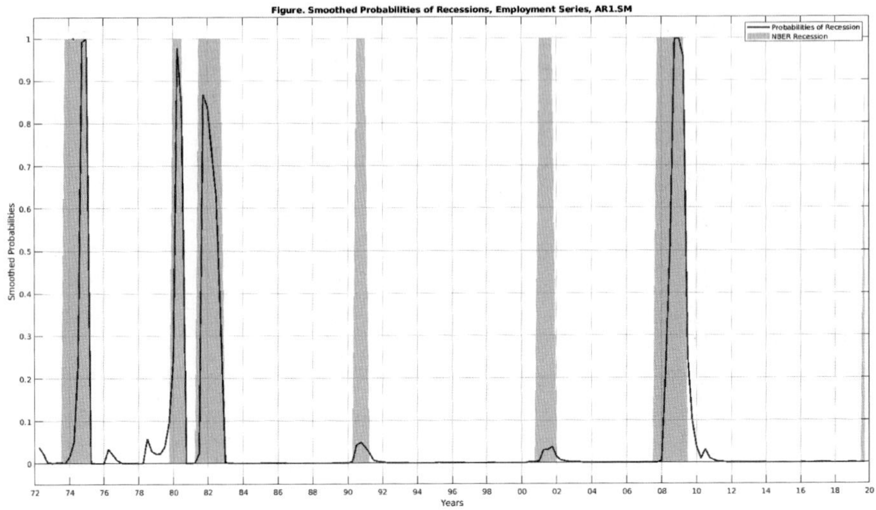

Figure 39.9. Smoothed probabilities of recessions: AR(1), switching in means.

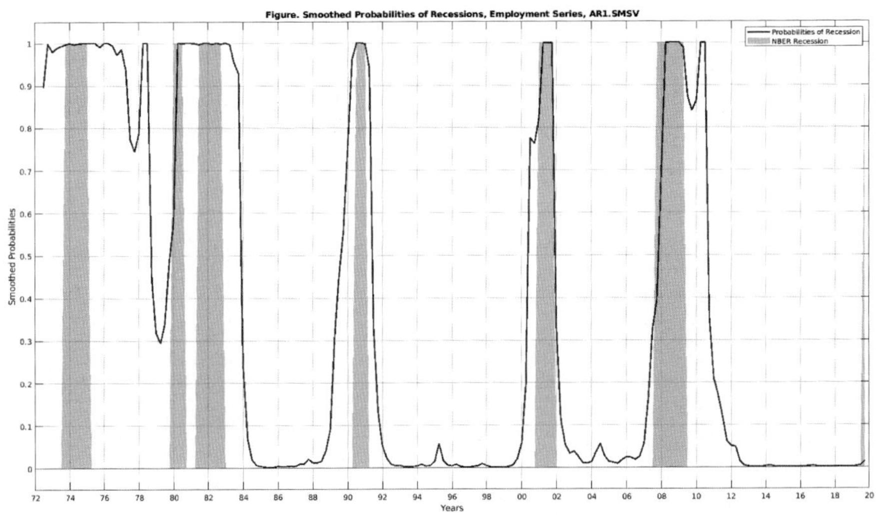

Figure 39.10. Smoothed probabilities of recessions: AR(1), switching in means and variances.

The features documented above point to two possible caveats. First, business cycles or recession periods are usually classified using a wide range of variables influencing aggregate economic activity; see the work of Burns and Mitchell (1946). Thus, we are unlikely to accurately identify recessions using a single time series. In practice, we can use high-dimensional and mixed-frequency datasets to improve upon the estimated smoothed recession probabilities. See the work of Qin and Qu (2021) for such an approach.

Second, the estimates are highly sensitive to whether dynamics are incorporated, here in the form of an $AR(1)$ component. This is an important and often overlooked feature of Markov-switching models. As an example, consider a simple stationary process fluctuating around some mean or trend, e.g., an $AR(2)$. This process is mean-reverting. Hence, it will have some parts above the mean (or trend) and some parts below, which can be viewed as expansions and recessions. A Markov-switching model can fit some average of these above and below means. The fit will not be perfect but the overall sum of squared residuals will be reduced. Hence, by not accounting properly for the dynamics of the process, it is possible to spuriously conclude that a Markov-switching model is appropriate, even if the mean is stable. This can explain why adding dynamics to a Markov-switching specification can reduce evidence for a Markov-switching model.

In light of the above discussion, what is needed is a proper testing procedure for the presence of changing means and variances allowing for dynamics in the form of lagged dependent variables. It turns out to be a quite challenging task. A likelihood-based testing procedure was developed by Qu and Zhuo (2020). Meitz and Saikkonen (2021) considered tests when the regime probabilities are time-varying and depended on the observations.

39.6.5 Extensions

We discuss three extensions of model (39.28).

Multiple Regimes and pth Autoregressive Order

For low-dimensional settings, we can easily extend the model (39.28) to multiple regimes with pth Autoregressive order, see the works of Hamilton (1989), Hamilton (1994), and Kim and Nelson (1999), among others. The general specification is as follows:

$$y_t = \mu_{S_t} + \sum_{i=1}^{p} \phi_i \left(y_{t-i} - \mu_{S_{t-i}}\right) + \epsilon_t, \quad \text{and} \quad \epsilon_t \sim N\left(0, \sigma_{S_t}^2\right),$$

where y_t is an $N \times 1$ vector with N small and S_t follows an S-state Markov chain with

$$\mu_{S_t} = \sum_{i=1}^{S} \mu_i \mathbf{1}_{\{S_t = i\}},$$

$$\sigma_{S_t}^2 = \sum_{i=1}^{S} \sigma_i^2 \mathbf{1}_{\{S_t = i\}}.$$

In applications, both S and p are small. For quarterly data, researchers often set $p = 4$. The number of regimes is often less than four since the complexity for computation increases exponentially. The maximum likelihood and Gibbs sampling methods discussed above can be extended straightforwardly.

High-dimensional Models

Since large datasets in fine detail are increasingly available across disciplines, it is natural to extend the classic low-dimensional Markov-switching models to high-dimensional settings. Qin and Qu (2021) proposed the following model:

$$y_{j,i,t} = \mu_{j,i,S_t} + \sum_{m=1}^{k} \phi_{j,m}(y_{j,i,t-m} - \mu_{j,i,S_{t-m}}) + e_{j,i,t},$$

with $e_{j,i,t} \sim N(0, \sigma_{j,i,S_t}^2)$, where the number of observable time series $y_{j,i,t}$ is large. They further extended the standard Gibbs sampling algorithm to deal with several high-dimensional issues and their algorithm can handle one thousand time series with reasonable computational time. By using disaggregated industrial production, capacity utilization, employment, and hours worked, their models can sharply identify US quarterly business cycles consistent with the NBER's dating.

Switching State-space Models

Technically, we can extend any time series models allowing switching parameters. For example, the parameters of the linear and Gaussian state-space models (38.1) and (38.2) can be regime dependent. Kim and Nelson (1998) studied a dynamic factor model with regime-switching. Fruhwirth-Schnatter (2001) labeled these types of models as switching state-space models and proposed various Monte Carlo Markov Chain (MCMC) methods for Bayesian estimation. The mixed-frequency Markov regime switching models proposed by Camacho (2013) can also be reformulated as switching state-space models and be analyzed using Gibbs sampling methods.

39.7 Exercises

Exercise 39.1. Suppose that a time series is generated by the following state-space model:

$$y_t = \mu + [1, \theta] x_t,$$
$$x_t = \begin{bmatrix} 0 & 0 \\ 1 & 0 \end{bmatrix} x_{t-1} + \begin{bmatrix} \epsilon_t \\ 0 \end{bmatrix},$$

where x_t is a 2×1 random vector, $\eta_t \sim i.i.d.\ N(0, \sigma_\eta^2)$, and μ and θ are scalar coefficients. (a) Derive the moving average representation for y_t. (b) Provide sufficient conditions under which y_t is invertible. What is the equivalent autoregressive representation for y_t under such conditions? (c) Is it possible to test whether the invertibility condition in (b) holds using observations on y_t? Explain.

Exercise 39.2. Derive the variance of the $AR(1)$ model $u_t = \alpha\rho u_{t-1} + e_t$, where $e_t \sim i.i.d.\ (0, 1)$ whose spectral density function is truncated by an ideal band-pass filter which eliminates all contributions outside the range $w^a = 2\pi/32$ to $w^b = 2\pi/6$.

Exercise 39.3 (Review). Suppose that a time series is generated by

$$y_t = \tau_t + c_t + \varepsilon_t,$$
$$\tau_t = \mu + \tau_{t-1} + \omega_t,$$
$$c_t = \phi_1 c_{t-1} + \phi_2 c_{t-2} + \epsilon_t,$$

with $\tau_0 \sim N(y_1, P_0)$, and

$$\begin{bmatrix} \omega_t \\ \epsilon_t \end{bmatrix} \sim i.i.d.\ N\left(\begin{bmatrix} 0 \\ 0 \end{bmatrix}, \begin{bmatrix} \sigma_\omega^2 & \sigma_{\omega\epsilon} \\ \sigma_{\omega\epsilon} & \sigma_\epsilon^2 \end{bmatrix}\right).$$

Here, τ_t is the trend function, c_t is the cyclical component, and $\varepsilon_t \sim i.i.d.\ N(0, \sigma_\varepsilon^2)$ is independent of ω_t and ϵ_t and is introduced to account for potential measurement errors. (a) Write this model in state-space form. (b) Describe the main steps involved to obtain the maximum likelihood estimates of the parameters. (No need for proofs, just give the main ingredients). (c) In many macroeconomic empirical analyses, theories are tested using the cyclical component of the time series. Discuss how to obtain an efficient estimate of the cyclical component assuming the series is generated by this model. (d) Describe various methods proposed to extract the cyclical or trend component of a univariate time series. Discuss their relative merits and drawbacks.

Chapter 40

DSGE Models

Dynamic Stochastic General Equilibrium (DSGE) models provide a unified framework for analyzing business cycles, evaluating monetary policies, and forecasting. This literature was, in great part, spurred by Lucas and Sargent (1979). An and Schorfheide (2007) provided a comprehensive survey of the application of Bayesian methods to the estimation and comparison of DSGE models. See the work of Fernández-Villaverde *et al.* (2016) for a very comprehensive review of solution and estimation methods. In this chapter, we discuss the basic ideas and main issues involved in specifying and estimating this class of models.

40.1 Motivation

As an illustrative example, we consider the analysis of Lubik and Schorfheide (2004). The model is given by

$$x_t = E_t\left[x_{t+1}\right] - \tau\left(R_t - E_t\left[\pi_{t+1}\right]\right) + g_t, \tag{40.1}$$

$$\pi_t = \beta E_t\left[\pi_{t+1}\right] + \kappa\left(x_t - z_t\right), \tag{40.2}$$

$$R_t = \psi \pi_t + e_t, \tag{40.3}$$

where R is the nominal interest rate, π is the inflation rate, x is output, $g_t \sim i.i.d.\, N(0, \sigma_g^2)$, $z_t \sim i.i.d.\, N(0, \sigma_z^2)$ captures exogenous shifts of the marginal costs of production, g_t captures the net effects of exogenous shifts, and $e_t \sim i.i.d.\, N(0, \sigma_e^2)$. The parameters are $\theta = (\tau, \beta, \kappa, \psi, \sigma_g^2, \sigma_z^2, \sigma_e^2)$ with the constraints: $\tau > 0$, $0 < \beta < 1$, and

$\psi > 1$. The first equation is an Euler-type equation for aggregate output x_t, the second a Phillips-type specification for inflation π_t, and the third a Taylor (1993) rule, with R_t, the nominal interest rate.

An interesting issue to address is as follows: "How are DSGE models different from standard simultaneous equations models?" DSGE models describe *general equilibrium* relationships derived from dynamic optimization problems. More specifically: (a) All variables are determined endogenously in DSGE models, while in simultaneous equations systems, they are classified somewhat arbitrarily into endogenous and exogenous variables. (b) The expectations are determined from optimizing behaviors and are rational. (c) The parameters are identified through cross equation restrictions, while in Keynesian models, they are identified through exclusion restrictions. Most importantly, DSGE models are *dynamic*. Both the past and the expectation about the future affect the state of the economy. Also, the equilibrium relationships in DSGE models are *stochastic*. The economy fluctuates while remaining in equilibrium.

DSGE models are fully parametric, meaning that all modeling aspects, from the utility to the production function, from the firm's price-setting behavior to the monetary policy rule, and from the exogenous shock processes to the types of inertia or frictions, need to be specified parametrically. There are two schools of thought about this essential feature. One school is skeptical because of potential model misspecification: What if the utility function is wrong; what if the actual disturbances are not normally distributed; what if the shocks are more general processes than the assumed $AR(1)$ or $ARMA(1,1)$ processes? Since different components of the model interact with each other, and the model is estimated using full information maximum likelihood, misspecification in one part of the model can propagate to other parts, potentially affecting the conclusion regarding the propagation mechanisms or the importance of shocks. The second school embraces the parametric structure as a strength. Their point is that, to make meaningful statements about the aggregate economy given limited data, strong parameter assumptions are indispensable. Only by making strong assumptions and attempting to falsify them can knowledge accumulate, and progress and consensus can take place. In other words, this is a "nothing goes in, nothing comes out" situation. There is some truth to both sides.

Nevertheless, irrespective of where one stands, it should be agreed upon that for DSGE models, model specification is a challenging issue that needs to be taken seriously econometrically. However, the specification analysis of DSGE models also happens to be one area in which econometrics has lagged behind.

DSGE models are micro-founded, meaning that the same parameter often shows up in multiple equations that characterize the market equilibrium. Subsequently, these equations need to be solved using numerical routines, which intensify the parameter interactions, resulting in complex cross-equation restrictions. This complexity leads to challenges when drawing conclusions from the model. In particular, it is often unclear whether the key policy or behavior parameters of interest are identified, and if they are identified, whether they are strongly or weakly identified. As we have seen in other contexts (e.g., weak IV), overlooking these identification issues can lead to over-confidence or even erroneous conclusions. The implications here are two-fold. First, drawing warranted conclusions from DSGE models is hard; mistakes are easy. Second, there is a need for formal econometric methods to adequately address the identification issues to lay solid statistical ground for these models.

As we can see from the above example, a small-scale DSGE model already consists of multiple sectors: consumer, final goods producer, intermediate goods producer, and the monetary policy authority. Medium scale models can have more sectors, with more elaborate structures, featuring more shocks and frictions. As a result, a large number of parameters emerge relative to the available sample size. This has two implications: First, there is simply not enough information in the aggregate time-series data to estimate all the parameters precisely. Second, because these parameters interact nonlinearly, the high-dimensional likelihood surface is not well behaved. To address these two issues, researchers have opted to place priors on parameters and use Monte Carlo Markov Chain (MCMC) methods to estimate them; see Chapter 52. There are two views on this: The first is that these priors genuinely reflect the researcher's knowledge about the problem, and the estimation and inference should be treated within the Bayesian realm only. The second is that, while some of the priors are genuine knowledge in an economic sense, in most cases, they serve as useful mechanisms to narrow down the parameter space and smooth out the likelihood surface. This viewpoint implies that frequentist methods are useful for understanding estimation and inference.

40.2 The main issues

The main steps when analyzing DSGE models are the following: (1) Obtain the optimality conditions that characterize the equilibrium, (2) approximate the dynamics of the model using log linearization or higher-order approximations around the steady state, (3) solve the model with forward/backward recursions, (4) construct the likelihood function, and (5) maximize it numerically (rarely practical) or apply a Bayesian procedure for estimation and inference.

To discuss how models are solved, we return to the example above. The system can be represented as

$$\begin{aligned} x_t &= E_t\left[x_{t+1}\right] - \tau\left(\psi\pi_t - E_t\left[\pi_{t+1}\right]\right) + g_t - \tau e_t, \\ \pi_t &= \beta E_t\left[\pi_{t+1}\right] + \kappa\left(x_t - z_t\right). \end{aligned} \tag{40.4}$$

It now involves only two endogenous variables. We have the equivalent representation:

$$\underbrace{\begin{bmatrix} 1 & \tau \\ 0 & \beta \end{bmatrix}}_{A} \begin{pmatrix} E_t\left[x_{t+1}\right] \\ E_t\left[\pi_{t+1}\right] \end{pmatrix} = \underbrace{\begin{bmatrix} 1 & \tau\psi \\ -\kappa & 1 \end{bmatrix}}_{B} \begin{pmatrix} x_t \\ \pi_t \end{pmatrix} + \underbrace{\begin{bmatrix} \tau & -1 & 0 \\ 0 & 0 & \kappa \end{bmatrix}}_{C} \begin{pmatrix} e_t \\ g_t \\ z_t \end{pmatrix}$$

or

$$\begin{pmatrix} E_t\left[x_{t+1}\right] \\ E_t\left[\pi_{t+1}\right] \end{pmatrix} = A^{-1}\left\{ B\begin{pmatrix} x_t \\ \pi_t \end{pmatrix} + C\begin{pmatrix} e_t \\ g_t \\ z_t \end{pmatrix} \right\}.$$

Simple algebra shows that the eigenvalues of $A^{-1}B$ are greater than 1. Therefore, the only way to obtain a stable solution is to have

$$B\left(x_t, \pi_t\right)' + C(e_t, g_t, z_t)' = 0.$$

This delivers

$$\begin{bmatrix} x_t \\ \pi_t \end{bmatrix} = \frac{1}{1+\kappa\tau\psi} \begin{bmatrix} -\tau & 1 & \kappa\tau\psi \\ -\kappa\tau & \kappa & -\kappa \end{bmatrix} \begin{pmatrix} e_t \\ g_t \\ z_t \end{pmatrix}.$$

Since $R_t = \psi\pi_t + e_t$,

$$R_t = \frac{1}{1+\kappa\tau\psi} \begin{bmatrix} 1 & \kappa\psi & -\kappa\psi \end{bmatrix} \begin{pmatrix} e_t \\ g_t \\ z_t \end{pmatrix}.$$

In summary, the law of motion for output, inflation, and the interest rate is given by

$$\begin{bmatrix} x_t \\ \pi_t \\ R_t \end{bmatrix} = \frac{1}{1+\kappa\tau\psi} \begin{bmatrix} -\tau & 1 & \kappa\tau\psi \\ -\kappa\tau & \kappa & -\kappa \\ 1 & \kappa\psi & -\kappa\psi \end{bmatrix} \begin{pmatrix} e_t \\ g_t \\ z_t \end{pmatrix}.$$

40.2.1 Solving the model: The general case using the GENSYS algorithm

A commonly applied method to solve such models uses the GENSYS algorithm of Sims (2002). The starting point is the following canonical form:

$$\Gamma_0 S_t = \Gamma_1 S_{t-1} + \Psi\varepsilon_t + \Pi\eta_t,$$

where (1) S_t is a vector of model variables that includes (a) the endogenous variables, (b) the conditional expectations, and (c) the variables from exogenous processes if they are serially correlated; (2) ε_t is a vector of exogenous disturbances; (3) η_t is a vector of expectation errors satisfying $E_{t-1}\eta_t = 0$ for all t; (4) Γ_0, Γ_1, Ψ, and Π are coefficient matrices. Note that in the working example, we have the following correspondence:

$$\begin{aligned} S_t &= (\pi_t, x_t, R_t, E_t[\pi_{t+1}], E_t[x_{t+1}])', \\ \varepsilon_t &= (g_t, z_t, e_t)', \\ \eta_t &= (\pi_t - E_{t-1}[\pi_t], x_t - E_{t-1}[x_t])'. \end{aligned}$$

By the generalized complex Schur decomposition (an upper-triangularization of two matrices, which is complex-valued), there exist Q, Z, Λ, and Ω satisfying

$$\begin{aligned} Q^*\Lambda Z^* &= \Gamma_0, \\ Q^*\Omega Z^* &= \Gamma_1, \end{aligned}$$

where "$*$" stands for conjugate transpose, Q and Z are unitary matrices satisfying $QQ^* = ZZ^* = I$, and Λ and Ω are upper triangular matrices. Let $w_t = Z^*S_t$ and pre-multiply the canonical form by Q:

$$\begin{bmatrix} \Lambda_{11} & \Lambda_{12} \\ 0 & \Lambda_{22} \end{bmatrix} \begin{bmatrix} w_{1,t} \\ w_{2,t} \end{bmatrix} = \begin{bmatrix} \Omega_{11} & \Omega_{12} \\ 0 & \Omega_{22} \end{bmatrix} \begin{bmatrix} w_{1,t-1} \\ w_{2,t-1} \end{bmatrix} + \begin{bmatrix} Q_{1.} \\ Q_{2.} \end{bmatrix} (\Psi\varepsilon_t + \Pi\eta_t), \tag{40.5}$$

where an ordering has been imposed for identification, such that the diagonal elements of Λ_{11} (Λ_{22}) are greater (smaller) than those of Ω_{11} (Ω_{22}) in absolute values. Assume the zero diagonal elements of Λ lie on different rows from those of Ω such that Ω_{22} is invertible. Since the generalized eigenvalues corresponding to Λ_{22} and Ω_{22} are unstable, the block of equations corresponding to $w_{2,t}$ has a stable solution if and only if $w_{2,0} = 0$, and

$$Q_{2.}\Pi\eta_t = -Q_{2.}\Psi\varepsilon_t \tag{40.6}$$

for all $t > 0$. The first condition, $w_{2,0} = 0$, requires $Z^*S_0 = 0$, thereby determining the initial condition of the system. The second condition determines $Q_{2.}\Pi\eta_t$. Meanwhile, the system also involves a different linear transformation of η_t, $Q_{1.}\Pi\eta_t$. If the solution exists and is unique, the row space of $Q_{1.}\Pi$ must be contained in that of $Q_{2.}\Pi$. In this case, we can write

$$Q_{1.}\Pi = \Phi Q_{2.}\Pi$$

for some matrix Φ. Pre-multiplying (40.5) by $[I, -\Phi]$ gives us a new set of equations, free of references to η_t, so that

$$\begin{aligned} &\begin{bmatrix} \Lambda_{11} & \Lambda_{12} - \Phi\Lambda_{22} \\ 0 & I \end{bmatrix} \begin{bmatrix} w_{1,t} \\ w_{2,t} \end{bmatrix} \\ &= \begin{bmatrix} \Omega_{11} & \Omega_{12} - \Phi\Omega_{22} \\ 0 & 0 \end{bmatrix} \begin{bmatrix} w_{1,t-1} \\ w_{2,t-1} \end{bmatrix} + \begin{bmatrix} Q_{1.} - \Phi Q_{2.} \\ 0 \end{bmatrix} \Psi\varepsilon_t. \end{aligned}$$

By construction, the first matrix on the left-hand side is invertible. Thus,

$$\begin{bmatrix} w_{1,t} \\ w_{2,t} \end{bmatrix} = \begin{bmatrix} \Lambda_{11} & \Lambda_{12} - \Phi\Lambda_{22} \\ 0 & I \end{bmatrix}^{-1} \begin{bmatrix} \Omega_{11} & \Omega_{12} - \Phi\Omega_{22} \\ 0 & 0 \end{bmatrix} \begin{bmatrix} w_{1,t-1} \\ w_{2,t-1} \end{bmatrix} + \begin{bmatrix} \Lambda_{11} & \Lambda_{12} - \Phi\Lambda_{22} \\ 0 & I \end{bmatrix}^{-1} \begin{bmatrix} Q_{1.} - \Phi Q_{2.} \\ 0 \end{bmatrix} \Psi\varepsilon_t.$$

Finally, multiply both sides of the above equation by Z so that

$$S_t = Z \begin{bmatrix} \Lambda_{11} & \Lambda_{12} - \Phi\Lambda_{22} \\ 0 & I \end{bmatrix}^{-1} \begin{bmatrix} \Omega_{11} & \Omega_{12} - \Phi\Omega_{22} \\ 0 & 0 \end{bmatrix} Z^* S_{t-1} + Z \begin{bmatrix} \Lambda_{11} & \Lambda_{12} - \Phi\Lambda_{22} \\ 0 & I \end{bmatrix}^{-1} \begin{bmatrix} Q_{1.} - \Phi Q_{2.} \\ 0 \end{bmatrix} \Psi\varepsilon_t.$$

More concisely, we can write

$$S_t = \Theta_1 S_{t-1} + \Theta_0 \varepsilon_t.$$

40.2.2 From model solution to likelihood

It is important to recall from the definition of S_t that it includes terms such as conditional expectations and variables from exogenous shock processes. Such variables are not observable to the econometrician. To conduct estimation and inference, we can define a selection matrix C, which includes zeros and ones, to single out the observables. This delivers the following representation for the dynamics of the observables:

$$\begin{aligned} Y_t &= CS_t, \\ S_t &= \Theta_1 S_{t-1} + \Theta_0 \varepsilon_t. \end{aligned} \tag{40.7}$$

The first equation is a measurement equation. The second is a transition equation. This is similar to the state-space model discussed in Chapter 39.

We now discuss the business cycle and policy implications. The system (40.7) has a vector moving average representation:

$$\begin{aligned} Y_t &= C\left(1-\Theta_1 L\right)^{-1}\Theta_0\varepsilon_t \\ &= C\Theta_0\varepsilon_t + C\Theta_1\Theta_0\varepsilon_{t-1} + C\Theta_1^2\Theta_0\varepsilon_{t-2} + \cdots . \end{aligned}$$

Hence, the tools that one can use to analyze the effect of a shock are the impulse response function and the variance decomposition; see Chapter 41. We consider four issues and the appropriate tools to address them: (1) How aggressive is the Fed toward inflation? This can be answered from the estimated model. (2) What is the most important factor affecting the monetary policy? This can be addressed via the variance decomposition of the effect of the shocks. (3) How do the policies affect the economy? This can be answered using the impulse response functions. (4) Counterfactual analysis: Economists are often interested in how the economy would have behaved if some economic policies were different, or if the shocks hitting the economy differed. Such counterfactual questions can be studied in a DSGE model framework because of its general equilibrium nature. For example, we can estimate the same DSGE model using pre- and post-1984 era data separately. Then, we replace the parameters of the post-1984 monetary rule by their pre-1984 values while keeping the shocks and other parameter values unchanged at their post-1984 levels. Subsequently, we simulate the model forward and compare the simulated outcomes with their historical values. This can reveal how the output growth and volatility would look after 1984 under the pre-1984 policy. Similarly, we can perturb the post-1984 economy with pre-1984 disturbances, keeping everything else unchanged, and compare the outcome. Exercises like these can contribute to the debate of whether the "great moderation" (a period starting from the mid-1980s until 2007 characterized by a reduction in the volatility of business cycle fluctuations) is more likely attributable to a better policy (an improved monetary policy rule) or better luck (i.e., smaller shocks).

40.3 Estimation

An early treatment of the methods used in this section is Watson (1989). The starting point for estimating the model is the DSGE solution:

$$Y_t = CS_t,$$
$$S_t = \Theta_1 S_{t-1} + \Theta_0 \varepsilon_t,$$

where $\varepsilon_t \sim i.i.d.\, N(0,Q)$. Note that this is the form of a state-space model discussed in Chapter 39. Hence, what is needed are the likelihood function expressed in terms of prediction errors and the Kalman filter to efficiently evaluate the likelihood for a set of values for the structural parameters of the model, which we continue to denote by θ. The likelihood function is $f(Y_T,\ldots,Y_1;\theta)$. Recall that

$$f(Y_T,\ldots,Y_1;\theta) = f(Y_T|Y_{T-1},\ldots,Y_1;\theta)\, f(Y_{T-1},\ldots,Y_1;\theta).$$

Iterating this formula, we find

$$f(Y_T,\ldots,Y_1;\theta) = \prod_{t=1}^{T} f(Y_t|Y_{t-1},\ldots,Y_1;\theta).$$

Under normality (typically assumed in DSGE models),

$$L = \log f(Y_T,\ldots,Y_1;\theta) = c - (1/2)\sum_{t=1}^{T} \ln|F_t| - (1/2)\sum_{t=1}^{T} v_t' F_t^{-1} v_t,$$

where

$$v_t = Y_t - E(Y_t|Y_{t-1},\ldots,Y_1),$$
$$F_t = E(v_t v_t'|Y_{t-1},\ldots,Y_1).$$

This is a multivariate version of the prediction error decomposition of the likelihood function discussed in Section (15.9). As discussed in Chapter 39, the Kalman filter provides an efficient way for computing v_t and F_t recursively. We discuss the main steps as they relate to this particular model.

We assume that the initial condition satisfies $S_0 \sim N(S_{0|0}, P_{0|0})$, where $S_{0|0}$ and $P_{0|0}$ are some parameters. For the predictions, starting with S_0, the optimal prediction of S_1 and the associated MMSE are

$$S_{1|0} = E\left[S_1\right] = \Theta_1 S_{0|0},$$
$$P_{1|0} = E\left[(S_1 - S_{1|0})(S_1 - S_{1|0})'\right] = \Theta_1 P_{0|0}\Theta_1' + \Theta_0 Q \Theta_0'.$$

The optimal prediction of Y_1 is then $Y_{1|0} = CS_{1|0}$. This implies

$$v_1 = Y_1 - Y_{1|0} = C\left(S_1 - S_{1|0}\right),$$
$$F_1 = CP_{1|0}C'.$$

The updating is performed as follows. Upon observing Y_1, S_1 can be updated using (see the proof in the appendix)

$$S_{1|1} = E[S_1|Y_1] = S_{1|0} + P_{1|0}C'F_1^{-1}v_1,$$
$$P_{1|1} = E[(S_1 - S_{1|1})(S_1 - S_{1|1})'|Y_1] = P_{1|0} - P_{1|0}C'F_1^{-1}CP_{1|0}. \tag{40.8}$$

For the recursions, we continue the predicting and updating steps for $t = 2, \ldots, T$. As a matter of notation, let

$$S_{t|t-1} = E\left[S_t|Y_{t-1}, \ldots, Y_1\right],$$
$$P_{t|t-1} = E\left[(S_t - S_{t|t-1})(S_t - S_{t|t-1})'|(Y_{t-1}', \ldots, Y_1)\right]$$

and

$$S_{t|t} = E[S_t|Y_t, \ldots, Y_1],$$
$$P_{t|t} = E[(S_t - S_{t|t})(S_t - S_{t|t})'|Y_t, \ldots, Y_1].$$

Then, in each recursion, the optimal prediction given $(Y_{t-1}, \ldots, Y_1)$ satisfies

$$S_{t|t-1} = \Theta_1 S_{t-1|t-1},$$
$$P_{t|t-1} = \Theta_1 P_{t-1|t-1}\Theta_1' + \Theta_0 Q \Theta_0'.$$

The forecast error given $(Y_{t-1}, \ldots, Y_1)$ is given by

$$v_t = Y_t - Y_{t|t-1} = C\left(S_t - S_{t|t-1}\right),$$
$$F_t = CP_{t|t-1}C'.$$

And the updating formulae given $(Y_t, \ldots, Y_1)$ are

$$\begin{aligned} S_{t|t} &= S_{t|t-1} + P_{t|t-1} C' F_t^{-1} v_t, \\ P_{t|t} &= P_{t|t-1} - P_{t|t-1} C' F_t^{-1} C P_{t|t-1}. \end{aligned} \tag{40.9}$$

40.4 Bayesian inference

Bayesian procedures are widely applied. The idea is to use information from economic theory or empirical evidence obtained elsewhere as priors to narrow down the possible sets of parameter values. Then, more informative results can be obtained (or we hope so). An excellent reference is the work of An and Schorfheide (2007). Bayesian inference treats the parameter as random. It supposes that there is a prior belief on its distribution and uses information from the observations to update the belief. The updated distribution is called the posterior distribution. The main ingredient is Bayes' law. To simplify matters, define $Y = (Y_T, \ldots, Y_1)$, then

$$p(\theta|Y) = \frac{p(Y|\theta)\pi(\theta)}{p(Y)},$$

where θ is the parameter and Y is the vector of observations, $p(Y|\theta)$ is the likelihood function, $\pi(\theta)$ is the prior, $p(Y)$ is the marginal distribution given by $p(Y) = \int p(Y|\theta)p(\theta)d\theta$, and $p(\theta|Y)$ is the posterior distribution. When the marginal distribution $p(Y)$ is not of interest, we often write

$$p(\theta|Y) \propto p(Y|\theta)\pi(\theta),$$

where $\propto$ means "proportional to", and the proportionality factor does not depend on θ. The above formula implies that to study the distribution of θ after observing the data, it is sufficient to know the likelihood and the prior. Since the likelihood function and the prior may be complicated, especially when the dimension of the parameter vector is high, we need efficient methods to evaluate them. The main methods used are the Gibbs sampler and the Metropolis–Hastings algorithms which are discussed in Sections 52.2.3 and 52.2.4.

40.5 Appendix

We provide a proof of (40.8) and (40.9). We have the following general result for multivariate normal distributions: If

$$\begin{pmatrix} z_1 \\ z_2 \end{pmatrix} \sim N\left(\begin{pmatrix} m_1 \\ m_2 \end{pmatrix}, \begin{bmatrix} \Sigma_{11} & \Sigma_{12} \\ \Sigma_{21} & \Sigma_{22} \end{bmatrix}\right),$$

then

$$(z_2|z_1) \sim N\left(m_2 + \Sigma_{21}\Sigma_{11}^{-1}(z_1 - m_1), \Sigma_{22} - \Sigma_{21}\Sigma_{11}^{-1}\Sigma_{12}\right).$$

From the definitions, we have

$$\begin{pmatrix} v_t \\ S_t \end{pmatrix}\Bigg|_{Y_{t-1},\ldots,Y_1} \sim N\left(\begin{pmatrix} 0 \\ S_{t|t-1} \end{pmatrix}, \begin{bmatrix} F_t & CP_{t|t-1} \\ P_{t|t-1}C' & P_{t|t-1} \end{bmatrix}\right).$$

Applying the general result to the above distribution. We obtain

$$\begin{aligned} &(S_t|v_t, Y_{t-1}, \ldots, Y_1) \\ &\quad \sim N\left(S_{t|t-1} + P_{t|t-1}C'F_t^{-1}v_t, P_{t|t-1} - P_{t|t-1}C'F_t^{-1}CP_{t|t-1}\right). \end{aligned}$$

This in particular implies

$$\begin{aligned} S_{t|t} &= S_{t|t-1} + P_{t|t-1}C'F_t^{-1}v_t, \\ P_{t|t} &= P_{t|t-1} - P_{t|t-1}C'F_t^{-1}CP_{t|t-1}. \end{aligned}$$

40.6 Exercises

Exercise 40.1. Explain how to compute the variance decomposition in DSGE models once the log-linearized solution is obtained.

Exercise 40.2 (Beyer and Farmer (2004)). The model is

$$u_t = E_t u_{t+1} + a_1(i_t - E_t\pi_{t+1}) + v_{1t}, \tag{40.10}$$

$$\pi_t = a_2 E_t\pi_{t+1} - a_3 u_t + v_{2t}, \tag{40.11}$$

$$i_t = a_4 E_t\pi_{t+1} + v_{3t}, \tag{40.12}$$

where u_t is the unemployment rate, π_t is the inflation rate, and i_t is the nominal interest rate. Equation (40.10) is an optimizing IS curve, (40.11) is a new-Keynesian aggregate supply curve, and (40.12) is a policy rule. The exogenous shocks v_{1t}, v_{2t}, and v_{3t} are mutually and serially independent with mean zero and standard deviations σ_u, σ_π, and σ_i. The parameter vector is

$$\theta = (a_1, a_2, a_3, a_4, \sigma_u, \sigma_\pi, \sigma_i).$$

Suppose the true parameter values are

$$\theta_0 = (0.05, 0.97, 0.5, 1.1, 1.55, 2.99, 3.4).$$

(a) Show that the solution of the model is given by

$$\begin{bmatrix} u_t \\ \pi_t \\ i_t \end{bmatrix} = \begin{bmatrix} 1 & 0 & a_1 \\ -a_3 & 1 & -a_1 a_3 \\ 0 & 0 & 1 \end{bmatrix} \begin{bmatrix} v_{1t} \\ v_{2t} \\ v_{3t} \end{bmatrix}.$$

(b) Which parameter is unidentified? What is the intuition behind the lack of identification? (c) Suppose someone runs a regression of i_t on π_t to measure the response of monetary policy to inflation. Explain why such a regression design is fundamentally flawed.

Chapter 41

Structural Vector Autoregressions

Following the work of Sims (1980b), vector autoregressions have been used extensively by economists for data description, forecasting, and structural inference. The discussion here focuses on structural inference. The key idea, as put forward by Sims (1980b), is to estimate a model with minimal parametric restrictions and then subsequently test economic hypotheses based on such a model. This idea has attracted a great deal of attention since it promises to deliver an alternative framework to testing economic theory without relying on elaborately parametrized dynamic general equilibrium models.

Some of the material in this chapter is based on the works of Watson (1994) and Fernández-Villaverde *et al.* (2007); see also the work of Lütkepohl (2006). Useful reviews are contained in the works of Amisano and Giannini (1997) and Kilian and Lütkepohl (2017). Interesting early applications include the works of Litterman and Weiss (1985), Blanchard (1989), and King *et al.* (1991).

We begin the discussion by introducing the structural moving average model and show that this model provides answers to the "impulse" and "propagation" questions often asked by macroeconomists. The relationship between the structural moving average model and structural VAR is then discussed in Section 41.1. The section discusses the conditions under which the structural moving average polynomial can be inverted so that the structural shocks can be recovered from a VAR. When this is possible, a structural VAR is obtained. Sections 41.2 and 41.3 show that the structural VAR can be interpreted as a dynamic simultaneous equation model and discuss econometric identification of the model's parameters. Section 41.4 discusses issues related to estimation and statistical inference. We also discuss the issue of structural VAR versus fully specified economic models, factor-augmented VAR, and Granger causality.

It is useful to put the work by Sims (1980b) into some historical context. In the 1960s and 1970s, almost all work done with macroeconomic modeling was carried using the simultaneous-equations system described in Chapter 22. This is often referred to as the Cowles Commission method since most of the tools (identification, 2SLS, 3SLS, FIML, and so on) were developed at the Cowles Foundation (first based at the University of Chicago until 1955 and since then at Yale University); see, e.g., Hood and Koopmans (1953). These methods are still heavily used for macroeconomic modeling, mostly outside academia, though certainly not exclusively. During the 1960s and early 1970s, the methods worked quite well. But then came the Oil Price Shock in 1973 and everything changed. It was a turbulent period in which macroeconomists (whether in academia or in Central Banks) had a hard time making decent forecasts. Sims' argument was that the models were flawed at their core. His two main objections were as follows: (1) We have no right to separate variables into endogenous and exogenous categories; all should be endogenous; (2) the required exclusion restrictions are *ad hoc* and should not be imposed. He then proposed that macroeconomic models should be based on VAR models.

As we see in the following, even VAR models require identification and this is usually achieved via exclusion restrictions that are motivated by contemporaneous exogeneity arguments. So, why did VAR models become some popular? It is in great part because they changed the focus of the analysis from analyzing "anticipated changes in policies" to assessing the impact of "unanticipated changes" or "shocks". This accorded well with the emerging rise of "rational expectations" models. The basic rational expectations models assert that pre-announced policies are already embedded in economic agents' actions right after the announcement. Hence, it is useless to ask what the effect of the implementation is. It is simply zero as all the action occurred at the time of the announcement, assuming it was itself not anticipated, i.e., it was a "shock".

This shift toward analyzing the effects of unanticipated shocks is the real revolution behind the use of the VAR methodology and, along with the belief in the usefulness of rational expectations models, the reason for its widespread use. It is not for us to decide whether this is good or bad. Researchers can have different views. Take the case of an announcement in tax policies, say a decrease in taxes. The rational expectation models state that you should adjust your consumption pattern at the time of the announcement. Surely, many would simply say "I'll make changes when I get the money". To be fair, macroeconomists have come to appreciate this and related issues (here, basically due to a lack of possibility to use the credit markets). They now call it frictions. But the important point is that the basic issue of the importance of unanticipated shocks remains even in such extended models.

We present various methods for the identification of structural VAR models and for the estimation of the parameters and, especially, the impulse response functions. In general, there is no agreement as to which types of restrictions for identification are "more reasonable" nor about which method of estimation performs best. For an interesting example of the various methods discussed in this chapter in the context of the effects of monetary policy shocks, see the work of Wolf (2020). The results obtained may, however, not translate to other problems of interest. Another interesting application is the work of Angeletos *et al.* (2020) about the nature of the business cycle.

41.1 The structural moving average model

Consider the vector moving-average (VMA) model, where we ignore deterministic components for simplicity:

$$Y_t = C(L)\varepsilon_t, \tag{41.1}$$

where Y_t is an $n_Y \times 1$ vector of variables all treated as being endogenous (e.g., quarterly GDP growth, inflation, and interest rate); ε_t is an $n_\varepsilon \times 1$ vector of shocks, where, for now, we allow the dimensions of Y_t and ε_t to be different; $C(L)$ is a matrix of lagged polynomials. It can be of infinite order, i.e., $C(L) = \sum_{j=0}^{\infty} C_j L^j$.

Equation (41.1) is called a structural moving average model since the elements of ε_t are given a structural economic interpretation. For example, one element of ε_t might be interpreted as an exogenous shock to technology, another as an exogenous shock to inflation (say an unexpected increase in oil price), another as an exogenous change in the quantity of money, and so forth. In the jargon developed for the analysis of dynamic simultaneous equation models, (41.1) is the final form of an economic model, in which the endogenous variables Y_t are expressed as a distributed lag of the exogenous variables, given here by the elements of ε_t.

It is assumed that the variables Y_t are observed but that the exogenous variables ε_t are not directly observed. Rather, the elements of ε_t are indirectly observed through their effect on the elements of Y_t. This assumption is made without loss of generality since any observed exogenous variables can always be added to the Y_t vector. The model (41.1) is considered to be general: If you log linearized a rational expectations model around its steady state, then the solution can almost always be represented as (41.1). Such a generality arises because the number of shocks is allowed to be different from the number of endogenous variables. For comprehensive reviews of structural VAR models, see the works of Ramey (2016) and Kilian and Lütkepohl (2017).

41.1.1 The impulse response function

We are interested in how the system's endogenous variables respond dynamically to the exogenous shocks. To continue, we suppose that the matrices C_j in the polynomial $C(L)$ are of dimension $n_Y \times n_\varepsilon$. Then,

$$\frac{\partial Y_t}{\partial \varepsilon_t'} = C_0, \frac{\partial Y_t}{\partial \varepsilon_{t-1}'} = C_1, \frac{\partial Y_t}{\partial \varepsilon_{t-2}'} = C_2, \dots .$$

Therefore, C_0 is the impact effect of ε_t on the endogenous variables, C_1 is the effect of ε_t one period later, C_2 corresponds to two periods later, and so on. This is similar to the univariate analysis discussed in Section 8.7. Consider an arbitrary column, say the jth column in C_k. It measures the effect of the jth element of ε_t on Y_{t+k}. Further, the (i, j)th element in C_k measures the effect of the jth element of ε_t on the ith element of Y_{t+k}. When this element is viewed as a function of k, it is called the impulse response function (henceforth IRF) of $\varepsilon_{j,t}$ on $Y_{i,t}$.

41.1.2 Variance decomposition

We are interested in measuring which shocks are the primary causes of variability in the endogenous variables. For example, is a technology or a monetary policy shock the main contributor to business cycle fluctuations? To answer this question, the probability structure of the model must be specified. We start with the following assumption:

Assumption 41.1. The shocks are $i.i.d.(0, \Sigma_\varepsilon)$.

The assumption implies that any serial correlation in the endogenous variables is captured by the lag polynomial $C(L)$. The assumption of zero mean is inconsequential since deterministic components such as constants and trends can always be added to (41.1). Viewed in this way, ε_t represents innovations or unanticipated shifts in the endogenous variables. The question concerning the relative importance of the shocks can be made more precise by casting it in terms of the h-step-ahead forecast errors of Y_t. Let

$$Y_{t|t-h} = E(Y_t|\,\{\varepsilon_s\}_{s=-\infty}^{t-h})$$

denote the h-step ahead forecast of Y_t, made at time $t-h$, and let

$$e_{t|t-h} = Y_t - Y_{t|t-h} = \sum_{k=0}^{h-1} C_k \varepsilon_{t-k}$$

denote the forecast error. For small values of h, $e_{t|t-h}$ can be interpreted as "short-run" movements in Y_t, while for large values of h, it is associated with "long-run" movements. In the limit as $h \to \infty$, we have $e_{t|t-h} = Y_t$. The importance of a specific shock can then be represented as the fraction of the variance in $e_{t|t-h}$ that is explained by that shock; it can be calculated for both short-run and long-run movements in Y_t by varying h. When the shocks are mutually correlated, there is no unique way to do this since the contributions must somehow be distributed across shocks. However, when the shocks are uncorrelated, the calculations are straightforward.

Assumption 41.2. Σ_ε is diagonal with diagonal elements σ_j^2 $(j = 1, \ldots, n_\varepsilon)$.

Under Assumptions 41.1 and 41.2, the variance of the ith element of $e_{t|t-h}$ is

$$\sum_{j=1}^{n_\varepsilon}\left[\sigma_j^2\sum_{k=0}^{h-1}c_{ij,k}^2\right],$$

where $c_{ij,k}$ is the (i,j)th element of C_k. The fraction of the h-step-ahead forecast error variance in $Y_{i,t}$ attributed to $\varepsilon_{j,t}$ is then given by

$$R_{ij,h}^2=\frac{\sigma_j^2\sum_{k=0}^{h-1}c_{ij,k}^2}{\sum_{j=1}^{n_\varepsilon}\left[\sigma_j^2\sum_{k=0}^{h-1}c_{ij,k}^2\right]}.$$

It is called the variance decomposition of $Y_{i,t}$ at horizon h.

41.2 The structural VAR representation

The structural moving average model (41.1) is useful but cannot be directly estimated since it involves an infinite number of parameters; even a finite long lag order would be problematic. Such long lags are expected since the effect of a shock can last up to 20 quarters or more. Then, the number of parameters to be estimated can easily exceed the number of observations. Hence, we need a parametric structure that involves few parameters. The typical one adopted is a Vector Autoregressive (VAR) model.

41.2.1 Connection between VAR and VMA: The invertibility requirement

If $C(L)$ is invertible, then

$$A(L)Y_t=\varepsilon_t, \tag{41.2}$$

where $A(L)=C(L)^{-1}=\sum_{j=0}^{\infty}A_jL^j$ is a one-sided matrix lag polynomial. We refer to (41.2) as the structural VAR representation of (41.1). It is useful for two reasons: First, when the model parameters are known, it can be used to construct the unobserved exogenous shocks as a function of current and lagged values of the observed variables Y_t, though this is rarely the case. Second, and more importantly, it provides a convenient framework for estimating the model parameters.

With $A(L)$ a finite order polynomial, (41.2) is a dynamic simultaneous equations model, and standard simultaneous equation methods can be used to estimate the parameters. However, a very important issue is the following. It is not always possible to invert $C(L)$ and move from the structural moving average representation (41.1) to the VAR representation (41.2). This requires some conditions, which we discuss next.

For invertibility, clearly we need $n_Y \geq n_\varepsilon$. This requirement has very important implications for the structural analysis using VAR models. In general, small scale VARs can only be used for structural analysis when the endogenous variables can be explained by a small number of structural shocks. For instance, this requirement implies that a bivariate VAR is not useful if there are more than two shocks affecting the variables. In what follows, we assume that $n_Y = n_\varepsilon$.

Assumption 41.3. $n_Y = n_\varepsilon = n$.

This rules out the simple cause of non-invertibility just discussed. It also assumes that any dynamic identities relating the elements of Y_t, when $n_Y > n_\varepsilon$, have been solved out of the model. However, Assumption 41.3 is insufficient to ensure invertibility. We also need the following.

Assumption 41.4. The determinantal polynomial $|C(z)|$ has all of its roots outside the unit circle.

Roots on the unit circle pose no special problems; they are evidence of over differencing and can be handled by appropriately transforming the variables. In any event, unit roots can be detected, at least in large samples, by appropriate statistical tests.

Roots of $|C(z)|$ that are inside the unit circle pose a much more difficult problem since models with roots inside the unit circle have the same second moments properties as models with roots outside the unit circle; see Section 8.4.10. The simplest example of this is the univariate $MA(1)$ model

$$y_t = (1 - cL)\varepsilon_t,$$

where ε_t is $i.i.d.(0, \sigma_\varepsilon^2)$. The same second moments of y_t is obtained for the model

$$y_t = (1 - \tilde{c}L)\tilde{\varepsilon}_t \quad \text{with } \tilde{c} = c^{-1},$$

where $\tilde{\varepsilon}_t \sim i.i.d.(0, c^2\sigma_\varepsilon^2)$.

This is important because it can lead to large specification errors in structural VAR models that cannot be detected from the data. For example, suppose that the true structural model is non-invertible and given by

$$y_t = (1 - cL)\varepsilon_t \quad \text{with } |c| > 1.$$

A researcher using the invertible model would not recover the true structural shocks but rather

$$\begin{aligned}
(1 - \tilde{c}L)^{-1}y_t &= (1 - \tilde{c}L)^{-1}(1 - cL)\varepsilon_t \\
&= (1 - \tilde{c}L)^{-1}(1 - \tilde{c}L + \tilde{c}L - cL)\varepsilon_t \\
&= \varepsilon_t + (\tilde{c} - c)(1 - \tilde{c}L)^{-1}\varepsilon_{t-1} \\
&= \varepsilon_t + (\tilde{c} - c)\sum_{i=0}^{\infty}(\tilde{c}L)^i\varepsilon_{t-1} \\
&= \varepsilon_t + (\tilde{c} - c)\sum_{i=0}^{\infty}\tilde{c}^i\varepsilon_{t-1-i}.
\end{aligned}$$

A general discussion of this subject is contained in the works of Hannan (1971) and Rozanov (1967). The implications of these results for the interpretation of structural VARs are discussed in the works of Hansen and Sargent (1990) and Lippi and Reichlin (1993). For related discussions, see the work of Quah (1987).

Hansen and Sargent (1990) provided a specific economic model in which non-invertible structural moving average processes arise. In the model, one set of economic variables, say X_t, are generated by an invertible moving average process. Another set, say Y_t, are expectation variables, formed as discounted sums of expected future X_ts. They then consider what would happen if only data about Y_t were available to the econometrician. They show that the implied moving average process of Y_t, written in terms of the structural shocks driving X_t, is not invertible. A simple version of the model is as follows: Let Y_t and X_t be two scalar time series, with X_t generated by the $MA(1)$ process $X_t = \varepsilon_t - \theta\varepsilon_{t-1}$. Suppose Y_t is related to X_t by the expectational equation

$$Y_t = E_t \sum_{i=0}^{\infty} \beta^i X_{t+i} = X_t + \beta E_t X_{t+1} = (1 - \beta\theta)\,\varepsilon_t - \theta\varepsilon_{t-1} = C(L)\varepsilon_t.$$

The root of $C(z)$ is $(1 - \beta\theta)/\theta$, which may be less than 1 even when the root of $(1 - \theta z)$ is greater than 1; for example, if $\theta = \beta = 0.8$.

This example provides an important and constructive lesson for researchers using structural VARs: It is important to include variables that are directly related to the exogenous shocks under consideration. If the only variables used in the model are indirect indicators with important expectational elements, severe misspecification may result. Put alternatively, the agents' information set consists of the history of X_t which, because X_t is invertible, is equivalent to the history of ε_t. When writing down a Wold decomposition, or the VAR representation, the econometrician's information set includes only lagged values of Y_t. The latter is strictly smaller than the former. Consequently, the two representations do not coincide. More generally, non-invertibility can be thought as a reduction in the information set available to the econometrician. Detailed cases of the importance of such features are presented in the work of Yang (2005) dealing with non-invertibility in a model with fiscal foresight and what is often called "Deaton's paradox"; see the works of Deaton (1987) and Quah (1990).

41.3 Identification of structural VAR

From now on, Assumptions 41.1, 41.3, and 41.4 are imposed. Assuming that the lag polynomial of $A(L)$ is of finite order p, then the structural VAR can be written as

$$A_0 Y_t = A_1 Y_{t-1} + A_2 Y_{t-2} + \cdots + A_p Y_{t-p} + \varepsilon_t, \tag{41.3}$$

where $\varepsilon_t \sim i.i.d.(0, \Sigma_\varepsilon)$ so that the shocks can be correlated. Note that the order p could be a function of the sample size T so that as T increases, we recover an arbitrary linear process (within some class).

We omit this potential dependence in what follows. In this section, we ask the following question: Under what conditions can we uniquely recover $A_0, A_1, \ldots, A_p$ and Σ_ε if we had a sample of infinite size generated from the above model? If we could recover these quantities, then because of the equivalence between the above representation and the vector moving average representation, we would be able to obtain the impulse responses and also the variance decomposition. With a finite sample, we would have consistent estimates of the relevant quantities.

Since A_0 is not restricted to be diagonal, equation (41.3) is a dynamic simultaneous equation model. It differs from standard representations of the simultaneous equation model because observable exogenous variables are not included in the equations. However, since exogenous and predetermined variables, i.e., lagged values of Y_t, are treated identically for purposes of identification, the estimation of equation (41.3) can be carried out using techniques developed for simultaneous equations; see Chapter 22. These techniques involve first estimating a reduced form model with a finite number of coefficients and then backing out the coefficients $A_0, A_1, \ldots, A_p$ and Σ_ε from them. The *reduced form* of (41.3) is

$$Y_t = \Phi_1 Y_{t-1} + \Phi_2 Y_{t-2} + \cdots + \Phi_p Y_{t-p} + e_t, \tag{41.4}$$

where

$$\begin{aligned} \Phi_i &= A_0^{-1} A_i \quad (i = 1, \ldots, p), \\ \Sigma_e &= A_0^{-1} \Sigma_\varepsilon \left(A_0^{-1}\right)'. \end{aligned} \tag{41.5}$$

With an infinite sample, Φ_i and Σ_e can be uniquely determined without error. Therefore, the identification question becomes as follows: Under what conditions can we uniquely determine $A_0, A_1, \ldots, A_p, \Sigma_\varepsilon$ from $\Phi_1, \ldots, \Phi_p, \Sigma_e$ using (41.5). This is a standard identification question in the simultaneous equation literature; see Section 22.3. Note that control variables can be added to the reduced form in order to improve the fit. These should be predetermined with respect to Y_t. Since this does not change in any way the issues to be discussed in the following, we omit such extensions.

41.3.1 The order condition

A necessary condition is the well-known "order" condition. We refer to the parameters in the reduced form as the "known parameters" since we are performing a thought experiment assuming an infinite sample. In practice, these "known" parameters are the estimated ones. We have the following:

1. Number of known parameters in the reduced form (41.4): There are pn^2 elements in $\Phi_1, \ldots, \Phi_p$ and $n(n+1)/2$ elements in Σ_e. These $[n^2p + n(n+1)/2]$ parameters completely characterize the second moments of the data;
2. Number of unknown parameters in the structural model (41.3): There are $(p+1)n^2$ elements in $A_0, A_1, \ldots, A_p$ and $n(n+1)/2$ elements in Σ_ε.

Since the difference between the "known" and unknown parameters is $n^2 > 0$, we need at least n^2 restrictions for identification. Setting the diagonal elements of A_0 equal to 1 gives the first n restrictions. Such restrictions are simply normalization restrictions. They are "free" provided that all the shocks have positive variances. This leaves $n(n-1)$ restrictions that must be deduced from economic considerations.

41.3.2 What should not be done

The identifying restrictions must be dictated by the economic model under consideration. It makes little sense to discuss the restrictions without reference to a specific economic system. An identification strategy that makes sense for one model can be nonsense for another. This is the first "what should not be done".

Here, we make some general remarks on identification in the context of a simple bivariate model explaining output and money. A more detailed discussion of identification in structural VAR models is presented in the work of Giannini (1991). Let the first element of Y_t, say y_{1t}, denote the rate of growth of real output, and the second element of Y_t, say y_{2t}, denote the rate of growth of money.

Writing the typical element of A as $a_{ij,k}$ (41.3) becomes

$$y_{1,t} = -a_{12,0}y_{2,t} + \sum_{i=1}^{p} a_{11,i}y_{1,t-i} + \sum_{i=1}^{p} a_{12,i}y_{2,t-i} + \varepsilon_{1,t}, \quad (41.6)$$

$$y_{2,t} = -a_{21,0}y_{1,t} + \sum_{i=1}^{p} a_{21,i}y_{1,t-i} + \sum_{i=1}^{p} a_{22,i}y_{2,t-i} + \varepsilon_{2,t}. \quad (41.7)$$

Equation (41.6) is interpreted as an output or "aggregate supply" equation, with $\varepsilon_{1,t}$ interpreted as an aggregate supply or productivity shock. Equation (41.7) is interpreted as a money supply "reaction function" showing how the money supply responds to contemporaneous output, lagged variables, and a money supply shock $\varepsilon_{2,t}$. Identification requires $n(n-1) = 2$ restrictions on the parameters of these two equations.

In the analysis of simultaneous equation models, identification is achieved by imposing zero restrictions on the coefficients for the predetermined variables. For example, the order condition is satisfied by imposing the two constraints $a_{11,2} = a_{12,1} = 0$. In this case, $y_{1,t-1}$ shifts the output equation but not the money equation, while $y_{2,t-1}$ shifts the money equation but not the output equation. This is a very odd restriction in the context of the output-money model since the lags in the equations capture expectation effects, technological and institutional inertia arising from production lags and sticky prices, information lags, etc. There is little basis for identifying the model with the restrictions $a_{11,2} = a_{12,1} = 0$.

Indeed, there is little basis for identifying the model with any zero restrictions on lag coefficients. Sims (1980b) persuasively made this argument in a more general context, and this has led structural VAR modelers to avoid imposing zero restrictions on lag coefficients. Instead, structural VARs have been identified using restrictions on the covariance matrix of structural shocks Σ_ε, the matrix of contemporaneous coefficients A_0, and the matrix of long-run multipliers $A(1) = A_0 - A_1 - \cdots - A_p$.

41.3.3 A common normalization

Restrictions on Σ_ε have generally taken the form that Σ_ε is diagonal so that the structural shocks are assumed to be uncorrelated.

In the example above, this means that the underlying productivity shocks and money supply shocks are uncorrelated, so that any contemporaneous cross-equation impact arises through nonzero values of $a_{12,0}$ and $a_{21,0}$. Some researchers have found this a natural assumption to make since it follows from a modeling strategy in which unobserved structural shocks are viewed as distinct phenomena which give rise to co-movements in observed variables only through the specific economic interactions studied in the model. Imposing diagonality on Σ_ε yields $n(n-1)/2$ restrictions on the model, leaving only $n(n-1)/2$ additional necessary restrictions. These additional restrictions can come from *a priori* knowledge about the A_0 or the $A(1)$ matrices. In particular, they are satisfied if one of these two matrices is triangular.

41.3.4 Identification through short-run restrictions

In (41.6) and (41.7), $n(n-1)/2 = 1$, so *a priori* knowledge of $a_{12,0}$ or $a_{21,0}$ will serve to identify the model. For example, if it was assumed that the money shocks affect output only with a lag, then $a_{12,0} = 0$ and this restriction identifies the model. The generalization of this restriction in the n-variable model produces the Wold causal chain; see the works of Wold (1954) and Malinvaud (1980) (pp. 605–608)) in which

$$\frac{\partial Y_{i,t}}{\partial \varepsilon_{j,t}} = 0 \quad \text{for } i < j.$$

This restriction leads to a recursive model with A_0 lower triangular, yielding the required $n(n-1)/2$ identifying restrictions:

$$A_0 = \begin{bmatrix} 1 & 0 & \dots & 0 \\ a_{21,0} & 1 & \ddots & 0 \\ \vdots & \ddots & \ddots & \vdots \\ a_{n1,0} & a_{n2,0} & a_{n3,0} & 1 \end{bmatrix} \tag{41.8}$$

This is essentially an ordering of the endogenous variables in Y_t. The most exogenous variable is ordered first. That is, contemporaneously $Y_{1,t}$ is uniquely determined by $\varepsilon_{1,t}$, therefore not affected by any $Y_{i,t}$ with $i > 1$. At the same time, $Y_{1,t}$ potentially affects all $Y_{i,t}$ with $i > 1$. This can be seen by setting $\varepsilon_{j,t} = 0$ for all $j > 1$ and only changing $\varepsilon_{1,t}$. Then, $Y_{1,t}$ moves. The other endogenous variables must also move accordingly because the remaining $n-1$ equations are now equality restrictions.

The restriction (41.8) was used in the work of Sims (1980b) and has become the "default" identifying restriction implemented automatically in commercial econometric software. Like any identifying restriction, it should never be used automatically. In the context of the output-money example, it is appropriate under the maintained assumption that exogenous money supply shocks, and the resulting change in interest rates, have no contemporaneous effect on output. This may be a reasonable assumption for data sampled at high frequencies but loses its appeal as the sampling interval increases.

The main reason this method of identification is so popular is that the estimation is very easy. Consider the reduced form (41.4). The goal is to transform this reduced form to obtain orthogonal residuals so that each shock can be given a structural interpretation. We first state a standard result in matrix algebra.

Lemma 41.1 (Gram–Schmidt Triangularization). *For any covariance matrix Σ_e (symmetric), there exists a unique matrix T which is triangular and with entries taking value one on the main diagonal, such that*

$$T\Sigma_e T' = D \quad \text{a diagonal matrix.} \tag{41.9}$$

Then, $\eta_t = Te_t$ is such that $\text{Var}(\eta_t) = D$ and the vector η_t is therefore called a vector of orthogonalized innovations. Hence, premultiplying the reduced form (41.4) by T, we have

$$TY_t = \sum_{i=1}^{p} T\Phi_i Y_{t-i} + \eta_t. \tag{41.10}$$

Comparing (41.3) and (41.10), we have the constraint that $T = A_0$ so that A_0 is triangular as discussed above and $n(n-1)/2$ restrictions are imposed.

The problem is that the decomposition is not unique. For any given Σ_e, it is unique, but we can change Σ_e arbitrarily by reordering the variables and a new $T = A_0$ matrix will be needed to orthogonalize the innovations. So, the identification procedure depends on the prior ordering of the variables in the VAR system. Sims' answer was to order the variables on *a priori* considerations according to causality criteria; i.e., put the variables considered exogenous first, and second, put a variable not caused by the 3rd, 4th, and so on. This implies a basic assumption of recursiveness in the system. Hence, we are still faced with the need to impose *a priori* restrictions and these are usually based on exogeneity type arguments; recall Sims' criticism of standard simultaneous equations models.

Other restrictions on A_0 can also be used to identify the model. Blanchard and Watson (1986), Bernanke (1986), and Sims (1986) present empirical models that are identified by zero restrictions on A_0 that do not yield a lower triangular matrix. Keating (1990) uses a related set of restrictions. Of course, non-zero equality restrictions can also be used; see the works of Blanchard and Watson (1986) and King and Watson (1994), for examples. But these types of restrictions lead to a different method of estimation, which is more complex. It is also possible to allow some correlation between the primitive shocks, which would then require more than $n(n-1)/2$ restrictions on the main parameters. This is, however, rarely done in practice. But all the ways of putting the zeros depend on *a priori* considerations and are exactly similar to the exclusion restrictions that are imposed in structural simultaneous equation systems of the "more traditional" type; i.e., the Cowles Commission method.

41.3.5 Identification through long-run restrictions

An alternative set of identifying restrictions relies on long-run relationships. In the context of structural VARs, these restrictions were used in the works of Blanchard and Quah (1989) and King *et al.* (1991), among many others. This involves restrictions on

$$A(1) = A_0 - \sum_{i=1}^{p} A_i$$

for identification. Since $C(1) = A(1)^{-1}$, these can alternatively be viewed as restrictions on the sum of impulse responses. To motivate these restrictions, consider the output-money example above. Using (41.1), the long-run cumulative effect of the jth element in ε_t on the

ith element in Y_t is

$$\sum_{k=0}^{\infty} c_{ij,k},$$

which is the (i, j)th element of $C(1)$. Now, suppose that money is neutral in the long run, in the sense that shocks to money have no permanent effect on the level of output. This means that $C(1)$ is a lower-triangular matrix. Since $A(1) = C(1)^{-1}$, this implies $A(1)$ is also lower triangular, and this yields the single extra identifying restriction that is required to identify the bivariate model. The analogous restriction in the general n-variables VAR is the long-run Wold causal chain in which $\varepsilon_{i,t}$ has no long-run effect on $Y_{j,t}$, for $j < i$. This restriction implies that $A(1)$ is lower triangular yielding the necessary $n(n-1)/2$ identifying restrictions.

As an illustration of the use of long-run restrictions to identify a VAR system, we consider the effect technology shocks on hours worked and productivity following the treatment in the work of Christiano *et al.* (2003), which was built upon by the work of Shapiro and Watson (1988). The bivariate system consists of the (log of the average) aggregate productivity f_t and hours worked h_t. There are two shocks in the model: (a) a technology shock, labeled ε_t^z, and a non-technology (or demand) shock, labeled ε_t^n. It is assumed that the following relationship holds:

$$\Delta f_t = \mu + \beta(L)\Delta f_{t-1} + \alpha(L)h_t + \varepsilon_t^z, \tag{41.11}$$

with $\beta(L)$ and $\alpha(L)$ lag order polynomials of orders $p-1$ and p, respectively.

The main assumptions are the following: (a) non-technology shocks have no long-run impact on productivity f_t, which is why only ε_t^z appears as the shock in (41.11); (b) ε_t^z and ε_t^n are uncorrelated; (c) Δf_t is covariance stationary; (d) hours worked h_t is a stationary process.

The latter two assumptions are very debatable. Christiano *et al.* (2003) tried to provide some evidence, but their argument is at best dubious for parts (c) and (d). Part (c) ignores the productivity slowdown in the mid 1970s, which would violate the covariance stationarity assumption, especially a stable mean. For part (d), the source of the problem is that they use a covariate-based augmented ADF unit root test as proposed by Hansen (1995) with the covariate being Δf_t assumed to be stationary. However, because productivity has a change in slope in 1973, Δf_t is not covariance stationary and this induces a bias so that the test rejects the null hypothesis of a unit root in h_t far too often under the null hypothesis. Nevertheless, we continue with these assumptions for the sake of illustration.

The reduced form for h_t in terms of the technology and non-technology shocks is given by

$$h_t = \gamma(L)\varepsilon_t^n + \phi(L)\varepsilon_t^z. \tag{41.12}$$

It is assumed that $\gamma(1) \neq 0$, i.e., the cumulative impact of non-technology shocks on hours worked is non-zero. The assumption that non-technology shocks have no long-run impact on productivity f_t implies that, using (41.11),

$$\alpha(L) = \alpha^*(L)(1 - L), \tag{41.13}$$

where $\alpha^*(L)$ is a lag order polynomial of order $p - 1$ with all roots outside the unit circle. To see why this needs to be the case, note that from (41.11), the only way non-technology shocks can have an impact on f_t is by their effect on h_t with the long-run impact of ε_t^n on f_t given by

$$\alpha(1)\gamma(1)/[1 - \beta(1)].$$

Given the assumptions imposed, this can be zero only if $\alpha(1) = 0$; hence, the decomposition is given by (41.13). Substituting (41.13) in (41.11), we have

$$\Delta f_t = \mu + \beta(L)\Delta f_{t-1} + \alpha^*(L)\Delta h_t + \varepsilon_t^z. \tag{41.14}$$

It then remains to estimate (41.14) to obtain estimates of the technology shocks ε_t^z. One problem is that, via the reduced form (41.12), ε_t^z is correlated with h_t. Hence, an instrumental variable (IV) method is used with lags of Δf_t and h_t as instruments. One then obtains an estimate of ε_t^z, say $\hat{\varepsilon}_t^z$.

Estimates of the dynamic response of ε_t^z on Δf_t and h_t can be obtained as follows. Let $Y_t = (\Delta f_t, h_t)$ and assume that it can be represented by the following bivariate VAR:

$$Y_t = c + B(L)Y_{t-1} + u_t, \tag{41.15}$$

where

$$E(u_t u_t') = V.$$

The system (41.15) can be estimated by OLS equation by equation specifying some order for the polynomial $B(L)$. The fundamental shocks are related to u_t via

$$\begin{bmatrix} u_{1t} \\ u_{2t} \end{bmatrix} = \begin{pmatrix} C_{11} & C_{12} \\ C_{21} & C_{22} \end{pmatrix} \begin{bmatrix} \varepsilon_t^z \\ \varepsilon_t^n \end{bmatrix},$$

with

$$E\left[\begin{pmatrix} \varepsilon_t^z \\ \varepsilon_t^n \end{pmatrix} \begin{pmatrix} \varepsilon_t^z & \varepsilon_t^n \end{pmatrix}\right] = I,$$

the identity matrix. Hence, what is required to evaluate the effect of ε_t^z on Δf_t and h_t are estimates of C_{11} and C_{21}. Let $\hat{u}_t$ be the OLS estimate of u_t obtained from (41.15). Then, estimates of C_{11} and C_{21} can be obtained via an OLS regression of $\hat{u}_t$ on $\hat{\varepsilon}_t^z$. The temporal effect of a technology shock ε_t^z on Δf_t and h_t can then be obtained using standard recursive methods.

41.3.6 Identification via sign restrictions

Uhlig (2005) and Rubio-Ramirez *et al.* (2010) considered identifying a structural VAR model via sign restrictions on the IRFs; see also the works of Blanchard *et al.* (1990), Faust (1998), Davis and Haltiwanger (1999), and Canova and de Nicolo (2002) for an early treatment. For a critical review of this approach, see the work of Fry and Pagan (2011) which, in particular, highlights the fact that a unique set of IRFs is not available. Hence, the IRFs are only set-identified. Only via further restrictions can one identify unique IRFs. Intuitively, this is due to the fact that the estimates are obtained via simulations keeping only the draws having the correct sign for the IRF targeted. For each such draw, there corresponds some IRFs for the effects of the other shocks on all variables. Hence, a set of IRFs are consistent with imposing only a sign restriction on the effect of one shock on one variable.

An example of such restrictions can be the assumption that the nominal interest rate r_t responds positively at all horizons to a monetary policy shock. Suppose that the monetary shock is ε_{1t}. It is related to the reduced form forecast error u_t via

$$\varepsilon_{1t} = b'u_t,$$

for some unknown vector b. To impose the sign restrictions, we search over all possible vectors b such that (a) the IRFs of r_t are positive at all horizons (up to some upper bound) and (b) the impulse response of r_t is normalized (usually to 1). Once the set of possible values for b is determined, one can use a VAR to compute the set of possible impulse responses of the full vector of variables in the system, say the vector y_t, with respect to the monetary shock $\varepsilon_{1t} = b'u_t$. Note, however, that this algorithm can be problematic. In practice, very few draws may satisfy the sign restrictions, especially if a large number is imposed. Then, the resulting estimates can be meaningless. For instance, simply changing the value of the initial seed to generate the random numbers can cause important conclusions to reverse; see the work of Baumeister and Hamilton (2024).

41.3.7 Identification using instruments

Identification using instrumental variables has been considered by the works of Stock (2008), Stock and Watson (2012a), and Mertens and Ravn (2013); see, in particular, the work of Stock and Watson (2018) for a comprehensive treatment. An instrumental variable is defined as an observed variable z_t that is contemporaneously correlated only with the shock of interest, say ε_{kt} (e.g., the money supply shock), but not with other shocks entering the structural model nor with leads and lags of the shocks of interest. Note that introducing some control variables can help make these conditions satisfied. This assumption requires that, controlling for all lagged data, the instrument is not affected by any shock, other than ε_{1t}, though it can be contaminated by some independent measurement error. This instrument is external to the model of interest.

To obtain instruments, one must think much in the same way as in the case when identifying causal effects with a random sample of data using instrumental variables; see Section 10.5. One needs a time series that represents a partial measure of the shock of interest. It will generally contain measurement errors, but that is no different from any of the IV applications. Examples of such instruments include the following (e.g., Stock and Watson (2018)): (a) the quantity of oil kept from going on the market because of political factors for an oil price shock, (b) changes in fiscal policy not related to business cycle conditions as a measure of the "fiscal" shock, and (c) monetary policy announcements set during regular announcement windows (e.g., the announcements of the Federal Open Market Committee) that reveal part of the monetary shock. Some of these will generate little controversy as being a valid instrument. Others such as changes in fiscal policy may be more troublesome if one believes that the effect takes some time. Under rational expectations, the market is supposed to react instantly to such announcements but households may face constraints such that they cannot act until the implementation. This would violate the requirement that the instrument be uncorrelated with the shocks at all leads and lags.

The IRF can be estimated using a VAR that orders the instrumental variable z_t first. The other variables can be in any order, though for the sake of exposition we will denote the first, i.e., $y_{1,t}$, as the variable of interest for which we wish to compute an IRF following a shock ε_{kt}. So, now we have a structural VAR of dimension $(n+1)$. Let $\hat{\varphi}_{y_1,h}$ be the implied IRF at horizon h of $y_{1,t}$ (the variable of interest) with respect to the first shock. Let $\hat{\varphi}_{y_k,0}$ be the implied "impact" (i.e., contemporaneous) impulse response of y_{kt} with respect to the first shock. Then, the impulse response function of interest is $\hat{\varphi}_{y_1,h}/\hat{\varphi}_{y_k,0}$. It is usually defined as a Local Projection IV estimate (see Section 41.6).

Note that this method does not require the concept of "invertibility", i.e., that using some restrictions one can infer the true structural model given some reduced form system. This is especially beneficial if there are more structural shocks than variables in the expended system (the variables y_t and the instrument z_t), i.e., $n_Y < n_\varepsilon$ in the notation of Section 41.2. The reason for this non-invertibility is the fact that the instrument z_t may be contaminated by measurement errors. But this leads to some bias that affects the estimates of the IRF at all horizons in the same way. In other words,

$\hat{\varphi}_{y_1,h}/\hat{\varphi}_{y_k,0}$ is simply a scaled version of the desired estimate of the IRFs $\hat{\varphi}_{y_1,h}$. Hence, what is obtained is a relative IRF.

An estimate of the absolute response function is possible if the model is invertible, i.e., $n_Y = n_\varepsilon$, and the model is identified. The procedure to obtain such estimate is usually called the SVAR-IV method (or proxy-SVAR). Let

$$\tilde{z}_t = \phi \varepsilon_{kt} + \nu_t$$

be the contaminated instrument with ν_t the measurement error. The procedure starts with an estimate of the shock of interest given by

$$\hat{\varepsilon}_{kt} = \tilde{z}_t^f / \sqrt{\mathrm{Var}(\tilde{z}_t^f)},$$

where $\tilde{z}_t^f$ is computed as a linear combination of the reduced form residuals u_t from a VAR involving only the vector of variables y_t (excluding the instrument), i.e., the best predictor of $\tilde{z}_t$ given all information available. This estimate removes the bias induced by the measurement errors and correctly identifies "absolute" IRFs.

As shown in the work of Plagborg-Møller and Wolf (2022) if the instruments are subject to measurement errors, the variance decompositions are only set-identified. They are point-identified only if the shock is spanned by current, past, and future values of the observed variables, a condition labeled "recoverability". This condition, however, holds as long as the model has the same number of shocks as the number of observables, i.e., $n_Y = n_\varepsilon$; see Assumption 41.3.

41.3.8 Identification using "narrative restrictions"

The use of so-called "narrative restrictions" is closely related to the use of instruments as discussed in the previous section. However, here the emphasis is on a few historical episodes that everybody (or almost everybody) can agree on what the IRF should look like. By a few we mean that it can be a very small number, even as small as one episode if the shock has a large enough effect. This is best explained using a few examples.

Antolin-Diaz and Rubio-Ramirez (2018) recognized that sign restrictions (discussed in Section 41.3.6) usually result in a set of structural parameters whose elements have very different implications for IRFs, forecasting error decompositions, and other measures of interest. The goal is to try to narrow the set of possible IRFs using external historical information so that implausible ones are ruled out and the set is substantially narrowed so as to be informative about economic implications.

There are two possible types of restrictions: (a) sign restrictions for shocks near particular historical events and (b) relative magnitude of shocks near some events; i.e., shocks widely perceived to be the main cause affecting some variable at some point in time. This ensures that near the selected events, the structural shocks agree with the established narrative, i.e., the way most would interpret such particular episodes.

Examples include the following. Concerning the first type, for oil price shocks, it is generally agreed that a negative supply shock occurred at the start of the Gulf War in August 1990. Hence, this suggests to impose a negative shock for that period. For the second type, it is widely believed that a monetary policy shock was the main driver of the increase in the federal funds rate in October 1979 (the Volcker period). Hence, in this case, one would like to impose both a sign restriction and the fact that the monetary policy shock was the most important determinant of the federal funds rate within the set of shocks considered for that particular event.

Such sign and relative magnitude restrictions can be imposed on the model via appropriate changes in the estimation method. One can also impose some trimming to allow weaker or stronger restrictions; e.g., the most important versus the overwhelming driver. Antolin-Diaz and Rubio-Ramirez (2018) used a Bayesian method of estimation. Then, sign restrictions truncate the support of the prior distribution, while "narrative restrictions" truncate the support of the likelihood function. For estimation, they modify the method of Rubio-Ramirez *et al.* (2010) and Arias *et al.* (2018). Since these methods are based on simulations involving draws to construct the likelihood function, the trick is basically to omit draws that do not satisfy the "narrative restrictions".

Ludvigson *et al.* (2020) took a more general approach beyond solely improving what can be done with sign restrictions. But again, the emphasis is on putting restrictions on the shocks justified by historical events; in this case, inequality restrictions. They refer to this class of model as "shock restricted SVAR". They focus on two possible sets of restrictions: (a) "event inequality constraints", which uses "historical narratives" to put constraints on various shocks, and (b) inequality restrictions that require the identified shocks to have some non-zero correlation with some external variables. Large threshold values can be used to focus on rare events, which should be particularly informative. The main drawback is that point identification is lost and the IRFs can only be set-identified. Examples include the following, among many others: (a) A large positive output shock in the 1982 recession should be dismissed and (b) uncertainty shocks negatively correlated with the value of a safe asset should be ruled out since uncertainty increases precautionary motives. The methodology allows the external variables not to be exogenous, as in the instrumental variable approach. A related application is contained in the work of Ludvigson *et al.* (2021).

Since the narrative restrictions usually apply to a few periods, fixed and small relative to the sample size, standard methods to construct confidence intervals are likely to perform poorly. This applies as well to methods tailored to handle standard weak instruments. These issues, and some recommendations, are discussed in the work of Giacomini *et al.* (2022).

This approach is interesting. It follows our view that one should look at the historical data first. Learn from them and use the salient features to inform models and estimation procedures to be used. Certainly, many would disagree that this is the right approach. A counterview is that a well-specified model should be able to exhibit all the features that are deemed necessary to impose *a priori*. There is certainly some validity to this point. On the other hand, the data are often noisy and not very informative. Hence, all the help we can get is welcomed. The use of sensible, well-agreed upon, restrictions seems a good way to extract more information from the data.

The narrative approach need not be restricted to some very few events. Romer and Romer (2023) used historical Minutes and Transcripts of Federal Reserve policymaking meetings to identify significant contractionary and expansionary changes in monetary policy not taken in response to current or prospective developments in real activity for the period 1946–2016. They found that such monetary shocks have large and significant effects on unemployment, output, and inflation.

41.3.9 Other types of restrictions

Many other types of restrictions are possible to identify a structural model. We discuss briefly a few others that have been proposed.

One is via heterogeneity; e.g., a change in the variance of the errors such as the one that occurred after the so-called "great moderation" around 1984; see the work of Rigobon (2003). Think about a demand and supply simultaneous equation model. The instrumental variable approach solves the problem of identification by finding a variable that shifts the supply schedule without affecting the demand curve, thus, measuring the slope of the demand. The heteroskedasticity of the structural shocks works in similar fashion, though in a more probabilistic manner. When the change is exogenous, it can act as a valid instrument. A useful extension is provided by Yamamoto and Hara (2022), which can deal with both observed and unobserved factors.

A second one is via structural change; see the work of Magnusson and Mavroeidis (2014). The idea is the following. Stability restrictions, e.g., immunity to the well-known Lucas (1976) critique, can be used as a source of identification of the stable structural parameters in economic models. The key insight is that changes in the distribution of the data induced by, for example, policy regime shifts provide additional exogenous variation that can be usefully exploited for inference.

A variation on these two approaches is provided by Mavroeidis (2021) who addressed the issue of the identification of the effect of monetary policy when the interest rate is near the zero lower bound (ZLB). Here, one can view the full sample as consisting of two regimes, namely ZLB and non-ZLB. If unconventional monetary policies (used at the ZLB) are as effective as conventional ones, one cannot infer any causal effect. However, if they are different, the response of the economy to shocks will change when the policy instrument hits the ZLB. Hence, the switch in this response across the two regimes can provide information about the causal effect of monetary policy. To deal with the problem of endogeneity, one can follow a Tobit-type approach for censored models; see Section 28.1. Here, regimes for which the ZLB is not binding induce the selection bias.

41.4 Estimation and inference

Estimating exactly identified models: The most commonly used method is based on least squares. It consists of two steps: (1) Estimate the reduced form model equation by equation using OLS and (2) estimate the structural parameters using $\Phi_i = A_0^{-1}A_i$ $(i = 1, \ldots, p)$, $\Sigma_e = A_0^{-1}\Sigma_\varepsilon \left(A_0^{-1}\right)'$, and additional appropriate identification restrictions.

Estimating over-identified models: Over-identified models can be estimated using GMM or quasi-maximum likelihood assuming normal errors. For GMM, let $Z_t = (Y_{t-1}', \ldots, Y_{t-p}')'$ denote the vector of predetermined variables in the model, and let θ denote the vector of unknown parameters in $A_0, A_1, \ldots, A_p$ and Σ_ε (imposing identification restrictions to reduce the parameter space). The population moment conditions that implicitly define the structural parameters are

$$E\left(\varepsilon_t Z_t'\right) = 0$$

and

$$E\left(\varepsilon_t \varepsilon_t'\right) = \Sigma_\varepsilon.$$

The GMM estimators are constructed choosing $\hat{\theta}$ such that the above two equations are satisfied (as closely as possible) with sample moments used in place of the population moments. This is a fairly standard GMM estimation problem. The theory and inferential procedures discussed in Chapter 23 apply. For MLE, the method is the same as FIML in standard simultaneous models, see Section 22.8.

Under the additional assumption that the variables involved are weakly stationary, conventional asymptotic theory can be used for inference. In many structural VAR applications, the IRFs and variance decompositions are of more interest than the parameters of the structural VAR. Since $C(L) = A(L)^{-1}$, the moving average parameters/impulse responses and the variance decompositions are differentiable functions of the structural VAR parameters. The continuous mapping theorem directly yields the asymptotic distribution of these parameters from the distribution of the structural VAR parameters.

Formulae for the resulting covariance matrix can be determined by delta method calculations. Convenient formulae for these covariance matrices can be found in the work of Hamilton (1994). These are, however, quite complex, and most applied researchers have instead relied on bootstrap methods to estimate the standard errors of the estimated impulse responses and the variance decompositions. A drawback of this standard procedure is that it does not recognize that we are dealing with a VAR process. In the following, we discuss various methods, their merits, and their drawbacks.

41.4.1 Standard errors for the impulse response functions

Suppose that the estimated structural model with the appropriate restrictions for identification is

$$\hat{A}(L)Y_t = \varepsilon_t$$

and the corresponding moving-average representation is

$$Y_t = \hat{A}(L)^{-1}\varepsilon_t = \sum_{i=0}^{\infty} \hat{\varphi}_i \varepsilon_{t-i},$$

where $\hat{\varphi}_i$ are $n \times n$ matrices. To construct confidence intervals about the IRFs, we need to enquire about the distribution of the estimates $\hat{\varphi}_i$ which are complicated functions of the estimates, $\hat{A}_i$ $(i = 1, \ldots, p)$.

The Asymptotic Distribution of $\hat{\varphi}_i$. For each lag i, define the following vector of estimates of dimension n^2:

$$\text{vec}(\hat{\varphi}_i) = f(\hat{A}_0, \hat{A}_1, \ldots, \hat{A}_p) = g(\text{vec}(\hat{A}^*)),$$

with $\hat{A}^* = [\hat{A}_0, \hat{A}_1, \ldots, \hat{A}_p]$. Hence, for each lag i, the matrix of estimates $\hat{\varphi}_i$ is a function of $(p+1)n^2$ estimates. With the assumption of stationarity, we have that

$$\sqrt{T}(\text{vec}(\hat{A}^*) - \text{vec}(A^*)) \xrightarrow{d} N(0, V),$$

for some matrix V of dimension $n^2(p+1) \times n^2(p+1)$. Hence, using the delta method,

$$\sqrt{T}(\text{vec}(\hat{\varphi}_i) - \text{vec}(\varphi_i)) \xrightarrow{d} N(0, \frac{\partial g}{\partial \alpha_i} V \frac{\partial g'}{\partial \alpha_i}), \qquad (41.16)$$

with the variance being an $n^2 \times n^2$ matrix. While this approach is the natural one to take, there are two problems with it: (1) In practice, obtaining the asymptotic covariance matrix in (41.16) can be very complicated and (2) even if it can be computed, the distribution can deliver a bad approximation if some roots are close to the unit circle. One can solve both problems using simulation methods.

Simulating the asymptotic distribution. To start with, one can think about simulating directly the asymptotic distribution of $\sqrt{T}(\hat{\varphi}_i - \varphi_i)$ from the asymptotic distribution of $\text{vec}(\hat{A}^*)$, which is easily obtained and is given by, say,

$$\sqrt{T}(\text{vec}(\hat{A}^*) - \text{vec}(A^*)) \xrightarrow{d} N(0, V). \tag{41.17}$$

The idea is to create artificial alternative histories for the estimates $\text{vec}(\hat{A}^*)$ and compute the corresponding estimates of the IRF. Now, from (41.17), we have

$$\text{vec}(A^*) \sim N(\text{vec}(\hat{A}^*), \hat{V}/T),$$

where $\hat{V}$ is a consistent estimate of V. To construct an alternative history for $\text{vec}(A^*)$, first simulate a vector of $(p+1)n^2$ independent $N(0,1)$, say $z^{(1)}$. Let Q be the Cholesky decomposition of $T^{-1/2}\hat{V}$ such that $Q'Q = T^{-1}\hat{V}$. Then, one can compute a first draw of $\text{vec}(A^*)$ as

$$\text{vec}(A^*)^{(1)} = \text{vec}(\hat{A}^*) + Qz^{(1)}$$

and the associated IRFs $\hat{\varphi}_i^{(1)}$ $(i = 1, \ldots, m)$ where m is the maximum lag considered. This process can be repeated a large number of times, say $N = 10{,}000$, and a 95% confidence interval can be obtained from the 2.5% and 97.5% quantiles of the simulated samples. Note that the asymptotic distribution is symmetric, but the finite sample distribution is usually not, especially when some roots are near unity. Hence, in many cases, the asymptotic distribution may not be a good approximation to the finite sample distribution. For instance, suppose one of the estimated roots is near 1, say 0.95. Then, using the asymptotic normal distribution implies that we draw values above and below 0.95 equally. This implies that draws of values above 1 (the explosive region) will be made. Hence, some simulated impulse responses will be nonsensical (i.e., rapidly explode to very large values). To alleviate this problem, an alternative simulation strategy is possible.

Simulating the finite sample distribution. The basic idea here is that, instead of creating alternative histories for the parameters from the asymptotic distribution of the estimates, we create alternative histories of the basic underlying shocks ε_t. From these alternative shock histories, we can create alternative data and parameter estimates $\text{vec}(\hat{A}^*)$ and the corresponding IRFs. Repeating this process many times, we can get a finite sample confidence interval. Let us first assume that the shocks are normally distributed, i.e., $\varepsilon_t \sim i.i.d.\ N(0, \Sigma_\varepsilon)$. Let S be the Cholesky decomposition of Σ_ε such that $S'S = \Sigma_\varepsilon$. To create an alternative history for the shocks ε_t, first generate a vector of dimension n of $i.i.d.\ N(0,1)$ random variables, say z_t. Then, construct $\varepsilon_t^{(1)} = Sz_t$ $(t = 1, \ldots, T)$ and using the parameter estimates $\{\hat{A}_0, \ldots, \hat{A}_p\}$ construct, recursively, a new history for the variables Y_t using the identified structural form so that

$$\hat{A}(L)Y_t^{(1)} = \varepsilon_t^{(1)}.$$

Using this new history for the data, re-estimate the model to get new coefficients with $\{\hat{A}_0^{(1)}, \ldots, \hat{A}_p^{(1)}\}$ and corresponding IRFs $\hat{\varphi}_i^{(1)}$ $(i = 1, \ldots, m)$. This process can be repeated a large number of times, say $N = 10{,}000$, and a 95% confidence interval can be obtained from the 2.5% and 97.5% quantiles of the simulated samples.

Simulating the finite sample distribution without normality. The normality assumption for the shocks may often be problematic. In such cases, an alternative simulation method called the bootstrap is available; see Section 9.2. Consider, the set of historical shocks that occurred with the given sample of data

$$\{\varepsilon_1, \varepsilon_2, \ldots, \varepsilon_{T-1}, \varepsilon_T\}.$$

These shocks are independent and identically distributed over time. Hence, the set of shocks that occurred in period 1 could as well have occurred in period 50, and the shocks that occurred in the last period could as well have occurred in period 1 or any other period.

Hence, instead of generating pseudo-random numbers from a specific distribution to create a new history for the shocks, one creates this new history by re-shuffling the error sequence in a random fashion. This can be done with or without re-sampling. With re-sampling, an easy way to do so is to generate a set of T *i.i.d.* uniform random variables, say h_i $(i = 1, \ldots, T)$. Then, we replace the shocks at position j by the shocks that occurred in position $\text{int}[Th_j] + 1$, where int[.] denotes the integer function. In practice, the true error sequence is unobserved. What is observed is the estimated residuals sequence

$$\{\hat{\varepsilon}_1, \hat{\varepsilon}_2, \ldots, \hat{\varepsilon}_{T-1}, \hat{\varepsilon}_T\}.$$

If the sample is large enough, re-sampling from the estimated residuals sequence instead of the true error sequence makes little difference (the difference becomes negligible as T increases; see the discussion in Section 9.2). To obtain a confidence interval for the IRFs, the remaining steps are as exactly as before. Such a procedure was advocated by Runkle (1987).

Kilian's modified bootstrap procedure. Kilian (1998) provided a bootstrap procedure that is tailored to the dynamic feature of the model. The main issue is that the autoregressive parameters estimated by OLS are well known to be biased in finite samples. Accordingly, the estimates of the moving-average coefficients are biased with distribution that is not scale invariant. This implies biased and skewed estimates of the IRFs. The method suggested by Kilian (1998) is to first apply a bootstrap procedure to remove the bias of the estimates of the parameters $\{\hat{A}_0, \ldots, \hat{A}_p\}$. This is achieved using a preliminary bootstrap correction, which follows the general procedure outlined in the work of Efron and Tibshirani (1994). It is labeled the bootstrap-after-bootstrap method and was shown to improve inference about the IRFs.

Remark 41.1. In practice, most applied work report 70% confidence intervals (or some number well below the usual 95%). This is essentially due to the fact that the data are often not very informative about the precise shape of the IRFs. Using a 95% confidence interval would often imply that none of the estimates are significant at any lag.

41.5 Structural VAR versus fully specified models

We now turn to a very basic question: Does it make sense to talk about impulse responses without specifying an economic model? Or more precisely, how informative are unrestricted VARs about how particular economic models respond to preference, technology, and information shocks? Is it possible to check whether a theoretical model has population properties so that it is possible to infer economic shocks and impulse responses from the innovations and the impulse responses associated with a VAR? The answer is yes for the simplest possible case, though no in general.

Suppose the equilibrium of an economic model or an approximation to it has the following representation:

$$\begin{aligned} X_t &= AX_{t-1} + B\eta_t, \\ Y_t &= CX_{t-1} + D\eta_t, \end{aligned} \tag{41.18}$$

where X_t is an $n_X \times 1$ vector of possibly unobserved state variables, Y_t is an $n_Y \times 1$ vector of variables observed by the econometrician (the same as those in the VAR), and η_t is an $n_\eta \times 1$ vector of economic shocks impinging on the states and observables (to be compared with ε_t in the VAR). Equilibrium representations of the form (41.18) are obtained in one of two widely used procedures. The first is to compute a linear or log linear approximation of a nonlinear model as discussed, for example, in the work of Uhlig (2000). It is straightforward to collect the linear or log linear approximations to the equilibrium decision rules and to arrange them into the state space form (41.18). A second way is to derive (41.18) directly as a representation of a member of a class of dynamic stochastic general equilibrium models with linear transition laws and quadratic preferences.

The question then is as follows: Under what conditions do the economic shocks in the state-space system (41.18) match with the shocks associated with a VAR? In other words, letting $\eta_t = \Omega\varepsilon_t$, where Ω depends on the structural parameters in (41.18), under what conditions can η_t be potentially uncovered by a "structural" VAR analysis? When (41.3) holds, i.e., $n_Y = n_\varepsilon$, impulse responses from the SVAR match the impulse responses from the economic model (41.18). Assume that the dimensions of ε_t and η_t are the same and D is non-singular, which is the simplest case. Then, the second equation in (41.18) implies

$$\eta_t = D^{-1}(Y_t - CX_{t-1}).$$

Substituting this into the first equation and rearranging gives

$$\left[I - \left(A - BD^{-1}C\right)L\right]X_t = BD^{-1}Y_t.$$

It will turn out that the answer depends on the eigenvalues of $A - BD^{-1}C$.

Case 1: The eigenvalues of $A - BD^{-1}C$ are strictly less than one in modulus. Then, we have

$$X_t = \left[I - \left(A - BD^{-1}C\right)L\right]^{-1} BD^{-1}Y_t.$$

Again, apply the second equation in (41.18),

$$Y_t = \left\{\left[I - \left(A - BD^{-1}C\right)L\right]^{-1} BD^{-1}\right\}Y_{t-1} + D\eta_t.$$

This equation defines a VAR for Y_t because $[I - (A - BD^{-1}C)L]^{-1}$ BD^{-1} is well defined and η_t is orthogonal to Y_{t-1}. Therefore, in this case, the answer is positive: The structural VAR can successfully uncover the economic shocks and impulse responses implied by the economic model.

Case 2: Some eigenvalues of $A - BD^{-1}C$ are greater than one in modulus. The most important difference from the previous case is that $\left[I - \left(A - BD^{-1}C\right)L\right]$ is not invertible, therefore X_t cannot be expressed as a linear function of Y_t and its lagged values. In other words, it is impossible to uniquely pin down the state variable X_t after observing the history $\{Y_t, Y_{t-1}, \ldots\}$. Therefore, Y_t is not a Markov process conditioning on its own past and $\eta_t \neq \Omega\varepsilon_t$ for any Ω. The detailed argument can be found in the work of Fernández-Villaverde *et al.* (2007). The popular DSGE model of Smets and Wouters (2007) is an example of this case.

Fernández-Villaverde *et al.* (2007) hesitated to draw sweeping conclusions about VARs. Some applications of VARs are informative about the shapes of impulse responses to some economic shocks that theories should attempt to match, while others are not. This follows the premise that one should seek to estimate the deep parameters of a complete and fully trusted model by likelihood-based methods. Of course, the caveat is whether we really fully trust complex behavioral models. The enterprise of identifying economic shocks and their impulse-response functions from VAR innovations aims, however, to infer interesting patterns from the data that will prevail across a set of incompletely specified and not fully trusted models. Despite pitfalls, it is easy to sympathize with the enterprise of identifying economic shocks from VAR innovations if one is not dogmatic in favor of a particular fully specified model. This yet another example of efficiency versus robustness.

41.6 Local projections

Jordà (2005) proposed an alternative method to construct IRFs and associated confidence intervals, labeled as "local projections". The work was in large part motivated by arguing that VAR models may be misspecified and that small departures from the true DGP may imply large differences between the estimated and true IRFs, especially at long horizons for which the effects of misspecifications are compounded; recall that the IRFs are obtained using recursions to solve for the moving-average representation of a VAR model. Also, it was argued that many realistic macroeconomic models imply a VARMA representation, thereby compounding the problems. However, Plagborg-Møller and Wolf (2021) showed that both methods estimate the same population IRFs, provided unrestricted lag structures are allowed in both. They imply two different procedures to estimate the same thing with different finite sample properties. Hence, working with one or the other is mostly a matter of convenience, especially with respect to how to impose identifying restrictions. We return to these issues later.

To start, we need to define the IRFs in a more general abstract way as stated in the following definition.

Definition 41.1. Let $Y_t = (y_{t-1}, \ldots, y_1)$ be an $n \times 1$ vector collecting all the data from some n-variable system up to time t, v_t be the $n \times 1$ vector of reduced-form disturbances, and D an $n \times n$ matrix whose columns d_i contain the relevant experimental shocks. The IRF at time t for a horizon s periods in the future is given by

$$IR(t, s, d_i) = E(y_{t+s}|v_t = d_i; Y_t) - E(y_{t+s}|v_t = 0; Y_t)$$

for $s = 0, 1, 2, \ldots$.

Remark 41.2. The matrix D dictates the identification problem. The paper is silent about the various possible specifications. However, as done above, using (41.9), one could let $D = T^{-1}$ such that $\Omega = TT'$, where Ω is the covariance matrix of the reduced form errors. In what follows, we assume that the model is properly identified. But we should stress the importance of how D is constructed. It dictates what ultimately is the shock of interest. Hence, proper identification is required.

Definition 41.1 shows that the IRFs can be calculated by recursive iteration to obtain the best (in a mean-squared sense) multi-step predictions. This involves a direct forecasting models re-estimated for each forecasting horizons. If one considers linear projections on the space generated by $(y_{t-1}, \ldots, y_{t-p})$, then the relevant regression to construct the best (linear) predictor is

$$y_{t+s} = c^s + B_1^{s+1} y_{t-1} + B_2^{s+1} y_{t-2} + \cdots + B_p^{s+1} y_{t-p} + u_{t+s}, \tag{41.19}$$

for $s = 0, 1, 2, \ldots, h$, where h is the maximal horizon for the IRFs. So, this involves running h regressions, labeled as local projections. With the estimates of the parameters denoted by $\hat{B}_i^s$, the estimates of the IRF are

$$\widehat{IR}(t, s, d_i) = \hat{B}_i^s d_i.$$

Note that in (41.19) the errors u_{t+s} are a moving-average of the forecast errors from time t to $t + s$ and therefore uncorrelated with the regressors. So, the OLS estimates are consistent and the confidence interval for an IRF can be computed using any of the heteroskedasticity and autocorrelation consistent (HAC) methods discussed in Chapter 11 to estimate (long-run) covariance matrices. That is, if $\hat{\Sigma}_i$ is a HAC estimate of $\hat{B}_i^s$, then a 95% confidence interval for $IR(t, s, d_i)$ is $\hat{B}_i^s d_i \pm 1.96 * \hat{\Sigma}_i$. Nonlinear projections can be used by adding nonlinear components in the regression (41.19), e.g., powers and cross-products of the variables. This may be useful to account for nonlinearities in the IRFs, e.g., non-symmetry between positive and negative shocks.

Plagborg-Møller and Wolf (2021) discussed how the various identification procedures discussed in this chapter can be implemented equally well using a Local Projection framework; i.e., recursive or short-run identification, long-run identification using sign restrictions, and the use of instruments. We refer the readers to their paper for a description of the various steps needed.

As mentioned, Plagborg-Møller and Wolf (2021) showed that the Local Projection and Structural VAR methods estimate the same population IRF. This result essentially says that if you can run an infinite order VAR for the reduced form and an infinite order version of the Local Projection (41.19), then the IRFs obtained are the same. This result holds for a wide class of models not restricted to linear ones. It is not surprising since a VAR model with a sufficiently long lag captures all covariance properties of the data; see the work of Lewis and Reinsel (1985) which makes this statement precise for "large enough p" in the abstract setting where p increases with the sample size T. Hence, iterated VAR(∞) forecasts coincide with direct Local Projection (with an infinite number of lags) forecasts since IRFs are linear forecasts conditional on some innovations. Hence, the two methods must yield the same result.

While the last result is interesting from a theoretical point of view, what is more revealing is what happens in finite samples when the lag orders p are severely constrained to be rather small (e.g., 4 for quarterly data and 12 for monthly data). Then, their results state that the IRFs are the same for horizons with values up to p, and after that they need not be the same. Hence, we are left in a limbo as to which is preferable. Jordà (2005) motivated Local Projections on the basis that it would be less subject to minor misspecifications given that a VAR approach implies computing IRFs via iterations of the estimated VAR, hence compounding minor misspecifications into possibly large biases for long horizons. However, note that the basic regression (41.19) involves y_{t+s} as the dependent variable. Hence, for large values of s, there is a considerable separation in time between this dependent variable and the regressors. If the model is misspecified, it is highly likely to imply that variables separated by long horizons are subject to different underlying stochastic structures, possibly due to misspecification or simply randomness in the data. Hence, it is not clear which effect dominates, namely the accumulation of possible misspecification induced by the recursion when using a VAR model or the randomness in the data induced by using a regression with a large time horizon between the dependent variable and the regressors. So far, there is no clear verdict as to which approach delivers the best estimates at medium to long horizons. Hence, for short horizons, the choice between the two methods is mostly a matter of taste and ease of implementation, while for long horizons, we still do not know.

Recently, Montiel Olea and Plagborg-Møller (2021) showed that inference based on local projections provides better coverage rates than standard methods based on inverting a VAR model. In particular, they showed that the coverage rates from local projections are valid uniformly over both stationary and nearly non-stationary data, i.e., nearly $I(1)$, though precluding the $I(1)$ case, and also over a wide range of response horizons. However, when the data are stationary and for short-horizons, the usual VAR-based methods perform better. Their results are, however, based on lag-augmented projections. This is similar to the approach used by Toda and Yamamoto (1995) to make Granger causality tests robust to unit roots; see Section 41.9.3. More importantly, the results only pertain to the coverage rates of confidence intervals, which are notoriously wide for IRFs. But we should care primarily about the precision of the estimates, e.g., the MSE or other measures of precision.

41.6.1 GLS estimation

Note that (41.19) can be written in the form

$$y_{t+s} = x_t'\beta + u_{t+s},$$

where $x_t = (y_{t-1}, \ldots, y_{t-p})'$ and u_{t+s} is an $MA(s-1)$ of the form

$$u_{t+s} = e_{t+s} + c_1 e_{t+s-1} + \cdots + e_t.$$

This is similar to the class of processes discussed in Remark 11.2.1. Hence, OLS is consistent since x_t is predetermined with respect to $\{e_t, \ldots, e_{t+s}\}$. However, as discussed in Section 12.2, GLS is also consistent and more efficient. Also, by construction, issues of exogeneity do not matter and the regressors are pre-determined by assumption. Hence, the method of Perron and González-Coya (2024) can be applied for this special case provided the roots of the MA polynomial are outside the unit circle, i.e., the MA process is invertible; see Section 13.4.1. Lusompa (2023) considers an alternative, more complex, GLS procedure tailored specifically to the local projections regressions, which is valid whether or not the MA process is invertible.

41.7 Bayesian VAR

In this book, we have not discussed Bayesian methods much. However, in dealing with VAR models, the Bayesian approach has become very popular. So, we try to explain why and discuss its relative merits and drawbacks.

41.7.1 The Bayesian method

Everything starts with Bayes rule, namely that for two events A and B:

$$P(A|B) = \frac{P(B|A)P(A)}{P(B)}.$$

The main difference between the so-called *frequentist and Bayesian* approaches is that the former treats the parameters of a model, say θ, as fixed unknown quantities, while the latter treats the parameters as random variables with some unknown distribution. Then, let $P(\theta)$ be some prior density about θ, $P(Y|\theta)$ be the likelihood function of the data conditional on the parameters θ, and $P(Y)$ the density function of the data. The latter is very difficult to compute in practice and is usually replaced by

$$\int P(Y|\theta)P(\theta)d\theta,$$

which can be evaluated by various numerical or simulation methods even for complex models. Then, the posterior density of θ given the data Y is given by

$$P(\theta|Y) = \frac{P(Y|\theta)P(\theta)}{\int P(Y|\theta)P(\theta)d\theta}.$$

Estimating this quantity gives us a likely distribution for the parameters given the likelihood function and the prior used. Note that using $\int P(Y|\theta)P(\theta)d\theta$ in the denominator ensures that the posterior density integrates to one. Then, an estimate of θ can be the mean or median of the posterior density $P(\theta|Y)$. Hence, what is needed for Bayesian inference is the likelihood function of the data and the prior distribution or density of the parameters.

The Bayesian method has been applied in a vast number of studies. The main reason is that even if the model is not identified, one can always obtain some posterior distribution and, hence, some estimates. The prior distribution acts as identifying restrictions, which is, indeed, convenient.

Some important papers that used a Bayesian method to estimate VAR models include the works of Doan *et al.* (1984), Sims and Zha (1998), Rubio-Ramirez *et al.* (2010), Granziera *et al.* (2018), and Arias *et al.* (2018), among many others. In the context of models with set identification, as when sign restrictions are applied, notable contributions include the works of Moon and Schorfheide (2012) and Arias *et al.* (2018). One issue of importance is the fact that the posterior distribution is, in most cases, quite difficult to evaluate (see Chapter 52 for some of the methods used). Hence, the prior is, in most cases, chosen with the intent to make the optimization problem tractable.

41.7.2 Issues of Bayesian inference related to VAR models

The following discussion draws heavily on the work of Baumeister and Hamilton (2015). Let us recall the structural VAR of interest given by

$$A_0 Y_t = A_1 Y_{t-1} + A_2 Y_{t-2} + \cdots + A_p Y_{t-p} + \varepsilon_t,$$

where $\varepsilon_t \sim i.i.d.(0, \Sigma_\varepsilon)$. Here are some facts that hold asymptotically and which are useful to lay out first. They may not hold exactly in finite samples but the departures should be minor. We assume stationary variables:

1. If the model is identified, the Bayesian method is equivalent to MLE, i.e., the prior plays no role.

2. Conditional on A_0, the estimates of A_i $(i = 1, \ldots, p)$ and Σ_ε are unaffected by the prior (Bayesian is the same as MLE), whether the model is identified or not.
3. Hence, Bayesian methods can play a role in estimating A_0. This is not unexpected as imposing restrictions on A_0 is the main way to achieve identification. This can occur whether the model is not identified or is set-identified, as when using sign restrictions.
4. There is no such thing as a prior that is uniformative. Even if one assigns a uniform prior on some parameter, it may imply a quite different prior (which imposes strict restrictions) on the parameters of interest, which are often non-linear transformations of the basic parameters; e.g., Datta and Ghosh (1996).
5. As is always the case, if the model is not identified, the prior will play a role in determining the posterior distribution even asymptotically, i.e., with an infinite amount of data.

The most important result of the work by Baumeister and Hamilton (2015) is the following:

- Consider some class of structures that is either not identified or set-identified, then in large samples, the height of the posterior distribution is simply the height of the prior distribution at that point when evaluated at any value A_0 that diagonalizes Σ_e in (41.4). More precisely, "as long as the prior assigns nonzero probability to a subset of A_0 that diagonalizes Σ_e, then in large samples the posterior density will be confined to that subset and at any point within the set will converge to some constant times the value of the prior density at that point" (pp. 1971–1972). To further quote them, "user of these methods can in some cases end up performing hundreds of thousands of calculations, ostensibly analyzing the data, but in fact doing nothing more than generating draws from a prior distribution that they never even acknowledged assuming" (p. 1965).

Does that mean that the Bayesian approach is doomed? No. Exclusion restrictions that exactly identify a model can be viewed as a very strong prior (with mass all on a few values). In this view, the Bayesian approach can be regarded as more flexible. But what must be recognized and made transparent to the readers is the exact form of the prior distribution on the parameters of interest, not simply those that enter the model, since the former may be some nonlinear transformation of the latter. A carefully constructed prior on the parameters of interest can indeed be beneficial in ruling out parameter configurations that are not credible. Previous work in the literature can help a lot in guiding the choice of the prior. Of course, this requires a lot of work to decide on which prior is reasonable and beneficial for the analysis. It cannot simply be dictated by considerations related to ease of implementation. Another illustration that no brain leads to no gain!

Baumeister and Hamilton (2024) made this point eloquently; see also the works of Baumeister and Hamilton (2018) and Baumeister and Hamilton (2019) for careful applications. Of particular interest is the following issue. Often, one is not interested in the structural parameter themselves but rather in some transformations, for example, elasticities which involve the ratio of more than one parameter. An interesting result is that one can impose parameter restrictions or prior distributions on the structural parameters that appear innocuous and reasonable. Yet, they can lead to widely implausible prior restrictions on the elasticities of interest. The message from this is that one has to be careful in imposing a prior on the structural parameters that translates into a reasonable prior on the parameters of interest. Commonly adopted methods can lead to outright inconsistent estimates of the elasticities of interest. In other words, the core issue is not the parameterization of the model but what aspects of the model we need to focus on when imposing prior information. Their discussion also has implications about the practice of using sign restrictions which only imply set identification. The common practice of reporting a single number as the best estimate can only be justified if the researcher's prior information about the structural model takes a particular form. It is argued that one should report and defend the source of this prior information. All this seems like a lot of work and far from the mechanical applications of imposing a convenient prior (for the sake of computation, say) that readily delivers estimates, a practice so often seen in the literature. But it is a step in the right direction: identification procedures must be made clear and be defended on the basis of their merits.

41.8 An introduction to factor augmented VAR

Following Stock and Watson (2005) with slightly different notation, the Factor Augmented VAR (FAVAR) is

$$Y_t = \lambda(L)f_t + D(L)Y_{t-1} + v_t,$$
$$f_t = \Gamma(L)f_{t-1} + \zeta_t,$$

where Y_t is an $n_Y \times 1$ vector of observables, f_t includes the latent factors, ζ_t and v_t are serially uncorrelated structural disturbances with $\text{Var}(\zeta_t) = I$, $\text{Var}(v_t) = \Sigma$, and $E(\zeta_t v_s') = 0$ for all t and s. The matrix lag polynomials $\lambda(L)$, $D(L)$, and $\Gamma(L)$ are finite order with $D(L)$ typically being diagonal. The structural parameter vector θ consists of the elements in $\lambda(L)$, $D(L)$, $\Gamma(L)$, and Σ. We typically assume f_t is of lower dimension than Y_t.

Extracting the factors is typically done using principal components applied to a pre-specified set of time series; see Chapter 31. The identification of $\lambda(L)$ parallels that of the SVAR. Suppose

$$\lambda(L) = \lambda_0 + \lambda_1 L + \cdots + \lambda_p L^p.$$

Then, this polynomial is identified under the restrictions that $[\lambda_0]_{i,i} > 0$ and $[\lambda_0]_{i,j} = 0$ for $j > i$. Stock and Watson (2005) discussed alternative identification restrictions. A good reference for estimation is the work of Bernanke *et al.* (2005). A survey with macroeconomic applications is contained in the work of Stock and Watson (2016). See also Section 42.4 for a more detailed analysis.

41.9 Granger causality

The concept of Granger causality is closely linked to the use of VAR models. The treatment in this section follows the original paper by Granger (1969). We start by the following definitions involving sets of stationary variables:

- $\bar{A}_t = \{A_{t-j};\ j = 1, 2, \ldots, \infty\}$, the past values of the variables in the set A;
- $\tilde{A} = \{A_{t-j};\ j = 0, 1, 2, \ldots, \infty\}$, the past and present values;
- $P_t(A|B)$ is the optimal predictor of the set A_t using the set B_t;

- $\varepsilon_t(A|B) = A_t - P_t(A|B)$ is the forecast error;
- $\sigma^2(A|B) = \text{Var}(\varepsilon_t(A|B))$ is the variance of the forecast error;
- U_t is all the information in the universe at time t and before;
- $U_t - Y_t$ is all the information in U_t except that contained in the group Y_t.

Definition 41.2 (Causality). Y causes X if

$$\sigma^2\left(X|\bar{U}\right) < \sigma^2\left(X|\overline{U-Y}\right),$$

i.e., Y causes X if we can better predict X using all past information over and above what we can do if we use all past information except that contained in Y. We use the notation $Y \Rightarrow X$.

Definition 41.3 (Feedback). There is feedback if

$$\sigma^2\left(X|\bar{U}\right) < \sigma^2\left(X|\overline{U-Y}\right)$$

and

$$\sigma^2\left(Y|\bar{U}\right) < \sigma^2\left(Y|\overline{U-X}\right),$$

i.e., if $X \Rightarrow Y$ and $Y \Rightarrow X$.

Definition 41.4 (Instantaneous Causality). Y causes X instantaneously if

$$\sigma^2(X|\bar{U},\tilde{Y}) < \sigma^2\left(X|\bar{U}\right),$$

i.e., if we can better predict X_t using the present value of Y_t.

These definitions cannot be used empirically. To do so, we must restrict them in the following way:

(1) Use a finite set of variables, D, instead of U, where Y and $X \subset D$.

Then, causality is defined with respect to this set D. As we see this restriction is empirically very important. First, D must be large enough to include the relevant variables, but since in the end we use a VAR system model to test the hypotheses of interest (see the following), it must be small enough so that the parameters can be estimated precisely and the tests have decent power.

(2) We consider only optimal predictors in the class of linear predictors.

The optimal linear predictor of X, given Y and Z, is

$$P_t\left(X|\bar{X},\bar{Y},\bar{Z}\right) = \sum_{j=1}^{\infty} a_j X_{t-j} + \sum_{j=1}^{\infty} b_j Y_{t-j} + \sum_{j=1}^{\infty} c_j Z_{t-j}, \qquad (41.20)$$

where a_j, b_j, c_j are chosen to minimize $\sigma^2\left(X|\bar{X},\bar{Y},\bar{Z}\right)$. Hence, Granger causality is **linear causality with respect to a given set D**. Of course, in practice, one cannot estimate (41.20). The relevant predictor of X_t can be obtained using the following regression estimated by OLS:

$$X_t = \sum_{j=1}^{m_1} a_j X_{t-j} + \sum_{j=1}^{m_2} b_j Y_{t-j} + \sum_{j=1}^{m_3} c_j Z_{t-j},$$

which is simply one of the equations in a trivariate VAR reduced-form system involving (X, Y, Z) assuming they are scalars, though this need not be the case. Note that m_1, m_2, and m_3 need not be the same, though in practice when using VAR systems, they are usually set to the same value.

The choice of *D*. The choice of D is very important and can lead to different results.

Example 41.1. Consider three variables X_t, Y_t, and Z_t given by

$$X_t = A_{t-1} + \varepsilon_t,$$
$$Y_t = A_t + \eta_t,$$
$$Z_t = A_t + \gamma_t,$$

where A_t is some stationary process and where $\varepsilon_t, \eta_t, \gamma_t$ are white noise and independent of each other. Consider the causality relation using the following different sets D:

- with $D = (X_t, Y_t)$; $Y_t \Rightarrow X_t$ and $X_t \nRightarrow Y_t$;
- with $D = (X_t, Z_t)$; $Z_t \Rightarrow X_t$ and $X_t \nRightarrow Z_t$;
- with $D = (X_t, Y_t, Z_t)$; $Y_t \nRightarrow X_t$ and $Z_t \nRightarrow X_t$.

To answer the causality relations, always ask the following question: "Can I better explain W_t, say, if I use the past of Q_t, over and above what I could do using the past of everything in D, except Q_t"? If the answer is yes, then we have Granger causality, otherwise, we do not. Here, the problem is that A_t causes Y_t and Y_t and Z_t have the same information about A_t. In practice, the choice of D is very important. For instance, Sims (1972) considered causality from the money supply to real output, with D restricted to these two variables. He found evidence of causality. Then, Sims (1980a) augmented D to include the interest rate. No more evidence of causality from money to real output. Here, the issue is that the effect of money on output was actually transmitted via the interest rate channel. So, with D restricted to money and output, this could not be accounted for.

Non-transitivity. The concept of causality is a statistical concept that does not share the same properties as the concept of causality in physics. The following example shows that it is non-transitive.

Example 41.2 (Non-transitivity). Consider three variables X_t, Y_t, and Z_t given by

$$\begin{aligned} X_t &= A_t + \varepsilon_t, \\ Y_t &= A_{t-1} + B_t + \eta_t, \\ Z_t &= B_{t-1} + \gamma_t, \end{aligned}$$

where A_t and B_t are some stationary processes and where $\varepsilon_t, \eta_t, \gamma_t$ are white noise and independent of each other. Consider the causality relation using the set $D = \{X_t, Y_t, Z_t\}$. We have

$$X_t \Rightarrow Y_t \quad \text{and} \quad Y_t \Rightarrow Z_t \quad \text{but} \quad X_t \nRightarrow Z_t.$$

Causality in bivariate models. Consider the following bivariate model:

$$\begin{bmatrix} A_{11}(L) & A_{12}(L) \\ A_{21}(L) & A_{22}(L) \end{bmatrix} \begin{bmatrix} X_t \\ Y_t \end{bmatrix} = \begin{bmatrix} U_{Xt} \\ U_{Yt} \end{bmatrix},$$

where U_{Xt}, U_{Yt} are uncorrelated white noise.

Theorem 41.1 (Granger's Theorem). *$Y \nRightarrow X$ iff $A_{12}(L) = 0$.*

Write the system as

$$X_t + b_0 Y_t = \sum_{j=1}^{m} a_j X_{t-j} + \sum_{j=1}^{m} b_j Y_{t-j} + \varepsilon_t,$$

$$Y_t + c_0 X_t = \sum_{j=1}^{m} c_j X_{t-j} + \sum_{j=1}^{m} d_j Y_{t-j} + \varepsilon_t,$$

then $Y \Rightarrow X$ if some $b_j \neq 0$. There is instantaneous causality if $b_0 \neq 0$. In practice, we must ensure white noise residuals in the regressions and adjust the lag length m accordingly.

Exogeneity. This leads us to the concept of exogeneity. We have the following definition within the context of a VAR system. For a more detailed treatment of issues related to exogeneity, see the work of Engle *et al.* (1983).

Definition 41.5. A group of k variables is exogenous with respect to the full set of n variables if we can write $A(L)$ as

$$A(L) = \begin{bmatrix} \underset{k\times k}{A_{11}(L)} & \underset{k\times(n-k)}{0} \\ \underset{(n-k)\times k}{A_{12}(L)} & \underset{(n-k)\times(n-k)}{A_{22}(L)} \end{bmatrix}$$

(here the first k variables are exogenous). Then, we can write

$$A_{11}(L) Y_t^* = \varepsilon_t^*,$$

where $Y_t^* = (y_1, \ldots, y_k)'$ and $\varepsilon_t^* = (\varepsilon_1, \ldots, \varepsilon_k)'$ so that the variables which are exogenous are not influenced by the innovations corresponding to the variables in the other group. The exogeneity concept is a property of a given variable (or a set of variables) with respect to a given full set of variables. It can change if we change the set. The exogeneity concept is closely linked to Granger causality.

41.9.1 Testing for Granger causality

If Granger causality exists, for example, $X \Rightarrow Y$ within a given information set D, then the prediction performance should improve if we include lagged values of X as regressors over and above what can be predicted using the past history of the other variables in the set D. This motivates a testing procedure for causality. We give some examples to highlight two important issues. The first is that the test and results may closely depend on the specification of the information set D. Second, causality may exist jointly, i.e., $(X, Y) \Rightarrow Z$, even if neither $X \Rightarrow Z$ nor $Y \Rightarrow Z$ holds.

Example 41.3. Consider an information set $D = (X, Y, Z)$. We want to test whether $X \Rightarrow Y$. We have $H_0 : X \not\Rightarrow Y$ and $H_1 : X \Rightarrow Y$. The regression will be

$$Y_t = \sum_{i=1}^{m_1} a_i X_{t-i} + \sum_{i=1}^{m_2} b_i Y_{t-i} + \sum_{i=1}^{m_3} c_i Z_{t-i} + e_t. \tag{41.21}$$

The relevant test is an F-test for the null hypothesis that $H_0 : a_1 = \cdots = a_{m_1} = 0$. Suppose now that the information set is $D = (X, Y)$ and we want to test the same hypotheses: $H_0 : X \not\Rightarrow Y$ and $H_1 : X \Rightarrow Y$. Here, the regression is different, namely:

$$Y_t = \sum_{i=1}^{m_1} a_i X_{t-i} + \sum_{i=1}^{m_2} b_i Y_{t-i} + e_t. \tag{41.22}$$

The relevant test is still the F-test to test the null hypothesis: $H_0 : a_1 = \cdots = a_{m_1} = 0$. It is easy to see that we may fail to reject $H_0 : a_1 = \cdots = a_{m_1} = 0$ in (41.22) and reject in (41.21) at the same time.

Example 41.4. Consider now three different tests using the same regression:

$$Y_t = \sum_{i=1}^{m_1} a_i X_{t-i} + \sum_{i=1}^{m_2} b_i Y_{t-i} + \sum_{i=1}^{m_3} c_i Z_{t-i} + e_t.$$

The first test pertains to the following specifications: $D = (X, Y, Z)$, $H_0 : X \not\Rightarrow Y$, and $H_1 : X \Rightarrow Y$. The relevant test is the F-test to test the null hypothesis: $H_0 : a_1 = \cdots = a_{m_1} = 0$. Consider now the following specifications: $D = (X, Y, Z)$, $H_0 : Z \not\Rightarrow Y$, $H_1 : Z \Rightarrow Y$. The relevant test is the F-test to test the null hypothesis: $H_0 : c_1 = \cdots = c_{m_3} = 0$. Suppose we do not reject the null hypothesis in both cases. The third test pertains to the specifications: $D = (X, Y, Z)$, $H_0 : (X, Z) \nRightarrow Y$, $H_1 : (X, Z) \Rightarrow Y$. The relevant test is the F-test to test the null hypothesis that

$$H_0 : a_1 = \cdots = a_{m_1} = c_1 = \cdots = c_{m_3} = 0.$$

It is possible that this third test allows a rejection of the null hypothesis while the first two do not. The reason is that there might exist a strong correlation between X and Z. Intuitively, X and Z would then contain similar information about Y. Hence, given X included as a regressor, including Z in the regression does not improve the prediction performance, i.e., Z does not cause Y, and vice versa. But X and Z may be jointly significant; see Section 4.4.

41.9.2 Sims' testing procedure

Another test procedure is due to the work of Sims (1972). We first state the following lemma:

Lemma 41.2. *Consider two stationary processes $\{X_t, Y_t\}$, then we have the relation*

$$X_t = \sum_{i=-\infty}^{\infty} c_i Y_{t-i} + u_t,$$

where $\{u_t\}$ is a stationary stochastic process, not necessarily serially uncorrelated, but uncorrelated with Y_{t-i} for all i.

Theorem 41.2 (Sims' Theorem). *If there is no instantaneous causality, then $Y \nRightarrow X$ if and only if*

$$Y_t = \sum_{i=-\infty}^{\infty} d_i X_{t-i} + \eta_t$$

with $d_i = 0$ for all $i < 0$, where η_t is uncorrelated with X_{t-k} for all k.

The intuition for this result is that if $Y \Rightarrow X$, then future values of X will contain some information about the present value of Y.

Based on this theorem, the relevant testing procedure is as follows. Estimate the following regression by least squares:

$$Y_t = \sum_{i=1}^{m_1} a_i X_{t+i} + bX_t + \sum_{j=1}^{m_2} c_j X_{t-j} + v_t,$$

and test the null hypothesis that $H_0 : a_1 = \cdots = a_{m_1} = 0$ versus the alternative hypothesis $H_1 : a_i \neq 0$ for some i. From Lemma 41.2, we know that generally v_t can be serially correlated. But here the least squares estimates are still consistent since the errors are uncorrelated with the regressors. In general, the F-test needs to be constructed using an estimate of the covariance matrix that is robust to serial correlation and heteroskedasticity; see Section 11.6. This bivariate framework can be extended to a multivariate setting quite easily.

For an alternative approach that includes the possibility of feedbacks, see the work of Geweke (1982).

41.9.3 A procedure valid with integrated variables

The discussion above assumes trend-stationary processes (including a trend in the regression if needed). If the variables are integrated, i.e., unit root processes, and possibly cointegrated, the limit distribution of the usual Wald tests, or F-tests, discussed above to test for Granger non-causality based on data in levels have non-standard distributions that depend on nuisance parameters; see the works of Toda and Phillips (1993) and Sims *et al.* (1990). Toda and Yamamoto (1995) presented a simple solution applicable when the multivariate process is a VAR of order p, with p fixed but potentially unknown. The process can be trend-stationary, integrated, and cointegrated of arbitrary order.

The idea is simply to estimate a VAR of order $p + d_{\max}$, where $d_{\max}$ is the maximum order of integration for the variables. In practice, $d_{\max} = 2$, which allows variables integrated up to order 2, which is sufficient for most applications. Even though the true coefficients of the added lags are zero, they act as a useful device to make inference possible and easy. Indeed, it is shown that the usual Wald tests for any hypothesis on the coefficients, including those used to test for Granger causality, have the usual chi-square distribution free of nuisance parameters. Toda and Yamamoto (1995) also showed how their results allow estimating the true order p of the VAR. The only issue is that often a VAR of order p is used as an approximation for a more general VARMA process. Then, there is no true autoregressive order p. Indeed, the best order (often selected via information criteria such as the AIC or BIC, see Section 36.4) implies an approximating order that depends on the sample size.

A similar procedure was suggested by Dolado and Lütkepohl (1996) to perform general types of Wald tests on the coefficients of a VAR process, valid with $I(0)$ or $I(1)$ regressors with any cointegrated rank.

41.10 Exercises

Exercise 41.1. Consider the structural VAR

$$y_t = a_1 y_{t-1} + a_2 m_{t-1} + \epsilon_{1,t}, \tag{41.23}$$

$$m_t + b_0 y_t = b_1 y_{t-1} + b_2 m_{t-1} + \epsilon_{2,t}. \tag{41.24}$$

Equation (41.23) is an aggregate supply equation with $\epsilon_{1,t}$ being a productivity shock. Equation (41.24) is a money supply reaction function with $\epsilon_{2,t}$ being a money supply shock. Assume $\epsilon_{1,t}$ and $\epsilon_{2,t}$ are independent of each other with $\epsilon_{1,t} \sim i.i.d.N(0, \sigma_1^2)$ and $\epsilon_{2,t} \sim i.i.d.N(0, \sigma_2^2)$. (a) Are the structural parameters identified? Justify your answer. (b) What are the immediate effects of a one unit change of $\epsilon_{1,t}$ on y_t and m_t? What are the effects one period later? (c) Explain how to use a bootstrap procedure to construct confidence intervals for the effects reported above. Be specific about how you generate your bootstrap sample and how you compute the relevant quantities. (d) One argues that the model given by (41.23)–(41.24) is misspecified and that the correct specification should be

$$y_t + \tilde{a}_0 m_t = \tilde{a}_1 y_{t-1} + \tilde{a}_2 m_{t-1} + \epsilon_{1,t},$$

$$m_t = \tilde{b}_1 y_{t-1} + \tilde{b}_2 m_{t-1} + \epsilon_{2,t},$$

where $\epsilon_{1,t}$ and $\epsilon_{2,t}$ have the same definition as before. Is it possible to test this hypothesis? Explain.

Exercise 41.2. Suppose you obtained the following estimated model:

$$\hat{A}_0 Y_t = \hat{A}_1 Y_{t-1} + \hat{A}_2 Y_{t-2} + \cdots + \hat{A}_p Y_{t-p} + \hat{e}_t,$$

where "^" stands for estimated values. Suppose the model satisfies Assumptions 41.1, 41.3, and 41.4. Explain how to compute IRFs and variance decomposition using the above model and the estimates.

Exercise 41.3. Suppose you consider the following stationary structural VAR:

$$A_0 Y_t = \mu + A_1 Y_{t-1} + A_2 Y_{t-2} + \cdots + A_p Y_{t-p} + e_t,$$

where μ is a vector of constants and $A_0, A_1, \ldots, A_p$ are coefficients matrices. (a) What is the effect of a unit increase in e_t on Y_t? What is the effect of a unit increase in e_t on Y_{t+2}? (b) What is the long run effect of a unit increase in e_t?

Exercise 41.4. Consider the following Bivariate VAR:

$$\begin{pmatrix} \Delta y_t \\ x_t \end{pmatrix} = B \begin{pmatrix} \Delta y_{t-1} \\ x_{t-1} \end{pmatrix} + \begin{pmatrix} u_{1t} \\ u_{2t} \end{pmatrix},$$

where y_t is the level of log output, x_t is the unemployment rate, and Δ is the first difference operator. There are two orthogonal structural shocks e_{1t} (technology shock) and e_{2t} (demand shock), which satisfy

$$\begin{pmatrix} u_{1t} \\ u_{2t} \end{pmatrix} = C \begin{pmatrix} e_{1t} \\ e_{2t} \end{pmatrix}.$$

The goal is to estimate the impulse response to e_{1t}. Write $u_t = (u_{1t}, u_{2t})'$ and $Eu_t u_t' = V$. Also, let $e_t = (e_{1t}, e_{2t})'$. The shocks are all normally distributed. (a) What are the reduced form parameters of the model? (b) Explain why C is unidentified without further restrictions. (c) What is the long run effect of e_{2t} on the *level* of log output? Express your answer in terms of elements of B and C. (d) Some macro theory implies that the long-run effect in part (c) equals zero and that the long-run effect of e_{1t} on the *level* of log output is positive. Show that incorporating these restrictions identifies C. (e) Explain how to estimate the impulse response to e_{1t} by building on your answer to part (d).

Exercise 41.5. Assume that $\varepsilon_t \in \mathbb{R}^2$ is *i.i.d.* $N(0, \Omega)$, where Ω is a positive definite, symmetric 2×2 covariance matrix and that $z_t' = (y_t, x_t)$ is the stationary solution to the structural model

$$A_0 z_t = A_1 z_{t-1} + \varepsilon_t,$$

with $z_0 = 0$. The coefficient matrices A_0 and A_1 are given by

$$A_0 = \begin{bmatrix} 1 & 0 \\ \alpha & 1 \end{bmatrix}, \quad A_1 = \begin{bmatrix} \phi & \beta \\ 0 & \theta \end{bmatrix}.$$

(a) Find the reduced form for z_t. Express the variance Σ of the reduced form innovations in terms of Ω, A_0, and A_1 and find the reduced form coefficients Π in terms of A_0 and A_1. (b) Write down the likelihood function of the reduced form parameters. (c) Find the maximum likelihood estimators of the reduced form parameters. (d) How would you test the hypothesis that $\beta = 0$. (e) Find the ML estimator for the restricted reduced form when $\beta = 0$. (f) Assume that the reduced form parameters Π and Σ are identified. Let the parameter space for $(\alpha, \beta, \phi, \theta)$ be $\mathbb{R}^4$. For which subsets of $\mathbb{R}^4$ are the structural parameters Ω, A_0, and A_1 identified? Do you need to impose restrictions on Ω ? How would you estimate the structural parameters?

Exercise 41.6. Assume that $\varepsilon_t \in \mathbb{R}^2$ is *i.i.d.* $N(0, I)$, where I is the 2×2 identity matrix. Assume that $z_t' = (y_t, x_t)$ is generated by the model

$$C_0 z_t = C(L)\varepsilon_t,$$

where $C(L) = I + \sum_{j=1}^{\infty} C^j L^j$ with the coefficient matrix C given by

$$C = \begin{bmatrix} \beta & \gamma \\ 0 & \phi \end{bmatrix},$$

and C_0 some 2×2 matrix. (a) Let $\theta = [\beta, \gamma, \phi] \in \mathbb{R}^3$. Find the subset $\Theta \subset \mathbb{R}^3$ such that $C(L)^{-1}$ exists. Find the reduced form (the VAR representation) of the model, i.e., find the polynomial $\Pi(L) = I - \sum_{i=1}^{p} \Pi_i L^i$ such that

$$\Pi(L) z_t = u_t.$$

Show how $\Pi(L)$ depends on the matrices C_0 and C. How is u_t related to the structural innovations ε_t? (b) Describe in detail how you would estimate the reduced form parameters Π. Derive the limiting distribution of your estimator. (c) Using your reduced form parameters, can you identify the structural form parameters C_0 and C? Do you need to impose additional restrictions on C_0? (d) Assuming that you have identified the structural model, find the impulse response function of a shock ε_t onto z_t.

Chapter 42

Linear Panel Data Models: Large N and T

This chapter provides an overview of the panel data literature. There is a vast literature on the subject and, therefore, our treatment is limited in scope and details. We focus on the main specifications of interest in applied work, focusing on methods and conditions under which they are valid instead of technical details. Panel data models typically involve data from various units (such as individuals, firms, and countries) that are different in some unobservable aspects to the researcher. Accordingly, there is a trade-off between using flexible methods to model the unobservable heterogeneity and using pooled models that avoid the heterogeneity by assuming to some extent homogeneous coefficients for all individual units.

Section 42.1 reviews linear homogeneous panels with exogenous regressors; the pooled-OLS, Fixed-Effects (FE), and Random-Effects (RE) estimators are discussed. In Section 42.3, we introduce the heterogeneous panel data models. As we argue, neither of these extremes offers completely satisfactory estimators. To overcome this challenge, recently, latent group structures in panel data models have received considerable attention; see Section 42.6. The most important advantage of the latent group structure is that unlike completely heterogeneous or fully homogeneous models, it allows panel units to be classified into groups, where the individuals within a group share the same slope parameters, while heterogeneity exists across the groups.

Many economic relationships are dynamic in nature, namely those for which the data-generating process is a panel containing lagged dependent variables. In Section 42.2, we consider dynamic panel data models. In this case, pooled-OLS, FE, and RE estimators are no longer consistent and thus we review estimators suited for this environment. We focus on the Arellano and Bond (1991) GMM estimator, the Ahn and Schmidt (1995) moment conditions, the Arellano and Bover (1995) estimator, and the Keane and Runkle (1992) estimator. For a greater degree of generalization, allowing cross-correlated errors and heterogeneous slopes, we discuss factor models for panel data in Section 42.4. For an introduction to factor models, see Section 31.5. For a deeper review of this literature, we refer the reader to the survey by Bai (2013). In Section 42.5, we consider spatial dependence in linear panel data regression models.

42.1 Linear panels with exogenous regressors

Note that most of the models covered in this section were introduced in Section 30.1 in the context of a large N and small T framework. Here, we extend the analysis to the case where the errors can be temporally serially correlated. Since we assume a large T framework, accounting for temporal dependence in the errors becomes feasible.

Let y_{it} be some variable to be explained for individual (or firm, country, etc.) i at time t, with $i = 1, \ldots, N$ and $t = 1, \ldots, T$, and assume that it is generated by the following panel data regression model:

$$y_{it} = \alpha_i + \beta' x_{it} + u_{it}, \tag{42.1}$$

where x_{it} is a $k \times 1$ vector of observed individual specific regressors for the ith cross-sectional unit at time t, u_{it} is the error term, β is a $k \times 1$ vector of unknown parameters, and α_i denotes an unobservable, time-invariant, individual-specific effect. Note that α_i accounts for any individual-specific effect not included in the regression; e.g., Mundlak (1978). We can rewrite model (42.1) in an individual-specific specification as follows for $i = 1, \ldots, N$:

$$y_i = \alpha_i \tau_T + X_i \beta + u_i, \tag{42.2}$$

where

$$y_i = \begin{pmatrix} y_{i1} \\ \vdots \\ y_{iT} \end{pmatrix}, \quad X_i = \begin{pmatrix} x_{i1}^{(1)} & x_{i1}^{(2)} & \dots & x_{i1}^{(k)} \\ \vdots & \vdots & \vdots & \vdots \\ x_{iT}^{(1)} & x_{iT}^{(2)} & \dots & x_{iT}^{(k)} \end{pmatrix},$$

$$u_i = \begin{pmatrix} u_{i1} \\ \vdots \\ u_{iT} \end{pmatrix}, \quad \tau_T = \begin{pmatrix} 1 \\ \vdots \\ 1 \end{pmatrix}.$$

We can also rewrite (42.1) in stacked form using a time-specific formulation given by

$$y_t = \begin{pmatrix} y_{1t} \\ \vdots \\ y_{Nt} \end{pmatrix}, \quad X_t = \begin{pmatrix} x_{1t}^{(1)} & x_{1t}^{(2)} & \dots & x_{1t}^{(k)} \\ \vdots & \vdots & \vdots & \vdots \\ x_{Nt}^{(1)} & x_{Nt}^{(2)} & \dots & x_{Nt}^{(k)} \end{pmatrix},$$

$$u_t = \begin{pmatrix} u_{1t} \\ \vdots \\ u_{Nt} \end{pmatrix}, \quad \alpha = \begin{pmatrix} \alpha_1 \\ \vdots \\ \alpha_N \end{pmatrix}.$$

Equation (42.1) can also be expressed in matrix form as

$$y = (\alpha \otimes \tau_T) + X\beta + u, \tag{42.3}$$

where $y = (y_1', \dots, y_N')'$, $X = (X_1, \dots, X_N)'$, $u = (u_1', \dots, u_N')'$, and $\otimes$ is the Kronecker product. Throughout this section, it is assumed that the regressors are exogenous, $E(u_{it}|X_i) = 0$, for all i and t.

42.1.1 Pooled OLS estimator

This estimator assumes that the individual-specific effects are homogeneous, namely $\alpha_i = \alpha$, for all i. In this case, the panel data model reduces to

$$y_{it} = \alpha + \beta' x_{it} + u_{it}, \tag{42.4}$$

and α and β can be estimated via an OLS procedure. The resultant estimator of β is referred to as the pooled OLS estimator and is given by

$$\hat{\beta}_{\text{OLS}} = \left[\sum_{i=1}^{N}\sum_{t=1}^{T}(x_{it}-\bar{x})(x_{it}-\bar{x})'\right]^{-1}\left[\sum_{i=1}^{N}\sum_{t=1}^{T}(x_{it}-\bar{x})(y_{it}-\bar{y})\right], \tag{42.5}$$

where

$$\bar{x} = (NT)^{-1}\sum_{i=1}^{N}\sum_{t=1}^{T}x_{it},,$$

$$\bar{y} = (NT)^{-1}\sum_{i=1}^{N}\sum_{t=1}^{T}y_{it},$$

assuming that $\sum_{i=1}^{N}\sum_{t=1}^{T}(x_{it}-\bar{x})(x_{it}-\bar{x})'$ is a non-singular matrix. Under the following assumptions, the pooled estimator is unbiased and consistent if x_{it} is exogenous and the individual-specific effects are homogeneous:

Assumption 42.1 (PD1). $E(u_{it}|x_{is}) = 0$, for all i, t, and s.

Assumption 42.2 (PD2). The regressors, x_{it}, are either deterministic and bounded, namely $\|x_{it}\| < K < \infty$, or they satisfy the moment conditions $E\left\|(x_{it}-\bar{x})(x_{js}-\bar{x})'\right\| < K < \infty$, for all i, j, t, and s, where $\|A\|$ denotes the Frobenius norm of matrix A, i.e., $\|A\| = trace(A'A)^{1/2}$.

Assumption 42.3 (PD3). The $k \times k$ matrix Q_{NT} defined by

$$Q_{NT} = (NT)^{-1}\sum_{i=1}^{N}\sum_{t=1}^{T}(x_{it}-\bar{x})(x_{it}-\bar{x})'$$

is positive definite for all fixed N and T, and also as N and/or $T \to \infty$.

Assumption 42.4 (PD4). The errors u_{it} are cross-sectionally independent.

Remark 42.1. The errors u_{it} are allowed to be cross-sectionally heteroskedastic and serially correlated

$$E\left(u_{it}u_{js}|X\right) = 0, \quad \text{if } i \neq j \quad \text{for all } t \text{ and } s,$$
$$E\left(u_{it}u_{js}|X\right) = \gamma_i\left(t,s\right), \quad \text{if } i = j, \quad \text{and} \quad t \neq s,$$
$$E\left(u_{it}u_{js}|X\right) = \sigma_i^2 < K < \infty, \quad \text{if } i = j, \quad \text{and} \quad t = s,$$

where $\gamma_i\left(t,s\right)$ is the auto-covariance function of u_{it}, which is assumed to be bounded.

Under Assumptions PD1–PD2, for any fixed T as $N \to \infty$,

$$\sqrt{NT}\left(\hat{\beta}_{\text{OLS}} - \beta\right) \overset{d}{\to} N(0, \Omega_{OLS}),$$

where $\Omega_{OLS} = plim_{T\to\infty}\Omega_{NT}$ and

$$\Omega_{NT} = Q_{NT}^{-1}V_{NT}Q_{NT}^{-1}$$

with

$$V_{NT} = N^{-1}\left[T^{-1}\sum_{i=1}^{N}\sum_{t=1}^{T}\sigma_i^2\left(x_{it}-\bar{x}\right)\left(x_{it}-\bar{x}\right)'\right.$$
$$\left.+T^{-1}\sum_{i-1}^{N}\sum_{t\neq s}^{T}\gamma_i\left(t,s\right)\left(x_{it}-\bar{x}\right)\left(x_{it}-\bar{x}\right)'\right].$$

Note that this approach is much like using OLS instead of GLS in the standard linear model. Hence, permitting and accounting for temporal dependence in the errors does not change the estimator, only the way the proper covariance matrix needs to be constructed. Not surprisingly, it is of the usual “sandwich form” as discussed in Section 11.3. Note also that, as before, this requires exogenous regressors, as specified by Assumption PD1.

Remark 42.2. When N is fixed and $T \to \infty$, then certain mixing or stationary conditions are required on the autocovariances $\gamma_i\left(t,s\right)$ for the pooled OLS estimator to remain consistent. A sufficient condition is given by

$$T^{-2}\sum_{t=1}^{T}\sum_{s=1}^{T}\gamma_i^2\left(t,s\right) \to 0,$$

for each i. This is the usual ergodicity condition and is met if the $T \times T$ autocovariance matrix Γ has bounded absolute row (column) sum norm. This condition is met, for example, if u_{it} is a short-memory stationary process for all i.

42.1.2 Fixed-effect specification

Under the Fixed-effect (FE) specification, no restrictions are imposed on the individual-specific effects α_i, besides boundedness, namely that $|\alpha_i| < K < \infty$, for all i, for some $K > 0$. Note that α_i is allowed to be correlated with both the regressors x_{it} and the error term u_{it}. The basic idea behind FE estimation is to estimate β after eliminating the individual effects, α_i. Averaging equation (42.1) over time yields

$$\bar{y}_i = \alpha_i + \beta' \bar{x}_i + \bar{u}_i, \tag{42.6}$$

where $\bar{y}_i, \bar{x}_i$, and $\bar{u}_i$ are time averages given by

$$\bar{y}_i = T^{-1} \sum_{t=1}^{T} y_{it}, \quad \bar{x}_i = T^{-1} \sum_{t=1}^{T} x_{it}, \quad \bar{u}_i = T^{-1} \sum_{t=1}^{T} u_{it}.$$

Subtracting (42.6) from (42.1) yields

$$y_{it} - \bar{y}_i = \beta' (x_{it} - \bar{x}_i) + (u_{it} - \bar{u}_i),$$

which is known as the FE or within transformation. The parameter β is now estimated by applying the method of pooled OLS to the above transformed regression to obtain

$$\hat{\beta}_{\mathrm{FE}} = \left[\sum_{t=1}^{T} \sum_{i=1}^{N} (x_{it} - \bar{x}_i)(x_{it} - \bar{x}_i)' \right]^{-1} \sum_{t=1}^{T} \sum_{i=1}^{N} (x_{it} - \bar{x}_i)(y_{it} - \bar{y}_i).$$

The estimator for α_i can be recovered from (42.6) via

$$\hat{\alpha}_i = \bar{y}_i - \hat{\beta}'_{FE} \bar{x}_i.$$

In what follows, we use the following modified versions of Assumptions PD2 and PD3.

Assumption 42.5 (PD2′). The regressors x_{it} are either deterministic and bounded, i.e., $\|x_{it}\| < K < \infty$, or they satisfy the moment conditions $E\left\|\left(x_{it}-\bar{x}_i\right)\left(x_{js}-\bar{x}_j\right)'\right\| < K < \infty$, for all i, j, t, and s.

Assumption 42.6 (PD3′). The $k \times k$ matrix $Q_{FE,NT}$ defined by

$$Q_{FE,NT} = (NT)^{-1}\sum_{i=1}^{N}\sum_{t=1}^{T}\left(x_{it}-\bar{x}_i\right)\left(x_{it}-\bar{x}_i\right)'$$

is positive definite for all fixed N and T, and also as N and/or $T \to \infty$.

Under Assumptions PD1, PD2′, PD3′, and PD4, the FE estimator is unbiased and consistent if x_{it} is exogenous, and, for any fixed T as $N \to \infty$, the FE estimator is asymptotically normal with a limiting distribution given by

$$\sqrt{NT}\left(\hat{\beta}_{\text{FE}}-\beta\right) \xrightarrow{d} N(0, \Omega_{FE}),$$

where $\Omega_{FE} = plim_{N\to\infty}\Omega_{FE,NT}$ and

$$\Omega_{FE,NT} = Q_{FE,NT}^{-1}V_{FE,NT}Q_{FE,NT}^{-1}$$

with

$$V_{FE,NT} = (NT)^{-1}\left[\sum_{i=1}^{N}\sum_{t=1}^{T}\sigma_i^2\left(x_{it}-\bar{x}_i\right)\left(x_{it}-\bar{x}_i\right)' + \sum_{i=1}^{N}\sum_{t\neq s}^{T}\gamma_i\left(t,s\right)\left(x_{it}-\bar{x}_i\right)\left(x_{it}-\bar{x}_i\right)'\right].$$

Remark 42.3. When both N and $T \to \infty$, a sufficient condition for the consistency of $\hat{\beta}_{\text{FE}}$ is given by

$$(NT)^{-2}\sum_{i=1}^{N}\sum_{t=1}^{T}\sum_{s=1}^{T}\gamma_i^2\left(t,s\right) \to 0,$$

which is trivially satisfied as $\gamma_i^2\left(t,s\right)$ is assumed to be bounded. However, when N is fixed and $T \to \infty$, then the short-memory stationary condition discussed in Remark 42.2 is required on the autocovariances $\gamma_i\left(t,s\right)$ for the FE estimator to remain consistent.

Remark 42.4. Here, we only discussed fully parametric methods. With large T, it is possible to take into account the large time dimension and consider non or semi-parametric models, which impose less restrictive conditions. For a review, see the work of Fernández-Val and Weidner (2018).

From Remark 42.1, we can write $E(u_i u_i') = \Omega_i$. Since for each individual we allow the errors to be serially correlated, Ω_i is not diagonal. Also, Ω_i is indexed by i since the serial correlation can vary across individuals. The matrix $E(uu'|X) = \Omega$ is block diagonal with Ω_i on the main diagonal blocks. Hence,

$$V_{FE,NT} = E[(NT)^{-1} X' Q \Omega Q X],$$

where $Q = I_{NT} - P$ with $P = I_N \otimes J_T/T$ and J_T a matrix with all entries equal to 1. Intuitively, the matrix P takes the average across time and the matrix Q demeans the observations. Given the block diagonality of Ω, we can write

$$\begin{aligned} E[X'Q\Omega QX] &= E\left[E\left[\sum_{i=1}^{N}(X_i' Q_T \Omega_i Q_T X_i)|X\right]\right] \\ &= \sum_{i=1}^{N} E(X_i' Q_T \Omega_i Q_T X_i). \end{aligned}$$

From Chapter 11, we know that we can consistently estimate each component $E(X_i' Q_T \Omega_i Q_T X_i)$ using

$$S_{i,T} = R_{i,T}(0) + \sum_{j=1}^{T-1} w_i(j,m)[R_{i,T}(j) + R_{i,T}(j)'],$$

where $R_{i,T}(j) = T^{-1}\sum_{j=1}^{T-j} \hat{v}_{it}\hat{v}_{it+j}$ with $\hat{v}_{it} = (x_{it} - \bar{x}_i)(\hat{u}_{it} - \bar{\hat{u}}_t)$. Note that $(\hat{u}_{it} - \bar{\hat{u}}_t) = (y_{it} - \bar{y}_i) - \hat{\beta}_{FE}(x_{it} - \bar{x}_i)$. Hence, a consistent estimate of $plim_{T\to\infty} V_{FE,NT}$ is

$$S_T = N^{-1}\sum_{i=1}^{N} S_{i,T}.$$

For refinements, such as small sample corrections and choices of the weighting function and the bandwidth m, see Chapter 11.

42.1.3 Random effect specification

The Random Effect (RE) specification assumes that the individual-specific effects α_i are independent of the regressors x_i. The model can then be written as

$$y_{it} = \beta' x_{it} + v_{it},$$

where

$$v_{it} = \alpha_i + u_{it}.$$

The full set of required conditions are the following:

Assumption 42.7 (RE.1). (a) $E(u_{it}|X_i, \alpha_i) = 0$. (b) $E(\alpha_i|X_i) = 0$, for all i and t.

Assumption 42.8 (RE.2). (a) $E(u_i u_i'|X_i, \alpha_i) = \sigma^2 I_T$. (b) $E(\alpha_i^2|X_i) = \sigma_\alpha^2$, for all i.

Note that Assumption RE.1 is more restrictive than needed for a pooled OLS analysis. However, the random effect approach is of interest as it exploits the cross-sectional correlation in the composite error, $v_{it} = \alpha_i + u_{it}$, in a generalized least squares (GLS) framework. It, however, does not exploit the temporal serial correlation in the errors u_{it}. Let $v_i = (v_{i1}, \ldots, v_{iT})'$. Note that under RE.2, we restrict the analysis to the case with no temporal serial correlation. This is relaxed later. The main distinction between fixed and random effects is whether the unobserved individual effects are composed of factors uncorrelated with the regressors, whether or not these effects are stochastic. An advantage of random effects is that one can include time-invariant variables (e.g., gender). In the fixed effects model such variables are absorbed by the intercept.

Under Assumptions RE.1 and RE.2, which abstract from temporal serial correlation in the errors:

$$E\left(v_{it}^2\right) = \sigma_\alpha^2 + \sigma^2 + 2\,\mathrm{Cov}\left(\alpha_i, u_{it}\right) = \sigma_\alpha^2 + \sigma^2$$

and

$$E\left(v_{it}v_{is}\right) = E\left[\left(\alpha_i + u_{it}\right)\left(\alpha_i + u_{is}\right)\right] = \sigma_\alpha^2, \quad \text{for } t \neq s.$$

Hence,

$$\Omega_v = E\left(v_i v_i'\right) = \left(\sigma_\alpha^2 + \sigma^2\right)\begin{pmatrix} 1 & \rho & \cdots & \rho \\ \rho & 1 & \cdots & \rho \\ \vdots & \vdots & \ddots & \vdots \\ \rho & \rho & \cdots & 1 \end{pmatrix}, \tag{42.7}$$

where

$$\rho = \frac{\sigma_\alpha^2}{\sigma_\alpha^2 + \sigma^2}.$$

Note that the presence of time-invariant effects, α_i, introduces contemporaneous correlation among regression errors belonging to the same individual i, although the errors between different individuals $j \neq i$ are independent. Thus, a GLS estimator needs to be used to obtain an efficient estimator of β, which is given by

$$\hat{\beta}_{RE} = \left(\sum_{i=1}^{N} X_i'\Omega_v^{-1}X_i\right)^{-1} \sum_{i=1}^{N} X_i'\Omega_v^{-1}y_i.$$

Feasible GLS

In order to ensure the consistency of the feasible GLS estimator, we need some form of strict exogeneity between the explanatory variables and the composite error. This is ensured by Assumption RE.1, which implies $E(v_{it}|X_t) = 0$, $t = 1, \ldots, T$, so that the regressors X_t are exogenous. A general estimator of Ω is

$$\hat{\Omega} = N^{-1}\sum_{i=1}^{N} \tilde{v}_i\tilde{v}_i',$$

where $\tilde{v}_i$ are the pooled OLS residuals. The resulting FGLS estimator is

$$\hat{\beta}_{RE} = \left(\sum_{i=1}^{N} X_i'\hat{\Omega}_v^{-1}X_i\right)^{-1}\sum_{i=1}^{N} X_i'\hat{\Omega}_v^{-1}y_i. \tag{42.8}$$

Under Assumption RE.1, the FGLS estimator (42.8) is consistent. If we further assume RE.2, then the FGLS estimator is asymptotically efficient and its asymptotic variance estimator takes the usual form, i.e.,

$$plim_{N\to\infty}\mathrm{Var}(\hat{\beta}_{RE}) = plim_{N\to\infty}\left(N^{-1}\sum_{i=1}^{N} X_i'\Omega_v^{-1}X_i\right)^{-1}.$$

Note that $\hat{\Omega}_v$ is robust in the sense that if Assumption RE.2 fails, and the errors u_{it} are heteroskedastic and serially correlated across t, $\hat{\Omega}_v$ remains consistent. Under Assumption RE.2, Ω_v given by (42.7) can be directly estimated using

$$\hat{\sigma}^2 = (NT-k)^{-1}\sum_{i=1}^{N}\sum_{t=1}^{T}\tilde{v}_i^2,$$

which is the usual variance estimator from the OLS regression on the pooled data. A consistent estimator of $\sigma_\alpha^2 = E(v_{it}v_{is})$, for all $t \neq s$, is

$$\hat{\sigma}_\alpha^2 = (NT(T-1)/2-k)^{-1}\sum_{i=1}^{N}\sum_{t=1}^{T-1}\sum_{s=t+1}^{T}\tilde{v}_{it}\tilde{v}_{is}. \tag{42.9}$$

The resulting estimate of Ω_v is $\tilde{\Omega}_v$. With large N asymptotics, the general FGLS estimator (42.8) is just as efficient as the RE estimator using $\tilde{\Omega}_v$ when Assumptions RE.1–RE.2 hold.

42.1.4 Testing for the presence of unobserved effects

If the random effect Assumptions RE.1–RE.2 hold but the model does not actually contain unobserved individual-specific effects, pooled OLS is efficient and its associated inference remains asymptotically valid. The absence of an unobserved effect is statistically equivalent to $H_0 : \sigma_\alpha^2 = 0$. We can construct a test of H_0 based on the estimate of σ_α^2 in equation (42.9). The test statistic is

$$\frac{\sum_{i=1}^{N}\sum_{t=1}^{T-1}\sum_{s=t+1}^{T}\tilde{v}_{it}\tilde{v}_{is}}{\left[\sum_{i=1}^{N}\left(\sum_{t=1}^{T-1}\sum_{s=t+1}^{T}\tilde{v}_{it}\tilde{v}_{is}\right)^2\right]}.$$

Under the null hypothesis that the v_{it} are serially uncorrelated, this statistic has a standard normal asymptotic distribution.

42.2 Dynamic panel data models

Many economic relationships are dynamic in nature, namely those for which the data generating process is a panel containing lagged dependent variables. One of the advantages of panel data is that they allow the researcher to better understand the dynamics of adjustment. Dynamic panels are used often; e.g., the work of Baltagi and Levin (1986) on dynamic demand for an addictive commodity like cigarettes, the work of Arellano and Bond (1991) on a dynamic model of employment, the work of Blundell *et al.* (1992) on a dynamic model of company investment, the work of Ziliak (1997) on a dynamic life cycle labor supply model, and the work of Acemoglu *et al.* (2005) on a dynamic model relating democracy to education.

The presence of lagged dependent variables as regressors creates some complications. Strict exogeneity of the regressors does not hold, and the pooled OLS and FE estimators are no longer consistent in the case of panel data models where the number of cross-section units, N, is large and T is small. The second complication arises due to the non-vanishing effects of the initial values and assumptions about these initial observations play a crucial role in interpreting the model and formulating consistent estimators. Note that some of the materials in this section were covered in Chapter 30; we include a brief discussion to ease the presentation.

In particular, some of the procedures discussed in this section were covered in Section 30.4. Here, we cover a more general class of estimators. Also, we highlight what can be done with arbitrary serial correlation in the errors, given that a large T framework allows us to account for such features.

42.2.1 Dynamic panels with small T and large N

Consider the dynamic panel model

$$y_{it} = \alpha_i + \lambda y_{it-1} + \beta' x_{it} + u_{it}, \quad i = 1, \dots, N; \;\; t = 1, \dots, T, \tag{42.10}$$

where the k-dimensional vector of regressors x_{it} is assumed to be exogenous, namely $E(u_{it}|x_{js}) = 0$, for all i, j, t, and s, and α_i are the individual-specific effects. Note that even if the error term u_{it} is not serially correlated, the fixed-effect (FE) estimator is inconsistent. To see this, note that $(y_{it-1} - \bar{y}_{i,-1})$, where $\bar{y}_{i,-1} = (T-1)^{-1} \sum_{t=2}^{T} y_{it-1}$ is correlated with $(u_{it} - \bar{u}_i)$ as y_{it-1} is correlated with $\bar{u}_i$. Moreover, u_{it} is also correlated with $\bar{y}_{i,-1}$ as y_{it} is contained in this average. Nickell (1981) showed that the FE estimator is biased of order $O(1/T)$ and it is inconsistent for N large and T small. However, as T gets large, the fixed-effect estimator becomes consistent.

To avoid the small T bias, alternative transformations of the regression equation for eliminating the individual-specific effects α_i are required. Anderson and Hsiao (1982) suggested first differencing the model to get rid of α_i and then using $\Delta y_{it-2} = (y_{it-2} - y_{it-3})$ or y_{it-2} as an instrument for Δy_{it-1}. Note that these instruments will not be correlated with Δu_{it} as long as u_{it} is not serially correlated. This instrumental variable (IV) estimation method leads to consistent but not necessarily efficient estimates of the parameters in the model because it does not make use of all the available moment conditions; see the work of Ahn and Schmidt (1995). It does not take into account the differenced structure on the errors Δu_{it}.

Arellano and Bond (1991) proposed a generalized method of moments (GMM) procedure that is more efficient than the Anderson and Hsiao (1982) estimator. Additional nonlinear moment restrictions were exploited by Ahn and Schmidt (1995). The GMM procedure has been widely generalized and extended in the literature; e.g., Arellano and Bover (1995) and Blundell and Bond (1998). Keane and

Runkle (1992) proposed an alternative method of estimation of the dynamic panel data model, based on a forward filtering.

42.2.2 The Arellano and Bond estimator

Arellano and Bond (1991) exploited orthogonality conditions that exist between lagged values of y_{it} and the disturbances u_{it}. They suggest using a GMM approach based on all available moment conditions. Write the dynamic panel as

$$y_{it} = \lambda y_{it-1} + \beta' x_{it} + \nu_{it}, \quad i = 1, \ldots, N; \;\; t = 1, \ldots, T,$$

where $\nu_{it} = \alpha_i + u_{it}$ with $\alpha_i \sim i.i.d.(0, \sigma_\alpha^2)$ and $u_{it} \sim i.i.d.(0, \sigma_u^2)$, independent of each other. It is also assumed that u_{it} is uncorrelated with y_{i0} for all t. The goal is to obtain a consistent estimate of λ as $N \to \infty$ with T fixed. The first step is to eliminate the individual-specific effects by taking first differences:

$$\Delta y_{it} = \lambda \Delta y_{it-1} + \beta' \Delta x_{it} + \Delta u_{it}, \quad i = 1, \ldots, N; \;\; t = 1, \ldots, T. \tag{42.11}$$

However, note that

$$E(\Delta y_{it-1} \Delta u_{it}) = E(\lambda \Delta u_{it-1} \Delta u_{it}) \neq 0,$$

and thus the OLS estimate of the first differenced model (42.11) would not be consistent. Moreover, note that even if the error term u_{it} is serially uncorrelated, Δu_{it} will be serially correlated since $E\left(\Delta u_{it} \Delta u_{i,t-s}\right) = -\sigma_u^2$, for $s = 1$ and 0, for $s > 1$. To deal with the problem of the correlation between Δy_{it-1} and Δu_{it}, Arellano and Bond (1991) suggested using an over-identified IV approach. To derive the moment conditions, note from the first differenced model (42.11) that for $t = 3$, we have

$$\Delta y_{i3} = \lambda \Delta y_{i2} + \beta' \Delta x_{i3} + \Delta u_{i3}, \quad i = 1, , \ldots, N.$$

In this case, y_{i1} is a valid instrument since it is highly correlated with Δy_{i2} and not correlated with Δu_{i3} as long as u_{it} is not serially correlated. For $t = 4$, we have

$$\Delta y_{i4} = \lambda \Delta y_{i3} + \beta' \Delta x_{i4} + \Delta u_{i4}, \quad i = 1, \ldots, N,$$

and in this case, y_{i2} as well as y_{i1} are valid instruments for Δy_{i3} since both y_{i2} and y_{i1} are not correlated with Δu_{i4}. In general, for period T, the set of valid instruments becomes $(y_{i1}, \ldots, y_{iT-2})$. Clearly, the appropriate instruments for Δx_{it} are themselves since it assumed that the regressors x_{it} are exogenous. Hence, there is a total of $T(T-1)/2$ available moment conditions for y_{it-1} that are given by

$$E\left[y_{is}\left(\Delta y_{it} - \lambda \Delta y_{i,t-1} - \beta' \Delta x_{it}\right)\right] = 0,$$
$$s = 0, 1, \ldots, t-2; \;\; t = 2, \ldots, T.$$

Write the first differenced model (42.11) as

$$\Delta y_i = \lambda \Delta y_{i,-1} + \Delta X_i \beta + \Delta u_i,$$

where

$$\Delta y_i = \begin{pmatrix} \Delta y_{i2} \\ \vdots \\ \Delta y_{iT} \end{pmatrix}, \quad \Delta X_i = \begin{pmatrix} \Delta x'_{i2} \\ \vdots \\ \Delta x'_{iT} \end{pmatrix},$$

$$\Delta y_{i,-1} = \begin{pmatrix} \Delta y_{i1} \\ \vdots \\ \Delta y_{i,t-1} \\ \vdots \\ \Delta y_{i,T-1} \end{pmatrix}, \quad \Delta u_i = \begin{pmatrix} \Delta u_{i2} \\ \vdots \\ \Delta u_{it} \\ \vdots \\ \Delta u_{iT} \end{pmatrix}.$$

Let

$$W_{Ni} = \begin{pmatrix} y_{i1} & 0 & \cdots & 0 \\ 0 & y_{i1}, y_{i2} & \cdots & 0 \\ \vdots & \vdots & \ddots & \vdots \\ 0 & 0 & \cdots & y_{i1}, \ldots, y_{i,T-2} \end{pmatrix}.$$

Then, the matrix of instruments is $W = [W'_1, \ldots, W'_N]'$ and the moment conditions can be expressed as

$$E\left(W_{N}{}'_{i} \Delta u_i\right) = 0.$$

These moment conditions have also been suggested by Holtz-Eakin *et al.* (1988) and Ahn and Schmidt (1995). The complete set of instruments is $Z = (W, \Delta X)$. Note that the moment conditions $E(Z'\Delta u) = 0$ still do not account for the serial correlation in the differenced error Δu. In fact,

$$E\left(Z'uu'Z\right) = Z'\left[\sigma_u^2\left(I_N \otimes A\right)\right] Z,$$

where

$$\underset{(T-2)\times(T-2)}{A} = \begin{pmatrix} 2 & -1 & \cdots & 0 & 0 \\ -1 & 2 & \cdots & 0 & 0 \\ \vdots & \ddots & \ddots & \ddots & \vdots \\ 0 & 0 & \cdots & 2 & -1 \\ 0 & 0 & \cdots & -1 & 2 \end{pmatrix}.$$

The Arellano and Bond (1991) optimal GMM consistent estimator for $\gamma = (\lambda, \beta)$ is

$$\hat{\gamma}_{GMM} = \left(G'ZS_NZ'G\right)^{-1} G'ZS_NZ'\Delta y, \tag{42.12}$$

where $G = (\Delta y_{-1}, \Delta X)$ and

$$S_N = \left(\sum_{i=1}^{N} Z_i'\tilde{u}_i\tilde{u}_i'Z_i\right),$$

with $\tilde{u}_i$ the residuals obtained from the following first-step consistent estimate:

$$\tilde{\gamma} = \left[G'Z(Z'(I_N \otimes A)Z)^{-1}Z'G\right]^{-1} G'Z(Z'(I_N \otimes A)Z)^{-1}Z'\Delta y.$$

Testing for Over-Identification Restrictions

Given the moment conditions $E(W_i'\Delta u_i) = 0$, Arellano and Bond (1991) suggested the following Sargan test for over-identifying restrictions:

$$M_N = \Delta\hat{u}'W\left[\sum_{i=1}^{N} W_i'\left(\Delta\hat{u}_i\right)\left(\Delta\hat{u}_i\right)' W_i\right]^{-1} W'(\Delta\hat{u}) \sim \chi^2_{p-K},$$

under the null hypothesis, where p refers to the number of columns of W and $\hat{u}_i$ are the residuals from the two-step Arellano and Bond estimator.

42.2.3 The Ahn and Schmidt moment conditions

Ahn and Schmidt (1995) showed that under the standard assumptions used in a dynamic panel data model, there are $T-2$ additional nonlinear moment conditions that were ignored by the Arellano and Bond (1991) estimator. These moment conditions are implied by the assumptions about the error term u_{it}: (i) $u_{it} \sim i.i.d.(0, \sigma_u^2)$, so that u_{it} is serially uncorrelated, and (ii) u_{it} is independent of α_i and y_{i0} for all t. Thus, the additional moment conditions are

$$E(\nu_{iT}\Delta\nu_{it}) = 0, \quad t = 2, \ldots, T-1.$$

These moments can be combined with the moment conditions already introduced by Arellano and Bond (1991), and further instruments can be added to Z. The computation of the GMM estimator (42.12) then proceeds exactly as described above.

42.2.4 The Arellano and Bover estimator

Arellano and Bover (1995) considered the Hausman and Taylor (1981) model, a general dynamic panel data model with time-invariant regressors,

$$y_{it} = \beta' x_{it} + \gamma' z_i + \nu_{it}, \quad i = 1, \ldots, N; \; t = 1, \ldots, T, \tag{42.13}$$

where $\nu_{it} = \alpha_i + u_{it}$, z_i is a vector of time-invariant regressors and x_{it} is allowed to contain lagged dependent variables. We can rewrite model (42.13) in vector form:

$$y_i = W_i\eta + \nu_i, \quad i = 1, \ldots, N, \tag{42.14}$$

where $\nu_i = \alpha_i\iota_T + u_i$, $W_i = (x_i, \iota_T z_i')$ and ι_T is a vector of ones of dimension T. The literature emphasizes two cases with cross-sectional homoskedasticity:

- Case 1: $E(\nu_i\nu_i') = \Omega$ independent of w_i, where allowance is made for an arbitrary covariance matrix Ω as long as it is the same across $i = 1, \ldots, N$.

- Case 2: The traditional error component model where $\Omega = \sigma_\alpha^2 I_T + \sigma_u^2 \iota_T \iota_T'$.

Arellano and Bover (1995) transformed the system of T equations in (42.13) using the non-singular transformation

$$H = \begin{bmatrix} C \\ \iota_T'/T \end{bmatrix},$$

where C is any $(T-1)\times T$ matrix of rank $(T-1)$ such that $C\iota_T = 0$. For example, C could be the first $(T-1)$ rows of the first difference operator. The transformed disturbances are

$$\nu_i^* = Hu_i = \begin{bmatrix} C\nu_i \\ \bar{\nu}_i \end{bmatrix}.$$

Note that the first $(T-1)$ elements of ν_i^* do not contain α_i. Hence, all exogenous variables are valid instruments for these first $(T-1)$ equations of the transformed model. Let $w_i = (x_i', z_i')'$ and let m_i denote the subset of variables of w_i assumed to be uncorrelated in levels with α_i and such that $rank(m_i) \geq rank(z_i)$. A valid matrix of instruments for the complete transformed system is given by

$$M_i = \begin{pmatrix} W_{Ni}' & 0 & \dots & 0 & 0 \\ 0 & W_{Ni}' & \dots & & \\ \vdots & \vdots & \ddots & \vdots & \vdots \\ & & \dots & W_{Ni}' & 0 \\ 0 & 0 & \dots & 0 & m_i' \end{pmatrix},$$

and the associated moment conditions are given by

$$E\left(M_i H \nu_i\right) = 0.$$

Let

$$\begin{aligned} H^* &= (I_N \otimes H), \\ \Omega^* &= (I_N \otimes \Omega), \\ W^* &= \left(W_1^{*\prime}, \dots, W_N^{*\prime}\right)', \\ M &= (M_1', \dots, M_N')'. \end{aligned}$$

Pre-multiplying (42.14) by $M'H^*$, we get

$$M'H^*y = M'H^*W\eta + M'H^*\nu. \tag{42.15}$$

The Arellano and Bover (1995) GMM estimator based on the above moment restrictions is the GLS estimator of equation (42.15):

$$\begin{aligned}\hat{\delta} &= \left[X^{*\prime}H^{*\prime}M\left(M'H^*\Omega^*H^{*\prime}M\right)^{-1}M'H^*X^*\right]^{-1} \\ &\quad \times \left[X^{*\prime}H^{*\prime}M\left(M'H^*\Omega^*H^{*\prime}M\right)^{-1}M'H^*y\right]. \end{aligned} \tag{42.16}$$

In practice, the covariance matrix of the transformed system, $S = H^*\Omega^*H^{*\prime}$, will be replaced by a consistent estimator of S, usually

$$\hat{S} = N^{-1}\sum_{i=1}^{N}\tilde{\nu}_i^*\tilde{\nu}_i^{*\prime},$$

where $\tilde{\nu}_i^*$ are the residuals from a consistent preliminary estimate. Arellano and Bover (1995) showed that since the set of instruments, M_i, is block-diagonal, the GMM estimator (42.16) is invariant to the choice of C.

42.2.5 The Keane and Runkle estimator

Keane and Runkle (1992) considered a dynamic panel data model in which the error term is allowed to be serially correlated and the instruments are simply required to be predetermined, i.e., without the need for an exogeneity assumption. The model is

$$\begin{aligned} y_{it} &= \beta' x_{it} + \nu_{it}, \\ \nu_{it} &= \alpha_i + u_{it}, \end{aligned} \tag{42.17}$$

where x_{it} is allowed to contain lagged dependent variables and

$$E\left(\nu_{it}|x_{it}\right) \neq 0.$$

The set of instruments, z_i, is required to be predetermined, i.e.,

$$\begin{aligned} E\left(\nu_{it}|z_{is}\right) &= 0, \quad \text{for } s \leq t, \\ E\left(\nu_{it}|z_{is}\right) &\neq 0, \quad \text{for } s > t. \end{aligned}$$

Note that z_{it} is thus allowed to contain lagged values of y_{it}. Let $\nu_i = (\nu_{i1}, \ldots, \nu_{iT})'$, with $\Sigma = E(\nu_i \nu_i')$ no longer constrained to be equal to A as in the case of the Arellano and Bond (1991) estimator. In this setting, 2SLS procedures will not be efficient. Keane and Runkle (1992) suggested an alternative efficient estimator by applying the forward filtering approach suggested by Hayashi and Sims (1983) (see Section 13.5) to the model:

$$y = X\beta + v, \tag{42.18}$$

where $y = (y_{1.,}, \ldots, y_N)'$ and $X = (x_1', \ldots, x_N')'$. Forward filtering eliminates the general serial correlation pattern in the data while preserving the use of predetermined instruments in obtaining consistent parameter estimates. The estimation procedure is as follows. First, using the Cholesky decomposition

$$\Sigma^{-1} = P'P,$$

where P is an upper triangular matrix. Next, we pre-multiply equation (42.18) by $Q = I_N \otimes P$, yielding

$$Qy = QX\beta + Qu.$$

Then, β is estimated by $2SLS$, using the untransformed instrument set Z, namely

$$\hat{\beta}_{KR} = \left(X'Q'P_z QX\right)^{-1} X'Q'P_z Qy, \tag{42.19}$$

where $P_z = Z(Z'Z)^{-1} Z'$ is the projection matrix for the set of instruments Z. The variance covariance matrix Σ can be estimated using consistent IV residuals from a preliminary estimation

$$\hat{\Sigma} = N^{-1} \sum_{i=1}^{N} \tilde{\nu}_i' \tilde{\nu}_i,$$

where $\tilde{\nu}_i$ are the preliminary IV residuals.

42.3 Heterogeneous panel data models

In the previous sections, we have assumed slope homogeneity across cross-sectional observations and that any remaining heterogeneity over the cross-sectional units can be modeled through an additive intercept and possibly heteroskedastic errors. This section extends the analysis to linear panel data models with slope heterogeneity. To deal with slope heterogeneity, especially in dynamic models, it is often necessary to assume that the number of time-series observations is relatively large.

Even with slope heterogeneity, the cross-sectional units could share common features of interest. For example, different countries or geographical regions may have different dynamics of adjustments toward equilibrium due to historical and cultural differences, but they could all converge to the same economic equilibrium in the long run. Other examples include cases where slope coefficients can be viewed as random draws from a distribution with a number of parameters that are bounded. Many panel datasets fit within this setup, where the cross-sectional units may be industries, regions, or countries, and we wish to identify common patterns of responses across otherwise heterogeneous units. The parameters of interest may be intercepts, short-run and long-run coefficients, or error variances.

42.3.1 The Swamy estimator

Suppose that the variable y_{it} for the ith unit at time t is specified as a linear function of k strictly exogenous variables, x_{kit} $(k = 1, \dots, k)$, is given by

$$y_{it} = \beta_{it}' X_{it} + u_{it}, i = 1, \dots, N, \quad t = 1, \dots, T, \tag{42.20}$$

where u_{it} denotes a serially uncorrelated random error term, x_{it} is a $k \times 1$ vector of exogenous variables, and β_{it} is a $k \times 1$ vector of coefficients. The above specification is very general and allows the coefficients to vary both across time and over individual units. As specified, it is too general and not estimable, as the number of parameters to be estimated exceeds the number of observations. For a model to become interesting and to acquire explanatory and predictive power, it is essential that some structure be imposed on the parameters.

One way to reduce the number of parameters in this model is to adopt a random coefficient approach, which assumes that the coefficients β_{it} are draws from probability distributions with a fixed number of parameters that do not vary with N and/or T. Depending on the type of assumption about the parameter variation, we can classify the models into one of two categories: stationary and non-stationary random-coefficient models.

The stationary random-coefficient models view the coefficients as having constant means and variance–covariances. Namely, the $k \times 1$ vector β_{it} is specified as

$$\beta_{it} = \beta + \eta_{it} \quad (i = 1, \ldots, N, \quad t = 1, \ldots, T),$$

where β is a $k \times 1$ vector of constants, and η_{it} is a $k \times 1$ vector of stationary random variables with zero means and constant variance–covariances. One widely used random coefficient specification is the Swamy (1970) model, which assumes that the randomness is time-invariant, in which case

$$\beta_{it} = \beta + \eta_i, \quad (i = 1, \ldots, N, \quad t = 1, \ldots, T)$$

and

$$\begin{aligned} E(\eta_i) &= 0, \\ E\left(\eta_i x'_{it}\right) &= 0, \quad \text{for all } t, \\ E(\eta_i \eta_j) &= \begin{cases} \Omega_\eta, & \text{if } i = j, \\ 0, & \text{if } i \neq j. \end{cases} \end{aligned}$$

Substituting $\beta_{it} = \beta + \eta_i$ in equation (42.20) yields

$$y_i = x_i \beta + v_i,$$

where $y_i = (y_{i1}, \ldots, y_{iT})'$ and $X_i = (x'_{i1}, \ldots, x'_{iT})'$, where the error term is

$$v_i = x\eta_i + \varepsilon_i.$$

The covariance matrix of v_i is

$$\Sigma_i = \mathrm{Var}(v_i) = \sigma_i^2 I_T + X_i \Omega_\eta X'_i.$$

For known values of Ω_η and σ_i^2, the best linear unbiased estimator of β is given by the generalized least squares (GLS) estimator, known in this case as the Swamy estimator:

$$\hat{\beta}_{SW} = \left(\sum_{i=1}^{N} X_i' \Sigma_i^{-1} X_i \right)^{-1} \sum_{i=1}^{N} X_i' \Sigma_i^{-1} y_i.$$

Under the assumption that Ω_η is non-singular, it can be shown that we can write the averaged Swamy estimator across individuals i as

$$\overline{\hat{\beta}}_{SW} = \sum_{i=1}^{N} R_i \hat{\beta}_i, \tag{42.21}$$

where

$$R_i = \left[\sum_{i=1}^{N} \left(\Omega_\eta + \Sigma_{\hat{\beta}_i} \right)^{-1} \right]^{-1} \left(\Omega_\eta + \Sigma_{\hat{\beta}_i} \right)^{-1}$$

and

$$\hat{\beta}_i = \left(X_i' X_i \right)^{-1} X_i' y_i,$$
$$\Sigma_{\hat{\beta}_i} = \mathrm{Var}(\hat{\beta}_i) = \sigma_i^2 \left(X_i' X_i \right)^{-1}.$$

This expression shows that the Swamy estimator is a matrix weighted average of the least squares estimator for each cross-sectional unit, with the weights inversely proportional to their covariance matrices. The covariance matrix of the estimator is

$$\mathrm{Var}(\overline{\hat{\beta}}_{SW}) = \left(\sum_{i=1}^{N} X_i' \Sigma_i^{-1} X_i \right)^{-1} = \left[\sum_{i=1}^{N} \left(\Omega_\eta + \Sigma_{\hat{\beta}_i} \right)^{-1} \right]^{-1}.$$

If the errors u_{it} and η_i are normally distributed, the SW estimator is the same as the maximum likelihood (ML) estimator of β conditional on Ω_η and σ_i^2. Without knowledge of Ω_η and σ_i^2, we can estimate β, Ω_η, and σ_i^2 $(i = 1, \ldots, N)$ simultaneously using a maximum likelihood procedure.

42.3.2 The mean group estimator

One alternative to Swamy's estimator of β given by (42.21) is the mean group (MG) estimator, proposed by Pesaran and Smith (1995) for the estimation of dynamic random coefficient models. The MG estimator is defined as the simple average of the OLS estimators, $\hat{\beta}_i$:

$$\hat{\beta}_{MG} = N^{-1} \sum_{i=1}^{N} \hat{\beta}_i,$$

where

$$\hat{\beta}_i = \left(X_i' X_i \right)^{-1} X_i' y_i.$$

MG estimation is possible when both T and N are sufficiently large and is applicable irrespective of whether the slope coefficients are random (in Swamy's sense), or fixed in the sense that the diversity in the slope coefficients across cross-sectional units cannot be captured by means of a finite parameter probability distribution. Let

$$Q_{iT} = \frac{X_i' X_i}{T\sigma_i^2} \quad \text{and} \quad q_{iT} = \frac{X_i' y_i}{T\sigma_i^2}.$$

To compute the variance of the MG estimator, first note that from (42.20),

$$\begin{aligned}
\hat{\beta}_i &= \left(X_i' X_i \right)^{-1} X_i' y_i \\
&= \left(X_i' X_i \right)^{-1} X_i' \left(X_i \beta + X_i \eta + \varepsilon_i \right) \\
&= \beta + \eta_i + \xi_i,
\end{aligned}$$

where

$$\xi_i = \left(X_i' X_i \right)^{-1} X_i' \varepsilon_i.$$

Thus, we can write

$$\hat{\beta}_{MG} = \beta + \bar{\eta} + \bar{\xi}, \tag{42.22}$$

with

$$\bar{\eta} = N^{-1}\sum_{i=1}^{N}\eta_i, \quad \bar{\xi} = N^{-1}\sum_{i=1}^{N}\xi_i.$$

Hence, when the regressors are strictly exogenous and the errors, u_{it}, are independently distributed, the variance of $\hat{\beta}_{MG}$ is

$$\begin{aligned}\text{Var}(\hat{\beta}_{MG}) &= \text{Var}(\bar{\eta}) + \text{Var}(\bar{\xi}) \\ &= N^{-1}\Omega_\eta + N^{-2}\sum_{i=1}^{N}\sigma_i^2 E\left[\left(T^{-1}X_i'X_i\right)^{-1}\right].\end{aligned}$$

An estimator of the covariance matrix of $\hat{\beta}_{MG}$ is given by

$$\widehat{\text{Var}}(\hat{\beta}_{MG}) = [N(N-1)]^{-1}\sum_{i=1}^{N}(\hat{\beta}_i - \hat{\beta}_{MG})(\hat{\beta}_i - \hat{\beta}_{MG})'.$$

The Swamy and MG estimators are algebraically equivalent when T is sufficiently large. First, note that we can write $\hat{\beta}_{SW}$ as

$$\begin{aligned}\hat{\beta}_{SW} = &\left\{\sum_{i=1}^{N}\left[Q_{iT} - \left(I_k + (\lambda/T)AQ_{iT}^{-1}\right)^{-1}Q_{jT}\right]\right\}^{-1} \\ &\times \sum_{i=1}^{N}\left[q_{iT} - \left(I_k + (\lambda/T)AQ_{iT}^{-1}\right)^{-1}q_{iT}\right],\end{aligned}$$

when we replace Ω_η^{-1} by

$$\Omega_\eta^{-1} = \lambda A,$$

where λ represents an overall index of parameter heterogeneity, such that $\lambda \to 0$ implies the highest degree of heterogeneity. For fixed N and T, and for a sufficiently small λ, we have

$$\left(I_k + (\lambda/T)AQ_{iT}^{-1}\right)^{-1} = I_k - (\lambda/T)G_{iT} + (\lambda/T)^2 G_{iT}^2 - \cdots,$$

where $G_{iT} = AQ_{iT}^{-1}$. Therefore,

$$\hat{\beta}_{SW} = \left\{ \sum_{i=1}^{N} \left[Q_{iT} - \left(I_k - (\lambda/T)G_{iT} + (\lambda/T)^2 G_{iT}^2 + \cdots \right) Q_{iT} \right] \right\}^{-1}$$

$$\times \sum_{i=1}^{N} \left[q_{iT} - \left(I_k - (\lambda/T)G_{iT} + (\lambda/T)^2 G_{iT}^2 + \cdots \right) q_{iT} \right]$$

$$= \left\{ \sum_{i=1}^{N} G_{iT}Q_{iT} - (\lambda/T) \sum_{i=1}^{N} G_{iT}^2 Q_{iT} + O\left[(\lambda/T)^2\right] \right\}^{-1}$$

$$\times \left\{ \sum_{i=1}^{N} G_{iT}q_{iT} - (\lambda/T) \sum_{i=1}^{N} G_{iT}^2 q_{iT} + O\left[(\lambda/T)^2\right] \right\}.$$

Hence, for any fixed $T > k$ and for any N, as $\lambda \to 0$,

$$\hat{\beta}_{SW} = \left(\sum_{i=1}^{N} G_{iT}Q_{jT} \right)^{-1} \sum_{i=1}^{N} G_{iT}q_{iT} + o_p(1).$$

However, note that

$$\left(\sum_{i=1}^{N} G_{iT}Q_{jT} \right)^{-1} \sum_{i=1}^{N} G_{iT}q_{iT} = \left(\sum_{i=1}^{N} AQ_{iT}^{-1}Q_{iT} \right)^{-1} \sum_{i=1}^{N} AQ_{iT}^{-1}q_{iT}$$

$$= N^{-1} \sum_{i=1}^{N} Q_{iT}^{-1}q_{iT} = N^{-1} \sum_{i=1}^{N} \hat{\beta}_i = \hat{\beta}_{MG},$$

from which it follows that

$$\lim_{\lambda \to 0} \hat{\beta}_{SW}(\lambda) = \hat{\beta}_{MG}$$

and, for all values of N and $\lambda > 0$,

$$\lim_{T \to \infty} \left(\hat{\beta}_{SW}(\lambda) - \hat{\beta}_{MG} \right) = 0.$$

42.3.3 The pooled mean group estimator

The pooled mean group (PMG) estimator proposed by Pesaran *et al.* (1999) allows the intercepts, short-run coefficients, and error variances to differ freely across groups but constrains the long-run coefficients to be the same. Consider an autoregressive distributed lag (ARDL) model:

$$y_{it} = \sum_{j=1}^{p} \lambda_{ij} y_{i,t-j} + \sum_{j=0}^{q} \delta'_{ij} x_{i,t-j} + \alpha_i + u_{it},$$
$$i = 1, \ldots, N, \;\; t = 1, \ldots, T. \tag{42.23}$$

It is convenient to work with the following reparameterization of (42.23):

$$\Delta y_{it} = \phi_i y_{i,t-1} + \beta'_i x_{it} + \sum_{j=1}^{p-1} \lambda^*_{ij} \Delta y_{i,t-j} + \sum_{j=0}^{q-1} \delta^{*\prime}_{ij} \Delta x_{i,t-j} + \alpha_i + u_{it}, \tag{42.24}$$

$i = 1, \ldots, N, t = 1, \ldots, T$, where

$$\phi_i = \sum_{j=1}^{p} \lambda_{ij} - 1,$$

$$\beta_i = \sum_{j-0}^{q} \delta_{ij},$$

$$\lambda^*_{ij} = - \sum_{m=j+1}^{p} \lambda_{im}, \quad j = 1, \ldots, p-1,$$

$$\delta^*_{ij} = - \sum_{m=j+1}^{q} \delta_{im}, \quad j = 1, \ldots, q-1.$$

When the ARDL model (42.23) is stable in the sense that the roots of $\sum_{j=1}^{p} \lambda_{ij} z^j = 1$ lie outside the unit circle for each $i = 1, \ldots, N$, there exists a long-run relationship between y_{it} and x_{it} defined by

$$y_{it} = -(\beta_i'/\phi_i)x_{it} + \eta_{it},$$

where η_{it} is a stationary process. Pesaran *et al.* (1999) assumed that the long-run coefficients on x_{it}, defined by $\theta_i = -\beta_i/\phi_i$, are the same across the groups, namely

$$\theta_i = \theta, \quad i = 1, \ldots, N.$$

Let $y_{i,-j}$, $\Delta y_{i,-j}$, $X_{i,-j}$, and $\Delta X_{i,-j}$ be j period lagged values of y_i, Δy_i, X_i, and ΔX_i, respectively. Then, (42.24) can be written more compactly as

$$\Delta y_i = \phi_i(y_{i,-1} - X_i\theta) + W_i\kappa_i + u_i, \quad i = 1, \ldots, N, \tag{42.25}$$

where

$$\begin{aligned} W_i &= (\Delta y_{i,-1}, \ldots, \Delta y_{i,-p+1}, \Delta X_i, \Delta X_{i,-1}, \ldots, \Delta X_{i,-q+1}, \tau_T), \\ \kappa_i &= (\lambda_{i1}^*, \ldots, \lambda_{i,p-1}^*, \delta_{i0}', \delta_{i1}', \ldots, \delta_{i,q-1}', \alpha_i)'. \end{aligned}$$

Pesaran *et al.* (1999) adopted a likelihood approach to estimate the model. They assumed that u_{it} are independent across i and t and independent of x_{it}. Moreover, u_{it} is normally distributed with mean 0 and variances $\sigma_i^2 > 0$, although normality is not required for the asymptotic results. Write $\varphi = (\theta', \phi', \sigma')'$, where $\phi = (\phi_1, \ldots, \phi_N)'$ and $\sigma = (\sigma_1^2, \ldots, \sigma_N^2)'$. Given normality, the concentrated log-likelihood function is

$$\begin{aligned} l_T(\varphi) = -(T/2)\sum_{i=1}^{N} \ln(2\pi\sigma_i^2) - (1/2)\sum_{i=1}^{N}(\Delta y_i - \phi_i(y_{i,-1} - X_i\theta))' \\ \times H_i(\Delta y_i - \phi_i(y_{i,-1} - X_i\theta))/\sigma_i^2, \end{aligned}$$

where $H_i = I_T - W_i(W_i'W_i)^{-1}W_i'$. The resulting maximum likelihood estimators of the long-run coefficients, θ, and the group-specific error-correction coefficients, ϕ_i, are termed the pooled mean group (PMG) estimators. These can be computed using the Newton–Raphson algorithm, which makes use of both the first and second derivatives, or a "back-substitution" algorithm that makes use of only the first derivatives.

For θ, the PMG estimator $\hat{\theta}$ is consistent as long as $T \to \infty$, irrespective of whether N is large or not. When N is large, the asymptotic distribution of $\hat{\theta}$ as $T \to \infty$ depends on whether the regressors are $I(0)$ or $I(1)$. When the regressors are $I(0)$, $\hat{\theta}$ asymptotically has a normal distribution, and the rate of convergence is $\sqrt{NT}$. When the regressors are $I(1)$, $\hat{\theta}$ asymptotically has a mixture-normal distribution, and the rate of convergence is $T\sqrt{N}$. On the other hand, for large N and large T, given the PMG estimators $\hat{\phi}_i$, the mean of ϕ_i can be estimated consistently by $N^{-1}\sum_{i=1}^{N}\hat{\phi}_i$. This is in line with the mean group estimator.

42.4 Factor models

In the previous sections, we assumed cross-sectionally independent errors and homogeneous slopes. A panel regression combined with a factor structure (see Section 31.5) provides a comprehensive framework to consistently estimate the parameters of a panel model with cross-correlated errors or heterogeneous slopes. The primary interest is the estimation of the following dynamic panel model augmented with a factor structure:

$$y_{it} = \rho y_{it-1} + x_{it}'\beta + \delta_t + \gamma_i' f_t + u_{it}, \tag{42.26}$$

where γ_i and f_t are each $m \times 1$ and both are unobservable, δ_t is the time effect, and u_{it} is the error term. Note that model (42.26) allows multiple individual effects ($m \geq 1$) and non-constant effects ($f_t \neq 1$). The regressors (y_{it-1}, x_{it}) can be correlated with the factor loadings γ_i and the factors f_t. The major challenge is to deal with this correlation and how to obtain consistent estimation of the unknown parameters. We seek suitable formulations under which consistent estimation and inference can be conducted. We consider both fixed and large T.

This section reviews econometric methods for large linear panel data models subject to cross-sectional error dependence. Treating the error term from model (42.26) as $\nu_t = \gamma_i' f_t + u_t$, each cross-section shares the same f_t, a source of cross-correlation. Cross-correlations of the errors could be due to omitted common effects, spatial effects, or could arise as a result of interactions within socioeconomic networks. Conventional panel estimators such as fixed or random effects can result in misleading inference and inconsistent estimators, depending on the extent of the cross-sectional dependence and on whether the source generating the cross-sectional dependence (such as an unobserved common shock) is correlated with regressors; see, e.g., Phillips and Sul (2003) and Sarafidis and Robertson (2009).

Remark 42.5. It is possible to cast factor models into a state-space framework and obtain maximum likelihood estimates via the Kalman filter; see, e.g., Engle and Watson (1987) and Stock and Watson (1991). However, when N is large, the computational burden is significant. Hence, principal component-based approaches have become the main tool for estimation and we focus on them.

42.4.1 Standard panels with a factor structure

We consider the static panel model augmented with a factor structure:

$$y_{it} = \gamma_i' f_t + e_{it}, \tag{42.27}$$

where γ_i and f_t are each $m \times 1$ and both are unobservable and e_{it} is the error term. This model can be written more compactly as

$$y_t = \Gamma f_t + e_t,$$

where $f_t = (f_{1t}, \ldots, f_{mt})'$, $e_t = (e_{1t}, \ldots, e_{Nt})'$, and $\Gamma = (\gamma_{ij})$, for $i = 1, \ldots, N$, $j = 1, \ldots, m$, is an $N \times m$ matrix of fixed coefficients, known as factor loadings; see also Section 31.5. The common factors f_t simultaneously affect all cross-sectional units but with different degrees as measured by the coefficients $\gamma_i = (\gamma_{i1}, \ldots, \gamma_{im})'$. The following assumptions are imposed:

Assumption 42.9 (CF.1). The $m \times 1$ vector f_t is a zero mean covariance stationary process, with absolutely summable autocovariances, distributed independently of e_{is} for all i, t, s, such that $E\left(f_{\ell t}^2\right) = 1$ and $E\left(f_{\ell t} f_{\ell' t}\right) = 0$, for $\ell \neq \ell' = 1, \ldots, m$.

Assumption 42.10 (CF.2). $\text{Var}(e_{it}) = \sigma_i^2 < K < \infty$, e_{it} and e_{jt} are independently distributed for all $i \neq j$ and for all t.

Assumption CF.1 is an identification condition since it is not possible to separately identify f_t and Γ. The above factor model with a fixed number of factors and cross-sectionally independent idiosyncratic errors is often referred to as an exact factor model. Under the above assumptions, the covariance matrix of y_t is given by

$$E\left(y_t y_t'\right) = \Gamma\Gamma' + V,$$

where V is a diagonal matrix with elements σ_i^2. The assumption that the idiosyncratic errors e_{it} are cross-sectionally independent is not necessary and can be relaxed. The factor model that allows the idiosyncratic shocks e_{it} to be cross-sectionally weakly correlated is known as the approximate factor model; see Chamberlain (1983). In general, the correlation patterns of the idiosyncratic errors can be characterized by

$$e_t = R\varepsilon_t,$$

where $\varepsilon_t = (\varepsilon_{1t}, \ldots, \varepsilon_{Nt})' \sim (0, I_N)$. With this formulation $V = RR'$, which is no longer diagonal when R is not diagonal, and further identification restrictions are needed so that the factor specification can be distinguished from the cross-sectional dependence assumed for the idiosyncratic errors.

Definition 42.1. Let $0 < K < \infty$, the factor $f_{\ell t}$ is said to be strong if

$$\lim_{N\to\infty} N^{-1} \sum_{i=1}^{N} |\gamma_{i\ell}| = K.$$

The factor $f_{\ell t}$ is said to be weak if

$$\lim_{N\to\infty} \sum_{i=1}^{N} |\gamma_{i\ell}| = K < \infty.$$

The factor $f_{\ell t}$ is said to be semi-strong if

$$\lim_{N\to\infty} N^{-\alpha_\ell} \sum_{i=1}^{N} |\gamma_{i\ell}| = K < \infty,$$

for some constant α_ℓ in the range $0 < \alpha_\ell < 1$.

Weak, strong, and semi-strong common factors may be used to represent very general forms of cross-sectional dependence. For example, as we see in Section 42.5, a factor process with an infinite number of weak factors and no idiosyncratic errors can be used to represent spatial processes. Strong factors can be used to represent the effect of the cross-sectional units that are "dominant" or pervasive, in the sense that they impact all units in the sample and their effect does not vanish as N tends to infinity; see Chudik and Pesaran (2013). The presence of weak or semi-strong factors in errors does not affect consistency of conventional panel data estimators but affects inference, as is evident from the following example.

Example 42.1. Consider the following panel data model:

$$y_{it} = \beta x_{it} + u_{it},$$
$$u_{it} = \gamma_i f_t + \varepsilon_{it},$$

where

$$x_{it} = \delta_i f_t + v_{it}.$$

For ease of exposition, assume that $\varepsilon_{it} \sim i.i.d.\left(0, \sigma_\varepsilon^2\right)$, $v_{it} \sim i.i.d.\left(0, \sigma_v^2\right)$, and $f_t \sim i.i.d.(0, 1)$. The pooled estimator of β satisfies

$$\sqrt{NT}\left(\hat{\beta}_P - \beta\right) = \frac{(NT)^{-1/2} \sum_{i=1}^{N} \sum_{t=1}^{T} x_{it} u_{it}}{(NT)^{-1} \sum_{i=1}^{N} \sum_{t=1}^{T} x_{it}^2},$$

where the denominator converges in probability to

$$\sigma_v^2 + \lim_{N\to\infty} N^{-1} \sum_{i=1}^{N} \delta_i^2 > 0,$$

while the numerator can be expressed, after substituting for x_{it} and u_{it}, as

$$\begin{aligned}
&(NT)^{-1/2}\sum_{i=1}^{N}\sum_{t=1}^{T} x_{it}u_{it} \\
&= (NT)^{-1/2}\sum_{i=1}^{N}\sum_{t=1}^{T}\gamma_i\delta_i f_t^2 \\
&\quad + (NT)^{-1/2}\sum_{i=1}^{N}\sum_{t=1}^{T}(\delta_i f_t\varepsilon_{it} + \gamma_i v_{it} f_t + v_{it}\varepsilon_{it}). \qquad (42.28)
\end{aligned}$$

Under the stated assumptions, it is now easily seen that the second term in the above expression is $O_p(1)$, but the first term can be written as

$$\begin{aligned}
(NT)^{-1/2}\sum_{i=1}^{N}\sum_{t=1}^{T}\gamma_i\delta_i f_t^2 &= \left(N^{-1/2}\sum_{i=1}^{N}\gamma_i\delta_i\right)\times\left(T^{-1/2}\sum_{t=1}^{T} f_t^2\right) \\
&= \left(N^{-1/2}\sum_{i=1}^{N}\gamma_i\delta_i\right)\times O_p\left(T^{1/2}\right).
\end{aligned}$$

Now suppose that f_t is a factor with loadings γ_i given by

$$\gamma_i = \begin{cases} \mu + v_i, & i = 1,\ldots,[N^{\alpha_\gamma}], \\ 0, & i = [N^{\alpha_\gamma}]+1,\ldots,N, \end{cases}$$

for some constant $0 \leq \alpha_\gamma \leq 1$, $\mu \neq 0$, and $v_i \sim i.i.d.(0,\sigma_v^2)$. The loadings δ_i are given by

$$\delta_i = \begin{cases} \mu + v_i, & i = 1,\ldots,[N^{\alpha_\delta}], \\ 0, & i = [N^{\alpha_\delta}]+1,\ldots,N, \end{cases}$$

for some constant $0 \leq \alpha_\delta \leq 1$, $\mu \neq 0$, and $v_i \sim i.i.d.(0,\sigma_s^2)$. Let $\alpha = \min(\alpha_\gamma,\alpha_\delta)$. It then follows that $\sum_{i=1}^{N}\gamma_i\delta_i = O_p(N^\alpha)$, and

$$(NT)^{-1/2}\sum_{i=1}^{N}\sum_{t=1}^{T}\gamma_i\delta_i f_t^2 = O_p\left(N^{\alpha-1/2}T^{1/2}\right).$$

Therefore, even if $\alpha < 1$, the first term in (42.28) diverges, and overall we have

$$\hat{\beta}_P - \beta = O_p\left(N^{\alpha-1}\right) + O_p\left(T^{-1/2}N^{-1/2}\right).$$

It is now clear that even if f_t is not a strong factor, the rate of convergence of $\hat{\beta}_P$ and its asymptotic variance will be affected by the factor structure of the error term.

42.4.2 Dynamic panels with a factor structure

We now consider a dynamic panel with a factor structure as in model (42.26), with no additional regressors:

$$y_{it} = \rho y_{it-1} + \delta_t + \gamma_i' f_t + u_{it}, \tag{42.29}$$

where δ_t are time effects and γ_i and f_t are $r \times 1$ with $r \geq 1$, all unobservable. We assume that $y_{i0} = 0$ for notational simplicity. The errors are assumed to be independent across i and over t and $E(u_{it}^2) = \sigma_t^2$. Let $\Phi = \mathrm{diag}(\sigma_1^2, \ldots, \sigma_T^2)$. Rewrite model (42.29) as

$$By_i = \delta + F\gamma_i + u_{it}, \tag{42.30}$$

where $\delta = (\delta_1, \ldots, \delta_T)'$ and $F = (f_1, \ldots, f_T)'$, both $T \times r$, and

$$\begin{gathered} B = \begin{bmatrix} 1 & 0 & \cdots & 0 \\ -\rho & 1 & \cdots & 0 \\ \vdots & \ddots & \ddots & \vdots \\ 0 & \cdots & -\rho & 1 \end{bmatrix}, \\ \Lambda = B^{-1} = \begin{bmatrix} 1 & 0 & \cdots & 0 \\ \rho & 1 & \cdots & 0 \\ \vdots & \ddots & \ddots & \vdots \\ \rho^{T-1} & \cdots & \rho & 1 \end{bmatrix}. \end{gathered} \tag{42.31}$$

We can rewrite model (42.30) as

$$y_i = \Lambda\delta + \Lambda F\gamma_i + \Lambda u_{it}. \tag{42.32}$$

The MLE of $\Lambda\delta$ is the sample mean $\bar{y}$. Let

$$S_N = (N-1)^{-1}\sum_{i=1}^{N}(y_i - \bar{y})(y_i - \bar{y})'$$

be the sample variance of y. Define the sample variance of γ_i as

$$\Psi_N = (N-1)^{-1}\sum_{i=1}^{N}(\gamma_i - \bar{\gamma})(\gamma_i - \bar{\gamma})'.$$

Bai (2009a) considered the fixed-effects setup so that γ_i and Ψ_N are non-random. Write

$$E(S_N) = \Sigma(\theta) = \Lambda F \Psi_N F'\Lambda' + \Lambda\Phi\Lambda' = \Lambda\Omega\Lambda',$$

where $\theta = (\rho, \Psi_N, F, \Phi)$ and $\Omega = F\Psi_N F' + \Phi$. We consider the likelihood function. It is not strictly a likelihood function under the fixed-effect setup, and we may call it a loss function. It is given by

$$\ell(\theta) = -(1/2)(N-1)^{-1}\log|\Sigma(\theta)| - (1/2)(N-1)^{-1}\mathrm{tr}\left[S_N\Sigma(\theta)^{-1}\right]. \tag{42.33}$$

We assume that the true parameter θ_N is an interior point of a compact set Θ. We let $\hat{\theta}$ be the estimator of θ_N obtained by minimizing the loss function over the compact set:

$$\hat{\theta} = \arg\min_{\theta} \ell(\theta).$$

Bai (2009a) imposed the following assumptions:

Assumption 42.11 (B1). u_i is *i.i.d.* over i; $E(u_{it}) = 0$, $\mathrm{Var}(u_{it}) = \sigma_t^2 > 0$, and u_{it} are independent across time t; $E(u_{it}^4) \leq M < \infty$ for all i and t; $|\rho| < 1$.

Assumption 42.12 (B2). The γ_i are fixed effects with $\Psi_n \to \Psi > 0$, as $N \to \infty$.

Assumption 42.13 (B3). There exist constants a and b such that $0 < a < \sigma_t^2 < b < \infty$ for all t:

$$T^{-1}F'\Phi^{-1}F = T^{-1}\sum_{t=1}^{T} f_t f_t'/\sigma_t^2 \to Q$$

and

$$T^{-1}\sum_{t=1}^{T} \sigma_t^{-4}(f_t f_t' \otimes f_t f_t') \to \Xi,$$

as $T \to \infty$, for some positive definite matrices Q and Ξ.

Since

$$F\Psi_N F' = FR\left(R^{-1}\Psi_N R'^{-1}\right)R'F',$$

for an arbitrary invertible $r \times r$ matrix R, the model is not identifiable without restrictions. Since an arbitrary $r \times r$ matrix has r^2 degrees of freedom, we need r^2 restrictions to make the parameters uniquely determined. Bai (2009a) considered two different sets of restrictions, referred to as IC1 and IC2:

- **Condition IC1:** Ψ_N unrestricted, $F = (I_r, F_2')$.
- **Condition IC2:** Ψ_N is diagonal and $T^{-1}F'\Phi^{-1}F = I_r$.

The restrictions imposed by Condition IC2 are similar to those used by Stock and Watson (2002) for the principal-component method. We assume that IC1 or IC2 holds for the true parameters, so we can estimate F and Ψ_N directly without rotation. Under fixed T, there are only a finite number of parameters and the standard arguments apply. That is, under Assumptions B1 and B2, and either condition IC1 or IC2,

$$\sqrt{N}\left(\hat{\theta} - \theta_N\right) \xrightarrow{d} N(0, V),$$

where

$$V = plim_{N\to\infty} N\left(\frac{\partial^2 \ell}{\partial\theta\partial\theta'}\right)^{-1}\left(E\frac{\partial \ell}{\partial\theta}\frac{\partial \ell}{\partial\theta'}\right)\left(\frac{\partial^2 \ell}{\partial\theta\partial\theta'}\right)^{-1}$$

and the derivatives are evaluated at θ_N. Assuming condition IC1 holds for the true parameters, then $\hat{\theta}$ is efficient among all estimators that are based on the second moments of the data, regardless of normality. Under condition IC2, we must impose random effects to prove efficiency. The details are provided in the work of Bai (2009a).

Under large T, the limiting distributions and convergence rates for a subset of the parameters depend on the identification conditions. Although estimating Ψ_N eliminates the incidental parameters in the cross-section, there are incidental parameters in the time dimension under large T. The matrices ϕ and F have an infinite number of parameters as T grows unbounded. Especially challenging is the analysis of consistency because of the high degree of nonlinearity of the objective function and the incidental-parameter problem. Bai (2009a) provided a detailed proof of consistency for the dynamic panels with factor errors. We state the result as the following lemma.

Lemma 42.1. *Under Assumptions B1–B3 and under either condition IC1 or IC2, as $N, T \to \infty$, we have $\hat{\rho} = \rho + o_p(1)$, $\hat{\Psi} = \Psi_n + o_p(1)$, and, for each t, $\hat{f}_t = f_t + o_p(1)$ and $\hat{\sigma}_t^2 = \sigma_t^2 + o_p(1)$.*

Bai (2009a) showed that all estimators with the possible exception of $\hat{\Psi}$ under condition IC2 are efficient under large T, despite non-normality and an increasing number of parameters.

42.4.3 Dynamic models with additional regressors

We now consider the most general version of model (42.26). In general, the regressors x_{it} are allowed to be correlated arbitrarily with γ_i and f_t. Bai (2009a) considered several cases regarding the assumptions made about the correlation of the regressors x_{it} with the regression error u_{it}. The regressors can be strictly exogenous, weakly exogenous, and non weakly exogenous with respect to u_{it}.

Panel VAR

We first consider the case of a panel vector-autoregressive models (panel VAR) given by

$$y_{it} = \rho y_{i,t-1} + \beta' x_{i,t-1} + \delta_{yt} + f_t' \gamma_i + \varepsilon_{it}, \tag{42.34}$$

and for the $p \times 1$ vector x_{it}:

$$x_{it} = \rho_x x_{i,t-1} + \beta_x y_{i,t-1} + \delta_{xt} + g_t' \gamma_i + \xi_{it}. \tag{42.35}$$

Here, we allow the errors ε_{it} to be correlated arbitrarily with the errors ξ_{it} in (42.35). We assume that $(\varepsilon_{it}, \xi'_{it})'$ are *i.i.d.* over i and are independent over t; δ_{yt} and δ_{xt} are the time effects. For simplicity, we also assume that the factor loadings γ_i are the same in both equations. Due to the correlation between ε_{it} and ξ_{it} and the common γ_i across equations, the regressor x_{it-1} is not exogenous, although it is predetermined with respect to ε_{it}. Rewrite model (42.34) in matrix form as

$$z_{it} = Az_{it-1} + \pi'_t\gamma_i + \zeta_{it},$$

where

$$z_{it} = \begin{bmatrix} y_{it} \\ x_{it} \end{bmatrix}, \quad A = \begin{bmatrix} \rho & \beta' \\ \beta_x & \rho_x \end{bmatrix},$$

$$\pi'_t = \begin{bmatrix} f'_t \\ g'_t \end{bmatrix}, \quad \zeta_{it} = \begin{bmatrix} \varepsilon_{it} \\ \xi_{it} \end{bmatrix}.$$

This model is a direct extension of the setup used by Holtz-Eakin *et al.* (1988) to multiple factors. Their GMM method requires the transformation of the variables (i.e., quasi-differencing) to eliminate the factor errors. The transformation becomes very complex with more than one factor. Also, the structural parameters cannot be directly estimated due to the transformation. Therefore, there is a need to recover the original parameters. In contrast, the factor approach allows a direct estimation of all structural parameters. It also allows the estimation of the covariance matrix of the factor loadings.

We let z_i be the $T(p+1)\times 1$ vector that stacks up z_{it} $(t = 1, \ldots, T)$ and Π be the $T(p+1)\times r$ matrix that stacks up the expanded factors π'_t. We define $B^\dagger$ in the same way as B in (42.31) by replacing the diagonal elements with I_{p+1}, and we replace ρ with the matrix A. We assume that the eigenvalues of A are strictly less than 1 in absolute value. We define

$$S_{zz} = N^{-1}\sum_{i=1}^{N}(z_i - \bar{z})(z_i - \bar{z})'.$$

Then, we have

$$E(S_{zz}) = \Sigma(\theta) = \Lambda^\dagger\left(\Pi\Psi_n\Pi' + \Phi^\dagger\right)\Lambda^{\dagger\prime},$$

where $\Lambda^\dagger$ is the inverse of $B^\dagger$ and $\Phi^\dagger$ is a block-diagonal matrix with blocks given by $\Sigma_t = E\left(\zeta_t\zeta_t'\right)$. We then consider the likelihood function as in the previous section. Using the same argument, the estimator $\hat{A}$ is $\sqrt{NT}$ consistent and asymptotically normal and is efficient, regardless of normality. All the parameters in $\hat{\Pi}$ and $\hat{\Phi}^\dagger$ are $\sqrt{N}$ consistent. The rate of convergence of $\hat{\Psi}_n$ is $N^{1/2}$ under IC1 and $\sqrt{NT}$ under IC2.

A Model of Common Shocks

We now consider the following dynamic panel model:

$$\begin{aligned} y_{it} &= \rho y_{it-1} + \beta x_{it-1} + \alpha_i + \delta_{yt} + \gamma_i' f_t + \varepsilon_{it}, \\ x_{it} &= \rho_x x_{it-1} + \beta_x y_{it-1} + v_i + \delta_{xt} + \tau_i' f_t + \xi_{it}. \end{aligned} \tag{42.36}$$

We assume that x_{it} is a scalar. This is a common-shock model because both y_{it} and x_{it} are driven by the same f_t; however, individual effects are present and the time effects in the two equations are allowed to be different. We consider a joint estimation method, i.e., we simultaneously estimate the parameters in both equations. This method is more efficient than single-equation approaches and there is no high-order asymptotic bias. We assume that $y_{i0} = 0$ and $x_{i0} = 0$. In matrix format, we have

$$\bar{B} z_i = \delta + \bar{F}\eta_i + \zeta_i$$

or

$$z_i = \bar{\Lambda}\delta + \bar{\Lambda}\bar{F}\eta_i + \bar{\Lambda}\zeta_i,$$

where

$$\bar{B} = \begin{bmatrix} B & -L\beta \\ -L\beta_x & B_x \end{bmatrix}, \quad z_i = \begin{bmatrix} y_i \\ x_i \end{bmatrix}, \quad \delta = \begin{bmatrix} \delta_y \\ \delta_x \end{bmatrix},$$

$$\bar{F} = \begin{bmatrix} 1_T & F & 0 & 0 \\ 0 & 0 & 1_T & F \end{bmatrix}, \quad \eta_i = \begin{bmatrix} \alpha_i \\ \gamma_i \\ v_i \\ \tau_i \end{bmatrix}, \quad \zeta_i = \begin{bmatrix} \varepsilon_i \\ \xi_i \end{bmatrix},$$

with

$$L = \begin{bmatrix} 1 & 0 & \cdots & 0 \\ \rho & 1 & \cdots & 0 \\ \vdots & \ddots & \ddots & \vdots \\ \rho^{T-2} & \cdots & \rho & 1 \end{bmatrix}. \tag{42.37}$$

B is defined in (42.31) and B_x is defined the same way but with ρ_x in place of ρ; δ_y and δ_x denote the vectors of the time effects. $\bar{\Lambda}$ is the inverse of $\bar{B}$. The matrix $\bar{B}$ is simply an orthogonal transformation of $B^{\dagger}$ with a known transformation matrix. We could have used the matrix $B^{\dagger}$; in this case, the matrix $\bar{F}$ must be replaced by the transpose of

$$F^{\dagger\prime} = \begin{bmatrix} 1 & 0 & 1 & 0 & \cdots & 1 & 0 \\ f_1 & 0 & f_2 & 0 & \cdots & f_T & 0 \\ 0 & 1 & 0 & 1 & \cdots & 0 & 1 \\ 0 & f_1 & 0 & f_2 & \cdots & 0 & f_T \end{bmatrix}$$

with other appropriate reordering of the variables. The common-shock model places many restrictions on the matrix $\bar{F}$. These imply more efficient estimates, and they can easily be incorporated in the maximum-likelihood estimator. In comparison, it would be more difficult for the principal-component method to impose these restrictions. We define

$$S_{zz} = N^{-1} \sum_{i=1}^{N} (\eta_i - \bar{\eta}) (\eta_i - \bar{\eta})',$$

with $x_c = (y_i', x_i')'$. Then,

$$E(S_{zz}) = \bar{\Sigma}(\theta) = \bar{\Gamma} \left(\bar{F} \bar{\Psi}_n \bar{F}' + \bar{\Phi} \right) \bar{\Gamma}',$$

where

$$\bar{\Psi}_n = N^{-1} \sum_{i=1}^{N} (\eta_i - \bar{\eta}) (\eta_i - \bar{\eta})',$$

and $\bar{\Phi}$ denotes the matrix $E(\zeta_i \zeta_i')$, which we assume to be a diagonal matrix for simplicity. We consider the likelihood function in equation

(42.33) with $\bar{\Sigma}(\theta)$ and S_{zz} replacing $\Sigma(\theta)$ and S_N, respectively. Using the same argument, we obtain the following result: The estimated parameters in the matrix $\bar{B}$ (ρ, β, ρ_x and β_x) are $\sqrt{NT}$ consistent; they also are asymptotically efficient within the class of estimators based on the second moment of the data. There are no asymptotic biases. The estimated parameters in $(F, \bar{\Phi})$ are $\sqrt{N}$ consistent. The matrix Ψ_n is estimated with $\sqrt{N}$ consistency or $\sqrt{NT}$ consistency, depending on the identification restrictions used.

42.4.4 Heterogeneous panels

We now consider a generalization of model (42.26) by allowing heterogeneous coefficients:

$$\begin{aligned} y_{it} &= \rho_i y_{it-1} + \beta_i' x_{it-1} + u_{it}, \\ u_{it} &= \gamma_i' f_t + e_{it}. \end{aligned} \tag{42.38}$$

In this case, ρ_i and β_i are randomly distributed across units and the objects of interest are the mean coefficients $\rho = E(\rho_i)$ and $\beta = E(\beta_i)$. Define the vector of regressors $\zeta_{it} = (y_{i,t-1}, x_{it}')'$ and the corresponding parameter vector $\pi_i = (\rho_i, \beta_i')'$ so that (42.38) can be written as

$$y_{it} = \pi_i' \zeta_{it} + u_{it}.$$

We first restrict our attention to a heterogeneous panel with a multifactor error structure with $\rho_i = 0$ for all i and we then generalize the results to the dynamic panel case.

Principal-Component Estimators

Consider the following heterogeneous panel data model:

$$\begin{aligned} y_{it} &= \beta_i' x_{it-1} + u_{it}, \\ u_{it} &= \gamma_i' f_t + e_{it}, \end{aligned} \tag{42.39}$$

where x_{it} is a $k \times 1$ vector of observed individual-specific regressors; f_t is an m-dimensional vector of unobservable common factors, we assume that $m << N$. Coakley *et al.* (2002) considered such a panel data model with strictly exogenous regressors and homogeneous slopes (i.e., $\beta_i = \beta$) and proposed a two-stage estimation procedure. In the first stage, the PCs are extracted from the OLS residuals as proxies for the unobserved variables, and in the second step, the estimated factors are treated as observable and the following augmented regression is estimated:

$$y_{it} = \beta' x_{it} + \gamma_i' \hat{f}_t + \varepsilon_{it}, \quad \text{for } i = 1, \ldots, N; \; t = 1, \ldots, T, \tag{42.40}$$

where $\hat{f}_t$ is an $m \times 1$ vector of principal components of the residuals computed in the first stage. The resultant estimator of β is consistent for N and T large, so long as f_t and the regressors x_{it} are uncorrelated. However, if the factors and the regressors are correlated, as is likely to be the case in practice, the two-stage estimator becomes inconsistent; see Pesaran (2006).

Building on the work of Coakley *et al.* (2002), Bai (2009b) proposed an iterative method which consists of alternating the PC method applied to OLS residuals and the least squares estimation of (42.40), until convergence. The least squares estimators of β and F are the solutions of the following set of equations:

$$\hat{\beta}_{PC} = \left(\sum_{i=1}^{N} X_i' M_{\hat{F}} X_i \right)^{-1} \sum_{i=1}^{N} X_i' M_{\hat{F}} y_i,$$

$$\hat{F}\hat{V} = (NT)^{-1} \sum_{i=1}^{N} \left(y_i - X_i \hat{\beta}_{PC} \right) \left(y_i - X_i \hat{\beta}_{PC} \right)',$$

where $X_i = (x_{i1}, \ldots, x_{iT})'$ is the matrix of observations of x_{it}, $y_i = (y_{i1}, \ldots, y_{iT})'$ is the vector of observations of y_{it}, $M_{\hat{F}} = I_T - \hat{F}(\hat{F}'\hat{F})^{-1}\hat{F}'$, with $\hat{F} = (\hat{f}_1, , \ldots, \hat{f}_T)'$, and $\hat{V}$ is a diagonal matrix with the m largest eigenvalues of the matrix

$$(NT)^{-1} \sum_{i=1}^{N} (y_i - X_i \hat{\beta}_{PC})(y_i - X_i \hat{\beta}_{PC})',$$

arranged in decreasing order. The solution $\hat{\beta}_{PC}$, $\hat{F}$, and

$$\hat{\gamma}_i = (\hat{F}'\hat{F})^{-1} \hat{F}'(y_i - X_i \hat{\beta}_{PC})$$

minimizes the sum of squared residual function:

$$\mathrm{SSR}_{NT}\Big(\beta, \{\gamma_i\}_{i=1}^{N}, \{f_t\}_{t=1}^{T}\Big) = \sum_{i=1}^{N}(y_i - X_i\beta - F\gamma_i)'(y_i - X_i\beta - F\gamma_i),$$

where $F = (f_1, \ldots, f_T)'$. This is a Gaussian quasi-maximum likelihood function of the model and, in this respect, the iterative principal-component estimator can also be seen as a quasi-maximum likelihood estimator.

Bai (2009b) showed that such an estimator is consistent even if the common factors are correlated with the explanatory variables. The estimate $\hat{\beta}_{PC}$ is consistent if $T, N \to \infty$ without any restrictions on the limit of the ratio T/N. When in addition $T/N \to c > 0$, $\hat{\beta}_{PC}$ converges at the rate $(NT)^{1/2}$; the limiting distribution of $\sqrt{NT}(\hat{\beta}_{PC} - \beta)$ is normal but it does not necessarily have a zero mean. Bai (2009b) showed that the asymptotic bias can be consistently estimated and proposed a bias corrected estimator. An alternative method based on maximum likelihood is considered in the work of Bai and Li (2014).

There is an extensive literature that considers the estimation of m, assuming all m factors to be strong. See, for example, Bai and Ng (2002), Bai and Ng (2007), Kapetanios (2010), Amengual and Watson (2007), Hallin and Liška (2007), Onatski (2010), Ahn and Horenstein (2013), and Breitung and Pigorsch (2013). There are also a number of useful surveys on dynamic panel data models, Bai and Ng (2008b), Breitung and Choi (2013), and Bai and Wang (2016), among others, that can be consulted for detailed discussions of these methods and additional references.

PC Estimators for Dynamic Panels

We first consider the quasi-maximum likelihood estimator suggested by Moon and Weidner (2015). They consider model (42.38) and assume homogeneous coefficients $\pi_i = \pi$ for all i and develop a Gaussian quasi-maximum likelihood estimator (QMLE) of the homogeneous coefficient vector π, given by

$$\hat{\pi}_{\mathrm{QMLE}} = \arg\min_{\pi \in \mathbb{B}} [L_{NT}(\pi)],$$

where $\mathbb{B}$ is a compact set assumed to contain the true parameter values, and

$$L_{NT}(\pi) = \min_{\{y_i\}_{i=1}^{N},\{f_t\}_{t=1}^{T}} (NT)^{-1} \sum_{i=1}^{N} (y_i - \Xi_i \pi - F\gamma_i)'(y_i - \Xi_i \pi - F\gamma_i),$$

where $y_i = (y_{i1}, \ldots, y_{iT})$ and

$$\Xi_i = \begin{pmatrix} y_{i0} & x'_{i,1} \\ y_{i,1} & x'_{i,2} \\ \vdots & \vdots \\ y_{i,T-1} & x'_{iT} \end{pmatrix}.$$

Moon and Weidner (2015) showed that $\hat{\pi}_{\text{QMLE}}$ is a consistent estimator of π as $N, T \to \infty$ without any restrictions on the ratio T/N. To derive the asymptotic distribution of $\hat{\pi}_{\text{QMLE}}$, we need $T/N \to c$, $0 < c < \infty$ as $N, T \to \infty$, and assume that the idiosyncratic errors e_{it} are cross-sectionally independent. Under some high-level assumptions, $\hat{\pi}_{\text{QMLE}}$ is asymptotically normal with a non-zero mean, which is due to two types of asymptotic biases. The first follows from the heteroskedasticity of the error terms, as in the work of Bai (2009b), and the second is due to the presence of weakly exogenous regressors. Moon and Weidner (2015) provided consistent estimators of these two components and proposed a bias-corrected QMLE.

Song (2013) extended Bai (2009b)'s approach to dynamic panels with heterogeneous coefficients. He proposed an iterated least squares estimator of π_i and showed, as in the work of Bai (2009b), that the solution can be obtained by alternating the PC method applied to the least squares residuals and the least squares estimation of (42.38) until convergence. The least squares estimators of π_i and F are the solution to the following set of nonlinear equations:

$$\hat{\pi}_{i,PC} = \left(\Xi_i' M_{\hat{F}} \Xi_i\right)^{-1} \Xi_i' M_{\hat{F}} y_i, \quad \text{for } i = 1, \ldots, N,$$

$$\hat{F}\hat{V} = (NT)^{-1} \sum_{i=1}^{N} \left(y_i - \Xi_i \hat{\pi}_{i,PC}\right)\left(y_i - \Xi_i \hat{\pi}_{i,PC}\right)' \hat{F}.$$

Song (2013) established consistency of $\hat{\pi}_{i,PC}$ when $(N,T) \to \infty$ without any restrictions on T/N. If in addition $T/N^2 \to 0$, $\hat{\pi}_{i,PC}$

is $\sqrt{T}$ consistent, and he derives the asymptotic distribution under some additional requirements including the cross-sectional independence of e_{it}. He also considered the following mean group estimator based on the individual estimates $\hat{\pi}_{i,PC}$

$$\hat{\pi}^s_{PCMG} = N^{-1} \sum_{i=1}^{N} \hat{\pi}_{i,PC}$$

in a Monte Carlo study and found that $\hat{\pi}^s_{PCMG}$ has satisfactory small sample properties in terms of bias and root mean squared error. However, no asymptotic distribution results for $\hat{\pi}^s_{PCMG}$ are given. Further, Monte Carlo studies presented in the work of Chudik and Pesaran (2015) suggested that $\sqrt{N}\,(\hat{\pi}^s_{PCMG} - \pi)$ is asymptotically normally distributed with mean zero and a covariance matrix that can be estimated by

$$\widehat{\text{Var}}\,(\hat{\pi}^s_{PCMG}) = [N(N-1)]^{-1} \sum_{i=1}^{N} (\hat{\pi}^s_i - \hat{\pi}^s_{MG})\,(\hat{\pi}^s_i - \hat{\pi}^s_{MG})'\,.$$

Remark 42.6. An extension of the factor models in the context of quantile regressions is contained in the work of Chen *et al.* (2021).

Remark 42.7. The analysis of factor models estimated via principal components can be sensitive to the nature of the data, i.e., whether they are stationary or unit root processes. Onatski and Wang (2021) showed that with high-dimensional non-stationary data having no common factors, a few of the principal components of such data absorb nearly all the data variation. This suggests the presence of common factors when none are warranted. They argue that this problem is similar to the spurious regression problem discussed in Section 21.6.2, namely finding a spurious correlation when regressing a random walk on another independent random walk. Accordingly, they label the problem as one of spurious factor analyses.

42.5 Spatial panel data models

This section provides a survey of econometric methods that address spatial dependence in linear panel data regression models. While cross-section correlation is typically not a concern in randomly drawn samples at the individual level, it becomes an issue when analyzing cross-sections of larger units, such as countries, regions, states, or counties. Spatial dependence can arise from localized interactions among units or from persistent unobserved characteristics that span over space or a network. To measure spatial correlation, a metric of distance between individuals is required, and the definition of "local" can vary, such as economic, policy, or social distance. Anselin (1988) provided a comprehensive introduction to this topic, and recent surveys of spatial panel models can be found in the works of Elhorst (2014) and Lee and Yu (2015).

Spatial models provide a straightforward way to incorporate spillover effects and externalities. In microeconomics, researchers have studied the decision-making process of agents in a system of social relations, where local interactions allow some behaviors to propagate throughout the population; see, e.g., Bala and Goyal (2001) and Brock and Durlauf (2001). In macroeconomics, various theories have suggested that strategic complementarity produce aggregate fluctuations. Input–output linkages, demand complementarity, and human capital spillover can explain comovements; see, e.g., Binder and Pesaran (1998). Additionally, the literature on endogenous growth has emphasized the significance of linkages between countries in the analysis of regional income growth; e.g., Rivera-Batiz and Romer (1991) and Arbia (2006).

Spatial correlation can also arise from measurement problems or sampling schemes that do not align with the spatial scope of the phenomenon under study. Anselin (1988) provided an example of this, where there is a lack of concordance between observed spatial units, such as the region or country, and the spatial scope of the analysis.

42.5.1 Spatial error component regression model

We can model the spatial correlation as well as the heterogeneity across cross-sectional observations (e.g. individuals and countries) using a spatial error component regression model, by allowing the disturbances to be spatially correlated:

$$y_{ti} = x'_{ti}\beta + u_{ti}, \quad (i = 1, \ldots, N; \quad t = 1, \ldots, T), \tag{42.41}$$

where y_{ti} is the observation of the ith cross-sectional unit at time period t, x_{ti} denotes the $k \times 1$ vector of observations on the regressors, and u_{ti} is the regression error. In vector form, the error term of (42.41) is assumed to have random individual effects as well as spatially autocorrelated disturbances. We model a spatial process for the error term using a matrix W_N, which relates each unit to its neighbors:

$$u_t = \mu + \epsilon_t, \tag{42.42}$$

with

$$\epsilon_t = \lambda W_N \epsilon_t + \nu_t, \tag{42.43}$$

where $\mu' = (\mu_1, \ldots, \mu_N)$ denote the vector of random individual effects which are assumed to be $i.i.d\ \left(0, \sigma_\mu^2\right)$. The parameter λ is the scalar spatial autoregressive coefficient with $|\lambda| < 1$. W_N is a known $N \times N$ spatial weight matrix whose diagonal elements are zero. W_N also satisfies the condition that $(I_N - \lambda W_N)$ is non-singular. The stochastic component $\nu_t' = (\nu_{t1}, \ldots, \nu_{tN})$, where ν_{ti} is assumed to be $i.i.d.\ \left(0, \sigma_\nu^2\right)$ and also independent of μ_i. One can then rewrite (42.43) as

$$\epsilon_t = (I_N - \lambda W_N)^{-1} \nu_t = B^{-1} \nu_t,$$

where $B - I_N - \lambda W_N$ and I_N is the identity matrix of dimension N. The model (42.41) can be rewritten in matrix notation as

$$y = X\beta + u,$$

where y is now of dimension $NT \times 1$, X is $NT \times k$, β is $k \times 1$, and u is $NT \times 1$. X is assumed to be of full column rank and its elements are assumed to be bounded in absolute value. Equation (42.42) can be written in vector form:

$$u = (\iota_T \otimes I_N)\, \mu + \left(I_T \otimes B^{-1}\right) \nu,$$

where $\nu' = (\nu_1', \ldots, \nu_T')$. Under these specifications, the covariance matrix of u is given by

$$\Omega = \sigma_\mu^2 \left(J_T \otimes I_N\right) + \sigma_\nu^2 \left(I_T \otimes \left(B'B\right)^{-1}\right),$$

which can be written as

$$\Omega = \sigma_\nu^2 \left[\bar{J}_T \otimes \left(T\phi I_N + (B'B)^{-1} \right) + E_T \otimes (B'B)^{-1} \right] = \sigma_\nu^2 \Sigma,$$

where $\phi = \sigma_\mu^2/\sigma_\nu^2$, $\bar{J}_T = J_T/T$, and $E_T = I_T - \bar{J}_T$. Using results in the work of Wansbeek and Kapteyn (1982), Σ^{-1} is given by

$$\Sigma^{-1} = \bar{J}_T \otimes \left(T\phi I_N + (B'B)^{-1} \right)^{-1} + E_T \otimes B'B.$$

Also,

$$|\Sigma| = \left| T\phi I_N + (B'B)^{-1} \right| \cdot \left| (B'B)^{-1} \right|^{T-1}.$$

Under the assumption of normality, the log-likelihood function for this model was derived by Anselin (1988), p. 154 as

$$\begin{aligned} L &= -(1/2)(NT)^{-1} \ln(2\pi\sigma_\nu^2) - (1/2) \ln |\Sigma| - (2\sigma_\nu^2)^{-1} u'\Sigma^{-1} u \\ &= -(1/2)(NT)^{-1} \ln(2\pi\sigma_\nu^2) - (1/2) \ln \left[\left| T\phi I_N + (B'B)^{-1} \right| \right] \\ &\quad + [(T-1)/2] \ln |B'B| - (2\sigma_\nu^2)^{-1} u'\Sigma^{-1} u, \end{aligned}$$

with $u = y - X\beta$. For a derivation of the first-order conditions of the MLE as well as the LM test for $\lambda = 0$ for this model, see the work of Anselin (1988).

42.5.2 Spatial autoregressive model

An alternative strategy is the spatial autoregressive (SAR) specification, proposed by Cliff and Ord (1973) and Cliff and Ord (1981). The SAR process is a variant of the model introduced by Whittle (1954) where the error term is modeled as

$$u_t = \lambda W_N + \nu_t, \tag{42.44}$$

where, again, W_N is a known $N \times N$ spatial weight matrix whose diagonal elements are zero. W_N also satisfies the condition that $(I_N - \lambda W_N)$ is non-singular; $\nu_t' = (\nu_{t1}, \ldots, \nu_{tN})$, where ν_{ti} is assumed to be *i.i.d.* $\left(0, \sigma_\nu^2\right)$ and also independent of μ_i. One can rewrite (42.44) as

$$u_t = \left(I_N - \lambda W_N\right)^{-1} \nu_t = B^{-1} \nu_t,$$

where $B = I_N - \lambda W_N$ and I_N is the identity matrix of dimension N. Under these assumptions, the variance–covariance matrix of u is given by

$$\Omega_{SAR} = \sigma_\nu^2 \left(I_T - \lambda W_N\right) \left(I_T - \lambda W_N'\right)^{-1}.$$

42.5.3 Spatial lag models

In a panel data model, spatial dependence can be incorporated by including spatial lags of the dependent variable among the regressors. Note that the terminology "lags" should not be confused with the more common time lag. Here, spatial lags consist of some neighbors, defined appropriately, e.g., nearby states or countries. The equation for this specification is given as follows:

$$y_{it} = \alpha_i + \rho \sum_{j=1}^{N} w_{ij} y_{it} + \beta' x_{it} + u_{it}, \quad (i = 1, \ldots, N; \quad t = 1, \ldots, T),$$

where y_{it} is the dependent variable for the ith cross-sectional unit at time t, α_i is the group or individual effect for the ith unit, that could be considered either fixed, unknown parameters to be estimated, or draws from a probability distribution. ρ and β are unknown parameters to be estimated, x_{it} is a $k \times 1$ vector of observed regressors on the ith unit at time t, and u_{it} is the error term. The sum in the equation represents the spatial lag of the dependent variable for the ith unit at time t, where w_{ij} represents the spatial weight between the ith and jth units. The model assumes that the regressors are strictly exogenous. The equation can be rewritten in stacked form as follows:

$$y_t = \alpha + \rho W_N y_t + X_t \beta + u_t, \tag{42.45}$$

where y_t is an $N \times 1$ vector of the cross-sectional units at time t, α is an $N \times 1$ vector of individual effects, W_N is an $N \times N$ matrix of spatial weights, X_t is an $N \times k$ matrix of observed regressors at time

t, β is a $k \times 1$ vector of unknown parameters, and u_t is an $N \times 1$ vector of error terms. The diagonal matrix D with elements $0 < \sigma_i^2 < K$ is used to represent the variance–covariance matrix of u_t.

Estimation of ρ and β by least squares applied to (42.45) can lead to biased and inconsistent estimates. This is because $\text{Cov}(\sum_{j=1}^{N} w_{ij} y_{it}, u_{it}) \neq 0$ when $\rho \neq 0$; see Kelejian and Prucha (2010). In order to solve the model, we need the following condition:

$$|\rho| < \max\left(1/||W_N||_1, 1/||W_N||_\infty\right),$$

which ensures that $I_N - \rho W_N$ is invertible. An alternative sufficient condition is $|\rho| < 1/\tau$, where $\tau = \min\left(||W_N||_1, ||W_N||_\infty\right)$. As conventional estimators of the parameters ρ and β, such as pooled OLS or FE, are inconsistent, an alternative estimation approach, such as maximum likelihood and generalized method of moments, is needed for consistent estimation of spatial lag models.

Spatial Lag Error Component Regression Model

Baltagi and Liu (2011) considered a panel data version of the cross-section spatial lag model considered by Kelejian and Prucha (1998):

$$\begin{aligned} y &= \lambda W y + X\beta + u, \\ u &= Z_\mu \mu + \nu, \end{aligned} \tag{42.46}$$

where y is of dimension $NT \times 1, X$ is $NT \times k, \beta$ is $k \times 1$, and u is $NT \times 1$. The regressors are assumed to be exogenous. We make the following assumption about the $(N \times N)$ spatial weight matrix $W = I_T \otimes W_N$:

SLEC1: All diagonal elements of the spatial weighting matrices W_N are zero.
SLEC2: The matrix $(I - \lambda W_N)$ is non-singular for all $|\lambda| < 1$.
SLEC3: The row and column sums of the matrices $W_N, (I - \lambda W_N)^{-1}$ are bounded uniformly in absolute value.

In practice, these assumptions are satisfied when the matrix W_N is row normalized with its entries usually declining with distance. The random error component structure implies $Z_\mu = \iota_T \otimes I_N$ denoting the selector matrix for the $(N \times 1)$ random vector of individual effects μ which is assumed to be *i.i.d.* $\left(0, \sigma_\mu^2 I_N\right)$. Recall that ι_T is a vector of ones of dimension T and I_N is the identity matrix of dimension N. The $NT \times 1$ vector ν is assumed to have mean 0 and variance $\sigma_\nu^2 I_{NT}$ so that all elements are *i.i.d.*. Also, μ and ν are independent of each other. Let $A = I_T \otimes A_N$, where $A_N = I_N - \lambda W_N$, then one can write

$$y = A^{-1}(X\beta + u).$$

Note that

$$E\left[Wyu'\right] = E\left[WA^{-1}(X\beta + u)u'\right] = WA^{-1}\Omega \neq 0,$$

where $\Omega = E(uu')$. Thus, the spatially lagged dependent variable Wy is correlated with the disturbance u and the OLS estimator is inconsistent. Let $Z = (X, Wy)$ and $\delta = (\beta, \lambda)'$, the model (42.46) can be written as

$$y = Z\delta + u. \tag{42.47}$$

In the cross-section spatial autoregressive model, Kelejian and Prucha (1998) suggested a two-stage least squares estimator (2SLS) based on the instruments $H = \left(X, WX, W^2X\right)$ which yields

$$\hat{\delta}_{2SLS} = \left[Z'P_H Z\right]^{-1} Z'P_H y,$$

where $P_H = H\left(H'H\right)^{-1} H'$ denotes the matrix that projects onto the space spanned by H. They show that this 2SLS estimator is consistent under some general regularity conditions.

Fixed Effects Estimator. Let $\bar{J}_T = J_T/T$, where J_T is a matrix of ones of dimension T. Also, let $E_T = I_T - \bar{J}_T$, and define P to be the matrix that projects onto the space spanned by Z_μ, i.e., $P = \bar{J}_T \otimes I_N$, and $Q = I_{NT} - P = E_T \otimes I_N$. Recall that $Z_\mu = \iota_T \otimes I_N$ is just a selector matrix with ι_T a vector of ones of dimension T and I_N the identity matrix of dimension N. Note that

$$\begin{aligned} QW &= (E_T \otimes I_N)(I_T \otimes W_N) = (E_T \otimes W_N) \\ &= (I_T \otimes W_N)(E_T \otimes I_N) = WQ. \end{aligned}$$

Hence, pre-multiplying equation (42.47) by Q we obtain

$$\tilde{y} = \lambda W\tilde{y} + \tilde{X}\beta + \tilde{u}.$$

Applying 2SLS to this Q transformed panel spatial lag model, we get the fixed-effect spatial 2SLS (FE-S2SLS) estimator of δ based on the instruments

$$\tilde{H} = \left(\tilde{X}, W\tilde{X}, W^2\tilde{X}\right) = (QX, QWX, QW^2X) = QH.$$

We denote this estimator by $\hat{\delta}_{FE-S2SLS}$. Note that the sum of squared residuals from the FE-S2SLS regression provides a consistent estimate $\hat{\sigma}_\nu^2$ of σ_ν^2.

Between Effects Estimator. We can also pre-multiply equation (42.47) by P to obtain

$$\bar{y} = \lambda W\bar{y} + \bar{X}\beta + \bar{u}.$$

This follows from the fact that

$$\begin{aligned} PW &= \left(\bar{J}_T \otimes I_N\right)(I_T \otimes W_N) = \left(\bar{J}_T \otimes W_N\right) \\ &= (I_T \otimes W_N)\left(\bar{J}_T \otimes I_N\right) = WP. \end{aligned}$$

Applying 2SLS to this P transformed panel spatial lag model, we get the Between Effects spatial 2SLS (BE-S2SLS) estimator of δ based upon the instruments

$$\bar{H} = \left(\bar{X}, W\bar{X}, W^2\bar{X}\right) = \left(PX, PWX, PW^2X\right) = PH.$$

We denote this estimator by $\hat{\delta}_{BE-S2SLS}$. Note that the sum of squared residuals provides a consistent estimate $\hat{\sigma}_1^2$ of $\sigma_1^2 = T\sigma_\mu^2 + \sigma_\nu^2$. The covariance matrix of u is

$$\Omega = E\left(uu'\right) = \sigma_1^2 P + \sigma_\nu^2 Q$$

and

$$\Omega^{-1/2} = \left(\sigma_1^{-1} P + \sigma_\nu^{-1} Q\right).$$

Random Effects Estimator. Alternatively, pre-multiply equation (42.47) by $\Omega^{-1/2}$ to obtain

$$y^* = Z^*\delta + u^*,$$

where $y^* = \Omega^{-1/2}y$, $u^* = \Omega^{-1/2}u$, and

$$Z^* = \Omega^{-1/2}Z = \Omega^{-1/2}(X, Wy) = (X^*, \Omega^{-1/2}Wy)$$
$$= \left(X^*, W\Omega^{-1/2}y\right) = (X^*, Wy^*).$$

The last expression follows from the fact that

$$\Omega^{-1/2}W = \left(\sigma_1^{-1}PW + \sigma_\nu^{-1}QW\right) = \left(\sigma_1^{-1}WP + \sigma_\nu^{-1}WQ\right) = W\Omega^{-1/2}.$$

Applying 2SLS to this $\Omega^{-1/2}$ transformed panel spatial lag model, we get the Random Effects spatial 2SLS estimator (RE-S2SLS) of δ given by

$$\hat{\delta}_{RE\text{-}S2SLS} = \left[Z^{*\prime}P_{H^*}Z^*\right]^{-1} Z^{*\prime}P_{H^*}y^*,$$

where

$$H^* = (X^*, WX^*, W^2X^*) = \left(\Omega^{-1/2}X, W\Omega^{-1/2}X, W^2\Omega^{-1/2}X\right)$$
$$= \left(\Omega^{-1/2}X, \Omega^{-1/2}WX, \Omega^{-1/2}W^2X\right) = \Omega^{-1/2}H.$$

42.6 Latent group structures in panel data

Although panel data presents many opportunities for empirical research, it often involves aggregate data from different units, such as workers, firms, and countries, that have unobservable differences. This poses a dilemma for researchers who must decide whether to use flexible methods to model the unobservable heterogeneity or pooled models that assume homogeneous coefficients for all individual units. Recently, the panel data literature has focused on addressing this challenge by exploring latent group structures. This approach offers the advantage of classifying panel units into groups based on individuals who share the same slope parameters while still allowing for heterogeneity across the groups. In contrast to completely heterogeneous or fully homogeneous models, this method strikes a balance between flexibility and homogeneity.

In panel data analyses, complete slope heterogeneity is a commonly assumed approach to model heterogeneity. Although it avoids misspecification, it may not take full advantage of panel data and may result in imprecise estimates, even with a long time dimension (Baltagi and Griffin, 1997). However, conventional panel data models often assume the same regression parameters for all individuals while modeling unobserved heterogeneity through individual-specific effects, such as fixed effect and random effect models. While this assumption exploits cross-section averaging and leads to higher efficiency, it comes at the cost of estimation bias and inconsistency, as supported by a growing number of studies (Maddala and Hu, 1996; and Baltagi and Griffin, 1997). Despite the better forecast performance of such estimators, justifying the slope homogeneity assumption can be challenging in empirical work, as noted by Hsiao and Tahmiscioglu (1997) and Phillips and Sul (2007a), among others. This discussion has motivated considerable research into latent group structures in panel data analysis, including studies by Sun (2005), Lin and Ng (2012), Deb and Trivedi (2013), Bonhomme and Manresa (2015), Sarafidis and Weber (2015), Ando and Bai (2016), Bester and Hansen (2016), Gu and Volgushev (2019), among others.

The latent group structure models partition individuals in different groups and allow the within group individuals to share common coefficients, while the groups are assumed to have slope heterogeneity. Since the group membership and the number of groups are unknown in these models, there are two critical issues about latent group structures in panel data analysis: How to determine the unknown number of groups, which is often referred to as convergence clubs in the economic growth literature, and how to identify the membership of each individual? These are long-standing questions of statistical classification in panel data, and although various approaches have been adopted in empirical research, no completely satisfactory solution has been found yet. For example, Bester and Hansen (2016) proposed a panel structure model where individuals are grouped according to some external classification such as geographic location or observable explanatory variables, while Ando and Bai (2015) considered a multifactor asset-pricing model with group-specific pervasive factors where the group membership is known. However, assuming the group structure is known to the researcher can be misleading when the number of groups and individual identities are incorrectly classified.

In modeling unobserved slope heterogeneity in panels, various approaches have been proposed to determine an unknown group structure. One approach applies finite mixture models, such as Sun (2005) who used a parametric finite mixture linear panel data model, as well as Kasahara and Shimotsu (2009) and Browning and Carro (2014) who studied identification in discrete choice panel data models using nonparametric discrete mixture distributions for a fixed number of groups. Another approach is based on the K-means algorithm in statistical cluster analysis. For example, Lin and Ng (2012) and Sarafidis and Weber (2015) modified the K-means algorithm to estimate linear panel data models with latent group structure for the slope coefficients, while Bonhomme and Manresa (2015) applied the K-means algorithm to estimate a linear panel data model with additive fixed effects having group structure and studied its asymptotic properties. Ando and Bai (2016) extended this approach to allow for group structure among the interactive fixed effects. Phillips and Sul (2007b) developed a nonlinear time varying factor model with individual heterogeneity for determining group cluster convergence. Club convergence is, however, determined by an unknown common growth component. Hahn and Moon (2010) argued for the sound foundations of the group structure in game theory or macroeconomic models, and they considered nonlinear panel data models where the parameter of interest is common across individuals, whereas the fixed effects have a finite group structure.

Su *et al.* (2016) introduced an automated data-driven method for identifying and estimating latent group structures in panel data using penalized profile likelihood (PPL), where the regression parameters vary across groups and the individual group membership is unknown. Unlike previous methods, it does not require specifying any modeling mechanism for the known group structure. In this section, we will briefly review the PPL estimation method for a linear model with exogenous regressors.

42.6.1 Identifying latent structures in linear panel data

We consider a linear panel model with exogenous regressors. This exposition is based on the penalized profile likelihood (PPL) estimation method of Su *et al.* (2016). It is convenient to assume first that the number of groups is known and later consider the determination of the number of groups. The linear panel structure model is

$$y_{it} = \beta_i' x_{it} + \mu_i + \varepsilon_{it}, \tag{42.48}$$

where x_{it} is a $p \times 1$ vector of exogenous or predetermined variables, μ_i is an individual fixed effect, β_i is a $p \times 1$ vector of slope parameters, and ε_{it} is the idiosyncratic error term with mean zero.

It is proposed to use fixed effects quasi-maximum likelihood to estimate the unknown parameters by solving the minimization problem

$$\min_{\{\beta_i,\mu_i\}} (NT)^{-1} \sum_{i=1}^{N} \sum_{t=1}^{T} \psi\left(w_{it}; \beta_i, \mu_i\right). \tag{42.49}$$

Here, $-\psi\left(w_{it}; \beta_i, \mu_i\right)$ denotes the logarithm of the pseudo-true conditional density function of y_{it} given x_{it}, the history of (y_{it}, x_{it}), and (μ_i, β_i), where μ_i are scalar individual effects and β_i are $p \times 1$ vectors of the parameters of interest. Before, we assumed that the β_i are common for all cross-sectional units (see Section 42.1), leading to a homogeneous panel with individual heterogeneity modeled through μ_i alone. At the other extreme, the β_i was assumed to differ across individuals and each is estimated at a slow convergence rate without pooling across sections; see Section 42.3. Su *et al.* (2016) allowed β_i to follow a group pattern of the general form

$$\beta_i = \sum_{k=1}^{K_0} \alpha_k 1\left\{i \in G_k\right\}.$$

Here, $\alpha_j \neq \alpha_k$ for any $j \neq k, \bigcup_{k=1}^{K} G_k = \{1, \ldots, N\}$, and $G_k \cap G_j = \emptyset$ for any $j \neq k$. Let $N_k = \#G_k$ denote the cardinality of the set G_k. In the economic growth literature (e.g., Phillips and Sul (2007a)), K_0 corresponds to the number of convergence clubs and countries (indexed by i) within the same kth club that share the same (slope) parameter vector α_k. In the market entry–exit example (e.g., Hahn and Moon, 2010), K_0 denotes the number of pure Nash equilibria and markets (indexed by i) selecting the same equilibrium over time that exhibit the same parameter vector.

For now, we assume that the number of groups K_0 is known and fixed but that each individual's group membership is unknown. In addition, following the works of Sun (2005) and Lin and Ng (2012), we implicitly assume that individual group membership does not vary over time. Let $\alpha \equiv (\alpha_1, \ldots, \alpha_{K_0})$ and $\beta \equiv (\beta_1, \ldots, \beta_N)$. The goal is to infer each individual's group identity and to estimate the group-specific parameters α_k. Gaussian quasi-maximum likelihood estimation (QMLE) of β_i and μ_i in the linear panel data model (42.48) is achieved by minimizing (42.49) with

$$\psi\left(w_{it};\beta_i,\mu_i\right)=(1/2)\left(y_{it}-\beta_i'x_{it}-\mu_i\right)^2$$

and $w_{it}=(y_{it},x_{it}')'$.

Following the works of Hahn and Newey (2004) and Hahn and Kuersteiner (2011), the profile log-likelihood function is

$$Q_{1,NT}(\beta)=(NT)^{-1}\sum_{i=1}^{N}\sum_{t=1}^{T}\psi\left(w_{it};\beta_i,\hat{\mu}_i\left(\beta_i\right)\right),$$

where

$$\hat{\mu}_i\left(\beta_i\right)=\arg\min_{\mu_i}T^{-1}\sum_{t=1}^{T}\psi\left(w_{it};\beta_i,\mu_i\right).$$

Motivated by the literature on group Lasso (e.g., Yuan and Lin, 2006), Su *et al.* (2016) proposed to estimate β and α by minimizing the following PPL criterion function:

$$Q_{1NT,\lambda_1}^{(K_0)}(\beta,\alpha)=Q_{1,NT}(\beta)+N^{-1}\lambda_1\sum_{i=1}^{N}\prod_{k=1}^{K_0}\|\beta_i-\alpha_k\|, \tag{42.50}$$

where $\lambda_1=\lambda_{1NT}$ is a tuning parameter. Minimizing the above criterion function produces classifier-Lasso (C-Lasso) estimates $\hat{\beta}$ and $\hat{\alpha}$ of β and α, respectively. Let $\hat{\beta}_i$ and $\hat{\alpha}_k$ denote the ith and kth columns of $\hat{\beta}$ and $\hat{\alpha}$, respectively, that is, $\hat{\alpha}\equiv(\hat{\alpha}_1,\ldots,\hat{\alpha}_K)$ and $\hat{\beta}\equiv(\hat{\beta}_1,\ldots,\hat{\beta}_N)$.

The C-Lasso method differs from the standard Lasso method of Tibshirani (1996) (see Chapter 33). The main purpose in the Lasso problem is to select relevant variables, while C-Lasso is designed to determine group membership for each individual. Both problems, however, enjoy the same motivation of parameter sparsity. C-Lasso has the additional motivation of classification of unknown parameters into *a priori* unknown groups each with their own parameters. The C-Lasso has N additive terms, each of which takes a multiplicative form as the product of K_0 separate penalties. We do not know *a priori* to which value, α_k, β_i should shrink, and all K_0 possibilities must be allowed.

Determination of the Number of Groups

In practice, the exact number of groups is typically unknown. We assume that K_0 is bounded from above by a finite integer $K_{\max}$ and study the determination of the number of groups via some information criterion (IC). By minimizing (42.50) with K_0 replaced by K, we obtain the C-Lasso estimates $\left\{\hat{\beta}_i(K,\lambda_1), \hat{\alpha}_k(K,\lambda_1)\right\}$ of $\{\beta_i, \alpha_k\}$. We classify individual i into group $\hat{G}_k(K,\lambda_1)$ if and only if $\hat{\beta}_i(K,\lambda_1) = \hat{\alpha}_k(K,\lambda_1)$, that is,

$$\hat{G}_k(K,\lambda_1) \equiv \left\{i \in \{1,,\ldots,N\} : \hat{\beta}_i(K,\lambda_1) = \hat{\alpha}_k(K,\lambda_1)\right\},$$

for $k = 1,\ldots,K$. Let $\hat{G}(K,\lambda_1) \equiv \{\hat{G}_1(K,\lambda_1),\ldots,\hat{G}_K(K,\lambda_1)\}$. The post-Lasso estimator of α_k is denoted as $\hat{\alpha}_{\hat{G}_k(K,\lambda_1)}$:

$$\hat{\alpha}_{\hat{G}_k(K,\lambda_1)} = \left(\sum_{i\in\hat{G}_k}\sum_{t=1}^{T}\tilde{x}_{it}\tilde{x}_{it}'\right)^{-1}\sum_{i\in\hat{G}_k}\sum_{t=1}^{T}\tilde{x}_{it}\tilde{y}_{it}.$$

The variance is

$$\hat{\sigma}^2_{\hat{G}(K,\lambda_1)} = (NT)^{-1}\sum_{k=1}^{K}\sum_{i\in\hat{G}_k(K,\lambda_1)}\sum_{t=1}^{T}\left(\tilde{y}_{it} - \hat{\alpha}'_{\hat{G}_k(K,\lambda_1)}\tilde{x}_{it}\right)^2.$$

Su *et al.* (2016) proposed to select K to minimize

$$\mathrm{IC}_1(K,\lambda_1) = \ln\left[\hat{\sigma}^2_{\hat{G}(K,\lambda_1)}\right] + \rho_{1NT}pK,$$

where ρ_{1NT} is a tuning parameter satisfying the following assumption as $(N,T)\to\infty$:

$$\rho_{1NT}\to 0 \quad \text{and} \quad \rho_{1NT}T\to\infty.$$

In practice, Su *et al.* (2016) found that $\rho_{1NT} = (2/3)(NT)^{-1/2}$ works fairly well in linear models. This requires that T goes to infinity faster than N.

Chapter 43

Continuous-time Processes and the FCLT

In this chapter, we briefly review some concepts related to continuous-time processes in order to better understand features of the limit distributions to be discussed when dealing with unit root processes and cointegration. Our emphasis is on understanding what are Wiener processes and Ito stochastic integrals. We also discuss stochastic differential equations, Ito's lemma and various other issues. The treatment is very informal. The aim is not to get all details precise but to gain a good enough understanding of some key concepts. For an accessible treatment of several issues discussed in this Chapter, see Arnold (2013)

43.1 Preliminaries

We consider a stationary stochastic process $x(t)$ in continuous time with autocorrelation function $\rho(\tau)$ for $\tau \geq 0$. Note that, as a matter of notation, we shall use $x(t)$ for a continuous-time process and x_t for a discrete-time one. We start with some definitions that will prove useful in subsequent discussions.

Definition 43.1 (Mean Square Convergence). A sequence X_T converges in mean square if and only if there exists a variable X such that $\lim_{T\to\infty} E[(X_T - X)^2] = 0$.

Lemma 43.1 (Stochastic Continuity). *$x(t)$ is stochastically continuous at $t = t_0$ if $\lim_{t \to t_0} E[\{x(t) - x(t_0)\}^2] = 0$, or if $\lim_{t \to t_0} \rho(t - t_0) = 1$ or if $\lim_{\tau \to 0} \rho(\tau) = 1$.*

Proof.

$$\begin{aligned} E\left[\{x(t) - x(t_0)\}^2\right] &= \mathrm{Var}(x(t)) + \mathrm{Var}(x(t_0)) - 2\mathrm{cov}(x(t), x(t_0)) \\ &= 2\sigma_x^2 \{1 - \rho(t - t_0)\} \to 0 \end{aligned}$$

if and only if $\rho(t - t_0) \to 1$ as $t \to t_0$. We can show that if $\rho(\tau)$ is continuous at $\tau = 0$, it is continuous everywhere.

Lemma 43.2 (Stochastic Differentiability). *$x(t)$ is stochastically differentiable at $t = t_0$ with derivative $\dot{x}(t_0)$ if and only if $\lim_{h \to 0} E[\{(x(t_0 + h) - x(t_0))/h\}^2]$ exists, or if $\lim_{h \to 0} (1 - \rho(h))/h^2$ exists, or if $\ddot{\rho}(0)$, the second derivative of $\rho(h)$ at $h = 0$ exists.*

Proof. This follows by the symmetry of $\rho(\tau)$. We have

$$\lim_{h \to 0} \frac{2(1 - \rho(h))}{h^2} = \lim_{h \to 0} \left[\frac{\{\rho(h) - \rho(0)\} - \{\rho(0) - \rho(-h)\}}{h^2}\right] = \ddot{\rho}(0).$$

Again, it is possible to prove that if $\ddot{\rho}(0)$ exists, $\ddot{\rho}(\tau)$ exists for all τ.

43.2 Purely random process in continuous time

We saw in Chapter 8 that a central result in time series analysis is Wold's theorem, which states that any stationary stochastic process can be represented as a linear combination of *i.i.d.* random variables. It is then natural to ask what happens if we try to adopt this starting point in continuous-time. We want to consider a random process in continuous time $\{\varepsilon(t)\}$ such that $\varepsilon(t_1), \ldots, \varepsilon(t_n)$ is a set of uncorrelated random variables for any subset $t_1, \ldots, t_n$. Let

$$E[\varepsilon(t)] = 0, \quad \mathrm{Var}(\varepsilon(t)) = \sigma_\varepsilon^2.$$

Then, the autocovariance function is

$$R_\varepsilon(\tau) = \begin{cases} \sigma_\varepsilon^2 & \tau = 0 \\ 0 & \tau \neq 0 \end{cases}$$

and the autocorrelation function is

$$\rho_e(\tau) = \begin{cases} 1 & \tau = 0 \\ 0 & \tau \neq 0. \end{cases}$$

We now argue that $\varepsilon(t)$ is a degenerate process in the sense that it is not well defined. Suppose that we construct a linear combination, i.e., an integral in continuous time,

$$U = \int_{t_1}^{t_2} g(t)\,\varepsilon(t)\,dt. \tag{43.1}$$

Then, assuming some regularity conditions for the function $g(t)$ (e.g., so that we can interchange the expectation operator with the integration), we have $E[U] = 0$, and

$$\begin{aligned} \text{Var}(U) &= \int_{t_1}^{t_2}\int_{t_1}^{t_2} g(u)\,g(v)\,\text{cov}\{\varepsilon(u),\varepsilon(v)\}\,dudv \\ &= \sigma_\varepsilon^2 \int_{t_1}^{t_2}\int_{t_1}^{t_2} g(u)\,g(v)\,\delta_{u,v}dudv, \end{aligned}$$

where

$$\delta_{u,v} = \begin{cases} 1 & \text{if } u = v \\ 0 & \text{if } u \neq v \end{cases}$$

is the Kronecker delta. Since the integrand is 0 everywhere except on the line $u = v$, the double integral must be 0. Therefore, for any choice of $g(t)$,

$$\text{Var}\left(\int_{t_1}^{t_2} g(t)\,\varepsilon(\tau)\,dt\right) = 0,$$

if σ_ε^2 is finite. Hence, such a construction for $\varepsilon(t)$ would be useless in generating a stationary process. One way out of the dilemma is to make σ_ε^2 infinite. This leads to a degenerate process for $\varepsilon(\tau)$ itself but any integral of the form (43.1) would be well defined, and since we are interested in such integrals, this will not pose a problem.

43.2.1 Example: An $AR(1)$ process

Here, we want to use the $AR(1)$ process to provide additional motivation for the fact that the white noise sequence in continuous time must have infinite variance. We start from the discrete time representation and construct the implied continuous time representation. The arguments presented are not rigorous but simply intended to convey the main idea. We are able to provide more rigorous results later when we have the necessary tools. Write the $AR\,(1)$ as

$$x_t = a x_{t-1} + e_t, \quad t = 0, 1, 2, \ldots, \tag{43.2}$$

or

$$x_t\,(1 - a) = -a\,(x_t - x_{t-1}) + e_t,$$

where $e_t \sim i.i.d.\ \left(0, \sigma_e^2\right)$. Let $\Delta x_t = x_t - x_{t-1}$. Then,

$$\Delta x_t + \left(\frac{1-a}{a}\right) x_t = \frac{e_t}{a}.$$

Suppose that the time interval between successive observations is Δt so $t = T\Delta t$. Then dividing by Δt,

$$\frac{\Delta x_t}{\Delta t} + \frac{1-a}{a\Delta t} x_t = \frac{e_t}{a\Delta t}\,. \tag{43.3}$$

Let $\alpha = (1-a)\,/(a\Delta t)$ and $\varepsilon\,(t) = e_t/(a\Delta t)$, and suppose that $\Delta x_t/\Delta t \to \dot{x}\,(t)$ as $\Delta t \to 0$. Then we can write, as $\Delta t \to 0$,

$$\dot{x}\,(t) + \alpha x\,(t) = \varepsilon\,(t), \tag{43.4}$$

which we can view as a stochastic differential equation. In going from (43.3) to (43.4), we implicitly assumed α to be fixed as $\Delta t \to 0$. For this to be true, we must have $a \to 1$ at the same rate as $\Delta t \to 0$. This is not obvious but will turn out to be true. Since a is the correlation coefficient of x_t and x_{t-1}, $a \to 1$ as $\Delta t \to 0$ makes sense since we expect closer observations to be more correlated. Note that $a = 1$ is the boundary of the stationary region, so as $\Delta t \to 0$, a moves to this boundary.

In stating that $\Delta x_t/\Delta t \to \dot{x}\,(t)$, we also assume that $x(t)$ is differentiable. This will turn out to be problematic, so we need to do something about it. For now, it shall cause no problem for the arguments put forward in this section.

We now consider the properties of $\varepsilon(t)$. In the discrete case, from (43.2),

$$\sigma_x^2 = \sigma_e^2 / \left(1 - a^2\right).$$

Note that σ_x^2 is the variance of the process, which is non-zero even with vanishingly small intervals. We have

$$\alpha = \frac{1-a}{a\Delta t} \Rightarrow a = \frac{1}{1+\alpha\Delta t} \sim 1 - \alpha\Delta t + o(\Delta t),$$

upon taking an expansion. Let us consider an expansion of the term $1 - a^2$. We have

$$\begin{aligned} 1 - a^2 = 1 - \left(\frac{1}{1+\alpha\Delta t}\right)^2 &= \frac{(1+\alpha\Delta t)^2 - 1}{(1+\alpha\Delta t)^2} \\ &= \frac{1 + 2\alpha\Delta t + \alpha^2\Delta t^2 - 1}{(1+\alpha\Delta t)^2} = \frac{2\alpha\Delta t + \alpha^2\Delta t^2}{(1+\alpha\Delta t)^2} \end{aligned}$$

so that

$$\frac{1-a^2}{\Delta t} = \frac{2\alpha + \alpha^2\Delta t}{(1+\alpha\Delta t)^2} \to 2\alpha,$$

as $\Delta t \to 0$. Hence,

$$1 - a^2 = 2\alpha\Delta t + o(\Delta t)$$

and

$$\sigma_x^2 = \frac{\sigma_e^2}{2\alpha\Delta t}\left(1 + O(\Delta t)\right).$$

So, for σ_x^2 to remain finite as $\Delta t \to 0$, we must have $\sigma_e^2 = o(\Delta t)$. From $\varepsilon(t) = e_t/(a\Delta t)$

$$\sigma_\varepsilon^2 = \frac{\sigma_e^2}{a^2(\Delta t)^2} \sim \frac{\sigma_e^2}{(\Delta t)^2} = O(1/\Delta t),$$

for small Δt, since $a \to 1$. Hence, $\sigma_\varepsilon^2 \to \infty$ as $\Delta t \to 0$. These arguments are meant to show that it makes sense to consider the variance of an *i.i.d.* process in continuous-time having infinite variance.

43.3 The Wiener process

Suppose in the $AR(1)$ model that $\alpha = 0$ which corresponds to the case of a random walk $(a = 1)$. Then,

$$\dot{x}(t) = \varepsilon(t)$$

or integrating

$$x(t) = \int_0^t \varepsilon(u)\, du. \tag{43.5}$$

Note that, with infinite variance errors $\varepsilon(u)$, the integral may be non-degenerate and well-defined, i.e., having finite and positive variance. Here, $x(t)$ in (43.5) is an important process called a Wiener process, denoted $W(t)$.

This is not the usual way of defining it, but it will prove useful to understand some of the properties more intuitively. See the work of Bergstrom (1976) for a treatment based on such infinite variance errors. Nevertheless, it will be convenient at time to view the Wiener process as the accumulation of *i.i.d.* errors with infinite variance just like a random walk in discrete time is the accumulation of *i.i.d.* errors with finite variance.

The usual way is to define the Wiener process as being a random variable satisfying a set of conditions and then proving that it exists and is well defined. This is outside the scope of our book. So, we simply state the following definition.

Definition 43.2 (Wiener Process). $W(t)$ is a (normalized) Wiener process if (1) $W(0) = 0$, (2) $E[W(t)] = 0$ for all t, (3) $W(t) \sim N(0, t)$ is normally distributed, and (4) $W(t)$ has stationary independent increments.

It is called a normalized of unit Wiener process since we impose the normalization $\text{Var}(W(1)) = 1$.

Remark 43.1. Since $W(t) = \int_0^t \varepsilon(u)\, du$, $\varepsilon(t)$ can be viewed as the derivative of the Wiener process $dW(t) = \varepsilon(t)\, dt$. Since the errors have infinite variance, this suggests that the Wiener process is not differentiable. This turns out to be the case. So, we need to explain why we so often use the notation $dW(t)$. Note also that by

Property (3), the Wiener process is non-stationary since its variance depends on the time index.

Property (4) merits some discussion to better understand what it means. The increments in question are simply the difference between the Wiener process at different time indices, say $W(t_1)$, $W(t_2)$, $W(t_3)$, and $W(t_4)$. The differences are called increments because, say,

$$W(t_2) - W(t_1) = \int_{t_1}^{t_2} \varepsilon(u)\, du$$

and

$$W(t_4) - W(t_3) = \int_{t_3}^{t_4} \varepsilon(u)\, du.$$

If $t_2 - t_1 = t_4 - t_3$, then $W(t_2) - W(t_1)$ and $W(t_4) - W(t_3)$ have the same distribution. This is the stationary part, i.e., invariance of the moments to a translation in time (up to order two is enough since it is normally distributed). This should make sense since then the two increments are the accumulation (or integration) of segments of the infinite variance *i.i.d.* errors having the same length. If $t_1 < t_2 < t_3 < t_4$, then the increments are integration of different segments of the *i.i.d.* errors, so they should be independent. This is the "independent increments" part.

We now discuss a useful property of the unit Wiener process, namely its covariance function. We have

$$\text{cov}\,(W\,(t), W\,(s)) = \min\,(t, s).$$

Proof. Let $s < t$

$$\begin{aligned}\text{cov}\,(W\,(s), W\,(t)) &= \text{cov}(W\,(s), [W\,(t) - W\,(s)] + W\,(s))\\ &= \text{cov}\,(W\,(s), [W\,(t) - W\,(s)]) + \text{Var}\,(W\,(s))\\ &= \text{Var}\,(W\,(s)) = s.\end{aligned}$$

The third equality follows from the assumption of independent increments, i.e., $W\,(s)$ and $(W\,(t) - W\,(s))$ are independent since they are the accumulation of different errors. The fourth equality follows from property (3). We can repeat the same argument with $t < s$ to get t and the result follows.

43.4 Back to the $AR(1)$ case

Let us go back to the $AR(1)$ case with discrete time representation

$$x_t = a x_{t-1} + e_t$$

and, in continuous time,

$$\dot{x}(t) = \alpha x(t) + \varepsilon(t).$$

In discrete time, the autocorrelation function of x_t is

$$\rho(r) = a^{|r|}.$$

Let $\tau = r\Delta t$ and recall that $a = 1/(1 + \alpha\Delta t)$, then

$$\rho(\tau) = (1 + \alpha\Delta t)^{-|(\tau/\Delta t)|}.$$

Let $\Delta t \to 0$, then

$$\rho(\tau) = \exp(-\alpha|\tau|).$$

This function is depicted in Figure 43.1 for $\alpha = 0.2$.

Recall that for a process $x(t)$ to be continuous, we need $\rho(\tau)$ to be continuous at $\tau = 0$. This is satisfied so the process is continuous. For stochastic differentiability, $\ddot{\rho}(0)$ must exist. It is clear here that $\ddot{\rho}(0)$ does not exist. So, $x(t)$ is not stochastically differentiable. This implies that we should not write

$$\dot{x}(t) = \alpha x(t) + \varepsilon(t)$$

(which does not exist). Somehow the literature has settled on writing such continuous-time stochastic differential equations as

$$dx(t) = \alpha x(t)\, dt + dW(t). \tag{43.6}$$

This is a special case of a diffusion process, called the Ornstein–Uhlenbeck process. Even the representation (43.6) is rather a shorthand for a solution that we now discuss.

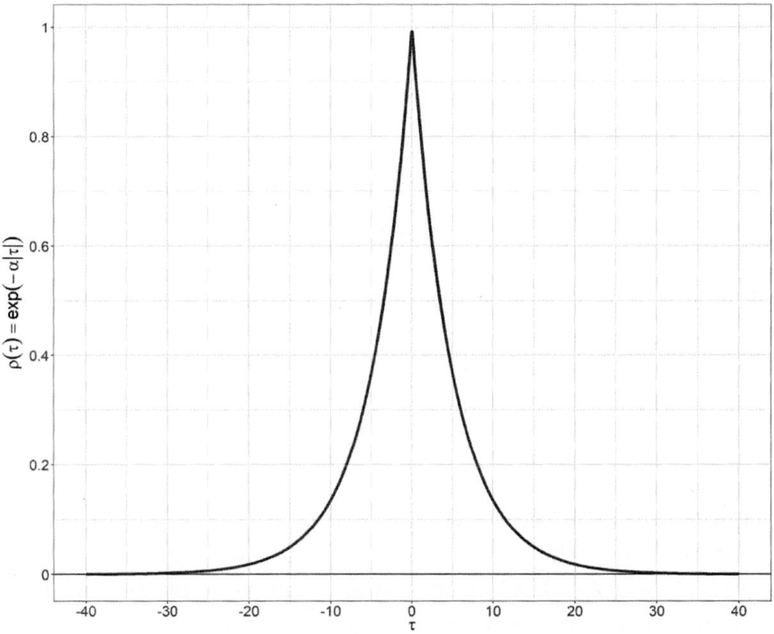

Figure 43.1. Autocorrelation function of a continuous-time $AR(1)$; $\alpha = 0.2$.

43.4.1 Basics of stochastic linear differential equations

Consider the class of scalar linear stochastic differential equations given by

$$dx(t) = (A\,(t)\,x(t) + a\,(t))\,dt + b\,(t)\,dW(t) \tag{43.7}$$

with initial condition $x_0 = c$. We seek a solution for $x(t)$.

Theorem 43.1 (Arnold (2013), p. 130). *By stating that* $x(t)$ *satisfies* (43.7), *we mean that it has the following solution:*

$$x(t) = \exp\left(\int_0^t A\,(s)\,ds\right)\left(c + \int_0^t \exp\left(-\int_0^s A\,(u)\,du\right)\right.$$
$$\left.\times\,(a\,(s)\,ds + b\,(s)\,dW(s))\right).$$

If $A(t) = a$, a constant, then

$$x(t) = \exp(at)\,c + \int_0^t \exp(a(t-s))\,(a(s)\,ds + b(s)\,dW(t)).$$

For the Ornstein–Uhlenbeck process,

$$dx(t) = \alpha x(t)dt + \sigma dW(t), \quad x(0) = c.$$

The solution is a special case with $A(t) = \alpha$, $a(s) = 0$, and $b(s) = \sigma$ given by

$$x(t) = x(0)\exp(\alpha t) + \sigma \int_0^t \exp(\alpha(t-s))\,dW(s).$$

In this book, we do not make use of general stochastic differential equations. The only one we use is the Ornstein–Uhlenbeck process, which is basically the continuous-time counterpart of the discrete-time $AR(1)$ process. For an accessible treatment of stochastic differential equations, see the work of Oksendal (1985).

43.5 Stochastic integrals

In general, we encounter expressions of the form

$$\int_0^t G(x(s), s)\,dW(s),$$

where $x(s)$ is itself a function of the Wiener process $W(s)$. This is called a stochastic integral. We need to spend some time on this before proceeding further. The problem is that we cannot interpret this as a Riemann–Stieltjes integral, basically because all sample functions of $W(s)$ are of unbounded variations (recall the interpretation in terms of infinite variance errors).

Definition 43.3. A Riemann–Stieltjes integral is defined as the mean-square limit of

$$\int_0^t G(s)\,dW(s) = \lim_{\max\{t_i, t_{i-1}\}\to 0} \sum_{i=1}^n G(\tau_i)\,(W(t_i) - W(t_{i-1}))$$

with $t_0 \leq t_1 \leq \ldots \leq t_n = t$ and $t_{i-1} \leq \tau_i \leq t_i$. It is well defined if for any choice of τ_i in (t_{i-1}, t_i), the limit is the same.

Remark 43.2. To illustrate this feature, consider integrating the simple function $f(x) = x$ in the interval $(0,1)$. Take equidistant intervals of length $(1/n)$, then

$$\int_0^1 x dx = \lim_{n\to\infty} \sum_{i=1}^{n} \tau_i (i/n - (i-1)/n)$$

for $(i-1)/n \leq \tau_i \leq i/n$. Consider the difference between evaluating the integrand at the upper limit and the lower limit of the rectangles. This is given by $\sum_{i=1}^{n}(1/n^2) = 1/n \to 0$, as $n \to \infty$. In general, the integral is the same whether the rectangles are constructed at any point in the interval $(t_{i-1} \leq \tau_i \leq t_i)$.

If G does not involve W, this is still the case. But if G involves W, the limit may depend on the particular choice of τ_i in the interval. The intuitive argument is that the Wiener process is not stochastically differentiable. Using the fact that

$$[W(t+h) - W(t)]/h \sim N(0, 1/h),$$

we have that, as $h \to 0$, the distribution diverges and

$$P\left[[W(t+h) - W(t)]/h \in B\right] \to 0,$$

as $h \to 0$ for any bounded set B. There are therefore enormous local fluctuations in $W(t)$. Each portion of almost every sample function of $W(t)$ is of unbounded variation in a finite interval of time.

Consider the following stochastic integral which plays a central role later:

$$\int_0^t W(s) dW(s).$$

If we use integration by parts $[\int f'\psi dx = f\psi - \int f\psi' dx]$, we have

$$\int_0^t W(s) dW(s) = \left(W(t)^2 - W(0)^2\right)/2 = W(t)^2/2$$

since $W(0) = 0$. But the validity of this solution presumes that

$$S_n = \sum_{i=1}^{n} W(\tau_i)\,(W(t_i) - W(t_{i-1}))$$

converges with finer partitioning and **any** choice of the intermediate points τ_i to a unique limit. Here, however, the limit depends **on the choice of the intermediate point**. Let

$$\tau_i = (1-a)\,t_{i-1} + at_i \quad 0 \leq a \leq 1 \quad i = 1, \ldots, n,$$

with $t_0 \leq t_1 \leq \ldots \leq t_n = t$. Consider evaluating the integral using the upper and lower limits for the integrand. For simplicity, suppose that $t = 1$ and that the rectangles are of equal length $1/n$. Then, the difference between the two is given by

$$\sum_{i=1}^{n} (W(i/n) - W((i-1)/n))^2, \tag{43.8}$$

whose expected value is 1 irrespective of n; see Exercise 43.1. Hence, evaluating the integrand at the upper or lower limits matters. In general, it can be shown (Arnold (2013)) that

$$\lim_{\max\{t_i - t_{i-1}\} \to 0} S_n = (1/2)W(t)^2 + (a - (1/2))\,t,$$

where the limit is in mean square.

43.6 The Ito integral

So what is the upshot of all this? First, the Riemann–Stieltjes integral theory breaks down. The usual rules of integration are no longer applicable; e.g., the chain rule or integration by parts. Second, we must choose an intermediate point at which to evaluate the integrand and once chosen, we must develop new rules. There is nothing that prevents us from using any intermediate point. The choice is simply a matter of convenience. It turns out that choosing the left point (i.e., $a = 0$) leads to simple and convenient properties. This was the choice made by Itô (1944). It is not the only one available; for instance, choosing $a = 1/2$ leads to what is called a Stratonovich integral (see Stratonovich, 1966), but it is far less convenient to work with.

For the example analyzed above, we then have

$$\int_0^t W(s)dW(s) = (1/2)[W(t)^2 - t],$$

or more generally,

$$\int_{t_0}^t W(s)dW(s) = (1/2)[(W(t)^2 - W(t_0)^2) - (t - t_0)].$$

This solution has the following properties:

1. $E[\int_{t_0}^t W(s)dW(s)] = 0$ since

$$E\left[\int_{t_0}^t W(s)dW(s)\right] = E\left[\frac{W(t)^2 - W(t_0)^2}{2}\right] - \left(\frac{t - t_0}{2}\right)$$
$$= \left(\frac{t - t_0}{2}\right) - \left(\frac{t - t_0}{2}\right) = 0.$$

2. $\int_{t_0}^t W(s)dW(s)$ is a martingale if and only if $a = 0$ (see the work of Arnold (2013) for a proof).

From now on, integrals of the form $\int_{t_0}^t G\left(W(s), s\right) dW(s)$ are to be understood as stochastic integrals of the Ito type. They have the following properties (for $G(s)$, $G_1(s)$ and $G_2(s)$ scalar functions and under some regularity conditions):

1. $$\int_{t_0}^t \left(aG_1\left(W(s), s\right) + bG_2\left(W(s), s\right)\right) dW(s)$$
$$= a\int_{t_0}^t G_1\left(W(s), s\right) dW(s) + b\int_{t_0}^t G_2\left(W(s), s\right) dW(s);$$

2. $E\left[\int_{t_0}^t G\left(W(s), s\right) dW(s)\right] = 0;$

3. $E\left[\int_{t_0}^t G\left(W(s), s\right) dW(s)\right]^2 = \int_{t_0}^t E\left[G\left(W(s), s\right)^2\right] ds.$

The first property is simply the usual additive property, so nothing new or special. What is of interest is especially the second one. All Ito stochastic integrals have mean zero. This is what makes the choice of the left point to evaluate the integrand so useful. This property is fairly easy to understand intuitively. If the integrand is evaluated at the left point, then the integral takes the form

$$\lim_{\max\{t_{i-1},t_i\}\to 0} \sum_{i=1}^{n} G\left(W(t_{i-1}), t_{i-1}\right)\left(W(t_i) - W(t_{i-1})\right).$$

Hence, the integrand depends on $W(t_{i-1})$ which is the integration of the *i.i.d.* errors from 0 to t_{i-1}. On the other hand, $W(t_i) - W(t_{i-1})$ is the integration of the *i.i.d.* errors from t_{i-1} to t_i. Since the segments are independent, the mean is 0. Property (3) is quite useful and applies even in the case of Riemann–Stieltjes integrals since the latter are valid for any choice of the intermediate point at which the integrand is evaluated.

43.7 Ito's lemma; scalar case

Ito's lemma is simply the chain rule for differentiation when the mean square limit of the Riemann–Stieltjes integral is evaluated at the intermediate point $a = 0$.

Theorem 43.2. *Suppose $u = u\,(t, x)$ is a continuous function with partial derivatives u_t, u_x, and u_{xx}. If $x(t)$ is defined according to the stochastic differential equation*

$$dx(t) = f\,(t)\,dt + G\,(t)\,dW(t),$$

then $y(t) = u\,(t, x(t))$ is represented by the stochastic differential equation

$$dy(t) = u_t\,(t, x(t))\,dt + u_x\,(t, x(t))\,dx(t) + (1/2)u_{xx}\,(t, x(t))\,G\,(t)^2\,dt.$$

Hence, $(1/2)u_{xx}\,(t, x(t))\,G\,(t)^2\,dt$ is the additional term to be added over the ordinary rule of differentiation.

We can also get an expression for the alternative formula for integration by parts in the case of stochastic integrals. We have the following result, with g' and g'', the first and second derivatives of g, respectively:

$$\int_{t_0}^{t_1} g(W(t),t)dW_t = g(W(t),t)W(t)|_{t_o}^{t_1} - \int_{t_0}^{t_1} g'(W(t),t)W(t)dW(t)$$
$$- (1/2)\int_{t_0}^{t_1} [g''(W(t),t)W(t) + 2g'(W(t))]dt.$$

Note that the last term is the additional one present in the case of stochastic integrals. To prove this, let $y(t) = g(W(t),t))W(t)$, then by Ito's lemma

$$dy(t) = d[g(W(t),t)W(t)] = [g'(W(t))W(t) + g(W(t))]dW(t)$$
$$+ (1/2)[g''(W(t),t)W(t) + 2g'(W(t),t)]dt.$$

Integrating both sides,

$$\int_{t_0}^{t_1} dy(t) = \int_{t_0}^{t_1} d[g(W(t),t)W(t)]$$
$$= \int_{t_0}^{t_1} g'(W(t),t)W(t)dW(t) + \int_{t_0}^{t_1} g(W(t),t)dW(t)$$
$$+ (1/2)\int_{t_0}^{t_1} g''(W(t),t)W(t)dt + \int_{t_0}^{t_1} g'(W(t),t)dt.$$

Rearranging gives the desired expression.

43.7.1 An application of Ito's lemma

Let us consider the evaluation of $\int_{t_0}^{t} W(s)dW(s)$. Let $y(t) = W(t)^2$ and $x(t) = W(t)$. Then, $f = 0, G = 1$, $u_t = 0$, $u_x = 2W(t)$, and $u_{xx} = 2$. Using Ito's lemma,

$$dy(t) = (1/2)2dt + 2W(t)dW(t) = dt + 2W(t)dW(t).$$

Integrate from t_0 to t:

$$\int_{t_0}^{t} dy(s) = \int_{t_0}^{t} dW(s)^2 = W(t)^2 - W(t_0)^2$$
$$= \int_{t_0}^{t} ds + 2\int_{t_0}^{t} W(s)dW(s),$$

which implies that

$$\int_{t_0}^{t} W(s)dW(s) = (1/2)[(W(t)^2 - W(t_0)^2) - (t - t_0)].$$

A special case that will be of interest later is

$$\int_{0}^{1} W(s)dW(s) = (1/2)[W(1)^2 - 1]. \tag{43.9}$$

43.8 The Ornstein–Uhlenbeck process

We go back to the stochastic differential equation defined by

$$dx(t) = \alpha x(t)dt + \sigma dW(t)$$

with solution

$$x(t) = x(0)\exp(\alpha t) + \sigma\int_{0}^{t} \exp(\alpha(t-s))\, dW(s). \tag{43.10}$$

We first consider the conditions for the process to be second-order stationary. We have

$$\operatorname{Var}(x(t)) = \operatorname{Var}(x(0))(\exp(2\alpha t)) + \sigma^2 \operatorname{Var}\left(\int_{0}^{t} \exp(\alpha(t-s))\, dW(s)\right) \tag{43.11}$$

since a stochastic integral has mean 0. Now,

$$\operatorname{Var}\left(\int_{0}^{t} \exp(\alpha(t-s))\, dW(s)\right) = (\exp(2\alpha t) - 1)/(2\alpha). \tag{43.12}$$

This is proved using the following developments, using property (3) of stochastic integrals:

$$\begin{aligned}\operatorname{Var}\left(\int_0^t \exp\left(\alpha\left(t-s\right)\right) dW\left(s\right)\right) &= \int_0^t E\left[\exp\left(\alpha\left(t-s\right)\right)\right]^2 ds \\ &= \int_0^t \exp\left(2\alpha\left(t-s\right)\right) ds \\ &= \left(\exp\left(2\alpha t\right)-1\right)/(2\alpha).\end{aligned}$$

after standard derivations. Using (43.11) and (43.12) and imposing stationarity,

$$\begin{aligned}\operatorname{Var}\left(x(t)\right) = \operatorname{Var}\left(x(0)\right) &= \frac{\sigma^2(\exp\left(2\alpha t\right)-1)}{2\alpha}\frac{1}{1-\exp\left(2\alpha t\right)} \\ &= \sigma^2/(-2\alpha).\end{aligned}$$

Hence, the required condition is that $\alpha < 0$ and $x_0 \sim N\left(0, \sigma^2/(-2\alpha)\right)$.

43.8.1 Discrete time representation

Let h denote the sampling interval and consider the sequence th for $t = 0, 1, \ldots, T$, where $Th = N$ is the span. We have from the solution (43.10)

$$\begin{aligned}x_{(t-1)h} &= x_0 \exp\left(\alpha\left(t-1\right)h\right) \\ &\quad + \sigma\int_0^{(t-1)h} \exp\left(\alpha\left(\left(t-1\right)h-s\right)\right) dW(s)\end{aligned}$$

and

$$\begin{aligned}x_{th} &= x_0\exp\left(\alpha th\right) + \sigma\int_0^{th} \exp\left(\alpha\left(th-s\right)\right) dW(s) \\ &= \exp\left(\alpha h\right)\left[x_0 \exp\left(\alpha\left(t-1\right)h\right)\right. \\ &\quad \left. + \sigma\int_0^{(t-1)h} \exp\left(\alpha\left(\left(t-1\right)h-s\right)\right) dW(s)\right] \\ &\quad + \sigma\int_{(t-1)h}^{th} \exp\left(\alpha\left(th-s\right)\right) dW(s),\end{aligned}$$

or

$$x_{th} = \exp(\alpha h)\, x_{(t-1)h} + u_{th}, \tag{43.13}$$

where

$$u_{th} = \sigma \int_{(t-1)h}^{th} \exp(\alpha(th - s))\, dW(s).$$

It is easy to show that (see Exercise 43.2)

$$u_{th} \sim N\left(0, \sigma^2(\exp(2\alpha h) - 1)/(2\alpha)\right). \tag{43.14}$$

The process (43.13) is simply an $AR(1)$ of the form

$$x_{th} = \beta_h x_{(t-1)h} + u_{th}, \tag{43.15}$$

where

$$\beta_h = \exp(\alpha h).$$

Remark that as $h \to 0$, $\beta_h \to 1$ and we have a random walk. Note that β_h approaches 1 at rate h^{-1}, in accordance with the stated conjecture (at the time) in Section 43.2.1. It is also easy to show that as $h \to 0$, $\text{Var}(u_{th}) \to 0$, as stated before using more heuristic arguments. The representation of an $AR(1)$ in discrete time given by (43.15) becomes useful later.

43.9 The functional central limit theorem

In what follows, we let u_t be the sequence of random variables of interest, for reasons that become clear in the following chapters. For now, it is a zero mean short-memory linear process generated by

$$u_t = C(L)\,\varepsilon_t = \sum_{j=0}^{\infty} c_j \varepsilon_{t-j},$$

where $\varepsilon_t \sim i.i.d.(0, \sigma_\varepsilon^2)$ and $\sum_{j=0}^{\infty} j|c_j| < \infty$ or $\sum_{j=0}^{\infty} j^2 c_j^2 < \infty$. We discussed earlier asymptotic tools such as the weak law of large numbers and the central limit theorem. In order to deal with unit root processes, we need another one: the Functional Central Limit Theorem (FCLT). Our discussion is again very intuitive and we do not deal with precise technical issues. For a rigorous treatment, see, e.g., the works of Billingsley (1999) or Bierens (1994) (Section 9.1) for a more accessible treatment; see also the work of Davidson (2006).

Consider the function

$$X_T(r) = T^{-1/2} \sum_{t=1}^{[Tr]} u_t,$$

where [.] is the operator that defines the greatest integer smaller than the argument. It is sometimes called the floor function in analogy with coding practices. For instance, if $T = 100$ and $r = 1/3$, then $[100 \times 1/3] = 33$. Here, u_t will again be a short-memory linear process with finite second moment, for simplicity. More general conditions are possible and we discuss some of those later. What is especially important to note here is that r is continuous and defined over the interval $[0, 1]$. This is what makes it a difficult problem because now we are asking questions about the limit of a whole random function as opposed to the limit of a single random variable as dealt with using a CLT. This will require some extra work and attention. We can depict the function as in Figure 43.2.

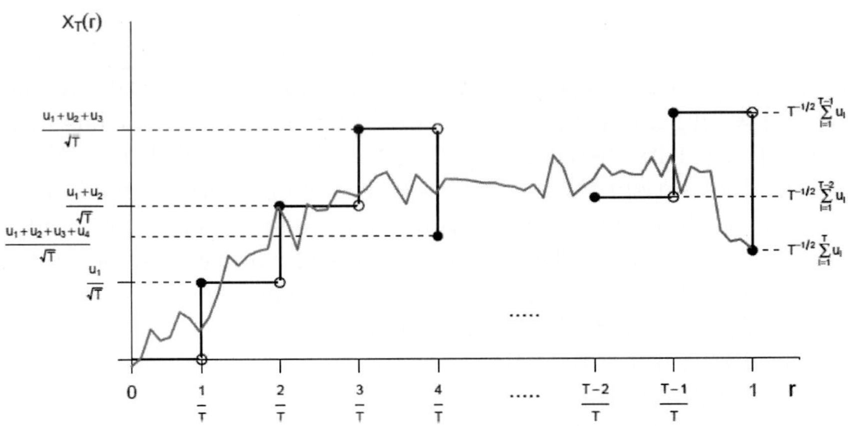

Figure 43.2. FCLT: $X_T(r)$, discontinuous line; $W(r)$, continuous line.

This function is called “càdlàg”, from the French for “continue à droite, limite à gauche”, which translates to a process being continuous to the right and having a limit to the left. The interesting thing is that when T increases, the width between the observations decreases, while the total length stays the same. Hence, we should expect a continuous process in the limit, represented by the solid thin line in the graph.

Let us first investigate what this process needs to satisfy at a bare minimum. Consider the limit for a given fixed r^*, in which case we are back to a single random variable (not a function). In order to alleviate the notation, we let $\sigma_u^2 = \text{Var}(u_t)$, the usual variance, and $\sigma^2 = 2\pi h_u(0)$, (2π) times the spectral density function of u_t at frequency zero, or the long-run variance. Recall that for a linear process $\sigma^2 = \sigma_u^2 C(1)^2$. Then,

$$\begin{aligned}
X_T(r^*) &= T^{-1/2} \sum_{t=1}^{[Tr^*]} u_t \\
&= \frac{[Tr^*]^{1/2}}{T^{1/2}} [Tr^*]^{-1/2} \sum_{t=1}^{[Tr^*]} u_t \\
&\xrightarrow{d} (r^*)^{1/2} N(0, \sigma^2) \\
&= \sigma N(0, r^*)
\end{aligned}$$

since $[Tr^*]/T \to r^*$ and $[Tr^*]^{-1/2} \sum_{t=1}^{[Tr^*]} u_t = n^{-1/2} \sum_{t=1}^{n} u_t \xrightarrow{d} N(0, \sigma^2)$ (setting $n = [Tr^*]$). The issue then is what function defined on $[0, 1]$ would satisfy: (a) It starts at 0 when $r = 0$; (b) it has mean 0 for all r; (c) its distribution is $N(0, r)$ for all r. Well, the Wiener process does satisfy these conditions and is obviously a good candidate for the limit random function that we seek. This turns out to be the correct “guess”. But we need to discuss a few more issues first to understand the main difference of the convergence concept used relative to the case with a single random variable.

The first issue is to define a topology, that is, a space for each function and a metric to measure the distance between the two. Now, $X_T(r)$ with $r \in [0, 1]$ is said to be an element of the space $D[0, 1]$, the space of discontinuous functions on the interval $[0, 1]$.

The Wiener process $W(r)$ for $r \in [0, 1]$ belongs to the space $C[0, 1]$, the space of continuous functions on $[0, 1]$.

When dealing with a single random variable, it is relatively easy to define a measure of distance between it and its candidate limit value, usually a mean-square deviation is enough. When dealing with a function, things are a bit more tricky. One candidate is the maximum (or supremum) deviation over the range $r \in [0, 1]$. This is a metric often adopted and called the sup-norm. There are many others. One often adopted is the Skorokhod topology. It allows some discontinuities in the process by somehow deforming the time index around such discontinuities and, hence, is more general than using the sup-norm.

The way one then proves convergence of a whole random function to some limit random function is to show two things: First, one establishes the finite-dimensional convergence (or fidi convergence). This involves showing that all moments of the finite sample random function converge to those of the limit random function. This is a bit what we have done above but only for the first moment. We could do it for the second- and higher-order moments (e.g., the covariances between two elements say) and we would still have obtained that the moments of $X_T(r)$ converge to those of $\sigma W(0, r)$. The second step is to show the so-called "tightness" property. In a nutshell, it says that in the limit, everything holds together. This is where the measure of distance plays a role. Namely, we must show that the distance (with respect to the norm used) converges to zero. This is usually the tougher part to prove.

The above discussion is meant to be a very intuitive and informal overview of the main issues. A precise technical treatment is outside the scope of this book. Useful references are the works of Davidson (1994) and Billingsley (1999). What matters to us is the end result, which in our context states that under the sup-norm or the Skorokhod topology, we have

$$X_T(r) \Rightarrow \sigma W(r), \tag{43.16}$$

where $W(r)$ is the Wiener process defined on $[0, 1]$ and "$\Rightarrow$" refers to weak (functional) convergence in distribution. We refer to it as the Functional Central Limit Theorem (FCLT). It is also often called an invariance principle.

Throughout this book, we assumed time series being generated by short-memory linear processes with *i.i.d.* errors. These can be generalized or weakened substantially but at the expense of introducing complexities without much added practical relevance. General results are available using so-called mixing-type assumptions, see, for example, the work of White (2001) for a discussion of law of large numbers and central limit theorems and the works of McLeish (1975a,b) and McLeish (1977) for FCLT.

For example, some mixing conditions measure the difference between the joint and the product of the marginal distributions of sets of events (sigma-fields) separated by, say, m periods and require this difference to vanish at some appropriate rate as m increases.

Despite their generality, the mixing-type conditions are often difficult to verify even for simple time-series models that are of direct interest here. Also, not all linear processes are strong-mixing and to analyze the simple first-order autoregressive model, one needs to consider functions of mixing processes to have a general theory in that case. Hence, we do not deal with them any further. See also the works of Bierens (1994) (Chapter 6) and Davidson (1994) for an extensive treatment.

One relaxation of the *i.i.d.* assumption that is useful and allows clearly more general models that are of relevance in practice is to allow a "martingale difference sequence" or "m.d.s.". None of the results are changed, we simply need to re-interpret some quantities in an appropriate way. In our context, these assumptions will pertain to the sequence u_t and will allow mild forms of heteroskedasticity and also conditional heteroskedasticity; e.g., ARCH, GARCH, see Chapter 48. We have the following definition:

Definition 43.4 (Martingale Difference Sequence). Let Φ_t be a filtration to which $\{\varepsilon_t\}$ is adapted, then $\{\varepsilon_t, \Phi_t\}$ is a martingale difference sequence if $E[\varepsilon_t|\Phi_{t-1}] = 0$.

For those not familiar with the measure-theoretic jargon, think about a filtration Φ_t as the information set available at time t. It is called a filtration because we assume that we do no lose any information as time goes by, i.e., a filtration is such that $\ldots, \Phi_{t-1} \subseteq \Phi_t \subseteq \Phi_{t+1} \ldots$. When we say that ε_t is adapted to Φ_t, we simply mean that it is in the information set at time t (in the jargon, it is measurable with respect to the sigma-field Φ_t). What is important is that for an m.d.s. sequence its conditional expectation using the information set available last period is zero. The substantial advantage it has over the *i.i.d.* assumption is that it only restricts the temporal dependence of the first moment. It forbids serial correlation in ε_t. To see this, note that

$$\begin{aligned} E\left[\varepsilon_t \varepsilon_{t-j}\right] &= E\left\{E\left[\varepsilon_t \varepsilon_{t-j} | \Phi_{t-j}\right]\right\} \\ &= E\left\{E\left[\varepsilon_t | \Phi_{t-j}\right] \varepsilon_{t-j}\right\} = 0. \end{aligned}$$

However, it does not restrict temporal dependence in the higher-order moments, in particular, the variance. This is important in practice since often macroeconomic or financial variables have time-varying variance or display conditional heteroskedasticity. Hence, following the work of Phillips and Solo (1992), we assume that

$$u_t = C(L)\varepsilon_t = \sum_{j=0}^{\infty} c_j \varepsilon_{t-j},$$

with

$$\sum_{j=1}^{\infty} j^2 c_j^2 < \infty,$$

and $\{\varepsilon_t\}$ a martingale difference sequence, strongly uniformly integrable with dominating random variable Z that satisfies $E\left[Z^{2+\eta}\right] < \infty$ for some $\eta > 0$, $E\left[Z^2 \ln^+ |Z|\right] < \infty$ and

$$\lim_{T\to\infty} T^{-1} \sum_{t=1}^{T} E(u_t^2 | \Phi_{t-1}) \equiv \sigma_u^2, \tag{43.17}$$

$$\lim_{T\to\infty} T^{-1} \sum_{t=1}^{T} E(\varepsilon_t^2 | \Phi_{t-1}) \equiv \sigma_\varepsilon^2, \tag{43.18}$$

where Φ_t is the filtration to which ε_t is adapted. Note that a sequence of random variables $\{Z_t\}$ is said to be strongly uniformly integrable if, for some dominating random variable Z with $E|Z| < \infty$, we have

$$\mathbb{P}(|Z_t| \geq x) \leq c\mathbb{P}(|Z| \geq x)$$

for all $x \geq 0, t \geq 1$ and for some constant c.

43.9.1 Summary

We then have the following results or tools:

1. Law of Large Numbers (LLN): $T^{-1}\sum_{t=1}^{T} u_t \xrightarrow{p} 0$; $T^{-1}\sum_{t=1}^{T} u_t^2 \xrightarrow{p} \sigma_u^2$ as defined by (43.17).
2. Central Limit Theorem (CLT): $T^{-1/2}\sum_{t=1}^{T} u_t \xrightarrow{d} N(0, \sigma_\varepsilon^2 C(1)^2) \equiv N(0, \sigma^2)$ with σ_ε^2 defined by (43.18), where

$$\begin{aligned}\sigma^2 &= \lim_{T\to\infty} T^{-1}E\left(\sum_{t=1}^{T} u_t\right)^2 \\ &= \lim_{T\to\infty} [T^{-1}\sum_{t=1}^{T} E\left(u_t^2\right) + 2\sum_{j=1}^{T-1}\sum_{t=j+1}^{T} E\left[u_t u_{t-j}\right]] \\ &= 2\pi h_u(0) \text{ when } u_t \text{ is stationary.}\end{aligned}$$

3. Functional Central Limit Theorem (FCLT): $X_T(r) = T^{-1/2} \sum_{t=1}^{[Tr]} u_t \Rightarrow \sigma W(r)$.
4. Continuous Mapping Theorem (CMT): If $g(.)$ is a function continuous almost everywhere (i.e., with a countable number of discontinuities), then $g(X_T(r)) \Rightarrow g(\sigma W(r))$.

These are all the tools we need to keep on going. Of course, other sets of conditions, potentially less restrictive, are possible. Our approach to this issue is the following. Assume anything you want so that conditions (1–4) stated above hold. All the estimates derived so far will remain consistent for the relevant quantities of interest. Then, go to work, which is what really matters as econometricians. We do so in the following chapter in the context of unit root processes.

43.10 Exercises

Exercise 43.1. Show that the limit of the expectation of (43.8) is 1 as $n \to \infty$.

Exercise 43.2. Prove the results stated in (43.14).

Exercise 43.3. Suppose that x_t satisfies the conditions for a functional central limit theorem to hold, i.e., $T^{-1/2}\sum_{t=1}^{[Tr]} x_t \Rightarrow \sigma W(r)$, where $\sigma^2 = \lim_{T\to\infty} T^{-1}E(\sum_{t=1}^{T} x_t)^2$. Derive the limiting distribution of $T^{-1/2}\sum_{t=1}^{[Tr]}(x_t - \bar{x})$, where $\bar{x} = T^{-1}\sum_{t=1}^{T} x_t$. State the limit distribution as, say, $\sigma B(r)$. What is the covariance function $E[B(r)B(s)]$?

Exercise 43.4. Suppose that $x_t = \mu + u_t$, where u_t is such that $T^{-1/2}\sum_{t=1}^{[Tr]} u_t \Rightarrow \sigma W(r)$ with $\sigma^2 = 2\pi h_u(0)$ and $W(r)$ is a standard Wiener process and $h_u(0)$ is the spectral density function of u_t at frequency 0. T is the size of the sample of data available. We also have $T^{-1}\sum_{t=1}^{T} u_t^2 \xrightarrow{p} \sigma_u^2 = var(u_t)$. You are interested in making inference about the mean of the process and accordingly run the following simple OLS regression:

$$x_t = \hat{\mu} + \hat{u}_t. \tag{43.19}$$

(a) Consider the standard t-statistic for testing the null hypothesis $H_0 : \mu = \mu_0$ versus the alternative $H_1 : \mu \neq \mu_0$. It is defined by

$$t_\mu = \frac{\hat{\mu} - \mu_0}{(s^2/T)^{1/2}},$$

where $s^2 = T^{-1}\sum_{t=1}^{T} \hat{u}_t^2$. Derive the limit distribution of t_μ. Is it free of nuisance parameters? If not, suggest a transformation that allows you to carry valid asymptotic inference. Call this statistic t_μ^*. What is the limit distribution of t_μ^*? (b) Instead of using the regression (43.19) as the basis to construct a test statistic to test H_0, consider a regression based on the partial sums from 1 to t of the variables on the left- and right-hand sides of (43.19), i.e.,

$$z_t = \mu t + S_t, \tag{43.20}$$

where $z_t = \sum_{j=1}^{t} x_j$ and $S_t = \sum_{j=1}^{t} u_j$. Let $\tilde{\mu}$ be the OLS estimate of μ from the regression (43.20) and t_z the associated usual t-statistic:

$t_z = (\tilde{\mu}-\mu_0)/(s^2(\sum_{t=1}^{T} t^2)^{-1})^{1/2}$, where $s^2 = T^{-1}\sum_{t=1}^{T} \hat{s}_t^2$. Derive the limit distribution of $T^{-1/2}t_z$. Is it free of nuisance parameters? What do you need to do to carry a valid asymptotic testing procedure? What advantage does $T^{-1/2}t_z$ have over t_μ^*? (c) Assume now that the errors are *i.i.d.* such that $\sigma^2 = \sigma_u^2$. Derive the local asymptotic power function of the tests t_μ and $T^{-1/2}t_z$ for a sequence of local alternative hypotheses of the form $\mu = \mu_0 + \delta/\sqrt{T}$.

Hint: Recall that $\lim_{T\to\infty} T^{-3}\sum_{t=1}^{T} t^2 = 1/3$.

Exercise 43.5. Suppose that $x_t = \mu + u_t$, where u_t is such that $T^{-1/2}\sum_{t=1}^{[Tr]} u_t \Rightarrow \sigma W(r)$ with $\sigma^2 = 2\pi h_u(0)$ and $W(r)$ is a standard Wiener process and $h_u(0)$ is the spectral density function of u_t at frequency 0. T is the size of the sample of data available. You are interested in making inference about the mean of the process and accordingly run the following simple *OLS* regression:

$$x_t = \hat{\mu} + \hat{u}_t.$$

As shown previously,

$$\sqrt{T}(\hat{\mu} - \mu_0) \xrightarrow{d} N(0, \sigma^2).$$

Hence, to construct a test one may use a consistent estimate of σ^2. One such estimate uses the Bartlett kernel and is given by

$$\hat{\sigma}^2 = \hat{R}(0) + 2\sum_{s=-(m_T-1)}^{m_T-1} (1 - s/m_T)\hat{R}(s),$$

where $\hat{R}(s) = T^{-1}\sum_{t=|s|+1}^{T} \hat{u}_t\hat{u}_{t-|s|}$. Recall that $\hat{\sigma}^2$ will be consistent for σ^2 if $m_T \to \infty$ and $m_T/T \to 0$ as $T \to \infty$. Now, let $S_t = \sum_{j=1}^{t} \hat{u}_j$ and $C_T = T^{-2}\sum_{t=1}^{T} S_t^2$. (a) Show that C_T is equal to the Bartlett estimate with bandwidth m_T equal to sample size T (this part is rather difficult but you can do the rest simply using the result). (b) Derive the limit of C_T. (c) Derive the limit distribution of the robust t-statistic

$$t^* = \frac{\sqrt{T}(\hat{\mu} - \mu_0)}{\sqrt{C_T}}$$

and show that it does not depend on nuisance parameters (beware, the numerator and denominator are not independent). (d) Since one can use simulations to obtain the critical values of the limit distribution (see Section 44.5), conclude that one can perform valid asymptotic hypothesis testing without the need for a consistent estimate of $\sigma^2 = 2\pi h_u(0)$ but simply one that is proportional to it. Why is the estimate not consistent? (e) Can you see any advantages or disadvantages in terms of size and power in using this approach instead of the usual one discussed in Chapter 38 (hint: for size, look at the relationship between C_T and the finite sample variance of $\hat{\mu}$; for power, look at the type of distribution found in part (3)).

Chapter 44

Unit Roots

We now consider processes with a unit root. We first assume the data are generated by, for $t = 1, \dots, T$,

$$\begin{aligned} y_t &= y_{t-1} + u_t, \\ u_t &= \sum_{i=0}^{\infty} c_i \varepsilon_{t-i} \ , \end{aligned} \tag{44.1}$$

with $\sum_{j=1}^{\infty} j^2 c_j^2 < \infty$ and $\{\varepsilon_t\}$ is a martingale difference sequence. We set $y_0 = O_p(1)$ so that the initial condition y_0 can be a fixed constant or some random variable. We then have conditions (1–4) of Section 43.9 satisfied, which we reproduce here for the sake of clarity of exposition:

1. Law of Large Numbers (LLN): $T^{-1} \sum_{t=1}^{T} u_t \xrightarrow{p} 0$; $T^{-1} \sum_{t=1}^{T} u_t^2 \xrightarrow{p} \sigma_u^2$ with

$$\sigma_u^2 \equiv \lim_{T \to \infty} T^{-1} \sum_{t=1}^{T} E(u_t^2 | \Phi_{t-1}).$$

2. Central Limit Theorem (CLT): $T^{-1/2} \sum_{t=1}^{T} u_t \xrightarrow{d} N(0, \sigma_\varepsilon^2 C(1)) \equiv N(0, \sigma^2)$ with

$$\sigma_\varepsilon^2 \equiv \lim_{T \to \infty} T^{-1} \sum_{t=1}^{T} E(\varepsilon_t^2 | \Phi_{t-1})$$

and

$$\sigma^2 = \lim_{T\to\infty} T^{-1} E\left(\sum_{t=1}^{T} u_t\right)^2$$
$$= \lim_{T\to\infty} \left[T^{-1} \sum_{t=1}^{T} E\left(u_t^2\right) + 2 \sum_{j=1}^{T-1} \sum_{t=j+1}^{T} E\left[u_t u_{t-j}\right]\right].$$

3. Functional Central Limit Theorem (FCLT): $X_T(r) = T^{-1/2} \sum_{t=1}^{[Tr]} u_t \Rightarrow \sigma W(r)$.
4. Continuous Mapping Theorem (CMT): If $g(.)$ is a function continuous almost everywhere (i.e., with a countable number of discontinuities), then $g(X_T(r)) \Rightarrow g(\sigma W(r))$.

Note that if u_t is stationary, then $\sigma_u^2 = \text{Var}(u_t)$ and $\sigma^2 = 2\pi h_u(0)$, where $h_u(0)$ is the spectral density function of u_t at frequency zero. Methods to construct consistent estimates for these quantities remain the same whether the process is stationary or more generally specified by conditions (1–4).

44.1 The sample mean of y_t and y_t^2

We start with the limit distribution of the sample mean of y_t and y_t^2. The easiest way to understand the results is to go back to Figure 43.2 (previous chapter), which we reproduce here.

For ease of notation, we simply assume $y_0 = 0$, without loss of generality. Also, we derive the limit of $T^{-3/2} \sum_{t=1}^{T} y_{t-1}$. This is the same as the limit of $T^{-3/2} \sum_{t=1}^{T} y_t$ since

$$T^{-3/2} \sum_{t=1}^{T} y_t = T^{-3/2} \sum_{t=1}^{T} y_{t-1} + T^{-3/2} y_T = T^{-3/2} \sum_{t=1}^{T} y_{t-1} + o_p(1)$$

since $y_T = \sum_{j=1}^{T} u_j = O_p(T^{1/2})$ using the CLT. By recursive substitution, we have

$$y_t = \sum_{j=1}^{t} u_j.$$

Hence, we can write $T^{-3/2}\sum_{t=1}^{T} y_{t-1}$ as

$$\frac{1}{T}0+\frac{1}{T}\left(\frac{u_1}{T^{1/2}}\right)+\frac{1}{T}\left(\frac{u_1+u_2}{T^{1/2}}\right)$$
$$+\frac{1}{T}\left(\frac{u_1+u_2+u_3}{T^{1/2}}\right)+\cdots+\frac{1}{T}\left(\frac{\sum_{j=1}^{T-1}u_j}{T^{1/2}}\right). \tag{44.2}$$

Making the correspondence between expression (44.2) and Figure 44.1, the T terms are the area of the T rectangles under the function $X_T(r)$, with $1/T$ being the width and $T^{-1/2}\sum_{j=1}^{i-1} u_j$ being the height for the ith rectangle for $i = 1, \ldots, T$. Hence,

$$T^{-3/2}\sum_{t=1}^{T} y_{t-1} = \int_0^1 X_T(r)dr \Rightarrow \sigma\int_0^1 W(r)dr, \tag{44.3}$$

using the FCLT $X_T(r) \Rightarrow \sigma W(r)$ and the continuous mapping theorem since the integral is a continuous function. To analyze the limit of $T^{-2}\sum_{t=1}^{T} y_{t-1}^2$, we can draw a graph for $X_T(r)^2$ similar to that of Figure 44.1, as depicted in Figure 44.2.

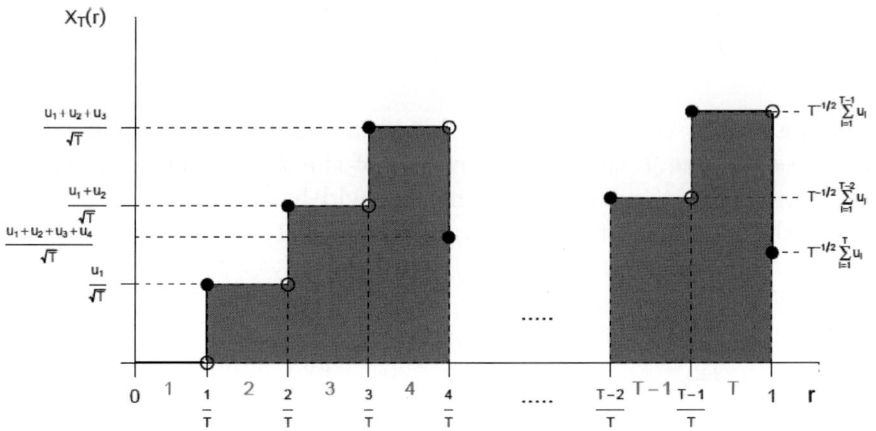

Figure 44.1. The integral of $X_T(r)$.

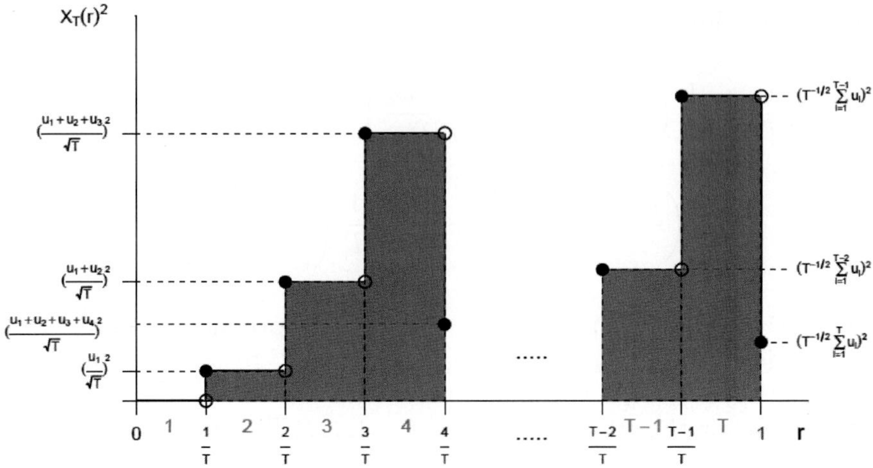

Figure 44.2. The integral of $X_T(r)^2$.

We can write $T^{-2}\sum_{t=1}^{T} y_{t-1}^2$ as

$$\frac{1}{T}0 + \frac{1}{T}\left(\frac{u_1}{T^{1/2}}\right)^2 + \frac{1}{T}\left(\frac{u_1+u_2}{T^{1/2}}\right)^2 + \frac{1}{T}\left(\frac{u_1+u_2+u_3}{T^{1/2}}\right)^2 + \cdots + \frac{1}{T}\left(\frac{\sum_{j=1}^{T-1} u_j}{T^{1/2}}\right)^2. \tag{44.4}$$

Making the correspondence between expression (44.4) and Figure 44.2, the T terms are the area of the T rectangles under the function $X_T(r)^2$, with $1/T$ being the width and $(T^{-1/2}\sum_{j=1}^{i-1} u_j)^2$ being the height for the ith rectangle for $i = 1, \ldots, T$. Hence,

$$T^{-2}\sum_{t=1}^{T} y_{t-1}^2 = \int_0^1 X_T(r)^2 dr \Rightarrow \sigma^2 \int_0^1 W(r)^2 dr, \tag{44.5}$$

using again the FCLT and the CMT.

44.2 The limit distribution of the OLS estimate in an AR(1)

Consider the following regression estimated by OLS:

$$y_t = \hat{\alpha} y_{t-1} + \hat{u}_t. \tag{44.6}$$

The OLS estimate is

$$\hat{\alpha} = \sum_{t=1}^{T} y_t y_{t-1} \Big/ \sum_{t=1}^{T} y_{t-1}^2,$$

and imposing the structure of the DGP (44.1)

$$T(\hat{\alpha} - 1) = T^{-1} \sum_{t=1}^{T} y_{t-1} u_t \Big/ \left(T^{-2} \sum_{t=1}^{T} y_{t-1}^2 \right).$$

We already have the limit of the denominator given by (44.5), hence we next consider the limit of the numerator. Start by squaring both sides of $y_t = y_{t-1} + u_t$:

$$y_t^2 = y_{t-1}^2 + 2 y_{t-1} u_t + u_t^2,$$

or

$$y_{t-1} u_t - (1/2)[y_t^2 - y_{t-1}^2 - u_t^2],$$

and

$$\begin{aligned} T^{-1} \sum_{t=1}^{T} y_{t-1} u_t &= (1/2) \left[T^{-1} y_T^2 - T^{-1} y_0^2 - T^{-1} \sum_{t=1}^{T} u_t^2 \right] \\ &\Rightarrow (1/2)[\sigma^2 W(1)^2 - \sigma_u^2] \\ &= (\sigma^2/2)(W(1)^2 - \sigma_u^2/\sigma^2) \\ &= (\sigma^2/2)(W(1)^2 - 1 + \left(\sigma^2 - \sigma_u^2\right)/\sigma^2) \end{aligned} \tag{44.7}$$

since $T^{-1} y_T^2 \Rightarrow \sigma^2 W(1)^2$ using the FCLT and $T^{-1} \sum_{t=1}^{T} u_t^2 \xrightarrow{p} \sigma_u^2$ using the LLN. Now, let

$$\delta = (\sigma^2 - \sigma_u^2)/(2\sigma^2). \tag{44.8}$$

Then, we can write (44.7) as

$$T^{-1}\sum_{t=1}^{T} y_{t-1}u_t \Rightarrow \sigma^2\left(\int_0^1 W(r)\,dW(r) + \delta\right) \tag{44.9}$$

from the fact that

$$\int_0^1 W(r)\,dW(r) = (W(1)^2 - 1)/2,$$

using Ito's lemma; see Section 43.7.1. Combining (44.5) and (44.9), we have

$$T(\hat{\alpha} - 1) \Rightarrow \frac{\int_0^1 W(r)\,dW(r) + \delta}{\int_0^1 W(r)^2 dr}$$

since the σ^2 terms cancel.

Remark 44.1. In this general case, the limiting distribution of $T(\hat{\alpha} - 1)$ depends on the nuisance parameter $\delta = \left(\sigma^2 - \sigma_u^2\right)/(2\sigma^2)$. When the sequence $\{u_t\}$ is uncorrelated, we have $\sigma^2 = \sigma_u^2$ and $\delta = 0$. To be more precise, $\delta = 0$ holds when the sequence $\{u_t\}$ is a martingale difference sequence. To see this, note that

$$\begin{aligned}
\sigma^2 &= \lim_{T\to\infty} T^{-1}E\left[\sum_{t=1}^{T} u_t\right]^2 \\
&= \lim_{T\to\infty}\left[T^{-1}\sum_{t=1}^{T} E\left(u_t^2\right) + 2\sum_{j=1}^{T-1}\sum_{t=j+1}^{T} E\left[u_t u_{t-j}\right]\right] \\
&= \sigma_u^2 + \lim_{T\to\infty}\left\{2\sum_{j=1}^{T-1}\sum_{t=j+1}^{T} E\left[u_t u_{t-j}\right]\right\}.
\end{aligned}$$

When $\{u_t\}$ is an *m.d.s.*, we have

$$\begin{aligned}
E\left[u_t u_{t-j}\right] &= E\left\{E\left[u_t u_{t-j} | \Phi_{t-j}\right]\right\} \\
&= E\left\{E\left[u_t | \Phi_{t-j}\right] u_{t-j}\right\} = 0.
\end{aligned}$$

Hence, $\sigma^2 = \sigma_u^2$.

Remark 44.2. When $\delta = 0$, the limiting distribution of $T(\hat{\alpha} - 1)$ is free of nuisance parameters and critical values can therefore be tabulated and used for inference. See the work of Fuller (1996). When $\delta \neq 0$, we need modifications to eliminate the effect of the nuisance parameters. We return to that issue after covering the cases with additional exogenous regressors (e.g., when a constant or a constant and a time trend are included).

The t-statistic for testing $\alpha = 1$ using the regression (44.6) can be written as

$$t_{\hat{\alpha}} = (\hat{\alpha} - 1) \Bigg/ \left[\hat{s}_u^2 \left(\sum_{t=1}^{T} y_{t-1}^2 \right)^{-1} \right]^{1/2},$$

where

$$\hat{s}_u^2 = T^{-1} \sum_{t=1}^{T} (y_t - \hat{\alpha} y_{t-1})^2 = T^{-1} \sum_{t=1}^{T} \hat{u}_t^2,$$

and imposing the DGP (44.1):

$$t_{\hat{\alpha}} = T^{-1} \sum_{t=1}^{T} y_{t-1} u_t / [\hat{s}_u^2 T^{-2} \sum_{t-1}^{T} y_{t-1}^2]^{1/2}.$$

Given the limiting results in (44.5) and (44.9), we only need to derive the limit of $\hat{s}_u^2$. We have

$$\begin{aligned}
\hat{s}_u^2 &= T^{-1} \sum_{t=1}^{T} (y_t - \hat{\alpha} y_{t-1})^2 \\
&= T^{-1} \sum_{t=1}^{T} (y_t - y_{t-1} - (\hat{\alpha} - 1) y_{t-1})^2 \\
&= T^{-1} \sum_{t=1}^{T} u_t^2 - 2(\hat{\alpha} - 1) T^{-1} \sum_{t=1}^{T} y_{t-1} u_t + T(\hat{\alpha} - 1)^2 T^{-2} \sum_{t=1}^{T} y_{t-1}^2 \\
&\xrightarrow{p} \sigma_u^2,
\end{aligned}$$

using (44.5) and (44.9), $(\hat{\alpha} - 1) = o_p(1)$, and the fact that $T^{-1} \sum_{t=1}^{T} u_t^2 \xrightarrow{p} \sigma_u^2$. Collecting results, we have

$$t_{\hat{\alpha}} \Rightarrow \sigma^2 \left(\int_0^1 W(r)\, dW(r) + \delta \right) \Big/ \left[\sigma_u^2 \sigma^2 \int_0^1 W(r)^2\, dr \right]^{1/2}$$

$$= \frac{\sigma}{\sigma_u} \left(\int_0^1 W(r)\, dW(r) + \delta \right) \Big/ \left[\int_0^1 W(r)^2\, dr \right]^{1/2}.$$

When $\delta = 0$, this reduces to

$$t_{\hat{\alpha}} \Rightarrow \int_0^1 W(r)\, dW(r) \Big/ \left[\int_0^1 W(r)^2\, dr \right]^{1/2},$$

for which critical values are tabulated in the work of Fuller (1996). Note that the limit distribution is clearly not normal. It is, nevertheless, simply a random variable for which quantiles of its distribution can be obtained.

44.2.1 The case with an intercept

We now consider the case where the data generating process is still given by (44.1) but the fitted regression includes a constant, that is, we estimate by *OLS* the regression

$$y_t = \mu + \alpha y_{t-1} + u_t.$$

We consider the limiting distribution of the *OLS* estimate of α which is given by (using Frisch–Waugh–Lovell's theorem; see Section 2.1.3):

$$\hat{\alpha} = \frac{\sum_{t=1}^{T} (y_t - \bar{Y})(y_{t-1} - \bar{Y}_{-1})}{\sum_{t=1}^{T} (y_{t-1} - \bar{Y}_{-1})^2},$$

where $\bar{Y} = T^{-1} \sum_{t=1}^{T} y_t$ and $\bar{Y}_{-1} = T^{-1} \sum_{t=1}^{T} y_{t-1}$. It is straightforward to show that under the stated DGP

$$T(\hat{\alpha} - 1) = \frac{T^{-1} \sum_{t=1}^{T} (y_{t-1} - \bar{Y}_{-1}) u_t}{T^{-2} \sum_{t=1}^{T} (y_{t-1} - \bar{Y}_{-1})^2}.$$

Consider first the limit of the numerator. We have

$$
\begin{aligned}
T^{-1}\sum_{t=1}^{T}&(y_{t-1}-\bar{Y}_{-1})u_t \\
&= T^{-1}\sum_{t=1}^{T} y_{t-1}u_t - \left(T^{-3/2}\sum_{t=1}^{T} y_{t-1}\right)\left(T^{-1/2}\sum_{t=1}^{T} u_t\right) \\
&\Rightarrow \sigma^2\left(\int_0^1 W(r)\,dW(r) + \delta - W(1)\int_0^1 W(r)\,dr\right).
\end{aligned}
$$

The limit of the denominator is given by

$$
\begin{aligned}
T^{-2}\sum_{t=1}^{T}(y_{t-1}-\bar{Y}_{-1})^2 &= T^{-2}\sum_{t=1}^{T} y_{t-1}^2 - \left(T^{-3/2}\sum_{t=1}^{T} y_{t-1}\right)^2 \\
&\Rightarrow \sigma^2\left(\int_0^1 W(r)^2\,dr - \left(\int_0^1 W(r)\,dr\right)^2\right).
\end{aligned}
$$

Hence, the limit of the normalized least-squares estimator is given by

$$
T(\hat{\alpha} - 1) \Rightarrow \frac{\int_0^1 W(r)\,dW(r) + \delta - W(1)\int_0^1 W(r)\,dr}{\int_0^1 W(r)^2\,dr - \left(\int_0^1 W(r)\,dr\right)^2}. \tag{44.10}
$$

The important thing to note is that this limiting distribution is different from the case where no intercept is included even if the data-generating process is the same. This holds even if the included regressor (the constant) is redundant, a feature completely different from that which applies in the stationary context or with a random sample of *i.i.d.* data. Additional terms are present in both the numerator and denominator. In fact, the limiting distribution will be different for different specifications of the deterministic components in the estimated autoregression.

We seek an expression for the limiting distribution that could encompass a general class of possible deterministic components. A general expression is derived in the following section but we provide an explicit treatment of the case with a fitted intercept here.

To provide some intuition, note that the normalized bias can be written as

$$T(\hat{\alpha}-1)=\frac{T^{-1}\sum_{t=1}^{T}y_{t-1}^{*}u_t}{T^{-2}\sum_{t=1}^{T}(y_{t-1}^{*})^2},$$

where $y_{t-1}^{*}=y_{t-1}-\bar{Y}_{-1}$ is the demeaned value of y_{t-1}. Hence, we can expect that the limit distribution could be expressed in terms of a demeaned Wiener process $W^{*}(r)$, that is,

$$T(\hat{\alpha}-1)\Rightarrow\frac{\int_0^1 W^{*}(r)\,dW(r)+\delta}{\int_0^1 W^{*}(r)^2\,dr}. \tag{44.11}$$

To see that this is indeed the case, we first need to define what we mean by a demeaned Wiener process. Consider a continuous time regression of the Wiener process on a constant where the span of the available data extends from time 0 to 1. The regression is of the form

$$W(r)=c+e(r),$$

say, for $r\in[0,1]$ where $e(r)$ is the error term. The least squares estimate of c solves the following minimization problem:

$$\min_{c}\int_0^1 (W(r)-c)^2dr$$

and the first-order condition is

$$2\int_0^1 (W(r)-c)dr=0$$

so that the estimate of c is given by the sample mean of the Wiener process, i.e.,

$$\hat{c}=\int_0^1 W(s)\,ds.$$

Hence, the estimated residual function $\hat{e}(r)$ is the demeaned Wiener process given by

$$W^{*}(r)=\hat{e}(r)=W(r)-\int_0^1 W(s)\,ds.$$

To see that the representations (44.10) and (44.11) are equivalent, note that

$$\begin{aligned}\int_0^1 W^*(r)\,dW(r) &= \int_0^1 [W(r) - \int_0^1 W(s)\,ds]dW(r)\\ &= \int_0^1 W(r)dW(r) - \int_0^1 dW(r)\int_0^1 W(s)\,ds\\ &= \int_0^1 W(r)dW(r) - W(1)\int_0^1 W(s)\,ds\end{aligned}$$

and

$$\begin{aligned}\int_0^1 W^*(r)^2\,dr &= \int_0^1 \left(W(r) - \int_0^1 W(s)\,ds\right)^2 dr\\ &= \int_0^1 W(r)^2 dr - 2\int_0^1 W(r)\int_0^1 W(s)\,dsdr\\ &\quad + \int_0^1 \left(\int_0^1 W(s)\,ds\right)^2 dr\\ &= \int_0^1 W(r)^2 dr - 2\left(\int_0^1 W(r)dr\right)^2 + \left(\int_0^1 W(r)dr\right)^2\\ &= \int_0^1 W(r)^2 dr - \left(\int_0^1 W(r)dr\right)^2.\end{aligned}$$

Remark 44.3. A similar result holds for the t-statistic and we have

$$t_{\hat{\alpha}} \to \frac{\sigma}{\sigma_u}\left(\int_0^1 W^*(r)\,dW(r) + \delta\right) / \left[\int_0^1 W^*(r)^2\,dr\right]^{1/2}.$$

The following section extends the results for a wide class of possible deterministic components including some that can be discontinuous.

44.3 Extensions to cases with deterministic components

In a first step, we still consider the same DGP as in the previous subsection. The regression, however, now includes a vector of deterministic variables $z_t' = (z_{1t}, \ldots, z_{kt})$ so that the regression estimated by OLS is

$$y_t = \alpha y_{t-1} + \beta z_t + u_t. \tag{44.12}$$

We can write the normalized bias as

$$T(\hat{\alpha} - 1) = \frac{T^{-1} \sum_{t=1}^{T} y_{t-1}^* u_t}{T^{-2} \sum_{t=1}^{T} (y_{t-1}^*)^2},$$

where y_{t-1}^* are the residuals from a projection of y_{t-1} on the components of z_t. We consider the general case where z_t contains both continuous and discontinuous functions of time. This is especially useful if one wants to allow for structural changes in the trend function of a series. We explicitly allow only for the possibility of a one-time change occurring at some date $[T\lambda]$, but the method extends immediately to the case of multiple discontinuities.

We separate the vector z_t as (z_t^A, z_t^B), where $z_t^A = (z_{1t}, \ldots, z_{pt})'$ and $z_t^B = (z_{p+1,t}, \ldots, z_{kt})'$. We assume

$$\begin{aligned} z_{it} &= g_i(t), & i &= 1, \ldots, p, \\ z_{it}(\lambda) &= g_i(t)\, 1(t > [\lambda T]), & i &= p+1, \ldots, k, \end{aligned}$$

and that there exists a diagonal matrix δ_T such that

$$\delta_T g([Tr]) \to g(r), \quad 0 \le r \le 1, \tag{44.13}$$

uniformly in r, where $g(\cdot) = (g_1(\cdot), g_2(\cdot), \ldots, g_k(\cdot))$. That is, we have convergence of $g(\cdot)$ under the sup norm, i.e.,

$$\sup_{r \in (0,1)} |\delta_{i,T} g_i([Tr]) - g_i(r)| \to 0 \quad \text{as } T \to \infty,$$

where $\delta_{i,T}$ is the ith diagonal element of δ_T. Note that we do not require that $\delta_T z_{[Tr]}$ converges uniformly, using the sup norm, to some limiting functions. We assume that the elements of the functions $g(r) = (g_1(r), \ldots, g_k(r))$ are differentiable.

Example 44.1. Consider the case of a linear trend with a change in intercept at date $[\lambda T]$. We have

$$z_t = (1, t, 1(t > [\lambda T]))$$

so that $g_1(t) = 1$, $g_2(t) = t$ and $g_3(t) = 1$. We have, with $\delta_T = (1, T^{-1}, 1)$,

$$\delta_T g([Tr]) \to (1, r, 1) \quad \text{as } T \to \infty,$$

under the sup norm. See also Exercise 44.3.

We have the following result proved in the work of Perron (1997a). Let

$$Pz_T(\lambda) = [Pz_{1,T}(\lambda), \ldots, Pz_{T,T}(\lambda)]$$

be the linear map projecting onto the space spanned by the columns of $z_T(\lambda)' = (z_1(\lambda), \ldots, z_T(\lambda))$. We introduce the argument λ to emphasize that the projection may depend on the location of the break point. By definition

$$Pz_T(\lambda) = z_T(\lambda)\left(z_T'(\lambda)\, z_T(\lambda)\right)^{-} z_T(\lambda)',$$

where $(\cdot)^{-}$ denotes a g-inverse.

Theorem 44.1. *If the DGP is given by* (44.1) *and the regression used is* (44.12). *We have, uniformly over* $\lambda \in [0,1]$ (*when a break is present in some of the regressors*),

(a) $Pz_T(\lambda)\, X_T(r) \Rightarrow \sigma Pz(\lambda)\, W(r)$ *with*

$$Pz(\lambda)\, W(r) \equiv Z(\lambda, r)' \left[\int_0^1 Z(\lambda, s)\, Z(\lambda, s)'\, ds\right]^{-} \times \int_0^1 Z(\lambda, s)\, W(s)\, ds;$$

(b) $\displaystyle\int_0^1 Pz_T(\lambda)\, X_T(r)\, dX_T(r) \to \sigma^2 \int_0^1 Pz(\lambda)\, W(r)\, dW(r)$;

(c) $\displaystyle T(\hat{\alpha} - 1) \Rightarrow \left[\int_0^1 W_z^*(r)\, dW(r) + \delta\right] \Big/ \int_0^1 W_z^*(r)^2\, dr$,

where $W_z^*(r) = W(r) - Pz(\lambda)\, W(r)$ *are the residuals from a projection of a Wiener process on the space spanned by the functions*

$$Z(\lambda, r)' = (g_1(r), \ldots, g_p(r), 1(r > \lambda)\, g_{p+1}(r), \ldots, 1(r > \lambda)\, g_k(r)).$$

(d) *Consider now the t-statistic for testing* $\alpha = 1$ *using the regression (44.12) defined by*

$$t_{\hat{\alpha}} = (\hat{\alpha} - 1) \Bigg/ \left[\hat{s}_u^2 \left(\sum_{t=1}^{T} (y_{t-1}^*)^2\right)^{-1}\right]^{1/2}.$$

We have

$$t_{\hat{\alpha}} \Rightarrow \left(\frac{\sigma}{\sigma_u}\right) \left[\int_0^1 W_z^*(r)\, dW(r) + \delta\right] \Bigg/ \left[\int_0^1 W_z^*(r)^2\, dr\right]^{1/2}.$$

Example 44.2. It is useful to illustrate this result returning to the example where $Z(\lambda, r) = (1, r, 1(r > \lambda))$. Note that

$$\int_0^1 Z(\lambda, s) Z(\lambda, s)' ds = \begin{bmatrix} 1 & 1/2 & (1-\lambda) \\ 1/2 & 1/3 & \left(1-\lambda^2\right)/2 \\ (1-\lambda) & \left(1-\lambda^2\right)/2 & (1-\lambda) \end{bmatrix}.$$

If $\lambda = 1$,

$$\int_0^1 Z(1, s) Z(1, s)' ds = \begin{bmatrix} 1 & 1/2 & 0 \\ 1/2 & 1/3 & 0 \\ 0 & 0 & 0 \end{bmatrix} \equiv A,$$

and if $\lambda = 0$,

$$\int_0^1 Z(0, s) Z(0, s)' ds = \begin{bmatrix} 1 & 1/2 & 1 \\ 1/2 & 1/3 & 1/2 \\ 1 & 1/2 & 1 \end{bmatrix} \equiv B.$$

A and B are obviously singular, but a common g-inverse of A is given by

$$A^{-} = 12 \begin{bmatrix} 1/3 & -1/2 & 0 \\ -1/2 & 1 & 0 \\ 0 & 0 & 0 \end{bmatrix}.$$

Since the choice of the g-inverse leaves a projection map unchanged, we have for $\lambda = 0, 1$

$$Pz(\lambda)W(r) = Z^{\perp}(r)' \left[\int_0^1 Z^{\perp}(s)Z^{\perp}(s)'ds\right]^{-1} \int_0^1 Z^{\perp}(s)W(s)ds,$$

where $Z^{\perp}(r)' = (1, r)$, in which case the limiting distribution of $T(\hat{\alpha} - 1)$ reduces to that in the case where no dummy for structural change is included.

Remark 44.4. The more usual case with $k = p$, i.e., with no discontinuous regressors, follows easily as a special case.

Critical values for inference: When $\sigma_u^2 = \sigma^2$, the limit distributions of $T(\hat{\alpha} - 1)$ and $t_{\hat{\alpha}}$ are invariant to nuisance parameters. Therefore, critical values can be constructed and used for inference about the null hypothesis that $\alpha = 1$. The limiting distributions depend, however, on the explicit structure of the deterministic components $\{z_t\}$ and, when dummy-type regressors are included, the value of λ if it is known. It is furthermore different if λ is treated as unknown. The following is a list of references where critical values can be found: (a) $z_t = \{\emptyset\}, \{1\}, \{1, t\}$: Dickey and Fuller (1979), Fuller (1996); (b) $z_t = \left\{1, t, t^2, \ldots, t^p\right\}$, $(p = 2, 3, 4, 5)$: Ouliaris *et al.* (1989); (c) $z_t = \{1, 1(t > \lambda T)\}$, λ known: Perron (1990a); (d) $z_t = \{1, t, 1(t > \lambda T)\}$, $\{1, t, 1(t > \lambda T), t1(t > \lambda T)\}$, λ known: Perron (1989b); (e) $z_t = \{1, t, t * 1(t > \lambda T)\}$, λ known: Perron and Vogelsang (1993a).

The same limiting result holds even with regressors that exhibit multiple discontinuities. The method of proof is exactly similar. The critical values depend, of course, on the precise structure. See Chapter 50 for the case with trend breaks at unknown dates.

44.4 Invariance to deterministic components

So far, we assumed that the DGP is (44.1), which has no deterministic component, and considered regressions of the form (44.12), which includes such deterministic components. We obviously need to extend the DGP. Suppose now that the data-generating process is

$$\begin{aligned} y_t &= \beta z_t + v_t, \\ v_t &= \alpha v_{t-1} + u_t, \end{aligned} \tag{44.14}$$

with v_0 some initial value and u_t satisfying the conditions stated above. We have the following facts:

1. The limiting distributions of $T(\hat{\alpha} - 1)$ and $t_{\hat{\alpha}}$ are asymptotically invariant to β and y_0 when $|\alpha| \leq 1$ (provided λ is treated as known and identical to the true date of change if breaks are present). If there are discontinuous regressors and the change point is unknown, this asymptotic invariance to β no longer holds when these regressors are trending. See the work of Vogelsang and Perron (1998).
2. The finite sample distributions of $T(\hat{\alpha} - 1)$ and $t_{\hat{\alpha}}$ (when λ is treated as known if discontinuous regressors are present) are invariant to β and y_0 if $\alpha = 1$ and only to β but not y_0 if $|\alpha| < 1$. For a proof in the case $z_t = \{1, t\}$, see Exercise 44.3.

The implication of these results is that all limit distributions that we derived under DGP (44.1), with no deterministic component, are still valid under the much more general DGP (44.14). This is so because, given the invariance of the OLS estimate to the value of β, we can, without loss of generality, set $\beta = 0$.

Remark 44.5. The DGP (44.14) is written in a so-called unobserved components framework with the trend βz_t and the noise v_t introduced additively and treated separately. It is inappropriate to write the DGP as

$$y_t = \beta z_t + \alpha y_{t-1} + u_t. \tag{44.15}$$

It makes no sense. For instance, if z_t is simply a constant, then

$$y_t = \beta + \alpha y_{t-1} + u_t.$$

If $|\alpha| < 1$, the process is stationary around a constant mean given by $\beta/(1 - \alpha)$. However, if $\alpha = 1$, the process is trending since, by recursive substitution, $y_t = y_0 + \beta t + \sum_{j=1}^{t} u_j$. It makes no sense to compare a process with a deterministic trend with one that is non-trending. One must make a decision about the trend component that applies in an equal fashion to both cases. This is yet another example of the importance of distinguishing between a DGP and a regression. Here, (44.15) is a regression, while the DGP is (44.14).

Remark 44.6. Note that the result discussed above holds only if there is no misspecification with respect to the included deterministic regressors. If one includes too many, the results go through but at the expense of power losses. However, if the deterministic components included in the regression omit some deterministic components present in the DGP driving the variable of interest, then everything changes. The limit distribution is, in general, different, especially if the excluded deterministic components are trending. For a general discussion of this issue, see the work of Campbell and Perron (1991). For instance, if the DGP is

$$y_t = a + bt + v_t,$$

and the regression is

$$y_t = c + \alpha y_{t-1} + u_t, \tag{44.16}$$

then a relevant trend component is omitted from the regression. In this case, the limit distribution of the t-statistic on α from estimating (44.16) by OLS is $t_\alpha \xrightarrow{d} N(0,1)$. However, under the alternative hypothesis that $|\alpha| < 1$, $t_\alpha \xrightarrow{p} 0$ so that the test has no power. See Exercise 44.9 and the work of Perron (1988). These results carry over to more general forms of misspecification when various trending deterministic components are incorrectly excluded, though the exact nature of the distributions may be different.

44.5 How to obtain critical values

When the nature of the deterministic components is simple, e.g., no more than a linear trend, it is possible to get closed-form expressions for the limit distribution of $T(\hat{\alpha} - 1)$, though not for the t-statistic. With no deterministic component, a closed-form expression was derived by Rao (1978) with corrections by Evans and Savin (1981a); see also the works of Chan and Wei (1988) and Abadir (1993). The expression is exceedingly complex.

A more friendly route is the following. In some cases, it is relatively easy to derive the joint characteristic function of the numerator ($\int_0^1 W^*(r)\,dW(r)+\delta$) and denominator ($\int_0^1 W^*(r)^2\,dr$). One can then use the following inversion formula due to the work of Gurland (1948) that relates the distribution and characteristic functions:

$$F(x) = (1/2) - (1/\pi)\int_0^\infty \frac{I\left[cf(\mu, -\mu x)\right]}{\mu}d\mu,$$

where $I(.)$ denotes the imaginary part of the complex number. Hence, one can use numerical integration techniques. This is the approach taken by Perron (1989b, 1991a,b, 1996), Nabeya and Perron (1994), and Nabeya and Sørensen (1994). An alternative approach is based on Fredholm determinants; see, e.g., the works of Nabeya and Tanaka (1990), Tanaka (1990), Tanaka (1993), and Nabeya and Perron (1995).

However, given the limited scope of the applicability of these methods, the most common technique to obtain quantiles of the limit distribution is to use simulation methods. The basic steps are the following. Suppose that the data generating process is given by (44.14). Consider an estimated autoregression of the form

$$y_t = \beta z_t + \alpha y_{t-1} + u_t.$$

Let $\hat{\alpha}$ be the least-squares estimate of α. Under the hypothesis that $\alpha = 1$, we have

$$T(\hat{\alpha} - 1) \Rightarrow \frac{\int_0^1 W^*(r)dW(r) + \delta}{\int_0^1 W^*(r)^2 dr},$$

with all terms as defined before. To simulate the asymptotic distribution of $T(\hat{\alpha} - 1)$, we use the following steps:

1. Approximate the integrals by $J = 1{,}000$ (or some other large number) steps and generate the Wiener process as the partial sums of *i.i.d.* $N(0,1)$ random variables (call them e_t). Hence, first generate $W_j = \sum_{t=1}^{j} e_t$, for $j = 1, \ldots, J$, where J is the number of steps.
2. When $z_t \neq 0$, an approximation to the detrended Wiener process is obtained using the residuals from a regression of W_j on z_t, denoted by W_j^*.

3. Then, the distribution of $\int_0^1 W^*(r)dW(r)$ is approximated by $N^{-1}\sum_{j=1}^{N} W_{j-1}^* e_j$ using the fact that $W_0 = 0$ and the distribution of $\int_0^1 W^*(r)^2 dr$ by $N^{-2}\sum_{j=1}^{N}(W_{j-1}^*)^2$.
4. Using N replications (e.g., 5,000), simulate the cdf of the limiting distribution of $T(\hat{\alpha}-1)$. Sort the values and take the $\beta\%$ quantile as the $[\beta * N]$th entry as the estimate.
5. The same applies to the t-statistic, except that one approximates $[\int_0^1 W^*(r)^2 dr]^{1/2}$ by $[N^{-2}\sum_{j=1}^{N}(W_{j-1}^*)^2]^{1/2}$.

44.6 Near-integrated processes

The usefulness of the near-integrated framework is due to the following features of the standard asymptotic distributions and their relations to the finite sample distributions. Let us consider, for ease of exposition, the simple first-order autoregressive process

$$y_t = \alpha y_{t-1} + e_t, \tag{44.17}$$

where $\{e_t\} \sim i.i.d.\ N(0,\sigma^2)$ and $y_0 = \kappa$, some constant. The OLS estimator of α is given by

$$\hat{\alpha} = \sum_{t=1}^{T} y_t y_{t-1} \Big/ \sum_{t=1}^{T} y_{t-1}^2.$$

The finite sample distribution of $\hat{\alpha}$ is a continuous function of the true value α. On the other hand, the asymptotic distribution is discontinuous at the boundary $\alpha = 1$. To be more precise, we have the followign:

(a) $T^{1/2}(\hat{\alpha}-\alpha)\left(1-\alpha^2\right)^{-1/2} \xrightarrow{d} N\left(0,\sigma^2\right)$ when $|\alpha| < 1$;
(b) $T(\hat{\alpha}-1) \Rightarrow \int_0^1 W(r)\,dW(r) / \int_0^1 W(r)^2\,dr$ when $\alpha = 1$;
(c) $|\alpha|^T\left(\alpha^2-\alpha\right)^{-1}(\hat{\alpha}-\alpha)$ has a limiting Cauchy distribution when $|\alpha| > 1$ provided $y_0 = 0$.

Part (a) follows from the Mann–Wald theorem, part (b) was discussed above and part (c) is due to White (1958) (see also White (1959)). Hence, not only are the limiting distributions different for the cases $|\alpha| < 1$, $|\alpha| = 1$ and $|\alpha| > 1$, but the rates of convergence are also different. Given the continuity of the finite sample distribution with respect to α, one could expect the limiting distribution to provide an inadequate approximation to the finite sample distribution when α is "near" but not equal to one. This has been documented, for example, in the work of Evans and Savin (1981b). A feature of interest is that, when α is close to 1, the unit root asymptotic distribution seems to provide a better approximation than the standard asymptotic distribution. Where α is further away from one, the usual asymptotic distribution provides a fairly accurate approximation for common sample sizes.

In an attempt to provide an asymptotic framework that provides a better approximation to the finite sample distribution when α is close to 1, various authors have considered the so-called near-integrated process. In this framework, the autoregressive parameter is modeled as local to unity by specifying

$$\alpha = \exp(c/T) \approx 1 + c/T. \tag{44.18}$$

Here, c, a real-valued constant, is a measure of the deviation from the unit root case. As the sample size increases, the autoregressive parameter converges to unity. Hence, the AR(1) process (44.17) with α described by (44.18) can be said to have a root that is local to unity. When c is negative, the process $\{y_t\}$ is said to be locally stationary, and when c is positive, it is said to be locally explosive.

The limiting distribution of $T(\hat{\alpha} - \alpha)$ in this near-integrated framework has been derived, using different approaches, by the works of Bobkoski (1983), Chan and Wei (1987), Chan (1988), Phillips (1988), and Jeganathan (1991). For an application, see the work of Stock (1991). Tabulations of this limiting distribution have been obtained by Bobkoski (1983), Nabeya and Tanaka (1990), Cavanagh (1986), Chan (1988), and Perron (1989a) through various methods. These studies also show the approximation to the finite sample distribution to be quite good when α is close to 1 and $y_0 = 0$. The main reason why this framework provides a better approximation is essentially because it provides an asymptotic distribution that is continuous in the parameter c which calibrates given pairs of T and α. In the following sections, we review the limiting results that are obtained in this near-integrated framework.

44.6.1 The data-generating process

The basic data-generating process is of the form

$$\begin{aligned} y_t &= \alpha y_{t-1} + u_t, \\ \alpha &= \exp(c/T) \approx 1 + c/T, \end{aligned} \tag{44.19}$$

and u_t satisfies the conditions for the application of a functional central limit theorem to the partial sums $X_T(r) = T^{-1/2} \sum_{j=1}^{[Tr]} u_j$. In particular, we have $X_T(r) \Rightarrow \sigma W(r)$, where $\sigma^2 = \lim_{T\to\infty} T^{-1} E[\sum_{j=1}^{T} u_j]^2$. As seen in the previous section, such conditions are general enough to allow for a wide class of linear processes and in particular all stationary and invertible $ARMA$ processes of finite order. We also assume that the conditions are such that

$$T^{-1} \sum_{t=1}^{T} u_t^2 \xrightarrow{p} \sigma_u^2 = \lim_{T\to\infty} T^{-1} \sum_{t=1}^{T} E\left[u_t^2 | \Phi_{t-1}\right] < \infty.$$

Going back to the discrete time representation of an Ornstein–Uhlenbeck process given by

$$x_{th} = \exp(\alpha h)\, x_{(t-1)h} + u_{th},$$

as derived in Section 43.8.1, we can see a similarity between a near-integrated process and this discrete-time representation of the Ornstein–Uhlenbeck process. Indeed, if we let $h = N/T$, where N is the fixed span of the data and T the number of observations, we have $\exp(\alpha h) = \exp(c/T)$ with $c = \alpha N$. Hence, it should come as no surprise that the limit of such near-integrated processes would involve the Ornstein–Uhlenbeck process. This is indeed the case.

44.6.2 Preliminary results

The basic ingredient in characterizing the asymptotic distribution in the near-integrated case is the continuous time version of the $AR(1)$ process, the so-called Ornstein–Uhlenbeck process. For reasons that become clear later, we denote this process by $W_c(r)$ where we explicitly denote the dependence of the process on the non-centrality parameter c. The stochastic process $W_c(r)$ is generated by the following stochastic differential equation:

$$dW_c(r) = cW_c(r)\,dr + dW(r),$$
$$W_c(0) = 0.$$

The solution to this stochastic differential equation is given by

$$W_c(r) = \int_0^r \exp(c(r-s))\,dW(s), \tag{44.20}$$

from which we deduce that

$$W_c(r) \sim N(0, (\exp(2cr) - 1)/(2c)).$$

Note that when $c = 0$, $W_0(r) = W(r)$ the standard Wiener process. Other relations are also useful. First, using integration by parts to solve (44.20),

$$W_c(r) = W(r) + c\int_0^r \exp(c(r-s))\,W(s)\,ds. \tag{44.21}$$

Second, applying Ito's formula to $\left\{\int_0^r \exp(-cs)\,dW(s)\right\}^2$, we have

$$W_c(1)^2 = 1 + 2c\int_0^1 W_c(r)^2\,dr + 2\int_0^1 W_c(r)\,dW(r). \tag{44.22}$$

See Exercise (44.1). We immediately deduce that when $c = 0$, $W_0(r) = W(r)$ and, solving (44.22) with $c = 0$

$$\int_0^1 W(r)\,dW(r) = (1/2)(W(1)^2 - 1),$$

consistent with our earlier derivations.

44.6.3 The limiting distribution of $T(\hat{\alpha} - \alpha)$

As a matter of notation, we define as before $X_T(r) = T^{-1/2}\sum_{t=1}^{[Tr]} u_t$. When the data generating process is given by (44.17) with α described by (44.18), we have the following limiting results for the sample moments of the data, whose proof is in the appendix.

Lemma 44.1. *If* $\{y_t\}$ *is generated by* (44.17) *and* α *by* (44.18), (a) $T^{-1/2}y_{[Tr]} \Rightarrow \sigma W_c(r)$, (b) $T^{-3/2}\sum_{t=1}^{T} y_t \Rightarrow \sigma \int_0^1 W_c(r)\,dr$, (c) $T^{-2}\sum_{t=1}^{T} y_t^2 \Rightarrow \sigma^2 \int_0^1 W_c(r)^2\,dr$, *and* (d) $T^{-1}\sum_{t=1}^{T} y_{t-1}u_t \Rightarrow \sigma^2\{\int_0^1 W_c(r)\,dW(r) + \delta\}$ *with* $\delta = (\sigma^2 - \sigma_u^2)/(2\sigma^2)$.

Using parts (c) and (d) of Lemma 44.1, we easily deduce the limiting distribution of $T(\hat{\alpha} - \alpha)$ in the near-integrated context:

$$T(\hat{\alpha} - \alpha) = \left(T^{-1}\sum_{t=1}^{T} y_{t-1}u_t\right) \Big/ \left(T^{-2}\sum_{t=1}^{T} y_{t-1}^2\right)$$

$$\Rightarrow \frac{\int_0^1 W_c(r)\,dW(r) + \delta}{\int_0^1 W_c(r)^2\,dr}, \tag{44.23}$$

where $\delta = (\sigma^2 - \sigma_u^2)/(2\sigma^2)$. If $\{u_t\}$ is a martingale difference sequence, or more simply *i.i.d.*, then $\sigma^2 = \sigma_u^2$ and

$$T(\hat{\alpha} - \alpha) \Rightarrow \frac{\int_0^1 W_c(r)\,dW(r)}{\int_0^1 W_c(r)^2\,dr}. \tag{44.24}$$

When $c = 0$, $\alpha = 1$ and this reduces to our earlier result in the unit root case with $W_c(r) = W(r)$ so that

$$T(\hat{\alpha} - 1) \Rightarrow \frac{\int_0^1 W(r)\,dW(r)}{\int_0^1 W(r)^2\,dr}. \tag{44.25}$$

44.6.4 A note on local asymptotic power

The limiting results (44.24) and (44.25) are useful to obtain the local asymptotic power function of a unit root test based on the statistic $T(\hat{\alpha} - 1)$. See Section 9.4 for a review of local asymptotic power. To be more explicit, we consider the following null and alternative hypotheses:

$$H_0\colon \alpha = 1,$$

$$H_{1,T}\colon \alpha_T = \exp(c/T) \approx 1 + c/T.$$

Under the sequence of alternative hypotheses, α_T is local to 1 and converges to this null value at rate T. This normalization is chosen to obtain a non-degenerate limiting power function. Note first that

$$T(\hat{\alpha}-1) = T(\hat{\alpha}-\alpha_T) + T(\alpha_T - 1).$$

Using (44.24) and the fact that $T(\alpha_T - 1) \to c$, we have, under the assumption of martingale difference errors,

$$T(\hat{\alpha}-1) \Rightarrow c + \frac{\int_0^1 W_c(r)\, dW(r)}{\int_0^1 W_c(r)^2\, dr} \equiv Z(c), \text{ say.} \tag{44.26}$$

Let $Z_\beta(0)$ be the β quantile of the distribution of $Z(0)$ (corresponding to the null hypothesis), then the local asymptotic power function of the test based on $T(\hat{\alpha}-1)$ is given by

$$\mathbb{P}\left[Z(c) < Z_\beta(0)\right]$$

for a one-sided left-tailed test with size β.

Plots of the cumulative distribution and probability density functions are presented in Figures 44.3 and 44.4 for various values of c. A striking feature is that the limiting density function of $T(\hat{\alpha}-\alpha)$ becomes more concentrated as c increases. For example, when $c = 5.0$, 90% of the density lies within the range $(-1.0, 0.25)$.

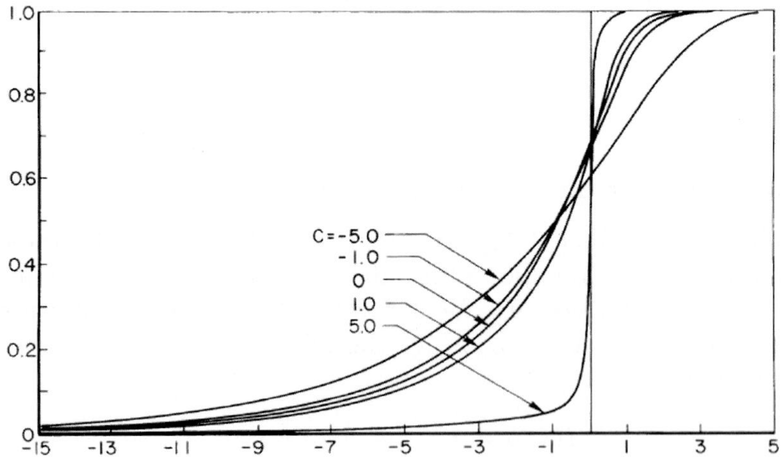

Figure 44.3. Cumulative distribution function of the limit distribution for near-integrated processes given by (44.26); $c = -5.0, -1.0, 0, 1.0, 5.0$.
Source: Perron (1989a). Reprinted with permission from Cambridge University Press.

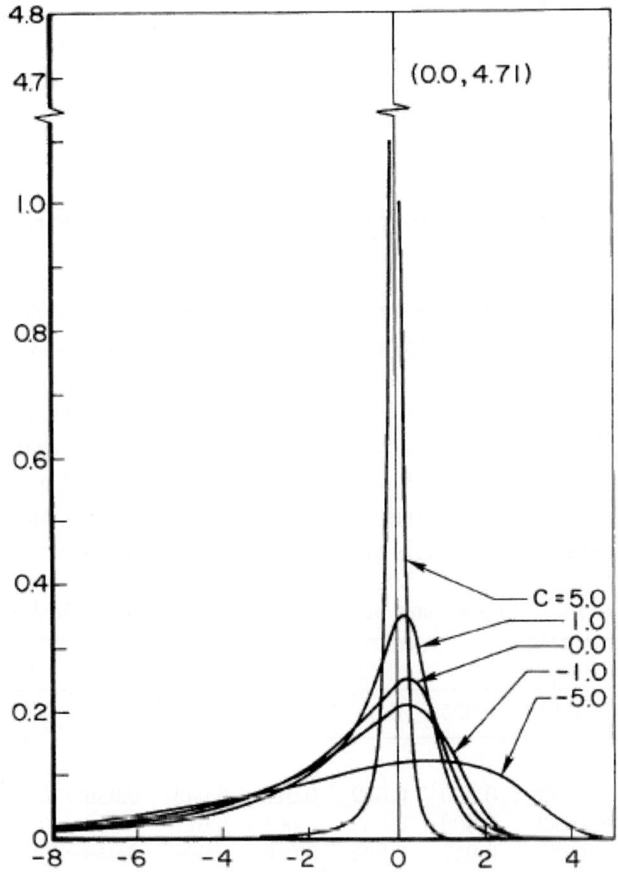

Figure 44.4. Probability density function of the limit distribution for near-integrated processes given by (44.26); $c = -5.0, -1.0, 0, 1.0, 5.0$.

Source: Perron (1989a). Reprinted with permission from Cambridge University Press.

When c is negative, the density is flatter and the tails are more important. As in the case of a (strict) unit root process, the distribution is skewed to the left. Although the median of the distribution is between -1.0 and 0.0 (closer to 0.0 as c increases), the peak in the density occurs between 0.0 and 1.0 (closer to 0.0 as c increases). Also to be noted is the sharp non-normality of the distribution, especially when $c = -5.0$. This feature makes apparent the difference between the usual asymptotic theory and the local asymptotic theory described here. The general pattern of these results points to the fact that $\hat{\alpha}$ converges faster to its true value α when the true value is greater than one. The greater concentration of the local asymptotic distribution around zero is a reflection of the greater precision of the estimates.

44.6.5 Approximation to the exact distribution of $T(\hat{\alpha} - \alpha)$

Using the asymptotic distribution of $T(\hat{\alpha} - \alpha)$ in this near-integrated framework, we have an alternative approximation to the exact distribution. For any pair of values of $\{T, \alpha\}$, we approximate the exact distribution of $T(\hat{\alpha} - \alpha)$ using the limiting distribution (44.24) with $c = T\ln(\alpha)$ since $\alpha = \exp(c/T)$. The exact distribution of $T(\hat{\alpha} - \alpha)$ can be obtained using the procedure developed by Imhof (1961) or directly integrating the relevant finite sample joint characteristic function, though most often one resorts to simulations.

Table 44.1. Exact size of tests using asymptotic critical values.

	Nominal Size							
	0.01	0.025	0.05	0.10	0.90	0.95	0.975	0.99
$c = -5.0$								
$T = 10$	0.000	0.000	0.002	0.018	0.943	0.986	0.998	1.000
$T = 25$	0.002	0.008	0.023	0.061	0.917	0.966	0.987	0.997
$T = 50$	0.005	0.015	0.035	0.080	0.908	0.958	0.981	0.994
$c = -1.0$								
$T = 10$	0.000	0.003	0.015	0.051	0.907	0.968	0.993	1.000
$T = 25$	0.004	0.014	0.035	0.080	0.902	0.956	0.981	0.995
$T = 50$	0.007	0.019	0.042	0.090	0.901	0.953	0.978	0.992
$c = 1.0$								
$T = 10$	0.001	0.009	0.029	0.078	0.907	0.965	0.990	0.999
$T = 25$	0.006	0.018	0.042	0.091	0.902	0.955	0.980	0.994
$T = 50$	0.008	0.022	0.046	0.096	0.901	0.952	0.977	0.992
$c = 5.0$								
$T = 10$	0.009	0.033	0.058	0.113	0.907	0.958	0.982	0.995
$T = 25$	0.009	0.028	0.053	0.104	0.904	0.953	0.978	0.992
$T = 50$	0.009	0.028	0.052	0.102	0.902	0.952	0.977	0.991

Source: Perron (1989a). Reprinted with permission from Cambridge University Press.

Table 44.1 presents the exact probability of obtaining a smaller value of $T(\hat{\alpha} - \alpha)$ when using the asymptotic critical values. These are from the work of Perron (1989a) obtained by integrating the relevant joint characteristic function. Results are presented for the cases where $c = \pm 5.0$, ± 1.0 and $T = 10$, 25, and 50. The values obtained can therefore be used to assess the adequacy of the approximation in the tails and evaluate the exact error in finite samples that would occur when performing a test using the asymptotic critical values.

Several interesting features emerge from the results of Table 44.1. First, the approximation is better as the non-centrality parameter c increases. It is not adequate for $T = 10$ or $T = 25$ when $c = -5.0$ but is very accurate when $c = 5.0$ for a sample size as small as 10, even in the extreme tail of the distribution. Second, the approximation is better for the right tail than the left (see, for example, the case with $c = -1.0$ and $T = 25$). Third, even if the approximation is not very adequate when $T = 10$ or $T = 25$ with negative values of c (stationary processes), the adequacy improves markedly as T increases to 50 suggesting a rapid convergence to the asymptotic distribution.

To give an idea of the fit for the whole distribution, Figure 44.5 compares the asymptotic and exact distributions for the case where $c = -5.0$ and $T = 10$, 25, and 50. The finite sample distributions of $T(\hat{\alpha} - \alpha)$ correspond to those of the pairs $\{T = 50, \alpha = 0.905\}$, $\{T = 25, \alpha = 0.819\}$, and $\{T = 10, \alpha = 0.607\}$. This figure illustrates the rapid convergence to the asymptotic distribution over the full range of support. This convergence is even more rapid for larger values of c.

The previous examples showed that the near-integrated asymptotic distribution is a good approximation to the finite sample distribution of $\hat{\alpha}$ (for α near one) *when* $y_0 = 0$. However, the exact distribution of $\hat{\alpha}$ is heavily influenced by the value of y_0 in finite samples especially when α is close to 1. The near-integrated asymptotic distribution theory is the same for all values of y_0 since the impact of y_0 vanishes in the limit. Hence, we need another approach that could incorporate the effect of y_0 on the asymptotic distribution. This was addressed in the works of Perron (1991b) and Perron (1991a) using a continuous-time asymptotic framework; see also the works of Perron and Vodounou (2001), Sørensen (1992), and Nabeya and Sørensen (1994). A treatment of this more general approach is outside the scope of this book.

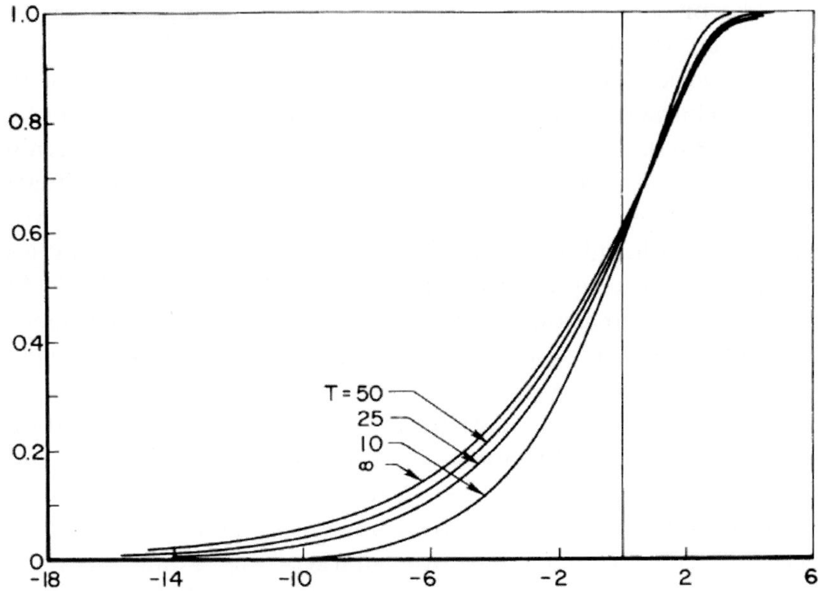

Figure 44.5. Asymptotic and exact distributions for the case where $c = -5.0$ and $T = 10$, 25, and 50. The finite sample distributions of $T(\hat{\alpha} - \alpha)$ correspond to those of the pairs $\{T = 50, \alpha = 0.905\}$, $\{T = 25, \alpha = 0.819\}$, and $\{T = 10, \alpha = 0.607\}$.

Source: Perron (1989a). Reprinted with permission from Cambridge University Press.

44.6.6 Extension to the t-statistic

It is straightforward to extend the limiting result to the case of the t-statistic defined by

$$t_{\hat{\alpha}} = (\hat{\alpha} - \alpha) \Bigg/ \left[\hat{\sigma}_u^2 \left(\sum_{t=1}^{T} y_{t-1}^2\right)^{-1}\right]^{1/2},$$

where

$$\hat{\sigma}_u^2 = T^{-1} \sum_{t=1}^{T} \hat{u}_t^2 = T^{-1} \sum_{t=1}^{T} (y_t - \hat{\alpha} y_{t-1})^2 .$$

It is easy to show that $\hat{\sigma}_u^2 \xrightarrow{p} \sigma_u^2$ under the conditions stated, and using the limits of $T^{-2}\sum_{t=1}^{T} y_{t-1}^2$ and of $T(\hat{\alpha}-\alpha)$, we obtain

$$t_{\hat{\alpha}} \Rightarrow \left(\frac{\sigma}{\sigma_u}\right) \frac{\int_0^1 W_c(r)\, dW(r) + \delta}{\left[\int_0^1 W_c(r)^2\, dr\right]^{1/2}},$$

where $\delta = \left(\sigma^2 - \sigma_u^2\right)/(2\sigma^2)$. When $\{u_t\}$ is a martingale difference sequence, we have

$$t_{\hat{\alpha}} \Rightarrow \frac{\int_0^1 W_c(r)\, dW(r)}{\left[\int_0^1 W_c(r)^2\, dr\right]^{1/2}}. \tag{44.27}$$

The limiting distribution (44.27) is free of nuisance parameters and quantiles can be obtained for various values of c. However, no exact solution useful for numerical integration exists. One therefore has to resort to simulation methods to obtain quantiles.

44.6.7 Extension to models with exogenous regressors

Suppose that the data generating process is again

$$y_t = \beta z_t + v_t,$$
$$v_t = \alpha v_{t-1} + u_t,$$

with v_0 some initial value and u_t satisfying the conditions stated above. Consider now the regression

$$y_t = \alpha y_{t-1} + \beta z_t(\lambda) + u_t, \tag{44.28}$$

where $z_t(\lambda)' = (z_{1t}, \ldots, z_{p,t}, z_{p+1,t}(\lambda), \ldots, z_{kt}(\lambda))$ is a vector of exogenous variables that satisfies the conditions discussed in Section 44.3. The derivation of the limiting distribution of $T(\hat{\alpha}-\alpha)$ and $t_{\hat{\alpha}}$ is basically identical to the case where $\{y_t\}$ is a unit root process

Again, we have

$$T(\hat{\alpha} - \alpha) = \left[T^{-2} Y_{-1}' M z_T(\lambda) Y_{-1}\right]^{-1} \left[T^{-1} Y_{-1}' M z_T(\lambda) U\right]$$

and

$$t_{\hat{\alpha}} = \left[T^{-2} Y_{-1}' M z_T(\lambda) Y_{-1}\right]^{-1/2} \left[T^{-1} Y_{-1}' M z_T(\lambda) U\right] / \hat{s}_T(\lambda),$$

where $U = (u_1, \ldots, u_T)'$, $Y_{-1} = (y_0, \ldots, y_{T-1})'$ and $Mz_T(\lambda) = (I - Pz_T(\lambda))$ is the matrix projecting orthogonally to the space spanned by the columns of $z_T(\lambda)' = (z_1(\lambda), \ldots, z_T(\lambda))$ (see Section 44.3 for details). Again,

$$\hat{s}_T^2(\lambda) = T^{-1} \sum_{t=1}^{T} \hat{u}_t^2 = T^{-1} \sum_{t=1}^{T} (y_t - \hat{\alpha} y_{t-1} - \hat{\beta} z_t(\lambda))^2.$$

As a matter of notation, let

$$X_{c,T}(r) = X_T(r) + c \int_0^r \exp(c(r-s)) X_T(s)\, ds, \qquad (44.29)$$

where, as before, $X_T(r) = T^{-1/2} \sum_{t=1}^{[Tr]} u_t$. We note that

$$y_{[Tr]} = X_{c,T}(r) + o_p(1),$$

where the term $o_p(1)$ is due to the initial condition. Using developments analogous to those used in Section 44.3, we have

$$T^{-2} Y_{-1}' M z_T(\lambda) Y_{-1} = \int_0^1 \{X_{c,T}(r) - Pz_T(\lambda) X_{c,T}(r)\}^2\, dr + o_{p\lambda}(1) \qquad (44.30)$$

and

$$T^{-1} Y_{-1}' M z_T(\lambda) U = \int_0^1 X_{c,T}(r)\, dX_T(r) - \int_0^1 Pz_T(\lambda) X_{c,T}(r)^2\, dX_T(r) + o_{p\lambda}(1), \qquad (44.31)$$

where the term $o_{p\lambda}(1)$ signifies a remainder that is $o_p(1)$ uniformly in λ. Hence, $T(\hat{\alpha}-1)$ and $t_{\hat{\alpha}}$ can be written as the following composite functionals:

$$T(\hat{\alpha}-1) = g_1\left\{X_{c,T}(r), \int_0^1 X_{c,T}(r)\, dX_T(r), Pz_T(\lambda)\, X_{c,T}(r)\right.$$
$$\left.\int_0^1 Pz_T(\lambda)\, X_{c,T}(r)\, dX_T(r)\right\}$$

and

$$t_{\hat{\alpha}} = g_2\left\{X_{c,T}(r), \int_0^1 X_{c,T}(r)\, dX_T(r), Pz_T(\lambda)\, X_{c,T}(r),\right.$$
$$\left.\int_0^1 Pz_T(\lambda)\, X_{c,T}(r)\, dX_T(r), \hat{s}_T(\lambda)\right\},$$

where

$$g_1 = h_1\left\{H_1\left[X_{c,T}(r), Pz_T(\lambda)\, X_{c,T}(r)\right],\right.$$
$$\left.H_2\left[\int_0^1 X_{c,T}(r)\, dX_T(r), \int_0^1 Pz_T(\lambda)\, X_{c,T}(r)\, dX_T(r)\right]\right\},$$

and

$$g_2 = h_2\left\{H_1\left[X_{c,T}(r), Pz_T(\lambda)\, X_{c,T}(r)\right],\right.$$
$$\left.H_2\left[\int_0^1 X_{c,T}(r)\, dX_T(r), \int_0^1 Pz_T(\lambda)\, X_{c,T}(r)\, dX_T(r)\right], \hat{s}_T(\lambda)\right\},$$

with $h_1\left[H_1(\cdot), H_2(\cdot)\right] = H_1(\cdot)^{-1} H_2(\cdot)$ and

$$h_2\left[H_1(\cdot), H_2(\cdot), \hat{s}_T(\cdot)\right] = H_1(\cdot)^{-1/2} H_2(\cdot)\, \hat{s}_T(\cdot)^{-1},$$

with H_1 and H_2 defined by (44.30) and (44.31). The weak convergence results for each of the elements are contained in the following lemma whose proof is omitted.

Lemma 44.2. *The following weak convergence results under the* sup *norm hold jointly (with* $\delta = \left(\sigma^2 - \sigma_u^2\right)/(2\sigma^2)$*):* (a) $X_{c,T}(r) \Rightarrow \sigma W_c(r)$; (b) $\int_0^1 X_{c,T}(r)\, dX_T(r) \Rightarrow \sigma^2(\int_0^1 W_c(r)\, dW(r) + \delta)$; (c) $Pz_T(\lambda) X_{c,T}(r) \Rightarrow \sigma P z_T(\lambda) W_c(r)$; (d)

$$Pz_T(\lambda) X_{c,T}(r)\, dX_T(r) \Rightarrow \sigma^2 \int_0^1 Pz_T(\lambda) W_c(r)\, dW(r).$$

It can be shown that the composite functionals $g_1(\cdot)$ and $g_2(\cdot)$ are continuous as in the standard unit root case. Hence, we have the following weak convergence results holding uniformly over $\lambda \in [0,1]$:

$$T(\hat{\alpha} - \alpha) \Rightarrow \left[\int_0^1 W_{c,z}^*(r)\, dW(r) + \delta\right] \Big/ \int_0^1 W_{c,z}^*(r)^2\, dr,$$

$$t_{\hat{\alpha}} \Rightarrow \left[\int_0^1 W_{c,z}^*(r)\, dW(r) + \delta\right] \Big/ \left[\int_0^1 W_{c,z}^*(r)^2\, dr\right]^{1/2},$$

where

$$W_{c,z}^*(r) = W_c(r) - Pz_T(\lambda) W_c(r)$$

and $\delta = \left(\sigma^2 - \sigma_u^2\right)/(2\sigma^2)$. The results for $t_{\hat{\alpha}}$ follow using the fact that $\hat{s}_T^2 \xrightarrow{p} \sigma_u^2$.

When the errors are martingale differences $\sigma^2 = \sigma_u^2$ and $\delta = 0$ and the asymptotic distributions are free of nuisance parameters. Therefore, for a given non-centrality parameter c, quantiles can be tabulated and used for asymptotic inference. As in the unit root case, no manageable expressions are available for the t-statistic. For the normalized bias $T(\hat{\alpha} - \alpha)$, one can use the inversion theorem discussed before based on the joint characteristic function of the pair $\{\int_0^1 W_{c,z}^*(r)\, dW(r),\ \int_0^1 W_{c,z}^*(r)^2\, dr\}$.

For the case with a constant and a linear time trend, the relevant characteristic function has been derived by Nabeya and Sørensen (1994) for the cases where (i) $z_t = \{1\}$, a constant, and (ii) $z_t = \{1, t\}$, a constant and a linear time trend. Hence, in those cases, the limit distribution of $T(\hat{\alpha} - \alpha)$ can be obtained using numerical integration via an inversion of the characteristic function. The relevant characteristic function is unknown for more complex forms of the deterministic component or for the t-statistics. Hence, in general, one resorts to simulation methods similar to those discussed in Section 44.5.

44.7 Appendix

Proof of Lemma 44.1. For part (a), write y_t as

$$y_t = \sum_{j=1}^{t} \exp\left((t-j)c/T\right) u_j + \exp(tc/T)y_0,$$

then

$$\begin{aligned}
T^{-1/2}y_{[Tr]} &= \sigma \sum_{j=1}^{[Tr]} \exp\left(([Tr]-j)c/T\right) \int_{\frac{j-1}{T}}^{j/T} dX_T(s) \\
&\quad + T^{-1/2}\exp([Tr]\,c/T)y_0 \\
&= \sigma \sum_{j=1}^{[Tr]} \int_{\frac{j-1}{T}}^{j/T} \exp\left((r-s)c\right) dX_T(s) + o(1) \\
&= \sigma \int_0^r \exp\left((r-s)c\right) dX_T(s) + o(1) \\
&= \sigma \left\{ X_T(r) + c\int_0^r \exp\left((r-s)c\right) X_T(s)\,ds \right\} + o(1) \\
&\Rightarrow \sigma \left\{ W(r) + c\int_0^r \exp\left((r-s)c\right) W(s)\,ds \right\} \\
&= \sigma W_c(r).
\end{aligned}$$

Parts (b) and (c) are proved analogously. To prove part (d), first square both sides of the equation

$$y_t = \exp\left(c/T\right) y_{t-1} + u_t$$

to obtain

$$y_t^2 = \exp\left(2c/T\right) y_{t-1}^2 + u_t^2 + 2\exp\left(c/T\right) y_{t-1}u_t$$

or

$$y_t^2 - y_{t-1}^2 = \left(\exp\left(2c/T\right) - 1\right) y_{t-1}^2 + u_t^2 + 2\exp\left(c/T\right) y_{t-1}u_t.$$

Summing each side over $t = 1, \ldots, T$

$$y_T^2 - y_0^2 = [\exp(2c/T) - 1] \sum_{t=1}^{T} y_{t-1}^2 + \sum_{t=1}^{T} u_t^2 + 2\exp(c/T) \sum_{t=1}^{T} y_{t-1}u_t$$

and, upon rearrangements

$$\begin{aligned} T^{-1} \sum_{t=1}^{T} y_{t-1}u_t &= (1/2)\exp(c/T) \Big\{ T^{-1} y_T^2 - T^{-1} \sum_{t=1}^{T} u_t^2 \\ &\quad - T(\exp(2c/T) - 1) T^{-2} \sum_{t=1}^{T} y_{t-1}^2 \Big\} \\ &\Rightarrow (1/2)\{\sigma^2 W_c(1)^2 - \sigma_u^2 - 2c\sigma^2 \int_0^1 W_c(r)^2 \, dr\} \\ &= \sigma^2 \int_0^1 W_c(r) \, dW(r) + \left(\sigma^2 - \sigma_u^2\right)/2 \end{aligned}$$

since $\exp(c/T) \to 1$, $T[\exp(2c/T) - 1] \to 2c$, $T^{-1}\sum_{t=1}^{T} u_t^2 \xrightarrow{p} \sigma_u^2$ and using parts (a) and (c) and (44.22).

44.8 Exercises

Exercise 44.1. Prove equations (44.21) and (44.22).

Exercise 44.2. Suppose that you have a unit root process given by $y_t = y_{t-1} + u_t$ where u_t is such that $T^{-1/2}\sum_{t=1}^{[Tr]} u_t \Rightarrow \sigma W(r)$ with $\sigma^2 = 2\pi h_u(0)$ and $W(r)$ is a standard Wiener process. For simplicity, $y_0 = 0$. Obtain the limit distribution and the limit variance of the following functionals: (a) $\sum_{t=1}^{T} t u_t$; (b) $\sum_{t=1}^{T} t^2 u_t$; (c) $\sum_{t=1}^{T} t y_{t-1}$. Be sure to state the appropriate scaling factor of T needed to get the results.

Exercise 44.3. Suppose that y_t is generated by

$$\begin{aligned} y_t &= a + bt + z_t, \\ z_t &= \alpha z_{t-1} + u_t, \end{aligned} \tag{44.32}$$

where $z_0 = 0$, with $\{u_t\}$ such that $T^{-1/2}\sum_{t=1}^{[Tr]} u_t \Rightarrow \sigma W(r)$ with

$$\sigma^2 = \lim_{T\to\infty} T^{-1}E\left(\sum_{t=1}^{T} u_t\right)^2.$$

Consider the following regression estimated by OLS:

$$y_t = \mu + \beta t + \alpha y_{t-1} + e_t.$$

(a) Show that the estimate $\hat{\alpha}$ of α is invariant with respect to a and b in (44.32). Is the estimate invariant to z_0? In Section 44.3, for $\alpha = 1$, we stated the limit distribution:

$$T(\hat{\alpha} - 1) \Rightarrow \frac{\int_0^1 W^*(r)dW(r) + \delta}{\int_0^1 W^*(r)^2 dr},$$

where $\delta = (\sigma^2 - \sigma_u^2)/2\sigma^2$, $\sigma_u^2 = \lim_{T\to\infty} T^{-1}\sum_{t=1}^{T} E(u_t^2)$, and $W^*(r)$ is a continuous time process defined on $[0,1]$ given by the residual function from a continuous time regression of $W(r)$ on $\{1, r\}$. (b) Derive an explicit expression for $W^*(r)$. (c) Using the expression derived in (b), show that the limit distribution of $T(\hat{\alpha} - 1)$ is equivalent to the expression stated in the works of Hamilton (1994) and Phillips and Perron (1988), namely

$$T(\hat{\alpha} - 1) \Rightarrow \left(\int_0^1 W(r)dW(r) + \delta + A\right)\Big/ D,$$

where

$$A = 12\left(\int_0^1 rW(r)dr - (1/2)\int_0^1 W(r)dr\right) \times \left(\int_0^1 W(r)dr - (1/2)W(1)\right) - W(1)\int_0^1 W(r)dr$$

and

$$D = \int_0^1 W(r)^2 dr - 12\left(\int_0^1 rW(r)dr\right)^2 + 12\int_0^1 W(r)dr\int_0^1 rW(r)dr - 4\left(\int_0^1 W(r)dr\right)^2.$$

Exercise 44.4. Suppose that you have an integrated process of the form

$$y_t = y_{t-1} + v_t, \tag{44.33}$$

for $t = 1, \ldots, T$ with $y_0 = 0$ and where $v_t = C(L)e_t$, $C(L) = \sum_{i=0}^{\infty} c_i L^i$, $\sum_{i=0}^{\infty} i^2 c_i^2 < \infty$, and $e_t \sim i.i.d.(0, \sigma_e^2)$. You suspect that the series might be contaminated by an outlier at some date T_o. To test for that, you run the following regression by OLS:

$$y_t = c + \delta D(T_o)_t + u_t,$$

where $D(T_o)_t = 1$ if $t = T_o$ and 0 otherwise. Your test is based on the t-statistic for testing that $\delta = 0$, denoted $t_{\hat{\delta}}$. Assuming that the position of the outlier is a some fixed proportion of the total sample size such that $T_o/T = \lambda$, derive the limit distribution of $t_{\hat{\delta}}$ under the null hypothesis of no outlier (i.e., with data generated by (44.33)).

Exercise 44.5. Suppose that we have the following data generating process:

$$\begin{aligned} y_t &= \beta t + z_t, \\ z_t &= \alpha z_{t-1} + e_t, \end{aligned} \tag{44.34}$$

where $e_t \sim i.i.d.(0, \sigma_e^2)$ and $z_0 = 0$. You have available a sample of T observations for the variable y_t. You are interested in making inference about the value of β, the slope of the trend function. Consider the following regression:

$$y_t = \mu + \beta t + z_t. \tag{44.35}$$

Let $\hat{\beta}_{ols}$ be the OLS estimate of β in the regression (44.35) and $\hat{\beta}_{gls}$ be the GLS estimate obtained supposing (correctly) that z_t is an $AR(1)$ process as defined by the system (44.34). (a) Suppose that $|\alpha| < 1$, derive the limit distribution of $\hat{\beta}_{ols}$ and $\hat{\beta}_{gls}$ and show that they are identical. (b) Suppose now that $\alpha = 1$, derive the limit distribution of $\hat{\beta}_{ols}$ and $\hat{\beta}_{gls}$ and show that $\hat{\beta}_{gls}$ is asymptotically more efficient than $\hat{\beta}_{ols}$.

Exercise 44.6. An issue of interest is to test whether there is or is not long range dependence in a time series x_t ($t = 1, \ldots, T$). A series with long range dependence has an autocorrelation function that does not decay exponentially (a fractionally integrated process or a unit root process). A statistic which has been suggested is the rescaled range statistic defined by

$$RS = (1/s)\left[\max_{1\le k\le T} T^{-1/2}\sum_{t=1}^{k}(x_t - \bar{x}) - \min_{1\le k\le T} T^{-1/2}\sum_{t=1}^{k}(x_t - \bar{x})\right],$$

where $\bar{x} = T^{-1}\sum_{t=1}^{T} x_t$ and $s^2 = T^{-1}\sum_{t=1}^{T}(x_t - \bar{x})^2$. (a) Assume that x_t is a stationary and invertible $ARMA(p,q)$ process, i.e., $A(L)x_t = B(L)e_t$, where the roots of $A(L)$ and $B(L)$ are outside the unit circle and $e_t \sim$ *i.i.d.* $(0,\sigma_e^2)$. Derive the limiting distribution of RS. (b) Suggest a transformation that yields a test statistic with an asymptotic distribution that is free of nuisance parameters. (c) Suppose now that x_t is an integrated process, i.e., there is a unit root in the autoregressive polynomial $A(L)$. What is the limiting distribution of RS? Is the test statistic consistent for testing the null hypothesis of stationarity versus the alternative hypothesis of a unit root?

Exercise 44.7. Assume that $x_t = x_{t-1} + \varepsilon_t$ and $\varepsilon_t \sim$ *i.i.d.* $N(0,1)$ and $x_0 = 0$. Consider a regression of x_t onto x_{t-2}, with the resulting estimate

$$\hat{\alpha} = \frac{\sum_{t=3}^{T} x_t x_{t-2}}{\sum_{t=3}^{T} x_{t-2}^2}.$$

(a) Is $\hat{\alpha}$ consistent for the parameter value $\alpha = 1$? Prove your answer. (b) Find the limiting distribution of a properly scaled and centered version of $\hat{\alpha}$. Could you use your result to test the hypothesis H : $x_t \sim I(1)$? If so, how would you construct the test? (c) Now assume that

$$y_t = \beta x_t + u_t + c\sum_{s=1}^{t-1} u_s,$$

where u_t is an *i.i.d.* $(0,1)$ sequence independent of ε_t and c is a constant. You run a regression of y_t on x_t. The residuals of this regression are denoted by $\hat{u}_t$. Find the limiting distribution of the OLS estimator of regressing $\hat{u}_t$ onto $\hat{u}_{t-1}$ assuming that $c \neq 0$. How can you use this estimator to test $H : c \neq 0$. (d) Discuss the behavior of your test under the alternative when $c = 0$ (i.e., derive the limiting distribution of the estimator under the alternative).

Exercise 44.8. Let

$$\lambda_x(\omega_j) = (2\pi T)^{-1/2} \sum_{t=1}^{T} x_t \exp(-it\omega_j)$$

be the discrete Fourier transform of some variable x_t at frequency $\omega_j = 2\pi j/T$ for $j = 1, \ldots, [T/2]$ (note that $i = \sqrt{-1}$). The periodogram is defined as the complex conjugate product of this quantity, i.e.,

$$I_T(\omega_j) = \frac{1}{2\pi T} \left(\sum_{t=1}^{T} x_t \exp(-it\omega_j) \right) \left(\sum_{t=1}^{T} x_t \exp(it\omega_j) \right).$$

(a) Discuss the properties of the periodogram $I_T(\omega_j)$ as an estimate of the spectral density function at frequency ω_j. (b) Discuss how the class of estimates of the spectral density function based on weighted sums of the autocovariances can be viewed as a weighted average of the periodogram, where the average is centered at the frequency of interest. Suppose now that x_t is a unit root process defined by $x_t = x_{t-1} + u_t$ ($x_0 = 0$) where u_t is a short-memory stationary process so that we have a functional central limit theorem of the form $T^{-1/2} \sum_{t=1}^{[Tr]} u_t \Rightarrow \sigma W(r)$, where $W(r)$ is a Wiener process and $\sigma^2 = 2\pi h_u(0)$ with $h_u(0)$ the spectral density function of u_t at frequency zero. (c) Show that, in this case, $\lambda_x(\omega_j)$, the discrete Fourier transform of x_t can be expressed as

$$\lambda_x(\omega_j) = \frac{1}{(1 - \exp(-i\omega_j))} \left[\lambda_u(\omega_j) - \frac{\exp(-i\omega_j)}{\sqrt{2\pi T}} x_T \right],$$

where $\lambda_u(\omega_j)$ is the discrete Fourier transform of u_t. (d) Use the representation in part (c) to show that the discrete Fourier transform of u_t at frequency zero affects the discrete Fourier transform of x_t at all frequencies. (e) Derive the limit distribution of $\lambda_x(\omega_j)$.
Hint: $\exp(-i\omega_j) = 1 + (2\pi ji/T) + O(j^2/T^2)$.

Exercise 44.9 (Difficult). Suppose that the data generating process is

$$y_t = a + bt + z_t,$$

$$z_t = \alpha z_{t-1} + e_t,$$

with $e_t \sim i.i.d.(0, \sigma_e^2)$, $z_0 = 0$ and $b \neq 0$. Consider a regression with only a constant included

$$y_t = \mu + \alpha y_{t-1} + u_t. \tag{44.36}$$

(a) Suppose that $\alpha = 1$, show that $t_\alpha \Rightarrow N(0,1)$, where t_α is the t-statistic for testing that $\alpha = 1$ in the regression (44.36) estimated by OLS. (b) Suppose now that $|\alpha| < 1$, show that $t_\alpha \xrightarrow{p} 0$. (c) What can you conclude from the results in (a) and (b) about trend specification in unit root testing?

Exercise 44.10 (Computer). Suppose that the data generating process is given by

$$y_t = y_{t-1} + u_t.$$

where u_t is a stationary process. Consider an estimated autoregression of the form

$$y_t = d_t + \alpha y_{t-1} + u_t,$$

where three cases are considered for d_t: (a) $d_t = 0$ (no deterministic component); (b) $d_t = c$ (a constant); (c) $d_t = c + \beta t$ (a linear trend). Let $\hat{\alpha}$ be the least-squares estimate of α. As discussed in this chapter, under the hypothesis that $\alpha = 1$, we have

$$T(\hat{\alpha} - 1) \Rightarrow \frac{\int_0^1 W^*(r)dW(r) + \delta}{\int_0^1 W^*(r)^2 dr},$$

where $\delta = (\sigma^2 - \sigma_u^2)/2\sigma^2$, $\sigma^2 = 2\pi h_u(0)$, and $\sigma_u^2 = var(u_t)$ with $h_u(0)$ the (non-normalized) spectral density function of u_t at frequency zero. $W^*(r)$ is the continuous time residual function from a projection of $W(r)$ on (a) nothing if $d_t = 0$, (b) $\{1\}$ if $d_t = c$ (a constant), and (c) $\{1, r\}$ if $d_t = c + \beta t$ (a linear trend). Consider first the case where u_t is $i.i.d.$ $N(0,1)$ in which case $\sigma^2 = \sigma_u^2$ and $\delta = 0$.

Using the method discussed in Section 44.5, simulate the asymptotic distribution of $T(\hat{\alpha}-1)$. (a) Using 5,000 replications, simulate the cdf of the limiting distribution of $T(\hat{\alpha}-1)$. Plot this cdf along with the finite sample cdf of $T(\hat{\alpha}-1)$ for $T = 10$, 25, 50, and 100. When is the asymptotic distribution a good approximation to the finite sample distribution? Consider now the case where u_t is an $MA(1)$ of the form $u_t = e_t + \theta e_{t-1}$ with $e_t \sim i.i.d.\ N(0,1)$. Consider two cases: $\theta = -0.8$ and $\theta = 0.8$. (b) Simulate the asymptotic distribution of $T(\hat{\alpha}-1)$. (c) Simulate the bias of $\hat{\alpha}$ and the finite sample distribution of $T(\hat{\alpha}-1)$ for $T = 100$, 500, and 1,000. (d) Compare the relation between the finite sample and asymptotic distributions via graphs of the cdf and interpret your results. Also discuss the extent of the bias of $\hat{\alpha}$ in relation to the parameters and the deterministic components included in the autoregression.

Exercise 44.11 (Computer). The data generating process is given by

$$y_t = \alpha y_{t-1} + e_t,$$

where $e_t \sim i.i.d.\ N(0,1)$. Consider estimating by OLS an autoregression with a constant, i.e.,

$$y_t = c + \alpha y_{t-1} + e_t. \tag{44.37}$$

Let $\hat{\alpha}$ be the OLS estimate. Using simulations with $N = 10{,}000$ replications, plot the cdf of $T(\hat{\alpha}-\alpha)$ for the following groups of values for T and α: (a) Group 1: $(T = 25, \alpha = 0.80)$, $(T = 50, \alpha = 0.90)$, $(T = 100, \alpha = 0.95)$, $(T = 500, \alpha = 0.99)$; (b) Group 2: $(T = 25, \alpha = 0.60)$, $(T = 50, \alpha = 0.80)$, $(T = 100, \alpha = 0.90)$, $(T = 500, \alpha = 0.98)$. Discuss your findings and give a theoretical explanation for your results.

Chapter 45

Testing for a Unit Root

There has been a flood of proposals to devise tests for a unit root; see the books by Patterson (2010) and Choi (2015), among others. Everyone seems to have their favorite test. We do not provide an exhaustive treatment. We simply cover what we think are the most important, mostly as judged by the number of citations; hence, how often practitioners use them. There are two landmark early generation tests: the so-called ADF (Augmented Dickey–Fuller) test (Dickey and Fuller, 1979) and the Phillips and Perron (1988) class of tests. We present these tests but argue that they both have been superseded by recent advances. One is the class of tests considered by Elliott *et al.* (1996) who argued for the use of a GLS detrending approach to devise more powerful tests. The other is the class of tests considered by Ng and Perron (2001) who devised methods to appropriately select the autoregressive lag length (among other things) to considerably minimize the size-distortions in finite samples as well as offering tests with improved power. This chapter also highlights the problems of the early generation tests and how they could be modified to achieve tests with better properties. In this chapter, we deal with a trend component that is linear, i.e., a constant or a constant and a time trend. In Chapter 50, we deal with the more complex issues arising when allowing for changes in the trend function, following the work by Perron (1989b).

The data-generating process is assumed to be

$$\begin{aligned} y_t &= \beta z_t + v_t, \\ v_t &= \alpha v_{t-1} + u_t, \end{aligned} \tag{45.1}$$

with $u_t = \sum_{j=0}^{\infty} c_j e_{t-j}$, $\sum_{j=0}^{\infty} j|c_j| < \infty$, $y_0 = O_p(1)$, where $\{e_t\}$ is a martingale difference sequence with respect to Φ_t, a filtration to which e_t is adapted, and $E(e_t^4) < \infty$. Also, $\sigma^2 = \lim_{T\to\infty} T^{-1}E(\sum_{t=1}^{T} u_t)^2$ is the "long run variance" or (2π) times the spectral density function at frequency zero of u_t (in the stationary case), and $\sigma_u^2 = \lim_{T\to\infty} T^{-1}\sum_{t=1}^{T} E(u_t)^2$ is the (average) variance. The vector z_t contains the deterministic components. As stated in Section 43.9, more general conditions are possible; for example, mixing-type conditions (see, e.g., the work of Phillips and Perron, 1988). The null and alternative hypotheses are $H_0 : \alpha = 1$, $H_1 : \alpha < 1$. Note that we may have $H_1 : \alpha \neq 1$ but this is rare in economics. The alternative $H_1 : \alpha > 1$ may sometimes be of interest; e.g., when trying to detect "bubbles" in financial time series.

45.1 Phillips–Perron (1988) unit root tests

The estimated regression is

$$y_t = \alpha y_{t-1} + \beta z_t + u_t. \tag{45.2}$$

Then, we have

$$T(\hat{\alpha} - 1) \Rightarrow \frac{\int_0^1 W^*(r)dW(r) + \delta}{\int_0^1 W^*(r)^2 dr},$$

where $W^*(r)$ is residual function from a regression of $W(r)$ on $g(r)$, as defined in (44.13), and $\delta = (\sigma^2 - \sigma_u^2)/(2\sigma^2)$. So, the asymptotic distribution of $T(\hat{\alpha} - 1)$ depends on the nuisance parameter δ. We need to construct a statistic whose asymptotic distribution is free of δ. Suppose that we have a variable X_T such that

$$X_T \Rightarrow \frac{\delta}{\int_0^1 W^*(r)^2 dr}.$$

Then, by the continuous mapping theorem,

$$\begin{aligned} T(\hat{\alpha} - 1) - X_T &\Rightarrow \frac{\int_0^1 W^*(r)dW(r) + \delta}{\int_0^1 W^*(r)^2 dr} - \frac{\delta}{\int_0^1 W^*(r)^2 dr} \\ &= \frac{\int_0^1 W^*(r)dW(r)}{\int_0^1 W^*(r)^2 dr} \end{aligned}$$

which is free of nuisance parameters and is only influenced by the nature of the deterministic components. The quantity X_T can be constructed as follows:

$$X_T = \frac{\hat{\sigma}^2 - \hat{\sigma}_u^2}{2T^{-2}\sum_{t=1}^T (y_{t-1}^*)^2},$$

where $\hat{\sigma}_u^2 = T^{-1}\sum_{t=1}^T \hat{u}_t^2$, with $\hat{u}_t$ the residual from (45.2) estimated by OLS. Again, y_{t-1}^* are the residuals from a regression of y_{t-1} on z_t. Also,

$$\hat{\sigma}^2 = T^{-1}\sum_{t=1}^T \hat{u}_t^2 + T^{-1}\sum_{j=1}^{T-1} \lambda(j, m_T) \sum_{t=j+1}^T \hat{u}_t\hat{u}_{t-j},$$

for some weight function $\lambda(j, m_T)$ and bandwidth m_T, though other estimators are possible. Under the stated data-generating process and upon some regularity conditions on $\lambda(j, m_T)$, we have $\hat{\sigma}_u^2 \xrightarrow{p} \sigma_u^2$, $\hat{\sigma}^2 \xrightarrow{p} \sigma^2$ and

$$2T^{-2}\sum_{t=1}^T (y_{t-1}^*)^2 \Rightarrow 2\sigma^2 \int_0^1 W^*(r)^2 dr.$$

Then, by continuous mapping theorem,

$$X_T \Rightarrow \frac{\delta}{\int_0^1 W^*(r)^2 dr},$$

and we can construct the transformed statistic for the normalized bias

$$\begin{aligned} Z_\alpha &= T(\hat{\alpha} - 1) - X_T \\ &= T(\hat{\alpha} - 1) - \frac{\hat{\sigma}^2 - \hat{\sigma}_u^2}{2T^{-2}\sum_{t=1}^T (y_{t-1}^*)^2} \\ &\Rightarrow \frac{\int_0^1 W^*(r) dW(r)}{\int_0^1 W^*(r)^2 dr}, \end{aligned}$$

which is free of nuisance parameters. Using similar arguments, we have the following transformation of the t-statistic:

$$Z_t = \left(\frac{\hat{\sigma}_u}{\hat{\sigma}}\right) t_{\hat{\alpha}} - \frac{\hat{\sigma}^2 - \hat{\sigma}_u^2}{2\hat{\sigma}(T^{-2}\sum_{t=1}^T (y_{t-1}^*)^2)^{1/2}}.$$

It is easy to show that

$$Z_t \Rightarrow \frac{\int_0^1 W^*(r)dW(r)}{\left(\int_0^1 W^*(r)^2 dr\right)^{1/2}},$$

which is again free of nuisance parameters. That's it!

45.2 The ADF test

We start by supposing that the DGP is an $AR(p)$ process of known order p, i.e.,

$$y_t = \sum_{i=1}^{p} a_i y_{t-i} + e_t$$

or $A(L)y_t = e_t$, with

$$A(L) = 1 - a_1 L - \cdots - a_p L^p.$$

If the process has an autoregressive unit root, then we can write

$$A(L) = (1 - L)A^*(L),$$

where $A^*(L)$ is a polynomial of order $p-1$ with all roots outside the unit circle. Hence, $A(1) = 0$, which implies that $\sum_{i=1}^{p} a_i = 1$. Now, reparameterize the model as

$$y_t = \alpha y_{t-1} + \sum_{i=1}^{p-1} d_i \Delta y_{t-i} + e_t, \tag{45.3}$$

with $\alpha = \sum_{i=1}^{p} a_i$ and $d_i = -\sum_{j=i+1}^{p} a_j$. The test is based on estimating (45.3) and using the t-statistic for testing the null hypothesis that $\alpha = 1$. More generally, in the presence of deterministic components, the regression is

$$y_t = \beta z_t + \alpha y_{t-1} + \sum_{i=1}^{p-1} d_i \Delta y_{t-i} + e_t.$$

The limit distribution of the t-statistic is then

$$t_{\hat{\alpha}} \Rightarrow \frac{\int_0^1 W^*(r)dW(r)}{\left(\int_0^1 W^*(r)^2 dr\right)^{1/2}}.$$

A test based on the normalized bias is also possible and is given by

$$\frac{T(\hat{\alpha}-1)}{(1-\sum_{i=1}^{p-1}\hat{d}_i)} \Rightarrow \frac{\int_0^1 W^*(r)dW(r)}{\int_0^1 W^*(r)^2 dr}.$$

It is rarely used since it requires the estimates of the nuisance parameters d_i, which can be tricky when dealing with linear processes as discussed in the following. The tests remain valid under the more general DGP (45.1). The idea is to approximate the process by an $AR(k_T)$ for k_T suitably chosen, i.e.,

$$y_t = \beta z_t + \alpha y_{t-1} + \sum_{i=1}^{k_T} d_i \Delta y_{t-i} + e_{tk},$$

so that the errors e_{tk} are approximately uncorrelated. The validity of the t-statistic was analyzed by Said and Dickey (1984) when the data are generated by an $ARMA(p,q)$ process of unknown order with $i.i.d.$ innovations. They established that

$$t_{\hat{\alpha}} \to \frac{\int_0^1 W^*(r)dW(r)}{\left(\int_0^1 W^*(r)^2 dr\right)^{1/2}}$$

provided $k_T \to \infty$,

$$k_T^3/T \to 0 \tag{45.4}$$

and

$$k_T > cT^a \tag{45.5}$$

for some $a > 0$ and $c > 0$. This is restrictive since it precludes the use of information criteria to select the lag order since the selected values of k_T are such that $k_T \propto \ln(T)$, which is slower than any polynomial rate. Ng and Perron (1995) showed that the lower bound (45.5) can be dispensed with, thereby allowing a logarithmic rate of increase for k_T. Chang and Park (2002) relaxed the upper bound condition

(45.4) to $k_T^2/T \to 0$, which is of no practical consequence.

45.3 Finite sample performance of default tests

Both the ADF and Phillips–Perron-type tests are widely used in practice and implemented in most statistical software, such as Stata, EViews, and so on. These software packages offer default values for the implementation of the tests. For the ADF, the crucial auxiliary parameter to choose is the truncation lag k_T. The default value in Stata is $k_T = int[4(T/100)^{2/9}]$, where $int[\cdot]$ denotes the greatest lower integer (the so-called "floor function"). For example, $k_T = 4$ if $T = 100$. For the Phillips–Perron-type tests, the default value in Stata and others is the Bartlett (or Newey–West) window: $w(j, m_T) = 1 - j/m_T$ if $j \leq m_T$ and 0 otherwise. Again m_T is chosen by the deterministic rule $m_T = int[4(T/100)^{2/9}]$.

To assess the finite sample performance of the tests, we consider data generated by

$$y_t = \alpha y_{t-1} + u_t$$

with a simple $MA(1)$ process for the errors u_t (see the work of Phillips and Perron (1988) for results with $AR(1)$ processes), i.e.,

$$MA(1) : u_t = e_t + \theta e_{t-1},$$

where $e_t \sim i.i.d.\ N(0,1)$. We consider the exact size and power of the test Z_α (we do not report results for the test Z_t as they are similar). The results are presented in Table 45.1. Here, $T = 100$ so the default values are $k_T = 4$ and $m_T = 4$. In the experiments, only a constant is included as a deterministic regressor and 2,000 replications are used. The nominal size of the test is set to 5%. The power is evaluated at $\alpha = 0.85$. We use the quadratic spectral window (with the method of Andrews (1991b) to select the bandwidth) to construct the long-run variance estimate.

The results show huge size distortions for the Z_α and ADF tests when θ is negative. A higher k_T would reduce size distortions for the ADF test with $\theta < 0$ but would reduce power with $\theta \geq 0$. A small k_T would be better with $i.i.d.$ errors and also with $AR(1)$ errors. With $\theta < 0$, no choice of m_T will yield Z_α tests with good size. These results

Table 45.1. (a) Size and power of the ADF$t_{\hat{\alpha}}$ test with fixed truncation. (b) Size and power of the Z_α test with fixed truncation.

(*a*)	Size						
θ	$k = 0$	$k = 1$	$k = 2$	$k = 4$	$k = 6$	$k = 8$	$k = 12$
0.0	0.056	0.055	0.068	0.064	0.078	0.086	0.106
0.5	0.025	0.099	0.052	0.064	0.071	0.085	0.102
0.8	0.026	0.129	0.037	0.051	0.072	0.082	0.109
−0.2	0.157	0.065	0.063	0.065	0.084	0.092	0.111
−0.5	0.597	0.227	0.116	0.076	0.073	0.086	0.105
−0.8	0.998	0.877	0.677	0.343	0.201	0.142	0.120
	Power						
0.0	0.634	0.562	0.557	0.472	0.406	0.354	0.303
0.5	0.097	0.764	0.378	0.411	0.377	0.348	0.308
0.8	0.052	0.837	0.267	0.302	0.313	0.308	0.273
−0.2	0.938	0.669	0.591	0.490	0.421	0.358	0.304
−0.5	1.00	0.973	0.868	0.626	0.512	0.434	0.350
−0.8	1.00	1.00	1.00	0.988	0.900	0.772	0.523

(*b*)	Size				
θ	$m = 2$	$m = 4$	$m = 6$	$m = 8$	$m = 12$
0.0	0.064	0.070	0.071	0.073	0.066
0.5	0.033	0.042	0.037	0.025	0.011
0.8	0.032	0.040	0.034	0.023	0.009
−0.2	0.125	0.127	0.153	0.176	0.195
−0.5	0.460	0.472	0.539	0.584	0.643
−0.8	0.985	0.986	0.993	0.996	0.999
	Power				
0.0	0.802	0.815	0.819	0.817	0.792
0.5	0.520	0.522	0.437	0.386	0.125
0.8	0.495	0.493	0.387	0.251	0.065
−0.2	0.953	0.963	0.972	0.979	0.983
−0.5	1.00	1.00	1.00	1.00	1.00
−0.8	1.00	1.00	1.00	1.00	1.00

point to two noteworthy features: (1) The PP test is severely size-distorted in the case of an $MA(1)$ process with a negative parameter. When $\theta = -0.8$, the test is basically useless as it always rejects. Here, the problem is not the choice of m_T or the window, there is something fundamentally problematic with the tests. (2) The ADF test has good size except for an MA process with negative parameter and k_T small, especially when $\theta = -0.8$. The size improves as k_T increases. (3) The power of the ADF test is very sensitive to k_T; it decreases noticeably as k_T increases. For instance, if the process is *i.i.d.*, the power is 0.634 when the correct value of $k_T = 0$ is used but drops to 0.472 when $k_T = 4$ and to 0.303 when $k_T = 12$.

The fixed rules were suggested by Schwert (1989a). He also suggested a more "conservative" rule given by $k_T = \text{int}[12(T/100)^{2/9}]$ so that $k_T = 12$ when $T = 100$. The idea was to ensure that the ADF test would have exact size close to the nominal level, across all parameters. The fact that these rules are so widely used in softwares is a great disservice to applied researchers. It focuses only on getting the size right without any concern for power. For instance, using any of these rules implies that we loose considerable power over what can be achieved when long lags are not needed to have adequate exact sizes. This encompasses most of the parameter space considered here except MA processes with $\theta = -0.8$. In a nutshell, such rules are useless. What we need are methods that select small lags when there is no need for a large lag to correct for size distortions and large lags when there is such a need. Hence, we need data-dependent rules, not fixed ones.

45.4 The ADF with data-dependent rules

Ng and Perron (1995) argued for the use of data-dependent methods to select the truncation lag in the ADF test. They considered four possibilities:

1. AIC: $k_T = \text{argmin}_k \ln(\hat{\sigma}_{ek}^2) + 2k/(T - k_{\max})$, where $\hat{\sigma}_{ek}^2 = (T - k_{\max})^{-1} \sum_{t=k_{\max}+1}^{T} \hat{e}_{tk}^2$ with $\hat{e}_{tk}$ the residuals from the Dickey–Fuller regression.
2. BIC: $k_T = \text{argmin}_k \ln(\hat{\sigma}_{ek}^2) + \ln(T - k_{\max})k/(T - k_{\max})$.

3. $t_{\text{sig}}(5)$: A general to specific testing procedure on the last autoregressive lag using 5% two-sided tests (starting at $k_{\max} = 10$, or some other value, and stopping when a rejection occurs).
4. $t_{\text{sig}}(10)$: The same except that a 10% two-sided test is used.

See Section 36.4 for the implementation of the AIC and BIC. The t_{sig} method is applied as follows. Start by estimating an $AR(k_{\max})$ and if the last lag is significant, choose $k_T = k_{\max}$, otherwise re-estimate an autoregression with $k_{\max} - 1$ lags and test whether the last lag is significant and so on until a rejection. In practice, one should assess the sensitivity of the results to different values of $k_{\max}$; e.g., try $k_{\max} = 5, 10, 15$ and see if the results are the same; if not, look carefully at the residuals to see if any of the selected models show signs of serial correlation in the residuals that is not accounted for. The limiting distribution of the estimates of the lagged coefficients is standard normal, so the usual two-sided t-tests can be used.

The results are presented in Tables 45.2 and 45.3 reproduced from the work of Ng and Perron (1995). Note that the results are based on a regression that includes no deterministic component.

We make the following observations: (1) With AIC and BIC, the size distortions are still very large in the negative MA case

Table 45.2. Size and power of the ADF test $MA(1)$ case, $T = 100$, $k_{\max} = 10$.

α	θ	$t_{\text{sig}}(10)$	$t_{\text{sig}}(5)$	AIC	BIC
1.0	0.00	0.063	0.059	0.052	0.046
1.0	−0.30	0.097	0.126	0.127	0.174
1.0	−0.50	0.116	0.158	0.167	0.244
1.0	−0.80	0.304	0.424	0.561	0.733
0.95	0.00	0.153	0.151	0.140	0.126
0.95	−0.30	0.228	0.292	0.294	0.393
0.95	−0.50	0.254	0.336	0.377	0.510
0.95	−0.80	0.534	0.704	0.877	0.963
0.85	0.00	0.486	0.540	0.580	0.575
0.85	−.30	0.555	0.682	0.758	0.859
0.85	−.50	0.627	0.753	0.860	0.936
0.85	−.80	0.825	0.908	0.996	1.000

Source: Ng and Perron (1995). Reproduced with permission from Taylor & Francis.

Table 45.3. Size of the ADF test $MA(1)$ case, $T = 200$, $k_{\max} = 12$.

α	θ	$t_{\text{sig}}(10)$	$t_{\text{sig}}(5)$	AIC	BIC
1.0	0.00	0.064	0.066	0.059	0.057
1.0	−0.30	0.067	0.076	0.076	0.102
1.0	−0.50	0.085	0.110	0.121	0.168
1.0	−0.80	0.177	0.250	0.366	0.557

Source: Ng and Perron (1995). Reproduced with permission from Taylor & Francis.

(especially BIC) and remain large even at $T = 200$. (2) The size distortions with information criteria arise because the chosen value of k_T is too small. Furthermore, k_T increases very slowly with T at a rate proportional to $\log(T)$. Recall that this rate was forbidden by the assumptions of Said–Dickey in their proof, which is why Ng and Perron (1995) relaxed the lower bound they had imposed to show the asymptotic validity of the tests with k_T selected using an information criterion. (3) Size distortions are smaller with t_{sig}, especially $t_{\text{sig}}(10)$ with $T = 200$. (4) These are vast improvements over the fixed rules; at least the power in the *i.i.d.* case is not destroyed. But in all cases, we are still far from the nominal 5% target. So, while these rules are still popular, especially the $t_{\text{sig}}(10)$, there is room for improvements. We come back to better methods later.

For the Phillips–Perron Z_α test (the same holds for the Z_t test), the "state of the art" data-dependent method to select the bandwidth would be to use the method advocated by Andrews (1991b), with the quadratic spectral window and an "optimal" method to select the bandwidth based on an $AR(1)$ approximation (denoted s^2_{WA}). Alternatively, one could use an autoregressive spectral density estimator based on the estimated residuals with the order selected using an information criterion, such as the BIC (denoted s^2_{AR}). The results are presented in Table 45.4 whose source is the work of Ng and Perron (1996). Also included in this table are the exact size of the tests when σ^2 is assumed known and not estimated. This is, of course, infeasible in practice but can offer some insights about the properties of the tests.

To summarize the results, the finite sample size is not improved. Furthermore, even if the true value of σ^2 is used with a large

Table 45.4. Exact size of the Z_α test 5% nominal size.

Estimate of σ^2	S^2_{WA}	S^2_{AR}	σ^2	S^2_{WA}	S^2_{AR}	σ^2
		$T = 200$			$T = 500$	
i.i.d. errors	0.044	0.079	0.039	0.051	0.073	0.055
MA(1): −0.800	0.983	0.736	0.687	0.971	0.631	0.623
−0.500	0.419	0.114	0.082	0.345	0.085	0.078
AR(1): 0.500	0.015	0.098	0.063	0.021	0.064	0.057
0.800	0.004	0.075	0.088	0.013	0.065	0.080

Source: Perron and Ng (1996). Reproduced with permission from Oxford University Press.

sample size, here $T = 500$, things are not better! So, trying to estimate the nuisance parameters in a better way would be of no help.

45.5 Source of the size distortions for the Z_α test

The basic problem with the PP tests is that with negative $MA(1)$ errors, the asymptotic distribution of $T(\hat{\alpha} - 1)$ is a very bad approximation to the finite sample distribution. In other words, even for very large T, $\hat{\alpha}$ is severely biased downward (away from the limit value 1). To understand why, consider a process generated by DGP (45.1) (e.g., a linear trend, $z_t = (1, t)$). The Phillips Perron test Z_α and its limit distribution are given by

$$\begin{aligned} Z_\alpha &= T(\hat{\alpha} - 1) - X_T \\ &\Rightarrow \frac{\int_0^1 W^*(r)dW(r) + \delta}{\int_0^1 W^*(r)^2 dr} - \frac{\delta}{\int_0^1 W^*(r)^2 dr} \\ &= \frac{\int_0^1 W^*(r)dW(r)}{\int_0^1 W^*(r)^2 dr}, \end{aligned}$$

where $\hat{\alpha}$ is the least-squares estimate in the regression

$$y_t = \gamma z_t + \alpha y_{t-1} + v_t.$$

Also,

$$X_T = (\hat{\sigma}^2 - \hat{\sigma}_u^2) \Big/ \left(2T^{-2} \sum_{t=1}^{T} (y_{t-1}^*)^2 \right)$$

and

$$\delta = (\sigma^2 - \sigma_u^2)/(2\sigma^2),$$

with σ^2 the so-called long-run variance of u_t (2π times the spectral density at frequency zero), σ_u^2 is the variance of u_t, with $\hat{\sigma}^2$ and $\hat{\sigma}_u^2$ consistent estimates, and y_{t-1}^* is the detrended version of y_{t-1}, while $W^*(r)$ is a detrended Wiener process.

The first step is to investigate the adequacy of the limit distribution. This was analyzed in the work of Perron (1996), who showed that

$$\left[\int_0^1 W^*(r) dW(r) + \delta \right] \Big/ \int_0^1 W^*(r)^2 dr$$

is a very bad approximation to $T(\hat{\alpha} - 1)$ when there is a negative moving-average component in v_t, while

$$\delta \Big/ \int_0^1 W^*(r)^2 dr$$

is a good approximation to X_T. Hence, the overall limit distribution provides a poor approximation which results in severe size distortions. The problem is that the standard functional central limit theorem underlying the derivations provides a poor approximation with a negative moving-average component; see the work of Perron and Mallet (2000). For alternative asymptotic frameworks that provide better approximation, see the work of Nabeya and Perron (1994, 1995).

Table 45.5 provides examples of the finite sample and limit distribution of $T(\hat{\alpha} - 1)$ when the deterministic components contain a linear trend. As an example, when $\theta = -0.90$, the 1% quantile of the

Table 45.5. The distribution of $T(\hat{\alpha} - 1)$; detrended case; MA(1) errors, $u_t = e_t + \theta e_{t-1}$.

	1.0%	5.0%	10.0%	50.0%	90.0%	95.0%	99.0%
$\theta = -0.90$							
$T = 50$	−69.99	−62.31	−59.65	−50.55	−41.35	−38.81	−33.44
$T = 100$	−120.76	−113.66	−110.15	−96.14	−81.92	−77.88	−70.61
$T = 500$	−481.24	−457.07	−442.54	−382.56	−298.77	−271.18	−218.21
$T = 1{,}000$	−872.31	−812.90	−780.05	−631.57	−417.01	−355.29	−263.09
$T = 5{,}000$	−2676.75	−2324.64	−2076.49	−1196.41	−601.78	−493.03	−348.43
$T = \infty$	−5377.20	−3883.05	−3252.54	−1629.49	−752.34	−600.56	−401.37
$\theta = -0.70$							
$T = 50$	−60.49	−54.52	−51.25	−39.76	−27.64	−24.12	−18.24
$T = 100$	−99.63	−89.58	−83.76	−62.40	−40.42	−34.77	−26.12
$T = 500$	−252.88	−210.87	−188.78	−115.11	−60.87	−49.59	−33.62
$T = 1, 000$	−347.75	−271.94	−238.93	−135.45	−61.02	−48.07	−31.97
$T = \infty$	−492.19	−355.00	−296.95	−149.05	−69.37	−55.83	−35.77

Source: Perron (1996). Reproduced with permission from Elsevier.

finite sample distribution when $T = 100$ corresponds to a quantile of the limit distribution above 99%!

45.6 Alternative unit root tests

The preceding section showed that the cause of the size distortions for the Phillips–Perron-type unit root tests is the severe bias of $\hat{\alpha}$ in the presence of strong serial correlation in the errors. This suggests, as an avenue to obtain better tests, to make Z_α not a function of $\hat{\alpha}$. The first step is to use

$$\tilde{\sigma}_u^2 = T^{-1} \sum_{t=1}^{T} (\Delta y_{t-1}^*)^2$$

instead of

$$\hat{\sigma}_u^2 - T^{-1} \sum_{t=1}^{T} \hat{u}_t^2,$$

i.e., construct an estimate of σ_u^2 using residuals obtained imposing the null hypothesis. A little algebra gives the following representation:

$$\begin{aligned} MZ_\alpha &= T(\hat{\alpha}-1) - \frac{s^2 - \tilde{\sigma}_u^2}{2T^{-2}\sum_{t=1}^T (y_{t-1}^*)^2} \\ &\approx Z_\alpha + T(\hat{\alpha}-1)^2 \\ &\approx \frac{T^{-1}(y_T^*)^2 - s^2}{2T^{-2}\sum_{t=1}^T (y_{t-1}^*)^2}. \end{aligned}$$

This statistic was originally proposed by Stock (1999). One problem is that we cannot get rid of the dependence of s^2 on $\hat{\alpha}$ (via $\hat{u}_t$) by using

$$\tilde{s}^2 = T^{-1}\sum_{t=1}^{T}(\Delta y_{t-1}^*)^2 + 2T^{-1}\sum_{j=1}^{T-1} w(j, m_T) \sum_{t=j+1}^{T} \Delta y_t^* \Delta y_{t-j}^*.$$

Under the null hypothesis $H_0 : \alpha = 1$, things are fine. We have

$$\begin{aligned} T^{-1}(y_T^*)^2 &\Rightarrow \sigma^2 W^*(1)^2, \\ T^{-2}\sum_{t=1}^{T}(y_{t-1}^*)^2 &\Rightarrow \sigma^2 \int_0^1 W^*(r)^2 dr \end{aligned}$$

and $\tilde{s}^2 \xrightarrow{p} \sigma^2$ so that

$$MZ_\alpha \approx \frac{T^{-1}(y_T^*)^2 - s^2}{2T^{-2}\sum_{t=1}^T (y_{t-1}^*)^2} \Rightarrow \frac{W^*(1)^2 - 1}{2\int_0^1 W^*(r)^2 dr} = \frac{\int_0^1 W^*(r)dW(r)}{\int_0^1 W^*(r)^2 dr}.$$

The problem is that under H_1,

$$T\tilde{s}^2 = O_p(1)$$

(see, e.g., the work of Phillips and Ouliaris, 1990) and the test would be inconsistent. To see this, write MZ_α as

$$MZ_\alpha = \frac{(y_T^*)^2 - Ts^2}{2T^{-1}\sum_{t=1}^T (y_{t-1}^*)^2}. \tag{45.6}$$

Then, under H_1, all terms are $O_p(1)$ and $MZ_\alpha = O_p(1)$ so that the test is inconsistent. The solution is to use the following autoregressive spectral density estimator of σ^2:

$$s_{AR}^2 = \frac{\hat{\sigma}_{ek}^2}{(1 - \sum_{i=1}^{k_T} \hat{b}_i)^2},$$

where

$$\hat{\sigma}_{ek}^2 = T^{-1} \sum_{t=k_T+1}^{T} \hat{e}_{tk}^2$$

with $\hat{b}_i$ and $\hat{e}_{tk}$ obtained from the following OLS regression:

$$\Delta y_t^* = \hat{b}_0 y_{t-1}^* + \sum_{i=1}^{k_T} \hat{b}_i \Delta y_{t-i}^* + \hat{e}_{tk}.$$

Note that this last equation is simply the ADF regression. Introducing the lagged level is necessary, otherwise, we still have $Ts_{AR}^2 = O_p(1)$ and an inconsistent test. But now $s_{AR}^2 \xrightarrow{p} \kappa > 0$, say. It does not matter what κ is as long as it is positive. Then, $Ts_{AR}^2 \to \infty$ and, in view of (45.6), $MZ_\alpha \to -\infty$ so that the test is consistent against stationary alternatives. More details about this estimator can be found in the work of Perron and Ng (1996).

Table 45.6 presents the size of MZ_α with s_{AR}^2. The source is the work of Perron and Ng (1996). The lag length is selected using the t_{sig} method with a carefully selected range of values for k_T. To summarize, we have the following results. The test has very good size if s_{AR}^2 is constructed with a "good" k_T. Hence, the key is to find a method that chooses a truncation lag k_T that yields good size without reducing power. If we solve the problem of selecting k_T in constructing s_{AR}^2, we also solve it for constructing the ADF test since the underlying OLS regression is the same. This is discussed in Section 45.9.

Table 45.6. Exact size of the MZ_α test with alternative estimate of σ^2 (5% nominal size).

Estimate of σ^2	$\tilde{s}^2$	s^2_{AR}	σ^2
		$T = 200$	
i.i.d. errors	0.037	0.072	0.034
MA(1): −0.800	0.981	0.089	0.000
−0.500	0.383	0.052	0.005
AR(1): 0.500	0.007	0.085	0.054
0.800	0.003	0.065	0.074
		$T = 500$	
i.i.d. errors	0.037	0.061	0.043
MA(1): −0.800	0.961	0.010	0.000
−0.500	0.304	0.042	0.021
AR(1): 0.500	0.013	0.048	0.039
0.800	0.009	0.046	0.063

Source: Perron and Ng (1996). Reproduced with permission from Oxford University Press.

45.7 GLS detrending

Elliott *et al.* (1996) addressed the issue of improved power. Suppose that

$$y_t = \gamma z_t + v_t, \tag{45.7}$$

where

$$v_t = \alpha v_{t-1} + u_t.$$

If the errors u_t are *i.i.d.* $N(0, \sigma_u^2)$, then, from the Neyman and Pearson (1933) lemma, the most powerful test of the null hypothesis $\alpha = 1$ versus the alternative hypothesis that $\alpha = \bar{\alpha}$ is given by the likelihood ratio test which, assuming normality, reduces to

$$L(\bar{\alpha}, 1) = S(\bar{\alpha}) - S(1),$$

where $S(\alpha)$ is the sum of squared residuals evaluated at α, defined in the following. Now, taking a quasi-difference, i.e., multiplying (45.7) by $(1-\alpha L)$, we have

$$(1-\alpha L)y_t = \gamma(1-\alpha L)z_t + u_t \tag{45.8}$$

for $t = 2, \ldots, T$, and

$$y_1 = \gamma z_1 + u_1.$$

Now, γ is a nuisance parameter which needs to be concentrated out. Let

$$y_t^\alpha = y_t - \alpha y_{t-1},$$
$$z_t^\alpha = z_t - \alpha z_{t-1},$$

for $t = 2, \ldots, T$ and $y_1^\alpha = y_1$, $z_1^\alpha = z_1$. These are usually called quasi-differenced data. Then, (45.8) can be expressed as

$$y_t^\alpha = \gamma z_t^\alpha + u_t. \tag{45.9}$$

Since $u_t \sim i.i.d.\ N(0, \sigma_u^2)$, the best estimate of γ is obtained by applying OLS to (45.9), which is equivalent to applying GLS to (45.7); see Section 13.2. Denote this estimate by $\hat{\gamma}^{GLS}$, which is implicitly a function of α. Then, the sum of squared residuals in terms of α only is

$$S(\alpha) = \sum_{t=1}^{T}(y_t^\alpha - \hat{\gamma}^{GLS} z_t^\alpha)^2.$$

Hence, the likelihood ratio test compares the sum of squared residuals from two GLS regressions with autoregressive parameters 1 and $\bar{\alpha}$. Assuming that the true value $\alpha = \bar{\alpha}$, and using the local to unity parameterization

$$\bar{\alpha} = 1 + \bar{c}/T,$$

the local asymptotic power function of the LR test for a range of values of $\bar{c}$ gives a local asymptotic power envelope, i.e., the maximum power that can be achieved under normal errors. This local asymptotic power envelope is a function of the deterministic components and the Ornstein–Uhlenbeck process since we are dealing with a near-integrated process under the sequence of local alternatives. See Exercise 45.7. For a review of local asymptotic power, see Section 9.4.

In practice, one does not know the true value of α. A sensible recommendation by Elliott *et al.* (1996) is to choose $\bar{\alpha} = 1 + \bar{c}/T$ such that the asymptotic power is 50% evaluated at $\bar{c}$. This implies $\bar{c} = -7.0$ when $z_t = 1$ and $\bar{c} = -13.5$ when $z_t = (1, t)$.

In the presence of serial correlation, a feasible point optimal test with the same asymptotic properties is

$$P_T = [S(\bar{\alpha}) - \bar{\alpha}S(1)]/s_{AR}^2. \tag{45.10}$$

Denote the GLS detrended data by

$$\tilde{y}_t = y_t - \hat{\gamma}^{GLS} z_t.$$

Consider the ADF test constructed with GLS detrended data, labeled ADF^{GLS}, i.e., the t-statistic for testing that $\alpha = 1$ in the OLS regression:

$$\tilde{y}_t = \alpha\tilde{y}_{t-1} + \sum_{i=1}^{k_T} b_i \Delta\tilde{y}_{t-i} + e_{tk}. \tag{45.11}$$

Elliott *et al.* (1996) found that it has an asymptotic power function very close to the power envelope, i.e., indistinguishable when looking at a graph. They also found the ADF^{GLS} and P_T tests to have local asymptotic power superior to the standard ADF, Z_t, and MZ_t (which share a common local asymptotic power function). The same applies to the Z_α and MZ_α tests, even though they theoretically have different local asymptotic power functions.

The only problem remaining in the analysis of Elliott *et al.* (1996) is that they fudge the simulations to some extent so that the tests seem to have decent (though still not very good) finite sample properties, especially in the case of a negative moving-average component. For the ADF^{GLS}, they used BIC but with a restricted range with $k_T \in [3, 6]$. This precluded the BIC from selecting low values, which would have increased substantially the exact size of the test. It also decreases the power of the test when there is little serial correlation and a small value of k_T is appropriate. Hence, a reliable method to select k_T remains to be derived.

Remark 45.1. When testing for a unit root, the finite sample distribution is invariant to the initial condition y_0 under the null hypothesis but not under the alternative; see Exercise 44.3. Müller and Elliott (2003) showed that if the initial condition is large, the advantage of the GLS approach is reduced. If it is very large, then the usual OLS detrended approach dominates. However, this result is of little practical relevance as the initial condition would need to be implausibly large for OLS to dominate; see the works of Perron and Rodríguez (2016) and Haldrup and Jansson (2006).

45.8 The M-tests with GLS detrending

Ng and Perron (2001) considered the MZ_α test constructed with GLS detrended data, i.e.,

$$MZ_\alpha^{GLS} = \frac{T^{-1}\tilde{y}_T^2 - s_{AR}^2}{2T^{-2}\sum_{t=1}^T \tilde{y}_{t-1}^2},$$

where s_{AR}^2 is constructed using the ADF autoregression with GLS detrended data (45.11). They also considered the following alternative tests:

$$MSB^{GLS} = \left(\frac{T^{-2}\sum_{t=1}^T \tilde{y}_{t-1}^2}{s_{AR}^2}\right)^{1/2}$$

and

$$MZ_t^{GLS} = MSB^{GLS} \times MZ_\alpha^{GLS}.$$

These tests are collectively referred to as the M^{GLS} tests though for illustration we use the MZ_α^{GLS}. Ng and Perron (2001) also considered a modified point-optimal test; see (45.10). It is given by

$$MP_T^{GLS} = \left[\bar{c}^2 T^{-2}\sum_{t=1}^T \tilde{y}_{t-1}^2 - \bar{c}T^{-1}\tilde{y}_T^2\right] \Big/ s_{AR}^2$$

if only a constant is included as deterministic regressor, while if a constant and a time trend are included, it is given by

$$MP_T^{GLS} = \left[\bar{c}^2 T^{-2}\sum_{t=1}^T \tilde{y}_{t-1}^2 + (1-\bar{c})T^{-1}\tilde{y}_T^2\right] \Big/ s_{AR}^2.$$

We have the following results concerning the asymptotic distributions of the tests.

Theorem 45.1. *If only a constant is included as a deterministic regressor,*

$$MZ_{\alpha}^{GLS} \Rightarrow \left(\int_0^1 W_c(r)dW(r)\right)\left(\int_0^1 W_c(r)^2dr\right)^{-1},$$

$$MSB^{GLS} \Rightarrow \left(\int_0^1 W_c(r)^2dr\right)^{1/2},$$

$$MP_T^{GLS} \Rightarrow \bar{c}^2\int_0^1 W_c(r)^2dr - \bar{c}W_c(1)^2.$$

If a constant and a time trend are included as deterministic regressors,

$$MZ_{\alpha}^{GLS} \Rightarrow 0.5(V_{c,\bar{c}}(1)^2 - 1)\left(\int_0^1 V_{c,\bar{c}}(r)^2dr\right)^{-1},$$

$$MSB^{GLS} \Rightarrow \left(\int_0^1 V_{c,\bar{c}}(r)^2dr\right)^{1/2},$$

$$MP_T^{GLS} \Rightarrow \bar{c}^2\int_0^1 V_{c,\bar{c}}(r)^2dr + (1-\bar{c})V_{c,\bar{c}}(1)^2,$$

where $W_c(r)$ is an Ornstein–Uhlenbeck process defined by

$$dW_c(r) = cW_c(r)dr + dW(r),$$

with $W_c(0) = 0$, and

$$V_{c,\bar{c}}(r) = W_c(r) - r[\lambda W_c(1) + 3(1-\lambda)\int_0^1 sW_c(s)ds],$$

$$\lambda = (1-\bar{c})/(1-\bar{c}+\bar{c}^2/3).$$

Results for MZ_t^{GLS} can be obtained in view of the fact that $MZ_t^{GLS} = MZ_{\alpha}^{GLS} \times MSB^{GLS}$. The limit distribution of the ADF^{GLS} (resp., P_T) is the same as that of MZ_t^{GLS} (resp., MP_T^{GLS}).

Remark 45.2. The results for the limit distribution under the null hypothesis of a unit root $\alpha = 1$ can be obtained by setting $c = 0$ in the expressions of the previous theorem.

Remark 45.3. The asymptotic distributions of the MZ_α^{GLS}, MZ_t^{GLS}, MSB^{GLS}, and ADF^{GLS} tests when only a constant is included do not depend upon $\bar{c}$. Furthermore, they are the same as would prevail with standard non-GLS detrended tests with no deterministic component; see Section 44.6.3 (with $\delta = 0$). This is because the GLS detrending device, with the AR parameter local to one, is nearly equivalent to taking first-differences of the data. Hence, the mean of the series gets eliminated. Since these tests are based on the data series, the limit distributions are then the same as when no constant is included in the standard procedures. This is not the case for the P_T test since it does not look at the data per se but rather at the local differences in the sum of squared residuals, in which case the effect of $\bar{c}$ remains. In other words, it is a finite sample counterpart of the infeasible LR tests whose power depends on both $\bar{c}$ and c. The same applies to the test MP_T^{GLS} since it is constructed to have the same limit distribution as the P_T test.

The finite sample performance of the various M tests (MZ_α^{GLS}, MZ_t^{GLS}, MSB^{GLS}, and MP_T^{GLS}) are very similar. The asymptotic critical values from Theorem 45.1 are presented in Table 45.7. Ng and Perron (2001) also showed that the local asymptotic power functions of the M-tests are close to the power envelope derived by Elliott

Table 45.7. Asymptotic critical values.

Percentile	MZ_α^{GLS}	MZ_t^{GLS}, ADF^{GLS}	MSB^{GLS}	P_T^{GLS}, MP_T^{GLS}
		Case: only a constant, $\bar{c} = -7.0$		
0.01	−13.8	−2.58	0.174	1.78
0.05	−8.1	−1.98	0.233	3.17
0.10	−5.7	−1.62	0.275	4.45
		Case: a constant and time trend, $\bar{c} = -13.5$		
0.01	−23.8	−3.42	0.143	4.03
0.05	−17.3	−2.91	0.168	5.48
0.10	−14.2	−2.62	0.185	6.67

Source: Ng and Perron (2001). Reproduced with permission from Wiley.

et al. (1996). Hence, the M^{GLS} tests are potential competitors in terms of power and may have better size in finite samples provided k_T is chosen adequately. For the MZ_α^{GLS}, MZ_t^{GLS}, and ADF^{GLS} with only a constant, the critical values are from the work of Fuller (1996). The other entries were obtained using 20,000 simulations and 5,000 steps to approximate the Wiener processes and reproduced from the work of Ng and Perron (2001).

45.9 The modified information criterion

We recall from Section 36.4 the justification for the penalty k_T for the AIC. Consider the linear model with k_T regressors:

$$y_t = x_t\beta + e_t.$$

An unbiased estimate of (twice) the expected log likelihood function (under normality) can be obtained by adjusting (twice) the likelihood function by the quadratic form

$$I_T(k_T) = (\hat{\beta} - \beta^0)'(X'X)(\hat{\beta} - \beta^0)/\hat{\sigma}_e^2,$$

i.e., the Wald test for testing that $\beta = \beta^0$. If

$$\sqrt{T}(\hat{\beta} - \beta^0) \xrightarrow{d} N(0, \sigma_e^2 V^{-1}),$$

where

$$V = plim_{T\to\infty}(X'X/T),$$

a fixed bounded positive definite matrix, then $I_T(k_T) \xrightarrow{d} \chi^2_{k_T}$ and $E(I_T(k_T)) \to k_T$. This is basically why all information criteria have k_T as the penalty factor. Our linear model is an autoregression of the form

$$\Delta\tilde{y}_t = b_0\tilde{y}_{t-1} + \sum_{i=1}^{k_T} b_i\Delta\tilde{y}_{t-i} + e_{tk}. \tag{45.12}$$

Let $\tilde{z}_t = (\Delta\tilde{y}_{t-1}, \ldots, \Delta\tilde{y}_{t-k_T})$, $\tilde{Z} = (\tilde{z}_1', \ldots, \tilde{z}_T')'$, $\beta' = (b_1, \ldots, b_{k_T})$, and $b_0 = (\alpha - 1)$, then

$$I_T(k_T) = (\hat{\sigma}_{ek}^2)^{-1}\left[(\hat{b}_0 - b_0)^2 T^{-2}\sum_{t=1}^{T}\tilde{y}_{t-1}^2 + (\hat{\beta} - \beta^0)'(\tilde{Z}'\tilde{Z})(\hat{\beta} - \beta^0)\right] + o_p(1).$$

The second term involves the unknown parameters β^0, hence to adjust the likelihood function, we need to resort to asymptotic approximations. We again have

$$(\hat{\beta} - \beta^0)'(\tilde{Z}'\tilde{Z})(\hat{\beta} - \beta^0) \xrightarrow{d} \chi_{k_T}^2$$

and

$$E[(\hat{\beta} - \beta^0)'(\tilde{Z}'\tilde{Z})(\hat{\beta} - \beta^0)] \to k_T.$$

For the first term, things are different. We can get rid of its dependence on unknown values by imposing the null hypothesis of a unit root $b_0 = 0$. There is then no need to resort to an asymptotic approximation to adjust the likelihood function and we can keep this term without further modifications. Hence, the penalty becomes

$$\tau_T(k_T) + k_T,$$

where

$$\tau_T(k_T) = (\hat{\sigma}_{ek}^2)^{-1}\hat{b}_0^2 \sum_{t=k_{\max}+1}^{T} \tilde{y}_{t-1}^2.$$

The modified information criterion is then

$$MIC(k_T) = \ln(\hat{\sigma}_{ek}^2) + C_T(\tau_T(k_T) + k_T)/(T - k_{\max}), \tag{45.13}$$

where

$$\hat{\sigma}_{ek}^2 = (T - k_{\max})^{-1} \sum_{t=k_{\max}+1}^{T} \hat{e}_{tk}^2.$$

The minimization is taken over the range $k_T \in [0, k_{\max}]$ and $\hat{e}_{tk}$ are obtained from a regression using the observations $t = k_{\max}+1, \ldots, T$

(see Section 36.4). We have the MAIC when $C_T = 2$ and the MBIC when $C_T = \ln(T)$.

The dependence of $\tau_T(k_T)$ on k_T is mainly through the estimate $\hat{b}_0$, the sum of the autoregressive coefficients. There is a lot of evidence that with negative MA errors; the bias of $\hat{b}_0$ is heavily dependent on k_T. It decreases as k_T increases. Hence, introducing $\tau_T(k_T)$ implies a nonlinear penalty function. If the decrease in the bias is strong enough, the penalty will initially decrease and then increase. When the errors are pure AR processes, the bias in $\hat{b}_0$ is little affected by k_T, hence $\tau_T(k_T)$ is a flat function and the MIC reduces to standard information criteria.

Also of importance is the fact that $\tau_T(k_T)$ is influenced by the nature of the deterministic components included. In particular, the decrease in $\tau_T(k_T)$ is sharper with a time trend than with a constant only. Hence, larger values of k_T will be selected with a time trend. This is useful and contrasts with standard information criteria which are basically invariant to the types of deterministic components included. Based upon an asymptotic analysis in which the MA parameter is made local to -1, Ng and Perron (2001) recommended the use of the MAIC with $C_T = 2$. They also showed some theoretical advantages for the MZ_α^{GLS} over the ADF^{GLS}.

There is one drawback in their analysis. Oftentimes practitioners test if both the level and the first-differences of the series are $I(1)$ or $I(0)$ to see whether two unit roots are present. Since the tests are based on local asymptotic arguments, they fail to deliver sensible results in this case. This is because if the process is $I(0)$ and one takes first-differences, the process is over-differenced. Hence, a very large k_T is selected and the test has no power. Perron and Qu (2007) proposed a simple remedy to address this problem: Estimate the lag length using the MIC (45.13) but with OLS-detrended data instead of GLS-detrended data. Once k_T is selected, construct the relevant test and estimate s_{AR}^2 using GLS-detrended data. See Section 45.11 for details.

45.10 Finite sample size and power

The simulation results are again based on simple $MA(1)$ and $AR(1)$ errors. Size-adjusted power is evaluated at $\bar{\alpha} = 1 + \bar{c}/T$ with $\bar{c} = -7$ when only a constant is included as a deterministic regressor, and $\bar{c} =$

Table 45.8. Size; constant only.

MA case: $v_t = e_t + \theta e_{t-1}, e_t \sim N(0,1)$								
T	θ/ρ	M_{mic}	M_{mic}^{GLS}	DF_{bic}	DF_{bic}^{GLS}	DF_t^{GLS}	DF_{mic}^{GLS}
100	−0.8	0.058	0.036	0.394	0.411	0.356	0.107
	−0.5	0.028	0.056	0.082	0.104	0.095	0.073
	0.0	0.018	0.043	0.072	0.077	0.072	0.050
250	−0.8	0.016	0.022	0.370	0.323	0.236	0.088
	−0.5	0.036	0.058	0.075	0.089	0.079	0.063
	0.0	0.021	0.047	0.059	0.062	0.062	0.045
AR case: $v_t = \rho v_{t-1} + e_t, e_t \sim N(0,1)$							
100	0.5	0.029	0.064	0.082	0.087	0.082	0.053
	0.8	0.047	0.090	0.091	0.081	0.077	0.053
250	0.5	0.028	0.052	0.056	0.061	0.061	0.045
	0.8	0.037	0.060	0.060	0.061	0.063	0.051

Source: Ng and Perron (2001). Reproduced with permission from Wiley.

−13.5 when a constant and time trend are included. Hence, the local asymptotic power is 50%. The results presented in Tables 45.8–45.11 are from the work of Ng and Perron (2001), where more extensive sets of simulations are reported. Here, we only report results for $T = 100$ and 250 and the most empirically relevant parameters for the $MA(1)$ and $AR(1)$ noise processes.

The tests considered are the following: (1) the MZ_α; since the numerical results for MZ_α, MZ_t, and MSB are similar, we use the label M in the tables. Three variants of the M tests are considered. The M_{mic} is the original MZ_α, the M_{mic}^{GLS} uses GLS detrended data to construct the statistic including s_{AR}^2, at $\bar{c} = -7.0$ (with a constant only), and $\bar{c} = -13.5$ (with a constant and a time trend). When the BIC is used, $k_{\max} = 6$ and $k_{\min} = 3$ as in the work of Elliott *et al.* (1996). For the MIC, $k_{\max} = int[12(T/100)^{1/4}]$, $k_{\min} = 0$, and $C_T = 2$ giving the MAIC. The DF_t^{GLS} is based on the 10% sequential t-test for the significance of the last lag. The results for the P_T test of Elliott *et al.* (1996) and its modification by Ng and Perron (2001) are similar to those of the M-tests. Hence, the results are not included.

To summarize the results:

1. The tests have, by far, better exact sizes when the MAIC is used and it is indeed close to 5% for all cases considered, a considerable

Table 45.9. Size-adjusted power; constant only.

T	θ/ρ	M_{mic}	M^{GLS}_{mic}	DF_{bic}	DF^{GLS}_{bic}	DF^{GLS}_{t}	DF^{GLS}_{mic}
MA case: $v_t = e_t + \theta e_{t-1}, e_t \sim N(0,1)$							
100	−0.8	0.193	0.311	0.241	0.419	0.412	0.385
	−0.5	0.253	0.344	0.191	0.448	0.429	0.385
	0.0	0.315	0.458	0.131	0.432	0.436	0.454
250	−0.8	0.190	0.334	0.287	0.441	0.420	0.437
	−0.5	0.264	0.396	0.201	0.477	0.455	0.428
	0.0	0.338	0.477	0.152	0.464	0.446	0.483
AR case: $v_t = \rho v_{t-1} + e_t, e_t \sim N(0,1)$							
100	0.5	0.279	0.368	0.115	0.338	0.330	0.385
	0.8	0.196	0.241	0.084	0.297	0.292	0.298
250	0.5	0.336	0.436	0.158	0.447	0.434	0.456
	0.8	0.279	0.366	0.131	0.386	0.382	0.381

Source: Ng and Perron (2001). Reproduced with permission from Wiley.

Table 45.10. Size; constant and time trend.

T	θ/ρ	M_{mic}	M^{GLS}_{mic}	DF_{bic}	DF^{GLS}_{bic}	DF^{GLS}_{t}	DF^{GLS}_{mic}
MA case: $v_t = e_t + \theta e_{t-1}, e_t \sim N(0,1)$							
100	−0.8	0.140	0.059	0.509	0.567	0.528	0.123
	−0.5	0.037	0.035	0.092	0.107	0.111	0.069
	0.0	0.011	0.018	0.075	0.074	0.078	0.039
250	−0.8	0.025	0.012	0.566	0.531	0.381	0.064
	−0.5	0.031	0.033	0.094	0.105	0.099	0.048
	0.0	0.023	0.029	0.056	0.059	0.065	0.038
AR case: $v_t = \rho v_{t-1} + e_t, e_t \sim N(0,1)$							
100	0.5	0.033	0.042	0.076	0.083	0.088	0.038
	0.8	0.081	0.093	0.081	0.086	0.091	0.043
250	0.5	0.037	0.044	0.059	0.063	0.068	0.039
	0.8	0.045	0.056	0.054	0.056	0.061	0.043

Source: Ng and Perron (2001). Reproduced with permission from Wiley.

improvement over what we reported before using other methods. For instance, if the BIC is used, even with a restricted range $k_{\text{max}} = 6$ and $k_{\text{min}} = 3$ as in the work of Elliott *et al.* (1996), the

Table 45.11. Size-adjusted power; constant and time trend.

MA case: $v_t = e_t + \theta e_{t-1}, e_t \sim N(0,1)$							
T	θ/ρ	M_{mic}	M_{mic}^{GLS}	DF_{bic}	DF_{bic}^{GLS}	DF_t^{GLS}	DF_{mic}^{GLS}
100	−0.8	0.296	0.348	0.283	0.398	0.414	0.357
	−0.5	0.320	0.300	0.258	0.421	0.420	0.324
	0.0	0.450	0.439	0.175	0.362	0.341	0.432
250	−0.8	0.247	0.296	0.371	0.460	0.430	0.375
	−0.5	0.308	0.366	0.278	0.459	0.441	0.392
	0.0	0.380	0.451	0.250	0.437	0.418	0.447
AR case: $v_t = \rho v_{t-1} + e_t, e_t \sim N(0,1)$							
100	0.5	0.235	0.270	0.133	0.262	0.264	0.286
	0.8	0.114	0.129	0.098	0.167	0.165	0.206
250	0.5	0.331	0.385	0.233	0.391	0.372	0.392
	0.8	0.259	0.288	0.189	0.314	0.292	0.289

Source: Ng and Perron (2001). Reproduced with permission from Wiley.

exact size is near 40% for the DF^{GLS} test when only a constant is included and between 50% and 55% when a constant and time trend are included. If the t_{sig} method is used (see DF_t^{GLS}), the corresponding numbers are 35% and 53%.

2. With MA errors, the M^{GLS} (any of the three versions) and the P_T^{GLS} have size closest to 5%. The DF_{mic}^{GLS} is somewhat liberal when $\theta = -0.8$ with an exact size around 10% when $T = 100$ and barely decreasing to 9% when $T = 250$. This can be explained using some of the theoretical results in the work of Ng and Perron (2001). Hence, the M^{GLS} tests have a slight advantage over the DF_{mic}^{GLS} test, when using the MAIC.
3. Of interest, though not reported here, the exact size of the M^{GLS} tests with k_T chosen by the MAIC is closer to the nominal 5% size compared to the exact size obtained using the best fixed k_T for a given DGP. This shows that the MAIC adapts to the information in a given sample very effectively.
4. Using GLS-detrended data improves the power of the tests considerably. It is close to the target asymptotic level 50% when the errors are *i.i.d.* or mildly correlated, though falls somewhat short when there is substantial correlation of either MA or AR type.
5. The size-adjusted power of the DF_{mic}^{GLS} test is, in general, slightly higher than that of the M_{mic}^{GLS}. So, there is a trade-off between

slightly higher size distortions for the DF_{mic}^{GLS} compared to M_{mic}^{GLS} and slightly higher power.

45.11 The importance of using OLS-detrending to select k_T

As noted above, a drawback of the tests constructed with the MAIC to select k_T is that for non-local alternatives, the power can be very small. In fact, for a given sample size T, the power can decrease as α gets further away from 1. An alternative specification considered by Ng and Perron (2001), which uses OLS detrended data instead of GLS detrended data in the autoregression (45.12) to construct the spectral density estimate, does not suffer much from this problem but it leads to tests that are too conservative in common sample sizes and, hence, was not recommended. The power problem is quite important. Indeed, if the underlying process is *i.i.d.*, the test has very low power (see the following). Hence, when dealing with a random walk and performing the test both in levels and first differences, one is likely to conclude that the series is integrated of order 2.

As shown by Perron and Qu (2007), there is an easy solution to this power reversal problem, which in addition leads to tests having an exact size even closer to nominal size for all specifications considered in the work of Ng and Perron (2001) (this is not shown here; see Perron and Qu, 2007, for details). The idea is to use a hybrid of the two specifications. The autoregressive spectral density estimate is still constructed using GLS detrended data as specified above, but the selection of the autoregressive order k_T uses the MAIC constructed with OLS detrended data, i.e., replacing $\tilde{y}_t$ by $\hat{y}_t$, the residuals from a regression of y_t on z_t and using the autoregression

$$\Delta y_t^* = \check{b}_0 y_{t-1}^* + \sum_{i=1}^{k_T} \check{b}_i \Delta y_{t-i}^* + \check{e}_{tk}. \tag{45.14}$$

One can also use a regression in levels with the deterministic components added as regressors, i.e.,

$$\Delta y_t = c + \delta t + \hat{b}_0 y_{t-1} + \sum_{i=1}^{k_T} \hat{b}_i \Delta y_{t-i} + \hat{e}_{tk}.$$

The results are virtually the same by the Frisch–Waugh–Lovell theorem 2.1.3. So, the modification involves a two-step procedure. First, use (45.14) to construct

$$MAIC(k_T) = \ln(\check{\sigma}_k^2) + 2(\tau_T(k_T) + k_T)/(T - k_{\max})$$

with

$$\tau_T(k_T) = (\check{\sigma}_k^2)^{-1}\check{b}_0^2 \sum_{t=k_{\max}+1}^{T} y_{t-1}^{*2}$$

and

$$\check{\sigma}_k^2 = (T - k_{\max})^{-1} \sum_{t=k_{\max}+1}^{T} \check{e}_{tk}^2.$$

Once the order is selected as the minimizer of $MAIC(k_T)$, say k_{MAIC}, estimate (45.12) with k_{MAIC} lags to construct s_{AR}^2 or the ADF^{GLS} test.

Consider now the power of the tests. We present simulations in Figure 45.1 for the case with *i.i.d.* errors $u_t \sim i.i.d.\ N(0,1)$. The value of α is varied between 1 and 0, and the graphs report results in terms of the value of $(1-\alpha)$. Three versions of the tests are considered: (a) the original procedure recommended by Ng and Perron (2001),

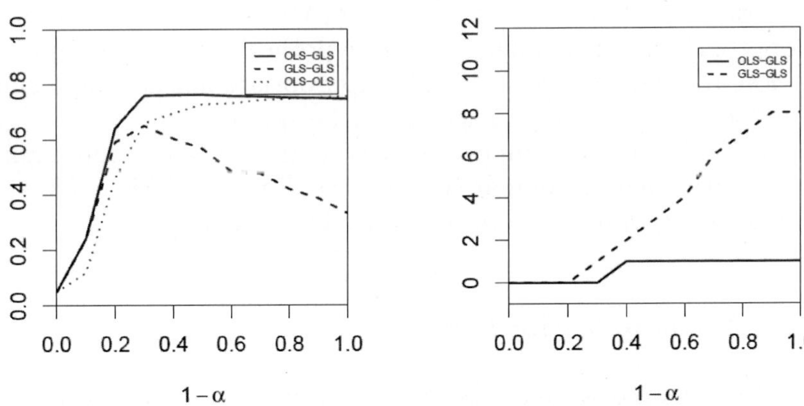

Figure 45.1. Power of the ADF test (left panel) and median of the lag order selected (right panel); $T = 100$, *i.i.d.* errors, constant and linear trend included. *Source*: Perron and Qu (2007). Reproduced with permission from Elsevier.

labeled GLS-GLS, (b) the modification discussed here labeled OLS-GLS, and (c) tests constructed using OLS detrended data throughout, labeled OLS-OLS, to assess the extent of the power gain of using GLS detrended data. The sample size is $T = 100$ and 50,000 replications were used. We present results for the ADF^{GLS} test for the case with a constant and a time trend. The results for the other tests and other cases are qualitatively similar; see Perron and Qu (2007). The left panel reports the power while the right panel reports the autoregressive order selected. Note that the lag selected is the same for the OLS-GLS and OLS-OLS procedures.

The results show that the original procedure recommended by Ng and Perron (2001) and the modification suggested here indeed have higher power than tests based on OLS detrended data when α is "local" to 1. But when α decreases, the original version has power that decreases rapidly. This reversal does not occur with the modification and the power for values of α away from 1 is close to what can be achieved using OLS detrended data throughout.

The reason for the difference in power when using OLS or GLS detrended data to construct the MAIC can be seen by looking at the right panel, which reports the autoregressive orders selected. When the MAIC is constructed with GLS detrended data, the value of k_T selected increases as α moves away from the null value 1. This is not the case when the MAIC is constructed with OLS detrended data. The choice of fewer lags translates into higher power. Hence, using OLS detrended data to construct the MAIC allows the selection of the appropriate order under the null hypothesis to achieve an exact size close to nominal size and is also appropriate in selecting a small lag under the alternative to achieve higher power.

This modification is important. Unfortunately, while the original tests are available in popular software, as of writing this book, they have not incorporated an option for it. They should.

45.12 Panel unit root tests

Panel unit root tests have become very popular in applied work. This is so despite the fact that it is very difficult to interpret what the results actually mean and under what conditions they offer any improvements in terms of power over simple univariate tests applied to each unit in the panel. Here, we provide a brief review of the main issues. The main motivation is the idea that using a panel should yield more information about the $I(1)$-$I(0)$ nature of the data, especially when T, the time dimension, is small, in which case univariate tests have low power. In other words, with N the number of cross-sectional units, it is hoped that when N is large and T is small, more useful information can be obtained. Useful references for the general concepts involved are the works of Pesaran (2012) and Im *et al.* (2023), on which this section draws heavily.

Suppose first that each series in the panel is an $AR(1)$ with *i.i.d.* errors $e_{i,t}$ given by

$$\begin{aligned} y_{i,t} &= \beta_i z_t + v_{i,t}, \\ v_{i,t} &= \alpha_i v_{i,t-1} + e_{i,t}, \end{aligned}$$

and the regression used is

$$y_{i,t} = \beta_i^* z_t + \alpha_i y_{i,t-1} + e_{i,t}, \tag{45.15}$$

for $i = 1, \ldots, N$ and $t = 1, \ldots, T$. It is first assumed that $e_{i,t}$ is independent across i as well as t. The variable z_t contains the deterministic components, usually only a constant or a constant an a time trend. We assume a balanced panel so that each unit has T observations. This can be relaxed at the expense of added notational complexities. The null hypothesis is

$$H_0\colon \alpha_i = 1,$$

for all $i = 1, \ldots, T$. Specifying the alternative hypothesis is more tricky. Early work started by considering

$$H_1^a\colon \alpha_i = \alpha \quad \text{with } |\alpha| < 1 \quad \text{for all } i$$

so that all series are stationary. The problem with this formulation is that most tests will reject the null hypothesis even if only some series are integrated, i.e., $\alpha_i = 1$ for some i. Hence, a rejection is not convincing evidence in favor of the alternative hypothesis. Also, the homogeneity assumption that $\alpha_i = \alpha$ for all i is unlikely to be relevant in practice. Another possible alternative hypothesis is

$$H_1^b\colon |\alpha_i| < 1 \text{ for one or more } i.$$

This is, however, only appropriate when N is fixed. The advantage of panel unit root tests relies on exploiting the large dimension of the panel in order to provide improvements over univariate tests. Also, with this alternative, if both N and T are large, the various tests proposed have low power. The literature seems to have settled on some middle-ground with the following alternative hypothesis:

$$H_1^c\colon |\alpha_i| < 1 \quad \text{for } i = 1, \ldots, M \quad \text{and} \quad \alpha_i = 1 \quad \text{for } i = M+1, \ldots, N,$$

where M is some number that can depend on the cross-section dimension N, i.e., $M = M_N$ such that

$$\lim_{N\to\infty} M_N/N = \delta.$$

Here, δ is interpreted as the proportion of units for which a rejection occurs. Then, the null and alternative hypotheses can be specified as

$$H_0\colon \delta = 0,$$
$$H_1^c\colon \delta > 0.$$

The most commonly used panel unit root test in the context of the simple example with no cross-sectional dependence, serially uncorrelated errors $e_{i,t}$, and H_1^c as the alternative hypothesis is that of Im *et al.* (2003). For each unit i, let the t-statistic for testing for a unit root using a sample of size T be denoted by $t_{i,T}$. Then, the test is simply the cross-sectional average of these t-statistics, i.e.,

$$\bar{t}_{i,T} = N^{-1}\sum_{i=1}^{N} t_{i,T}.$$

Consider the case with a small time dimension, say $T = 6$ (or 7) depending on the nature of the deterministic components. The latter is needed to ensure finite moments of the relevant quantities so that a central limit theorem can be applied. Then, under additional regularity conditions,

$$\sqrt{N}(\bar{t}_{i,T} - E(t_{i,T}))/\sqrt{\mathrm{Var}(t_{i,T})} \xrightarrow{d} N(0,1),$$

as $N \to \infty$. Expressions for the mean and variance of $t_{i,T}$ under the null hypothesis are provided in the work of Im *et al.* (2003). The test is consistent against the alternative H_1^c and it has higher power than applying individual unit root tests to each unit. However, it applies to a very restrictive DGP. This is labeled as a unit root test in heterogenous panels because the alternative H_1^c allow heterogeneity in the value of α_i across units.

One issue is the assumption that $e_{i,t}$ is uncorrelated in the time dimension. It is possible to relax this assumption, even allowing different serial correlation structures across units. This, however, requires the time dimension T to increase to infinity, i.e., both N and T need to be sufficiently large. This is obvious when allowing $e_{i,t}$ to be a general linear process that is usually approximated an autoregressive process of increasing order. But it also applies when considering a finite order AR process since the limit distribution of the $\bar{t}_{i,T}$ statistics when T is fixed depends on nuisance parameters associated with the correlation structure under the null hypothesis. These are usually unknown in practice. However, one can get rid of this dependence provided $T \to \infty$.

So far, we assumed that the errors $e_{i,t}$ are uncorrelated in the cross-section dimension. This is most often unrealistic. Hence, a second generation of procedures proposed tests that allow for cross-sectional dependence. Some used bootstrap procedures. A popular approach is to use a factor model structure. For instance, Bai and Ng (2004) considered a multi-factor model with the possibility of unit roots in both the latent factors and the unit-specific component. Their test, however, requires $N/T \to 0$ as $N, T \to \infty$ implying that the time dimension is larger than the cross-sectional dimension. This is undesirable since as stated above, panel unit root tests should offer improvements over univariate tests, when T is smaller than N.

A method that has become widely applied is that of Pesaran (2007). It requires only that $\sqrt{N}/T \to 0$ as $N, T \to \infty$, thereby allowing N to be larger than T. In a nutshell, it builds on the work of Im *et al.* (2003) by augmenting the regression (45.15) with cross-sectional averages $\bar{y}_{t-1} = N^{-1} \sum_{i=1}^{N} y_{i,t-1}$ and the first differences $\Delta\bar{y}_t = \bar{y}_t - \bar{y}_{t-1}$. The same modification applies when accounting for serial correlation in the time dimension, i.e., when using an ADF regression with additional lagged values of $y_{i,t}$ in (45.15). This simple modification ensures that the test is robust to cross-sectional dependence. The test is labeled as the CADF, where the "C" stands for Cross-section. In order to achieve a nuisance parameter free distribution, the CADF test is truncated to avoid influences of extreme outcomes when T is small (in the range of 10–20). The derivation of the test is based on a one-factor residual model which could be restrictive.

An important issue is how to interpret a rejection of the null hypothesis. To be useful, the method should provide an estimate of δ. In other words, are the series in the panel almost all stationary or almost all unit roots or somewhere in between? This can only be achieved if both N and T are large. A commonly suggested procedure is to apply unit root tests to each unit. Other procedures have been proposed but they cannot identify which units have a unit root and which do not. To quote Pesaran (2012) (p. 546): "To identify the exact proportion of the sample for which the null hypothesis is rejected, one requires country-specific data sets with T sufficiently large. But if T is large enough for reliable country-specific inferences to be made, then there seems little justification for pooling countries into a panel."

45.13 Exercises

Exercise 45.1. Researchers want to analyze the properties of the French inflation rate for the period 1960:1–1999:12 (monthly data). They start by doing a standard Augmented Dickey–Fuller (ADF) test. To choose the lag length, they use the BIC which selects three lags. The associated ADF test is -4.5, which is a significant evidence against the unit root in favor of stationarity (the 5% left tail critical value is -2.86 since only a constant was included in the regression). To assess whether their finding is reasonable, they run a small Monte Carlo experiment. They first estimate an $ARMA(1,1)$ which suggests an AR coefficient below but not far from 1 and an MA coefficient around -0.7. Since they want to assess whether the ADF test has the right size in finite samples, the Data Generating Process (DGP) they select is an $MA(1)$ in first differences with MA parameter -0.7. They use 1,000 replications of this DGP and construct the associated ADF test with the number of lags fixed at 3 (the value selected by

BIC). They do this for sample sizes of $T = 50, 100, 200$, and 500. The exact size of the tests for a nominal size 5% are as follows:

T	50	100	250	500
size	0.26	0.35	0.37	0.40

Since the simulations show that the ADF test is substantially liberal, they conclude that the French inflation series is integrated (has a unit root). Also, because the exact size of the test moves away from the nominal size as the sample size increases, they also conclude that the ADF test has serious problems and should not be used. Comment on their stated conclusions. Are they warranted? Why? Justify your answer carefully.

Exercise 45.2. Suppose that a series y_t is generated by a unit root process contaminated by random outliers, i.e.,

$$y_t = z_t + \phi d_t,$$

where $z_t = z_{t-1} + e_t$ with $e_t \sim i.i.d.(0, \sigma_e^2)$, i.e., z_t is a random walk, and d_t is an *i.i.d.* Bernoulli process with

$$d_t = \begin{cases} 1, & \text{with probability } \kappa/2, \\ 0, & \text{with probability } 1-\kappa, \\ -1, & \text{with probability } \kappa/2. \end{cases}$$

Consider the data-generating process for y_t written as

$$y_t = y_{t-1} + u_t.$$

(a) Show that u_t has a linear representation given by an $MA(1)$ process of the form

$$u_t = v_t + \theta v_{t-1},$$

where $v_t \sim i.i.d.(0, \sigma_v^2)$. Show what sets of conditions σ_v^2 and θ must satisfy in terms of σ_e^2, ϕ and κ (but do not try to solve explicitly). (b) What is the sign of θ? What is the effect of increasing ϕ or κ on the magnitude of θ? Explain intuitively why. Consider now a least-squares regression of the form

$$y_t = \hat{\alpha} y_{t-1} + \hat{u}_t.$$

(c) Express the limiting distribution of $T(\hat{\alpha}-1)$ in terms of functionals of a Wiener process and the parameters σ_e^2, ϕ, and κ. (d) Discuss the effect of the presence of outliers on the adequacy of the limiting distribution of $T(\hat{\alpha}-1)$ as an approximation to the corresponding finite sample distribution. (e) Discuss the effect of outliers on the size of popular unit root tests such as the Phillips–Perron Z_α and the Dickey–Fuller ADF tests. Explain your assertions. (f) What can be done to have unit root tests that are less affected by the presence of outliers?

Exercise 45.3. Consider the following $AR(1)$ process subject to measurement errors:

$$y_t = x_t + v_t,$$

where

$$x_t = \alpha x_{t-1} + e_t,$$

with $e_t \sim i.i.d.\ N(0, \sigma_e^2)$, $v_t \sim i.i.d.\ N(0, \sigma_v^2)$, and e_t is independent of v_t. (a) Explain how you can obtain maximum likelihood estimates of the parameters of the model. (b) Show that y_t has an equivalent representation in terms of an ARMA(1,1) of the form

$$y_t = \alpha y_{t-1} + u_t + \theta u_{t-1},$$

where $u_t \sim i.i.d.\ N(0, \sigma_u^2)$. Express θ and σ_u^2 in terms of σ_e^2 and σ_v^2. What is the sign of θ and what determines its magnitude? Provide an intuitive explanation for your assertions. Consider now a least-squares regression of the form

$$y_t = \hat{\alpha} y_{t-1} + \hat{u}_t.$$

(c) Assuming that $\alpha = 1$, express the limiting distribution of $T(\hat{\alpha}-1)$ in terms of functionals of a Wiener process and the parameters σ_e^2 and σ_v^2. (d) Discuss the potential effects of measurement errors on the size of popular unit root tests, such as the Phillips–Perron Z_α and the Dickey-Fuller *ADF* tests. Explain your assertions. (f) What can be done to have unit root tests that are less affected by measurement errors?

Exercise 45.4. Consider the problem of testing for a unit root using the so-called GLS detrending procedure. Suppose we have data generated under the null hypothesis by a random walk $y_t = y_{t-1} + e_t$ $(t = 2, \ldots, T)$ with $e_t \sim i.i.d.N(0, \sigma^2)$ and y_1 a fixed constant. (a) Consider including only a constant as deterministic component (i.e., $z_t = \{1\}$) and let $y_t^{\bar{\alpha}}$ be the quasi-differenced data with a non-centrality parameter $\bar{c}$, i.e., $y_t^{\bar{\alpha}} = y_t - \bar{\alpha} y_{t-1}$ with $\bar{\alpha} = (1 + \bar{c}/T)$. Define $z_t^{\bar{\alpha}}$ similarly. Consider the *OLS* regression

$$y_t^{\bar{\alpha}} = \hat{\delta} z_t^{\bar{\alpha}} + \hat{v}_t.$$

Show that $\hat{\delta} \xrightarrow{p} y_1$. (b) Consider now the regression

$$\tilde{y}_t = \tilde{\alpha} \tilde{y}_{t-1} + \tilde{u}_t,$$

where $\tilde{y}_t = y_t - \hat{\delta} z_t$ are GLS-detrended data. Using the result in part (a), show that the limit distribution of $T(\tilde{\alpha} - 1)$ under the null hypothesis stated above is the same as that of $T(\hat{\alpha} - 1)$ with $\hat{\alpha}$ obtained from the regression

$$y_t = \hat{\alpha} y_{t-1} + \hat{u}_t,$$

i.e., from a regression using the original data with no deterministic component.

Exercise 45.5. When testing for a unit root, we usually consider a process that can be written in the form $y_t = \alpha y_{t-1} + \sum_{i=1}^{\infty} d_i \Delta y_{t-i} + e_t$, with α the sum of the autoregressive coefficients. The null hypothesis is then H_0: $\alpha = 1$ and the alternative hypothesis of stationarity is H_1: $|\alpha| < 1$. Suppose that you wish to test the null hypothesis of stationarity versus the alternative hypothesis of a unit root. The use of the sum of the autoregressive coefficients would then imply a composite null versus a point alternative, which leads to complications. Suggest an alternative way of testing the null of stationarity versus the alternative of a unit root such that the problem can be specified as a point null versus a composite alternative. You need not state the exact form of the statistic but make sure you specify the appropriate null and alternative hypotheses.

Exercise 45.6. Consider a unit root process with $MA(1)$ errors. We wish to get an approximation when the MA coefficient is close to -1. So, let the data-generating process be

$$y_t = y_{t-1} + u_t,$$
$$u_t = e_t + \theta_T e_{t-1},$$
$$\theta_T = -1 + \delta T^{-1/2},$$

for some $\delta > 0$ and $e_t \sim i.i.d.\ (0, \sigma_e^2)$, and for simplicity, $y_0 = e_0 = 0$. T is the sample size. (a) Show that y_t can equivalently be expressed as

$$y_t = -\theta_T e_t + \delta T^{-1/2} X_t,$$

where $X_t = \sum_{j=1}^{t} e_j$ is a random walk. (b) Consider the least squares estimate in a first order autoregression defined by

$$\hat{\alpha} = \frac{\sum_{t=1}^{T} y_t y_{t-1}}{\sum_{t=1}^{T} y_{t-1}^2}.$$

Using the result in part (a), derive the limit distribution of $\hat{\alpha}$. (c) Describe how you can obtain the quantiles of the limit distribution derived in part (b). (d) Show how you can use the limit distribution in part (b) to provide an approximation to the exact distribution of $\hat{\alpha}$ for various values of the MA coefficient and the sample size. (e) Compare the limit distribution found in part (b) with the limit distribution that applies when the MA coefficient $\theta_T = \theta$ is some fixed value in the interval $(-1, 1)$. Discuss how this comparison can explain results to the effect that the limit distribution of $T(\hat{\alpha} - 1)$ is a very bad approximation to the exact distribution when the MA coefficient is large and negative (see Exercise 44.10).

Exercise 45.7. Consider data generated by

$$y_t = \alpha_c y_{t-1} + u_t, \quad u_t \sim i.i.d.\ N(0, \sigma^2),$$
$$\alpha_c = 1 + c/T, \quad y_0 = 0.$$

(a) Derive the Gaussian local asymptotic power envelope for the testing problem H_0: $\alpha = 1$ versus H_1: $\alpha_c = 1 + c/T$. (b) Show that if the DGP is $y_t = \gamma z_t + v_t$, where $v_t = \alpha v_{t-1} + u_t$ and only a constant is included in z_t, the same results holds. (c) Derive the local asymptotic power envelope when a constant and a trend are included as regressors.

Exercise 45.8. Suppose that $y_t = \alpha y_{t-1} + e_t + \theta e_{t-1}$, where $|\theta| < 1$ and $e_t \sim i.i.d.\ (0, \sigma_e^2)$. For simplicity, assume $y_0 = 0$. Consider a regression of y_t on y_{t-1} with the corresponding estimate

$$\hat{\alpha} = \frac{\sum_{t=1}^{T} y_t y_{t-1}}{\sum_{t=1}^{T} y_{t-1}^2}.$$

(a) Assume that $|\alpha| < 1$. Is $\hat{\alpha}$ a consistent estimate of α? Explain. What is the limit distribution of $\hat{\alpha}$? (b) Assume now that $\alpha = 1$. Is $\hat{\alpha}$ a consistent estimate of α? Explain. What is the limit distribution of $\hat{\alpha}$? Be careful to express your results in terms of the basic parameters of the model. (c) Still with $\alpha = 1$, is the limit distribution stated in part (b) a good approximation to the finite sample distribution of $\hat{\alpha}$? Explain. Consider now an instrumental variable estimator using y_{t-2} as an instrument, i.e.,

$$\hat{\alpha}_{IV} = \frac{\sum_{t=2}^{T} y_t y_{t-2}}{\sum_{t=2}^{T} y_{t-1} y_{t-2}}.$$

(d) When $|\alpha| < 1$, is $\hat{\alpha}_{IV}$ a consistent estimate of α? What is its limit distribution? (e) When $\alpha = 1$, is $\hat{\alpha}_{IV}$ a consistent estimate of α? What is its limit distribution? Prove your result. (f) Still with $\alpha = 1$, given your answer in part (c), would you expect the limit distribution obtained in part (e) to be a good approximation to the finite sample distribution of $\hat{\alpha}$? Explain carefully your assertions (hint: look at the proof of part (e)).

Exercise 45.9. Suppose that you have a trending series with a first-order autoregressive noise function

$$y_t = \mu + \beta t + z_t,$$

$$z_t = \alpha z_{t-1} + v_t,$$

where $v_t \sim i.i.d.\ N(0, \sigma_e^2)$ and $z_0 = \kappa$, some constant. You want to test the null hypothesis that $\alpha = 1$ versus the alternative hypothesis that $\alpha \neq 1$. Let $\hat{\alpha}$ be the *OLS* estimate of α in the regression

$$y_t = \mu + \beta t + \alpha y_{t-1} + u_t.$$

What is the local asymptotic power function of the test $T(\hat{\alpha}-1)$? Suppose now that we have the same data-generating process but that v_t is a stationary process of the form $v_t = \sum_{i=0}^{\infty} g_i e_{t-i}$ with $g_0 = 1$, $\sum_{i=0}^{\infty} i|g_i| < \infty$, and $e_t \sim i.i.d.(0, \sigma_e^2)$. Show that the Phillips–Perron Z_α test has the same local asymptotic power function.

Exercise 45.10. Suppose the data are generated by $y_t = y_{t-1} + u_t$ where u_t is such that a functional central limit theorem holds, i.e., $T^{-1/2}\sum_{t=1}^{[Tr]} u_t \Rightarrow \sigma W(r)$ with $\sigma^2 = 2\pi h_u(0)$ where $h_u(0)$ is the spectral density function at frequency zero of u_t. Consider the first-order autoregression

$$y_t = \alpha y_{t-1} + u_t.$$

An estimate of α that has been proposed is the "symmetric least squares" estimate given by

$$\hat{\alpha}_S = \frac{\sum_{t=2}^{T} y_t y_{t-1}}{\sum_{t=2}^{T-1} y_t^2 + (y_1^2 + y_T^2)/2}.$$

(a) Derive the limit distribution of $T(\hat{\alpha}_S - 1)$ under the stated data generating process and show that asymptotically it takes a negative value with probability one. (b) Derive the local asymptotic power function of this test. Be sure to specify the relevant sequence of local alternatives.

Exercise 45.11 (Computer; Continuation of the Empirical Exercise 36.6). The exercise is to perform various unit root tests on the 7 inflation rate series for the G7 countries following up on Exercise 36.6. The model is

$$y_t = \mu + \alpha y_{t-1} + u_t \tag{45.16}$$

(only a constant included). The null hypothesis is $\alpha = 1$ and the alternative is $\alpha < 1$. In all tests, except the ADF, a consistent estimate of $2\pi h_u(0)$ is needed where $h_u(0)$ is the non-normalized spectral density function at frequency 0 of u_t. Let $\hat{u}_t$ be the OLS residuals obtained from estimating regression (45.16). Consider the following estimates (when using an information criterion set $k_{\max} = int(12(T/100)^{1/4})$): (i) $s^2_{sc,1} = \sum_{j=-(T-1)}^{(T-1)} w(j, m_T)\hat{R}_u(j)$, where $\hat{R}_u(j) = T^{-1}\sum_{t=1}^{T-j} \hat{u}_t\hat{u}_{t-j}$ with $w(j, m_T)$ the quadratic spectral window and m_T chosen using Andrews (1991b) data-dependent method with an $AR(1)$ approximation. (ii) $s^2_{AR,\Delta y}(BIC) = \hat{\sigma}^2_{ek}/(1 - \sum_{i=1}^{k_T} \hat{b}_i)^2$, where $\hat{\sigma}^2_{ek} = T^{-1}\sum_{t=k_T+1}^{T} \hat{e}^2_t$ and $\hat{e}_t$ and $\hat{b}_i$ are obtained from the following regression estimated by OLS:

$$\Delta y_t = \mu + b_0 y_{t-1} + \sum_{i=1}^{k_T} b_i \Delta y_{t-i} + e_t, \tag{45.17}$$

with k_T selected using the BIC. (iii) $s^2_{AR,\Delta y}(MAIC)$, same as $s^2_{AR,\Delta y}(BIC)$ except that k_T is selected using the $MAIC$. (a) Construct the original Phillips–Perron Z_α test with the three methods to estimate $\sigma^2 = 2\pi h_u(0)$. (b) Construct the Phillips–Perron Z_α test with GLS detrended data (using $\bar{c} = -7$) with the three methods to estimate $\sigma^2 = 2\pi h_u(0)$ (note that in this case regression (45.16) is replaced by $\tilde{y}_t = \alpha\tilde{y}_{t-1} + u_t$ and regression (45.17) by $\Delta\tilde{y}_t = b_0\tilde{y}_{t-1} + \sum_{i=1}^{k_T} b_i\Delta\tilde{y}_{t-i} + e_t$ where $\tilde{y}_t$ are GLS detrended data with $\bar{c} = -7$). (c) Construct the MZ_α^{GLS} test with GLS detrended data and the three methods to estimate $\sigma^2 = 2\pi h_u(0)$ (the comments in (b) also apply). (d) Construct the ADF and ADF^{GLS} with k_T selected by (i) BIC and (ii) $MAIC$. In all cases, state the values of m_T or k_T selected. In each case, state whether the null hypothesis can be rejected at the 10%, 5%, or 1% level. Discuss the merits and/or potential drawbacks of the tests and the reasons for differences and similarities in the outcomes. For each series which conclusion (to reject or not to reject the unit root), do you think is more appropriate?

Chapter 46

Cointegration

In this chapter, we discuss the concept of cointegration due to the work of Engle and Granger (1987), following the works by Granger (1981) and Granger (1983). We start with basic definitions and important results and then turn to single equation estimation methods and finally to multiple VAR-based estimation procedures. We conclude by addressing the implications of imposing cointegrating relationships to help (or not) identify structural Vector Autoregressive (VAR) models. Useful references for more details are the works of Campbell and Perron (1991), Watson (1994), and Johansen (2006).

46.1 Basic issues and results

The material in this section borrows heavily from the work of Campbell and Perron (1991). We start by defining an n-dimensional vector of time series generated by, for $i = 1, \ldots, n$,

$$y_{it} = \kappa_i + \delta_i t + v_{it}.$$

In vector format, let

$$\begin{aligned} y_t &= (y_{1t}, \ldots, y_{nt})', \\ v_t &= (v_{1t}, \ldots, v_{nt})', \\ \kappa &= (\kappa_1, \ldots, \kappa_n)', \\ \delta &= (\delta_1, \ldots, \delta_n)', \\ e_t &= (e_{1t}, \ldots, e_{nt})' \sim i.i.d.(0, \Sigma), \end{aligned}$$

where Σ need not be diagonal. Then,

$$y_t = \kappa + \delta t + v_t. \tag{46.1}$$

It is assumed that there exists an autoregressive representation so that

$$A(L)v_t = e_t, \tag{46.2}$$

where

$$A(L) = [A_1(L), \dots, A_n(L)]$$

with $A(L) = \sum_{j=0}^{\infty} A_j L^j$ and $A_0 = I_n$, the identity matrix of order n. It is not assumed that $A_i(L)$ has a root on the unit circle, though multiple roots on the unit circle are ruled out. This means that each variable y_{it} can be either $I(0)$ or $I(1)$. Note also that we restrict the analysis to a trend function being linear of the form $\kappa + \delta t$. We could extend the analysis to more general trend specifications at the expense of added complexities. Nevertheless, this is by far the most common specification used. We now define the concept of cointegration.

Definition 46.1 (Cointegration). A vector of variables y_t defined by (46.1) is said to be cointegrated if there exists at least one n-element vector β_j such that $\beta_j' y_t$ is trend-stationary (see Section 21.2) with β_j labeled as a cointegrating vector. If there exist r such linearly independent vectors β_j $(j = 1, \dots, r)$, we say that y_t is cointegrated with cointegrating rank r. The $n \times r$ matrix $\beta = (\beta_1, \dots, \beta_r)$ is the matrix of cointegrating vectors or the cointegrating matrix. The r elements of the vector $\beta' y_t$ are trend-stationary.

Remark 46.1. The cointegrating vectors are identifiable at most up to a scale transformation. See also Remark 46.2.

The definition provided is different in some aspects from the usual treatment. First, the variables can be all $I(0)$, all $I(1)$, or a mixture of both, with or without trends. This will prove useful when considering the types of cointegration considered and what regression system is then appropriate. We have the following two sub-cases.

Definition 46.2 (Stochastic Cointegration). The vector y_t is "stochastically cointegrated" if the linear combinations $\beta' y_t$ are trend-stationary but not necessarily without trends. That is, $\beta' y_t \sim I(0)$ but $\beta'\delta \neq 0$. Then, the cointegrating vectors eliminate the non-stationarity potentially present in the stochastic component v_t (because of the presence of unit roots) but not the non-stationarity due to the deterministic component δt, i.e., the trends.

Definition 46.3 (Deterministic Cointegration). The vector y_t is "deterministically cointegrated" if the linear combinations $\beta' y_t$ are $I(0)$ without trends. That is, $\beta' v_t \sim I(0)$ and $\beta'\delta = 0$. Then, the cointegrating vectors eliminate the non-stationarity potentially present in both the stochastic component v_t (because of the presence of unit roots) and the non-stationarity due to the deterministic component δt, i.e., the trends.

We first state the following lemma that is useful in subsequent developments. See Exercise 46.1 for a proof.

Lemma 46.1. (a) *If at least one trend-stationary variable is present, the system is trivially cointegrated (the cointegrating vector then simply picks the relevant trend-stationary variable).* (b) *If at least one $I(1)$ variable is present in the system, there cannot exist more than $n-1$ independent cointegrating vectors.*

46.1.1 The autoregressive and error correction representations

In what follows, we assume that y_t is specified by (46.1) with the elements of v_t given by

$$A(L)v_t = e_t,$$

where

$$A(L) = I - \sum_{j=1}^{k+1} A_j L^j$$

so that the noise component is a finite-order VAR. Of course, this should be viewed as an approximation. Methods to select k in the context of hypothesis testing have been proposed by Qu and Perron (2007b). Hence,

$$\begin{aligned} y_t &= \kappa + \delta t + v_t, \\ A(L)v_t &= e_t, \end{aligned} \tag{46.3}$$

or (see Exercise 46.2)

$$\begin{aligned} \Delta y_t &= \mu + \Pi(y_{t-1} - \delta(t-1)) + \sum_{j=1}^{k} \Gamma_j \Delta y_{t-j} + e_t \\ &= \mu + \Pi v_{t-1} + \sum_{j=1}^{k} \Gamma_j \Delta y_{t-j} + e_t, \end{aligned} \tag{46.4}$$

where $\Pi = \sum_{j=1}^{k+1} A_j - I_n$, with I_n the identity matrix, $\Gamma_j = -\sum_{i=j+1}^{k+1} A_i$, and μ is a vector of constants not necessarily the same across equations and also not necessarily the same throughout this section, for the sake of simplifying notation. Since Δy_t and e_t are $I(0)$, in order to have a balanced equation, we must have that Πv_{t-1} is stationary irrespective of the nature of the noise component v_t, i.e., $I(0)$ or $I(1)$. There are three possible cases depending on the rank of Π:

1. rank(Π) $= n$, i.e., Π is of full rank. Hence, there exist n cointegrating relationships. According to Lemma 46.1, this implies that all variables are trend-stationary and the model corresponds to a standard VAR system in level, i.e.,

$$y_t = \mu + \delta^* t + \sum_{j=1}^{k+1} \Gamma_j^* y_{t-j} + e_t.$$

2. rank(Π) $= 0$, in which case $\Pi = 0$ and there are no cointegrating relations. According to Lemma 46.1, this implies that all variables are integrated and the model corresponds to a standard VAR system in first differences, i.e.,

$$\Delta y_t = \mu + \sum_{j=1}^{k} \Gamma_j \Delta y_{t-j} + e_t.$$

3. rank(Π) = r with $0 < r < n$. Then, there exist $n \times r$ matrices α and β such that

$$\Pi = \alpha\beta'.$$

Hence, $\beta' v_{t-1}$ (or $\beta' v_t$) is stationary. The columns of β are the cointegrating vectors and the system has cointegrating rank r. The appropriate regression system to use depends on the assumed nature of the cointegration, i.e., stochastic or deterministic. In the case of deterministic cointegration, we have $\beta'\delta = 0$ since the same cointegrating vectors eliminate both types of non-stationarity coming from the trend or the unit roots. Hence, the appropriate system does not include a time trend since (46.4) reduces to

$$\Delta y_t = \mu + \alpha\beta' y_{t-1} + \sum_{j=1}^{k} \Gamma_j \Delta y_{t-j} + e_t. \tag{46.5}$$

In the case of stochastic cointegration, $\beta'\delta \neq 0$ and a time trend must be included in the system, which is then given by

$$\Delta y_t = \mu^* + \delta^* t + \alpha\beta' y_{t-1} + \sum_{j=1}^{k} \Gamma_j \Delta y_{t-j} + e_t, \tag{46.6}$$

where $\delta^* = -\alpha\beta'\delta$. In both cases, a VAR in first differences is misspecified since the component $\alpha\beta' y_{t-1}$ is omitted. A VAR in level is not misspecified but is inefficient since the appropriate restrictions on Π are not imposed.

Remark 46.2. The parameters α and β are not identified since for any non-singular matrix F, the matrices αF and $\beta(F')^{-1}$ yield the same matrix Π. This implies that the data can only provide information about the space spanned by the columns of β (the cointegrating space) and the space spanned by the columns of α. This is an important fact. It implies that care must be taken to impose restrictions in order to identify the cointegrating vectors. Otherwise, tests of hypotheses about the cointegrating vectors are not well defined.

46.1.2 The error-correction representation

Let

$$z_{t-1} = \beta'(y_{t-1} - \delta(t-1))$$

if stochastic cointegration is allowed or

$$z_{t-1} = \beta' y_{t-1}$$

if deterministic cointegration is imposed. The linear combinations $\beta' y_{t-1}$ are called the disequilibrium errors. If y_t is $I(1)$, then the requirement that $\beta' y_{t-1}$ be $I(0)$ means that the linear combinations $\beta' y_t$ are the target long-run equilibrium. Any deviation from 0 means that the system is out of long-run equilibrium. Then, (46.5) or (46.6) can be written as

$$\Delta y_t = \mu + \alpha z_{t-1} + \sum_{j=1}^{k} \Gamma_j \Delta y_{t-j} + e_t. \tag{46.7}$$

This is often referred to as an error-correction model or, maybe more precisely, a (long-run) disequilibrium correction model. It states that, apart from dynamics inherent to the model (i.e., the lagged values of Δy_t), the changes in the variables, Δy_t, depend on how far from equilibrium the system was the previous period. The system then adjusts to revert back to long-run equilibrium depending on the magnitudes and signs of the coefficients in the matrix α. The model will be stable given proper restrictions on α; see the discussion in Section 21.6.

46.1.3 The conditional error correction model

For exposition, let $y_t = (y_{1t}, x_t')'$, where y_{1t} is a scalar variable and x_t is the vector of the remaining $n-1$ variables. We wish to find a model of y_{1t} conditional on x_t and the past values of Δy_t (including y_0). For simplicity, we deal with the model without a trend given by

$$\Delta y_t = \mu + \Pi y_{t-1} + \sum_{j=1}^{k} \Gamma_j \Delta y_{t-j} + e_t. \tag{46.8}$$

Start by partitioning the vector of innovations as $e_t = (e_{yt}, e_{xt}')'$ where similarly e_{yt} is a scalar and e_{xt} is a $(n-1)$ vector. Denote the covariance matrix of e_t as

$$\Sigma = \begin{pmatrix} \sigma_{yy} & \sigma_{yx} \\ \sigma_{xy} & \Sigma_{xx} \end{pmatrix}.$$

We can express e_{yt} conditionally in terms of e_{xt} as

$$e_{yt} = \sigma_{yx}\Sigma_{xx}^{-1}e_{xt} + u_t,$$

where $u_t \sim i.i.d.\ N(0, \sigma_{uu})$,

$$\sigma_{uu} = \sigma_{yy} - \sigma_{yx}\Sigma_{xx}^{-1}\sigma_{xy},$$

and u_t is independent of e_{xt}. Partition the coefficients of (46.8) as follows: $\mu = (\mu_y, \mu_x')'$, $\Pi = (\pi_y', \Pi_x')'$, $\Gamma_i = (\gamma_{yi}', \Gamma_{xi}')'$. The conditional ECM of y_{1t} conditional on x_t and the past values of Δy_t is then given by

$$\Delta y_{1t} = c + \pi_{y,x}y_{t-1} + \sum_{j=1}^{k} \psi_j'\Delta y_{t-j} + \omega'\Delta x_t + u_t,$$

where $\omega = \Sigma_{xx}^{-1}\sigma_{xy}$, $c = \mu_y - \omega'\mu_x$, $\psi_i' = \gamma_{yi} - \omega'\Gamma_{xi}$ $(i = 1, \ldots, k)$, and $\pi_{y,x} = \pi_y - \omega'\Pi_x$.

Often, we may wish to impose some exogeneity type assumption on x_t so that x_t has a long-run effect on y_{1t} but there is no feedback. Let

$$\Pi = \begin{pmatrix} \pi_{yy} & \pi_{yx} \\ \pi_{xy} & \Pi_{xx} \end{pmatrix},$$

then the relevant condition for this assumption is that $\pi_{xy} = 0$. It imposes the existence of at most one conditional relationship between y_{1t} and x_t irrespective of whether x_t is $I(1)$ or $I(0)$. The conditional ECM is then

$$\Delta y_{1t} = c + \pi_{yy}y_{1t-1} + \pi_{yx,x}x_{t-1} + \sum_{j=1}^{k} \psi_j'\Delta y_{t-j} + \omega'\Delta x_t + u_t,$$

where $\pi_{yx,x} = \pi_{yx} - \omega'\Pi_{xx}$.

46.1.4 The moving-average representation

Since the elements of y_t have at most one autoregressive unit root, the following representation holds for the first differences Δy_t since it is a stationary process:

$$\Delta y_t = \delta + \Phi(L)e_t.$$

Using a multivariate version of the Beveridge–Nelson decomposition (see Section 8.7),

$$y_t = \mu + \delta t + \Phi(1)S_t + \Phi^*(L)e_t, \tag{46.9}$$

where

$$\Phi^*(L) = (1 - L)^{-1}[\Phi(L) - \Phi(1)]$$

and $S_t = \sum_{j=1}^{t} e_j$, a vector of n independent random walks. Now, pre-multiply (46.9) by β', then, with $z_t = \beta' y_t$, the disequilibrium error is

$$z_t = \beta'\mu + \beta'\Phi(1)S_t + \beta'\Phi^*(L)e_t$$

assuming deterministic cointegration, i.e., $\beta'\delta = 0$. Since z_t and $\beta'\Phi^*(L)e_t$ are stationary, we must have $\beta'\Phi(1) = 0$ in order to have a balanced equation. Hence, $\Phi(1)$ is of rank $n - r$.

46.1.5 The long-run covariance matrix

We now consider the spectral density matrix of Δy_t evaluated at frequency zero, denoted by $h_{\Delta y}(0)$. Note that using standard results for linear processes as in Section 37.4.2 extended to a multivariate setting, we have

$$h_{\Delta y}(0) = \Phi(1)\Sigma\Phi(1)'.$$

Since $\beta'\Phi(1) = 0$, we have $\beta' h_{\Delta y}(0) = 0$ so that $h_{\Delta y}(0)$ is of rank $n - r$. $h_{\Delta y}(0)$ is of full rank only if no cointegration relation exists among the variables y_t.

46.1.6 The common trend representation

Suppose first that we deal with deterministic cointegration so that $\beta'\delta = 0$. Since $\beta'\Phi(1) = 0$ and $\beta'\delta = 0$, we have $\delta = \Phi(1)\delta^*$ and then

$$y_t = \mu^* + \Phi(1)S_t^* + \Phi^*(L)e_t,$$

where

$$S_t^* = \delta^* t + \sum_{j=1}^{t} e_t.$$

Since $\Phi(1)$ is not of full rank, but with rank $n-r$, y_t can be represented as the sum of (a) $n-r$ deterministic trends, (b) $n-r$ random walks, and (c) n stationary components.

If we consider stochastic cointegration, (a) is replaced by n deterministic trends.

46.2 Single-equation estimation

We start with a discussion of the asymptotic distribution of the OLS estimate. Useful references are the works of Stock (1987), Phillips and Durlauf (1986), and Sims *et al.* (1990). Consider the following cointegrated model, where for simplicity we assume x_t to be a scalar:

$$\begin{aligned} y_t &= a x_t + u_{1t}, \\ x_t &= x_{t-1} + u_{2t}. \end{aligned} \tag{46.10}$$

Let

$$u_t = (u_{1t}, u_{2t})',$$

and assume that the conditions on u_t are such that we can apply a functional central limit theorem. We define

$$\Omega_0 = \lim_{T\to\infty} T^{-1} \sum_{t=1}^{T} E(u_t u_t'),$$

$$\Omega_1 = \lim_{T\to\infty} T^{-1} \sum_{j=1}^{T-1} \sum_{t=j+1}^{T} E(u_j u_{t-j}'),$$

$$\Omega = \lim_{T\to\infty} E(T^{-1} S_T S_T') = \Omega_0 + \Omega_1 + \Omega_1',$$

where $S_T = \sum_{t=1}^{T} u_t$. When u_t is stationary, Ω_0 is the variance of the bivariate process and Ω is (2π times) the spectral density function at frequency zero of u_t. If u_t is a martingale difference sequence, then $\Omega_1 = 0$ and $\Omega_0 = \Omega$. Let

$$\Omega_0 = \begin{bmatrix} \sigma_1^2 & \sigma_{12} \\ \sigma_{12} & \sigma_2^2 \end{bmatrix}.$$

If $\sigma_{12} = 0$, we have that x_t is exogenous, otherwise there is endogeneity since u_{1t} is correlated with x_t in (46.10).

The OLS estimate of a using (46.10) as the regression is given by

$$\hat{a} = \sum_{t=1}^{T} x_t y_t \Big/ \sum_{t=1}^{T} x_t^2$$

and

$$T(\hat{a} - a) = T^{-1} \sum_{t=1}^{T} x_t u_{1t} \Big/ T^{-2} \sum_{t=1}^{T} x_t^2.$$

Now, define

$$q_t = q_{t-1} + u_t = \sum_{j=1}^{t} u_j.$$

Here, q_t is a 2×1 vector with $q_0 = 0$. Then,

$$T^{-2} \sum_{t=1}^{T} q_t q_t' \Rightarrow \Omega^{1/2} \int_0^1 W(t) W(t)' dt \Omega^{1/2} \tag{46.11}$$

and

$$T^{-1} \sum_{t=1}^{T} q_{t-1} u_t' \Rightarrow \Omega^{1/2} \int_0^1 W(t) dW(t) \Omega^{1/2} + \Omega_1, \tag{46.12}$$

where $W(t)$ is a two-dimensional Wiener process, i.e., $W(t) = (W_1(t), W_2(t))$, with $W_1(t)$ and $W_2(t)$ independent. The results

(46.11) and (46.12) are straightforward extensions of the univariate case. For a proof, see the work of Phillips and Durlauf (1986). From (46.12), we have

$$
\begin{aligned}
T^{-1}\sum_{t=1}^{T} q_t u_t' &= T^{-1}\sum_{t=1}^{T} q_{t-1}u_t' + T^{-1}\sum_{t=1}^{T} u_t u_t' \\
&\Rightarrow \Omega^{1/2}\int_0^1 W(t)dW(t)\Omega^{1/2} + \Omega_1 + \Omega_0
\end{aligned}
$$

since

$$
T^{-1}\sum_{t=1}^{T} u_t u_t' \xrightarrow{p} \Omega_0.
$$

Now, note that $q_{2,t} = x_t$, hence,

$$
T^{-2}\sum_{t=1}^{T} q_t q_t' = T^{-2}\begin{pmatrix} \sum_{t=1}^{T} q_{1,t}^2 & \sum_{t=1}^{T} q_{1,t}x_t \\ \sum_{t=1}^{T} x_t q_{1,t} & \sum_{t=1}^{T} x_t^2 \end{pmatrix}.
$$

Also,

$$
T^{-1}\sum_{t=1}^{T} q_t u_t' = T^{-1}\begin{pmatrix} \sum_{t=1}^{T} q_{1,t}u_{1,t} & \sum_{t=1}^{T} q_{1,t}u_{2,t} \\ \sum_{t=1}^{T} x_t u_{1,t} & \sum_{t=1}^{T} x_t u_{2,t} \end{pmatrix}.
$$

Hence,

$$
T^{-2}\sum_{t=1}^{T} x_t^2 = \left\{T^{-2}\sum_{t=1}^{T} q_t q_t'\right\}_{22}
$$

and

$$
T^{-1}\sum_{t=1}^{T} x_t u_{1,t} = \left\{T^{-1}\sum_{t=1}^{T} q_t u_t'\right\}_{21},
$$

where the indices "*ab*" refers to the entry from the *a*th row and *b*th column. Hence,

$$
T(\hat{a} - a) \Rightarrow \frac{\left\{\Omega^{1/2}\int_0^1 W(t)dW(t)\Omega^{1/2} + \Omega_1 + \Omega_0\right\}_{21}}{\left\{\Omega^{1/2}\int_0^1 W(t)W(t)'dt\Omega^{1/2}\right\}_{22}}.
$$

So, the limiting distribution depends on (1) serial correlation in either $u_{1,t}$ or $u_{2,t}$ and (2) correlation between $u_{1,t}$ and $u_{2,t}$ (the endogeneity issue). Suppose there is no serial correlation, then

$$\Omega_1 = 0 \quad \text{and} \quad \Omega = \Omega_0$$

so that

$$T(\hat{a} - a) \Rightarrow \frac{\left\{\Omega_0^{1/2} \int_0^1 W(t)dW(t)\Omega_0^{1/2} + \Omega_0\right\}_{21}}{\left\{\Omega_0^{1/2} \int_0^1 W(t)W(t)'dt\Omega_0^{1/2}\right\}_{22}}.$$

The limiting distribution still depends on nuisance parameters if $\sigma_{12} \neq 0$. This is the traditional endogeneity problem, where the regressors are correlated with the errors. With stationary variables, the OLS estimate would be inconsistent. Here, the estimate is still consistent, but the correlation affects the limiting distribution. Hence, the endogeneity issue has no first-order effect (consistency with the same fast rate of convergence) but has a second-order effect by impacting the limit distribution.

If $\sigma_{12} = 0$, then x_t is weakly exogenous and there is no correlation between the regressors and errors. Then, we have

$$\begin{aligned}
&\left\{\Omega_0^{1/2} \int_0^1 W(t)dW(t)\Omega_0^{1/2} + \Omega_0\right\}_{21} \\
&= \left\{\begin{pmatrix}\sigma_1 & 0 \\ 0 & \sigma_2\end{pmatrix}\begin{pmatrix}\int_0^1 W_1(t)dW_1(t) & \int_0^1 W_1(t)dW_2(t) \\ \int_0^1 W_2(t)dW_1(t) & \int_0^1 W_2(t)dW_2(t)\end{pmatrix}\right. \\
&\quad \left. \times \begin{pmatrix}\sigma_1 & 0 \\ 0 & \sigma_2\end{pmatrix} + \begin{pmatrix}\sigma_1^2 & 0 \\ 0 & \sigma_2^2\end{pmatrix}\right\}_{21} \\
&= \left\{\begin{pmatrix}\sigma_1^2 \int_0^1 W_1(t)dW_1(t) & \sigma_1\sigma_2 \int_0^1 W_1(t)dW_2(t) \\ \sigma_1\sigma_2 \int_0^1 W_2(t)dW_1(t) & \sigma_2^2 \int_0^1 W_2(t)dW_2(t)\end{pmatrix}\right. \\
&\quad \left. + \begin{pmatrix}\sigma_1^2 & 0 \\ 0 & \sigma_2^2\end{pmatrix}\right\}_{21} \\
&= \sigma_1\sigma_2 \int_0^1 W_2(t)dW_1(t).
\end{aligned}$$

Similarly,

$$\left\{\begin{pmatrix}\sigma_1 & 0\\ 0 & \sigma_2\end{pmatrix}\begin{pmatrix}\int_0^1 W_1(t)^2dt & \int_0^1 W_1(t)W_2(t)dt\\ \int_0^1 W_2(t)W_1(t)dt & \int_0^1 W_2(t)^2dt\end{pmatrix}\begin{pmatrix}\sigma_1 & 0\\ 0 & \sigma_2\end{pmatrix}\right\}_{22}$$

$$= \sigma_2^2\int_0^1 W_2(t)^2dt.$$

Hence,

$$T(\hat{a}-a) \Rightarrow \left(\frac{\sigma_1}{\sigma_2}\right)\frac{\int_0^1 W_2(t)dW_1(t)}{\int_0^1 W_2(t)^2dt}. \tag{46.13}$$

Consider now the t-statistic defined by

$$t_{\hat{a}} = \frac{T(\hat{a}-a)}{\left[\hat{s}^2(T^{-2}\sum_{t=1}^T x_t^2)^{-1}\right]^{1/2}}$$

$$= \frac{1}{\hat{s}}\frac{T^{-1}\sum_{t=1}^T x_t u_{1,t}}{(T^{-2}\sum x_t^2)^{1/2}},$$

where

$$\hat{s}^2 = T^{-1}\sum_{t=1}^T \hat{u}_{1,t}^2 = T^{-1}\sum_{t=1}^T (y_t - \hat{a}x_t)^2.$$

It is easy to show that $\hat{s}^2 \xrightarrow{p} \sigma_1^2$ since $T(\hat{a}-a) = O_p(1)$. Hence,

$$t_{\hat{a}} \Rightarrow \frac{1}{\sigma_1}\frac{\sigma_1\sigma_2\int_0^1 W_2(t)dW_1(t)}{\left(\sigma_2^2\int_0^1 W_2(t)^2dt\right)^{1/2}}$$

$$= \frac{\int_0^1 W_2(t)dW_1(t)}{\left(\int_0^1 W_2(t)^2dt\right)^{1/2}} \equiv H.$$

Consider the distribution of H conditional upon a particular realization of $W_2(t) = W_2^*(t)$, say. Then, $\int_0^1 W_2^*(t)dW_1(t)$ is a linear combination of normals and so is a normal random variable. It has mean zero and variance $\int_0^1 W_2^*(t)^2dt$; see Property #3 of Ito integrals stated in Section 43.6. Hence, conditional on $W_2(t) = W_2^*(t)$,

$$H \sim \frac{1}{\left(\int_0^1 W_2^*(t)^2dt\right)^{1/2}} N(0, \int_0^1 W_2^*(t)^2dt) = N(0,1).$$

Since the conditional distribution does not depend on what we condition upon, it is also the unconditional distribution. Hence,

$$t_{\widehat{a}} \Rightarrow N(0,1). \tag{46.14}$$

The same kind of argument holds in the multivariate case with more than one regressor. Then, the tests of hypotheses on the coefficients have an asymptotic chi-square distribution.

When the estimate of the cointegrating vector has a limiting distribution such as (46.13) (and the t-test has a normal asymptotic distribution), it was shown by Saikkonen (1991) that the estimates are, in some well-defined sense, optimal.

In the general case where serial correlation and correlation between the regressors and the errors are allowed, a strategy is then to modify the estimate such that the transformation has an asymptotic distribution similar to (46.13). These transformed estimates can then be viewed as asymptotically optimal.

46.2.1 Dynamic OLS

We now discuss a method of estimation that provides asymptotically efficient estimates when there is serial correlation and endogeneity. The number of proposed methods to achieve that aim is very large, much larger than warrants space in such a book. We focus on what we think is the most appealing method given its simplicity and its good properties in finite samples. A fully non-parametric modification in the spirit of the Phillips and Perron (1988) test was suggested by Phillips and Hansen (1990), but its finite-sample performance is not good for the same reasons as those discussed for the Phillips and Perron (1988) unit root test.

The Dynamic OLS (DOLS) method was proposed by Saikkonen (1991) (see also the work of Stock and Watson (1993) for a similar approach). In what follows, x_t can be an m-vector of variables.

We first need the following result. Consider two stationary stochastic process (w_{1t}, w_{2t}), then we have the following representation (see the work of Brillinger (2001)):

$$w_{1t} = \sum_{j=-\infty}^{\infty} d_j w_{2t-j} + \eta_t,$$

where η_t is a stationary stochastic process possibly serially correlated but uncorrelated with w_{2t}, contemporaneously and at all leads and lags. Using this result, the errors from (46.10) can be related via

$$u_{1,t} = \sum_{j=-\infty}^{\infty} d_j u_{2t-j} + \eta_t,$$

and using the fact that $\Delta x_t = u_{2,t}$, we have

$$u_{1,t} = \sum_{j=-\infty}^{\infty} d_j \Delta x_{t-j} + \eta_t.$$

Then, we can write, where a constant is now added,

$$y_t = c + a x_t + \sum_{j=-\infty}^{\infty} d_j \Delta x_{t-j} + \eta_t.$$

This is an alternative regression with current, future, and past values of Δx_t, where now the errors are uncorrelated with the regressors. In practice, we need to truncate the infinite sum so that the regression estimated is

$$y_t = c + a x_t + \sum_{j=-m_1}^{m_2} d_j \Delta x_{t-j} + \eta_t. \tag{46.15}$$

This "parametric transformation" corrects for the presence of correlation between the regressors and the errors. To correct for serial correlation, two approaches have been suggested:

1. Construct heteroskedasticity and autocorrelation consistent standard errors for $\hat{a}$ using a kernel-based method or an autoregressive spectral density estimator at frequency zero; see Chapter 38.

2. Introduce lags of the disequilibrium errors in the regression as suggested by Phillips and Loretan (1991), i.e.,

$$y_t = c + ax_t + \sum_{j=1}^{m_3} f_j(y_{t-j} - ax_{t-j}) + \sum_{j=-m_1}^{m_2} d_j \Delta x_{t-j} + e_t,$$

by selecting m_3 large enough so that the errors e_t are approximately uncorrelated. This second approach leads to a nonlinear regression and is, hence, less popular in applied work.

The estimates will be consistent and have a standard asymptotic distribution (e.g., the t-statistics of the elements of a have a standard asymptotic normal distribution). This will be asymptotically valid provided m_1, m_2, and m_3 increase at some appropriate rate as T increases. For the method based on (46.15) suggested by Saikkonen (1991), Kejriwal and Perron (2008a) relaxed the theoretical conditions imposed by Saikkonen (1991) to show that information criteria (e.g., AIC or BIC) can be used to select m_1 and m_2 and in doing so, the estimate of the cointegrating vector has good finite sample properties.

The use of single-equation methods raises the issue as to what variable to put as the "dependent" variable. In principle, any $I(1)$ variable part of the cointegrating relationship is admissible. This issue was analyzed by Ng and Perron (1997). They suggest to first rank the spectral density at frequency zero of the first differenced series, then the variable with the smallest value is used as the dependent variable, i.e., the "less integrated one". This is desirable from the point of view of both estimation and hypothesis testing. The main reason why this works well is that using the "more integrated" variables as regressors amounts to putting the variables with more variability on the right-hand side of the regression. As is well known, the greater the variations in the regressors, the more precise the parameter estimates; see Section 4.4.

Finally, when considering a system of variables possibly subject to multiple cointegrating vectors, an issue that arises is which of the cointegrating vectors is picked up when using a single equation method. From basic least-squares theory, the answer is quite obvious, namely the one that yields the smallest sum of squared residuals.

Here, this translates into the cointegrating vector having the smallest disequilibrium error.

46.2.2 Testing for cointegration

A myriad of proposals have been suggested to test for cointegration within a single-equation framework. It is not our goal to provide an extensive review. Instead, we simply discuss a popular approach followed by related recent extensions. Let the n-variable system be decomposed as $y_t = (y_{1t}, x_t)$, where y_{1t} is a scalar and x_t an m-element vector of $I(1)$ variables. Then, the regression of interest is

$$y_{1t} = \tau' z_t + \beta' x_t + u_t, \tag{46.16}$$

where z_t is the vector of deterministic components. Here, we consider only $z_t = \{0\}$, $\{1\}$, $\{1, t\}$, though more general specifications are possible. Note that $I(0)$ regressors could be included in (46.16) without changing the asymptotic distribution of the test. Still, it is advisable to include only the $I(1)$ regressors to ensure higher power, in general.

An assumption made is that if there exists a cointegrating relationship, then y_t has a non-zero coefficient in the cointegrating vector $(1, -\beta)$. An another assumption is that the vector x_t is not cointegrated. This assumption is quite strong and implies that only one cointegrating vector is present. To see this in an intuitive manner, take an old-fashioned money demand function

$$M_t = \tau + \beta_0 P_t + \beta_1 r_t + \beta_2 i_t + u_t,$$

where M_t is the (log) money supply, P_t is the (log) aggregate price level, r_t is the nominal interest rate, and i_t is the inflation rate. Suppose that there is a cointegrating vector involving all variables, i.e., $(1, -\beta_0, -\beta_1, -\beta_2)$. There cannot exist a cointegrating relation between (M, r_t, i_t) since, otherwise, the system is unbalanced. Suppose there is a second cointegrating vector. From standard monetary theory, M_t and P_t should be cointegrated. Then, write the relation as

$$M_t - \beta_0 P_t = \tau + \beta_1 r_t + \beta_2 i_t + u_t$$

since the left-hand side is $I(0)$ then so must be the right-hand side and (r_t, i_t) need to be cointegrated. This would violate the assumption that the right-hand-side variables are not cointegrated. Hence, we can only have a single cointegrating vector in the whole system. While this might seem restrictive, there are many applications in which a single cointegrating vector is present.

The null hypothesis is that there is no cointegration, while the alternative hypothesis is that cointegration holds in the single equation (46.16). If cointegration holds, then the parameter estimates are consistent, the cointegrating vector is consistently estimated, and, most importantly the errors are $I(0)$. Under the null hypothesis of no cointegration, the regression is labeled as spurious, the parameter estimates converge to some random variables (see the discussion in Section 21.6), and most importantly, the errors are $I(1)$ for any parameter values.

Hence, a natural testing strategy is the following: estimate (46.16) by OLS and use any unit root test applied to the estimated OLS residuals $\hat{u}_t$. This leads to the so-called OLS residual-based cointegration tests. This was the approach taken by Phillips and Ouliaris (1990) using "old-generation" unit root tests; e.g., ADF, Phillips–Perron, and others.

The limit null distribution depends on (a) the number, m, of $I(1)$ variables included as regressors, (b) the nature of the deterministic components in z_t, and (c) the nature of the deterministic components in the true data generating process, which becomes irrelevant if the deterministic components are correctly specified. For example, when testing for stochastic cointegration, a trend must be included, otherwise the limit distribution depends on nuisance parameters. (d) When testing for deterministic cointegration, one needs to set $z_t = \{1\}$, but then the limit distribution is not invariant to having trending or non-trending data; see the work of Hansen (1992a). While for theoretical interest, the latter issue has little impact in practical applications since the critical values are virtually the same with data that are trending or not. The asymptotic critical values are present in Table 46.1.

In the case of testing for a unit root, we discussed methods based on GLS detrending that permit constructing tests that have a local asymptotic power function nearly identical to the Gaussian local power envelope. A relevant question to ask is whether a similar

Table 46.1. Critical values of OLS-based cointegration tests. m is the number of $I(1)$ right-hand-side variables.

		No constant/trend			Constant			Constant plus time trend		
	m	10%	5%	1%	10%	5%	1%	10%	5%	1%
Z_α	1	−12.54	−15.64	−22.83	−17.04	−20.49	−28.32	−23.19	−27.09	−35.42
	2	−18.18	−21.48	−29.27	−22.20	−26.09	−34.17	−27.78	−32.22	−40.34
	3	−23.92	−27.85	−36.16	−27.59	−32.06	−41.14	−33.16	−37.73	−47.36
	4	−28.85	−33.48	−42.87	−32.74	−37.15	−47.51	−37.74	−42.46	−53.61
	5	−33.80	−38.09	−48.52	−37.00	−41.94	−52.17	−42.32	−47.38	−58.16
Z_t, ADF	1	−2.45	−2.76	−3.39	−3.07	−3.37	−3.96	−3.52	−3.80	−4.36
	2	−2.99	−3.27	−3.84	−3.45	−3.77	−4.31	−3.84	−4.16	−4.65
	3	−3.45	−3.74	−4.30	−3.83	−4.11	−4.73	−4.20	−4.49	−5.04
	4	−3.81	−4.13	−4.67	−4.16	−4.45	−5.07	−4.46	−4.74	−5.36
	5	−4.14	−4.40	−4.99	−4.43	−4.71	−5.28	−4.73	−5.03	−5.59

Source: Phillips and Ouliaris (1990).

approach is possible when testing for cointegration. After all, cointegration tests are basically unit root tests on some OLS residuals. It turns out that this is still an unresolved issue. The problem is the difficulty (maybe impossibility) of deriving the local Gaussian power envelope of cointegration tests given that the cointegrating vector β is not identified under the null hypothesis of no cointegration. However, as a second best option, it seems that using GLS-detrended data along with tests that are nearly optimal in the unit root context can deliver power gains when testing for cointegration. This is indeed the case as shown in the work of Perron and Rodríguez (2016).

Consider regression (46.16), written in a slightly different way with z_t^y the deterministic component included in the regression, while z_t^x are the deterministic components affecting the variables x_t. For instance, if one tests for deterministic cointegration with trending variables, $z_t^y = \{1\}$ and $z_t^x = \{1, t\}$. Then,

$$y_t = \tau_y' z_t^y + \beta' x_t + u_t, \tag{46.17}$$

where $u_t = \overline{\rho} u_{t-1} + e_t$, with $\overline{\rho} = 1 + \overline{c}/T$ and, for simplicity, $e_t \sim i.i.d.\ (0, \sigma_e^2)$. In this setup, y_t and x_t are cointegrated for any finite samples but not cointegrated in the limit as $T \to \infty$. Hence, this is a case of a nearly non-cointegrated process similar to the nearly integrated framework used by Elliott *et al.* (1996). Let $w_t = (x_t', y_t)'$

and $w_t^{\overline{\rho}} = (1 - \overline{\rho}L)w_t$, $z_t^{y\overline{\rho}} = (1-\overline{\rho}L)z_t^y$. Ignoring the first observation, we can apply a GLS transformation and write (46.17) as

$$y_t^{\overline{\rho}} = \tau_y' z_t^{y\overline{\rho}} + \beta' x_t^{\overline{\rho}} + e_t. \tag{46.18}$$

Concentrating out τ_y, we can write (46.18) as

$$\begin{aligned} y_t^{\overline{\rho}} - \hat{\tau}_y' z_t^y &= \beta'(x_t^{\overline{\rho}} - \hat{\tau}_x' z_t^y) + e_t, \\ (\hat{\tau}_y', \hat{\tau}_x')' &= (Z_y^{\overline{\rho}\prime} Z_y^{\overline{\rho}})^{-1} Z_y^{\overline{\rho}\prime} W^{\overline{\rho}}. \end{aligned} \tag{46.19}$$

with

$$\begin{aligned} W^{\overline{\rho}} &= [w_1^{\overline{\rho}}, \ldots, w_T^{\overline{\rho}}]', \\ Z_y^{\overline{\rho}} &= [z_1^{y\overline{\rho}}, \ldots, z_T^{y\overline{\rho}}]'. \end{aligned}$$

Let the GLS-detrended data be defined by

$$\begin{aligned} y_t^d &= y_t - \hat{\tau}_y' z_t^y, \\ x_t^d &= x_t - \hat{\tau}_x' z_t^y, \end{aligned}$$

then (46.19) can be written as

$$y_t^d = \beta' x_t^d + u_t^d, \tag{46.20}$$

where

$$u_t^d = u_t - (\hat{\tau}_y - \tau_y)' z_t^y + \beta' \hat{\tau}_x' z_t^y. \tag{46.21}$$

This implies that each series is "detrended" separately by an OLS regression on quasi-differenced data with differencing parameter $\overline{\rho}$. Accordingly, the method to construct the test statistic is one that provides, via the GLS transformation, a better method to concentrate out the parameter τ_y of the cointegrating regression and not better estimates of the coefficients of the trend function of the variables of the system, e.g., β for the regressors x_t. For instance, when $z_t^y = \{1\}$, the quasi-differenced data only "quasi-demean" whether the data are trending or not. The use of GLS detrended data does not arise from a concern to get better estimates of the coefficients of the trend functions of the variables in the system.

As mentioned above, it seems sensible to argue that tests that perform best in the unit root case would also allow power gains in the cointegration context. Hence, the approach taken is to consider nearly optimal tests for unit roots and apply them in the cointegration context. The tests are then based on the OLS residuals $\hat{u}_t$ using GLS-detrended data:

$$\hat{u}_t = y_t^d - \hat{\beta}' x_t^d, \tag{46.22}$$

where $\hat{\beta}$ is the OLS estimate obtained from (46.20). The tests considered by Perron and Rodríguez (2016) are the same as those described in Sections 45.7 (ADF^{GLS}) and 45.8 (the various M^{GLS} tests). These lead to considerable power gains over the standard OLS residual-based tests for cointegration proposed by Phillips and Ouliaris (1990).

Of importance for the implementation of the tests is the choice of $\bar{c}$. Those suggested by Perron and Rodríguez (2016) are presented in Table 46.2 for $m = 1, \ldots, 5$ and various scenarios for the deterministic components. The asymptotic critical values of the tests are presented in Table 46.3. As a matter of notation, we use (a) $p_x = 0$, $p_y = 0$, when the data are not trending and there is only a constant in the regression, (b) $p_x = 1$, $p_y = 0$, when the data are trending and there is only a constant in the regression (deterministic cointegration), and (c) $p_x = 1$, $p_y = 1$, when the data are trending and both a constant and time trend are included in the regression (stochastic cointegration).

Table 46.2. Optimal Value of $\bar{c}$.

m	$p_x = 0$, $p_y = 0$	$p_x = 1$, $p_y = 0$	$p_x = 1$, $p_y = 1$
$x = 1$	−13.75	−13.50	−20.50
$x = 2$	−18.25	−18.00	−23.75
$x = 3$	−22.25	−23.00	−27.25
$x = 4$	−26.25	−26.00	−30.75
$x = 5$	−30.00	−29.75	−33.75

Source: Perron and Rodríguez (2016). Reproduced with permission of Oxford University Press.

Table 46.3. Critical values of GLS-based cointegration tests. m is the number of $I(1)$ right-hand-side variables.

		$p_x = 0,\ p_y = 0$			$p_x = 1,\ p_y = 0$			$p_x = 1,\ p_y = 1$		
	m	10%	5%	1%	10%	5%	1%	10%	5%	1%
MP_T	1	7.88	6.33	4.35	7.18	5.86	4.10	11.35	9.50	7.21
	2	9.33	4.86	5.82	8.84	7.47	5.49	11.89	10.16	7.89
	3	10.44	8.92	6.89	11.14	9.54	7.31	12.76	11.00	8.78
	4	12.03	10.56	8.27	11.82	10.22	8.00	13.94	12.41	9.62
	5	13.28	11.66	9.50	13.04	11.47	9.06	14.50	12.89	10.28
MSB	1	0.193	0.174	0.146	0.187	0.170	0.143	0.160	0.147	0.127
	2	0.161	0.147	0.128	0.158	0.146	0.125	0.141	0.131	0.115
	3	0.141	0.131	0.114	0.140	0.130	0.114	0.128	0.119	0.107
	4	0.128	0.120	0.107	0.128	0.119	0.106	0.119	0.112	0.099
	5	0.119	0.111	0.100	0.118	0.111	0.099	0.110	0.104	0.093
Z_α, MZ_α	1	−12.57	−15.60	−22.66	−13.45	−16.51	−23.55	−18.88	−22.55	−29.88
	2	−18.50	−22.01	−29.95	−19.09	−22.59	−31.11	−24.35	−28.50	−36.74
	3	−24.39	−28.61	−37.16	−24.42	−28.63	−37.17	−29.77	−34.48	−43.30
	4	−29.37	−33.63	−42.78	−29.62	−34.18	−43.60	−34.76	−38.94	−50.39
	5	−34.64	−39.53	−48.84	−34.99	−39.87	−50.10	−43.31	−45.07	−56.94
Z_t, MZ_t	1	−2.42	−2.74	−3.32	−2.55	−2.84	−3.43	−3.05	−3.32	−3.87
ADF	2	−2.97	−2.35	−3.79	−3.03	−3.32	−3.90	−3.46	−3.73	−4.32
	3	−3.43	−3.71	−4.24	−3.45	−3.73	−4.26	−3.81	−4.09	−4.61
	4	−3.77	−4.03	−4.58	−3.78	−4.06	−4.64	−4.10	−4.38	−4.95
	5	−4.08	−4.37	−4.89	−4.11	−4.39	−4.94	−4.40	−4.69	−5.20

Source: Perron and Rodríguez (2016). Reproduced with permission of Oxford University Press.

46.3 System-based methods

We now cover system-based methods of estimation. Think about the distinction between, say, 2SLS and FIML when estimating a simultaneous-equation system. The same pros and cons apply for single-equation versus system-based methods to estimate cointegrating vectors. The former may be more robust but less efficient, provided the whole system is correctly specified. By far the most popular system-based method stems from the work of Soren Johansen. We present the main outline of his proposed estimation method and test statistics. We also cover briefly a method suggested by Ahn and Reinsel (1990) which assumes a triangular system. The implications of imposing cointegrating relations and the identification assumptions underlying each method have implications for the identification of structural VAR models discussed in Chapter 41.

46.3.1 Johansen's FIML method

The method proposed by Johansen in a series of papers is by far the most widely used method to estimate systems of equations with integrated variables that are cointegrated; see, in particular, the works of Johansen (1988), Johansen (1991), Johansen and Juselius (1990), Johansen (1995), and Johansen (2006). Consider the following representation of a cointegrating system with y_t a vector of dimension n:

$$\Delta y_t = u + \Pi y_{t-1} + \sum_{i=1}^{k} \Gamma_i \Delta y_{t-i} + e_t, \tag{46.23}$$

where $e_t \sim i.i.d.\ N(0, \Sigma)$. Note that, as before, not all elements of y_t need to be $I(1)$, though when considering test statistics for the cointegrating rank, this will be assumed to hold. As usual, the normality assumption is imposed to derive a closed form solution to the likelihood function. The parameter estimates remain consistent and have the same limit distribution without imposing it. The same applies to the tests proposed. Suppose that the system is cointegrated so that

$$\text{rank}(\Pi) = r,$$

with $0 < r < n$. Then,

$$\Pi = \alpha\beta', \tag{46.24}$$

with α and β being $n \times r$ matrices. We consider several cases depending on the nature of the deterministic component and the type of cointegration assumed (i.e., deterministic or stochastic).

Case (1): Deterministic Cointegration Without Restrictions

We make extensive use of the Frisch–Waugh–Lovell theorem (see Section 2.1.3). Let

- R_{0t}: residuals from a regression of Δy_t on a constant and the lagged values $\{\Delta y_{t-i}; i = 1, \ldots, k\}$;
- R_{1t}: residuals from a regression of y_{t-1} on a constant and on the lagged values $\{\Delta y_{t-i}; i = 1, \ldots, k\}$;
- $S_{ij} = T^{-1} \sum_{t=1}^{T} R_{it} R'_{jt}$.

Then, the model (46.23) becomes

$$R_{0t} = \Pi R_{1t} + e_t. \tag{46.25}$$

The unrestricted MLE of Π is then simply the multivariate OLS estimate given by

$$\hat{\Pi} = S_{01} S_{11}^{-1}.$$

However, we wish to impose the cointegrating restriction specified (46.24). Start by assuming that β is known, then (46.25) is such that

$$R_{0t} = \alpha(\beta' R_{1t}) + e_t.$$

The MLE of α is the OLS estimate given by

$$\hat{\alpha}(\beta) = S_{01}\beta(\beta' S_{11}\beta)^{-1}$$

and the estimate of the covariance matrix of the residuals is

$$\hat{\Sigma}(\beta) = S_{00} - \hat{\alpha}(\beta)\beta' S_{11}\beta\hat{\alpha}(\beta)' = S_{00} - S_{01}\beta(\beta' S_{11}\beta)^{-1}\beta' S_{10}.$$

The MLE of β minimizes $|\hat{\Sigma}(\beta)|$ or, see Exercise 46.3,

$$\begin{aligned}|S_{00} - S_{01}\beta(\beta' S_{11}\beta)^{-1}\beta' S_{10}| \\ = |S_{00}||\beta' S_{11}\beta - \beta' S_{10} S_{00}^{-1} S_{01}\beta| / \left|\beta' S_{11}\beta\right|.\end{aligned} \tag{46.26}$$

Now, recall that the cointegrating vectors are not identified, only the space spanned by them is. Hence, to obtain estimates, we need to impose some restrictions; in fact, $r(r+1)/2$ restrictions. For example, if $r = 2$, we need 3 restrictions, 2 of which would specify the length of each vector in the space spanned by the cointegrating vectors and one which would set the angle between each. Johansen (1988) considered imposing the restrictions

$$\beta' S_{11}\beta = I_r, \tag{46.27}$$

which effectively impose $r(r+1)/2$ restrictions on β. These may seem strange at first sight since they depend on the data via the matrix S_{11}. The reason for adopting these restrictions is that it permitted using some well-established result by Anderson (1958) in the context of Limited Information Maximum Likelihood (LIML) estimation. The relevant result states that minimizing

$$|\beta' S_{11}\beta - \beta' S_{10} S_{00}^{-1} S_{01}\beta|$$

with respect to β, subject to the restrictions (46.27), implies that the estimates of the cointegrating vector contained in the cointegrating matrix β are the eigenvectors corresponding to the largest r eigenvalues of the determinantal system

$$\left|\lambda S_{11} - S_{10} S_{00}^{-1} S_{01}\right| = 0. \tag{46.28}$$

The system (46.28) has n eigenvalues, each associated with an eigenvector. Label the eigenvalues by $\hat{\lambda}_i$ $(i = 1, \ldots, n)$ and arrange then in decreasing order such that

$$\hat{\lambda}_1 \geqslant \hat{\lambda}_2 \geqslant \cdots \geqslant \hat{\lambda}_r \geqslant \hat{\lambda}_{r+1} \geqslant \cdots \geqslant \hat{\lambda}_n.$$

Under the hypothesis that $\mathrm{rank}(\Pi) = r$, the population values of $(\lambda_1, \lambda_2, \ldots, \lambda_r)$ are non-zero, while those of $(\lambda_{r+1}, \lambda_{r+2}, \ldots, \lambda_n)$ are zero. The columns of β are the eigenvectors corresponding to $(\hat{\lambda}_1, \hat{\lambda}_2, \ldots, \hat{\lambda}_r)$.

With these results, it is then straightforward to construct test statistics. Consider first the following null and alternative hypotheses:

$$H_0\colon \text{rank}(\Pi) = r,$$
$$H_1\colon \text{rank}(\Pi) > r.$$

Under the null hypothesis, the population values of $(\lambda_{r+1}, \lambda_{r+2}, \ldots, \lambda_n)$ are zero, while under the alternative hypothesis, some are non-zero. Hence, a sensible choice is to look at whether the sample values $(\hat{\lambda}_{r+1}, \hat{\lambda}_{r+2}, \ldots, \hat{\lambda}_n)$ are close to zero. This is the basis of the likelihood ratio test, which takes the form

$$T \sum_{i=r+1}^{n} \ln(1 - \hat{\lambda}_i).$$

This is called the "trace statistic" because its limit distribution can be expressed as the trace of some matrix involving functions of a vector Wiener process. See the work of Johansen and Juselius (1990) for a tabulation of the critical values, which depend on n and r. They are reproduced in the following.

Consider now the following null and alternative hypotheses:

$$H_0\colon \text{rank}(\Pi) = r,$$
$$H_1\colon \text{rank}(\Pi) = r + 1.$$

Under the null hypothesis, the population value of λ_{r+1} is zero, while under the alternative hypothesis, it is non-zero. Hence, a sensible choice is to look at whether the sample value of $\hat{\lambda}_{r+1}$ is close to zero. This is the basis of the likelihood ratio test, which takes the form

$$T \ln(1 - \hat{\lambda}_{r+1}).$$

This is called the "maximal eigenvalue" statistic because the limit distribution of the test can be expressed as the maximal eigenvalue of some matrix involving a vector Wiener processes. See the work of Johansen and Juselius (1990) for a tabulation of the critical values, which depend on n and r. They are reproduced in the following; see Table 46.4.

Case (2): Deterministic Cointegration Imposing Non-trending Variables

Case (1) dealt with estimation and tests for deterministic cointegration without imposing the appropriate constraints on the constant u in the regression when the variables are non-trending. Let us go back to the model:

$$\Delta y_t = u + \alpha\beta' y_{t-1} + \sum_{i=1}^{k} \Gamma_i \Delta y_{t-i} + e_t. \tag{46.29}$$

Take expectations on both sides and let $\delta = E(\Delta y_t)$. Then,

$$(I_n - \Gamma_1 \cdots - \Gamma_k)\delta = u + \alpha b^*,$$

where

$$b^* = E(\beta' y_{t-1}) = E z_{t-1}.$$

No drift or trend in any of the variables implies $\delta = 0$, hence

$$u = -\alpha b^*. \tag{46.30}$$

How can we impose the restriction (46.30) in the estimation procedure? Basically, we want to impose that u is some linear combination of α. Write (46.29) as

$$\Delta y_t = \alpha(-b^*, \beta' y_{t-1}) + \sum_{i=1}^{k} \Gamma_i \Delta y_{t-i} + e_t. \tag{46.31}$$

Let

$$y^*_{t-1} = (1, y_{t-1})_{(n+1)\times 1}.$$

Applying the Frisch–Waugh–Lovell theorem, let

- R^*_{0t}: residuals from a regression of Δy_t on the lagged values $\{\Delta y_{t-i}; i = 1, \ldots, k\}$ (no constant);
- R^*_{1t}: residuals from a regression of y^*_{t-1} on the lagged values $\{\Delta y_{t-i}; i - 1, \ldots, k\}$ (no constant).

Repeat the same steps as above to get the system

$$\left|\lambda S_{11}^{*} - S_{10}^{*} S_{00}^{*-1} S_{01}^{*}\right| = 0 \tag{46.32}$$

where we use the following notation: $S_{ij}^{*} = T^{-1}\sum_{t=1}^{T} R_{it}^{*}R_{jt}^{*\prime}$ so that S_{11}^{*} is $(n+1)\times(n+1)$, S_{10}^{*} is $(n+1)\times n$, S_{00}^{*} is $n\times n$, and S_{01}^{*} is $n\times(n+1)$.

The system (46.32) has $(n+1)$ solutions. Then, the MLE of $(-b^{*},\beta)$ is the matrix of the $(r+1)$ eigenvectors corresponding the $(r+1)$ largest eigenvalues of (46.32). The test statistics are similar (based on the largest eigenvalues) but the limiting distributions change. See the work of Johansen and Juselius (1990) for a tabulation of the critical values, which depend on n and r.

Case (3): Testing for Stochastic Cointegration

When considering stochastic cointegration, we should include a time trend in the regression so that the regression model is

$$\Delta y_t = u + \rho t + \alpha\beta' y_{t-1} + \sum_{i=1}^{k}\Gamma_i \Delta y_{t-i} + e_t.$$

The analysis is the same as in Case (1) but adding a time trend when applying the Frisch–Waugh–Lovell theorem. The asymptotic distributions of the tests are different; see the work of Perron and Campbell (1993) for the relevant asymptotic critical values.

Summary

In all cases, the resulting estimates of the cointegrating vectors may be meaningless since they are highly dependent on the normalization (46.27). Hence, a rotation is needed to obtain economically meaningful estimates. This sometimes can be achieved by simple re-normalizations. Also, note that the usual F-tests applied to the vector β have the standard chi-square asymptotic distribution.

The critical values of all three versions of both tests are presented in Table 46.4.

Table 46.4. Critical values of cointegration tests.

	$n-r$	80%	90%	95%	97.5%	99%
	Maximal Eigenvalue					
	1	4.91	6.69	8.08	9.66	11.58
	2	10.67	12.78	14.60	16.40	18.78
	3	16.52	18.96	21.28	23.36	26.15
	4	22.34	24.92	27.34	29.60	32.62
(1) Constant	5	27.95	30.82	33.26	35.70	38.86
Only	Trace					
	1	4.91	6.69	8.08	9.66	11.58
	2	13.04	15.58	17.84	19.61	21.96
	3	25.45	28.44	31.26	34.06	37.29
	4	41.62	45.25	48.42	51.80	55.55
	5	61.57	65.96	69.98	73.03	77.91
	Maximal Eigenvalue					
	1	5.88	7.56	9.09	10.71	12.74
	2	11.63	13.78	15.75	17.62	19.83
	3	17.47	19.80	21.89	23.84	26.41
	4	22.94	25.61	28.17	30.26	33.12
(2) Restricted	5	28.64	31.59	34.40	36.63	39.67
Constant	Trace					
	1	5.88	7.56	9.09	10.71	12.74
	2	15.36	17.96	20.17	22.20	24.99
	3	28.77	32.09	35.07	37.60	40.20
	4	45.64	49.93	53.35	56.45	60.05
	5	66.62	71.47	75.33	78.86	82.97
	Maximal Eigenvalue					
	1	7.76	9.75	11.62	13.43	15.74
	2	13.90	16.20	18.33	20.34	22.83
	3	19.85	22.51	24.79	27.02	29.76
	4	25.66	28.51	31.07	33.41	36.40
(3) Constant	5	31.44	34.45	37.09	39.51	42.78
and time	Trace					
trend	1	7.76	9.75	11.62	13.43	15.74
	2	18.44	21.22	23.65	26.03	28.83
	3	32.98	36.52	39.67	42.55	46.06
	4	51.22	55.57	59.44	62.81	67.06
	5	73.38	78.40	82.68	86.68	91.39

Source: Johansen and Juselius (1990); (cases 1–2); Perron and Campbell (1993) (Case 3).

46.3.2 An alternative method based on a triangular system

Let us go back to the concentrated regression

$$R_{0t} = \Pi R_{1t} + e_t,$$

and suppose instead of the restrictions $\beta' S_{11} \beta = I_r$, we impose the restrictions

$$\beta' = [I_r, \beta_0'].$$

By doing this, we impose $r \times r$ restrictions in such a way that the system becomes triangular and given by

$$y_{1t} = -\beta_0' y_{2t} + u_t,$$

where $y_{2t} \sim I(1)$ and is not affected by y_{1t}, while $u_t \sim I(0)$. Such models were analyzed by Ahn and Reinsel (1990); see also the work of Phillips (1991). This is a different type of *a priori* restriction guided by exogeneity principles. Whether it is reasonable to do so is case dependent. Note that in this case,

$$\Pi = (\Pi_1, \Pi_2) = \alpha\beta' = \alpha(I_r, \beta_0') = (\alpha, \alpha\beta_0')$$

so that

$$\alpha = \Pi_1,$$
$$\alpha\beta_0' = \Pi_2.$$

The OLS estimate consistent for Π is

$$\hat{\Pi} = S_{01} S_{11}^{-1}.$$

Hence,

$$\hat{\alpha} = \hat{\Pi}_1,$$

the first r columns of $\hat{\Pi}$. Using the relation

$$\Pi_2 = \alpha\beta_0' = \Pi_1 \beta_0',$$

consider the regression

$$\hat{\Pi}_2 = \hat{\Pi}_1 \beta_0' + v_t.$$

We can apply GLS to obtain

$$\beta_0' = [\hat{\Pi}_1' \hat{\Omega}_e^{-1} \hat{\Pi}_1]^{-1} \hat{\Pi}_1' \hat{\Omega}_e^{-1} \hat{\Pi}_2,$$

where

$$\hat{\Omega}_e = T^{-1} \sum_{t=1}^{T} (R_{0t} - \hat{\Pi} R_{1t})(R_{0t} - \hat{\Pi} R_{1t})'.$$

46.4 Identification of VAR models

Recall the structural from of a VAR given by

$$A(L) y_t = \varepsilon_t,$$

where

$$A(L) = A_0 - A_1 L - \cdots - A_k L^k,$$

with

$$\varepsilon_t \sim i.i.d.(0, \Sigma),$$

and Σ usually assumed to be a diagonal matrix. The reduced form is

$$y_t = \sum_{i-1}^{k} B_i y_{t-i} + u_t$$

with

$$u_t \sim i.i.d.(0, \Omega).$$

Suppose that the diagonal elements of A_0 are set to 1 as normalizations. Then, we need $n(n-1)/2$ restrictions to identify the model. The presence of cointegrating relationships can allow some long-term restrictions, though they can also induce additional parameters in the structural form so that even more restrictions are needed. We discuss these issues in the following.

Write the structural form as

$$\Delta y_t = \Pi y_{t-1} + \sum_{i=1}^{k} \Gamma_i \Delta y_{t-i} + \varepsilon_t^*,$$

where $\Pi = \sum_{i=1}^{k} A_0^{-1} A_i - I$, $\Gamma_j = -\sum_{i=j+1}^{k} A_0^{-1} A_i$ $(j = 1, \ldots, k-1)$, and $\varepsilon_t^* \sim i.i.d.(0, \Sigma^*)$ with $\Sigma^* = A_0^{-1}\Sigma(A_0^{-1})'$. With no constraint on Σ^*, the model is identified if $n(n-1)/2$ constraints are imposed on Π. Whether imposing cointegrating relationships achieves this goal depends on the precise structure of the model:

- Suppose that $r = 0$ so that $\Pi = 0$. This amounts to imposing unit root constraints. The model is identified since the n^2 elements of Π are constrained.
- Suppose that $r = n$ so that no cointegrating relationship holds and all variables are $I(0)$, then we are back to the standard case since no restrictions are imposed and we need $n(n-1)/2$ restrictions.
- Suppose that $0 < r < n$. Then, $\Pi = \alpha\beta'$, which involves $2nr$ coefficients instead of n^2. Hence, cointegration imposes restrictions if $r < n/2$. More precisely, (a) if $r < n/2$, we need less than $n(n-1)/2$ further additional restrictions to identify the model; (b) however, if $r > n/2$, we need more than $n(n-1)/2$; (c) if $r = n/2$, no gains nor losses, we still need $n(n-1)/2$ restrictions.

Case with $r = 1$. Here, $\Pi = \alpha\beta'$ has $2n$ coefficients. Hence, $n(n-2)$ restrictions are imposed.

The estimation methods of Johansen (1988) and Ahn and Reinsel (1990) impose one additional restriction, either $|\beta' S_{11} \beta| = 1$ with the former, which normalizes the cointegrating vector, or setting one coefficient to 1 with the latter. Hence, we have $n(n-2)+1$ restrictions which is weakly greater than $n(n-1)/2$ if $n \geqslant 2$. So, the model is identified if $n \geqslant 2$ since then enough restrictions are imposed.

Case with $r > 1$. Here things are more complex. We consider the problem of identifying α and β separately.

(a) Identification of β: Since β depends on the long-run properties of the data, we can abstract from the short-term components and write the system as

$$\beta' y_t = w_t,$$

where $w_t \sim I(0)$. We can view this as a standard simultaneous equation model with r equations. Hence, a necessary condition is that there be r^2 constraints (the sufficient conditions are given by the usual rank conditions). If $r = 1$, a simple normalization will do. However, if $r > 1$, additional restrictions are necessary. Since the method of Ahn and Reinsel (1990) imposes r^2 restrictions, the cointegrating vector is identified. However, the method of Johansen (1988) imposes $r(r+1)/2$ restrictions, in which case additional restrictions are needed if $r > 1$.

(b) Identification of α: Given the number of restrictions to identify β, the number of restrictions needed to identify α is

$$n(n-1)/2 - (n^2 - 2nr) - r^2,$$

provided this number is positive. If it is 0 (e.g., $n = 2$ and $r = 1$), α is just-identified, while if it is less than 0 it is overidentified. The result follows since $(n^2 - 2nr)$ restrictions are imposed via cointegration, and r^2 restrictions are imposed for the identification of β.

If the model is not identified, tests of hypotheses about β are inconsistent since the limit of the estimates are then random variables. We can test hypotheses about the space spanned by the cointegrating vector but these are of limited economic interest. So, to test hypotheses about cointegrating vectors, we need to have an identified model. When using Johansen's method, this implies the need to impose more constraints. A method of estimation using FIML with constraints has been considered by Johansen and Juselius (1992).

46.5 Exercises

Exercise 46.1. Prove Lemma 46.1.

Exercise 46.2. Show that (46.4) follows from (46.3).

Exercise 46.3. Prove the statement in equation (46.26).

Exercise 46.4. Suppose y_t and x_t are two unit root processes, satisfying

$$y_t = y_{t-1} + \varepsilon_t,$$
$$x_t = x_{t-1} + \eta_t,$$

where

$$\begin{bmatrix} \varepsilon_t \\ \eta_t \end{bmatrix} \sim i.i.d.N\left(\begin{bmatrix} 0 \\ 0 \end{bmatrix}, \begin{pmatrix} \sigma_\varepsilon^2 & 0 \\ 0 & \sigma_\eta^2 \end{pmatrix}\right)$$

with $\sigma_\varepsilon^2 > 0$ and $\sigma_\eta^2 > 0$. (a) Are y_t and x_t cointegrated? Explain. (b) Suppose we run the following regression

$$y_t = \alpha x_t + e_t.$$

Derive the asymptotic distribution of the OLS estimator $\hat{\alpha}$. (c) Show that the t-statistic for testing $\alpha = 0$ diverges.

Exercise 46.5. Suppose that the two-dimensional vector of series $y_t = \{y_{1t}, y_{2t}\}$ is generated by $y_t = y_{t-1} + u_t$, with $y_0 = 0$ and where $u_t = \{u_{1t}, u_{2t}\}$ is a stationary process such that $T^{-1/2}\sum_{t=1}^{[Tr]} u_t \Rightarrow \Omega^{1/2}W(r)$, with

$$\Omega = \begin{bmatrix} \sigma_1^2 & 0 \\ 0 & \sigma_2^2 \end{bmatrix} = 2\pi h_u(0) = \lim_{T\to\infty} T^{-1}E\left(\sum_{t=1}^{T} u_t\right)^2,$$

and $W(r) = \{W_1(r), W_2(r)\}$ is a two-dimensional vector of independent Wiener processes. Since Ω is of full rank, the two series are not cointegrated. (a) Derive the limit of the *OLS* estimate $\hat{\beta}$ from the regression

$$y_{1t} = \beta y_{2t} + v_t. \tag{46.33}$$

(b) Consider the t-statistic for testing the null hypothesis that $\beta = 0$. Show that, as the sample size increases to infinity, it diverges. (c) Recall that the Durbin–Watson statistic is

$$DW = \frac{\sum_{t=2}^{T}(\hat{v}_t - \hat{v}_{t-1})^2}{\sum_{t=1}^{T}\hat{v}_t^2},$$

where $\hat{v}_t$ are the least-squares residuals from regression (46.33). Show that, as $T \to \infty$, $DW \xrightarrow{p} 0$. (d) Interpret the relevance of regression (46.33) in light of the results obtained in parts (a)–(c).

Exercise 46.6. Suppose that the two-dimensional vector $z_t = \{y_t, x_t\}$ is generated by

$$z_t = z_{t-1} + u_t$$

with $z_0 = 0$ and where $u_t = \{u_{yt}, u_{xt}\}$, $u_{yt} \sim i.i.d.(0, \sigma_y^2)$, $u_{xt} \sim i.i.d.(0, \sigma_x^2)$, $E(u_{xt}^4) < \infty$, $E(u_{yt}^4) < \infty$, and $E(u_{yt}u_{xs}) = 0$ for all t and s (hence, y_t and x_t are uncorrelated). Now, consider a regression of y_t on x_t (with a constant included). Denote the least squares estimate of the coefficient on x_t by $\hat{\beta}$, the t-statistic for testing the null hypothesis that $\beta = 0$ by $t_{\hat{\beta}}$, and the R^2 of the regression given by

$$R^2 = \frac{\hat{\beta}^2 \sum_{t=1}^{T}(x_t - \bar{x})^2}{\sum_{t=1}^{T}(y_t - \bar{y})^2},$$

with $\bar{x} = T^{-1}\sum_{t=1}^{T} x_t$ and $\bar{y} = T^{-1}\sum_{t=1}^{T} y_t$. (a) Derive the limit of $\hat{\beta}$, $t_{\hat{\beta}}$ and the R^2 as $T \to \infty$. (b) Suppose that the data are generated by

$$y_t = \delta_y t + u_{yt},$$

$$x_t = \delta_x t + u_{xt},$$

with $u_t = \{u_{yt}, u_{xt}\}$ as defined in part (a). Note that, again, y_t and x_t are uncorrelated. Consider again a regression of y_t on x_t (with a constant included). Derive the limit of $\hat{\beta}$, $t_{\hat{\beta}}$ and the R^2 as $T \to \infty$. (*Hint*: Remember that $\lim_{T\to\infty} T^{-3}\sum_{t=1}^{T} t^2 = 1/3$ and $\lim_{T\to\infty} T^{-2}\sum_{t=1}^{T} t = 1/2$.) (c) Compare and discuss the results obtained in parts (a) and (b). Give an intuitive explanation for them. (d) Discuss the relevance of using the t-statistic and the R^2 to assess the relationship between two series. For each case discussed in parts (a) and (b), discuss alternative statistics or procedures that could deliver a more sensible conclusion. (e) Suppose now that x_t and y_t generated by

$$y_t = \beta_0 x_t + u_{yt},$$

$$x_t = x_{t-1} + u_{xt},$$

with $u_t = \{u_{yt}, u_{xt}\}$ as defined in part (a). Consider again a regression of y_t on x_t (with a constant included). What is the limit distribution of $T(\hat{\beta} - \beta_0)$ and $t_{\hat{\beta}}$, the t-statistic for testing the null hypothesis that $\beta = \beta_0$? Does your result for the limit distribution of $t_{\hat{\beta}}$ change if u_{yt} and u_{xt} are serially correlated and/or correlated with each other? Are nuisance parameters involved in the limit distribution? If so, describe procedures that would deliver asymptotically valid inference on β.

Exercise 46.7. Consider y_t a random walk defined by $y_t = y_{t-1}+u_t$, where u_t is such that $T^{-1/2}\sum_{t=1}^{[Tr]} u_t \Rightarrow \sigma W(r)$ with $\sigma^2 = 2\pi h_u(0)$ and $W(r)$ is a standard Wiener process and $h_u(0)$ is the spectral density function of u_t at frequency zero. T is the size of the sample of data available. We also have $T^{-1}\sum_{t=1}^{T} u_t^2 \xrightarrow{p} \sigma_u^2 = var(u_t)$. Consider a least squares regression of y_t on a time trend, i.e.,

$$y_t = \hat{\beta}t + \hat{u}_t. \tag{46.34}$$

Show that

$$T^{1/2}\hat{\beta} \Rightarrow 3\sigma^2 \int_0^1 rW(r)dr,$$

and derive the mean and variance of this limit random variable. (b) Consider now the usual t-statistic. Show that it is unbounded as T increases. (c) Consider the usual R^2 as a measure of the goodness of fit of regression (46.34). Derive its limit distribution. (d) Compare the results obtained with those from the so-called spurious regression problem where a random walk is regressed on an independent random walk. Explain intuitively why similar results hold.

Exercise 46.8. Consider testing the null hypothesis of no cointegration. (a) Describe how to implement an augmented Dickey–Fuller type test. (b) In the case of non-trending data, describe the limit distribution of that test. Do not attempt to prove or derive it; simply use heuristic arguments based on methods used in Chapter 44.

Exercise 46.9. Let $x_t = \sum_{s=1}^{t} \varepsilon_s$ and $\varepsilon_s \sim i.i.d.\ N(0,1)$ and $y_t = \sum_{s=1}^{t} v_s$ with $v_s \sim i.i.d.\ N(0,1)$. Assume that $E(\varepsilon_s v_t) = 0$ for all t and s. (a) Are x_t and y_t stationary? (b) Consider a regression of y_t on x_t. Let $\hat{\beta}$ be the OLS estimator of that regression defined by

$$\hat{\beta} = \frac{\sum_{t=1}^{T} y_t x_t}{\sum_{t=1}^{T} x_t^2}.$$

Show that

$$\hat{\beta} \Rightarrow \frac{\int_0^1 W_1(r) W_2(r) dr}{\int_0^1 W_2(r)^2 dr},$$

where $W_1(r)$ and $W_2(r)$ are two independent standard Brownian motions on $C[0,1]$. (c) Let the R^2 of the regression be given as

$$R^2 = \frac{\hat{\beta}^2 \sum_{t=1}^{T} (x_t - \bar{x})^2}{\sum_{t=1}^{T} (y_t - \bar{y})^2},$$

with $\bar{x} = T^{-1} \sum_{t=1}^{T} x_t$ and $\bar{y} = T^{-1} \sum_{t=1}^{T} y_t$. Find an expression for R^2 as $T \to \infty$. (d) Discuss the implications of your result for a standard F-test of the hypothesis $\beta = 0$. (e) Now, assume that $x_t = \sum_{s=1}^{t} \varepsilon_s$ and $\varepsilon_s \sim i.i.d.\ N(0,1)$ and that

$$y_t = x_t + v_t,$$

where $v_t \sim i.i.d.\ N(0,1)$ and $E(\varepsilon_s v_t) = 0$ for all t and s. Consider the OLS estimator $\hat{\beta}$ from the regression of y_t on x_t where $\hat{\beta} = \sum_{t=1}^{T} y_t x_t / \sum_{t=1}^{T} x_t^2$. Is $\hat{\beta}$ consistent? Can you find a limit distribution for $\hat{\beta}$ after appropriate scaling and centering? (f) Continue to maintain the assumptions under part (e). How would you test the hypothesis that $\beta = 1$? Construct a test and indicate how you would obtain critical values under H_0: $\beta = 1$.

Exercise 46.10 (Review). You have at your disposition the major macroeconomic variables (such as real GNP, price indices, interest rates, consumption, exchange rate, and money supply). You are asked to quantify the effect of a shock (or innovation) to money supply (e.g., to M1) on the level of real GNP for various horizons in the future. Describe the various steps that you would need to do to obtain estimates and confidence intervals based on using a vector autoregressive system. Describe these steps for the following cases: (1) supposing all variables to have a stochastic component that is stationary and (2) supposing all variables to have a stochastic component with an autoregressive unit root ($I(1)$ variables). Make sure to discuss the main features of each step (modeling, estimation, confidence intervals, etc.).

Chapter 47

Long-Memory Processes

Processes that are persistent in the sense that the correlation between distant observations decays hyperbolically are called long-memory processes. They have found extensive use in capturing the behavior of many observed series since their introduction by Hurst (1951). There has long been an interest in long-memory models, especially with applications to financial time series. For reviews of the literature, see the works of Robinson (1994), Beran (1994), Baillie (1996), and Pipiras and Taqqu (2017).

Of interest in econometrics is the fractionally integrated model (Granger (1981), Granger and Joyeux (1980), and Hosking (1981)) whose difference of order d is a short-memory process often modeled as an $ARMA$ process for which the autocorrelations decay exponentially. The parameter d can be non-integer-valued and when $0 < d < 1$, the autocorrelations decay very slowly, a characteristic of long-memory processes. For a review, see the work of Hualde and Nielsen (2023) which also covers cointegration between fractionally integrated series. This occurs when a vector of variables are, say, $I(d)$ and some linear combinations are $I(d^*)$ with $d^* < d$. This is a generalization of the usual concept of cointegration in which the variables are $I(1)$ and some linear combinations are $I(0)$. For an example of a general estimation procedure, see the work of Andersen and Varneskov (2021). The literature on this topic is quite technical and the applications are few, so we do not cover it.

Various methods have been proposed to estimate the long-memory parameter d. The estimators of the memory parameter are divided into parametric and semi-parametric ones. The theory of parametric estimators was developed by Fox and Taqqu (1986) and Dahlhaus (1989), among others. Semi-parametric estimators of the memory parameter have become popular since they do not require knowing the specific form of the short-memory structure. They are based on the periodograms of the series and can be categorized into two types. A popular method is the log periodogram (LP) regression proposed by Geweke and Porter-Hudak (1983), whose large sample distribution was analyzed by, among others, Robinson (1995b) and Hurvich *et al.* (1998) as well as Phillips (2007) who covers the unit root case $d = 1$.

Another popular method is the local Whittle (LW) estimator which is credited to Kunsch (1987). The LP estimator is akin to OLS and the LW estimator to the MLE in the frequency domain. Robinson (1995a) and Robinson (1995b) analyzed the asymptotic properties of these two types of estimators. He showed that they are asymptotically normal and have the same convergence rate and that the asymptotic variance of the LW estimator is smaller than that of the LP estimator. Applications to macroeconomics, international trade and finance are numerous. For example, Ding *et al.* (1993) argued that stock return volatility is well described by a long-memory process.

47.1 Basic definitions

We start with some basic definitions of a long-memory process. Let $\{x_t\}_{t=1}^{T}$ be a stationary time series with spectral density function $f_x(w)$ at frequency w given by

$$f_x(w) = G(w)w^{-2d} \quad \text{as } w \to 0, \tag{47.1}$$

with $G(w)$ a slowly varying function as $w \to 0$ (i.e., for any real t, $G(tw)/G(w) \to 1$ as $w \to 0$). When $d > 0$, x_t is a long-memory process with a spectral density function that increases for frequencies getting closer to zero. The rate of divergence to infinity depends on the parameter d. Under some general conditions, this low-frequency definition is equivalent to the following long-lag autocorrelation definition from Beran (1994). Let $\gamma_x(\tau)$ be the autocorrelation function of x_t at lag τ. If

$$\gamma_x(\tau) = c(\tau)\tau^{2d-1}$$

as $\tau \to \infty$, with $c(\tau)$ a slowly varying function as $\tau \to \infty$, the process is said to have long memory. For $0 < d < 1/2$, this implies that the autocorrelations decrease to zero at a slow hyperbolic rate which depends on the parameter d, in contrast to the fast geometric rate of decay that applies to a short-memory process. When $d = 0$, x_t is a short-memory process.

For an integer d, the operator $\Delta^d = (1 - L)^d$ denotes the differencing operator with the usual lag operator L. For a non-integer real number $d > -1$, the difference operator $\Delta^d = (1 - L)^d$ is defined by means of the binomial expansion:

$$\Delta^d = \sum_{k=0}^{\infty} \binom{d}{k} (-L)^k = \sum_{k=0}^{\infty} \phi_k(d) L^k,$$

where

$$\binom{d}{k} \equiv \frac{d!}{k!(d-k)!} = \frac{d \times (d-1) \times \cdots \times (d-k+1)}{k \times (k-1) \times \cdots \times 2 \times 1},$$

$$\phi_k(d) \equiv (-1)^k \binom{d}{k} = \prod_{s=1}^{k} \frac{s-1-d}{s} = \frac{\Gamma(k-d)}{\Gamma(k+1)\Gamma(-d)},$$

with $\Gamma(\cdot)$ the gamma function so that

$$\phi_k(d) = \binom{k-d-1}{k},$$

and $\phi_0(d) = 1$. Recall that $z! \equiv \Gamma(z+1)$, $z = 0, 1, \ldots$, and for any integer $k > 0$, $0 < z < 1$, $\Gamma(z-k)$ is defined as

$$\Gamma(z) = (z-1)\Gamma(z-1) = \cdots = (z-1)\cdots(z-k)\Gamma(z-k).$$

To define a fractional process, we use the notation of Robinson (2005). Let $\{\eta_t, t = 0, \pm 1, \ldots\}$ be a short-memory zero-mean covariance stationary process, with spectral density that is finite and bounded away from zero. For $d \in (-0.5, 0.5)$,

$$\zeta_t = \Delta^{-d}\eta_t, \quad t = 0, \pm 1, \ldots,$$

is covariance stationary and invertible. The truncated version of ζ_t is defined as

$$\zeta_t^{\#} = \zeta_t \mathbf{1}_{t \geq 1}, \quad t = 0, \pm 1, \ldots,$$

where $\mathbf{1}_A$ is the indicator function for the event A. For an integer $m \geq 0$,

$$x_t = \Delta^{-m}\zeta_t^{\#}, \quad t = 0, \pm 1, \ldots, \tag{47.2}$$

is called a type I $I(m+d)$ process.

Let $\mathcal{D}[0,1]$ be the space of functions on $[0,1]$ which are right continuous and have left limits, equipped with the Skorohod topology (or the sup norm). Denote by $[a]$ the integer part of $a \in \mathbb{R}$. The order of integration is $d_0 = d + m$ with $d \in (-0.5, 0.5)$ and $m \in \{0, 1\}$. The restriction that $d_0 \neq 0.5$ is standard in the long-memory literature. Tanaka (1999) showed that the case with $d_0 = 0.5$ needs to be treated separately from the case with $d_0 \neq 0.5$. We omit the case $d_0 = 0.5$ in this chapter. For theoretical results about this boundary case (and others), see the work of Duffy and Kasparis (2021).

A type II long-memory process is defined by

$$x_t^* = \Delta^{-m-d}\eta_t^{\#}, \quad t = 0, \pm 1, \ldots,$$

where $\eta_t^{\#} = \eta_t \mathbf{1}_{t \geq 1}$ $(t = 0, \pm 1, \ldots)$. When $d = 0$, the two types are identical so that the processes are the same for stationary processes $(m = 0)$ or ones having one or multiple unit roots $(m > 0)$. They, however, differ when $d \neq 0$. For details about the differences, see the works of Robinson (2005) and Marinucci and Robinson (1999). In practice, it is difficult to reliably determine if a process is type I or II. Hence, the choice mostly pertains to theoretical convenience. Robinson (2005) and Davidson and Hashimzade (2009) pointed out that asymptotic results vary depending on the definition of fractional Brownian motions considered. When $m = 0$ and for $d \in (-0.5, 0.5)$, we have the following weak convergence results on $\mathcal{D}[0,1]$: (a) for type I processes,

$$T^{-1/2-d}\sum_{t=1}^{[Tr]} x_t \Rightarrow B_I(t)$$
$$= \frac{1}{\Gamma(d+1)}\left\{\int_{-\infty}^{0}[(t-s)^d-(-s)^d]dW(s)\right.$$
$$\left.+\int_0^t (t-s)^d dW(s)\right\},$$

and (b) for type II processes,

$$T^{-1/2-d}\sum_{t=1}^{[Tr]} x_t^* \Rightarrow B_{II}(t) = \frac{1}{\Gamma(d+1)}\left\{\int_0^t (t-s)^d dW(s)\right\},$$

where $W(\cdot)$ denotes the standard Wiener process. Davidson and Hashimzade (2009) discussed methods to simulate each of the two stated distributions. Unless stated otherwise, the results stated in this chapter are valid for both types of processes and we simply refer to x_t for the observed data.

A commonly used class of parametric models is the so-called $ARFIMA(p,d,q)$ given by, see the work of Granger and Joyeux (1980),

$$A(L)(1-L)^d(x_t-\mu) = B(L)e_t,$$

where

$$A(L) = 1 - \sum_{j=1}^{p} a_j L^j,$$
$$B(L) = 1 + \sum_{j=1}^{q} b_j L^j,$$

μ is the unknown mean of x_t and $e_t \sim i.i.d.\ (0, \sigma_e^2)$.

47.2 The log-periodogram estimate of *d*

The log-periodogram (LP) regression estimator of the memory parameter d was proposed by Geweke and Porter-Hudak (1983). It is a semi-parametric method which uses only frequencies near zero to avoid possible misspecification caused by high-frequency movements. Let $I_{x,T}(w_j)$ be the sample periodogram of x_t at the jth Fourier frequency $w_j = 2\pi j/T$ ($j = 1, \ldots, [T/2]$), i.e., see Section 38.1,

$$\begin{aligned} I_{x,T}(w_j) &= (2\pi T)^{-1} \left| \sum_{t=1}^{T} x_t \exp(-iw_j t) \right|^2 \\ &= (2\pi T)^{-1} \left(\sum_{t=1}^{T} x_t \exp(-iw_j t) \right) \left(\sum_{t=1}^{T} x_t \exp(iw_j t) \right). \end{aligned}$$

An estimate of d can be obtained using the theoretical relation (47.1), taking the logarithm and replacing $f_x(\lambda)$ by its empirical counterpart $I_{x,T}(w_j)$. This leads to the following regression estimated by least squares:

$$\log(I_{x,T}(w_j)) = c + dX_t + \varepsilon_j,$$

where

$$X_t = -2\log(2\sin(w_j/2)) = -\log(2 - 2(w_j/2)) \approx -\log(w_j^2),$$

with observations pertaining to frequencies ranging from $j = 1$ to m. Here, m acts as an upper bound on the number of frequencies used. So long as $m/T \to 0$, this approximating relation holds asymptotically. A popular rule of thumb is $m = T^{1/2}$. As a matter of notation, let

$$a_j = -\log(2\sin(w_j/2)) + (1/m)\sum_{k=1}^{m} \log(2\sin(w_k/2))$$

and $S_T = \sum_{k=1}^{m} a_j^2$. The estimate of d is then

$$\hat{d} = (2S_T)^{-1} \sum_{j=1}^{m} a_j \log(I_x(w_j)).$$

Under some conditions, the limit distribution of the estimate is given by (see Robinson (1995b) and Hurvich *et al.* (1998))

$$m^{1/2}(\hat{d} - d) \xrightarrow{d} N(0, \pi^2/24). \tag{47.3}$$

For this result to hold, some conditions needed on the spectral density function are purely technical. Of more practical relevance, what is needed is (a) $m = o(T^{4/5})$ and $\log^2(T) = o(m)$ and (b) the data are normally distributed. The first requirement pertains to the rate of increase of m as T increases. Hurvich *et al.* (1998) provided a plug-in method that provides an estimate of m which minimizes the mean-square error using some expansion that neglects higher-order terms. The second requirement is much stronger and important for practical applications. The existing literature on LP estimators does not cover the non-Gaussian case without necessitating one to "pool" observations across adjacent Fourier frequencies; see the work of Velasco (2000). The assumption of Gaussianity may appear strong since processes in economics and finance most frequently thought to exhibit long-memory are volatility processes. Nevertheless, simulation evidence indicates that this assumption could be relaxed; i.e., non-Gaussian errors induce no important deviations from the stated asymptotic distribution.

47.3 The local Whittle estimate of *d*

The local Whittle (LW) estimation method of Kunsch (1987) and Robinson (1995a) has become popular because of its likelihood interpretation, nice asymptotic properties (smaller asymptotic variance compared to the log-periodogram estimator), mild assumptions (e.g., no need for a normality assumption), and also the possibility to easily modify it to accommodate the presence of contaminations (see Section 47.4). It is defined as the minimizer of the (negative) local Whittle likelihood function in the frequency domain

$$Q(G_0, d) = m^{-1} \sum_{j=1}^{m} [\log(G_0 w_j^{-2d}) + I_{x,T}(w_j)/(G_0 w_j^{-2d})],$$

where $G_0 = G(0)$, as defined by (47.1), $m = m(T)$ is the bandwidth which goes to infinity as $T \to \infty$ but at a slower rate than T, and

$w_j = 2\pi j/T$ are the Fourier frequencies. Concentrating with respect to G_0, the estimator of d is

$$\hat{d}_{LW} = \arg\min_d \left[\log \hat{G}_0(d) - 2dm^{-1} \sum_{j=1}^{m} \log w_j \right],$$

where

$$\hat{G}_0(d) = m^{-1} \sum_{j=1}^{m} w_j^{2d} I_{x,T}(w_j).$$

Under some technical conditions, the limit distribution of the estimate is

$$m^{1/2}(\hat{d}_m - d_0) \xrightarrow{d} N(0, 1/4) \tag{47.4}$$

as $T \to \infty$. Hence, it is more efficient than the LP estimator since the asymptotic variance is smaller. It, however, requires a nonlinear estimation method.

47.4 Dealing with finite sample contaminations

There are so-called contaminations that have an effect on the bias and efficiency of these semi-parametric estimators, either in finite samples or even asymptotically. Part of the literature has focused on providing methods to mitigate the effect of additive noise and/or short-memory dynamics, which have only a finite sample effect.

In the case of additive noise or so-called perturbed fractional processes, although both the LW and LP estimators preserve consistency and asymptotic normality, as shown by Deo and Hurvich (2001) and Arteche (2004), they can be severely biased. Hurvich and Ray (2003), Hurvich *et al.* (2005), and Arteche (2006), among others, have proposed estimators that can reduce the effect of noise by introducing an additive constant or polynomial term in the spectral density function. These methods are all based on local Whittle estimators, given their flexibility in accommodating more structures in the specified data-generating process. For example, for the case with additive noise, suppose we observe

$$x_t = c + y_t + \varepsilon_t, \tag{47.5}$$

where y_t is a long-memory component and the additive noise ε_t is a zero mean white noise with variance σ_ε^2, such that for each $s \neq t$, $E[\varepsilon_s y_t] = 0$ and for each t, $E[\varepsilon_t y_t] = \rho_\varepsilon \sigma_\varepsilon$, where ρ_ε is the correlation between ε_t and y_t, assumed to be constant. Following the work of Hurvich *et al.* (2005), we add a constant term into the spectral density function so that the modified pseudo spectral density function is

$$\begin{aligned} f_k \triangleq f_x(w_k) &= G_0 w_k^{-2d} + G_\varepsilon = G_0(w_k^{-2d} + (G_\varepsilon/G_0)) \\ &= G_0(w_k^{-2d} + \theta_\varepsilon) = G_0 g_k, \end{aligned} \tag{47.6}$$

where $g_k = w_k^{-2d} + \theta_\varepsilon$ and the (approximate) frequency domain Quasi-Maximum Likelihood Function (QMLF) is

$$\varphi(G, d, \theta) = m^{-1} \sum_{k=1}^{m} \varphi_k(G, d, \theta_\varepsilon).$$

Concentrating G out of the QMLF, the estimate of G is

$$\hat{G} = m^{-1} \sum_{k=1}^{m} (I_k/g_k)$$

and the local Whittle QMLE estimator under noise perturbations is

$$(\hat{d}_m, \hat{\theta}_m) = \arg\min_{(d,\theta)} J_m(d, \theta),$$

where

$$J_m(d, \theta) = \log\left(m^{-1} \sum_{k=1}^{m} I_k/g_k\right) + m^{-1} \sum_{k=1}^{m} \log(g_k).$$

For reasons discussed by Hurvich *et al.* (2005), this approach is expected to work when d_0 is not too close to zero. When $d_0 = 0$, the process is short-memory. We then have a combination of two additive short-memory processes which cannot be identified separately.

Hence, if the true value of d is 0, the estimate performs badly and has a very large mean squared error.

The standard LP and LW estimators are also strongly biased when substantial short-memory dynamics are present, i.e., strong positive serial correlation. Among others, Andrews and Sun (2004) considered an adaptive local polynomial Whittle estimator adding a polynomial structure into G_0, i.e., replacing G_0 in (47.6) by

$$G_0 \exp(-p_r(\lambda_j, \theta)),$$

where

$$p_r(\lambda_j, \theta) = \sum_{s=1}^{r} \theta_s \lambda_j^{2s}$$

and $\theta = (\theta_1, \ldots, \theta_r)$. By substituting a polynomial structure for the constant term used to approximate the behavior of the short-memory component near frequency zero in the local Whittle estimator, they showed that their estimator has considerable efficiency gains compared to standard LW and LP estimators under the presence of strong short-memory dynamics. This somewhat increases the variance of the estimate but in such a way as to reduce the overall MSE.

To deal with both additive noise and short-memory dynamics, one can follow the approach of Frederiksen *et al.* (2012) who add polynomials and a constant as additive terms in the quasi-maximum likelihood function. One drawback is that the increase in the number of parameters can induce an important increase in variance resulting in increased mean squared error for the estimate of d. In both cases, the limit distribution remains the same, as stated in (47.4).

47.5 Dealing with asymptotic contaminations

There are other low-frequency contaminations that can have a more serious effect causing outright inconsistent estimates. They may be important enough to induce researchers to mistakenly conclude that a short-memory process with low-frequency contaminations is a long-memory process. Such an effect is often called “spurious long-memory”. These low-frequency contaminations include but are not confined to random level shifts, deterministic level shifts, and deterministic trends. A short-memory process contaminated by these components will exhibit hyperbolically decaying autocorrelations as well as a pole in its spectral density function at frequency zero, which are characteristics of a long-memory process.

Among others, Diebold and Inoue (2001), Granger and Hyung (2004), Mikosch and Stărică (2004), and Perron and Qu (2010) provided theoretical explanations for and simulation evidence of this spurious long-memory effect.

It has also been argued that models incorporating a short-memory process with such low-frequency contaminations provide a better in-sample fit and, in particular, forecast better compared to models assuming a pure long-memory process. Various studies reported evidence that these forms of data contaminations are in fact likely present in the volatility of asset prices and considerably weaken the evidence of pure long-memory; see, e.g., the works of Granger and Hyung (2004), Mikosch and Stărică (2004), Stărică and Granger (2005), Perron and Qu (2010), Lu and Perron (2010), Qu and Perron (2013), Perron and Varneskov (2017), Xu and Perron (2014), and Casini *et al.* (2024).

Ohanissian *et al.* (2008), Perron and Qu (2010), and Qu (2011) proposed tests in both the time and frequency domain with varying degrees of success. Many have argued that the long-memory properties of many economic time series are indeed spurious. These tests focus on distinguishing between a short-memory process affected by low-frequency contaminations from a true long-memory process. They do not offer methods to estimate the memory parameter in the presence of low-frequency contaminations when the true signal may be of long or short memory.

47.5.1 Low-frequency contaminations

The DGP is now

$$x_t = c + y_t + u_t + \varepsilon_t,$$

where the low-frequency component u_t is independent of the additive noise ε_t and the long-memory process y_t.

The types of processes considered by Hou and Perron (2014) for the low-frequency contamination (LFC) component u_t are laid out in the following definition.

Definition 47.1. The low-frequency contamination component u_t is generated by one of the following processes:

1. Random level shifts (RLS): $u_t = \Sigma_{t=1}^{T} \delta_{T,t}$, where $\delta_{T,t} = \pi_{T,t}\eta_t$ with $\eta_t \sim i.i.d.\ N(0, \sigma_\eta^2)$ and $\pi_{T,t} \sim i.i.d.\ Bernoulli(p/T, 1)$ for some $p \geq 0$. The components $\pi_{T,t}$, η_t are mutually independent.
2. Deterministic level shifts: $u_t = \Sigma_{i=1}^{B} c_i 1(T_{i-1} < t \leq T_i)$, where B is the (fixed) number of regimes ($B - 1$ is the number of breaks), $0 < |c_i| < \infty$, $1(\cdot)$ is the indicator function, $0 = T_0 < T_1 < \cdots < T_{B-1} < T_B = T$, and $T_i/T \to \tau_i$ with $0 < \tau_1 < \cdots < \tau_{B-1} < 1$.
3. Deterministic trends: $u_t = h(t/T)$, where $h(\cdot)$ is a deterministic non-constant function on $[0, 1]$ that is either Lipschitz continuous or monotone with $h(1) = 0$. This includes all cases for which $h(\cdot)$ is monotonic and bounded because we can simply subtract $h(1)$ from $h(\cdot)$ and add $h(1)$ to c in (47.5) to have the same DGP.
4. Fractional trends: $u_t = O((t + 1)^{\phi - 1/2})$, $u_0 = 0$, $|u_{t+1} - u_t| = O(|u_t|/t)$, where $\phi \in (-1/2, 1/2)$.

Note that the probability of a level shift in the RLS model is sample size dependent. If this were not the case, u_t would have properties similar to that of a random walk. A defining characteristic of the RLS model is that the average number of level shifts p remains constant as the sample size grows. Note that p can be zero so that the assumption nests the no level shift or no contamination case as well. Perron and Qu (2010) considered the asymptotic properties of the periodogram for this type of process contaminating a short-memory process and showed that, for any $k = 1, \ldots, [T/2]$,

$$(k^2/T)E(I_{u,k}) \to (p\sigma_\eta^2)/(4\pi^3),$$

as $T \to \infty$. Mikosch and Stărică (2004) considered the asymptotic properties of the periodogram for a deterministic level shift component when $B = 2$ (one level shift), with the addition of a short-memory component, and showed that $E(I_{u,k}) = O(T/k^2)$. Kunsch (1987) (Lemma 2) considered the asymptotic properties of the periodogram of a short-memory process contaminated by a bounded monotone trend. Qu (2011) (Lemma 1) extended Kunsch's results to the Lipschitz continuous case and showed that $E(I_{u,k}) = O(T/k^2)$. Iacone (2010) discussed the order of the periodogram in the case of a fractional trend and showed that $E(I_{u,k}) = O_p(T/k^2)$.

The common feature of these contaminating processes is that the mean of their periodograms near frequency zero is of order $O(T/k^2)$, or equivalently of order $O(T^{-1}\lambda_k^{-2})$ since $\lambda_k = 2\pi k/T$ (note that the O term could be o since it is possible that $E[(I_{u,k})/(T/k^2)] \to 0$).

Processes with such LFC as additive components are non-stationary so they do not have the traditionally defined spectral density function. Following common practice in such cases, we define their spectral density function to be the expectation of their periodogram. Since the spectral density function of a long-memory process near frequency zero is of order $O(\lambda_k^{-2d})$, in general, the spectral density function of such contaminating components dominates that of a long-memory process at low frequencies and vice-versa at high frequencies. Note that in the representation (47.1), when the process is contaminated by such LFC, we have

$$G_u \equiv G_u(0) = \lim_{T\to\infty} (k^2/T)E(I_{u,k}).$$

Remark 47.1. Definition 47.1 could be replaced by the condition

$$E(I_{u,k}) = G_u(k)(T/k^2)(1 + O(1)),$$

with $G_u(k) \leq B$, where B is a fixed bounded positive constant. Hence, $E(I_{u,k})/(T/k^2)$ need not converge to a constant, it only needs to be bounded as $T \to \infty$. All LFC in Definition 47.1 satisfy this property and all results to be discussed in the following remain valid under this general condition.

Unlike short-memory dynamics or contaminating noise, which cause only finite sample biases to the memory parameter estimator, the bias caused by LFC usually remains asymptotically. To see when this applies, let

$$A_k = (k^2/T)E(I_{u,k}).$$

Then, one can show that

$$\lambda_k^{2d} I_k = \lambda_k^{2d} I_{y,k} + A_k O_p(T^{1-2d}/k^{2-2d}).$$

So, the bias introduced by LFC is of order

$$O_p(m^{-1}T^{1-2d}\sum_{k=1}^{m}(A_k/k^{2-2d})).$$

The following definition is useful.

Definition 47.2. A LFC is said to be non-degenerate if $\lim_{T\to\infty}$ $\{(k^2/T)E(I_{u,k})\} > 0$ for every k. Otherwise, it is said to be degenerate.

An example of a non-degenerate LFC is an RLS model, in which case

$$\lim_{T\to\infty}(k^2/T)E(I_{u,k}) = (p\sigma_\eta^2)/(4\pi^3).$$

An example of a degenerate LFC is a monotone deterministic trend. The bias caused by a non-degenerate LFC remains asymptotically while the bias caused by a degenerate LFC can either remain or vanish asymptotically, with the degree of the (potentially asymptotic or finite sample) bias depending on d and the bandwidth m.

47.5.2 Estimation robust to low-frequency contaminations

For estimation, much of the work focused on providing modified LP or LW estimators to account for low-frequency contaminations. McCloskey and Perron (2013) proposed trimmed LP estimators that have desirable asymptotic and finite sample properties in the presence of low-frequency contaminations, though their method is not robust to large additive noise. It amounts to the standard LP estimator but with a lower bound truncation so that

$$\hat{d} = (2S_T)^{-1}\sum_{j=l}^{m} a_j \log(I_x(w_j)).$$

Conditions on the rate of increase of l and m are provided. The limit distribution remains the same, as stated in (47.3). The main idea is the following. Although both a level shift (or deterministic trend) process and a long-memory process tend to have poles in their periodograms at the zero frequency as the sample size increases, these poles essentially taper off differently. The pole induced by level shifts is steeper and tapers off more quickly than the pole induced by a long-memory process. Hence, by excluding a few frequencies near zero, the low-frequency contaminations have no (or little) effect on the estimate of d. In related work, McCloskey and Hill (2017) considered a trimmed frequency domain quasi-maximum likelihood estimator that can be used to consistently estimate the parameters of a long-memory stochastic volatility model in the presence of low-frequency contamination assuming the signal to be an $ARFIMA(p, d, q)$ process.

Iacone (2010) considered a trimmed local Whittle estimator, though under a more restrictive setting. The idea is the same, namely to exclude the very low-frequency components. Hence, the estimate takes the form

$$\hat{d}_{LW} = \arg\min_{d} \left[\log{(m-l-1)^{-1}} \sum_{j=l}^{m} w_j^{2d} I_{x,T}(w_j) \right. \\ \left. - 2d(m-l-1)^{-1} \sum_{j=l}^{m} \log w_j \right],$$

where $l \leq T/2$. A general treatment was provided by Hou and Perron (2014). Following the work of Hurvich *et al.* (2005), they add a constant term into the spectral density function to account for the noise component. However, they also added a component $G_u(\lambda_k^{-2}/T)$ to account for the LFC so that the modified pseudo-spectral density function is

$$\begin{aligned} f_k \triangleq f_x(w_k) &= G_0 w_k^{-2d} + G_\varepsilon + G_u(w_k^{-2}/T) \\ &= G_0(w_k^{-2d} + (G_\varepsilon/G_0) + (G_u/G_0)(w_k^{-2}/T)) \\ &= G_0(w_k^{-2d} + \theta_\varepsilon + (\theta_u/T)w_k^{-2}) = G_0 g_k, \end{aligned}$$

where, with a slight abuse of notation relabeling $\theta_u = G_u/G_0$,

$$g_k = (w_k^{-2d} + \theta_\varepsilon + (\theta_u/T)w_k^{-2}),$$

and the (approximate) frequency domain QMLF is

$$\varphi(G, d, \theta) = m^{-1} \sum_{k=1}^{m} \varphi_k(G, d, \theta),$$

with $\theta = (\theta_w, \theta_u)'$. Concentrating G out of the QMLF, the estimate of G is

$$\hat{G} = m^{-1} \sum_{k=1}^{m} (I_k/g_k),$$

and the local Whittle QMLE estimator under noise perturbations and low-frequency contaminations is

$$(\hat{d}_m, \hat{\theta}_m) = \arg\min_{(d,\theta)} J_m(d, \theta), \tag{47.7}$$

where

$$J_m(d, \theta) = \log\left(m^{-1} \sum_{k=1}^{m} I_k/g_k\right) + m^{-1} \sum_{k=1}^{m} \log(g_k).$$

Again, this approach is expected to work when d_0 is not too close to zero. When $d_0 = 0$, the process is short-memory. We then have a combination of two additive short-memory processes which cannot be identified separately.

Note that the estimate is robust to strong short-run dynamics even though no corrections are made to account for this feature. As stated above, one could follow the approach of Andrews and Sun (2004) who added a polynomial structure into G_0, i.e., replace G_0 by $G_0 \exp(-p_r(\lambda_j, \theta))$, where $p_r(\lambda_j, \theta) = \Sigma_{s=1}^{r} \theta_s \lambda_j^{2s}$ and $\theta = (\theta_1, \ldots, \theta_r)$. However, Hou and Perron (2014) argued that doing so does not offer any gain in performance when a relatively small value of the bandwidth is used. This feature can be explained as follows. Under strong short-memory dynamics and LFC, the estimator (47.7) constructed with a large bandwidth has substantial bias but very small variance so that the overall MSE is almost entirely due to the bias. When a polynomial component is added, the upward bias is reduced but the variance is increased considerably so that the overall MSE is almost the same or larger. With no LFC, the increased variance is smaller so that the MSE is indeed reduced as reported by Andrews and Sun (2004). At the root of the issue is the fact that both LFC and strong short-memory dynamics cause upward biases in the estimate of the memory parameter. Hence, there is a confounding effect so that the QMLF is flat with respect to the correction factors for strong short-memory dynamics and LFC. Hence, the best way to account for short-memory dynamics and LFC is to use the estimator (47.7) with a small bandwidth.

In all cases, the limit distribution remains the same, as stated in (47.4). Hence, there is no loss in asymptotic efficiency.

Chapter 48

Volatility Models

We mainly deal with conditional heteroskedasticity and stochastic volatility models. This literature is mostly a concern in financial econometrics for the purpose of modelling the volatility of asset returns. However, it is also useful in a variety of other contexts in macroeconomics and other financial applications. A good reference for some of the material in this chapter is the work of Taylor (2011).

A popular method to model volatility in finance is to use the so-called "realized volatility" based on high-frequency data (say, minute by minute or transactions data within a day). For n trading periods, some asset returns r_t, and $\{r_t\}_{t=1}^{n}$ denoting a sequence of continuously compounded returns within a day, whose average is $\bar{r}$, an estimate of the realized volatility is given by

$$s = \left(\sum_{t=1}^{n} (r_t - \bar{r})^2 \right)^{1/2}.$$

In this chapter, we do not deal with such estimates. They involve high-frequency data, which entail a host of issues that are specific to the pricing of asset returns; for example, taking care of the bid-ask spread or what to do with issues related to the opening of the market often characterized by a sudden jump due to the arrival of information overnight and the lack of trading.

An alternative measure used in finance is the so-called "implied volatility". It is the level of volatility consistent with an option price (or a set of option prices) given some spot prices for the assets and a theoretical model, such as that of Black and Scholes (1973). In practice, the Black–Scholes formula is often inverted to calculate implied volatility. However, there is inconsistency involved since the Black–Scholes framework assumes a constant volatility. The implied volatility will be different from the realized volatility if the volatility risk is priced. Empirical estimates suggest that the implied volatility is often higher.

In this chapter, we deal with common volatility models applicable using standard time-series data sampled at a daily or lower frequency. Oftentimes, it is useful to think about the linear model

$$y_t = \beta x_t + u_t, \quad (t = 1, \dots, T),$$

and the issue is to model the time-series dependence in the variance of u_t. Of course, everything will apply to more general nonlinear models. Henceforth, the object of interest is the volatility structure of y_t, conditional on x_t. When applied to asset returns, think of u_t as being the demeaned returns, i.e., y_t is the returns series and x_t is simply a constant. We refer to y_t as the series of interest for which our aim is to model its volatility. This could be the dependent variable or the errors.

The issue of why volatility may change over time is largely still an open debate; see the work of Schwert (1989b) for some discussion. Qu and Perron (2013) suggested that one should look at low-frequency events for explanations, whether they be macroeconomic, financial, or political.

48.1 Some definitions

We start with some basic definitions to set the stage for subsequent discussions. Two types of models are most often used in theoretical and applied work: (a) conditional heteroskedasticity and (b) stochastic volatility.

Definition 48.1 (Conditional Volatility). The conditional volatility of y_t is the standard deviation of y_t conditional on known information such as the history of past errors and data. The leading example is the *ARCH* model introduced by Engle (1982). The simplest case is the $ARCH(1)$ model specified by

$$y_t = \mu + h_t^{1/2}\varepsilon_t, \quad \varepsilon_t \sim i.i.d.\ N(0,1),$$

$$h_t = \omega + \alpha(y_{t-1} - \mu)^2.$$

Then, the conditional volatility of y_t is simply $h_t^{1/2}$.

Definition 48.2 (Stochastic Volatility). Stochastic volatility models specify the volatility as a latent process. A simple standard stochastic volatility model is

$$y_t = \mu + \exp(h_t/2)\,\varepsilon_t,$$

$$h_t = \omega + \rho h_{t-1} + \eta_t,$$

$$\varepsilon_t \sim i.i.d.\ N(0,1),$$

$$\eta_t \sim i.i.d.\ N(0,\sigma_\eta^2),$$

with η_t independent of ε_s for all t, s.

Remark 48.1. In both cases, μ can be replaced by some parametric specification, e.g., βx_t in the linear case, or some nonlinear counterpart. The results to be discussed remain the same with some obvious modifications, provided we condition on the covariates x_t.

48.2 The family of ARCH-type models

The simplest example of an *ARCH* process is the $ARCH(1)$ specification presented by Engle (1982):

$$y_t = \mu + h_t^{1/2}\varepsilon_t, \quad \varepsilon_t \sim i.i.d.\ N(0,1),$$

and

$$h_t = \omega + \alpha(y_{t-1} - \mu)^2. \tag{48.1}$$

The volatility parameters are $\omega > 0$ and $\alpha \geq 0$. Thus, the volatility in period t depends solely on the previous observation. Hence, it is deterministic (i.e., non-stochastic) conditional on the data. The error at time t is

$$e_t = y_t - \mu,$$

and the forecast error when predicting the squared errors is

$$v_t = e_t^2 - E\left[e_t^2 | y_{t-1}, y_{t-2}, \ldots\right] = e_t^2 - h_t.$$

Replacing h_t in (48.1) by $e_t^2 - v_t$ gives

$$e_t^2 = \omega + \alpha e_{t-1}^2 + v_t,$$

where v_t is uncorrelated with e_{t-1}^2. Hence, the squared errors follow an $AR(1)$ process. Note that $\mathrm{Var}\left(e_t^2\right) < \infty$ requires $3\alpha^2 < 1$ (given the normality assumption). The $ARCH(1)$ model is covariance stationary when $\alpha < 1$, in which case the squared returns have autocorrelations $\rho_\tau = \alpha^\tau$. This geometric rate of decay is often too fast in many applications (e.g., asset returns). It also imposes quite stringent conditions about skewness and kurtosis. Hence, a huge literature has sought to expand the simple $ARCH(1)$ model to allow more flexibility in modeling various time series. The extent of the literature and the various acronyms proposed is simply mind-boggling, see the work of Bollerslev (2010) for an extensive description. For a review of applications to finance, see the work of Bollerslev *et al.* (1992) and, for a more technical treatment, see the work of Bollerslev *et al.* (1994).

Since an $ARCH(1)$ model implies an $AR(1)$ representation for the squared errors, a natural starting point is to have a model that implies an $ARMA$ structure. This is provided by the class of $GARCH$ models introduced in the work of Bollerslev (1986).

48.3 GARCH models

We start with the simplest $GARCH(1,1)$ model specified by

$$y_t = \mu + h_t^{1/2}\varepsilon_t, \quad \varepsilon_t \sim i.i.d.\ N(0,1),$$

and

$$h_t = \omega + \alpha(y_{t-1} - \mu)^2 + \beta h_{t-1}, \tag{48.2}$$

where we impose the conditions $\omega > 0$, $\alpha \geq 0$, and $\beta \geq 0$ to ensure a non-negative variance. The process is covariance stationary if $\alpha + \beta < 1$, in which case the process can be inverted to obtain the following $ARCH(\infty)$ representation:

$$\begin{aligned} h_t = {} & \frac{\omega}{1-\beta} + \alpha(y_{t-1} - \mu)^2 + \alpha\beta(y_{t-2} - \mu)^2 \\ & + \alpha\beta^2(y_{t-3} - \mu)^2 + \alpha\beta^3(y_{t-4} - \mu)^2 + \cdots . \end{aligned} \tag{48.3}$$

Hence, the conditional variance at period t is a linear function of the past squared errors $(y_{t-\tau} - \mu)^2$. The weights decay exponentially depending on β^τ. The model is symmetric in the sense that the signs of the past returns do not directly affect volatility, a feature of importance that we discuss further in the following.

The representation (48.3) makes clear that what generates persistence is the component associated with β. In other words, $ARCH(1)$ processes have very little persistence even for large values of α. On the other hand, moderate values of β in a $GARCH(1,1)$ model generate substantial persistence.

As an example of the implications, consider a testing procedure whose limit distribution depends on the nature of the conditional heteroskedasticity and for which a correction needs to be applied to obtain a pivotal limit distribution. One example is the work of Perron *et al.* (2020) who considered, among other things, testing for changes in variance allowing for changes in regression coefficients. Under the null hypothesis of no change in variance, the limit distribution depends on the nature of the conditional heteroskedasticity. If the process is an $ARCH(1)$, the impact on the size of the test is negligible, i.e., the persistence is so small that there is nothing to correct in practice. However, with a $GARCH(1,1)$ process, the size distortions (without corrections) are substantial. Hence, to evaluate whether the correction built in the test works well, it is much more informative to adopt a $GARCH(1,1)$ process rather than an $ARCH(1)$. Fortunately, the correction proposed by Perron *et al.* (2020) yields tests with no (or very minor) size distortions.

We next consider more technical issues about the properties of $GARCH(1,1)$ processes. The derivations are left as exercises. For the moments, we have:

1. $E(y_t) = \mu$;
2. $\sigma^2 = \text{Var}\,(y_t) = E\,(y_t - \mu)^2 = E(h_t)E(\varepsilon_t^2) = E(h_t) = \omega/(1 - \alpha - \beta)$. Hence, the process is unconditionally homoskedastic. The conditional variance equation (48.2) can be rewritten as

$$h_t = (1 - \alpha - \beta)\,\sigma^2 + \alpha(y_{t-1} - \mu)^2 + \beta h_{t-1}.$$

3. The unconditional fourth-order moment is finite if and only if

$$2\alpha^2 + (\alpha + \beta)^2 < 1,$$

and then

$$E(y_t - \mu)^4 = E(h_t^2)E(\varepsilon_t^4) = 3E(h_t^2).$$

Let $e_t = y_t - \mu$ so that $e_t = h_t^{1/2}\varepsilon_t$, then

$$\begin{aligned} h_t &= \omega + \alpha e_{t-1}^2 + \beta h_{t-1} \\ &= \omega + \alpha(h_{t-1}^{1/2}\varepsilon_{t-1})^2 + \beta h_{t-1} \\ &= \omega + (\alpha\varepsilon_{t-1}^2 + \beta)h_{t-1}. \end{aligned}$$

This leads to the following result for the kurtosis (kur):

$$kur(y_t) = \frac{3E(h_t^2)}{\sigma^4} = 3\left[\frac{1 - (\alpha + \beta)^2}{1 - 2\alpha^2 - (\alpha + \beta)^2}\right] > 3.$$

Hence, the kurtosis is higher than that for the normal distribution, which is a consequence of the unconditional distribution being a mixture of normals. By this, we mean that $y_t \sim N(\mu, h_t)$ with h_t random.

For the autocorrelations, let $e_t = y_t - \mu$ and $s_t = e_t^2 = h_t\varepsilon_t^2$. The autocorrelations of s_t are defined when the kurtosis is finite.

Let v_t be the forecast error when predicting squared errors:

$$v_t = e_t^2 - h_t.$$

Then,

$$s_t = \omega + (\alpha + \beta)\, s_{t-1} + v_t - \beta v_{t-1}, \tag{48.4}$$

which is an $ARMA(1,1)$ process. Note that the autocorrelation at delay τ of the process (48.4) is

$$\mathrm{Cor}\,(s_t, s_{t+\tau}) = C(\alpha+\beta)\,(\alpha+\beta)^{\tau}\,,$$
$$C(\alpha+\beta) = \frac{\alpha\left(1-\alpha\beta-\beta^2\right)}{(\alpha+\beta)\,(1-2\alpha\beta-\beta^2)}.$$

Thus, the autocorrelations of the squared errors decrease exponentially, depending on $(\alpha+\beta)^{\tau}$. In practice, when applied to daily stock returns, the estimates of β are usually very close to 1 indicating a (nearly) non-stationary process.

Remark 48.2. The $GARCH(1,1)$ model is not a simple extension of the $ARCH(1)$ like the $ARMA(1,1)$ is an extension of the $AR(1)$. The two have very different persistence. In fact, an $ARCH(1)$ has almost no persistence, somewhat like the $AR(1)$, but a $GARCH(1,1)$ has substantial persistence, almost similar to a long-memory process. To illustrate this feature, we estimated parameter values using models fitted to the daily SP500 stock returns from 2010 to 2021. The sample size is $T = 2000$. The fitted $ARCH(1)$ process has value $\alpha = 0.646$. The $GARCH(1,1)$ process has values $\alpha = 0.212$ and $\beta = 0.751$. Both are in the stationary region and in both cases the fitted constant is 0.005. Figure 48.1 presents the autocorrelation function of the two processes. It is clear that the $GARCH(1,1)$ implies much higher persistence with autocorrelations that decay very slowly. On the other hand, the $ARCH(1)$ process has autocorrelations that decay very fast, much like an $AR(1)$. The results remain the same, qualitatively if we increase the value of the parameter α; what drives the substantial correlation is the value β.

We now turn to forecasts. First, note that a $GARCH(1,1)$ specification implies that the level y_t is not predictable, while the variance

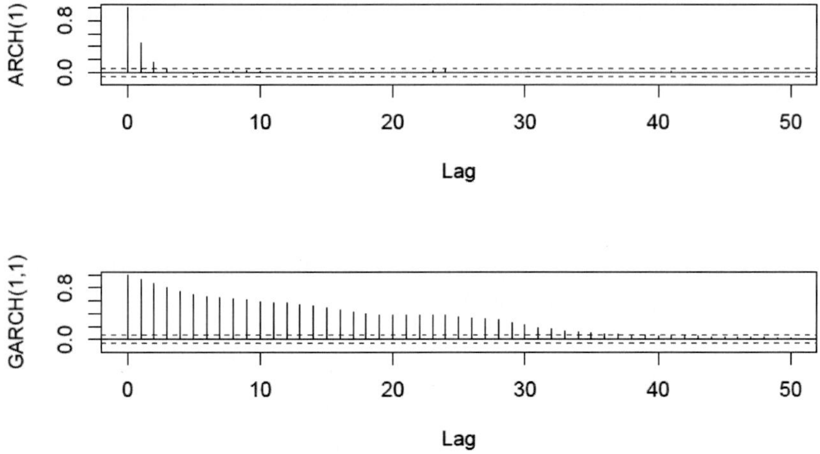

Figure 48.1. Autocorrelation function of $ARCH(1)$ and $GARCH(1,1)$ processes. See Remark 48.2 for details.

of y_t is. The best predictor for the variance is given by

$$\text{Var}(y_{t+1}|y_t, y_{t-1}, \ldots) = E(s_{t+1}|y_t, y_{t-1}, \ldots) = h_{t+1}$$

and

$$\begin{aligned}\text{Var}(y_{t+2}|y_t, y_{t-1}, \ldots) &= E\left(s_{t+2}|y_t, y_{t-1}, \ldots\right)\\ &= E\left(h_{t+2}|y_t, y_{t-1}, \ldots\right)\\ &= \sigma^2 + (\alpha+\beta)\left(h_{t+1} - \sigma^2\right).\end{aligned}$$

In general, for all $n \geq 1$,

$$\text{Var}(y_{t+n}|y_t, y_{t-1}, \ldots) = \sigma^2 + (\alpha+\beta)^{n-1}\left(h_{t+1} - \sigma^2\right).$$

Since returns are conditionally uncorrelated, the conditional variance for the n-period sum of y_t (think about the variance of n-period returns) is

$$\text{Var}(y_{t+1} + \cdots + y_{t+n}|y_t, y_{t-1}, \ldots) = n\sigma^2 + \frac{1-(\alpha+\beta)^n}{1-\alpha-\beta}\left(h_{t+1} - \sigma^2\right).$$

To estimate the parameters, one applies a maximum likelihood procedure. The likelihood function can be decomposed as (see Section 15.9)

$$\mathcal{L}(\theta) = f(y_1;\theta)\, f(y_2|y_1;\theta)\, f(y_3|y_2,y_1;\theta)\cdots f(y_T|y_{T-1},\ldots,y_1;\theta).$$

Taking the logarithm,

$$\begin{aligned}\log \mathcal{L}(\theta) &= \sum_{t=1}^{T} \log f(y_t|y_{t-1};\theta),\\ &= \sum_{t=1}^{T}\left[(-1/2)\log(2\pi) - (1/2)\log h_t - (y_t-\mu)^2/2h_t\right]\\ &= (-1/2)\left[T\log(2\pi) + \sum_{t=1}^{T}\log h_t + \varepsilon_t^2\right],\end{aligned}$$

which can be maximized numerically.

Remark 48.3. The $ARCH(1)$ and $GARCH(1,1)$ processes can easily be extended to $ARCH(p)$ and $GARCH(p,q)$ processes just as for the class of $ARMA$ processes for the level of the series. The main features are similar with more or less obvious modifications. Hence, we skip detailed descriptions. In any event, it is often found that a $GARCH(1,1)$ specification is appropriate and that adding more lags yields little in-sample fit or forecast improvements. For example, Hansen and Lunde (2005) compared 330 $ARCH$ type models (some to be discussed in the following and many other extensions) in their ability to describe the conditional variance (mostly using a forecast accuracy criterion) for some specific asset returns and exchange rates. They find no evidence that a simple $GARCH(1,1)$ model can be outperformed by more sophisticated versions.

48.3.1 Some extensions

In this section, we briefly describe some extensions of the $ARCH$ and $GARCH$-type processes, motivated by various features encountered when dealing with actual time series of data, often in finance with asset returns.

The t-GARCH(1, 1). This extension is motivated by the fact that the errors from a normally distributed $GARCH(1,1)$ model still have kurtosis much greater than 3. It also allows more flexibility in accounting for fat-tail distributions (e.g., induced by outliers). The only change is in the specification of the distribution of the errors, which is replaced by

$$\varepsilon_t \sim i.i.d.\ t_v,$$

where t_v stands for the t distribution with v degrees of freedom. Then, v becomes an additional parameter to be estimated via MLE. The rest remains the same. The fitted volatility from a t-$GARCH(1,1)$ is usually more persistent than that from a $GARCH(1,1)$ model with normal errors.

ARCH-M models. This extension introduces the conditional standard deviation as a component of the mean of the level of the series. This is often used to model weak correlation in asset returns. Hence, we have instead of μ

$$\mu_t = \xi + \lambda h_t^{1/2}.$$

This is an example of the $ARCH$-in-mean model of Engle *et al.* (1987). Any model that represents μ_t as a function of h_t is called an $ARCH$-M model.

Asymmetric *GARCH* models. Researchers beginning with Black (1976) have found a negative correlation between current asset returns and future returns volatility, i.e., volatility tends to rise in response to "bad news" (excess returns lower than expected) and to fall in response to "good news" (excess returns higher than expected). $GARCH$ models, however, assume that only the magnitude and not the sign of unanticipated excess returns determines the features of volatility. Hence, modeling may be improved by adopting a model that explicitly accounts for this asymmetry. One such model is the popular $EGARCH$ proposed by Nelson (1991). It takes the form

$$\log h_t = \mu + \beta\left(\log h_{t-1} - \mu\right) + g\left(\varepsilon_t\right),$$
$$g\left(\varepsilon_t\right) = v + \gamma\left(\left|\varepsilon_t\right| - E\left|\varepsilon_t\right|\right).$$

Another advantage of the $EGARCH$ model is that it guarantees a non-negative estimate of h_t by construction. $GARCH$ models impose parameter restrictions that are sometimes violated by estimated coefficients and that may unduly restrict the dynamics of the conditional variance process. These non-negativity constraints can create difficulties in estimating $GARCH$ models. Also, interpreting whether shocks to conditional variance "persist" or not is difficult in $GARCH$ models because the usual norms measuring persistence often do not agree.

Another class of asymmetric model is the GJR-$GARCH$ proposed by Glosten *et al.* (1993). The specification for h_t is given by

$$h_t = \omega + \alpha_1 e_{t-1}^2 + \alpha_2 S_{t-1} e_{t-1}^2 + \beta h_{t-1},$$

where $S_{t-1} = 1$ when the return is below its conditional expectation, and 0 otherwise.

Long-memory GARCH models. The preceding $GARCH$-type models all have short memory, i.e., the autocorrelations of the squared returns decay exponentially. In practice, it is often the case that volatility exhibits long memory (hyperbolic rate of decay for the autocorrelations) or even that shocks may be persistent. As discussed above, measures of persistence can be problematic when adopting a $GARCH$ model. Hence, we describe the extensions pertaining to the class of $EGARCH$ models, labeled $FIEGARCH(1, d, 1)$, for long-memory fractionally integrated $EGARCH(1, 1)$ model with long-memory parameter d. These mimic the class of $ARFIMA$ models described in Chapter 47. The conditional variance equation is given by

$$\begin{aligned} \log h_t &= \mu + (1 - \alpha L)^{-1} (1 - L)^{-d} (1 + \psi L) g(\varepsilon_t) \\ g(\varepsilon_t) &= \upsilon + \gamma (|\varepsilon_t| - E|\varepsilon_t|), \end{aligned}$$

where the fractional differencing operator is such that

$$(1 - L)^d = 1 - dL + \frac{d(d-1)}{2!} L^2 - \frac{d(d-1)(d-2)}{3!} L^3 + \cdots .$$

As discussed in Chapter 47, y_t is covariance stationary if $0 \leq d < 1/2$. The unconditional variance is infinite if $d > 1/2$. The weights in the expansion of $(1-L)^d$ decrease slowly. Note that

$$(1-L)^d = 1 - \sum_{j=1}^{\infty} a_j L^j,$$

$$a_1 = d,$$

$$a_j = j^{-1}(j-d-1)a_{j-1},$$

which implies

$$a_j \propto j^{d-1}.$$

For most asset returns, the empirical studies using equity indices usually report estimates of d in the range $(1/2, 1)$, which would suggest a misspecification. Realized volatility estimates suggest values of d less than 0.5 for the volatility of both exchange rates and equity indices. More research is needed to obtain a coherent picture, though the random level shift model discussed in Chapter 47 is able to resolve this problem, at least to some extent.

48.4 Stochastic volatility models

We now consider stochastic volatility models. The main difference with the $GARCH$-type models is that the volatility is modeled as a latent process. A common specification is the following:

$$\begin{aligned} y_t &= \mu + \sigma_t \varepsilon_t, \\ \log \sigma_t &= \omega + \rho \log \sigma_{t-1} + \eta_t, \\ \varepsilon_t &\sim i.i.d.\ N(0,1), \\ \eta_t &\sim i.i.d.\ N(0, \sigma_\eta^2), \end{aligned} \tag{48.5}$$

where ε_t and η_s are mutually independent for all t,s. The method of estimation is based on MLE. The likelihood function is the product of the conditional densities $f(y_t|y_{t-1},\ldots)$, but tractable expressions for these densities are not available because the process is only partially Gaussian. More specifically, we have

$$L(y_1, \ldots, y_T|\theta) = \int_{\sigma_1} \int_{\sigma_2} \cdots \int_{\sigma_T} f(y_1, \ldots, y_T|\sigma_1, \ldots, \sigma_T)$$
$$\times f(\sigma_1, \ldots, \sigma_T|\theta) d\sigma_1, \ldots, d\sigma_T.$$

Both terms inside the integral can be evaluated with ease, but the exact value of the integral cannot be evaluated analytically. However, it can be evaluated using either numerical methods, see the work of Fridman and Harris (1998), or Monte Carlo methods, see the works of Danielsson (1994) and Sandmann and Koopman (1998). An alternative method of estimation is to adopt a Bayesian approach, which requires the use of Monte Carlo Markov Chain (MCMC) techniques; see the work of Jacquier and Rossi (1994) and Chapter 52.

An alternative is to use the simulated maximum likelihood method. The basic idea is the following. Start by taking the logarithm of the square of (48.5) so that

$$\log (y_t - \mu)^2 = \log \sigma_t^2 + \log \varepsilon_t^2,$$
$$\log \sigma_t = \omega + \rho \log \sigma_{t-1} + \eta_t.$$

Or, equivalently, in state-space form (see Chapter 39),

$$x_t = c + 2h_t + v_t,$$
$$h_t = \omega + \rho h_{t-1} + \eta_t,$$

where $c = E(\log \varepsilon_t^2)$. The transition equation is Gaussian but the measurement equation is not because v_t is a re-centered log chi-square random variable. Let $Y_t = \{y_t, y_{t-1}, \ldots\}$ and collect all the parameters in the vector θ. Then,

$$\log L(y_1, \ldots, y_T|\theta) = \sum_{t=1}^{T} \log f\,(y_t|Y_{t-1}; \theta),$$

where

$$\begin{aligned} f\left(y_t|Y_{t-1};\theta\right) &= \iint f\left(y_t, h_t, h_{t-1}|Y_{t-1};\theta\right) dh_t dh_{t-1} \\ &= \iint f\left(y_t|h_t;\theta\right) f(h_t|h_{t-1};\theta) f(h_{t-1}|Y_{t-1};\theta) dh_t dh_{t-1}. \end{aligned}$$

Thus, $f\left(y_t|Y_{t-1};\theta\right)$ can be estimated as follows:

1. Sample from $f(h_{t-1}|Y_{t-1};\theta)$ to obtain $f(h_{t-1}^{(s)}|Y_{t-1};\theta)$.
2. Sample from $f(h_t|h_{t-1}^{(s)};\theta)$ to obtain $f(h_t^{(s)}|h_{t-1}^{(s)};\theta)$.
3. Calculate $f(y_t|h_t^{(s)};\theta)$.
4. Repeat steps 1–3 S times, and compute

$$\hat{f}\left(y_t|Y_{t-1};\theta\right) = S^{-1}\sum_{s=1}^{S} f(y_t, |h_t^{(s)};\theta).$$

To obtain $\hat{f}\left(y_t|Y_{t-1};\theta\right)$ for $t = 2, \ldots, T$, we need to be able to sample sequentially from $f(h_{t-1}|Y_{t-1};\theta)$. This is feasible since $f(h_t|Y_t;\theta)$ is related to $f(h_{t-1}|Y_{t-1};\theta)$ via

$$f(h_t|Y_t;\theta) = \frac{f(y_t|h_t;\theta)}{f(y_t|Y_{t-1};\theta)} f(h_t|Y_{t-1};\theta) \tag{48.6}$$

and

$$\begin{aligned} f(h_t|Y_{t-1};\theta) &= \int f(h_t, h_{t-1}|Y_{t-1};\theta) dh_{t-1} \\ &= \int f(h_{t-1}|Y_{t-1};\theta) f(h_t|h_{t-1};\theta) dh_{t-1}. \end{aligned} \tag{48.7}$$

The equation (48.6) implies that to sample from $f(h_t|Y_t;\theta)$ we can sample from $f(h_t|Y_{t-1};\theta)$ and re-weight the draws by $f(y_t|h_t;\theta)/f(y_t|Y_{t-1};\theta)$. Equation (48.7) implies that the latter can be obtained by sampling from $f(h_{t-1}|Y_{t-1};\theta)$ followed by $f(h_t|h_{t-1};\theta)$. The currently used methods are largely refinements, in various dimensions, of the above procedure to improve computational efficiency.

48.5 Exercises

Exercise 48.1 ($ARCH(1)$ stochastic process). In conventional econometric models, the variance of the disturbance term is assumed to be constant. However, many economic time series exhibit periods of unusually large volatility followed by periods of relative tranquility. In such circumstances, the assumption of a constant variance is inappropriate. Consider the following:

$$\epsilon_t = u_t h_t^{1/2},$$
$$h_t = \alpha_0 + \alpha_1 \epsilon_{t-1}^2,$$
$$u_t \sim N(0,1), \quad \text{independent of } \epsilon_{t-1}.$$

(a) Compute the unconditional expectation, the unconditional variance, and the autocovariances of ϵ_t. For which values of α_0 and α_1 is ϵ_t white noise? Now, compute the conditional mean of ϵ_t, $E(\epsilon_t|\epsilon_{t-1}, \epsilon_{t-2}, \ldots)$, and its conditional variance. Do we have to restrict further the values of α_0 and α_1? (b) Assume you are interested in the following stationary $ARMA$ model:

$$y_t = a_0 + a_1 y_{t-1} + \epsilon_t.$$

Compute the unconditional mean and variance of y_t. (c) Now, consider

$$x_t = \epsilon_t^2 - E(\epsilon_t^2).$$

Is x_t covariance stationary? If so, compute the autocovariance function.

Chapter 49

Structural Change

In this chapter, we discuss issues related to estimation and inference about the break dates in a linear regression framework. The emphasis is on describing methods that are most useful in applied econometrics, explaining the relevance of the conditions imposed, and explaining the main steps used depending on the nature of the data. For useful reviews, see the works of Perron (2006) and Casini and Perron (2019), on which this chapter is mostly based. We focus on methods relevant to econometrics. Readers interested in a more theoretical perspective with a statistical approach can consult the work of Csörgö and Horváth (1997).

Following the works of Bai (1997b) and Bai and Perron (1998), the main framework of analysis can be described by the following multiple linear regression with m breaks (or $m+1$ regimes):

$$y_t = x_t'\beta + z_t'\delta_j + u_t, \quad t = T_{j-1}+1, \ldots, T_j, \tag{49.1}$$

for $j = 1, \ldots, m+1$. In this model, y_t is the observed dependent variable at time t; both x_t ($p \times 1$) and z_t ($q \times 1$) are vectors of covariates and β and δ_j ($j = 1, \ldots, m+1$) are the corresponding vectors of coefficients; u_t is the disturbance at time t. The indices $(T_1, \ldots, T_m)$, or the break points, are explicitly treated as unknown with the convention that $T_0 = 0$ and $T_{m+1} = T$. The purpose is to estimate the unknown regression coefficients together with the break points when T observations on (y_t, x_t, z_t) are available.

This is a partial structural change model since the parameter vector β is not subject to shifts. When $p = 0$, we obtain a pure structural change model where all the model's coefficients are subject to change. Note that using a partial structural change model where only some coefficients are allowed to change can be beneficial both in terms of obtaining more precise estimates and also in having more powerful tests. The multiple linear regression system (49.1) may be expressed in matrix form as

$$Y = X\beta + \bar{Z}\delta + U,$$

where $Y = (y_1, \ldots, y_T)', X = (x_1, \ldots, x_T)'$, $U = (u_1, \ldots, u_T)'$, $\delta = (\delta_1', \ldots, \delta_{m+1}')'$, and $\bar{Z}$ is the matrix which diagonally partitions Z at $(T_1, \ldots, T_m)$, i.e., $\bar{Z} = \text{diag}(Z_1, \ldots, Z_{m+1})$ with $Z_i = (z_{T_{i-1}+1}, \ldots, z_{T_i})'$. We denote the true value of a parameter with a 0 superscript. In particular, $\delta^0 = (\delta_1^{0'}, \ldots, \delta_{m+1}^{0'})'$ and $(T_1^0, \ldots, T_m^0)$ are used to denote, respectively, the true values of the parameters δ and the true break points. The matrix $\bar{Z}^0$ is the one which diagonally partitions Z at $(T_1^0, \ldots, T_m^0)$. Hence, the data-generating process is assumed to be

$$Y = X\beta^0 + \bar{Z}^0\delta^0 + U. \tag{49.2}$$

49.1 Estimation of the break dates

The method of estimation considered is based on the least-squares principle (or MLE with normal *i.i.d.* errors). For each m-partition $(T_1, \ldots, T_m)$, the least-squares estimates of β and δ_j are obtained by minimizing the sum of squared residuals

$$(Y - X\beta - \bar{Z}\delta)'(Y - X\beta - \bar{Z}\delta) = \sum_{i=1}^{m+1} \sum_{t=T_{i-1}+1}^{T_i} [y_t - x_t'\beta - z_t'\delta_i]^2.$$

Let $\hat{\beta}(\{T_j\})$ and $\hat{\delta}(\{T_j\})$ denote the estimates based on the m-partition $(T_1, \ldots, T_m)$ denoted $\{T_j\}$. Substituting these in the objective function and denoting the resulting sum of squared residuals as $S_T(T_1, \ldots, T_m)$, the estimated break points $(\hat{T}_1, \ldots, \hat{T}_m)$ are

$$(\hat{T}_1, \ldots, \hat{T}_m) = \underset{(T_1,\ldots,T_m)}{\text{argmin}}\ S_T(T_1, \ldots, T_m), \tag{49.3}$$

where the minimization is taken over some set of admissible partitions (see the following). Thus, the break-point estimators are global minimizers of the objective function. The regression parameter estimates are the estimates associated with the m-partition $\{\hat{T}_j\}$, i.e., $\hat{\beta} = \hat{\beta}(\{\hat{T}_j\})$, $\hat{\delta} = \hat{\delta}(\{\hat{T}_j\})$.

This framework includes many contributions made in the literature as special cases depending on the assumptions imposed; e.g., single change and changes in the mean of a stationary process. However, the fact that the method of estimation is based on the least-squares principle implies that, even if changes in the variance of u_t are allowed, provided they occur at the same dates as the breaks in the parameters of the regression, such changes are not exploited to increase the precision of the break date estimators. This is due to the fact that the least-squares method imposes equal weights on all errors. Allowing different weights, as needed when accounting for changes in variance, requires adopting a quasi-likelihood framework, see Section 49.6.10.

49.1.1 Allowing for restrictions on the parameters

Perron and Qu (2006) approached issues related to multiple structural changes in a broader framework whereby arbitrary linear restrictions on the parameters of the conditional mean can be imposed in the estimation. The class of models considered is

$$y = \bar{Z}\delta + u,$$

where $R\delta = r$, with R a k by $(m+1)q$ matrix with rank k, and r a k dimensional vector of constants. This is a useful generalization since it permits a wider class of models of practical interests; for example, a model which specifies a number of states less than the number of regimes (with two states, the coefficients would be the same in odd and even regimes). Or it could be the case that the value of the parameters in a specific segment is known. Also, a subset of coefficients may be allowed to change over only a limited number of regimes.

Perron and Qu (2006) showed that the same consistency and rate of convergence results hold. Moreover, an interesting result is that the limit distribution (discussed in Section 49.2.2) of the estimates of the break dates is unaffected by the imposition of valid restrictions. But the main advantage of imposing restrictions is that much more powerful tests are possible.

49.1.2 Method to compute global minimizers

To estimate models with multiple breaks, what are needed are global minimizers of the objective function (49.3). A standard grid search procedure would require least squares operations of order $O(T^m)$ and become prohibitive when the number of breaks is greater than 2, even for relatively small samples. Bai and Perron (2003a) discussed a method based on a dynamic programming algorithm that is very efficient. Indeed, the additional computing time needed to estimate more than two break dates is marginal compared to the time needed to estimate a two-break model. The method is indeed very fast since it requires only the inversion of matrices of order T, the rest is simply updating formulae and a dynamic programming algorithm. The basis of the method, for specialized cases, was considered by Guthery (1974), Bellman and Roth (1969), and Fisher (1958). An early comprehensive treatment was also presented in the work of Hawkins (1976).

Consider the case of a pure structural change model. The basic idea of the approach becomes fairly intuitive once it is realized that, with a sample of size T, the total number of possible segments is at most $T(T+1)/2$ and is therefore of order $O(T^2)$. One then needs a method to select which combination of segments (i.e., which partition of the sample) yields a minimal value of the objective function. This is achieved efficiently using a dynamic programming algorithm. For models with restrictions (including the partial structural change model), an iterative procedure is available, which in most cases requires very few iterations (see Bai and Perron, 2003a; Perron and Qu, 2006). Hence, even with large samples, the computing cost to estimate models with multiple structural changes should be considered minimal.

The Triangular Matrix of Sums of Squared Residuals. Figure 49.1 presents the possible segments for the special case with $T = 25$ and $m = 2$ where the vertical axis represents the initial date of a segment and the horizontal axis the ending date. Each entry represents an estimated sum of squared residuals corresponding to

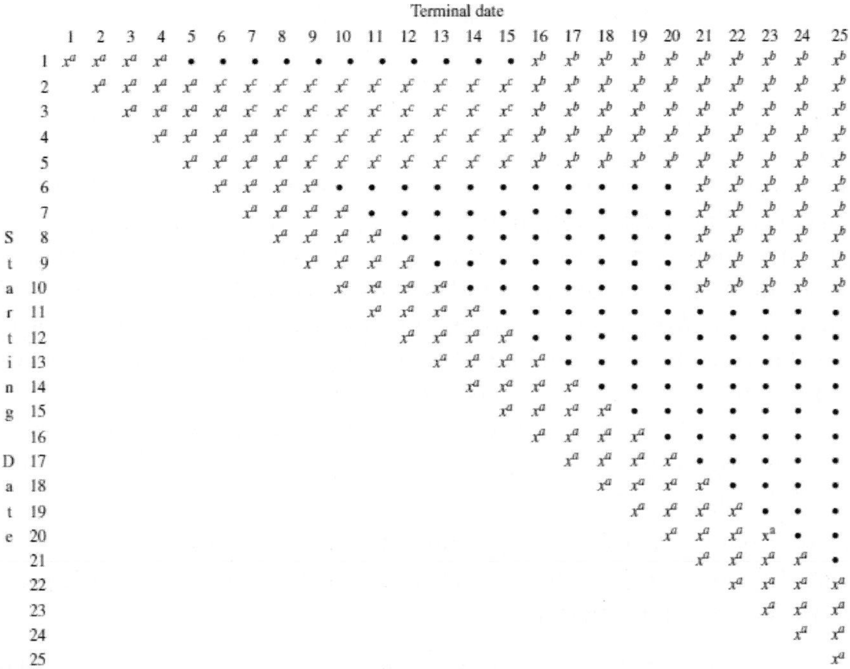

Figure 49.1. Example of the triangular matrix of sums of squared residuals with $T = 25$, $h = 5$, and $m = 2$. The row number indicates the initial date of a segment while the horizontal number indicates the terminal date. For example, the entry (4,10) indicates a segment that starts at date 4 and ends at date 10, hence having 7 observations; x^a indicates a segment not considered since it must be at least of length 5; x^b indicates a segment not considered since otherwise there would be no place for 3 segments of length 5; x^c indicates a segment not considered since otherwise there would be no place for a segment of length 5 prior to it. A $\bullet$ indicates an admissible segment.

Source: Bai and Perron (2003a). Reproduced with permission from Wiley.

the associated segment. The global sum of squared residuals for any m-partition $(T_1, \ldots, T_m)$ and for any value of m must necessarily be a particular linear combination of these $T(T+1)/2$ sums of squared residuals. The estimates of the break dates, the m-partition $(\hat{T}_1, \ldots, \hat{T}_m)$, correspond to this linear combination with a minimal value. The dynamic programming algorithm can be seen as an efficient way to compare possible combinations (corresponding to different m-partitions) to achieve a minimum global sum of squared residuals.

It is useful to note that, in practice, less than $T(T+1)/2$ segments are permissible. First, some minimum distance between each break is usually imposed, especially when considering testing. Let this minimum distance be denoted by h, i.e., each segment contains at least h ($\geq q$) observations. This implies a reduction in the number of segments to be considered. Other reductions are possible. The largest segment must still be short enough to allow m other segments before or after. For example, when the segment starts at a date between 1 and h, the maximal length of this segment is $T - hm$ when m breaks are allowed (i.e., $m+1$ regimes). We therefore need to evaluate the sum of squared residuals for segments starting at dates $i = \ell h + 1, \ldots, (\ell+1)h$ and ending at dates $j = h + i - 1, \ldots, T - (m-\ell)h$, for $\ell = 1, \ldots, m-1$, as well as starting at dates $i = hm + 1, \ldots, T - h + 1$ and ending at dates $j = h + i - 1, \ldots, T$.

The Case of a Pure Structural Change Model. To begin, we consider the case of a pure structural change model, i.e., with $p = 0$ and the regression model:

$$Y = \bar{Z}\delta + U. \tag{49.4}$$

In such a case, the computation of the estimates $\hat{\delta}$, $\hat{u}_t$ and $S_T(T_1, \ldots, T_m)$ can be done applying OLS segment by segment without constraints among them. The computation of the triangular matrix of sums of squared residuals can be achieved using standard updating formulae to calculate recursive residuals; see Section 4.9. Indeed, all the relevant information can be calculated from $T-hm+1$ sets of recursive residuals. Let $v(i,j)$ be the recursive residual at time j obtained using a sample that starts at date i, and let $\text{SSR}(i,j)$ be the sum of squared residuals obtained by applying least squares to a segment that starts at date i and ends at date j. We have the following recursive relation (e.g., Brown *et al.*, 1975):

$$\text{SSR}(i,j) = \text{SSR}(i,j-1) + v(i,j)^2.$$

All the relevant information is contained in the values $\text{SSR}(i,j)$ for the combinations (i,j) indicated above. Note that the number of matrix inversions needed is simply of order $O(T)$.

The Dynamic Programming Algorithm. Once the sums of squared residuals (SSR) of the relevant segments have been computed and stored, a dynamic programming approach can be used to evaluate which partition achieves a global minimization of the overall sum of squared residuals. This method essentially proceeds via a sequential examination of optimal one-break (or two segments) partitions. Let $\mathrm{SSR}(\{T_{r,n}\})$ be the sum of squared residuals associated with the optimal partition containing r breaks using the first n observations. The optimal partition solves the following recursive problem:

$$\mathrm{SSR}(\{T_{m,T}\}) = \min_{mh \le j \le T-h} [\mathrm{SSR}(\{T_{m-1,j}\}) + \mathrm{SSR}(j+1, T)]. \quad (49.5)$$

It is useful to expand this algorithm as follows:

$$\begin{aligned} &\mathrm{SSR}(\{T_{m,T}\}) \\ &\quad = \min_{mh \le j_1 \le T-h} [\mathrm{SSR}(j_1 + 1, T) \\ &\qquad + \min_{(m-1)h \le j_2 \le j_1 - h} [\mathrm{SSR}(j_2 + 1, j_1) \\ &\qquad + \min_{(m-2)h \le j_3 \le j_2 - h} [\mathrm{SSR}(j_3 + 1, j_2) \\ &\qquad \vdots \\ &\qquad + \min_{h \le j_m \le j_{m-1} - h} [\mathrm{SSR}(1, j_m) + \mathrm{SSR}(j_m + 1, j_{m-1})] \ldots]]]. \end{aligned}$$

The method can therefore be viewed as a sequential updating of $T - (m+1)h + 1$ segments into optimal one, two, and up to $m-1$ break partitions (or into two, three, and up to m sub-segments); the last step is simply creating a single optimal m breaks (or $m+1$ segments) partition.

It is important to note that, in practice, this method is very fast even with very large sample sizes. Indeed, the major computation cost is the construction of the triangular matrix of sums of squared residuals for all possible segments. The search for the optimal m-partition represents a marginal addition to the total computing time. This means that it is only marginally longer to obtain global minimizers with five or ten breaks as it is with two. The only constraint is one of memory space. The procedure requires to store a vector of dimension proportional to $T(T+1)/2$.

The Case of a Partial Structural Change Model. This dynamic programming method to obtain global minimizers of the sum of squared residuals cannot be applied directly to the case of a partial structural change model ($p > 0$). This is because we cannot concentrate out the parameters β without knowing the appropriate partition, i.e., the estimate of β associated with a global minimization depends on the optimal partition which we are trying to obtain. Unlike for the pure structural change model for which we can write the regression in the form (49.4), each element of the triangular matrix of sums of squared residuals depends on the final optimal m-partition that we search.

However, a simple iterative procedure is possible. Let $\theta = (\delta, T_1, \ldots, T_m)$, we can write the sum of squared residuals as a function of the vectors β and θ, i.e., $\text{SSR}(\beta, \theta)$. As discussed in the work of Sargan (1964), we can minimize $\text{SSR}(\beta, \theta)$ in an iterative fashion as follows. First, minimize with respect to θ keeping β fixed and then minimize with respect to β keeping θ fixed, and iterate. Each iteration ensures a decrease in the objective function. Of course, convergence to the global minimum is not guaranteed and a proper choice of the initial value of β might be important to avoid a local minimum.

We discuss the details of this method in the structural change context with a slight modification that permits a very rapid convergence. Note that the first step, minimizing with respect to θ keeping β fixed, amounts to applying the dynamic programming algorithm discussed above with $y_t - x_t'\beta$ as the dependent variable. Since β is fixed, this is, indeed, a step involving a pure structural change model. Let $\theta^* = (\delta^*, \{T^*\})$ be the associated estimate from this first stage (with $\{T^*\} = (T_1^*, \ldots, T_m^*)$). The application of Sargan's method suggests that the second step be a simple linear regression with $y_t - z_t'\delta_j^*$ being the dependent variable for t in regime j ($j = 1, \ldots, m+1$), the regimes being defined by the partition $\{T^*\}$.

Important efficiency gains can be obtained making a slight modification to the second step. The idea is to only keep $\{T^*\}$ fixed and to maximize again with respect to δ and β simultaneously. Hence, δ is updated at each of the two steps. The reason why this leads to important efficiency gains can be explained as follows. In general, the values $\{T^*\}$ obtained at the first iteration will be quite close to the values $\{\hat{T}\}$ that correspond to the global minimum. Intuitively, this is so because a misspecification in the initial value of β has little effect on the estimates $\{T^*\}$ since the latter depend mostly on the changes in the coefficients δ (associated with the z_t variables) across regimes. Consider a second step which applies the OLS regression

$$Y = X\beta + \bar{Z}^*\delta + U,$$

with $\bar{Z}^*$, the diagonal partition of Z at the m-partition $\{T^*\} = (T_1^*, \ldots, T_m^*)$. If the values $\{T^*\}$ are equal to the values $\{\hat{T}\}$ corresponding to the global minimum, the estimates of β and δ from this second step are then automatically those that correspond to the global minimum. The convergence criterion adopted is that the change in the objective function $S_T(T_1, \ldots, T_m)$ be smaller than some arbitrary ε. Using the iterative method suggested, it is possible to specify $\varepsilon = 0$ because of the discrete nature of the variables $(T_1, \ldots, T_m)$. Indeed, in most of the experiments performed by Bai and Perron (2003a) and Bai and Perron (2006), the minimum was attained after the first iteration and the second one only verified that there was effectively no change in the objective function.

49.2 Asymptotic distributions

In this section, we first review the standard assumptions imposed on the regressors, errors, and break dates as they relate to the works of Bai and Perron (1998) and Perron and Qu (2006) that apply for stationary type regressors, or more precisely short memory and mixing. We then cover the limit distribution of the estimates of the break dates and the parameters of the model.

49.2.1 The assumptions for "stationary" type regressors

To obtain theoretical results about the consistency and limit distribution of the estimates of the break dates, some conditions need to be imposed on the regressors, the errors, the set of admissible partitions, and the break dates. We start with the case of weakly stationary or mixing processes. This is the leading case of interest. However, in many cases, these are not satisfied and alternative procedures are discussed.

To our knowledge, the most general set of assumptions, as far as applications are concerned, are those in the work of Perron and Qu (2006) following the work of Bai and Perron (1998). Some are simply technical (e.g., invertibility requirements), while others restrict the potential applicability of the results. Hence, it is useful to discuss the latter:

- The regressors $w_t = (x_t', z_t')'$ satisfy some law of large numbers within each segment $i = 0, \ldots, m$, given by

$$(1/l_i) \sum_{t=T_i^0+1}^{T_i^0+[l_i v]} w_t w_t' \xrightarrow{p} Q_i(v),$$

  a non-random positive definite matrix uniformly in $v \in [0, 1]$.

This assumption allows the distribution of the regressors to vary across regimes. It, however, requires the data to be weakly stationary short-memory processes. This can be relaxed substantially, though the technical proofs then depend on the nature of the relaxation. For instance, the scaling used forbids trending regressors, unless they are of the form $\{1, (t/T), \ldots, (t/T)^p\}$, say, for a polynomial trend of order p. Casting trend functions in this form can deliver useful results in many cases. However, there are instances where specifying trends in unscaled form, i.e., $\{1, t, \ldots, t^p\}$, can deliver much better results, especially if level and trend slope changes occur jointly. Results using unscaled trends with $p = 1$ are presented in the work of Perron and Zhu (2005). A comparison of their results with other trend specifications is presented in the work of Deng and Perron (2006).

Another important restriction is implied by the requirement that the limit be a fixed matrix, as opposed to permitting it to be stochastic. This, along with the scaling, precludes integrated processes as regressors (i.e., unit roots). In the single break case, this has been relaxed by Bai *et al.* (1998) who considered, among other things, structural changes in cointegrated relationships. Consistency still applies but the rate of convergence and limit distributions of the estimates are different. A comprehensive treatment of structural change in single-equation cointegrated models is presented in the work of Kejriwal and Perron (2008b, 2010b), discussed in Section 49.6.11. Another context in which integrated regressors play a role is the case of changes in persistence. This is addressed in the work of Kejriwal *et al.* (2013), see Section 49.6.13:

- The sequences $\{w_t u_t\}$ and $\{u_t\}$ satisfy some mixing-type conditions; see the work of Perron and Qu (2006) for details.

The formal assumptions are quite technical and their precise statement is not essential. They impose mild restrictions on the vector $w_t u_t$ and permit a wide class of potential correlation and heterogeneity (including conditional heteroskedasticity) and also allow lagged dependent variables. They rule out errors having unit roots. In this latter case, if the regressors are "stationary", the estimates of the break dates are inconsistent (see the work of Nunes *et al.*, 1996). However, unit root errors can be of interest; for example, when testing for a change in the deterministic component of the trend function for an integrated series, in which case the estimates are consistent (see the work of Perron and Zhu, 2005). Technically, what is important is to be able to establish a generalized Hájek and Rényi (1955)-type inequality for the zero mean variables $z_t u_t$, as well as a functional central limit theorem and a law of large numbers. Note that $\sum_{i=1}^{k} z_i u_i$ satisfies the generalized Hajek and Renyi inequality when there exists an $L > 0$ such that for every $c > 0$ and $m > 0$,

$$P\left(\sup_{k \geq m} \frac{1}{k}\left\|\sum_{i=1}^{k} z_i u_i\right\| > c\right) \leq \frac{L}{c^2 m}.$$

This result is very useful to bound various terms and allows deriving the relevant results:

- (Minimization problem): The minimization problem defined by (49.3) is taken over all possible partitions such that $T_i - T_{i-1} \geq \epsilon T$ for some $\epsilon > 0$.

There is a vast amount of work in the statistics literature, which dispenses with this assumption when considering testing, i.e., they allow searching over the whole sample. For an application in econometrics, see the work of Hidalgo and Seo (2013). The problem is that the tests then diverge, though at a slow rate $\log(T)$. This complicates inference and the finite sample properties are not improved. Though, allowing to search over the whole sample may be of theoretical interest, in practice, there is virtually no advantage as the trimming parameter ϵ can be made arbitrarily small:

- (Break dates): $T_i^0 = [T\lambda_i^0]$, where $0 < \lambda_1^0 < \cdots < \lambda_m^0 < 1$.

This condition specifies that the break dates are asymptotically distinct, in particular, the break cannot occur too close to the beginning or end of the sample. It also dictates the asymptotic framework adopted. With this condition, when the sample size T increases, all segments increase in length in the same proportions to each other. Oftentimes, an asymptotic analysis is viewed as a thought experiment about what would happen if we were able to collect more and more data in the future. If one adheres to this view, then the last regime should increase in length (assuming no other break will occur in the future) and all other segments then become a negligible proportion of the total sample. Hence, as T increases, we would find ourselves with a single segment, in which case the framework becomes useless.

The fact is that any asymptotic analysis is simply a device to enable us to get useful information about the structure, which can help us understand the finite sample distributions, and hopefully to deliver good approximations. The adoption of any asymptotic framework should only be evaluated on this basis, no matter how *ad hoc* it may seem at first sight. Here, with, say, a sample of size 100 and 3 breaks occurring at dates 25, 50, and 75, all segments are a fourth of the total sample. It therefore makes sense to use an asymptotic framework whereby this feature is preserved. Having said that, it does not mean that the asymptotic framework adopted in this literature is the only one useful or even the best. For example, it is conceivable that an asymptotic theory whereby more and more data are added keeping a fixed span of data would be useful as well. This is indeed the case and is covered in Section 49.3, following the work of Casini and Perron (2021).

Under these conditions, the main theoretical results are that the break fractions λ_i^0 are consistently estimated, i.e., $\hat{\lambda}_i \equiv (\hat{T}_i/T) \xrightarrow{p} \lambda_i^0$, and that the rate of convergence is T. More precisely, for every $\varepsilon > 0$, there exists a $C < \infty$, such that for large T,

$$P(|T(\hat{\lambda}_i - \lambda_i^0)| > C\Delta_i^{-2}) < \varepsilon, \tag{49.6}$$

for every $i = 1, \ldots, m$, where $\Delta_i = \delta_{i+1} - \delta_i$. Note that the estimates of the break dates are not consistent themselves, but the differences between the estimates and the true values are bounded by some constant, in probability. Also, this implies that the estimates of the other parameters have the same distribution as would prevail if the break dates were known. Kurozumi and Arai (2007) and Kejriwal and Perron (2008a) obtained a similar result with $I(1)$ regressors for a cointegrated model subject to a change in some parameters of the cointegrating vector.

49.2.2 The limit distribution of the estimates

With the assumptions on the regressors, the errors, and given the asymptotic framework adopted, the limit distributions of the estimates of the break dates are independent of each other. Hence, for each break date, the analysis becomes exactly the same as if a single break occurred. The intuition behind this feature is first that the distance between each break increases at rate T as the sample size increases. Also, the conditions on the regressors and errors impose a short memory property so that events that occur a long enough time apart are nearly independent. We do not reproduce the results in details but simply describe the main qualitative features and the practical relevance of the required assumptions. The reader is referred to the works of Bai (1997b) and Bai and Perron (1998, 2003a), in particular. Also, confidence intervals for the break dates need not be based on the limit distributions of the estimates. Other approaches are possible.

The limit distribution of the estimates of the break dates depends on the following: (a) The magnitude of the change in coefficients (with larger changes leading to higher precision, as expected), (b) the (limit) sample moment matrices of the regressors for the segments prior to and after the true break date (which are allowed to be different), (c) the so-called 'long-run' variance of $\{w_t u_t\}$, which involves potential serial correlation in the errors (also allowed to be different across segments), and (d) whether the regressors are trending or not. In all cases, all relevant nuisance parameters can be consistently estimated and the appropriate confidence intervals constructed. A feature of interest is that the confidence intervals need not be symmetric given that the data and errors can have different properties before and after the break.

To get an idea of the importance of particular assumptions needed to derive the limit distribution, it is instructive to look at a simple case with *i.i.d.* errors u_t and a single break (for details, see the work of Bai, 1997b). Then, the estimate of the break date satisfies

$$\hat{T}_1 = \arg\min_{T_1} \text{SSR}(T_1) = \arg\max_{T_1} \left[\text{SSR}(T_1^0) - \text{SSR}(T_1)\right].$$

Using the fact that, given the rate of convergence result (49.6), the inequality $|\hat{T}_1 - T_1^0| < C\Delta^{-2}$ is satisfied with probability one in large samples (here, $\Delta = \delta_2 - \delta_1$). Hence, we can restrict the search over the compact set

$$S(\Delta) = \{T_1 : |T_1 - T_1^0| < C\Delta^{-2}\}.$$

Then, after some derivations, for $T_1 < T_1^0$,

$$\text{SSR}(T_1^0) - \text{SSR}(T_1) = -\Delta' \sum_{t=T_1+1}^{T_1^0} z_t z_t' \Delta + 2\Delta' \sum_{t=T_1+1}^{T_1^0} z_t u_t + o_p(1) \tag{49.7}$$

and, for $T_1 > T_1^0$,

$$\text{SSR}(T_1^0) - \text{SSR}(T_1) = -\Delta' \sum_{t=T_1^0+1}^{T_1} z_t z_t' \Delta - 2\Delta' \sum_{t=T_1^0+1}^{T_1} z_t u_t + o_p(1). \tag{49.8}$$

The problem is that, with $|T_1 - T_1^0|$ bounded, we cannot apply a law of large numbers or a central limit theorem to approximate the sums above with something that does not depend on the exact distributions of z_t and u_t. Furthermore, the distributions of these sums depend on the exact location of the break. It is possible to obtain a limit distribution assuming strict stationarity but then it depends on the exact distributions of the errors and regressors, which are unknown in practice.

Note that for the difference $T_1 - T_1^0$ to increase as the sample size increases, then a law of large numbers and a functional central limit theorem can be applied. The trick is to realize that from the convergence rate result (49.6), the rate of convergence of the estimate will be slower if the change in the parameters Δ_i gets smaller as the sample size increases but does so slowly enough for the estimated break fraction to remain consistent. Early applications of this framework are the work of Yao (1987) in the context of a change in distribution for a sequence of *i.i.d.* random variables and the work of Picard (1985) for a change in an autoregressive process.

Letting $\Delta = \Delta_T$ to highlight the fact that the change in the parameters depends on the sample size, this leads to the specification $\Delta_T = \Delta_0 v_T$, where v_T is such that $v_T \to 0$ and $T^{(1/2)-\alpha} v_T \to \infty$ for some $\alpha \in (0, 1/2)$. Under these specifications, we have from (49.6) that $\hat{T}_1 - T_1^0 = O_p(T^{1-2\alpha})$. Hence, we can restrict the search to those values T_1 such that $T_1 = T_1^0 + [s v_T^{-2}]$ for some fixed s. We can write (49.7) as

$$\mathrm{SSR}(T_1^0) - \mathrm{SSR}(T_1) = -\Delta_0' v_T^2 \sum_{t=T_1+1}^{T_1^0} z_t z_t' \Delta_0 + 2\Delta_0' v_T \sum_{t=T_1+1}^{T_1^0} z_t u_t + o_p(1).$$

Without trending regressors, the following assumptions are usually imposed:

- (Limit distribution). Let $\Delta T_i^0 = T_i^0 - T_{i-1}^0$, then as $\Delta T_i^0 \to \infty$, the following hold uniformly in s: (a) $(\Delta T_i^0)^{-1} \sum_{t=T_{i-1}^0+1}^{T_{i-1}^0+[s\Delta T_i^0]} z_t z_t' \xrightarrow{p} sQ_i$, (b) $(\Delta T_i^0)^{-1} \sum_{t=T_{i-1}^0+1}^{T_{i-1}^0+[s\Delta T_i^0]} u_t^2 \xrightarrow{p} s\sigma_i^2$, (c) $\Omega_i = plim_{T\to\infty}$ $(\Delta T_i^0)^{-1} \sum_{r=T_{i-1}^0+1}^{T_i^0} \sum_{t=T_{i-1}^0+1}^{T_i^0} E(z_r z_t' u_r u_t)$.

  These imply that

$$(\Delta T_i^0)^{-1/2} \sum_{t=T_{i-1}^0+1}^{T_{i-1}^0+[s\Delta T_i^0]} z_t u_t \Rightarrow B_i(s),$$

where $B_i(s)$ is a multivariate Gaussian process on $[0, 1]$ with mean zero and covariance $E[B_i(s)B_i(u)] = \min\{s, u\}\sigma_i^2 Q_i$. Here, and throughout the chapter, "$\Rightarrow$" denotes weak convergence in distribution as discussed in Section 43.9. Hence, for $s < 0$,

$$\begin{aligned}
&\text{SSR}(T_1^0) - \text{SSR}(T_1^0 + [sv_T^{-2}]) \\
&\quad = -|s|\Delta_0' Q_1 \Delta_0 + 2(\Delta_0' Q_1 \Delta_0)^{1/2} W_1(-s) + o_p(1),
\end{aligned}$$

where $W_1(-s)$ is a Wiener process defined on $(0, \infty)$. A similar analysis holds for the case $s > 0$ and for more general assumptions on u_t. But this suffices to make clear that under these assumptions, the limit distribution of the estimate of the break date no longer depends on the exact distribution of z_t and u_t but only on quantities that can be consistently estimated. For details, see the works of Bai (1997b) and Bai and Perron (1998, 2003a).

The limit distribution is given by (the derivations are quite tedious; see the work of Bai and Perron (1998)).

$$\frac{(\Delta_i' Q_i \Delta_i)^2}{(\Delta_i' \Omega_i \Delta_i)} (\hat{T}_i - T_i^0) \Rightarrow \arg\max{}_s V^{(i)}(s), \quad (i = 1, \ldots, m), \tag{49.9}$$

where

$$V^{(i)}(s) = \begin{cases} W_1^{(i)}(-s) - |s|/2, & \text{if } s \leq 0, \\ \sqrt{\xi_i}(\phi_{i,2}/\phi_{i,1}) W_2^{(i)}(s) - \xi_i |s|/2, & \text{if } s > 0, \end{cases}$$

and

$$\begin{aligned}
\xi_i &= \Delta_i' Q_{i+1} \Delta_i / \Delta_i' Q_i \Delta_i, \\
\phi_{i,1}^2 &= \Delta_i' \Omega_i \Delta_i / \Delta_i' Q_i \Delta_i, \\
\phi_{i,2}^2 &= \Delta_i' \Omega_{i+1} \Delta_i / \Delta_i' Q_{i+1} \Delta_i.
\end{aligned}$$

Also, $W_1^{(i)}(s)$ and $W_2^{(i)}(s)$ are independent standard Wiener processes defined on $[0, \infty)$, starting at the origin when $s = 0$. These processes are also independent across i. The cumulative distribution function of $\text{argmax}_s V^{(i)}(s)$ is derived in the work of Bai (1997b) and all that is needed to compute the relevant critical values are estimates of Δ_i, Q_i, and Ω_i in order to construct confidence intervals. These are given by

$$\hat{\Delta}_i = \hat{\delta}_{i+1} - \hat{\delta}_i,$$

$$\hat{Q}_i = (\Delta\hat{T}_i)^{-1} \sum_{t=\hat{T}_{i-1}+1}^{\hat{T}_i} z_t z_t',$$

and an estimate of Ω_i can be constructed using an HAC estimator applied to the vector $\{z_t\hat{u}_t\}$ and using data over segment i only. In practice, one may want to impose some constraints on this general framework related to the distribution of the errors and regressors across segments. See the work of Bai and Perron (2003a) for details.

So, what do we learn from these asymptotic results? First, for large shifts, the distributions of the estimates of the break dates depend on the exact distributions of the regressors and errors even if the sample is large. When shifts are not too large, we can expect the distributions of the estimates of the break dates to be insensitive to the exact nature of the distributions of the regressors and errors. The question is then as follows: How small do the changes have to be? There is no clear cut solution to this problem and the answer is case specific. The simulations in the work of Bai and Perron (2006) show that the shrinking shifts asymptotic framework provides useful approximations to the finite sample distribution of the estimated break dates, but their simulation design uses normally distributed errors and regressors. The coverage rates are adequate, in general, unless the shifts are quite small in which case the confidence interval is too narrow.

The method of Elliott and Müller (2007), based on inverting a test, works better in the case with *i.i.d.* errors and no lagged dependent variables but fail miserably otherwise; their method can yield a confidence interval equal to the total sample even when the break magnitude is very large; see the work of Chang and Perron (2018). Yamamoto (2018) proposed a modification of the long-run variance estimator that alleviates this problem, though the method does not apply when lagged dependent variables are present; see also the work of Kurozumi and Yamamoto (2015). Kurozumi and Yamamoto (2015) proposed confidence sets obtained by inverting a test that maximizes some weighted average power function. The fact that the method of Bai and Perron (1998) provides a poor approximation when the magnitude of the break is small is of little practical concern since the answer remains the same as with a method that provides a good coverage rate, namely that the data are not informative about the location of the break date. Still, it would be nice from a theoretical point of view to have a method that is accurate for all break magnitudes.

Deng and Perron (2006) showed that the shrinking shift asymptotic framework leads to a poor approximation in the context of changes in a linear trend function and that the limit distribution based on a fixed magnitude of shift is highly preferable. Eo and Morley (2015) generalized the method of Siegmund (1988) inverting the likelihood-ratio statistic of Qu and Perron (2007a). The confidence sets proposed by Eo and Morley (2015) display a coverage probability often above the nominal level and this results in an average length larger than the Bai (1997b) method. Overall, the findings suggest a need for a method that provides over a wide range of empirically relevant models both good coverage probabilities and reasonable lengths of confidence sets, especially for all break sizes, whether large or small. See Section 49.3 for a recent alternative using a continuous time asymptotic framework. Chang and Perron (2018) presented a bootstrap method to construct the confidence intervals.

49.3 Continuous record asymptotic distributions

Casini and Perron (2021) considered an asymptotic framework based on a continuous-time approximation, i.e., T observations with a sampling interval h over a fixed time span $[0, N]$, where $N = Th$, with $T \to \infty$ and $h \to 0$ with N fixed. They consider the following partial structural change model with a single break point:

$$\begin{aligned} Y_t &= D_t'\pi^0 + Z_t'\delta_1^0 + e_t, \quad (t \le T_b^0), \\ Y_t &= D_t'\pi^0 + Z_t'\delta_2^0 + e_t, \quad (t > T_b^0), \end{aligned} \tag{49.10}$$

where $\{D_s, Z_s, e_s\}_{s\ge 0}$ are continuous-time processes and we observe realizations at discrete points of time, namely $\{Y_{kh}, D_{kh}, Z_{kh}; k = 0, \dots, T = N/h\}$. They consider the least-squares estimator of the break point and the analysis is valid for general time series regression models including errors with correlation and/or heteroskedasticity and lagged dependent variables. Besides the usual small shifts assumption, the limiting distribution is derived under the additional assumption of increasing local variances around the true break date. The continuous record asymptotic distribution of the least-squares estimator is then given by

$$Th(\hat{\lambda}_b - \lambda_0) \Rightarrow \underset{v\in A}{\operatorname{argmax}}\{-\left(\delta^0\right)' \langle Z_\Delta,\, Z_\Delta\rangle\,(v)\,\delta^0 + 2\left(\delta^0\right)' W\,(v)\},$$

where

$$A = [-N_b^0/(||\delta^0||^{-2}\bar{\sigma}^2),\ \left(N - N_b^0\right)/(||\delta^0||^{-2}\bar{\sigma}^2)]$$

and with $\langle Z_\Delta,\, Z_\Delta\rangle\,(v)$ the predictable quadratic variation process of Z_t, $W\,(v)$ a two-sided centered Gaussian process, and $\bar{\sigma}^2$ is the limit of an estimate of the error innovation variance over $[0,\, N]$. It is shown that the continuous record asymptotic distribution provides a much better approximation to the finite-sample distribution of the least-squares estimator, with small or large magnitude of breaks. The former is highly non-standard and captures the main properties of the latter, such as tri-modality, asymmetry, and skewness. Casini and Perron (2021) proposed constructing confidence sets by computing the Highest Density Regions (HDR) of the density of the continuous record limiting distribution. Their confidence sets are shown to provide accurate converge rates and relatively short length of the confidence sets across different break magnitudes and break locations.

49.4 Estimating breaks one at a time

Bai (1997a) and Bai and Perron (1998) showed that it is possible to consistently estimate all break fractions sequentially, i.e., one at a time. This is due to the following result. When estimating a single break model in the presence of multiple breaks, the estimate of the break fraction will converge to one of the true break fractions, the one that is dominant in the sense that taking it into account allows the greatest reduction in the sum of squared residuals. Then, allowing for a break at the estimated value, a second one-break model can be applied to the estimated sub-samples which will consistently estimate the second dominating break, and so on (in the case of two breaks that are equally dominant, the estimate will converge with probability 1/2 to either break). Fu and Curnow (1990) presented an early account of this property for a sequence of Bernoulli random variables when the probability of obtaining a 0 or a 1 is subject to multiple structural changes (see also the work of Chong, 1995). Interestingly, Yang (2017) showed that this is not the case when testing for changes in the slope of a trend function; hence, care must be applied with trending regressors.

Bai (1997a) considered the limit distribution of the estimates and showed that they are not the same as those obtained when estimating all break dates simultaneously. To remedy this problem, he suggested a procedure called 'repartition'. This amounts to re-estimating each break date conditional on the adjacent break dates. For example, let the initial estimates of the break dates be denoted by $(\hat{T}_1^a, \ldots, \hat{T}_m^a)$. The second round estimate for the ith break date is obtained by fitting a one break model to the segment starting at date $\hat{T}_{i-1}^a + 1$ and ending at date $\hat{T}_{i+1}^a$ (with the convention that $\hat{T}_0^a = 0$ and $\hat{T}_{m+1}^a = T$). The estimates obtained from this repartition procedure have the same limit distributions as those obtained simultaneously, as discussed above.

49.5 Estimation in a system of regressions

Bai *et al.* (1998) considered asymptotically valid inference for the estimate of a single break date in multivariate time series allowing stationary or integrated regressors as well as trends. They show that the width of the confidence interval decreases in an important way when series having a common break are treated as a group and estimation is carried using a quasi maximum likelihood (QML) procedure. Also, Bai (2000) considered VAR models estimated again by QML when the breaks can occur in the parameters of the conditional mean, the covariance matrix of the error term, or both.

A general framework is that of Qu and Perron (2007a) who consider models of the form

$$y_t = (I \otimes z_t')S\beta_j + u_t,$$

for $T_{j-1} + 1 \leq t \leq T_j$ $(j = 1, \ldots, m + 1)$, where y_t is an n-vector of dependent variables and z_t is a q-vector that includes the regressors from all equations. The vector of errors u_t has mean 0 and covariance matrix Σ_j. The matrix S is of dimension nq by p with full column rank. Though, in principle, it is allowed to have entries that are arbitrary constants, it is usually a selection matrix involving elements that are 0 or 1 and, hence, specifies which regressors appear in each equation. The set of basic parameters in regime j consists of the p vector β_j and of Σ_j. They also allow for the imposition of a set of r restrictions of the form $g(\beta, \text{vec}(\Sigma)) = 0$, where $\beta = (\beta_1', \ldots, \beta_{m+1}')'$, $\Sigma = (\Sigma_1, \ldots, \Sigma_{m+1})$, and $g(\cdot)$ is an r-dimensional vector. Both within- and cross-equation restrictions are allowed, and in each case, within or across regimes. The assumptions on the regressors z_t and the errors u_t are similar to those discussed in Section 49.2.1 (properly extended for the multivariate nature of the problem). Hence, the framework permits a wide class of models including VAR, SUR, linear panel data, change in means of a vector of stationary processes, etc. Models with integrated regressors (i.e., models with cointegration) are not permitted.

Allowing for general restrictions on the parameters β_j and Σ_j permits a very wide range of special cases that are of practical interest: (a) partial structural change models where only a subset of the parameters are subject to change, (b) block partial structural change models where only a subset of the equations are subject to change, (c) changes in only some element of the covariance matrix Σ_j (e.g., only variances in a subset of equations), (d) changes in only the covariance matrix Σ_j, while β_j is the same for all segments, (e) ordered break models where one can impose the breaks to occur in a particular order across subsets of equations, etc.

The method of estimation is again QML (based on normal errors) subject to the restrictions. They derive the consistency, rate of convergence, and limit distribution of the estimated break dates. They obtain a general result stating that, in large samples, the restricted likelihood function can be separated in two parts: one that involves only the break dates and the true values of the coefficients so that the estimates of the break dates are not affected by the restrictions imposed on the coefficients; the other involving the parameters of the model, the true values of the break dates, and the restrictions, showing that the limiting distributions of these estimates are influenced by the restrictions but not by the estimation of the break dates.

The limit distribution results for the estimates of the break dates are qualitatively similar to those discussed above, in particular, they depend on the true parameters of the model. Though only root-T consistent estimates of (β, Σ) are needed to construct asymptotically valid confidence intervals, it is likely that more precise estimates of these parameters will lead to better finite sample coverage rates. Hence, it is recommended to use the estimates obtained imposing the restrictions even though imposing restrictions does not have a first-order effect on the limiting distributions of the estimates of the break dates. To make estimation possible in practice, for any number of breaks, they present an algorithm which extends the one discussed in the work of Bai and Perron (2003a) using, in particular, an iterative GLS procedure to construct the likelihood function for all possible segments.

The theoretical analysis shows how substantial efficiency gains can be obtained by casting the analysis in a system of regressions. All that is needed is that the correlation between the errors be non-zero. This result is *ex post* fairly intuitive since a poorly estimated break in one regression affects the likelihood function through both the error variance of that equation and the correlation with the rest of the regressions. Hence, by including ancillary equations without breaks, additional forces are in play to better pinpoint the break dates. The result is also similar to that obtained when using a Seemingly Unrelated Regression (SUR) model as discussed in Section 14.1.

Qu and Perron (2007a) also considered a novel aspect to the problem of multiple structural changes labeled "locally ordered breaks". Suppose one equation is a policy-reaction function and the other is some market-clearing equation whose parameters are related to the policy function. According to the Lucas critique, if a change in policy occurs, it is expected to induce a change in the market equation but the change may not be simultaneous and may occur with a lag, say, because of some adjustments due to frictions or incomplete information. However, it is expected to take place soon after the break in the policy function. Here, the breaks across the two equations are "ordered" in the sense that we have the prior knowledge that the break in one equation occurs after the break in the other. The breaks are also "local" in the sense that the time span between their occurrence is expected to be short. Hence, the breaks cannot be viewed as occurring simultaneously nor can the break fractions be viewed as asymptotically distinct.

An algorithm to estimate such models is presented. Also, a framework to analyze the limit distribution of the estimates is introduced. Unlike the case with asymptotically distinct breaks, here the distributions of the estimates of the break dates need to be considered jointly. Their results have been extended in the work of Li and Perron (2017) which allows (a) the covariates to be any mix of trends and stationary or integrated regressors, (b) for breaks in the variance–covariance matrix of the errors, and (c) multiple locally ordered breaks, each occurring in a different equation within a subset of equations in the system.

49.6 Testing for structural change

In this section, we review testing procedures related to structural changes. The following issues are covered: some historical notes, tests obtained without modeling any break, the problem of non monotonic power functions, tests for a single structural change obtained by explicitly modeling a break, locally optimal tests allowing breaks, tests for multiple structural changes, double maximum tests, sequential tests, tests for restricted structural changes, joint tests for changes in coefficients and variance, tests valid with $I(1)$ regressors, tests for a change in slope valid allowing the noise component to be $I(0)$ or $I(1)$, and tests for changes in persistence.

49.6.1 Introductory historical notes

It is instructive to start with some interesting historical notes concerning early tests for structural change. Consider a univariate time series, y_t, which under the null hypothesis is independently and identically distributed with mean μ and finite variance. Under the alternative hypothesis, y_t is subject to a one-time change in mean at some unknown date T_b, i.e.,

$$y_t = \mu_1 + \mu_2 1(t > T_b) + e_t, \tag{49.11}$$

where $e_t \sim i.i.d.\ (0, \sigma_e^2)$ and $1(\cdot)$ denotes the indicator function. Quandt (1958, 1960) introduced what is now known as the *Sup-F* test (assuming normally distributed errors), i.e., the likelihood ratio test for a change in parameters evaluated at the break date that maximizes the likelihood function. However, the limit distribution was then unknown. Following earlier works by Chernoff and Zacks (1964) and Kander and Zacks (1966), an alternative approach was advocated by Gardner (1969) stemming from a suggestion by Page (1955, 1957) to use partial sums of demeaned data to analyze structural changes. The test considered is Bayesian in nature and, under the alternative, assigns weights p_t as the prior probability that a change occurs at date t ($t = 1, \ldots, T$). With a prior that assigns equal weight to all observations, i.e., $p_t = 1/T$, and assuming normal errors, this strategy leads to the test

$$Q = \hat{\sigma}_e^{-2} T^{-2} \sum_{t=1}^{T} \left[\sum_{j=t+1}^{T} (y_j - \bar{y}) \right]^2,$$

where $\bar{y} = T^{-1} \sum_{t=1}^{T} y_t$ is the sample average and $\hat{\sigma}_e^2 = T^{-1} \sum_{t=1}^{T} (y_t - \bar{y})^2$ is the sample variance of the data. The limit distribution of the statistic Q, valid with non-normal errors, was analyzed by MacNeill (1974). He showed that (see Exercise 49.1)

$$Q \Rightarrow \int_0^1 B_0(r)^2 dr,$$

where

$$B_0(r) = W(r) - rW(1)$$

is a Brownian bridge, and noted that percentage point had already been derived by Anderson and Darling (1952) in the context of goodness of fit tests. MacNeill (1978) extended the procedure to test for a change in a polynomial trend function of the form

$$y_t = \sum_{i=0}^{p} \beta_{i,t} t^i + e_t,$$

where $\beta_{i,t} = \beta_i + \delta_i 1(t > T_b)$. The test of no change ($\delta_i = 0$ for all i) is then

$$Q_p = \hat{\sigma}_e^{-2} T^{-2} \sum_{t=1}^{T} \left[\sum_{j=t+1}^{T} \hat{e}_j \right]^2,$$

with $\hat{\sigma}_e^2 = T^{-1} \sum_{t=1}^{T} \hat{e}_t^2$ and $\hat{e}_t$ the residuals from a regression of y_t on $\{1, t, \ldots, t^p\}$. The limit distribution is given by

$$Q \Rightarrow \int_0^1 B_p(r)^2 dr,$$

where $B_p(r)$ is a generalized Brownian bridge. MacNeill (1978) computed the critical values by exact numerical methods up to six decimals accuracy (showing, for $p = 0$, the critical values of Anderson and Darling (1952) to be very accurate). The test was extended to allow dependence in the errors e_t by Perron (1991d) (published as Perron (2019)) and Tang and MacNeill (1993) (see also the works of Kulperger 1987a,b, Jandhyala and MacNeill 1989, Jandhyala and Minogue 1993, and Antoch *et al.* 1997). In particular, Perron (1991d) showed that, under general conditions with serially correlated errors, the same limit distribution obtains using the statistic

$$Q_p^* = \hat{h}_e(0)^{-1} T^{-2} \sum_{t=1}^{T} \left[\sum_{j=t+1}^{T} \hat{e}_j \right]^2,$$

where $\hat{h}_e(0)$ is a consistent estimate of (2π times) the spectral density function at frequency zero of e_t.

Even though, little of this filtered through the econometrics literature, the statistic Q_p^* is well known to applied economists. It is the so-called KPSS test for testing the null hypothesis of stationarity versus the alternative of a unit root, see the work of Kwiatkowski *et al.* (1992). In the econometrics literature, several extensions of this test have been proposed, in particular, for testing the null hypothesis of cointegration versus the alternative of no cointegration (Nyblom and Harvey, 2000) and testing whether any part of a sample shows a vector of series to be cointegrated (Qu, 2007). Note also that the same test can be given the interpretation of a locally best invariant test for parameter constancy versus the alternative that the parameters follow a random walk (e.g., Nyblom and Mäkeläinen, 1983, Nyblom, 1989, Nabeya and Tanaka, 1988, Jandhyala and MacNeill, 1992, and Hansen, 1992b). The same statistic is also the basis for a test of the null hypothesis of no-cointegration when considering a functional of its reciprocal (Breitung, 2002).

So, what are we to make of all of this? The important message to learn from the fact that the same statistic can be applied to tests for stationarity versus either unit root or structural change is that the two issues are linked in important ways. Evidence in favor of unit roots can be a manifestation of structural changes and vice versa. This was indeed an important message of Perron (1989b, 1990a). We return to this problem and see how it introduces severe complications; see Chapter 50.

It is also of interest to go back to the work by Page (1955, 1957) who had proposed to use partial sums of demeaned data to test for structural change. Let

$$S_r = \sum_{j=1}^{r} (y_j - \bar{y}).$$

His procedure for a two-sided test for change in the mean is based on the following quantities

$$\max_{0 \le r \le T} \left[S_r - \min_{0 \le i < r} S_i \right] \quad \text{and} \quad \max_{0 \le r \le T} \left[\min_{0 \le i < r} S_i - S_r \right]$$

and looks whether either exceeds a threshold (which, in the symmetric case, is the same). So, we reject the null hypothesis if the partial sum rises enough from its previous minimum or falls enough from its previous maximum. Nadler and Robbins (1971) showed that this procedure is equivalent to looking at the statistic

$$RS = \left[\max_{0 \le r \le T} S_r - \min_{0 \le r \le T} S_r \right],$$

i.e., to assess whether the range of the sequence of partial sums is large enough. But this is also exactly the basis of the popular rescaled range procedure used to test the null hypothesis of short memory versus the alternative of long memory; see, in particular, the works of Hurst (1951), Mandelbrot and Taqqu (1979), Bhattacharya *et al.* (1983), and Lo (1991).

This is symptomatic of the same problem discussed above from a slightly different angle; structural change and long memory imply similar features in the data and, accordingly, are hard to distinguish. In particular, evidence for long memory can be caused by the presence of structural changes, and vice versa. The intuition is basically the same as the message in the work of Perron (1990a), i.e., level shifts induce persistent features in the data. This problem has received a lot of attention, especially in the finance literature concerning the characteristics of stock returns volatility (see, in particular, the works of Diebold and Inoue, 2001, Gouriéroux and Jasiak, 2001, Granger and Hyung, 2004, Lobato and Savin, 1998, and Perron and Qu, 2010). This was discussed in details in Chapter 47.

49.6.2 Tests for a single change without modeling the break

Historically, tests for structural change were first devised based on procedures that did not estimate a break point explicitly. The main reason is that the distribution theory for the estimates of the break dates (obtained using a least-squares or likelihood principle) was not available and the problem was solved only for few special cases (see, e.g., the works of Hawkins, 1977; Kim and Siegmund, 1989). Most tests proposed were of the form of partial sums of residuals. Besides the Q test based on the average of partial sums of residuals and the rescaled range test based on the range of partial sums of demeaned data, discussed above, another statistic which has played an important role in theory and applications is the CUSUM test proposed by Brown *et al.* (1975). This test is based on the maximum of partial sums of recursive residuals. For a linear regression with k regressors

$$y_t = x_t'\beta + u_t,$$

it is defined by

$$CUSUM = \max_{k+1<r\leq T} \left| \frac{\sum_{t=k+1}^{r} \tilde{v}_t}{\hat{\sigma}\sqrt{T-k}} \right| \Big/ \left(1 + 2\frac{r-k}{T-k}\right),$$

where $\hat{\sigma}^2$ is a consistent estimate of the variance of u_t (usually, the sum of squared OLS residuals although, to increase power, one can use the sum of squared demeaned recursive residuals, as suggested by Harvey (1975)) and $\tilde{v}_t$ are the recursive residuals defined by (see Section 4.9)

$$\tilde{v}_t = (y_t - x_t'\hat{\beta}_{t-1})/f_t,$$
$$f_t = (1 + x_t'(X_{t-1}'X_{t-1})x_t)^{1/2},$$

where X_{t-1} contains the observations on the regressors up to time $t-1$ and $\hat{\beta}_{t-1}$ is the OLS estimate of β using data up to time $t-1$. The limit distribution of the CUSUM test can be expressed in terms of the maximum of a weighted Wiener process, i.e.,

$$CUSUM \Rightarrow \sup_{0 \le r \le 1} |W(r)/(1+2r)|,$$

where $W(r)$ is a unit Wiener process defined on $(0,1)$, see the work of Sen (1982) and Exercise (49.3). Also, it was shown by Krämer *et al.* (1988) that the limit distribution remains valid even if lagged dependent variables are present as regressors. Furthermore, Ploberger and Krämer (1992) showed that using OLS residuals instead of recursive residuals yields a valid test, though the limit distribution under the null hypothesis is different (expressed in terms of a Brownian bridge, $W(r) - rW(1)$, instead of a Wiener process). An alternative, also suggested by Brown *et al.* (1975), is the CUSUM of squares test. It takes the form

$$CUSSQ = \max_{k+1<r\le T} \left| S_T^{(r)} - (r-k)/(T-k) \right|,$$

where $S_T^{(r)} = (\sum_{t=k+1}^{r} \tilde{v}_t^2)/(\sum_{t=k+1}^{T} \tilde{v}_t^2)$. Ploberger and Krämer (1990) considered the local power functions of the CUSUM and CUSUM of squares. The former has non-trivial local asymptotic power unless the mean regressor is orthogonal to all structural changes. On the other hand, the latter has only trivial local power (i.e., power equal to size) for local changes that specify a one-time change in the coefficients (see also the work of Deshayes and Picard, 1986). This suggests that the CUSUM test should be preferred, a conclusion we revisit in the following.

49.6.3 Non-monotonic power functions in finite samples

All tests discussed above are consistent for given fixed values in the relevant set of alternative hypotheses. All (except the CUSUM of squares) are, however, subject to the following problem. For a given sample size, the power function can be non-monotonic in the sense that it can decrease and even reach a zero value as the alternative considered becomes further away from the null value. This was shown by Perron (1991, 2019) for the Q statistic and extended to a wide range of tests in Vogelsang (1999). See also the work of Deng and Perron (2008) for a treatment related to the CUSUM and CUSUM of squares tests and the work of Kim and Perron (2009a) for a theoretical analysis of the sup $Wald$, LM, and LR tests.

This was illustrated using a basic shift in mean process or a shift in the slope of a linear trend (for some statistics designed for that alternative). In the change in mean case, with a single shift occurring, it was shown that the power of the tests discussed above eventually decreases as the magnitude of the shift increases and can reach zero. This decrease in power can be especially pronounced even with smaller mean shifts when a lagged dependent variable is included as a regressor to account for potential serial correlation in the errors.

The basic reason for this feature is first the need to estimate the variance of the errors, or the spectral density function at frequency zero when correlation in the errors is allowed, to properly scale the statistics. Since no break is directly modeled, one needs to estimate this variance using least squares or recursive residuals that are 'contaminated' by the shift under the alternative. As the shift gets larger, the estimate of the scale gets inflated with a resulting loss in power. With a lagged dependent variable, the problem is exacerbated because the shift induces a bias of the autoregressive coefficient toward one (Perron, 1989a, 1990a). Crainiceanu and Vogelsang (2007) also showed how the problem is exacerbated when using estimates of the scale factor that allow for correlation, e.g., weighted sums of the autocovariance function. The usual methods to select the bandwidth (see the work of Andrews, 1991b) will choose a value that is severely biased upward and lead to a decrease in power. This is again due to the fact that the method to choose the bandwidth m is usually based on estimating an $AR(1)$ approximation.

For instance, when using the quadratic spectral kernel (see Section 38.9),

$$\hat{m}_T = 1.3221(\hat{\alpha}T)^{1/5}.$$

If a change is present, the autoregressive parameter is biased toward one (see Section 50.2) and more so as the magnitude of the change increases. This leads to a very large value of m selected, thereby further inflating the estimate of the long-run variance. With a change in slope, the bandwidth increases at rate T and the tests become inconsistent. The results are similar using any other kernel.

This is a troubling feature since tests that are consistent and have good local asymptotic properties can perform rather badly globally. In simulations reported in the work of Deng and Perron (2008), this feature does not occur for the CUSUM of squares test. This leads us to the curious conclusion that the test with the worst local asymptotic property has a better global behavior.

So, the message to retain from this is as follows:

- Beware of anyone telling you they have an optimal test. The optimality criterion adopted is almost always a local asymptotic one, which is tailored for small shifts. In structural change problems, it is useless unless breaks are accounted for under both the null and alternative hypotheses.

Accordingly, there are problems with tests based on some local asymptotic arguments (e.g., LM or CUSUM) or that do no try to model the breaks explicitly. An example is the test of Elliott and Müller (2006) which is deemed optimal for a class of models involving "small" non-constant coefficients. The suggested procedure does not explicitly model breaks and the test is then akin to a 'partial sums type' test. Perron and Yamamoto (2016) show that their test suffers from severe non-monotonic power, while offering only modest gains for small breaks. Methods to overcome non-monotonic power problems have been suggested. Some solve the problem caused by the inflated estimate of the scaling factor but there is currently no reliable method to appropriately deal with dynamic models involving lagged dependent variables.

Recently, work has been done on "self-normalized" tests. These do not model any change but estimate the relevant variance or long-run variance in such a way that it is consistent under the null hypothesis and bounded under the alternative hypothesis even for large break sizes. The types of changes allowed are quite general. Given the robustness, there is an inevitable loss in power and it is unclear how they perform in time-series models with lagged dependent variables. See, in particular, the works of Shao and Zhang (2010), Zhang and Lavitas (2018), Chan (2022), Zhao *et al.* (2022), Wang *et al.* (2022), and Cheng and Chan (2024); for an early review of self-normalization, see the work of Shao (2015). An extension to multivariate non-parametric regressions is presented in the work of Bai and Wu (2024).

49.6.4 Tests that allow for a single break

The discussion above suggests that to have better tests for the null hypothesis of no structural change versus the alternative hypothesis that changes are present, one should consider statistics that are based on a regression that allows for a break (or multiple breaks). As discussed, the suggestion by Quandt (1958, 1960) was to use the likelihood ratio test evaluated at the break date that maximizes this likelihood function. This is a non-standard problem since one parameter is only identified under the alternative hypothesis, namely the break date (see the works of Andrews and Ploberger, 1994; Davies, 1977, 1987; Hansen, 1996; King and Shively, 1993). The problem raised by Quandt was treated under various degrees of specificity by Deshayes and Picard (1984a), Worsley (1986), James *et al.* (1987), Hawkins (1987), Kim and Siegmund (1989), and Horváth (1995) and generalized by Andrews (1993b). The basic method advocated by Davies (1977), for the case in which a nuisance parameter is present only under the alternative, is to use as a test statistic the maximum of the likelihood ratio test over all possible values of the parameter in some pre-specified set. In the case of a single structural change occurring at some unknown date, this translates into the following statistic:

$$\sup_{\lambda_1 \in \Lambda_\epsilon} LR_T(\lambda_1),$$

where $LR(\lambda_1)$ denotes the value of the likelihood ratio evaluated at some break point $T_1 = [T\lambda_1]$ and the maximization is restricted over break fractions that are in the set $\Lambda_\epsilon = [\epsilon_1, 1-\epsilon_2]$, a subset of the unit interval $[0,1]$ with ϵ_1 being the lower bound and $1-\epsilon_2$ the upper bound. The limit distribution of the statistic is given by

$$\sup_{\lambda_1 \in \Lambda_\epsilon} LR_T(\lambda_1) \Rightarrow \sup_{\lambda_1 \in \Lambda_\epsilon} G_q(\lambda_1),$$

where

$$G_q(\lambda_1) = \frac{[\lambda_1 W_q(1) - W_q(\lambda_1)]'[\lambda_1 W_q(1) - W_q(\lambda_1)]}{\lambda_1(1-\lambda_1)}, \tag{49.12}$$

with $W_q(\lambda)$ a vector of independent Wiener processes of dimension q, the number of coefficients that are allowed to change (this result holds with non-trending data). Not surprisingly, the limit distribution depends on q and also on Λ_ϵ. This is important since the restriction that the search for a maximum value be restricted is not simply a technical requirement. It influences the properties of the test. In particular, Andrews (1993b) showed that if $\epsilon_1 = \epsilon_2 = 0$ so that no restrictions are imposed, the test diverges to infinity under the null hypothesis (an earlier statement of this result in a more specialized context can be found in the work of Deshayes and Picard, 1984b). This means that critical values grow and the power of the test decreases as ϵ_1 and ϵ_2 get smaller. Hence, the range over which we search for a maximum must be small enough for the critical values not to be too large and for the test to retain descent power, yet large enough to include break dates that are potential candidates. In the single break case, a popular choice is $\epsilon_1 = \epsilon_2 = 0.15$. Andrews (1993b) tabulated critical values for a range of dimensions q and for intervals of the form $[\epsilon, 1-\epsilon]$. This does not imply, however, that one is restricted to imposing equal trimming at both ends of the sample. This is because the limit distribution depends on ϵ_1 and ϵ_2 only through the parameter $\gamma = \epsilon_2(1-\epsilon_1)/(\epsilon_1(1-\epsilon_2))$. Hence, the critical values for a symmetric trimming are also valid for some asymmetric trimmings. To be fair, the divergence stated by Andrews (1993b) is of the $\log(T)$-type rate, very slow. It is related to the fact that for a sequence of stationary random variables, z_t say, over $t = 1, \ldots, T$, we have

$$\sup_{t=1,\ldots,T} z_t = O_p(\ln(T)).$$

Hence, it is more of a technical issue and, in practice, one can safely use a very small trimming, even as small as 1%. In finite samples, the critical values may change slightly but the size of the test will remain adequate.

To better understand these results, it is useful to look at the simple one-time shift in mean of some variable y_t specified by

$$y_t = \mu_1 + \mu_2 1(t > T_b) + e_t. \tag{49.13}$$

For a given break date $T_1 = [T\lambda_1]$, the Wald test is asymptotically equivalent to the LR test and is given by

$$W_T(\lambda_1) = \frac{\mathrm{SSR}(1,T) - \mathrm{SSR}(1,T_1) - \mathrm{SSR}(T_1+1,T)}{[\mathrm{SSR}(1,T_1) + \mathrm{SSR}(T_1+1,T)]/T},$$

where $\mathrm{SSR}(i,j)$ is the sum of squared residuals from regressing y_t on a constant using data from date i to date j, i.e.,

$$\mathrm{SSR}(i,j) = \sum_{t=i}^{j}\left(y_t - (j-i)^{-1}\sum_{t=i}^{j} y_t\right) = \sum_{t=i}^{j}\left(e_t - (j-i)^{-1}\sum_{t=i}^{j} e_t\right).$$

Then, we have, see Exercise 49.2,

$$W_T(\lambda_1) \Rightarrow [\lambda_1 W(1) - W(\lambda_1)]^2 / [\lambda_1(1-\lambda_1)],$$

which is equivalent to (49.12) for $q = 1$.

Andrews (1993b) also considered tests based on the maximal value of the Wald and LM tests and showed that they are asymptotically equivalent, i.e., they have the same limit distribution under the null hypothesis and under a sequence of local alternatives. All tests are also consistent and have non-trivial local asymptotic power against a wide range of alternatives, namely for which the parameters of interest are not constant over the interval specified by Λ_ϵ. This does not mean, however, that they all have the same behavior in finite samples. Indeed, the simulations of Vogelsang (1999) for the special case of a change in mean showed the $\sup LM_T$ test to be seriously affected by the problem of non-monotonic power, in the sense that, for a fixed sample size, the power of the test can rapidly decrease to zero as the change in mean increases. See also the work of Kim and Perron (2009b). This is again because the variance of the errors is estimated under the null hypothesis of no change. Hence, we do not discuss it any further.

Consider now a partial structural change model. In the context of Model (49.1) with *i.i.d.* errors and a single change, i.e.,

$$y_t = x_t'\beta + z_t'\delta_j + u_t, \quad t = T_{j-1}+1, \ldots, T_j,$$

for $j = 1, 2$, the LR and Wald tests have similar properties, so we discuss the Wald test. For a single change, it is defined by (up to a scaling by q)

$$\sup_{\lambda_1 \in \Lambda_\epsilon} W_T(\lambda_1; q) = \sup_{\lambda_1 \in \Lambda_\epsilon} \left(\frac{T-2q-p}{k}\right) \frac{\hat{\delta}' H'(H(\bar{Z}' M_X \bar{Z})^{-1} H')^{-1} H\hat{\delta}}{\mathrm{SSR}_k}, \tag{49.14}$$

where H is a matrix such that $(H\delta)' = (\delta_1' - \delta_2')$ and $M_X = I - X(X'X)^{-1}X'$. Here, SSR_k is the sum of squared residuals under the alternative hypothesis, which depends on the break date T_1.

One thing that is very useful with the $\sup W_T$ test is that the break point that maximizes the Wald test is the same as that obtained by minimizing the sum of squared residuals provided the minimization problem (49.3) is restricted to the set Λ_ϵ, i.e.,

$$\sup_{\lambda_1 \in \Lambda_\epsilon} W_T(\lambda_1; q) = W_T(\hat{\lambda}_1; q).$$

When serial correlation and/or heteroskedasticity in the errors are permitted, things are different since the Wald test must be adjusted to account for this. In this case, it is defined by

$$W_T^*(\lambda_1; q) = \frac{1}{T}\left(\frac{T-2q-p}{k}\right) \hat{\delta}' H'(H\hat{V}(\hat{\delta})H')^{-1} H\hat{\delta}, \tag{49.15}$$

where $\hat{V}(\hat{\delta})$ is an estimate of the covariance matrix of $\hat{\delta}$ that is robust to serial correlation and heteroskedasticity; i.e., a consistent estimate of

$$V(\hat{\delta}) = plim_{T\to\infty} T(\bar{Z}'M_X\bar{Z})^{-1}\bar{Z}'M_X\Omega M_X\bar{Z}(\bar{Z}'M_X\bar{Z})^{-1}. \quad (49.16)$$

Note that it can be constructed allowing identical or different distributions for the regressors and the errors across segments. This is important because if a variance shift occurs at the same time and is not taken into account, inference can be distorted; see the works of Pitarakis (2004) Perron and Yamamoto (2019a).

The computation of the robust version of the Wald test (49.15) can be involved especially if a data-dependent method is used to construct the robust asymptotic covariance matrix of $\hat{\delta}$. Since the estimates of the break fractions are T-consistent even with correlated errors, an asymptotically equivalent version is to first take the supremum of the original Wald test, as in (49.14), to obtain the break points, i.e., imposing $\Omega = \sigma^2 I$. The robust version of the test is obtained by evaluating (49.15) and (49.16) at these estimated break dates, i.e., using $W_T^*(\hat{\lambda}_1; q)$ instead of $\sup_{\lambda_1\in\Lambda_\epsilon} W_T^*(\lambda_1; q)$, where $\hat{\lambda}_1$ is obtained by minimizing the sum of squared residuals over the set Λ_ϵ. This is especially helpful in the context of testing for multiple structural changes.

49.6.5 Locally optimal tests allowing breaks

The sup-LR or sup-Wald tests are not optimal, except in a very restrictive sense. Andrews and Ploberger (1994) considered a class of tests that are optimal, in the sense that they maximize a weighted average power. Two types of weights are involved. The first applies to the parameter that is only identified under the alternative. It assigns a weight function $J(\lambda_1)$ that can be given the interpretation of a prior distribution over the possible break dates or break fractions. The other is related to how far the alternative value is from the null hypothesis within an asymptotic framework that treats alternative values as being local to the null hypothesis. The dependence of a given statistic on this weight function occurs only through a single-scalar parameter c. The higher the value of c, the more distant is the alternative value from the null value, and vice versa.

The optimal test is then a weighted function of the standard Wald, LM, or LR statistics for all permissible fixed break dates. Using either of the three basic statistics leads to tests that are asymptotically equivalent. Here, we proceed with the version based on the Wald test (and comment briefly on the version based on the LM test).

The class of optimal statistics is of the following exponential form:

$$\text{Exp-}W_T(c) = (1+c)^{-q/2} \int \exp\left\{\frac{1}{2}\frac{c}{1+c} W_T(\lambda_1)\right\} dJ(\lambda_1),$$

where we recall that q is the number of parameters that are subject to change and $W_T(\lambda_1)$ is the standard Wald test defined in our context as in (49.14). To implement this test in practice, one needs to specify $J(\lambda_1)$ and c. A natural choice for $J(\lambda_1)$ is to specify it so that equal weights are given to all break fractions in some trimmed interval $[\epsilon_1, 1-\epsilon_2]$. For the parameter c, one version sets $c = 0$ and puts greatest weight on alternatives close to the null value, i.e., on small shifts; the other version specifies $c = \infty$, in which case the greatest weight is put on large changes. This leads to two statistics that have found wide appeal. When $c = \infty$, the test is of an exponential form:

$$\text{Exp-}W_T(\infty) = \log\left(T^{-1} \sum_{T_1=[T\epsilon_1]+1}^{T-[T\epsilon_2]} \exp\left(W_T\left(T_1/T\right)/2\right)\right).$$

When $c = 0$, the test takes the form of an average of the Wald tests and is often referred to as the Mean-W_T test. It is given by

$$\text{Mean-}W_T = \text{Exp-}W_T(0) = T^{-1} \sum_{T_1=[T\epsilon_1]+1}^{T-[T\epsilon_2]} W_T\left(T_1/T\right).$$

The limit distributions of the tests are

$$\text{Exp-}W_T(\infty) \Rightarrow \log\left(\int_{\epsilon_1}^{1-\epsilon_2} \exp\left(G_q(\lambda_1)/2\right) d\lambda_1\right),$$

$$\text{Mean-}W_T \Rightarrow \int_{\epsilon_1}^{1-\epsilon_2} G_q(\lambda_1) d\lambda_1,$$

where $\mathrm{G}_q(\lambda_1)$ is defined in (49.12).

Andrews and Ploberger (1994) presented critical values for both tests for a range of values for symmetric trimmings $\epsilon_1 = \epsilon_2$, though as stated above they can be used for some non-symmetric trimmings as well. Relative to other tests discussed above, the Mean-W_T has the highest power for small shifts, though the test Exp-$W_T(\infty)$ performs better for moderate to large shifts. None of them uniformly dominates the Sup-W_T test and they recommend the use of the Exp-$W_T(\infty)$ form of the test, referred to as the Exp-Wald test in the following.

As mentioned above, both tests can equally be implemented (with the same asymptotic critical values) with the LM or LR tests replacing the Wald test. As noted by Andrews and Ploberger (1994), the Mean-LM test is closely related to Gardner's test (discussed above in Section 49.6.1). This is because, in the change in mean case, the LM test takes the form of a scaled partial sums. Given the poor properties of this test, especially with respect to large shifts when the power can reach zero, we do not recommend the tests based on the LM version. In our context, tests based on the Wald or LR statistics have similar properties.

The Sup-Wald and Exp-Wald tests have monotonic power when only one break occurs under the alternative. As shown in the work of Vogelsang (1999), the Mean-Wald test can exhibit a non-monotonic power function, though the problem has not been shown to be severe. All of these, however, suffer from some important power problems when the alternative is one that involves two breaks. Simulations to that effect are presented in the work of Vogelsang (1997) in the context of testing for a shift in trend. This suggests that, even though a single break test is consistent against multiple breaks, substantial power gains can result from using tests for multiple structural changes.

49.6.6 Tests for multiple structural changes

The literature on tests for multiple structural changes is relatively scarce. Andrews *et al.* (1996) studied a class of so-called optimal tests. However, the Avg-W and Exp-W tests require the computation of the W-test over all permissible partitions of the sample, hence the number of tests that need to be evaluated is of the order $O(T^m)$, which is already very large with $m = 2$ and prohibitively large when $m > 2$.

Consider instead the Sup-W test. With *i.i.d.* errors, maximizing the Wald statistic with respect to admissible break points is equivalent to minimizing the sum of squared residuals when the search is restricted to the same possible partitions of the sample. As discussed in Section 49.1.2, this maximization problem can be solved with a very efficient algorithm. This is the approach taken by Bai and Perron (1998) (also used with two breaks in the work of Garcia and Perron, 1996). A method to efficiently evaluate the Avg-W test was proposed by Kurozumi (2015). None so far are available for the Exp-W test.

In the context of the linear model (49.1) with *i.i.d.* errors, the Wald test for testing the null hypothesis of no change versus the alternative hypothesis of k changes is given by

$$W_T(\lambda_1, \ldots, \lambda_k; q) = \left(\frac{T-(k+1)q-p}{k}\right)\frac{\hat{\delta}'H'(H(\bar{Z}'M_X\bar{Z})^{-1}H')^{-1}H\hat{\delta}}{\mathrm{SSR}_k},$$

where H now is the matrix such that $(H\delta)' = (\delta_1' - \delta_2', \ldots, \delta_k' - \delta_{k+1}')$ and $M_X = I - X(X'X)^{-1}X'$. Here, SSR_k is the sum of squared residuals under the alternative hypothesis, which depends on $(T_1, \ldots, T_k)$. Note that one can allow different variance across segments when constructing SSR_k, see the work of Bai and Perron (2003a) for details. The sup-W test is defined by

$$\sup_{(\lambda_1,\ldots,\lambda_k)\in\Lambda_{k,\epsilon}} W_T(\lambda_1, \ldots, \lambda_k; q) = W_T(\hat{\lambda}_1, \ldots, \hat{\lambda}_k; q),$$

where

$$\Lambda_\epsilon = \{(\lambda_1, \ldots, \lambda_k); |\lambda_{i+1} - \lambda_i| \geq \epsilon, \lambda_1 \geq \epsilon, \lambda_k \leq 1-\epsilon\},$$

and $(\hat{\lambda}_1, \ldots, \hat{\lambda}_k) = (\hat{T}_1/T, \ldots, \hat{T}_k/T)$, with $(\hat{T}_1, \ldots, \hat{T}_k)$ the estimates of the break dates obtained by minimizing the sum of squared residuals searching over partitions defined by the set Λ_ϵ. When serial correlation and/or heteroskedasticity in the residuals is allowed, the test is

$$W_T^*(\lambda_1, \ldots, \lambda_k; q) = \frac{1}{T}\left(\frac{T-(k+1)q-p}{k}\right)\hat{\delta}'H'(H\hat{V}(\hat{\delta})H')^{-1}H\hat{\delta},$$

with $\hat{V}(\hat{\delta})$ as defined by (49.16). Again, the asymptotically equivalent version with the Wald test evaluated at the estimates $(\hat{\lambda}_1, \ldots, \hat{\lambda}_k)$ is used to make the problem tractable. The limit distribution of the tests under the null hypothesis is the same in both cases, namely

$$\sup W_T(k; q) \Rightarrow \sup W_{k,q} \stackrel{\text{def}}{=} \sup_{(\lambda_1,\ldots,\lambda_k)\in\Lambda_\epsilon} W(\lambda_1, \ldots, \lambda_k; q),$$

with

$$W(\lambda_1, \ldots, \lambda_k; q) \stackrel{\text{def}}{=} (1/k) \sum_{i=1}^{k} \frac{[\lambda_i W_q(\lambda_{i+1}) - \lambda_{i+1} W_q(\lambda_i)]'[\lambda_i W_q(\lambda_{i+1}) - \lambda_{i+1} W_q(\lambda_i)]}{\lambda_i \lambda_{i+1}(\lambda_{i+1} - \lambda_i)},$$

again, assuming non-trending data. Critical values are presented the work of in Bai and Perron (1998, 2003b). The importance of the choice of ϵ for the size and power of the test is discussed in the work of Bai and Perron (2003a, 2006). Also discussed in the work of Bai and Perron (2003a) are variations in the exact construction of the test that allow one to impose various restrictions on the nature of the errors and regressors, which can help improve power. Boldea *et al.* (2019) presented a bootstrap procedure in order to achieve better size in finite samples.

49.6.7 Double maximum tests

Often, one may not wish to pre-specify a particular number of breaks to make inference. Then, a test of the null hypothesis of no structural break against an unknown number of breaks given some upper bound M can be used. These are called the 'double maximum tests'. The first is an equal-weight version defined by

$$UD\max W_T(M, q) = \max_{1\leq m\leq M} W_T(\hat{\lambda}_1, \ldots, \hat{\lambda}_m; q),$$

where $\hat{\lambda}_j = \hat{T}_j/T$ $(j = 1, \ldots, m)$ are the estimates of the break points obtained using the global minimization of the sum of squared residuals. The second test applies weights to the individual tests such that the marginal p-values are equal across values of m and is denoted $WD\max F_T(M, q)$ (see the work of Bai and Perron, 1998, for details). The choice $M = 5$ should be sufficient for most applications. In any event, the critical values vary little as M is increased beyond 5.

The double maximum tests can play a significant role in testing for structural changes and are arguably the most useful tests to apply when trying to determine if structural changes are present. While the test for one break is consistent against alternatives involving multiple changes, its power in finite samples can sometimes be poor. First, there are types of multiple structural changes that are difficult to detect with a test for a single change (for example, two breaks with the first and third regimes the same). Second, as discussed above, tests for a particular number of changes may have non-monotonic power when the number of changes is greater than specified. Third, the simulations of Bai and Perron (2006) show that the power of the double maximum tests is almost as high as the best power that can be achieved using the test that accounts for the correct number of breaks. All these elements strongly point to their usefulness.

49.6.8 Sequential tests

Bai and Perron (1998) also discussed a test of ℓ versus $\ell + 1$ breaks, which can be used as the basis of a sequential testing procedure to estimate the number of breaks. For the model with ℓ breaks, the estimated break points denoted by $(\hat{T}_1, \ldots, \hat{T}_\ell)$ are obtained by a global minimization of the sum of squared residuals. The strategy proceeds by testing for the presence of an additional break in each of the $(\ell+1)$ segments, obtained using the estimated partition $(\hat{T}_1, \ldots, \hat{T}_\ell)$. The test amounts to the application of $(\ell + 1)$ tests of the null hypothesis of no structural change versus the alternative hypothesis of a single change. It is applied to each segment containing the observations $\hat{T}_{i-1} + 1$ to $\hat{T}_i$ $(i = 1, \ldots, \ell + 1)$. We conclude for a rejection in favor of a model with $(\ell + 1)$ breaks if the overall minimal value of the sum of squared residuals (over all segments where an additional break is included) is sufficiently smaller than the sum of squared residuals from the ℓ breaks model. The break date thus selected is the one associated with this overall minimum. More precisely, the test is defined by

$$W_T(\ell+1|\ell) = \left\{ S_T(\hat{T}_1, \ldots, \hat{T}_\ell) - \min_{1 \le i \le \ell+1} \right.$$
$$\left. \times \inf_{\tau \in \Lambda_{i,\eta}} S_T(\hat{T}_1, \ldots, \hat{T}_{i-1}, \tau, \hat{T}_i, \ldots, \hat{T}_\ell) \right\} / \hat{\sigma}^2, \tag{49.17}$$

where $S_T(\cdot)$ denotes the sum of squared residuals,

$$\Lambda_{i,\epsilon} = \{\tau; \hat{T}_{i-1} + (\hat{T}_i - \hat{T}_{i-1})\epsilon \le \tau \le \hat{T}_i - (\hat{T}_i - \hat{T}_{i-1})\epsilon\}, \tag{49.18}$$

and $\hat{\sigma}^2$ is a consistent estimate of σ^2 under the null hypothesis and also, preferably, under the alternative. Note that for $i = 1$, $S_T(\hat{T}_1, \ldots, \hat{T}_{i-1}, \tau, \hat{T}_i, \ldots, \hat{T}_\ell)$ is understood as $S_T(\tau, \hat{T}_1, \ldots, \hat{T}_\ell)$ and for $i = \ell+1$ as $S_T(\hat{T}_1, \ldots, \hat{T}_\ell, \tau)$. It is important to note that one can allow different distributions across segments for the regressors and the errors. The limit distribution of the test is related to the limit distribution of a test for a single change.

Bai (1999) considered the same problem of testing for ℓ versus $\ell+1$ breaks while allowing the breaks to be global minimizers of the sum of squared residuals under both the null and alternative hypotheses. This leads to the likelihood ratio test defined by

$$\sup LR_T(\ell+1|\ell) = \frac{S_T(\hat{T}_1, \ldots, \hat{T}_\ell) - S_T(\hat{T}_1^*, \ldots, \hat{T}_{\ell+1}^*)}{S_T(\hat{T}_1^*, \ldots, \hat{T}_{\ell+1}^*)/T},$$

where $\{\hat{T}_1, \ldots, \hat{T}_\ell\}$ and $\{\hat{T}_1^*, \ldots, \hat{T}_{\ell+1}^*\}$ are the sets of ℓ and $\ell+1$ breaks obtained by minimizing the sum of squared residuals using ℓ and $\ell+1$ break models, respectively. The limit distribution of the test is different and is given by

$$\sup LR_T(\ell+1|\ell) \Rightarrow \max\{\xi_1, \ldots, \xi_{\ell+1}\},$$

where $\xi_1, \ldots, \xi_{\ell+1}$ are independent random variables with the following distribution:

$$\xi_i = \sup_{\eta_i \le s \le 1-\eta_i} \sum_{j=1}^{q} [B_{i,j}(s)]/[s(1-s)],$$

with $B_{i,j}(s)$ independent standard Brownian bridges on $[0,1]$ and $\eta_i = \epsilon/(\lambda_i^0 - \lambda_{i-1}^0)$. Bai (1999) discussed a method to compute the asymptotic critical values and also extended the results to the case of trending regressors.

These tests can form the basis of a sequential testing procedure. One simply needs to apply the tests successively starting from $\ell = 0$, until a non-rejection occurs. The estimate of the number of breaks thus selected will be consistent provided the significance level used decreases at an appropriate rate. The simulation results of Bai and Perron (2006) show that such an estimate of the number of breaks is much better than those obtained using information criteria as suggested by, among others, Liu *et al.* (1997) and Yao (1988) (see also the work of Perron, 1997b). But such a sequential procedure should not be applied mechanically. It is easy to have cases where the procedure stops too early. The recommendation is to first use a double maximum test to ascertain if any break is at all present. The sequential tests can then be used starting at some value greater than 0 to determine the number of breaks.

49.6.9 Tests for restricted structural changes

Perron and Qu (2006) analyzed the estimation of structural change models subject to restrictions. Consider testing the null hypothesis of 0 break versus an alternative with k breaks, with the restrictions $R\delta = r$. Define

$$W_T(\lambda_1, \ldots, \lambda_k; q) = \tilde{\delta}' H' (H \tilde{V}(\tilde{\delta}) H')^- H \tilde{\delta}, \tag{49.19}$$

where $\tilde{\delta}$ is the restricted estimate of δ obtained using the partition $\{\lambda_1, \ldots, \lambda_k\}$, and $\tilde{V}(\tilde{\delta})$ is an estimate of the variance covariance matrix of $\tilde{\delta}$ that may be constructed to be robust to heteroskedasticity and serial correlation in the errors. As usual, for a matrix A, A^- denotes the generalized inverse of A. Such a generalized inverse is needed since, in general, the covariance matrix of $\tilde{\delta}$ will be singular given that restrictions are imposed. The restrictions can alternatively be parameterized by the relation

$$\delta = S\theta + s,$$

where S is a $q(k+1)$ by d matrix, with d the number of basic parameters in the column vector θ, and s is a $q(k+1)$ vector of constants. Then,

$$W_T(\hat{\lambda}_1, \ldots, \hat{\lambda}_k; q, S) \Rightarrow \sup_{|\lambda_i - \lambda_{i-1}| > \varepsilon} W(\lambda_1, \ldots, \lambda_k; q, S)$$

with

$$\begin{aligned} &W(\lambda_1, \ldots, \lambda_k; q, S) \\ &\quad = W^{*\prime} S[S'(\Lambda \otimes I_q)S]^{-1} S' H' [HS(S'(\Lambda \otimes I_q)S)^{-1} H' S']^{-} \\ &\quad\quad \times HS[S'(\Lambda \otimes I_q)S]^{-1} S' W^*, \end{aligned}$$

where

$$\Lambda = \mathrm{diag}(\lambda_1, \lambda_2 - \lambda_1, \ldots, 1 - \lambda_k),$$

I_q is the standard identity matrix of dimension q and the $q(k+1)$ vector W^* is defined by

$$W^* = [W_q(\lambda_1), W_q(\lambda_2) - W_q(\lambda_1), \ldots, W_q(1) - W_q(\lambda_k)],$$

with $W_q(r)$ a q vector of independent unit Wiener processes. The limit distribution depends on the exact nature of the restrictions so that it is not possible to tabulate critical values that are valid in general. Perron and Qu (2006) discussed a simulation algorithm to compute the relevant critical values given some restrictions. Imposing valid restrictions results in tests with much improved power.

49.6.10 Joint tests for changes in coefficients and variance

The framework of Bai (2000) and Qu and Perron (2007a) permits testing for changes in the covariance matrix of the errors. However, the limit distributions are only valid assuming a normal distribution for these errors. Perron *et al.* (2020) generalized the analysis to allow multiple tests for changes in coefficients and variances of the errors allowing the errors to be non-normal and conditionally heteroskedastic (e.g., ARCH or GARCH processes). Their analysis is, however, restricted to a single equation. For estimation, the algorithm of Qu and Perron (2007a) is used.

They proposed tests for changes in the variances of the errors allowing for changes in the parameters of the regression. They also considered various extensions including testing for changes in the parameter allowing for change in variances and testing for joint changes. Both problems of changes in the distribution of the regressors and the variance of the errors can be handled using the framework of Perron *et al.* (2020). If a change in the variance of the residuals is a concern, one can perform a test for no change in some parameters of the conditional model allowing for a change in variance.

An important advantage of the general framework analyzed by Perron *et al.* (2020) is that it allows studying changes in the variance of the errors in the presence of simultaneous changes in the parameters of the conditional mean, thereby avoiding inference problem when changes in variance are studied in isolation. Also, it allows for the two types of changes to occur at different dates, thereby avoiding problems related to tests for changes in the parameters when, for example, a change in variance occurs at some other date; see, e.g., the works of Hansen (2000), Pitarakis (2004), and Perron and Yamamoto (2019a).

49.6.11 Tests valid with I(1) regressors

With $I(1)$ regressors, the case of interest is that of a system of cointegrated variables. The goal is then to test whether the cointegrating relationship has changed and to estimate the break dates and form confidence intervals for them.

Consider, for simplicity, the following case with an intercept and m $I(1)$ regressors y_{2t}:

$$y_{1t} = a + \beta y_{2t} + u_t, \tag{49.20}$$

where u_t is $I(0)$ so that y_{1t} and y_{2t} are cointegrated with cointegrating vector $(1, -\beta)$. An early contribution concerning the consistency and limit distribution of the estimates of the break dates is that of Bai *et al.* (1998); see also Hansen (1992b) and Kuo (1998) who considered the sup and Mean LM tests directed against an alternative of a one-time change in the coefficients.

Kejriwal and Perron (2010b) provided a comprehensive treatment of issues related to testing for multiple structural changes at unknown dates in cointegrated regression models using the Sup-Wald test. They allowed both $I(0)$ and $I(1)$ variables and derived the limiting distribution of the Sup-Wald test for some given number of cointegrating regimes. They also considered the double maximum tests and provided critical values for a wide variety of models that are expected to be relevant in practice. The asymptotic results have important implications for inference. It is shown that in models involving both $I(1)$ and $I(0)$ variables, inference is possible as long as the intercept is allowed to change across regimes. Otherwise, the limiting distributions of the tests depend on nuisance parameters. They propose a modified Sup-Wald test that has good size and power properties. Note, however, that the Sup and Mean-Wald test will also reject when no structural change is present and the system is not cointegrated. Hence, the application of such tests should be interpreted with caution.

An interesting related contribution is the work of Qu (2007). He recognized that regime changes may mask cointegration relationships, rendering cointegration tests uninformative. He proposed tests to detect whether a cointegration relationship holds in any one or more parts of the sample. Specifically, he tested the null hypothesis of r_0, which can be zero, stable cointegrating vectors against the alternative hypothesis of more than r_0 cointegrating vectors existing in some sub-sample. The tests proposed follow the work of Breitung (2002). A distinctive feature is that they allow us to detect the hidden cointegration when the system is affected by an unknown number of regime changes at unknown dates.

Consider now a cointegrated VAR system written in the following error correction format with $y_t' = (y_{1t}, y_{2t}')'$ of dimension $n = m + 1$,

$$\Delta y_t = \mu + \alpha\beta' y_{t-1} + \sum_{i=1}^{p} \Gamma_i \Delta y_{t-i} + u_t, \qquad (49.21)$$

where β $(n \times r)$ is the cointegrating matrix and α $(n \times r)$ the adjustment matrix (hence, there are r cointegrating vectors). Under the null hypothesis, both are assumed constant, while under the alternative, either one or both are assumed to exhibit a one-time change at some unknown date T_1. For the case of a triangular system with the restriction that $\beta' = [I_r, \beta^*]$, Seo (1998) considered the Sup, Mean, and Exp versions of the LM test for the following three cases: (1) the constant vector μ is excluded (and the data are assumed non-trending), (2) the constant μ is included but the data are not trending, and (3) the constant μ is included and the data are trending. The Sup and Mean LM tests in this cointegrated VAR setup are shown to have a similar asymptotic distribution as the Sup and Mean LM tests of Hansen (1992b) for the case of a change in all coefficients. See also the work of Hao (1996) which also considers the an extension of the test of Hansen (1992b) to test for no cointegration allowing for a one-time change in intercept at some unknown date using the maximal value overall possible break dates.

Hansen and Johansen (1999) also considered a VAR process. Then, the MLE (based on normal errors) of the cointegrating matrix β are the eigenvectors corresponding to the r largest eigenvalues of the system:

$$|\lambda S_{11} - S_{10} S_{00}^{-1} S_{01}| = 0,$$

where $S_{ij} = T^{-1} \sum_{j=1}^{T} R_{it} R_{jt}$ with R_{0t} (resp., R_{1t}) the residuals from a regression of Δy_t (resp., y_{t-1}) on a constant and lags of Δy_t; see Section 46.3.1. Hansen and Johansen (1999) showed that instability in α and/or β will manifest themselves in the form of instability in the eigenvalues' estimates when evaluated using different samples. They therefore suggest the use of the recursive estimates of λ. Their test takes the form of the fluctuations test of Ploberger *et al.* (1989) and will have power when either α or β change (see also the work of Quintos, 1998). They also suggest a test that allows the detection of changes in β, an extension of the test of Hansen (1992b) that can be constructed using recursive estimates of λ. Interestingly, Quintos (1998) documented that such tests over-reject the null hypothesis of no structural change when the cointegrating rank is over specified, i.e., when the number of stochastic trends, or unit root components, is under-specified. This is the multivariate equivalent of the problem discussed earlier, namely that structural change and unit roots can easily be confounded. She proposes a test for the stability of the cointegrating rank. However, when the alternative hypothesis is of a greater rank (less unit roots), the tests will not have power if structural change is present. This is the dilemma faced when trying to assess jointly the correct rank of a cointegrating system and whether structural change is present in the cointegrating vectors.

From this brief review, most tests available, except those of the work of Kejriwal and Perron (2010b), are seen to be of the LM type. Given our earlier discussion, these can be expected to have non-monotonic power since they do not explicitly allow for any break. Also, these tests are valid if the cointegrating rank is well specified. As discussed above, a rejection can be due to an over specification of this rank. The problem of jointly determining whether the cointegrating rank is appropriate and whether the system is structurally stable is an important issue still unresolved.

49.6.12 Tests for changes in trend with $I(0)$ or $I(1)$ noise

As a starting point, we consider some results from the work of Perron and Zhu (2005) which considered the properties of the least-squares estimate of the break date in a simple first-order polynomial regression, whether a change in intercept is allowed or not. Consider the regression

$$y_t = \beta_0 + \beta_1 t + \gamma DT_t^* + u_t, \tag{49.22}$$

where $DT_t^* = 1(t > T_1)(t - T_1)$. When estimating the break date by minimizing the SSR from (49.22), assuming u_t is $I(0)$, we have the following results. Denote the resulting estimate by $\hat{T}_1$ and the associated estimate of the break fraction by $\hat{\lambda} = \hat{T}_1/T$. The limit distribution of the break fraction $\hat{\lambda}$ is

$$T^{3/2}(\hat{\lambda} - \lambda) \xrightarrow{d} N\left(0, \frac{4\sigma^2}{[\lambda_0(1-\lambda_0)(\gamma^0)^2]}\right),$$

where γ^0 is the true value of the change in the slope parameter, λ_0 is the true break fraction, and σ^2 is the long-run variance of u_t (or 2π times the spectral density function at frequency zero of u_t). Hence, it is straightforward to construct a confidence interval using estimates of σ^2, β_b^0, and λ_0. Note that in this case, the break dates themselves are consistent unlike in the case with stationary regressors.

This result is of independent interest and has been applied in a variety of contexts; e.g., Estrada *et al.* (2013), Estrada and Perron (2019), and Kim *et al.* (2020) in the context of climate change. Note that the limiting distribution of the break date does not depend on the structure of the errors (except from the long-run variance term σ^2).

Interestingly, suppose that one includes an irrelevant intercept change so that the regression is

$$y_t = \beta_0 + \beta_1 t + \gamma_1 DU_t + \gamma_2 DT_t^* + u_t, \tag{49.23}$$

where $DU_t = 1(t > T_1)$. Then, the OLS estimate of the break fraction converges at the slower rate T with a complex limit distribution that depends on the exact distribution of the regressors and errors. This is because the level shift dummy allows one to pick up extra variation around the true break date making the estimate less precise. When u_t is $I(1)$ in (49.22), the rate of convergence of the estimated break fraction is $T^{1/2}$, much slower than with $I(0)$ errors.

The problem of testing for structural changes in a linear model with errors that are either $I(0)$ or $I(1)$ is of substantial interest when the regression is a polynomial time trend. The leading case is testing for changes in the mean or slope of a linear trend, a question of substantial interest with economic data. We use this example to illustrate the main issues involved. Consider the specification (49.23) with the errors following a (possibly non-stationary) $AR(k)$ process $A(L)u_t = e_t$, with $A(L) = (1 - \alpha L)A^*(L)$ and the roots of $A^*(L)$ all outside the unit circle. The tests advocated by Andrews and Ploberger (1994) have different rates of convergence under the hypothesis of $I(0)$ and $I(1)$ errors when based on regression (49.23).

Perron and Yabu (2009b), following the work of Perron and Yabu (2009a) which dealt with inference about the slope of a time trend, proposed an approach which leads to powerful tests. We present the case of a model with a one-time structural break in the slope of the trend function with an autoregressive noise component of order one ($AR(1)$). A more detailed presentation of this case and of other structural change models and extensions can be found in the work of Perron and Yabu (2009b). As an example, consider the following data generating process:

$$y_t = x_t'\Psi + u_t; \quad u_t = \alpha u_{t-1} + e_t, \tag{49.24}$$

for $t = 1, \ldots, T$, $e_t \sim i.i.d.\left(0, \sigma^2\right)$. The initial condition u_0 is assumed to be bounded in probability. The autoregressive coefficient is such that $|\alpha| \leq 1$ and therefore, both integrated and stationary errors are allowed. The model to test for a one-time change in the slope of the trend function is specified with

$$x_t = (1, t, DT_t)',$$

and $\Psi = (\mu_0, \beta_0, \beta_1)'$, where

$$DT_t = 1\,(t > T_1)\,(t - T_1)$$

so that the trend function is joined at the time of the break. The hypothesis of interest is $\beta_1 = 0$.

The testing procedure is based on a quasi feasible generalized least squares approach that uses a superefficient estimate of the sum of the autoregressive parameters α when $\alpha = 1$. The estimate of α is the OLS estimate obtained from an autoregression applied to detrended data and is truncated to take a value 1 when the estimate is in a $T^{-\delta}$ neighborhood of 1. This makes the estimate "super-efficient" when $\alpha = 1$ (see Exercises 15.8 and 15.9) and implies that in the case of a known break date, inference on the slope parameter can be performed using the standard normal or chi-square distribution whether $\alpha = 1$ or $|\alpha| < 1$. Theoretical arguments and simulation evidence show that $\delta = 1/2$ is the appropriate choice.

When the break date are unknown, the limit distribution is nearly the same in the $I(0)$ and $I(1)$ cases when considering the Exp functional of the Wald test across all permissible dates for a specified equation, see the work of Andrews and Ploberger (1994). Hence, it is possible to have tests with nearly the same size in both cases. To improve the finite sample properties of the test, they also use a bias-corrected version of the OLS estimate of α as suggested by Roy and Fuller (2001). The testing procedure suggested is ass follows:

1. For any given break date, detrend the data by Ordinary Least Squares (OLS) to obtain the residuals $\hat{u}_t$.
2. Estimate an AR(1) model for $\hat{u}_t$ yielding the estimate $\hat{\alpha}$.

3. Use $\hat{\alpha}$ to get the Roy and Fuller (2001) biased corrected estimate $\hat{\alpha}_M$, see Remark 49.2.
4. Apply the truncation

$$\hat{\alpha}_{MS} = \begin{cases} \hat{\alpha}_M & if\ |\hat{\alpha}_M - 1| > T^{-1/2}, \\ 1 & if\ |\hat{\alpha}_M - 1| \leq T^{-1/2}. \end{cases}$$

5. Apply a Generalized Least Squares (GLS) procedure with $\hat{\alpha}_{MS}$ to obtain the estimates of the coefficients of the trend and the variance of the residuals and construct the standard Wald statistic W_{FMS}.
6. Since the break date are assumed to be unknown, the above five steps must be repeated for all permissible break dates to construct the Exp functional of the Wald test denoted by

$$\text{Exp-}W_{FS} = \log\left[T^{-1}\sum_{\Lambda}\exp\left((1/2)W_{FMS}(\lambda)\right)\right], \tag{49.25}$$

where $\Lambda = \{\lambda; \epsilon \leq \lambda \leq 1-\epsilon\}$ for some $\epsilon > 0$. A value $\epsilon = 0.15$ is common in the literature, though others are certainly possible.

Remark 49.1. To illustrate the problem and the need for a super-efficient estimate when $\alpha = 1$, consider the simple case with $x_t = DT_t$ and $\Psi = \beta_1$. Also suppose that the date of the break point is known. When $|\alpha| < 1$, it is easy to show that the limit distribution of the t-statistic for testing $\beta_1 = 0$ is $N(0,1)$ and that of the Wald test is $\chi^2(1)$. However, when $\alpha = 1$, the limit distribution is given by (see Exercise 49.7)

$$t_F \Rightarrow \frac{\begin{array}{l} W(1) - W(\lambda_1) - \kappa\int_{\lambda_1}^1 W(r)dr \\ \quad - \kappa[\int_{\lambda_1}^1 (r-\lambda_1)dW(r) - \kappa\int_{\lambda_1}^1 (r-\lambda_1)W(r)dr] \end{array}}{[(1-\lambda_1) - \kappa(1-\lambda_1)^2 + \kappa^2(1-\lambda_1)^3/3]^{1/2}}, \tag{49.26}$$

where κ is defined by

$$T(\hat{\alpha}-1) \Rightarrow \int_0^1 W^*(r)dW(r) \Big/ \int_0^1 W^*(r)^2 dr \equiv \kappa,$$

with $W^*(r)$, $0 \leq r \leq 1$, the continuous time residual function from a projection of a Wiener process $W(r)$ on the continuous-time version of the deterministic components, here $\{1(r > \lambda_1)\}$. This is different from a standard normal distribution. Accordingly, the limit of the Wald statistic, $W_F = {t_F}^2$, is no longer chi-square distributed. Suppose now that κ, the limit of $T(\hat{\alpha} - 1)$, was zero, then,

$$t_F \Rightarrow [W(1) - W(\lambda_1)]/(1 - \lambda_1)^{1/2} \stackrel{d}{=} N(0, 1),$$

and, hence,

$$W_F \Rightarrow [W(1) - W(\lambda_1)]^2/(1 - \lambda_1) \stackrel{d}{=} \chi^2(1).$$

We would then recover in the unit root case the same limiting distribution as in the stationary case and no discontinuity would be present. Perron and Yabu (2009b) exploited this fact to derive a testing procedure with the same limit distribution in both the $I(0)$ and $I(1)$ cases. This is achieved using the super-efficient estimator when $\alpha = 1$. Then,

$$\hat{\alpha}_{MS} \stackrel{p}{\to} 0.$$

When the break date is unknown, this equivalence no longer holds for various functionals of the limit distribution, even though for each fixed break point the limit is $\chi^2(1)$ whether the noise is $I(0)$ or $I(1)$. However, the limit distribution of the test $Exp\text{-}W_{FS}$ defined by (49.25) is nearly the same in both cases. While theoretically they are different, the quantiles are very close so that inference can be carried out with minimal size distortions.

Remark 49.2. The truncated weighted symmetric least-squares estimate. The weighted symmetric least-squares estimate of the autoregressive parameter α is defined by

$$\hat{\alpha}_W = \left[\sum_{t=2}^{T-1} \hat{u}_t^2 + T^{-1} \sum_{t=1}^{T} \hat{u}_t^2\right]^{-1} \sum_{t=2}^{T} \hat{u}_t \hat{u}_{t-1}.$$

An estimate of its variance is given by

$$\hat{\sigma}_W^2 = \left[\sum_{t=2}^{T-1} \hat{u}_t^2 + T^{-1} \sum_{t=1}^{T} \hat{u}_t^2\right]^{-1} (T-3)^{-1} \sum_{t=2}^{T} (\hat{u}_t - \hat{\alpha}_W \hat{u}_{t-1})^2,$$

and the associated t-ratio for testing that $\alpha = 1$ is

$$\hat{\tau}_W = (\hat{\alpha}_W - 1)/\hat{\sigma}_W.$$

The modification proposed by Roy and Fuller (2001) is similar in spirit to the Perron and Yabu (2009a) superefficient estimate in that it also replaces estimates which are in a $T^{1/2}$ neighborhood of one. The modification is, however, discontinuous and depends on the value of the t-ratio $\hat{\tau}_W$, making the procedure explicitly dependent on some pre-test. The modified value is given by

$$\hat{\alpha}_{TW} = \hat{\alpha}_W + C(\hat{\tau}_W)\hat{\sigma}_W,$$

where

$$C(\hat{\tau}_W) = \begin{cases} -\hat{\tau}_W & \text{if } \hat{\tau}_W > \tau_{pct} \\ T^{-1}\hat{\tau}_W - 3[\hat{\tau}_W + k(\hat{\tau}_W + 5)]^{-1} & \text{if } -5 < \hat{\tau}_W \leq \tau_{pct} \\ T^{-1}\hat{\tau}_W - 3[\hat{\tau}_W]^{-1} & \text{if } -(3T)^{1/2} < \hat{\tau}_W \leq -5 \\ 0 & \text{if } \hat{\tau}_W \leq -(3T)^{1/2} \end{cases}$$

with $k = [3T - \tau_{pct}^2(I_p + T)][\tau_{pct}(5 + \tau_{pct})(I_p + T)]^{-1}$, where in the case of a general noise component with an $AR(p)$ structure, I_p is the integer part of $(p+1)/2$, and τ_{pct} is the percentile of the limiting distribution of $\hat{\tau}_W$ when $\alpha = 1$. The form of the WSLS estimator for an $AR(p)$ process is given in the work of Fuller (1996, p. 572). If $\tau_{pct} = -1.96$, the median of the distribution of $\hat{\tau}_W$ when $\alpha = 1$, $\hat{\alpha}_{TW}$ is approximately median unbiased, in the sense that it is nearly unbiased when $\alpha < 1$ and has a median of 1 when $\alpha = 1$.

Another proposal is that of Harvey *et al.* (2009a) building on the work of Harvey *et al.* (2007). It suffers from the same drawback as that of Vogelsang (2001), namely that under $I(1)$ errors the statistics is a random version of the best test (the one applied to first differences), thereby considerably reducing power in that case. This is not the case with the approach of Perron and Yabu (2009a) since when either $\alpha = 1$ or $|\alpha| < 1$, the optimal test is applied. This argument, however, holds only point-wise in α, not uniformly. Hence, some size distortions are expected and, indeed, the test is conservative when α is local to one. The Perron and Yabu (2009a) test has greater power overall; see the work of Chun and Perron (2013). Kejriwal and Perron (2010a) extended the results to show that their can be applied in a sequential manner using the same critical values. An alternative perspective was provided by Sayginsoy and Vogelsang (2011) who use a fixed-bandwidth asymptotic theory. Extensions that allow the errors to be fractionally integrated have been considered by Iacone *et al.* (2013a,b). Carrion-i Silvestre and Gadea (2023) considered testing for multiple level shifts with an integrated or stationary noise component.

49.6.13 Testing for change in persistence

A problem involving structural change and the presence of $I(0)$ and $I(1)$ processes relates to the literature on change in persistence. What is meant, in most cases, by this is that a process can switch at some date from being $I(0)$ to being $I(1)$, or vice versa. This has been an issue of substantial empirical interest, especially concerning inflation rate series (e.g., Barsky, 1987; Burdekin and Siklos, 1999), short-term interest rates (e.g., Mankiw *et al.*, 1987), government budget deficits (e.g., Hakkio and Rush, 1991), and real output (e.g., De Long *et al.*, 1988). Chong (2001) derived the limit distribution of the estimate of the break date obtained by minimizing the sum of squared residuals from a regression that allows the coefficient on the lagged dependent variable to change at some unknown date; see also the work of Kejriwal and Perron (2012). However, he provided no procedure to test whether a change has occurred and in which direction.

As discussed, tests for structural change started with statistics based on partial sums of the data (or some appropriate residuals, in general) as in the Q test of Gardner (1969), and tests of the null hypothesis of stationarity versus a unit root process started with the same statistic. Interestingly, we are again back to the work of Gardner (1969) when devising procedures to test for a change in persistence. Kim (2000) and Busetti and Taylor (2005) consider testing the null hypothesis that the series is $I(0)$ throughout the sample versus the alternative that it switches from $I(0)$ to $I(1)$ or vice versa. The statistic used is the ratio of the unscaled Gardner (1969) Q test over the post- and pre-break samples. Busetti and Taylor (2005) suggested using the maximum of the test and its reciprocal (whether the sup, Mean, or Exp functional is used). Interestingly, Leybourne and

Taylor (2004) suggested a scaling so that the test is then exactly the ratio of the Q tests applied to each sub-samples. An issue related to this class of tests is the fact that they reject the null hypothesis often when the process is actually $I(1)$ throughout the sample. Harvey *et al.* (2006) used the same device suggested by Vogelsang (1998, 2001) to solve the problem. Busetti and Taylor (2005) also considered locally best invariant (LBI) tests. As discussed previously, this class of test has important problems (e.g., non-monotonic power) and here is no exception.

Kejriwal *et al.* (2013) proposed sup-Wald tests of the null hypothesis that the process is $I(1)$ against the alternative hypothesis that the process alternates between stationary and $I(1)$ regimes. The tests are based on the difference between the sum of squared residuals from the unit root model and those from a model that allows shifts in persistence between stationary and non-stationary regimes. They considered tests for both single and multiple changes in persistence. The limit distributions of the tests are derived under the null and their consistency is established under the relevant alternatives. They further show that the tests are inconsistent when directed against the incorrect alternative, thereby allowing the researcher to identify the nature of persistence in the initial regime. Also proposed is a hybrid testing procedure that allows ruling out stable stationary processes or ones that are subject to only stationary changes under the null, thereby aiding the researcher interpret a rejection as emanating from a switch between a unit root and stationary regime. The tests can be used to distinguish between persistence breaks and pure level or trend breaks. The computation of the test statistics as well as asymptotic critical values is facilitated by the dynamic programming algorithm proposed in the work of Perron and Qu (2006) which allows the minimization of the sum of squared residuals under the alternative hypothesis while imposing within and cross regime restrictions on the parameters. Estimators for the break dates are also proposed, which can be used once evidence against a stable persistence parameter is obtained. Simulations show that the tests perform well and offer improvements over previously suggested procedures. One drawback is that it assumes constant variance in the errors. Kejriwal *et al.* (2020) proposed a bootstrap method to have tests valid under nonstationary variance.

49.7 Endogenous regressors

Consider a model with errors correlated with the regressors:

$$y = \bar{X}\delta + u, \tag{49.27}$$

where $\bar{X} = \text{diag}(X_1, \ldots, X_{m+1})$, a T by $(m+1)p$ matrix with $X_i = (x_{T_{i-1}+1}, \ldots, x_{T_i})'$ $(i = 1, \ldots, m+1)$. This includes partial structural change models imposing $R\delta = r$ with R a k by $(m+1)p$ matrix.

When the regressors are correlated with the errors, we assume a set of q variables w_t that can serve as instruments and define the T by q matrix $W = (w_1, \ldots, w_T)'$. We consider a reduced form linking W and X that itself exhibits m_w changes so that

$$X = \bar{W}^0\theta^0 + v,$$

with

$$\bar{W}^0 = \text{diag}(W_1^0, \ldots, W_{m_w+1}^0),$$

the diagonal partition of W at the break dates $(T_1^{z0}, \ldots, T_{m_w}^{z0})$ and $\theta^0 = (\theta_1^0, \ldots, \theta_{m_w+1}^0)$. Also, $v = (v_1, \ldots, v_T)'$ is a T by q matrix, which can be correlated with u_t but not with w_t. Given estimates $(\hat{T}_1^z, \ldots, \hat{T}_{m_w}^z)$ obtained using the method of Bai and Perron (2003a), one constructs

$$\hat{W} = \text{diag}(\hat{W}_1, \ldots, \hat{W}_{m_w+1}),$$

a T by $(m_w + 1)q$ matrix with $\hat{W}_l = (w_{\hat{T}_{l-1}^z+1}, \ldots, w_{\hat{T}_l^z})'$ for $l = 1, \ldots, m_w + 1$. Let $\hat{\theta}$ be the OLS estimate in a regression of X on $\hat{W}$. The instruments are

$$\hat{X} = \hat{W}\hat{\theta} = \text{diag}(\hat{X}_1', \ldots, \hat{X}_{m_z+1}')',$$

where

$$\hat{X}_l = \hat{W}_l(\hat{W}_l'\hat{W}_l)^{-1}\hat{W}_l'\tilde{X}_l$$

with

$$\tilde{X}_l = (x_{\hat{T}^z_{l-1}+1}, \ldots, x_{\hat{T}^z_l})'.$$

The instrumental variable (IV) regression is

$$y = \bar{X}^* \delta + \tilde{u}, \tag{49.28}$$

subject to the restrictions $R\delta = r$, where

$$\bar{X}^* = \text{diag}(\hat{X}_1, \ldots, \hat{X}_{m+1}),$$

a T by $(m+1)p$ matrix with $\hat{X}_j = (\hat{x}_{T_{j-1}+1}, \ldots, \hat{x}_{T_j})'$ $(j = 1, \ldots, m+1)$. Also, $\tilde{u} = (\tilde{u}_1, \ldots, \tilde{u}_T)'$ with

$$\tilde{u}_t = u_t + \eta_t,$$

where

$$\eta_t = (x_t' - \hat{x}_t')\delta_j,$$

for $T^0_{j-1} + 1 \leq t \leq T^0_j$. The estimates of the break dates are

$$(\hat{T}_1, \ldots, \hat{T}_{m_x}) = \arg \min_{T_1, \ldots, T_{m_x}} \text{SSR}^R_T(T_1, \ldots, T_m),$$

where $\text{SSR}^R_T(T_1, \ldots, T_m)$ is the SSR from (49.28) evaluated at $\{T_1, \ldots, T_m\}$. Perron and Yamamoto (2014) provided a simple proof of the consistency and limit distribution of the estimates of the break dates showing that using generated (or second stage) regressors implies that the assumptions of Perron and Qu (2006) are satisfied. For an earlier, more elaborate though less comprehensive treatment, see the works of Hall *et al.* (2012) and Boldea *et al.* (2012). Hence, all results of Bai and Perron (1998) carry through but care must be applied when the structural and reduced forms contain non-common break.

Of substantive interest is that the IV approach is not necessary as discussed in the work of Perron and Yamamoto (2015); one can simply still use OLS applied to (49.27). First, except for a knife-edge case, changes in the true parameters imply a change in the probability limits of the OLS estimates, which is equivalent in the leading case of regressors and errors having a homogenous distribution across segments. Second, one can reformulate the model with those limits as the basic parameters so that the regressors and errors are uncorrelated. We are then back to the standard framework.

Importantly, using OLS involves the original regressors while IV the second-stage regressors, which have less quadratic variation since $||P_W X|| \leq ||X||$. Hence, in most cases, a given change in the parameters will cause a larger change in the conditional mean of the dependent variable using OLS compared with IV. It follows that using OLS delivers consistent estimates of the break fractions and tests with the usual limit distributions and also improves on the efficiency of the estimates and the power of the tests in almost all cases. Also, OLS avoids weak identification problems inherent when using IV methods.

Some care must, however, be exercised. Upon a rejection, one should verify that the change in the probability limit of the OLS parameter estimates is not due to a change in the bias terms. In most applications, there will be no change in the bias but still one should be careful to assess the source of the rejection. This is easily done since after obtaining the OLS-based estimates of the break dates one would estimate the structural model based on such estimates.

The relevant quantities needed to compute the change in bias across segments are then directly available. To elaborate, assume known break dates and let

$$\underset{T\to\infty}{plim}(\Delta T_i^0)^{-1}\sum_{t=T_{i-1}^0+1}^{T_{i-1}^0+[s\Delta T_i^0]} x_t x_t' = Q_{XX}^i$$

and

$$\lim_{T\to\infty} E(X_i u) = \phi_i \quad (i = 1, \ldots, m+1),$$

the probability limit of the OLS estimate is

$$\delta^* = \delta^0 + [(Q_{XX}^1)^{-1}\phi_1, \ldots, (Q_{XX}^{m+1})^{-1}\phi_{m+1}]'.$$

Any change in δ^0 implies a change in δ^*, except for a knife-edge case when the change in the bias exactly offsets the change in δ^0. Hence, one can still identify parameter changes using OLS and a change in δ^0 will, in general, cause a larger change in the conditional mean of

y_t. Consider writing (49.27) as

$$\begin{aligned} y &= \bar{X}_0\delta^0 + P_{\bar{X}_0}u + (I - P_{\bar{X}_0})u \\ &= \bar{X}_0[\delta^0 + (\bar{X}_0'\bar{X}_0)^{-1}\bar{X}_0'u] + (I - P_{\bar{X}_0})u = \bar{X}_0\delta_T^* + u^*, \end{aligned}$$

where

$$u^* = (I - P_{\bar{X}_0})u$$

and

$$\delta_T^* = [\delta^0 + (\bar{X}_0'\bar{X}_0)^{-1}\bar{X}_0'u],$$

for which $\delta_T^* \xrightarrow{p} \delta^*$. So, we can consider a regression in terms of the population value of the parameters. Now, $\bar{X}_0$ is uncorrelated with u^* so that the OLS estimate, say $\hat{\delta}^*$, is consistent for δ^*. This suggests estimating the break dates by minimizing the SSR from the regression

$$y = \bar{X}\delta^* + u^*.$$

OLS dominates IV except for a narrow case, unlikely in practice. The loss in efficiency when using IV can be especially pronounced when the instruments are weak as is often the case.

Of course, the ultimate goal is not to get estimates of the break dates *per se* but of the parameters within each regime, one should then use an IV regression but conditioning on the estimates of the break dates obtained using the OLS-based procedure. Their limit distributions will, as usual, be the same as if the break dates were known.

Using the same logic, tests for structural change are more powerful when based on OLS rather than IV. This follows since the break dates and the changes in the parameters are more precisely estimated. This idea was used by Kurozumi (2017) to show that, with endogenous regressors, using OLS is better when monitoring online for a structural change using a CUSUM-type method.

Yu (2015) and Yu and Phillips (2018) used the idea advanced by Perron and Yamamoto (2015) to analyze the consistency of the least-squares estimator in threshold regressions with endogeneity. Their results are as expected since estimating a threshold model is similar to estimating a structural change model when the time index is replaced by the ordered variable that index the threshold.

49.8 Extensions

In this section, we discuss methods that have been proposed to estimate and test for structural change outside the frameworks considered earlier. These include the following: testing for common breaks, using band-spectral regressions, quantile regressions, LASSO, factor models, panel data models, and testing for changes in forecast performance. This section borrows heavily from the work of Casini and Perron (2019).

49.8.1 Testing for common breaks

Oka and Perron (2018) considered testing for common breaks across or within equations in a multivariate system. The framework is very general and allows stationary or integrated regressors and trends. The null hypothesis is that breaks in different parameters occur at common locations or are separated by some positive fraction of the sample size. Under the alternative hypothesis, the break dates are not the same and need not be separated by a positive fraction of the sample size across parameters. A quasi-likelihood ratio test assuming normal errors is used. The quantiles of the limit distribution need to be simulated and an efficient algorithm is provided. Kim *et al.* (2020) extended this work to cover the case of testing for common breaks in a system of equations involving joint-segmented trends. The motivation was spurred by a need to test whether the breaks in the slope of the trend functions of temperatures and radiative forcing, occurring in 1960, are common (see the work of Estrada *et al.*, 2013).

49.8.2 Band spectral regressions and low-frequency changes

Yamamoto and Perron (2013) considered the issue of testing for structural change using a band-spectral analysis. They allow changes over time within some frequency bands, permitting the coefficients to be different across frequency bands. Using standard assumptions, the limit distributions obtained are similar to those in the time-domain counterpart.

They show that when the coefficients change only within some frequency band (e.g., the business cycle), we can have increased efficiency of the estimates of the break dates and increased power for the tests provided, of course, that the user chosen band contains the band at which the changes occur.

They also discuss a very useful application in which the data are contaminated by some low-frequency process and that the researcher is interested in whether the original non-contaminated model is stable. For example, the dependent variable may be affected by some random-level shift process (a low-frequency contamination), but at the business cycle frequency, the model of interest is otherwise stable. They show that all that is needed to obtain estimates of the break dates and tests for structural changes that are not affected by such low-frequency contaminations is to truncate a low-frequency band that shrinks to zero at rate $\log(T)/T$. Simulations show that the tests have good sizes for a wide range of truncations. The exact truncation does not really matter, as long as some of the very low frequencies are excluded. Hence, the method is quite robust. They also show that the method delivers more precise estimates of the break dates and tests with better power compared to using filtered series via a band-pass filter or with a Hodrick and Prescott (1997) filter. This work is related to a recent strand in the literature that attempts to deliver methods robust to low-frequency contaminations. See Chapter 47.

49.8.3 Quantile regressions

Following the work of Oka and Qu (2011), assume that the τth conditional quantile function of y_t given x_t is linear in the parameters and given by

$$Q_{y_t}(\tau|x_t) = F^{-1}_{y_t|x_t}(\tau|x_t) = x_t\beta(\tau).$$

The population coefficient $\beta(\tau)$ is the minimizer of the criterion function

$$Q_\tau(\beta) = E[\rho_\tau(y - x'\beta)],$$

where $\rho_\tau(a)$ is the check function given by $\rho_\tau(a) = a(\tau - 1(a < 0))$; see the work of Koenker (2005) and Chapter 25. Without structural changes, the quantile regression estimator of $\beta(\tau)$ is the minimizer of the empirical analog

$$\hat{Q}_\tau(\beta) = \sum_{t=1}^{T} \rho_\tau(y_t - x_t'\beta).$$

Suppose that the τth quantile has m structural changes, occurring at unknown dates $(T_1, \ldots, T_m)$, such that

$$Q_{y_t}(\tau|x_t) = x_t'\theta_j(\tau), \quad t = T_{j-1} + 1, \ldots, T_j, \tag{49.29}$$

for $j = 1, \ldots, m + 1$. The vectors $\theta_j(\tau)$ are the quantile dependent unknown parameters, with possible restrictions to allow for partial structural changes. Qu (2008) proposed a fluctuation-type statistic based on the sub-gradient and a Wald-type statistic based on comparing parameter estimates from different sub-samples. They can be used to test for changes occurring in a prespecified quantile, or across quantiles. The limiting distributions under the null is nuisance parameter free and can be simulated. Oka and Qu (2011) considered the estimation of multiple structural changes at unknown dates in one or multiple conditional quantile functions. A procedure to determine the number of breaks is also discussed.

Of particular interest, there is an interesting difference between quantile regressions and the usual least-squares method when conducting tests for structural change. As discussed in Section 49.6.3, the CUSUM test or more generally any test based on partial sums of residuals estimated under the null hypothesis of no change is prone to be affected by problems of non-monotonic power, i.e., power that declines as the magnitude of the change increases for some given fixed sample size T. On the other hand, in the standard linear model, Wald-type tests are easy to construct and do not suffer from this problem. Hence, in least-squares-type problems, there is a clear advantage in using a test that explicitly models the change under the alternative. Here, the opposite is the case. The main reason is the following. First, least-squares methods are ultimately based on the following functional central limit theorem for the score function:

$$T^{-1/2} \sum_{t=1}^{[Tr]} x_t u_t \Rightarrow \sigma^2 W(r),$$

with $W(r)$ the unit Wiener process and σ^2 the long-run variance of $\{x_t u_t\}$. Hence, one cannot simply look at fluctuations in the partial sums of $\{x_t u_t\}$ without a proper re-scaling for σ^2. Since estimates of this quantity are constructed under the null hypothesis, whenever there is a change they get inflated and lead to non-monotonic power functions. However, following the same approach, the score (or sub-gradient) of interest in quantile regressions is

$$T^{-1/2} \sum_{t=1}^{[Tr]} x_t \psi_\tau(y_t - x_t'\beta),$$

where $\psi_\tau(a) = 1(a < 0) - \tau$. The key observation is that under the null hypothesis of no structural change, $\psi_\tau(y_t - x_t'\beta)$ is a pivotal statistic, i.e., a sequence of independent binary random variables with mean 0 and variance $\tau(1-\tau)$. Hence, no rescaling for the variance is needed. The intuition here is that what matters in quantile regressions is the relative position of some quantity with respect to the distribution function, not the absolute level. Hence, scaling is irrelevant. Qu (2008) proposed a fluctuation-type statistic based on this sub-gradient. It is given by

$$\begin{aligned} SQ_\tau &= \sup_{\lambda \in [0,1]} ||(\tau(1-\tau))^{-1/2}[H_{\lambda,T}(\hat{\beta}(\tau)) - \lambda H_{1,T}(\hat{\beta}(\tau))||_\infty \\ &\Rightarrow \sup_{\lambda \in [0,1]} ||B(\lambda)||_\infty, \end{aligned}$$

where $B(r) = W(r) - \lambda W(1)$ is a Brownian Bridge, $||\cdot||_\infty$ the sup-norm, and

$$H_{\lambda,T}(\hat{\beta}(\tau)) = (X'X)^{-1/2} \sum_{t=1}^{[T\lambda]} x_t \rho_\tau(y_t - x_t'\hat{\beta}(\tau)).$$

What is important is that no re-scaling for the variance or long-run variance is needed. The test is automatically self-normalized.

The usual Wald test is still applicable. However, one needs to construct a consistent estimate of the limiting variance of the changes in the parameters. This turns out to be more complex. The variation in the estimates $\hat{\beta}(\tau)$ now depends on the shape of the distribution function via the conditional density $f(y_t|x_t)$, which needs to be estimated using non-parametric methods. This invariably introduces extra complications and also more sampling uncertainty. For this reason, Qu (2008) and Oka and Qu (2011) recommended the fluctuations-type test SQ_τ to test for structural changes at some given quantile of the distribution and also to estimate the number of breaks.

Note that, so far, we assumed that the analysis is carried for a particular user-chosen value of the quantile τ. It is very easy to construct an extended statistic that searches for breaks across some grid values of possible quantiles, say $\tau \in \mathcal{T} = [0.1, .0.2, \ldots, 0.9\}$, for example. Then, the test is simply analogous to the UDmax test of Bai and Perron (1998), namely

$$DQ_\tau = \sup_{\tau \in \mathcal{T}} SQ_\tau.$$

The relevant quantiles of the limit distribution can easily be obtained via simulations but depend on the choice of $\mathcal{T}$. The method can easily be extended to test for multiple structural change.

49.8.4 Lasso

A growing literature uses Lasso-type methods to address structural change problems, which can estimate the location and number of breaks simultaneously. Estimating structural changes can be viewed as a variable selection problem and Lasso estimates the regression coefficients by minimizing the usual Sum of Squared Residuals (SSR) with a penalty for model complexity through the sum of the absolute values of the coefficients. Assume, for simplicity, $p = 0$ and $q = 1$, i.e., a pure structural change model with a single regressor. When $m = 1$, the model is

$$y_t = z_t\delta_1 + (\delta_2 - \delta_1)z_t\mathbf{1}(t \geq T_1 + 1) + u_t.$$

When there is a break at $t = T_1$, then $\delta_2 \neq \delta_1 \neq 0$, otherwise $\delta_2 = \delta_1$. Using a set of regressors

$$g(z_t) = \{z_t\mathbf{1}(t \geq \tilde{t}), \forall \tilde{t} \in [\underline{t}, \bar{t}], 1 < \underline{t} < \bar{t} < T\},$$

we can express the model as

$$\begin{aligned} y_t &= z_t\delta_1 + b_1 z_t \mathbf{1}(t \geq \underline{t}) + \cdots + b_{\bar{t}-\underline{t}} z \mathbf{1}(t \geq \bar{t}) + u_t \\ &= \underbrace{z_t}_{w_{0,t}} \delta_1 + \underbrace{(z_t \mathbf{1}(t \geq \underline{t}))}_{w_{1,t}} b_1 + \cdots + \underbrace{(z_t \mathbf{1}(t \geq T_1 + 1))}_{w_{(T_1-\underline{t}+2),t}} \underbrace{b_{T_1-\underline{t}+2}}_{\delta_2-\delta_1} \\ &\quad + \cdots + \underbrace{(z_t \mathbf{1}(t \geq \bar{t}))}_{z_{(\bar{t}-\underline{t}+1),t}} b_{\bar{t}-\underline{t}+1} + u_t \\ &= w_{0,t}\theta_0 + g(w_{0,t})\theta_1 + u_t = w_t'\theta + u_t, \end{aligned}$$

with $b_i = 0$, $i = 1, \ldots, T_1 - \underline{t} + 1, T_1 - \underline{t} + 3, \ldots, \bar{t} - \underline{t} + 1$, and $b_{T_1-\underline{t}+2} = |\delta_2 - \delta_1| \neq 0$. Denote by

$$g(x_{0,t}) = \{w_{1,t}, \ldots, w_{(\bar{t}-\underline{t}+1),t}\}$$

the transformed regressors generated from $w_{0,t} = z_t$ whose coefficient is subject to change. Then,

$$w_t = \{w_{0,t}, g(w_{0,t})\}$$

is the complete set of regressors. If we can consistently estimate the coefficients associated with $g(x_{0,t})$ that are greater than zero, we can date the break point. OLS would not provide consistent estimates because the number of regressors is too large.

The method is flexible; e.g., if one has some prior knowledge that a change has occurred at some date, a dummy variable can be added without the associated generated regressors. A model with multiple structural changes in many regressors can be obtained as an extension. One simply lets $w_{0,t}$ be the vector of regressors whose coefficients are subject to change and $g(w_{0,t})$ be the vector of artificially constructed regressors obtained from the original ones. In general, the number of regressors is $n = p + q(\ddot{r} + 1)$, where $\ddot{r} = \bar{t} - \underline{t} + 1$ is the number of transformed regressors associated with the original regressors whose coefficients are allowed to change (fewer are possible if there is prior information about where the breaks cannot occur). Hence, n can be very large, much larger than T. The structural break model has a sparse pattern since few coefficients are non-zero, namely

$s = p + q(m+1)$. The Lasso estimator for sparse models is

$$\hat{\theta} = \arg\min_{\theta \in \mathbb{R}^q} \hat{Q}(\theta) + (\lambda/T)\|\hat{\Upsilon}\theta\|_1,$$

where λ is the penalty level,

$$\hat{Q}(\theta) = \sum_{t=1}^{T}(y_t - w_t'\theta)^2,$$

and

$$\hat{\Upsilon} = \text{diag}(\hat{\gamma}_1, \ldots, \hat{\gamma}_p)$$

is a diagonal matrix with the penalty loadings and

$$\|\hat{\Upsilon}\theta\|_1 = \sum_{j=1}^{p} |\hat{\gamma}_j\theta_j|$$

is the ℓ_1-norm. Ideally, these are adapted to information about the error term, which is not feasible since u_t is not observed. In practice, we can use the estimated residuals and proceed via iterations or simply assume homoskedastic Gaussian errors, in which case $\hat{\Upsilon}$ is the identity matrix.

Often, additional thresholding is applied to remove regressors with small estimated coefficients which may have been included due to estimation error. Then, the thresholded Lasso estimator is

$$\hat{\theta}(t_L) = \hat{\theta}_j 1\{|\hat{\theta}_j| > t_L\} \; (j = 1, \ldots, q),$$

where $t_L \geq 0$ is the threshold level. The problem is in the choice of λ and t_L. Results are well established for a random sample of data. With serially correlated series, things are more complex.

The following is a partial list of some relevant papers using Lasso for models with structural changes. Harchaoui and Lévy-Leduc (2010) proposed a total variation penalty to estimate changes in the mean of a sequence of independent and identically distributed (*i.i.d.*) Gaussian random variables. Bleakley and Vert (2011) proposed a group-fused Lasso method for changes in the mean of a vector of *i.i.d.* Gaussian random variables assumed to share common break points. Chan *et al.* (2014) considered using a group Lasso method for changes in an autoregressive model with heteroskedastic errors. They suggested a two-step method involving the use of an information criterion to select the number of break points. Ciuperca (2014) considered multiple changes in a linear regression model with *i.i.d.* errors using Lasso with an information criterion or adaptive Lasso. Rojas and Wahlberg (2014) used penalized maximum likelihood estimator for changes in the mean of a sequence of *i.i.d.* Gaussian random variables. Aue *et al.* (2014) considered structural breaks in conditional quantiles using the minimum description length principle. While the framework is quite general, the method cannot consistently estimate the number of breaks jointly with their location. Qian and Su (2016) considered estimation and inference of common breaks in panel data models with endogenous regressors. The regressors and errors are, however, restricted to be *i.i.d.* processes, a common feature in this literature up to now. Allowing for general mixing regressors and errors is still work in progress to achieve the level of generality available using standard procedures. Nevertheless, it remains a promising approach, especially in the context of very large datasets.

49.8.5 Factor models

The issue of structural breaks in factor models has recently received considerable attention; for a more detailed survey, see the work of Bai and Han (2016). We first discuss in some detail the methods of Baltagi *et al.* (2021) and Bai *et al.* (2017) and then briefly mention other works. The high-dimensional factor model with m changes in the factor loadings considered by Baltagi *et al.* (2021) is given by

$$y_{it} = f_t'\phi_i + f_{b,t}'\phi_{i,j} + u_{it}, \quad (t = T_{j-1}^0 + 1, \dots, T_j^0)$$

for $j = 1, \dots, m + 1$, $i = 1, \dots, N$, and $t = 1, \dots, T$ where f_t and $f_{b,t}$ are vectors of factors without and with changes in the loadings, respectively, ϕ_i and $\phi_{i,j}$ are the factor loadings of unit i corresponding to f_t and $f_{b,t}$ in the jth regime, respectively, and u_{it} is a disturbance term which can have serial and cross-sectional dependence as well as heteroskedasticity.

The problem is to estimate the break points, determine the number of factors, and estimate the factors and loadings in each regime.

We first discuss a procedure when the number of breaks is known. It first estimates the break points using a simultaneous or sequential method, which leads to consistent estimates for $\lambda_b^0 = T_b^0/T$, though not for T_b^0. Second, it involves plugging-in the break point estimates and estimating the number of factors and the factor space in each regime. Since the factors are latent, one has to determine the number of pseudo factors which is akin to selecting moment conditions, whereas in the work of Bai and Perron (1998), the model is parametric and the moment conditions are known *a priori*.

Baltagi *et al.* (2021) proposed to convert the statistical problem from estimating multiple changes in the loadings to estimating changes in the pseudo factors. This relies on the fact that the mean of the second moment matrix of the pseudo factors changes at the same dates as the loadings. After this conversion, the data become fixed-dimensional with observable regressors and conceptually the problem becomes similar to that of Qu and Perron (2007a).

Estimation of the break points involves three steps: (1) ignoring breaks, use any consistent estimator $\tilde{r}$ to estimate the number of factors; (2) estimate the first $\tilde{r}$ factors $\tilde{g}_t$ using the Principal Component (PC) method (see Chapter 31); (3) for any partition $(T_1, \ldots, T_m)$, split the sample into $m+1$ sub-samples, estimate

$$\tilde{\Sigma}_j = (T_j - T_{j-1})^{-1} \sum_{t=T_{j-1}+1}^{T_j} \tilde{g}_t \tilde{g}_t',$$

and calculate the SSR:

$$\tilde{S}(T_1, \ldots, T_m) = \sum_{j=1}^{m+1} \sum_{t=T_{j-1}+1}^{T_j} [\text{vec}(\tilde{g}_t \tilde{g}_t' - \tilde{\Sigma}_j)]' [\text{vec}(\tilde{g}_t \tilde{g}_t' - \tilde{\Sigma}_j)].$$

The estimates of the break points are the minimizer of $\tilde{S}(T_1, \ldots, T_m)$. The motivation is that the second moment matrix of g_t has breaks at the same dates as the factor loadings. The results are valid under general high-level conditions on the errors and the factors are allowed to be dynamic and to include lags. To estimate the number of factors, these can be correlated with the errors. The limiting distributions of $\hat{T}_b - T_b^0$ $(b = 1, \ldots, m)$ have the same form as the one for the single break case derived in the work of Baltagi *et al.* (2021).

Consider now testing for multiple changes in the factor loadings. Following the work of Bai and Perron (1998), Baltagi *et al.* (2021) proposed two different tests: no change versus a fixed number of changes and l versus $l+1$ changes. The limit distributions follow those in the work of Bai and Perron (1998). The first test loses power when the number of changes is misspecified. They proposed adapting the UDmax and WDmax tests of Bai and Perron (1998) allowing an unknown number of changes (up to some upper bound). For the test of $m = l$ versus $m = l+1$, one first estimates the break points, and once they are plugged in, testing for $m = l$ versus $m = l+1$ changes becomes equivalent to testing no change versus a single change in each regime jointly. The null limiting distribution is obtained by simulations and depends on the number of factors in each regime. When this number is stable, it is similar to that in the work of Bai and Perron (1998).

Bai *et al.* (2017) studied the properties of the least-squares estimator of the single break point in a high-dimensional factor model. The model is given by

$$y_{it} = \phi_{ij}' f_t + u_{it}, \quad \text{for } t = 1, \ldots, T_b^0,$$
$$\text{if } j = 1, \quad \text{and} \quad t = T_b^0 + 1, \ldots, T, \quad \text{if } j = 2,$$

for $i = 1, \ldots, N$ where $T_b^0 = T\lambda_b^0$ is the unknown common break point. The estimation of T_b^0 involves the estimated latent factors. The model in matrix format is

$$\begin{bmatrix} Y_{T_b^0}^{(1)} \\ Y_{T_b^0}^{(2)} \end{bmatrix} = \begin{bmatrix} F^{(1)} & 0_{T_b^0 \times r} \\ 0_{(T-T_b^0)\times r} & F^{(2)} \end{bmatrix} \begin{bmatrix} \Lambda_1' \\ \Lambda_2' \end{bmatrix} + \begin{bmatrix} u_{T_b^0}^{(1)} \\ u_{T_b^0}^{(2)} \end{bmatrix} \equiv G\Theta' + u. \quad (49.30)$$

Model (49.30) is an observationally equivalent factor model, where the number of factors is doubled and the factor loadings are time invariant. Under (49.30), the factor process has structural breaks, which was the basis for the framework of Baltagi *et al.* (2017). The estimates of the break points are the minimizer of

$$\text{SSR}(T_b, \tilde{F}) = \sum_{i=1}^{N}\sum_{t=1}^{T_b}(y_{it} - \tilde{f}_t'\tilde{\phi}_{i1})^2 + \sum_{i=1}^{N}\sum_{t=T_b+1}^{T}(y_{it} - \tilde{f}_t'\tilde{\phi}_{i2})^2$$

over $T\lambda_1 \leq T_b \leq T\lambda_2$, where $\tilde{f}$ are estimates of f_t using a principal component method. Since the factors are estimated by a principle component method, they are not efficient. However, the efficiency loss relative to the maximum likelihood estimator vanishes as $N, T \to \infty$. The errors are assumed to be independent from the factors and loadings; however u_{it} can be weakly correlated in both cross-sectional and time dimensions. There can be dependence between $\{f_t\}$ and $\{\phi_{i1}, \phi_{i2}\}$ and the break magnitudes $\phi_{i2} - \phi_{i1}$ can be dependent on the factors.

Theoretical results are provided under both large and small breaks where the latter are modeled in two ways: (1) The magnitude of the change in each factor loading is of order $N^{\frac{\nu-1}{2}}$ for some $0 < \nu \leq 1$ and (2) the magnitude of the change is fixed but only $O(N^{\nu})$ units have a break for some $0 < \nu \leq 1$. The case $\nu = 1$ corresponds to large breaks studied by Chen *et al.* (2014), Han and Inoue (2015), Cheng *et al.* (2016), Baltagi *et al.* (2015), and Baltagi *et al.* (2021).

For small breaks, $\tilde{T}_b$ is consistent for T_b^0 as $N, T \to \infty$ provided conditions on the ratio N/T are satisfied. The consistency result for $\tilde{T}_b$ is strong and different from the univariate case for which only the break fraction is consistently estimated. The framework under small breaks allows a non-degenerate asymptotic distribution similar to that of the OLS break point estimator in panel models (cf. the work of Bai (2010) and Section 49.8.6). It does not depend on the exact distribution of the errors but on the distribution of the factors f_t, being the same whether f_t is observable or not. Hence, evaluating the limit distribution using the plug-in approach, replacing population quantities with consistent estimates, is not applicable due to rotations. Bai *et al.* (2017) proposed a bootstrap method, which, however, lacks robustness to cross-sectional correlation. Duan *et al.* (2023) proposed a quasi-maximum likelihood estimator of the break point when the covariance matrix of the pre- or post-break factor loading (or both) is singular. Singularity occurs for most types of structural changes, except for a rotational change. Even for a rotational change, the estimator is still T-consistent in terms of the break fraction.

Bai *et al.* (2024) noted that a factor model with a break in its factor loadings is observationally equivalent to a model without changes in the loadings but with a change in the variance of its factors.

This feature allows transforming a high-dimensional structural change problem into a low-dimensional problem. They considered the likelihood ratio test for a variance change in the estimated factors, which exploits a special feature of the estimated factors, namely that the pre-break and post-break variances can be a singular matrix under the alternative hypothesis, making the LR test diverging faster and thus more powerful than Wald-type tests.

49.8.6 Panels data models

Panel data studies have become increasingly popular including inference about breaks. The literature on estimating panel structural breaks can be categorized by whether the parameters of interest are allowed to be heterogenous across units or not. We focus on heterogeneous panels since they are more relevant in practice and refer the reader to the works of De Wachter and Tzavalis (2012) and Qian and Su (2016) for corresponding methods for homogeneous panels.

Bai (2010) considered the problem of estimating a common break point in a panel with N units and T observations for each unit. The model takes the form

$$y_{it} = \mu_{ij} + u_{it},$$

for $t = 1, \ldots, T_b^0$, if $j = 1$, and $t = T_b^0 + 1, \ldots, T$, if $j = 2$, where $i = 1, \ldots, N$, and u_{it} is a disturbance term. The common break specification means that each unit has a break point at T_b^0. The model allows for heterogeneous means and break magnitudes $\mu_{i2} - \mu_{i1}$. Bai (2010) provided results for both fixed T and T going to infinity.

Unlike in the univariate model where the break point is assumed to correspond to a positive fraction of the total sample size, the panel setup allows one to consider also the case where T_b^0 can take any value in $[1, T - 1]$. The latter case can be studied under the asymptotic framework with $N \to \infty$ and T fixed or $N, T \to \infty$ such that $T/N \to 0$. Importantly, only consistency can be established under the latter scenario. For the derivation of the limiting distribution, one needs the standard assumption $T_b^0 = T\lambda_0$. Turning to the assumptions on the errors, Bai (2010) required stationarity of $\{u_{it}\}$ in the time dimension and independence over i. It is argued that it can be relaxed without affecting the consistency result, though for the asymptotic distribution one requires the cross-sectional dependence to be not too strong.

The assumption on the break sizes is

$$\lim_{N\to\infty} N^{-1/2}\sum_{i=1}^{N}(\mu_{i2}-\mu_{i1})^2=\infty.$$

To understand this, note that if $\mu_{i2}-\mu_{i1}$ were *i.i.d.* random variables with positive variance, then the above limit with N^{-1} replacing $N^{-1/2}$ should converge to a positive constant. Thus, the condition does not require every unit to have a break. The estimation method involves least squares. For a given $1\le T_b\le T-1$, define

$$\bar{y}_{i1}=T_b^{-1}\sum_{t=1}^{T_b}y_{it}$$

and

$$\bar{y}_{i2}=(T-T_b)^{-1}\sum_{t=T_b+1}^{T}y_{it},$$

which are the estimates of μ_{i1} and μ_{i2}, respectively. Define the sum of squared residuals for the *ith* equation as

$$S_{iT}(T_b)=\sum_{t=1}^{T_b}(y_{it}-\bar{y}_{i1})^2+\sum_{t=T_b+1}^{T}(y_{it}-\bar{y}_{i2})^2,$$

for $T_b=1,\ldots,T-1$, and

$$S_{iT}(T_b)=\sum_{t=1}^{T}(y_{it}-\bar{y}_i)^2,$$

for $T_b=T$, where $\bar{y}_i$ is the whole sample mean. The least-squares estimator of the break point is defined as

$$\hat{T}_b=\underset{1\le T_b\le T-1}{\operatorname{argmin}}\ \mathrm{SSR}(T_b),$$

where

$$\mathrm{SSR}\left(T_b\right)=\sum_{i=1}^{N} S_{iT}\left(T_b\right).$$

The availability of panel data leads to a stronger result about the rate of convergence. In the univariate case, we have $\hat{T}_b = T_b^0 + O_p(1)$. For panel data, under either fixed T or $T \to \infty$, $\hat{T}_b = T_b^0 + o_p(1)$, and results show that with $N \to \infty$ the common break point can be estimated precisely even with a regime having a single observation.

The limiting distribution is derived under a small shift assumption with $\mu_{i2} - \mu_{i1} = N^{-1/2}\Delta_i$, $\Delta_i > 0$. Construction of the confidence intervals requires simulations of the derived limiting distribution. Unlike in the univariate case, a change in variable allowing to express it as a function of quantities that can be consistently estimated cannot be immediately carried out. Nonetheless, noting that a Gaussian random walk and a standard Wiener process have the same distribution at integer times, one can apply the change in variable argument leading to the same inference procedure as in the univariate case, which now only holds approximately, so that inference works as in the univariate setting. Finally, Bai (2010) further considered the case of (possibly) simultaneous break in mean and variance and proposed a QML method.

Kim (2011) studied the least-squares estimation of a common deterministic time trend break in large panels with a break either in the intercept, slope, or both with a general dependence structure in the errors. He modeled cross-sectional dependence with a common factor structure and allowed the errors to be serially correlated in each equation:

$$u_{it} = \gamma_i' f_t + e_{ti},$$

where f_t is a vector of latent common factors, γ_i is a factor loading, and e_{it} is a unit specific error. Under joint asymptotics $(T, N) \to \infty$, serial correlation and cross-sectional dependence are shown to affect the rate of convergence and the limiting distribution of the break point estimator. As in the work of Bai (2010), $\hat{T}_b$ can be consistent for T_b^0 even when T is fixed, though it only holds when the u_{it} are independent across both i and t. When the e_{it} are serially correlated and there are no common factors, the rate of convergence depends on N and is faster than in the univariate case. With common factors generating strong cross-sectional dependence, the rate of convergence does not depend on N and reduces to the univariate case (cf Perron and Zhu, 2005). For fixed shifts, the limiting distribution depends on many elements, e.g., the form of the break, the presence of common factors, and stationary versus integrated errors. For a joint broken trend, it can be normal. To obtain a limit theory not depending on the exact distribution of the errors, the break magnitudes need to converge to zero at a rate $N^{-1/2}$, in which case asymptotically valid confidence intervals can be computed via simulations.

Results pertaining to regression models using stationary panels were obtained by Baltagi *et al.* (2016). They considered large heterogeneous panels with common correlated effects (CCE) and allowed for unknown common structural breaks in the slopes. The CCE setting takes the following form:

$$y_{it} = x_{it}'\beta(T_b^0) + u_{it},$$

where

$$\begin{aligned} u_{it} &= \gamma_i' f_t + e_{it}, \\ x_{it} &= \Gamma_i' f_t + v_{it}, \end{aligned}$$

with e_{it}, v_{it} idiosyncratic errors and where some or all components of $\beta(T_b^0)$ can differ pre- and post-break. Due to the correlation between x_{it} and u_{it}, least squares for each cross-sectional regression could be inconsistent. They use a least-squares method using augmented data and confirm the result in the work of Bai (2010) that the break point T_b^0 can be consistently estimated as both N and T go to infinity. Common breaks in panels were also considered by Qian and Su (2016) and Li *et al.* (2016) who studied estimation and inference with and without interactive fixed effects using Lasso methods. Kim (2014) generalized Kim (2011) by allowing a factor structure in the error terms. Baltagi *et al.* (2016) studied structural breaks in a heterogeneous large panel with interactive fixed effects. They showed the consistency of the estimated break fraction and break date under some conditions. Okui and Wang (2021) approached the issue of heterogeneity via a group structure whereby the breaks in a given group are common, while they may differ in timing, number, and size across groups. An adaptive Lasso procedure is used for estimation.

Most of the work on structural breaks in panels focused on common breaks, in which case T_b^0 itself can be consistently estimated and not only λ_b^0. One may infer that simply adding a cross-sectional dimension yields more information and precise estimates. This is misleading because the result crucially relies on the assumption that the break is common to all units. Although this may be relevant in practice, the results should be interpreted carefully.

49.9 Exercises

Exercise 49.1. Consider a stationary stochastic process described by

$$y_t = \mu + v_t,$$

where $A(L)v_t = B(L)e_t$, with $A(L) = 1 + a_1L + \cdots + a_pL^p$, $B(L) = 1 + b_1L + \cdots + b_qL^q$, and $e_t \sim i.i.d.\ N(0, \sigma_e^2)$. The roots of $A(z) = 0$ and $B(z) = 0$ are assumed to be strictly outside the unit circle. A statistic that has been suggested for testing the null hypothesis of the absence of structural change versus the alternative hypothesis of a change in mean is

$$Q_T = (\hat{\sigma}^2)^{-1}T^{-2}\sum_{t=1}^{T}\left(\sum_{j=1}^{t}(y_j - \bar{Y})\right)^2,$$

where $\hat{\sigma}^2 = T^{-1}\sum_{t=1}^{T}(y_t - \bar{Y})^2$ and $\bar{Y} = T^{-1}\sum_{t=1}^{T} y_t$. (a) Derive the limiting distribution of the statistic Q_T under the null hypothesis. (b) Propose a transformed version of Q_T whose limiting distribution is free of nuisance parameters. (c) Discuss how you could obtain critical values of the limiting distribution of the transformed statistic obtained in (b). (d) Suppose now that one of the roots of $A(z) = 0$ is one. What is the limit of Q_T? (e) Discuss the implications of your results for the problem of distinguishing between processes with a unit root and processes that exhibit a structural change in the trend function (here the mean).

Exercise 49.2. The interest is in testing whether the mean of a stationary stochastic process has changed at a particular date. Let the process $\{y_t;\ t = 1, \ldots, T\}$ be defined by

$$y_t = c_1 + u_t \quad \text{for } t \leq T_b,$$
$$y_t = c_2 + u_t \quad \text{for } t > T_b,$$

where T_b is some break date that is assumed to be a fixed proportion of the sample size T, such that $\lambda = T_b/T$. The stochastic part u_t is defined by $u_t = \varphi(L)e_t$ where $e_t \sim i.i.d.(0, \sigma^2)$ and $\varphi(L) = \sum_{j=0}^{\infty} \varphi_j L^j$ (with L, the lag operator) and $\sum_{j=0}^{\infty} j^2 \varphi_j^2 < \infty$. The interest is in testing the null hypothesis $H_0 : c_1 = c_2 = c$ versus the alternative hypothesis $H_1 : c_1 \neq c_2$. To that effect, the statistic considered is the Wald test defined, for a given break fraction λ, by

$$W_T(\lambda) = [\mathrm{SSR}_R - \mathrm{SSR}_U]/\hat{\sigma}_u^2,$$

where SSR_R is the restricted sum of squared residuals, SSR_U is the unrestricted sum of squared residuals, and $\hat{\sigma}_u^2 = \mathrm{SSR}_R/T$. (a) Show that, under H_0, $W_T(\lambda)$ can be expressed as

$$W_T(\lambda) = \left[\frac{T_b}{T}\left(1 - \frac{T_b}{T}\right)\right]^{-1} \times \left(\frac{T_b}{T} T^{-1/2} \sum_{t=T_b+1}^{T} u_t - \frac{T - T_b}{T} T^{-1/2} \sum_{t=1}^{T_b} u_t\right)^2 \Big/ \hat{\sigma}_u^2.$$

(b) It is often the case that the date of change is unknown. Then, a popular procedure is to reject the null hypothesis if the statistic $\sup W_T = \sup_{\lambda \in (\varepsilon, 1-\varepsilon)} W_T(\lambda)$ is large (where ε is some small positive number). Derive the limiting distribution of $\sup W_T$ under the null hypothesis of no change. (c) Propose a modification of the $\sup W_T$ statistic whose limit distribution is free of nuisance parameters. Be specific as to how you would construct estimates of the various quantities involved in the transformation. (d) If the break point is known to occur at say $\lambda^* = T_b^*/T$, one can simply reject the null hypothesis if the statistic $W_T(\lambda^*)$ (appropriately transformed as in (c)) is large. Using the result obtained in part (b), show that the limit distribution of (the transformed) $W_T(\lambda^*)$ is χ_1^2 (a chi-square with 1 degree of freedom). (e) What happens to the result in part (b) if, instead, the stochastic component u_t is $I(1)$? (i.e., $u_t = u_{t-1} + v_t$, where v_t is a stationary process which satisfies the conditions stated above for u_t). Is it possible to have a consistent test for a change in mean if the stochastic component is $I(1)$?

Exercise 49.3. Consider the linear model

$$y_t = x_t'\beta + u_t, \quad (t = 1, \ldots, T), \tag{49.31}$$

where $u_t \sim i.i.d.\ (0, \sigma_u^2)$ and x_t is a vector of k regressors such that $T^{-1}\sum_{t=1}^T x_t \xrightarrow{p} \mu_x$ and $T^{-1}\sum_{t=1}^T x_t x_t' \xrightarrow{p} Q_x$ as $T \to \infty$. Consider the recursive residuals

$$\hat{v}_t = (y_t - \hat{\beta}_{t-1}x_t)/f_t,$$

where $\hat{\beta}_{t-1}$ is the OLS estimate of β using observations up to time $t-1$, and

$$f_t = \left(1 + x_t'\left(X_{t-1}'X_{t-1}\right)^{-1} x_t\right),$$

with $X_{t-1} = (x_1, x_2, \ldots, x_{t-1})'$. The recursive residuals have the property that they are independent and identically distributed. A popular statistic to test for structural change is the CUSUM test defined by

$$CS = \max_{k<r\le T}\left|(T-k)^{-1/2}\sum_{t=k+1}^{r}\hat{v}_t \Big/ \left[\hat{\sigma}\left(1 + 2\frac{r-k}{T-k}\right)\right]\right|,$$

where $\hat{\sigma}^2 = T^{-1}\sum_{t=k+1}^T \hat{v}_t^{\,2}$. (a) Derive the limiting distribution of CS under the null hypothesis of no structural change (i.e., under the hypothesis that the model (49.31) is well specified). (b) To investigate power, consider the special case where, under the null hypothesis, the process is simply $y_t = u_t$, i.e., $\beta = 0$ for the whole sample. Under a sequence of local alternative hypotheses, y_t is generated by

$$y_t = T^{-1/2}\gamma 1(t > T_b)x_{1t} + u_t,$$

where $1(t > T_b) = 1$ if $t > T_b$ and 0, otherwise. Derive the limit of CS under this sequence of local alternatives and explain why the test has no power if the mean of the regressor x_{1t} is 0.

Exercise 49.4. A useful test for a change in variance is the CUSUM of squares test. Suppose for simplicity that y_t is a series with mean zero, then it is defined by $CUSQ = \max_{1\le r\le T} T^{1/2}|S_T^{(r)} - (r/T)|$, with $S_T^{(r)} = (\sum_{t=1}^{r} y_t^2)/(\sum_{t=1}^{T} y_t^2)$ or equivalently by

$$CUSQ = \max_{1\le r\le T} \left| T^{-1/2}\left[\sum_{t=1}^{r} y_t^2 - (r/T)\sum_{t=1}^{T} y_t^2\right]\right| \Big/ T^{-1}\sum_{t=1}^{T} y_t.$$

Under the null hypothesis of no change, we make the following assumptions on y_t: (a) The partial sums of y_t satisfy a functional central limit theorem such that

$$T^{-1/2}\sum_{t=1}^{[Ts]} y_t \Rightarrow \sigma_2 W_2(s),$$

where $\sigma_2^2 = \lim_{T\to\infty} T^{-1}E(\sum_{t=1}^{T} y_t)^2$ and (b) with $\xi_t = y_t^2/\sigma_y^2 - 1$, the partial sums of ξ_t satisfy a functional central limit theorem such that

$$T^{-1/2}\sum_{t=1}^{[Ts]} \xi_t \Rightarrow \sigma_3 W_3(s),$$

where $W_3(s)$ is independent of $W_2(s)$ and

$$\sigma_3^2 = \lim_{T\to\infty} T^{-1}E\left(\sum_{t=1}^{T}(y_t^2/\sigma_y^2 - 1)\right)^2,$$

$$\sigma_y^2 = \lim_{T\to\infty} T^{-1}\sum_{t=1}^{T} E(y_t^2) = \underset{T\to\infty}{plim}\, T^{-1}\sum_{t=1}^{T} y_t^2.$$

(a) Derive the limit distribution of $CUSQ$ under H_0. (b) Show that the limit distribution depends on the exact distribution of y_t. What is the limit distribution when y_t is *i.i.d.* Normally distributed? (recall that $E(y_t^4) = 3\sigma_y^4$ if $y_t \sim N(0, \sigma_y^2)$). (c) Suppose that you want to allow for non-normal errors but you assume that there is no serial correlation in y_t^2. Suggest a transformation of the statistic that has the same limit distribution as in the case when y_t is *i.i.d.* normally distributed. (d) Would the transformation suggested in part (c) yield a test that is asymptotically invariant to the presence of conditional heteroskedasticity in y_t? If not what would need to be done to have such an invariance?

Exercise 49.5. Consider the linear regression model given by

$$y_t = X_t'\beta_t + u_t, \tag{49.32}$$

for $t = 1, \ldots, T$. Under the null hypothesis, the parameter vector β is constant throughout the sample, i.e., $H_0 : \beta_t = \bar{\beta}$ for all t, while under the alternative hypothesis, there is at least one change in β occurring within the sample, i.e., $H_1 : \beta_t \neq \bar{\beta}$ for some t. The conditions on the errors are: u_t is stationary such that $T^{-1/2}\sum_{t=1}^{[Tr]} u_t \Rightarrow \sigma W(r)$ with $\sigma^2 = 2\pi h_u(0)$, where $h_u(\omega)$ is the spectral density function of u_t. A locally best invariant test for parameter variation is Nyblom's test defined by

$$N_T = \frac{1}{T^2\hat{\sigma}^2} tr\left[Q^{-1}\sum_{t=1}^{T} S_t S_t'\right],$$

where $S_t = \sum_{j=1}^{t} X_j\hat{u}_j$, $Q = T^{-1}\sum_{t=1}^{T} X_t X_t'$, and $\hat{u}_t$ are the OLS estimates of the errors from estimating regression (49.32). For simplicity, assume that there is only a constant regressor, i.e., $X_t = 1$ for all t, so that we are testing for changes in mean. Also, we consider, for simplicity that $\hat{\sigma}^2$, the estimate of σ^2 is based on the truncated window so that

$$\hat{\sigma}^2 = \hat{R}(0) + 2\sum_{j=1}^{m_T} \hat{R}(j),$$

where $\hat{R}(j) = T^{-1}\sum_{t=j+1}^{T} \hat{u}_t\hat{u}_{t-j}$. We also suppose that the bandwidth m_T is chosen using Andrews' method so that $m_T = c(\hat{\alpha}T)^{1/5}$, where $\hat{\alpha} = 4\hat{\rho}^2/(1-\hat{\rho})^4$ with $\hat{\rho}$ the estimate in a regression of $\hat{u}_t$ on $\hat{u}_{t-1}$. (a) Derive the limit distribution of the test under the null hypothesis of no change. Suppose now that the alternative hypothesis specifies a one-time change in mean so that $\beta_t = 0$ for $t \leq [T\lambda]$

and $\beta_t = \theta$ for $t > [T\lambda]$, where $[T\lambda]$ is the date of break and λ is the break fraction. (b) Derive the probability limit of $\hat{R}(j)$ under the alternative hypothesis. (c) Using the result in part (b), show that $\hat{\rho}$ converges to 1 as θ increases and that $\hat{\alpha} = O_p(\theta^8)$ so that $m_T = O_p(\theta^8 T)^{1/5}$. (d) Using the result in parts (b) and (c), show that $\hat{\sigma}^2 = O_p(\theta^{8/5+2}T^{1/5})$. (e) Derive the limit of

$$T^{-3} tr \left[Q^{-1} \sum_{t=1}^{T} S_t S_t' \right]$$

and show that it is $O_p(\theta^2)$. (f) Using these results, show that for any fixed θ, N_T is consistent but that its power goes to zero as the magnitude of the change increases.

Exercise 49.6 (Review). Discuss the interplay between structural change in the trend (mean and/or slope changes) and unit roots. What are the properties of unit root tests if a change in trend is present? What are the properties of structural change tests if the noise is $I(1)$? When both changes in trend and $I(1)$ or $I(0)$ noise are possibilities: (a) How can you decide whether the noise is $I(0)$ or $I(1)$? (b) How can you decide if there is actually a change in trend?

Exercise 49.7. Prove equation (49.26).

Chapter 50

Unit Root and Trend Breaks

As discussed in Section 21.5 and Chapter 49, structural changes and unit root non-stationarity share similar features in the sense that most tests for structural changes will reject in the presence of a unit root in the errors, and vice versa, tests of stationarity versus unit root will reject in the presence of structural changes. We now discuss methods to test the null hypothesis of a unit root in the presence of structural changes in the trend function. The motivation for doing so was discussed in Section 21.5 and some of the needed limit distribution results were covered in Chapter 44. This chapter uses material from the work of Perron (2006).

50.1 The framework

We start with a brief review of the specifications proposed by Perron (1989b, 1990a). When allowance is made for a one-time change in the trend function, Perron (1989b, 1990a) specified two versions of four different structures: (1) a change in level for a non-trending series and, for trending series, (2) a change in level, (3) a change in slope, and (4) a change in both level and slope. For each of the four cases, two different versions allow for different transition effects. Following the terminology in the work of Box and Tiao (1975), the first is labeled the "additive outlier model" and specifies that the change to the new trend function occurs quickly. The second is labeled the "innovational outlier model" and specifies that the change to the new trend function is gradual.

Of course, in principle, there is an infinity of ways to model gradual changes following the occurrence of a "big shock". One way out of this difficulty is to suppose that the variables respond to the "big shocks" the same way as they respond to so-called "regular shocks" (shocks associated with the stationary noise component of the series). This is the approach taken in the modelization of the "innovational outlier model", following the treatment of intervention analyses in the work of Box and Tiao (1975). The distinction between the additive and innovational outlier models is important not only because the assumed transition paths are different but also because the statistical procedures to test for unit roots are also different.

The additive outlier models for each of the four specifications for the types of changes occurring at a break date T_1 are specified as follows:

Model (AO-0): $$y_t = \mu_1 + (\mu_2 - \mu_1)\, DU_t + u_t,$$

Model (AO-A): $$y_t = \mu_1 + \beta t + (\mu_2 - \mu_1)\, DU_t + u_t,$$

Model (AO-B): $$y_t = \mu_1 + \beta_1 t + (\beta_2 - \beta_1)\, DT_t^* + u_t,$$

Model (AO-C): $$y_t = \mu_1 + \beta_1 t + (\mu_2 - \mu_1)\, DU_t + (\beta_2 - \beta_1)\, DT_t^* + u_t,$$

where

$$DU_t = 1, \quad DT_t^* = t - T_1, \quad \text{if } t > T_1 \text{ and 0 otherwise}$$

and u_t is specified by

$$\Delta u_t = C(L) e_t.$$

Under the null hypothesis $C(1) \neq 0$, while under the alternative hypothesis, $C(1) = 0$. Alternatively, one can define the autoregressive polynomial $A(L) = (1-L)C(L)^{-1}$. The null hypothesis then specifies that a root of the autoregressive polynomial is one, i.e., that we can write $A(L) = (1 - L)A^*(L)$ where all the roots of $A^*(L)$ are outside the unit circle. Under the alternative hypothesis of stationary fluctuations around the trend function, all the roots of $A(L)$ are strictly outside the unit circle.

Model (AO-B) was found to be useful for the analysis of postwar quarterly real GNP for the G7 countries and Model (AO-0) for some exchange rate series as well as the US real interest rate, among others. It is important to note that changes in the trend function are allowed to occur under both the null and alternative hypotheses.

The innovational outlier models are easier to characterize by describing them separately under the null and alternative hypotheses. Note also that the innovational outlier versions have been considered only for Models (A) and (C) in the case of trending series. The basic reason is that the innovational outlier version of Model (B) does not lend itself easily to empirical applications using linear estimation methods. Under the null hypothesis $C(1) \neq 0$, we have

Model (IO-0-UR): $$y_t = y_{t-1} + C(L)(e_t + \delta D(T_1)_t),$$

Model (IO-A-UR): $$y_t = y_{t-1} + b + C(L)(e_t + \delta D(T_1)_t),$$

Model (IO-C-UR): $$y_t = y_{t-1} + b + C(L)(e_t + \delta D(T_1)_t + \eta DU_t),$$

where b is the slope of the deterministic trend function and

$$D(T_1)_t = 1 \quad \text{if } t = T_1 + 1 \text{ and } 0 \text{ otherwise.}$$

Under this specification, the immediate impact of the change in the intercept is δ while the long run impact is $C(1)\delta$. Similarly, under Model (IO-C), the immediate impact of the change in slope is η while the long run impact is $C(1)\eta$. Under the alternative hypothesis of stationary fluctuations, the specifications are

Model (IO-0-TS): $$y_t = \mu + C(L)^*(e_t + \theta DU_t),$$

Model (IO-A-TS): $$y_t = \mu + \beta t + C(L)^*(e_t + \theta DU_t),$$

Model (IO-C-TS): $$y_t = \mu + \beta t + C(L)^*(e_t + \theta DU_t + \gamma DT_t^*),$$

where

$$C(L)^* = (1 - L)^{-1}C(L).$$

The immediate impact of the change in the intercept of the trend function is θ while the long run impact is $C(1)^*\theta$, and the immediate impact of the change in slope is γ while the long run impact is $C(1)^*\gamma$.

50.2 The effect of change in trend on unit root tests

Consider the augmented Dickey and Fuller (1979) (ADF) test, which is based on the t-statistic for testing that $\alpha = 1$ in the following regression:

$$y_t = \mu + \beta t + \alpha y_{t-1} + \sum_{i=1}^{k} c_i \Delta y_{t-i} + e_t,$$

with the trend regressor excluded when dealing with non-trending series. A central message of the work by Perron (1989b, 1990a) is that, when the true process involves structural changes in the trend function, the power of such unit root tests can be dramatically reduced. In particular, it was shown that if a level shift is present, the estimate of the autoregressive coefficients (α when $k = 0$) is asymptotically biased toward 1. If a change in slope is present, its limit value is 1. It was shown that this translates into substantial power losses. Simulations presented in the work of Perron (1994b) show the power reduction to increase as k is increased; see also the theoretical analysis of Montañés and Reyes (2000), which also shows that the power problem remains with the Phillips and Perron (1988)-type unit root test. For a more precise and complete theoretical analysis, see the work of Montañés and Reyes (1998, 1999).

Under the null hypothesis, the large sample distribution is unaffected by the presence of a level shift (Montañés and Reyes, 1999) and the test is asymptotically conservative in the presence of a change in slope. It can, however, have a liberal size if the break occurs very early in the sample ($\lambda_1 < .15$) as documented by Leybourne *et al.* (1998) and Leybourne and Newbold (2000). Intuitively, the latter result can be understood by thinking about the early observations as outliers such that the series reverts back to the mean in effect for the rest of the sample. The latter problem is, however, specific to the Dickey and Fuller (1979)-type unit root test, which is based on the conditional likelihood function, discarding the first observations (see the work of Lee, 2000).

It has also been documented that the presence of structural breaks in trend affects tests of the null hypothesis of stationarity by inducing size distortions toward rejecting the null hypothesis too often (e.g., Lee *et al.*, 1997). This is consistent with the effect on unit root tests in the sense that when trying to distinguish the two hypotheses, the presence of structural changes induces a bias in favor of the unit root representation.

It is important to discuss these results in relation to the proper way to specify alternative unit root tests. The main result is that large enough changes in level and/or slope will induce a reduction in the power of standard unit root tests. Small shifts, especially in level, are likely to reduce power only slightly. Hence, what is important is to account for the large shifts, not all of them if the others are small. Consider analyzing the US real GDP over, say, the period 1900–1980. Within this sample, one can identify two shifts related to the 1929 crash (change in level) and the post 1973 productivity slowdown (change in slope). However, the post 73 sample would, here, consist of only a small proportion of the total sample and the shift in slope in this period is unlikely to induce a bias and need not be accounted for. Hence, the testing strategy discussed in the following need not make a statement about the precise number of changes. It should rather be viewed as a device to remove biases induced by shifts large enough to cause an important reduction in power.

50.3 Unit root tests with changes at known dates

The IO models under the null and alternative hypotheses can be nested in a way which specifies the regression from which the statistics will be constructed as follows:

$$y_t = \mu + \theta DU_t + \beta t + \gamma DT_t^* + \delta D\left(T_1\right)_t + \alpha y_{t-1} + \sum_{i=1}^{k} c_i \Delta y_{t-i} + e_t, \tag{50.1}$$

for a value of the truncation lag parameter k chosen to be large enough as to provide a good approximation; for methods on how to choose k, see the work of Ng and Perron (1995, 2001). For Model (IO-0), the regressors (t, DT_t^*) are not present, while for Model (IO-A), the regressor (DT_t^*) is not present.

The null hypothesis imposes the following restrictions on the coefficients. For Model (IO–0), these are $\alpha = 1$, $\theta = \mu = 0$ and, in general, $\delta \neq 0$ (if there is a change in the intercept). For Model (IO-A), the restrictions are $\alpha = 1$, $\beta = \theta = 0$ and again, in general, $\delta \neq 0$, while for Model (IO-C), $\alpha = 1$, $\beta = \gamma = 0$. Under the alternative hypothesis, we have the following specifications: $|\alpha| < 1$ and, in general, $\delta = 0$. These restrictions are, however, not imposed by most testing procedures.

The test statistic used is the t-statistic for testing the null hypothesis that $\alpha = 1$ versus the alternative hypothesis that $|\alpha| < 1$, denoted $t_\alpha(\lambda_1)$ with $\lambda_1 = T_1/T$. It is important to note that, provided the specified break date corresponds to the true break date, the statistic is invariant to the parameters of the trend function, including those related to the changes in level and slope. For an analysis of the case when the break date is misspecified, see the works of Hecq and Urbain (1993), Montañés (1997), Montañés and Olloqui (1999), and Montañés *et al.* (2005), which also considered the effect of choosing the wrong specification for the type of break. Following the analysis in Chapter 44, the limit distribution of the test under the null hypothesis is

$$t_\alpha(\lambda_1) \Rightarrow \frac{\int_0^1 W^*(r,\lambda_1)dW(r)}{\left[\int_0^1 W^*(r,\lambda_1)^2 dr\right]^{1/2}}, \tag{50.2}$$

where $W^*(r,\lambda_1)$ is the residual function from a projection of a Wiener process $W(r)$ on the relevant continuous time versions of the deterministic components: ($\{1, 1(r > \lambda_1)\}$ for Model (IO-0), $\{1, 1(r > \lambda_1), r\}$ for Model (IO-A), and $\{1, 1(r > \lambda_1), r, 1(r > \lambda_1)(r - \lambda_1)\}$ for Model (IO-C)). Tabulated critical values can be found in the work of Perron (1989b, 1990a). See also the work of Carrion-i-Silvestre *et al.* (1999).

For the additive outlier models, the procedures are different and consist of a two-step approach. In the first step, the trend function of the series is estimated and removed from the original series via the following OLS regressions for Model (AO-0) to (AO-C), respectively:

$$y_t = \mu + \gamma DU_t + \tilde{y}_t,$$

$$y_t = \mu + \beta t + \gamma DU_t + \tilde{y}_t,$$

$$y_t = \mu + \beta t + \gamma DT_t^* + \tilde{y}_t,$$

$$y_t = \mu + \beta t + \theta DU_t + \gamma DT_t^* + \tilde{y}_t,$$

where $\tilde{y}_t$ is accordingly defined as the detrended series. The next step differs according to whether or not the first step involves DU_t, the dummy associated with a change in intercept. For Models (AO-0), (AO-A), and (AO-C), the test is based on the value of the t-statistic for testing that $\alpha = 1$ in the following autoregression:

$$\tilde{y}_t = \alpha \tilde{y}_{t-1} + \sum_{j=0}^{k} d_j D(T_1)_{t-j} + \sum_{i=1}^{k} a_i \Delta \tilde{y}_{t-i} + e_t.$$

Details about the need to introduce the current value and lags of the dummies $D(T_b)_t$ can be found in Perron and Vogelsang (1992b). The limit distributions of the tests are then the same as for the IO case. There is no need to introduce the dummies in the second step regression for Model (AO-B) where no change in level is involved and the two segments of the trend are joined at the time of break. The limit distribution is, however, different; see the work of Perron and Vogelsang (1993a,b). Again, in all cases, the tests are invariant to the change in level or slope provided the break date is correctly specified.

These unit root tests with known break dates have been extended in the following directions. Kunitomo and Sato (1995) derived the limit distribution of the likelihood ratio tests for multiple structural changes in the AO case. Amsler and Lee (1995) considerd an LM-type test in the context of a shift in level of the AO type. Saikkonen and Lütkepohl (2001) also considered cases with a level shift of the AO type, though they allow for general forms of shifts which can be indexed by some unknown parameter to be estimated. Following Elliott *et al.* (1996), they propose a GLS-type detrending procedure, which is, however, based on an $AR(p)$ process for the noise. On the basis of simulation results, they recommend using GLS detrending under the null hypothesis instead of a local alternative as done in the work of Elliott *et al.* (1996). Lanne *et al.* (2002) proposed a finite sample modification which is akin to a pre-whitening device. Let the detrended series be

$$y_t^{GLS} = y_t - \tilde{\mu} - \tilde{\gamma} DU_t - \tilde{\beta} t$$

and the estimate of the autoregressive polynomial of the first difference Δu_t be $\tilde{b}(L)$ (all estimates being obtained from the GLS procedure). With the filtered series defined as $\tilde{w}_t = \tilde{b}(L) y_t^{GLS}$, the test is then the t-statistic for testing that $\alpha = 1$ in the regression

$$\tilde{w}_t = \mu + \alpha\tilde{w}_{t-1} + \pi\tilde{b}(L)D\left(T_1\right)_t + \sum_{i=1}^{k} a_i \Delta y_{t-i}^{GLS} + e_t.$$

Note that the limit distribution does not depend on the break date. This is because the data are detrended using a GLS approach under the null hypothesis of a unit root (or more generally under a sequence of alternatives that are local to a unit root) and the level shift regressor is, in the terminology of Elliott *et al.* (1996), a slowly evolving trend, in which case, the limit distribution is the same as when no deterministic regressor is present (loosely speaking, the level shift becomes a one-time dummy). Hence, the limit distribution of the test is the same as that of Elliott *et al.* (1996) for their unit root test when only a constant is included as a deterministic regressor. Lanne and Lütkepohl (2002) showed that this test has better size and power than the test proposed in the work of Perron (1990a) and the LM test of Amsler and Lee (1995). A similar procedure for level shifts of the IO type is presented in the work of Müller *et al.* (2001).

50.4 Tests allowing for changes at unknown dates

As stated in Section 21.5, the methodology adopted by Perron (1989b, 1990a) was criticized by, among others, Christiano (1992), on the grounds that using a framework where the break is treated as fixed is inappropriate. An avenue taken by Banerjee *et al.* (1992) was to consider rolling and recursive tests. Asymptotically, such procedures will correctly reject the null hypothesis if the alternative is true but the fact that all tests are based on sub-samples means that not all information in the data is used and consequently one can expect a loss of power.

An alternative strategy, more closely related to the methodology of Perron (1989b), was adopted by Zivot and Andrews (1992) as well as Banerjee *et al.* (1992). They considered the IO-type specification and a slightly different regression that does not involve the one-time dummy when a shift in level is allowed under the alternative hypothesis. For example, for Model C, the regression is

$$y_t = \mu + \theta DU_t + \beta t + \gamma DT_t^* + \alpha y_{t-1} + \sum_{i=1}^{k} c_i \Delta y_{t-i} + e_t \qquad (50.3)$$

and the test considered is the minimal value of the t-statistic for testing that $\alpha = 1$ over all possible break dates in some pre-specified range for the break fraction $\lambda_1 \in [\epsilon, 1-\epsilon]$ where a popular choice for ϵ is 0.15. Denote the resulting test by

$$t_\alpha^* = \inf_{\lambda_1 \in [\epsilon, 1-\epsilon]} t_\alpha(\lambda_1),$$

where $t_\alpha(\lambda_1)$ is the t-statistic for testing $\alpha = 1$ in (50.3) when the break date $T_1 = [T\lambda_1]$ is used. The limit distribution of the test is

$$t_\alpha^* \Rightarrow \inf_{\lambda_1 \in [\epsilon, 1-\epsilon]} \frac{\int_0^1 W^*(r, \lambda_1) dW(r)}{\left[\int_0^1 W^*(r, \lambda_1)^2 dr\right]^{1/2}}, \qquad (50.4)$$

with $W^*(r, \lambda_1)$ as defined in (50.2). Perron (1997a) extended their theoretical results by showing, using projection arguments, that trimming for the possible values of λ_1 was unnecessary so that one could minimize over all possible break dates.

For the Nelson and Plosser (1982) dataset, Zivot and Andrews (1992) reported fewer rejections compared to what was reported in the work of Perron (1989b) using a known break date assumption. These rejections should be viewed as providing stronger evidence against the unit root but a failure to reject does not imply a reversal of the conclusions of Perron (1989b). This is a commonly found misconception in the literature, which overlooks the fact that a failure to reject may simply be due to tests with low power.

The extension by Zivot and Andrews (1992) involves, however, a substantial methodological difference. The null hypothesis considered is that of a unit root process with no break, while the alternative hypothesis is a stationary process with a break. Hence, there is an asymmetric treatment of the specification of the trend under the null and alternative hypotheses. In particular, their limit result (50.4) is not valid if a break is present under the null hypothesis.

Vogelsang and Perron (1998) showed that, in this case, t_{α}^{*} diverges to $-\infty$ when a shift in slope is present. This implies that a rejection can be due to the presence of a unit root process with a breaking trend. The reason for this is the following. With a fixed break date, the statistic $t_{\alpha}(\lambda_1)$ from regression (50.1) is invariant to the values of the parameters of the trend function under both the null and alternative hypotheses. When searching over a range of values for the break date (only one of which corresponds to the true value), this invariance no longer holds.

In the case of Model A with only a level shift and for non-trending series with a change in mean considered by Perron and Vogelsang (1992a), the statistic t_{α}^{*} is asymptotically invariant to the value of the level shift but not in finite samples. Simulations reported by Perron and Vogelsang (1992b) showed size distortions that increase with the magnitude of the level shift. They argued, however, that substantial size distortions are in effect only when implausibly large shifts occur and that the problem is not important in practice. Vogelsang and Perron (1998) showed, however, that things are quite different in the case of a shift in slope. Here, when using the IO models, the tests can diverge under the null hypothesis of a unit root. This is a problematic feature of this approach.

Perron and Vogelsang (1992a), for the non-trending case, and Perron (1997a), for the trending case, extended the analysis of Zivot and Andrews (1992). They consider tests for both the IO and AO cases based on the minimal value of the t-statistic for testing that $\alpha = 1$ and also tests based on $t_{\alpha}(\lambda_1)$ with T_1 selected by maximizing the absolute value of the t-statistic on the coefficient of the appropriate shift dummy, DU_t if only a level shift is present and DT_t^{*} if a slope change is present (see also the works of Banerjee *et al.*, 1992; Christiano, 1992). For the IO case, they also suggested using regression (50.1) instead of (50.3) which includes the one-time dummy $D\left(T_b\right)_t$ since that would be the right regression to use with a known break date. They derived the limit distribution under the null hypothesis of a unit root and no break (in which case it does not matter if the one-time dummy $D\left(T_b\right)_t$ is incorporated).

Perron (1997a) also considered tests where the break date is selected by minimizing or maximizing the value of the t-statistic on the slope dummy, which allows one to impose *a priori* the restriction of a direction for the change in slope and provides a more powerful test. This approach is more sensible since it is basically equivalent to selecting the break date by minimizing the sum of squared residuals of the appropriate regression. Carrion-i Silvestre and Sansó (2006) considered statistics which jointly test the null hypothesis and the zero value of appropriate deterministic regressors, extending the likelihood ratio test of Dickey and Fuller (1981).

Generalizations to multiple breaks include the following. Ohara (1999) extended the Zivot and Andrews (1992) approach to the general case with m breaks, though only critical values for the two break case are presented. Ohara (1999) also proved an interesting generalization of a result in the work of Perron (1989b) to the effect that if a unit root test allowing for m_1 changes in slope is performed on a series having m_0 changes with $m_0 > m_1$, then the least-squares estimate of α converges to one. This provides theoretical support for Rule 6 stated in the work of Campbell and Perron (1991), which states that "a non-rejection of the unit root hypothesis may be due to misspecification of the deterministic components included as regressors".

Kapetanios (2005) also dealt with the multiple break case but considered the following strategy, based on the sequential method of the works of Bai (1997a) and Bai and Perron (1998) (see Section 49.4). Saikkonen and Lütkepohl (2002) extended their tests for a level shift with a known break date to the case of a shift occurring at an unknown date. It can be performed in both the AO and IO frameworks and the resulting procedure is basically the same as for the known break date case. This is because, with a GLS detrending procedure based on a specification that is local to a unit root, the limit distribution of the test is the same whatever the break point is selected to be. They recommend first-differencing for the detrending. Of course, power is highly sensitive to an incorrectly estimated break date.

The issue of unit roots and trend breaks has also been addressed using a Bayesian framework with results that are generally in agreement with those of the work of Perron (1989b); see the works of Zivot and Phillips (1994), Wang and Zivot (2000), and Marriott and Newbold (2000). For the non-trending case, Clemente *et al.* (1998) extended the results of Perron and Vogelsang (1992a) to the case with two breaks. A similar extension is provided by Lumsdaine and Papell (1997) for the case of trending series.

Perron and Rodríguez (2003) considered tests for trending series with a shift in slope in the AO framework. Following the work of Elliott *et al.* (1996), they derived the asymptotic local power envelope and showed that using GLS detrended series (based on a local alternative) yields tests with power close to the envelope. Since the limit distributions are different whether a break is present or not, they use the limit distribution assuming no break in order to construct test statistics for inference. Hence, asymptotically the procedures have the correct size under no break but are conservative when a break is present provided the break date is estimated by minimizing the sum of squared residuals or relevant t-statistic. Hence, a loss of power is incurred.

50.5 Problems and recent proposals

Theoretical results by Vogelsang and Perron (1998) and simulation results reported in the works of Perron and Vogelsang (1992a), Lee and Strazicich (2001), Harvey *et al.* (2001), and Nunes *et al.* (1997) yield the following conclusions about the tests when a break is present under the null hypothesis. For the IO case when a slope shift is present, both versions using the break date obtained by minimizing the unit root test or maximizing the absolute value of the t-statistic on the coefficient of the slope dummy yield tests with similar features, namely an asymptotic size of 100%. In the presence of a level shift, the asymptotic size is correct but liberal distortions occur in finite samples when the level shift is large.

When the one-time dummy $D(T_1)_t$ is included in the regression, the source of the problem is that the break point selected with highest probability (which increases as the magnitude of the break increases) is T_1^0-1, i.e., one period before the true break, and it is for this choice of the break date that the tests have largest size distortions. Lee and Strazicich (2001) showed that the problem is the same as if the one-time dummy $D(T_1)_t$ was excluded when considering the known break date case. Their result also implies that, when unit root tests are performed using a regression of the form (50.3) without the one time dummy $D(T_1)_t$, the correct break date is selected but the tests are still affected by size distortions. In cases with only a level shift, Harvey *et al.* (2001) suggested evaluating the unit root t-statistic at the break date selected by maximizing the absolute value of the t-statistic on the coefficient of the level shift plus one and showed that the tests then have correct size even for large breaks.

For the AO-type models, the following features apply. When the break date is selected by minimizing the unit root test, similar size distortions apply. However, when the break date is selected by maximizing the absolute value of the t-statistic on the relevant shift dummy, the tests have the correct size even for large breaks, and the correct break date is selected in large samples. Vogelsang and Perron (1998) argued that the limit distribution of the unit root tests is then that corresponding to the known break date case. They suggested, nevertheless, to use the asymptotic critical values corresponding to the no break case since this leads to a test having asymptotic size no greater than that specified for all magnitudes of the break, even though this implies a conservative procedure when a break is present.

An alternative testing procedure, which naturally follows from the structural change literature, is to evaluate the unit root test at the break date selected by minimizing the sum of squared residuals from the appropriate regression. Interesting simulations pertaining to the IO case are presented in the work of Lee and Strazicich (2001). They showed that if one uses the usual asymptotic critical values that apply for the no break case under the null hypothesis, the tests are conservative when a break is present (provided the one-time dummy $D(T_1)_t$ is included in the regression). They correctly note, however, that the limit null distribution when no break is present depends on the limit distribution of the estimated break date which may depend on nuisance parameters.

Hatanaka and Yamada (1999) presented useful theoretical results for the IO regression (though they specify the data generating process to be of the AO type). They showed that, when a change in slope is present, the estimate of the break fraction λ_1, obtained by minimizing the sum of squared residuals, is consistent and that the rate of convergence is T in both the $I(1)$ and $I(0)$ cases. They also showed that this rate of convergence is sufficient to ensure that the null limit distribution of the unit root test is the same as when the break date is known. The test accordingly has more power since the critical values are smaller in absolute value. The problem, however, is that the results apply provided there is a break in the slope under the null hypothesis. Indeed, if no break is present, the known break date limit distribution no longer applies, and if the break is small, it is likely to provide a poor approximation to the finite sample distribution.

50.5.1 The Kim and Perron test

As Vogelsang and Perron (1998) showed, if the noise component has a unit root and a break occurs in the trend function, the tests of Zivot and Andrews (1992) often diverge or are not invariant to break parameters. This is a natural consequence of not permitting a break under the null hypothesis. An added consequence is that these types of tests have substantially less power than those of Perron (1989b) because they do not fully utilize the information about the break, when one is present. It is clear that the tests of Perron (1989b, 1990a) have the most desirable properties with respect to allowing a break under both the null and alternative hypotheses and having tests that are invariant to parameters of the trend function. This robustness is attained at the cost of the need to assume a known break date.

This motivated Kim and Perron (2009b) to develop new test procedures, which allow a break in the trend function at an unknown time under both the null and alternative hypotheses. Also, when a break is present, the limit distribution of the test is the same as in the case of a known break date, thereby allowing increased power while maintaining the correct size. It is important to remark that this work is not an extension of the work of Zivot and Andrews (1992). On the contrary, the testing problem they considered is inadequate and can lead to misleading results.

In order to allow the possibility of a break under both the null and alternative hypotheses, a completely different approach is required. To achieve this, Kim and Perron (2009b) used advances related to structural change problems in models with trending variables, in particular, those of Perron and Zhu (2005) and Perron and Yabu (2009b). We discuss their method in details as it is, at least for now, the most appropriate approach to the problem of unit root tests with a trend break. Alternative procedures were suggested by Harris *et al.* (2009). Extensions of this work to the multiple break case were considered by Carrion-i Silvestre *et al.* (2009), though we do not discuss the details. These should not be viewed as a complement to the test of Zivot and Andrews (1992) but as superseding it, however popular it has become.

The Kim and Perron (2009b) procedure is based on a pre-test for a change in the trend function, namely the Perron and Yabu (2009b) test. If this pre-test rejects, the limit distribution of the unit root test is then the same as if the break date was known (Perron and Vogelsang, 1993a). This is very advantageous since when a break is present the test has much greater power. It was also shown in simulations to maintain good size in finite samples and that it offers improvements over other commonly used methods. The testing procedure under the additive outlier approach starts with the following changing growth model estimated by OLS:

$$y_t = \mu + \beta t + \gamma DT_t^* + \tilde{y}_t, \tag{50.5}$$

where $\tilde{y}_t$ is accordingly defined as the detrended series. Also,

$$DT_t^* = (t - T_1) \quad \text{if } t > T_1 \text{ and } 0 \text{ otherwise.}$$

The testing procedure consists of the following steps:

1. Obtain an estimate of the break date $\hat{T}_B = \hat{\lambda} T$ by minimizing the sum of squared residuals using regression (50.5). Then, construct a window around that estimate defined by a lower bound T_l and an upper bound T_h. A window of 6 observations is often used. The results are not sensitive to this choice.
2. Create a new dataset $\{y^n\}$ by removing the data from to $T_l + 1$ to T_h and shifting down the data after the window by $S(T) = y_{T_h} - y_{T_l}$; hence,

$$y_t^n = \begin{cases} y_t & \text{if } t \leq T_l \\ y_{t+t_h-t_l} - S(T) & \text{if } t > T_l. \end{cases}$$

3. Perform the unit root test using the break date T_l. This is the t-test statistic for testing that $\tilde{\alpha} = 1$ in the following regression estimated by OLS, denoted by $t_\alpha(\hat{\lambda}_{tr}^{AO})$:

$$\ddot{y}_t^n = \ddot{\alpha} \ddot{y}_{t-1}^n + \sum_{i=1}^{k} c_i \Delta \ddot{y}_{t-i}^n + \ddot{e}_t, \tag{50.6}$$

where $\hat{\lambda}_{tr}^{AO} = T_l/T_r$, $T_r = T - (T_h - T_l)$, and $\tilde{y}_t^n$ is the detrended value of y^n using model (50.5) with T_r instead of T_1 and y_t^n instead of y_t.

The number of lags in (50.1) and (50.6) can be chosen using the Schwarz Information Criterion (BIC) but the results are robust to alternative methods such as the Akaike Information Criterion (AIC). After choosing the lag length, it is advisable to apply a test for serial correlation on the residuals. It is important that there be no evidence of remaining autocorrelation.

The reason for the trimming of the data is as follows. Recall from Section 49.6.12 that if u_t is $I(1)$ in (50.5), then the rate of convergence of the OLS estimate of the break fraction is $T^{1/2}$. Kim and Perron (2009b) showed that to obtain the same limiting distribution for the unit root test using $\hat{\lambda}$ as an estimate compared to using the true break date λ^0, $(\hat{\lambda} - \lambda^0) = o_p(T^{-1/2})$ is needed. When this condition holds, one can use the critical values corresponding to the case of a known break date conditioning on the break date being $\hat{\lambda}$. The trimming device ensures that this condition holds. It effectively eliminates noise around the OLS estimate of the break date (or break fraction) so that a faster rate of convergence can be achieved. The same essential ingredients are used in the work of Carrion-i Silvestre *et al.* (2009) for the multiple break case with the addition of the GLS-detrending device to obtain higher power. Methods applicable to models other than the "changing growth" model are discussed in the work of Kim and Perron (2009b).

The tests of Kim and Perron (2009b) and Carrion-i Silvestre *et al.* (2009) depend on the "super-efficient estimate" of the sum of the autoregressive parameters, α, proposed by Perron and Yabu (2009a) and used in the test for changes in slope proposed by Perron and Yabu (2009b). It is to be noted that the estimate proposed by Perron and Yabu (2009a) is not uniformly normally distributed when $|\alpha| < 1$. When α is local to one, the limit distribution is different and implies conservative tests. This creates a power valley when α is near one. Harvey *et al.* (2013) proposed some remedy, which, however, comes at the expense of important power losses when $\alpha = 1$.

50.6 Summary

Let us summarize the above discussion. First, in the unknown break date case, the invariance properties with respect to the parameters of the trend no longer apply as in the known break date case. Popular methods based on evaluating the unit root test at the value of the break date that minimizes it suffer from problems of liberal size distortions when a large break is present and little if any when the break is small. When the break is large, evaluating the unit root test at the break date that minimizes the sum of squared residuals leads to a procedure with correct size and better power. So, this suggests a procedure that requires in the first step a test for a change in the trend function that is valid whether a unit root is present or not, i.e., under both the null and alternative hypotheses. In this context, the work of Perron and Yabu (2009b) is especially relevant. It is applied by Kim and Perron (2009b) and extended the multiple break case by Carrion-i Silvestre *et al.* (2009). They used a pre-test for a change in trend valid whether the series is I(1) or I(0). Upon a rejection, the unit root test is evaluated at the estimate of the break date that minimizes the sum of squared residuals from the relevant regression. If the test does not reject, a standard Dickey–Fuller test is applied. This is shown to yield unit root tests with good size properties overall and better power. In cases where only level shifts are present, similar improvements are possible even though, with a fixed magnitude of shift, the estimate of the break date is not consistent under the null hypothesis of a unit root.

Chapter 51

Forecasting

Forecasting is a difficult and messy business. We try to address various issues that are relevant in practice. We assume that one has relevant models in mind and the appropriate data to yield useful forecasts. The choice of models is highly specific to the particular variable one is trying to forecast. For an extensive list of potential applications, see the work of Petropoulos *et al.* (2022) and various papers in the collections of the Handbook of Economic Forecasting. We have nothing to say about this in this chapter. There are a number of issues that need to be addressed prior to constructing a forecast and also when evaluating the forecasting performance of various methods. For an interesting overview and applications, see the work of Camacho *et al.* (2013). There are a few issues worth pointing out, mostly related to the fact that most often what is of interest is "real-time" forecasts, i.e., forecasting now given whatever available information is available this period, be it a month or a quarter, or some other sampling period. Let us take the case of trying to forecast GDP (or inflation or other macroeconomic variables) this quarter for the next few quarters (one quarter ahead or four, say). Then, one is faced with the following problems:

1. Many variables this quarter are not yet available, or are imprecisely estimated. This is especially the case with GDP and many other non-financial variables. These are measured based on sampling methods that apply some kind of incomplete survey each month or each quarter. Given this feature, they are constantly being revised as further information gets accumulated.

2. When forecasting at the quarterly level, say, some components may be available (at least in preliminary form) at the monthly level. How should we combine all this information? In other words, the construction of estimates of many variables often involves data sampled at different frequencies. This is the case especially for GDP. How can we use this information efficiently?
3. If one wants to forecast multi-periods ahead, should a direct or iterative procedure be adopted?
4. While most of the releases of preliminary estimates of important macroeconomic variables are done on a fixed regular schedule, the timing can be quite different across variables. For instance, variables like GDP have a long reporting lag, opinion surveys are available scheduled at the same time within the month, and financial variables are readily available on an almost daily basis.
5. Given the vast number of variables available to forecast a single one of interest, what should be done? For instance, a VAR model incorporating data sampled at different frequencies might be appealing, but it rapidly involves a curse of dimensionality, i.e., too many parameters to estimate. An alternative could be to use a state-space model which allows imputing missing observations as state variables.
6. How do we evaluate the forecasting performance of various models? Most studies use the usual posted final estimates as published by various agencies. But this in fact misses an important feature. Forecasts are made in real time with whatever information is available when the forecast is made. Sometimes, these are referred to as "time-t vintage data". Here, the use of a state-space model can help since it can deliver a time-t estimate of the state vector. But most importantly, some vintage estimates are now available; see https://alfred.stlouisfed.org/.

Given space constraints and the fact that these issues are highly variable specific, we do not discuss much these important issues. Issue (1) points to the importance of using real time vintage data. Issue (2) can partially be addressed using a so-called MIDAS approach; see, e.g., the work of Ghysels *et al.* (2007) for a review. Issue (3) is discussed briefly in Section 51.2. Issue (4) is more difficult to handle but can be done using an extensive updating algorithm. For an interesting application, see the work of Bianchi *et al.* (2022). We do not address this problem in detail since the issues to be dealt with are highly variable specific. One interesting thing to note, however, is the fact that, for some variables (e.g., GDP), even the current date t value is only measured with very incomplete data. This usually also applies to few previous data points depending on the context. Since this variable and many others are of utmost interest for the practice of economic policy, this has led to an extensive literature on what is called "nowcasting", i.e., predicting (or estimating) the current value. For reviews, see the works of Banbura (2013) and Bok *et al.* (2018).

We address issue (5) briefly. When faced with a very large set of data, the issue is then about doing aggregation or dimension reduction; see Section 51.8. Again, because of the date-specific nature of the problem, we do not say much about issue (6), though we believe that most forecasting exercises and comparisons across models should be done with real time-t vintage data, at least whenever possible. So, basically, we assume that the practitioner has some models to produce forecasts and discuss various theoretical issues pertaining to (a) obtaining better forecasts in the presence of some problems (e.g., structural change) and (b) comparing the forecasting accuracy of various forecasting models.

In this chapter, we cover the following topics. First, in Section 51.1, we briefly discuss loss functions and optimal forecasts, followed by some remarks about the merits and drawbacks of direct versus iterated forecasts in Section 51.2. Section 51.3 deals with various methods advocated to produce forecasts when the model is subject to structural changes. In Section 51.4, we discuss techniques to compare the predictive performance of two or more forecasts. Section 51.5 discusses the concept of forecast failure (or breakdown) and describes methods proposed to detect changes in the forecasting performance over time. We consider various methods to combine different forecasting models to produce better forecasts in Section 51.6. Section 51.7 discusses the model confidence set, a method advocated by Hansen *et al.* (2011) to sort out which, among many possible models, could be viewed as most useful for forecasting. Section 51.8 discusses issues related to forecasting when a very large dataset is available.

We focus on point forecasts and not density forecasts. The latter are of interest in some contexts but most of the empirical (and theoretical) work relates to point forecasts. Useful surveys include the works of Stock and Watson (2006), Timmermann (2006), Elliott and Timmermann (2008), Clark and McCracken (2013), Ng (2013), among others.

51.1 Loss functions and optimal forecasts

It is important to note that the problem of forecasting goes hand-in-hand with the loss function an individual may have. In the vast majority of cases, the loss function adopted is the Mean Squared Forecast Error (MSFE). This makes things easier. For instance, if the model is linear, then the optimal predictor is simply that obtained using a least-squares estimation method. However, in several cases, one may have an asymmetric loss function. Then, the optimal estimator differs. For example, if there is a large cost for a positive forecast error, then the best estimator would be larger and in fact, related to the quantile function associated with the loss function; see the work of Koenker and Bassett (1978).

If the loss function is the MSFE, then the optimal forecast is the conditional mean. If it is the mean absolute error, then it is the conditional median. Elliott *et al.* (2005) considered a flexible class of loss functions and derived the associated optimal loss function. A somewhat popular asymmetric loss function is the so-called linex function; see, e.g., the works of Zellner (1986) and Christoffersen and Diebold (1997), given by, with e_{t+h} the h-period ahead forecast error,

$$\exp(\alpha e_{t+h}) - \alpha e_{t+h} - 1,$$

where α dictates the degree of the asymmetry. For instance, if $\alpha > 0$, large underpredictions are costlier than overpredictions of the same magnitude. The loss function can also be a very simple sign function where only the direction of the forecast error matters, which is often encountered in financial applications; see the work of Christoffersen and Diebold (2006). For a review and additional references on the importance of asymmetric loss functions, see Section 4 in the work of Elliott and Timmermann (2008) and the various papers referenced therein.

Given that there exist so many possible loss functions, each of which is associated with a particular problem or variable being forecasted, we restrict our attention to the most commonly used MSFE loss function. In this case, the conditional mean is the optimal forecast, and if the model is linear, simple least-squares procedures are sufficient. Still, even in this standard case, the construction of optimal forecasts involves a host of issues: (a) which variables to use to produce the forecasts; (b) what model to use, and if many models are available should we try to sort out the best one or average the forecasts from some subsets of the models; (c) how to track the performance of the forecasting model in the presence of instabilities, i.e., structural changes. These issues are addressed.

An issue of interest is how accurate a model is in forecasting. In order to answer these questions, we need to specify a measure to evaluate the accuracy of the predictions. Such measures are functions $g(\cdot)$ of the forecast errors e_{t+h}. The most often used measures of forecast accuracy in the literature are (1) Mean Square Forecast Error (MSFE): $g(e_{t+h}) = e_{t+h}^2$, (2) bias: $g(e_{t+h}) = e_{t+h}$, (3) mean absolute error: $g(e_{t+h}) = |e_{t+h}|$, and (4) serial correlation: $g(e_{t+h}) = e_{t+h}e_{t+h-1}$.

By far, the most popular measure used to compare models is the MSFE. Of course, one often also reports the bias. The mean absolute error is useful when outliers are of concern. Since optimal single-step forecasts should be uncorrelated, the serial correlation is also a useful metric to gauge departures from efficient use of information, instabilities or misspecifications. There are many other measures that can be used depending on the context. For instance, in finance, an utmost concern is the probability of large negative returns. Then, one should adopt an asymmetric loss function. For an extensive treatment of other measures, see the work of West (2006). In general, depending on the loss function, a forecast need not minimize the MSFE, bias, or MAE. In what follows, we concentrate on evaluating models according to the MSFE criterion with the caveat that it may not be the appropriate measure in a variety of cases. A complete treatment is well outside the scope of this chapter.

Under an MSFE loss function, a seminal contribution to assessing whether forecasts are good is that of Mincer and Zarnowitz (1969). Suppose that you wish to forecast some variable y_{t+1} using a model

$f(x_t, \beta)$, where $f(\cdot)$ is some functional form, x_t the variables used to construct the forecasts, and β the parameters of the model. Consider the regression equation

$$y_{t+1} = \alpha_0 + \alpha_1 f(x_t, \beta) + e_{t+1},$$

where $E(e_{t+1}|\Phi_t) = 0$ so that the forecast errors are uncorrelated. Here, Φ_t denotes the information set available at time t, which, in particular, includes x_t. The forecast will be unbiased if $\alpha_0 = 0$ and $\alpha_1 = 1$. This is a testing framework often used to evaluate the reliability of forecasting models. However, recall that a rejection may not be due to inefficient use of information but rather because the individual may have a loss function different from the MSFE, especially if asymmetric. This framework can be extended to evaluating and comparing multiple models as discussed in Section 51.4.

51.2 Direct versus iterated forecasts

This section discusses a simple problem related to forecasting when models contain lagged dependent variables. When producing one-step ahead forecasts, the standard method simply estimates the model and use the fitted value as the forecast. However, when forecasting multi-periods ahead, then one is faced with two possible approaches: (a) direct forecasts and (b) iterated one-step forecasts. We review the pros and cons of both methods. For simplicity, we consider a single variable with no covariates, so we have a time series $(y_1, \ldots, y_T)$ and we would like to forecast $(y_{T+1}, \ldots, y_{T+H})$. To make things even simpler and transparent suppose that the forecasting model is an AR(1) given by

$$y_t = \rho y_{t-1} + \varepsilon_t. \tag{51.1}$$

- **Iterated:** One way to construct multi-period forecasts is to use an iterative method. We start by estimating (51.1) (usually by OLS) and obtain an estimate $\hat{\rho}$ of the autoregressive coefficient. We then construct the forecasts in the following way:

$$\hat{y}_{t+1} = \hat{\rho} y_t,$$
$$\hat{y}_{t+2} = \hat{\rho} \hat{y}_{t+1} = \hat{\rho}^2 y_t,$$
$$\dots$$
$$\hat{y}_{t+H} = \hat{\rho} \hat{y}_{t+H-1} = \hat{\rho}^H y_t.$$

Hence, the iterated forecasts are constructed by estimating a one-period ahead model and obtaining the h-step ahead forecast by iteratively substituting the one-period ahead forecast for different horizons.

- **Direct:** An alternative approach is "direct forecasting". We then need to estimate H models, one for each forecast horizon $h = 1, \dots, H$, given by

$$y_t = \rho_h y_{t-h} + \varepsilon_t,$$

to obtain an estimate of the H autoregressive coefficients associated with the H different models $(\rho_1, \dots, \rho_H)$ and we construct the forecasts in the following way:

$$\hat{y}_{t+1} = \hat{\rho}_1 y_t,$$
$$\dots$$
$$\hat{y}_{t+h} = \hat{\rho}_h y_t,$$
$$\dots$$
$$\hat{y}_{t+H} = \hat{\rho}_H y_t.$$

Hence, with a direct forecasting approach, the forecast for each horizon h is constructed by estimating a specific model where the dependent variable is lagged h periods.

In general, the iterated forecast is believed to be more efficient if the estimated model is correctly specified while it can lead to an amplification of any bias as h increases if the estimate of the autoregressive coefficient is biased. The direct forecast is less efficient but provides more robustness in case of misspecification. Marcellino *et al.* (2006) compared the performance of the two methods using 170 U.S. monthly macroeconomic time series spanning 1959–2002. The iterated forecast is constructed estimating the parameters $\alpha, \rho_1, \ldots, \rho_p$ in the forecasting equation

$$y_t = \alpha + \sum_{i=1}^{p} \rho_i y_{t-i} + \varepsilon_t,$$

and the forecast is given by

$$\hat{y}_{t+h} = \hat{\alpha} + \sum_{i=1}^{p} \hat{\rho}_i \hat{y}_{t+h-i},$$

estimated by OLS, where $\hat{y}_j = y_j$ for $j \leq t$. The direct forecast is constructed estimating, for each horizon $h = 1, \ldots, H$, the parameters $\alpha, \rho_h, \ldots, \rho_{p+h-1}$ of the model

$$y_t = \alpha + \sum_{i=h}^{p+h-1} \rho_i y_{t-i} + \varepsilon_t,$$

and the forecast is given by

$$\hat{y}_{t+h} = \hat{\alpha} + \sum_{i=1}^{p} \hat{\rho}_i y_{t+1-i}.$$

The lag length p is usually determined using one of the common information criteria (e.g., AIC or BIC). The empirical results of the study clearly show the superiority of the iterated forecast method, which on average leads to lower out of sample mean square error. The relative performance of the direct forecast deteriorates with the number of steps ahead showing that the lack of robustness of the direct forecast is outweighed by its efficiency when the forecast horizon increases. They argue that these findings are in contrast with the idea that there exists an efficiency-robustness trade-off between these two procedures.

51.3 Forecasting under structural breaks

A key challenge in forecasting is the fact that economic relationships modeled via simple models may be unstable over time, i.e., they may exhibit structural changes whether abrupt or gradual. There is indeed substantial evidence of the presence of structural breaks in simple models describing macroeconomic and financial data as highlighted by, e.g., Stock and Watson (1996). This is an important problem that has received substantial attention from both theoretical and applied perspectives.

One way to hope avoiding biases induced by such structural changes is to adopt a rolling window to estimate the model, hoping that the most recent window is not affected by structural changes. Another avenue is to test for structural changes in the pre-forecasting sample. One can then simply use the sample associated with the last stable regime. This, however, is not optimal, in general. Using some pre-break data in addition to all the post-break data may reduce the MSFE. It depends on the magnitude of the break, the variance of the shocks, and the lengths of the regimes. This is a reflection of the standard bias versus variance trade-off. We review such issues. However, many other approaches are available to mitigate the effect of breaks. Several are outlined in this section.

We start in Section 51.3.1 with a description of the types of breaks that may lead to changes in the MSFE of forecasts for a simple linear regression model. For simplicity, throughout this section, we assume a single break. This is basically without loss of generality since in practice one cares about the position of the last break date.

Depending on the type of break considered, the literature has developed various methods which improve the forecasts in terms of the MSFE criterion. We can classify these methods in two categories, those which require a pre-test of the time of the break T_1 and those that do not. As a preview, there is no clear ranking between the methods proposed: The usual trade-off between efficiency and robustness is present. Some methods produce satisfactory forecasts for some types of breaks but may be severely biased under other specifications of the instabilities. In general, when the break is large and away from the extremes of the sample, the break date can be precisely estimated and the methods based on some pre-test seem to perform better. On the other hand, when the break is small, close to the end of the sample or there are other types of misspecification in the model, the methods that do not require a pre-test of the time of the break T_1 are more robust. While one can think that the consistency at rate T of the estimator of the break fraction allows establishing a distribution theory as if the date break was known *a priori* (see Section 49.2.1), Koo and Seo (2015) showed that misspecification of the model can result in a slower convergence rate. Section 51.3.2 describes various methods based on some estimate of the last break, while Section 51.3.3 considers methods that make no such attempt. Section 51.3.4 also briefly discusses methods that also attempt to forecast breaks in the out-of-sample period.

51.3.1 Types of breaks

To begin, it is useful to have an idea of the types of structural breaks in the parameters the literature has covered. These are not exhaustive but serve as simple illustrations to motivate the development of more robust forecasting methods. Consider a structural linear model of the following type:

$$y_{t+1} = x_t'\beta_t + \sigma_t\varepsilon_t, \quad t = 1, \ldots, T_1, \ldots, T,$$

where x_t is a $k \times 1$ vector of stationary regressors, $\varepsilon_t \sim i.i.d.(0, 1)$, and T_1 is the time of the break, which can be either known or unknown. The most common breaks considered are as follows:

1. A single break in the coefficient β_t:

$$\beta_t = \begin{cases} \beta^{(1)} & \text{if } 1 < t \leq T_1, \\ \beta^{(2)} & \text{if } T_1 < t \leq T. \end{cases}$$

2. A break in the variance σ_t:

$$\sigma_t = \begin{cases} \sigma^{(1)} & \text{if } 1 < t \leq T_1, \\ \sigma^{(2)} & \text{if } T_1 < t \leq T. \end{cases}$$

3. A combination of both a break in the coefficient and the variance.
4. Multiple breaks in either the coefficients or the variance occurring at dates $\{T_1, \ldots, T_m\}$, where m is the number of breaks.
5. A smooth continuous change in the coefficient β_t:

$$\beta_t = \beta(t/T),$$

   where $\beta : [0, 1] \to \mathbb{R}^q$ is a continuous function.

6. A random walk process where at every period β_t differs from the previous value by an error $v_t \sim i.i.d.(0, V)$ so that

$$\beta_t = \beta_{t-1} + v_t.$$

To keep the exposition simple, we focus on a single break and provide references that consider smooth continuous changes.

Under the assumption of a single break in the coefficients β_t and σ_t at time T_1, we can rewrite the model as

$$\begin{aligned} y_{t+1} = {} & 1(t \leq T_1)\left[x_t'\beta^{(1)} + \sigma^{(1)}\varepsilon_t\right] \\ & + 1(t > T_1)\left[x_t'\beta^{(2)} + \sigma^{(2)}\varepsilon_t\right], \quad t = 1, \ldots, T_1, \ldots, T, \end{aligned}$$

or, in matrix notation,

$$\begin{aligned} (Y^{(1)\prime}, Y^{(2)\prime})' = {} & 1(t \leq T_1)[X^{(1)\prime}\beta^{(1)} + \sigma^{(1)}\varepsilon^{(1)}] \\ & + 1(t > T_1)[X^{(2)\prime}\beta^{(2)} + \sigma^{(2)}\varepsilon^{(2)}], \end{aligned}$$

where $X^{(1)} = (x_1', \ldots, x_{T_1}')$, $X^{(2)} = (x_{T_1+1}', \ldots, x_T')$, and $Y^{(1)}, Y^{(2)}$, $\varepsilon^{(1)}, \varepsilon^{(2)}$ are defined in a similar way.

Remark 51.1. Changes in only the variance of the shocks may have practical implications for forecasting when the model is otherwise stable and one uses the high-variance regime. However, it can also be beneficial when the variance decreases, in which case the forecasts are more precise. This is often referred to as the "good luck" scenario. Either way, they induce a change in the forecasting performance; hence, we include such cases. Also, when associated with breaks in coefficients, they have an effect on the reliability of some of the procedures discussed.

51.3.2 Methods based on an estimate of the break date

The first methods discussed assume that one has an estimate $\hat{T}_1$ of the break date T_1 which can be obtained from standard methods in the literature such as the works of Bai (1997b), Bai and Perron (1998), and Bai and Perron (2003a). A comprehensive treatment was provided by Pesaran and Timmermann (2007) who suggested the following procedures:

- **Post-break.** This is the simplest method which consists of using only the post-break observations:

$$\hat{\beta}^{PB} = (X^{(2)\prime} X^{(2)})^{-1} X^{(2)\prime} Y^{(2)},$$

where we used the estimate $\hat{T}_1$ to define $X^{(2)} = (x'_{\hat{T}_1+1}, \ldots, x'_T)$. Here, with a slight abuse of notation, we are using $X^{(2)}$ to define the post-break sample defined by the estimate $\hat{T}_1$ instead of the the true break date T_1. The resulting forecast is given by

$$\hat{y}^{PB}_{T+1} = x'_T \hat{\beta}^{PB}.$$

- **Trade-off.** This method is based on choosing the optimal window size by minimizing the conditional MSFE given $(X^{(1)}, X^{(2)})$. The motivation of this approach is that the estimator that minimizes the bias is not always the one that minimizes jointly the bias and variance, which is what we are interested in, namely the MSFE. Given the starting point m of the window, define $X^{(m)} = (x'_m, \ldots, x'_T)$, the vector of the observations from m onward. The trade-off method consists in choosing the m that minimizes the MSFE. This method relies on some expression of the bias variance trade-off. More formally, let $\lambda = v_1/v$, where $v_1 = T_1 - m + 1$ is the number of pre-break observations and $v = T - m + 1$ is the total number of observations. The optimal value of λ minimizes the sum of the bias $B_m(v_1)$ and the estimation error $E_m(v_1)$ in which the conditional MSFE can be decomposed:

$$\hat{\lambda} = \arg \min_{0 \leq \lambda < 1} [B_m(v_1) + E_m(v_1)].$$

The exact expressions for $B_m(v_1)$ and $E_m(v_1)$ depend on various nuisance parameters, which can be consistently estimated. We refer the reader to the work of Pesaran and Timmermann (2007) for a complete description. As mentioned before, this method relies on an estimate of the unknown break date T_1. Furthermore, consistency requires an especially large relative post-break window size $v - v_1$ which is not always available in applications. From $\hat{\lambda}$, we can recover a good estimate of the best window length m^* and the resulting parameter estimate is given by

$$\hat{\beta}^{TO} = (X^{(m^*)'}X^{(m^*)})^{-1}X^{(m^*)'}Y^{(m^*)}$$

so that the forecast is

$$\hat{y}_{T+1}^{TO} = x_T'\hat{\beta}^{TO}.$$

An extension with less restrictive assumptions is provided by Inoue *et al.* (2017).

- **Cross-validation.** This method consists of using the last $\bar{\omega}$ observations to perform an out-of-sample cross-validation to obtain the optimal estimation window starting point m. Given an estimate based on observations from m to τ,

$$\hat{\beta}^{(m:\tau)} = (X^{(m:\tau)'}X^{(m:\tau)})^{-1}X^{(m:\tau)'}Y^{(m:\tau)},$$

with $X^{(m:\tau)} = (x_m', \ldots, x_\tau')$, and similarly for $Y^{(m:\tau)}$, we define the out of sample MSFE in the following way:

$$\text{MSFE}(m|T,\bar{\omega}) = \bar{\omega}^{-1}\sum_{\tau=T-\bar{\omega}}^{T-1}(y_{\tau+1} - x_\tau'\hat{\beta}^{(m:\tau)})^2.$$

Then, we choose

$$m^* \in M = [1, \ldots, \min\{\hat{T}_1 + 1, \underline{\omega} + \bar{\omega}\}]$$

to minimize $\text{MSFE}(m|T,\bar{\omega})$. The maximum of the set M is the smallest between $\hat{T}_1 + 1$ and $\underline{\omega} + \bar{\omega}$ since it is not efficient to use a sub-sample of the post-break data. Also, $\underline{\omega} + \bar{\omega}$ is the minimum number $\underline{\omega}$ of observations required to estimate the parameters plus the final observations set aside for the out-of-sample validation $\bar{\omega}$. Note that this maximum depends on the estimated time of the break $\hat{T}_1$, so whenever this break date is poorly estimated, it may be reflected in a choice of m that does not minimize the MSFE.

Accordingly,

$$m^* = \arg \min_{m \in [1,\ldots,\min\{\hat{T}_1+1,\underline{\omega}+\bar{\omega}\}]} \text{MSFE}(m|T,\bar{\omega}),$$

and the resulting parameter estimate is given by

$$\hat{\beta}^{CV} = (X^{(m^*:T)\prime} X^{(m^*:T)})^{-1} X^{(m^*:T)\prime} Y^{(m^*:T)}$$

so that the forecast is

$$\hat{y}_{T+1}^{CV} = x_T' \hat{\beta}^{CV}.$$

It is possible to avoid using an estimate of the break date with a slight modification. One simply minimizes the MSFE over $m^* \in M = [1, \ldots, \underline{\omega} + \bar{\omega}]$, i.e., treating $\hat{T}_1$ as unknown. Then,

$$m^* = \arg \min_{m \in [1,\ldots.,\underline{\omega}+\bar{\omega}]} \text{MSFE}(m|T,\bar{\omega}).$$

- **Laplace Cross-validation.** This method builds upon the cross-validation procedure previously discussed. The intuition is that in the standard method of cross-validating the estimates uses a limited time span so that the cross validation criterion can be noisy due to estimation uncertainty. To account for this, Hirano and Wright (2022) proposed a pseudo-Bayesian alternative. Define

$$L(m) = \exp\left(-\frac{1}{2}\frac{\text{MSFE}(m|T,\bar{\omega})}{\hat{\sigma}^2}\right),$$

and compute the start date m^* as the pseudo-posterior mean

$$m^* = \frac{\int mL(m)dm}{\int L(m)dm},$$

which assumes a flat prior. By integrating over all possible values of m, the method based on the entire cross-validation function, and not just the minimizer, takes into account the asymmetry of the MSFE. Once we get m^*, we proceed as before to find the forecast. The authors show by simulations that this method gives smaller MSFE than the ordinary cross-validation procedure.

- **Weighted Combination.** This procedure is motivated by the fact that, as mentioned before, $\hat{T}_1$ can be a poor estimate of the true break date. Hence, the idea is to use a combination of forecasts weighted by a function proportional to the inverse of the associated out-of-sample MSFE. Given an estimate of the break date $\hat{T}_1$, which is assumed not too close to the end of the sample (i.e., with $\hat{T}_1 + 1 < T - \underline{\omega} - \bar{\omega}$), we compute the estimate $\hat{\beta}^{(m:T)}$ and the forecast $\hat{y}_{T+1}^{(m:T)} = x_T'\hat{\beta}^{(m:T)}$ for all $m = 1, \ldots, \hat{T}_1 + 1$. Then, we construct the weights as the inverse of the relative MSFE

$$w_{m,T} = \frac{\text{MSFE}(m|T, \bar{\omega})^{-1}}{\sum_{m=1}^{\hat{T}_1+1} \text{MSFE}(m|T, \bar{\omega})^{-1}},$$

and the forecast is

$$\hat{y}_{T+1}^{WC} = \sum_{m=1}^{\hat{T}_1+1} w_{m,T}\hat{y}_{T+1}^{(m:T)}.$$

Again, it is possible to avoid using an estimate of the break date. Instead of averaging forecasts from $m = 1$ to $\hat{T}_1 + 1$, we change the maximum to $T - \underline{\omega} + \bar{\omega}$ which is the minimal sample size required to estimate the parameters and compute the associated MSFE. The weights will be

$$w_{m,T} = \frac{\text{MSFE}(m|T, \omega)^{-1}}{\sum_{m=1}^{T-\underline{\omega}+\bar{\omega}} \text{MSFE}(m|T, \bar{\omega})^{-1}},$$

and the forecast is

$$\hat{y}_{T+1}^{WC} = \sum_{m=1}^{T-\underline{\omega}+\omega} w_{m,T}\hat{y}_{T+1}^{(m:T)}.$$

- **Simple or Pooled Combination.** This method is a special case of the weighted combination where the weights are equal for every observation so that the forecast is

$$\hat{y}_{T+1}^{PO} = (\hat{T}_1 + 1)^{-1} \sum_{m=1}^{\hat{T}_1+1} \hat{y}_{T+1}^{(m:T)}.$$

Here also, it is possible to avoid using an estimate of the break date. One simply sets the weights equal for every observation so the forecast will be

$$\hat{y}_{T+1}^{POL} = \frac{1}{T - \underline{\omega} + \bar{\omega}} \sum_{m=1}^{T-\underline{\omega}+\bar{\omega}} \hat{y}_{T+1}^{(m:T)}.$$

See the work of Pesaran and Pick (2011) for the theoretical properties and some applications.

- **Optimal Weights.** This procedure, suggested by Pesaran *et al.* (2013), uses the whole sample to estimate the parameter β by assigning different weights to each observation to obtain the optimal estimator that minimizes the MSFE:

$$\hat{\beta}^{PPP} = (X'WX)^{-1}X'WY,$$

where W is the matrix of weights which is chosen to minimize the MSFE. In the case of a single break, given an estimate $\hat{T}_1$, the optimal weighting matrix is of the form $W = \text{diag}(w^{(1)}, \ldots, w^{(1)}, w^{(2)}, \ldots, w^{(2)})$ with

$$w^{(1)} = \frac{1}{T}\frac{1}{b_1 + (1 - b_1)(q^2 + Tb_1\phi^2)},$$

$$w^{(2)} = \frac{1}{T}\frac{q^2 + Tb_1\phi^2}{b_1 + (1 - b_1)(q^2 + Tb_1\phi^2)},$$

where $b_1 = T_1/T$ is the proportion of observations before the break, $q = \sigma^{(1)}/\sigma^{(2)}$ is the break in the error variance, and

$$\phi = \frac{x'_{T+1}(\beta^{(1)} - \beta^{(2)})}{\sigma^{(2)}\sqrt{x'_{T+1}E(x_t x'_t)x_{T+1}}}.$$

It can be rewritten as a combination of the pre-break and post-break estimators

$$\hat{\beta}^{PPP} = \Lambda\hat{\beta}^{(1)} + (1 - \Lambda)\hat{\beta}^{(2)},$$

where $\hat{\beta}_1$ and $\hat{\beta}_2$ are the estimators constructed using pre and post-break data, respectively. The weight Λ is given by

$$\Lambda = \left(\frac{w^{(1)}}{w^{(2)}} X^{(1)\prime} X^{(1)} + X^{(2)\prime} X^{(2)}\right)^{-1} \frac{w^{(1)}}{w^{(2)}} X^{(1)\prime} X^{(1)}.$$

We refer to the work of Pesaran *et al.* (2013) for the formula of the optimal weighting matrix for the case of a smooth continuous change in the parameters. Lee *et al.* (2022) revisited this method and suggested using a kernel weighting function which facilitates the implementation of this approach.

- **Stein-like Combined.** Lee *et al.* (2022) proposed a Stein-like estimator which linearly combines the post-break estimate $\hat{\beta}^{(2)}$ and the full sample estimate $\hat{\beta}^{(full)}$ via

$$\hat{\beta}_\alpha = \alpha\hat{\beta}^{(full)} + (1-\alpha)\hat{\beta}^{(2)}.$$

The weight α is a function of the Hausman statistics H_T (see Section 18.3) and a parameter τ that governs the shrinkage of the estimator. The Hausman statistic H_T is constructed to test the null hypothesis of $\beta^{(2)} = \beta^{(full)}$. Under the null of no break, both the full sample estimator $\hat{\beta}^{(full)}$ and the post-break estimator $\hat{\beta}^{(2)}$ are consistent but only the former is efficient. On the other hand, when the null does not hold, $\hat{\beta}^{(2)}$ remains consistent while $\hat{\beta}^{(full)}$ is inconsistent. The Hausman statistic takes the following form:

$$H_T = \left(\hat{\beta}^{(2)} - \hat{\beta}^{(full)}\right)' \left[\hat{V}_{\beta^{(2)}} - \hat{V}_{\beta^{(full)}}\right]^{-} \left(\hat{\beta}^{(2)} - \hat{\beta}^{(full)}\right),$$

with $\hat{V}_{\beta^{(2)}}$ and $\hat{V}_{\beta^{(full)}}$ consistent estimators of the respective asymptotic variances; e.g., when the errors are assumed to be *i.i.d.*, they are given by

$$\hat{V}_{\beta^{(2)}} = \frac{\hat{u}'_{(2)}\hat{u}_{(2)}}{T - T_1 - k}(X^{(1)\prime}X^{(1)})^{-1}, \quad \hat{u}_{(2)} = y - x'\hat{\beta}^{(2)},$$

$$\hat{V}_{\beta^{(full)}} = \frac{\hat{u}'_{(full)}\hat{u}_{(full)}}{T - k}(X^{(2)\prime}X^{(2)})^{-1}, \quad \hat{u}_{(full)} = y - x'\hat{\beta}^{(full)}.$$

Finally, the weight α is given by

$$\alpha = \begin{cases} \tau H_T^{-1}, & \text{if } H_T \geq \tau, \\ 1, & \text{if } H_T < \tau, \end{cases}$$

where τ governs the shrinkage of the estimator. The idea behind this approach is that when the Hausman statistic is small, it means that the break is small, so the bias of the full sample estimate is negligible. Hence, more weight would be assigned to the full sample estimate. On the other hand, when the Hausman statistic is large, it means that the break is substantial, so the bias of the full sample estimate is no longer negligible. In this case, a larger weight is assigned to the post-break estimate which is consistent. Lee *et al.* (2022) showed via simulations that this estimator never performs worse than the post-break estimate.

51.3.3 Breaks not explicitly modeled

The following methods do not require the estimation of a break date T_1. Hence, they are more robust since they can be reliable when there are continuous breaks, a small undetectable (by standard tests) break, or when the break is close to the end of the sample.

- **Reverse order CUSUM** (Pesaran and Timmermann (2002)). This method does not require an estimate of $\hat{T}_1$ as the other methods previously discussed. The reason is that it is a two-step procedure where one initially estimates the last break point with a reverse CUSUM test and then uses the selected post-break observations to estimate the parameters. The reverse CUSUM test starts with the reversed dataset, from the most recent observations moving to the past. Given $\bar{w}$ the minimum estimation window, define $x'_{T:\tau} = (x_T, \ldots, x_\tau)$ $y'_{T:\tau} = (y_T, \ldots, y_\tau)$ with $\tau = T-1, \ldots, 1$ and compute

$$\hat{\beta}^R_{T:\tau} = \left(x'_{T:\tau} x_{T:\tau}\right)^{-1} x'_{T:\tau} y_{T:\tau},$$

and the standardized associated recursive residuals (see Section 4.9):

$$v_t = \frac{y_t - x'_t \hat{\beta}^R_{T:t}}{\sqrt{1 + x'_t (x'_t x_t)^{-1} x_t}}.$$

The reverse order CUSUM statistic s_τ is given by

$$s_\tau = \frac{\sum_{t=\tau}^{T-\bar{w}} v_t^2}{\sum_{t=1}^{T-\bar{w}} v_t^2}, \quad \text{with } \tau = T - \bar{w}, \ldots, 1.$$

The critical values of the CUSUM statistics are tabulated by Brown *et al.* (1975) who originally suggested the procedure. Call m^* the first value of τ for which the null of no break is rejected. Pesaran and Timmermann (2002) proposed to use all the observations starting from m^*, detected above, to estimate the parameters

$$\hat{\beta}^{ROC} = (X^{(m^*)\prime} X^{(m^*)})^{-1} X^{(m^*)\prime} Y^{(m^*)},$$

and the forecast will be

$$\hat{y}_{T+1}^{ROC} = x_T' \hat{\beta}^{ROC}.$$

This method is especially appealing because the CUSUM test is especially tailored to detect some forecast breakdown. Applying it in reverse order allows us to obtain an estimate of the point at which there is enough evidence to suggest that a forecasting breakdown occurred. It will not correspond to the true break date (even in large samples), but that may be viewed as beneficial since the optimal window to be used usually involves some observations that precede the break date.

- **Weighted reverse order CUSUM.** Tian and Anderson (2014) proposed a modification of the reverse CUSUM discussed previously that uses all the data available. Basically, it considers all the forecasts, obtained by starting from the shortest window $\tau = T - \bar{w}$ and expanding until $\tau = 1$, and averages them using weights proportional to the CUSUM statistic s_τ. So, for $\tau = T - \bar{w}, \ldots, 1$, we need to compute

$$\hat{\beta}^{(\tau)} = \left(X^{(\tau)\prime} X^{(\tau)}\right)^{-1} X^{(\tau)\prime} Y^{(\tau)}$$

and the CUSUM statistic s_τ. Define the weight cw_τ for the forecast $\hat{y}_{T+1}^{(\tau+1)} = x_{T+1}' \hat{\beta}^{(\tau+1)}$ as

$$cw_\tau = \frac{\left| s_\tau - \left(\frac{T-\bar{w}-\tau-1}{T-\bar{w}}\right)\right|}{\sum_{\tau=1}^{T-\bar{w}} \left| s_\tau - \left(\frac{T-\bar{w}-\tau-1}{T-\bar{w}}\right)\right|},$$

where

$$\left(\frac{T-\bar{w}-\tau-1}{T-\bar{w}}\right)=E(s_\tau),$$

under the null of no structural change. It is then suggested to apply proportionally higher weight to larger deviations of s_τ from the mean. The weighted reverse order CUSUM forecast is then

$$\hat{y}_{T+1}^{WROC}=\sum_{\tau=1}^{T-\bar{w}}cw_\tau\hat{y}_{T+1}^{(\tau+1)}.$$

Tian and Anderson (2014) claimed that this method works especially well when the time of the break is early and the sample size is small. They also proposed a modification of the weights to give relatively more weight to the last observations. Intuitively, a deviation from the trend is more informative when it happens at the end of the sample rather than at the beginning. To account for this, they modified the weights introducing a weight adjustment variable l_τ:

$$cw_\tau^l=\frac{\left|s_\tau-\left(\frac{T-\bar{w}-\tau-1}{T-\bar{w}}\right)\right|l_\tau}{\sum_{\tau=1}^{T-\bar{w}}\left|s_\tau-\left(\frac{T-\bar{w}-\tau-1}{T-\bar{w}}\right)\right|l_\tau}.$$

When $l_\tau=1$, we recover the previous weighting, while when $l_\tau=\tau$, we are modifying the weights to increase the importance of the forecasts based on the last observations in the sample. Clearly, this weighting scheme dominates the one above when the break is at the end of the sample, given that the forecasts based on the last observations are relatively more important.

- **A simple autoregressive process.** It has been argued that in many actual forecasting exercises it is difficult to beat simple autoregressive processes with enough lags, most often selected via some information criterion. Suppose that one is faced with the case of a change in the parameter associated with a regressor having a non-zero mean. Then, this translates into a change in the mean of the dependent variable y_t. Hence, if one considers an autoregression of the form

$$y_t = \mu + \sum_{i=1}^{k} \alpha_i y_{t-i} + e_t,$$

the change in structure can be associated with a change in the intercept μ. As shown in the work of Perron (1990a), for the case of an $AR(1)$ regression, the autoregressive parameter is biased toward one, and in the limit, the estimate approaches one as the magnitude of change increases. Perron (1994b) showed via simulations that this bias is even more pronounced when considering longer autoregressive processes in the sense that the sum of the autoregressive coefficients is even more biased towards one as more lags are included. Hence, with a change in the conditional mean of y_t (induced by whatever source), the fitted process is akin to a random walk or integrated progress. This induces the forecast to follow the post-break mean. Demetrescu and Hassler (2016) used this insight to advocate such a forecasting procedure. They showed that the forecasts obtained are consistent for the true values. In other words, the induced unit-root-like behavior allows achieving the right mean. The correlation structure may be distorted but this only has a lower-order impact. Of course, if the change is in the autoregressive parameters (not the conditional mean), then the methods break down and the forecasts are biased even in large samples. Some have argued that even if a test indicates a structural break in the forecasting model, this does not imply that it is relevant for forecasting; see, e.g., the work of Boot and Pick (2020). However, their empirical evidence is related to forecasting models using simple autoregressions. Their results may simply be a reflection of the arguments discussed here. This method has been extended to the multivariate VAR context by Demetrescu and Salish (2024).

The above is just a snapshot of some procedures that have been suggested. The list is not exhaustive. Other procedures suggested include the following, among many others: (a) the use of robust weights, i.e., obtained by integrating the optimal weights with respect to a uniformly distributed break date over a possible range; see the work of Pesaran *et al.* (2013); (b) using the average of the inverted likelihood ratio test, suggested by Koo and Seo (2015); (c) a time-varying jackknife model averaging, which selects the optimal time-varying weights by minimizing a local jackknife criterion; see the work of Sun *et al.* (2021); (d) the use of exponential smoothing; see the work of Hirano and Wright (2022).

In our opinion, the most promising and effective methods, among those reviewed so far, are the simplest: (a) using only the post-break sample based on the last estimate, (b) the simple reverse-order CUSUM-based method, and (c) a simple autoregressive model with the lag length selected via some information criterion. These also offer more robustness as very few extraneous parameters need to be estimated.

51.3.4 Methods that model possible breaks in the post-forecasting period

Additional work that relates to the issue of forecasting allowing for possible in- and out-of-sample changes is quite sparse as it is quite challenging, see, e.g., the work of Clements and Hendry (2006). Some Bayesian models have been proposed to address this problem; see, e.g., the works of Cogley and Sargent (2005), Pesaran *et al.* (2006), Koop and Potter (2007), Maheu and Gordon (2008), and Maheu and McCurdy (2009). The advantage of the Bayesian approach stems from the fact that it treats the parameters as random, and by imposing a prior (or meta-prior) distribution, one can model the breaks and allow them to occur out-of-sample with some probability. Such methods can, however, be sensitive to the prior distributions used.

Xu and Perron (2023) took a different frequentist approach, i.e., non-Bayesian. They considered a forecasting model in which the changes in the parameters have a probabilistic structure so that the estimates can help forecast future out-of-sample breaks. The approach is best suited to the case for which breaks occur both in- and out-of-sample, which in particular avoids the problematic use of a trimming window assumed to have a stable structure. The method will work best indeed if there are many in-sample breaks so that a long span of data is beneficial. This is unavoidable since good out-of-sample forecasts of breaks require in-sample information about the process generating such breaks, the more such information the more efficient the forecasts will be. The same applies to previously proposed Bayesian methods, though the use of tight priors can partially substitute for the lack of precise in-sample information. Having said that, their method still yields considerable improvements even if relatively few breaks are present in-sample.

The approach is similar in spirit to unobserved component models in which the parameters are modeled as random walk processes. There are, however, important departures. Most importantly, a shift need not occur every period. It does so with some probability dictated by a Bernoulli process for the occurrence of shifts and a normal random variable for its magnitude. This leads to a specification in which the parameters evolve according to a random level shift process. Some or all of the parameters of the model can be allowed to change and the latent variables that dictate the changes can be common or different for each parameter. Also, the variance of the errors may change in a similar manner. To improve the forecasting performance, they augment the basic model in two directions. First, the probability of shifts is modeled as a function of some covariates which can be forecasted. Second, a mean-reversion mechanism is allowed such that the parameters tend to revert back to the pre-forecast average. This last feature is especially influential in providing good forecasts at long horizons. Functional forms for these two modifications are suggested for which the parameters can be estimated and incorporated into the forecast scheme to model the future path of the parameters. The model can be cast into a nonlinear non-Gaussian state space framework for which standard Kalman filter-type algorithms cannot be used. A full description of the estimation method is described in Chapter 52. Simulations show that the estimation method provides reliable results in finite samples. The parameters are estimated precisely and the filtered estimates of the time path of the parameters follow the true process closely. More importantly, it provides improved forecasts over commonly used methods. Given the availability of the proper code for estimation and forecasting, the method is very flexible and easy to implement. For a given forecasting model, all that is required by the users are (1) which parameters (including the variance of the errors if desired) are subject to change, (2) whether the same or different latent Bernoulli processes dictates the timing of the changes in each parameter, and (3) which covariates are potential explanatory variables to model the probability of shifts. Even though the method is more complex to implement, few extraneous parameters need to be estimated. Hence, it is also quite robust. In order to increase efficiency by incorporating breaks in the out-of-sample period, a drawback is the need to have a relatively large number of in-sample breaks. Still, the method remains effective with few in-sample breaks; it then simply does not predict any out of sample breaks and relies on the full sample estimates allowing for whatever number of breaks is present in the in-sample period.

51.4 Forecast comparisons

There are three main issues related to choosing which forecast method to use: (1) whether the null hypothesis is set in terms of the population value of the parameters or the estimates based on a finite sample, (2) whether one accounts for estimation uncertainty or not, and (3) whether the models being compared are nested or not. In this section, we illustrate the techniques to compare the predictive performance of two or more forecasts. Important references for the material covered in this section are the works of West (2006) and Clark and McCracken (2013).

51.4.1 Types of estimators and measures of forecast accuracy

When comparing forecasting models, it is useful to try to follow typical procedures used in practice. There are three main such procedures depending on the window used to compute the forecasts: recursive, rolling, and fixed. The recursive method implicitly assumes a stable model and, accordingly, uses all observations up to the forecast period. The rolling method tries in a crude way to account for potential parameter instability or changes in the structure of the appropriate model; hence, it uses only the most recent observations. The fixed scheme uses only some initial window hoping that it corresponds to a stable period. We describe each in what follows.

Consider a sample (y_t, x_t) of T observations and divide it into two groups: the in-sample group that spans from 1 to R and the out-of-sample group that spans from $R+h$ to T, with h being the forecast horizon. Suppose we have one or more models of the form

$$y_t = x_t\beta + \epsilon_t,$$

where β is an unknown k-vector of coefficients. Our aim is to forecast y_{t+h} using the model

$$y_{t+h} = x_t\beta + \epsilon_{t+h}.$$

To do so, we have three possible ways to estimate the unknown parameters β at each point in time $t = R, \ldots, T - h$ and obtain a sequence of estimators $\hat{\beta}_R, \ldots, \hat{\beta}_{T-h}$, with $\hat{\beta}_t$ a function of the data up to time t: $(y_1, \ldots, y_t, x_1, \ldots, x_t)$. Note that in what follows ϵ_t refers to the population value of the forecast errors, while e_t denote an estimate.

1. **Recursive:** The idea is to estimate β using all the observations available up to time t. Hence, in every period, the additional observation (y_{t+1}, x_{t+1}) is effectively used in the estimation procedure. The recursive estimate $\hat{\beta}_t^{\text{Rec}}$ is the solution to the following minimization problem:

$$\hat{\beta}_t^{\text{Rec}} = \arg\min_{\beta} \sum_{i=1}^{t-h} (y_{i+h} - x_i\beta)^2, \quad t = R, \ldots, T.$$

   It minimizes the sum of squared residuals where the summation is over $t - h$ terms. Note that the number of terms summed is increasing in t. This means that any change in two subsequent elements of the sequence of estimates $\hat{\beta}_R, \ldots, \hat{\beta}_{T-h}$ is due to the new observation used in the following estimation.
2. **Rolling:** The idea of the rolling window is to use a fixed number R of the most recent observations to estimate β at each point in time. This means that from one period t to the next one $t + 1$, we are adding the new observation (y_{t+1}, x_{t+1}) that has become available and removing the oldest one (y_{t-R}, x_{t-R}). The rolling estimate $\hat{\beta}_t$ is the solution to the following minimization problem:

$$\hat{\beta}_t^{\text{Rol}} = \arg\min_{\beta} \sum_{i=t+1-R-h}^{t-h} (y_{i+h} - x_i\beta)^2, \quad t = R, \ldots, T.$$

   It minimizes the sum of squared residuals where the summation is over R terms $(t - h - [t + 1 - R - h] + 1 = R)$, which is not increasing in t.

3. **Fixed:** The fixed scheme uses the same first R observations to estimate β. Hence, we are not using the new information (y_{t+1}, x_{t+1}) that becomes available from one period to another. The fixed estimate $\hat{\beta}_t$ is the solution to the following minimization problem:

$$\hat{\beta}_t^{\text{Fix}} = \arg\min_{\beta} \sum_{i=1}^{R-h} (y_{i+h} - x_t\beta)^2, \quad t = R, \dots, T.$$

Note that $\hat{\beta}_t$ is constant since it does not depend on t, i.e., $\hat{\beta}_t = \hat{\beta}_{t+1}$ for all $t \geq R$.

Example 51.1. Suppose we have a simple univariate model and we would like to forecast two steps ahead:

$$y_{t+2} = x_t\beta + \varepsilon_{t+2}.$$

The three estimators of β are

$$\hat{\beta}_t^{\text{Rec}} = \left(\sum_{i=1}^{t-2} x_i^2\right)^{-1} \sum_{i=1}^{t-2} x_i y_{i+2},$$

$$\hat{\beta}_t^{\text{Rol}} = \left(\sum_{i=t+1-R}^{t-2} x_i^2\right)^{-1} \sum_{i=t+1-R}^{t-2} x_i y_{i+2},$$

$$\hat{\beta}_t^{\text{Fix}} = \left(\sum_{i=1}^{R-2} x_i^2\right)^{-1} \sum_{i=1}^{R-2} x_i y_{i+2}.$$

Let $Y_{i:j} = (y_i, \dots, y_j)'$ and $X_{i:j} = (x_i, \dots, x_j)'$ for $i < j$. In matrix notation, we have

$$\hat{\beta}_t^{\text{Rec}} = (X_{1:t-2}'X_{1:t-2})^{-1}X_{1:t-2}'Y_{3:t},$$

$$\hat{\beta}_t^{\text{Rol}} = (X_{t+1-R:t-2}'X_{t+1-R:t-2})^{-1}X_{t+1-R:t-2}'Y_{t-R+3:t},$$

$$\hat{\beta}_t^{\text{Fix}} = (X_{1:R-2}'X_{1:R-2})^{-1}X_{1:R-2}'Y_{3:R}.$$

At each point in time $t = R, \ldots, T$, once we have an estimate of β, we can construct the forecast

$$\hat{y}_{t+h} = x_t \hat{\beta}_t,$$

and the forecast error is

$$e_{t+h} = y_{t+h} - \hat{y}_{t+h}.$$

Issues of interest are how accurate a model is in forecasting and, in the case of two or more competing models, which one performs better. In order to answer these questions, we need to specify a measure to evaluate the accuracy of the prediction. Such measures are functions $g(\cdot)$ of the forecast errors e_{t+h} or, more generally, functions of $y_{t+h}, x_t, \hat{\beta}_t$ as well. The most often used measures of forecast accuracy in the literature are, as stated in Section 51.1: (1) Mean Square Forecast Error (MSFE): $g(e_{t+h}) = e^2_{t+h}$, (2) bias: $g(e_{t+h}) = e_{t+h}$, (3) mean absolute error: $g(e_{t+h}) = |e_{t+h}|$, and (4) serial correlation: $g(e_{t+h}) = e_{t+h} e_{t+h-1}$.

As discussed before, the most popular measure used to compare models is the MSFE. Hence, in what follows, we concentrate on evaluating models according to the MSFE criterion with the caveat that it may not be the appropriate measure in a variety of cases. A complete treatment is well outside the scope of this chapter. For simplicity, we mostly compare two models. For multiple models, see Section 51.7. When comparing models, it is important to distinguish between the cases in which they are nested or not.

Definition 51.1. Given two parametric models, A and B, model A is nested in model B if we can recover A from B by imposing some restrictions on the parameters of B.

To better understand this definition, consider the following simple example.

Example 51.2. Consider the following two models:

$$\begin{aligned} \text{Model A}: &\quad y_{t+h} = \beta_0 + \beta_1 x_{1,t} + \epsilon_{t+h}, \\ \text{Model B}: &\quad y_{t+h} = \beta_0 + \beta_1 x_{1,t} + \beta_2 x_{2,t} + \epsilon_{t+h}. \end{aligned}$$

We see that model A is nested in model B since the latter coincides with the former when $\beta_2 = 0$.

Of course, non-nested models are such that the conditions in Definition 51.1 are not satisfied. It turns out that comparing non-nested models is much easier than comparing nested models. Hence, we start with a treatment of the former case.

51.4.2 Testing for unconditional equal predictive performance

Suppose we are interested in comparing the population-level predictive performance of two models. We can specify the null hypothesis as

$$H_0 : E[g(\epsilon_{1,t+h}) - g(\epsilon_{2,t+h})] = 0.$$

For convenience, define the function f_{t+h} which embeds the g functions. Moreover, since $\epsilon_{1,t+h}$ and $\epsilon_{2,t+h}$ are functions of β_1 and β_2, we can write f_{t+h} in the following way:

$$g(\epsilon_{1,t+h}) - g(\epsilon_{2,t+h}) = f_{t+h}(\beta_1, \beta_2).$$

In light of this, for simplicity, we define $\beta := (\beta_1', \beta_2')'$ so that we can write more compactly $f_{t+h}(\beta) = f_{t+h}(\beta_1, \beta_2)$ and the null hypothesis becomes

$$H_0 : E[f_{t+h}(\beta)] = 0.$$

As a matter of notation, we let R be the size of the window used to estimate the models and P be the number of forecasts produced so that $P = T - R - h$. Thus, $R + P - 1 + h = T - 1$ is the total sample size available to conduct the forecasting comparisons.

51.4.3 Comparing two non-nested models

The simplest and, arguably, the most popular test for this null hypothesis is due to the work of Diebold and Mariano (1995). It simply consists in testing whether the sample average of the difference in the loss functions is different from zero. Let P be the length of the forecasting horizon, which can vary depending on whether one uses a rolling, recursive of fixed forecasting scheme. Assuming some parameter estimate $\hat{\beta}$, the test is

$$DM = P^{-1} \sum_{t=1}^{P} f_{t+h}(\hat{\beta})/\hat{V}_f,$$

where $\hat{V}_f$ is a consistent estimate of the long-run variance of $f_{t+h}(\beta)$ $(t = 1, \ldots, P)$, i.e., (2π) times the spectral density function at frequency zero of the sequence $f_{t+h}(\beta)$ in the stationary case. See Section 38.9 for various estimation methods. Note that the DM test is only valid for non-nested models and when the estimation uncertainty about the parameter is either irrelevant or negligible. This is usually not the case with a rolling window approach for the estimation of the model, when the size of the window R is fixed, or small relative to the sample size. Clark and West (2006) provided an interesting example where a true model involving many parameters can perform poorly in forecasting compared to a more parsimonious, though biased, model. This can occur unless the extra components of the larger model have sufficient additional predictive power.

Diebold and Mariano (1995) argued that their test can be extended to test for conditional predictive performance but provided no details; see the following. This avenue was extended by White (2000) and Hansen (2005). The idea here is then to compare multiple models and see if any one of the models has superior unconditional predictive ability; see also Section 51.7.

In this section, we analyze in more detail the issues discussed above in the context of simple models when comparing the population-level predictive performance of non-nested models. We start with the description of the comparison between two models and then move to the more general framework where one compares $m \geq 2$ models. Consider two simple linear non-nested models to forecast h-steps ahead:

$$y_{t+h} = x'_{1,t}\beta_1 + \epsilon_{1,t+h}, \tag{51.2}$$

$$y_{t+h} = x'_{2,t}\beta_2 + \epsilon_{2,t+h}, \tag{51.3}$$

where $x'_{1,t} \neq x'_{2,t}$ are $k_1 \times 1$ and $k_2 \times 1$ vectors and $E(\epsilon_{1,t}) = \sigma_1^2$, $E(\epsilon_{2,t}) = \sigma_2^2$.

Example 51.3. If we use the mean square forecast error as a measure of the predictive ability of 2-steps ahead forecasts, the null hypothesis is

$$H_0\colon E[f_{t+h}(\beta)] = E[g(\epsilon_{1,t+2}) - g(\epsilon_{2,t+2})] = E[\epsilon_{1,t+2}^2 - \epsilon_{2,t+2}^2] = 0,$$

while, if we use the mean absolute forecast error (MAFE), we have

$$H_0\colon E[f_{t+h}(\beta)] = E[g(\epsilon_{1,t+2}) - g(\epsilon_{2,t+2})] = E[|\epsilon_{1,t+2}| - |\epsilon_{2,t+2}|] = 0.$$

It is important to stress the fact that in example (51.3) we are testing if the population-level MSFE of the errors, $\epsilon_{i,t+h}(\beta_i)$, are identical for both models. We are not testing if the MSFE of the estimated *residuals*, $e_{i,t+h}(\hat{\beta}_i)$, are identical. This second hypothesis pertains to the finite-sample-level predictive ability. We comment on this problem later. Note that the population-level errors depend on the population parameter β while the finite-sample-level residuals depend on the estimate $\hat{\beta}$. This means that at the population level, we are not testing which of the two estimated models generates the lower MSFE, but we are trying to say something about the predictive performance of the theoretical models as if we have an infinite sample that allows estimating parameters without uncertainty. In practice, in finite samples, it can happen that a richer, but correctly specified, theoretical model is poorly estimated and results in a larger MSFE compared to a misspecified but more parsimonious model.

Given the number of steps ahead h, let β^* be the population parameter, i.e., the probability limit of the estimate. Define the errors, the function f_{t+h}, and the sample mean $\bar{f}_h(\beta^*)$ of f_{t+h} in the following way:

$$\begin{aligned} \epsilon_{i,t+h} &= y_{t+h} - x_{i,t}'\beta_i^*, \quad i \in \{1,2\}, \\ f_{t+h}(\beta^*) &= g(\epsilon_{1,t+h}) - g(\epsilon_{2,t+h}), \quad t = R, \ldots, T-h, \\ \bar{f}_h(\beta^*) &= (P-h+1)^{-1} \sum_{t=R}^{T-h} f_{t+h}(\beta^*). \end{aligned} \tag{51.4}$$

It is convenient to look at an illustrative example where we assume the parameter β^* is known.

Example 51.4. Consider the models (51.2)–(51.3) and the null hypothesis for the MAFE described in Example (51.3):

$$H_0\colon E[f_{t+2}(\beta^*)] = E[|\epsilon_{1,t+2}| - |\epsilon_{2,t+2}|] = 0.$$

Assume that f_{t+2} is covariance stationary. For simplicity, suppose we have $T = P + 1$. Since we are not estimating any parameter, we would have in principle T observations. In order to avoid confusion, it is easier to think about having $P + 1$ observations. Then,

$$f_{t+2}(\beta^*) = g(\epsilon_{1,t+2}) - g(\epsilon_{2,t+2}) = |\epsilon_{1,t+2}| - |\epsilon_{2,t+2}|,$$
$$\bar{f}_2(\beta^*) = (P-1)^{-1} \sum_{t=R}^{T-2} (|\epsilon_{1,t+2}| - |\epsilon_{2,t+2}|).$$

Using a central limit theorem (assuming the proper regularity conditions hold),

$$\sqrt{P-1}\left(\bar{f}_2(\beta^*) - E[f_{t+2}(\beta^*)]\right) \xrightarrow{d} \mathcal{N}(0, \Omega^*),$$

where

$$\Omega^* = \sum_{j=-\infty}^{\infty} E[(f_{t+2} - Ef_{t+2})(f_{t+2-j} - Ef_{t+2})].$$

Given a consistent estimator $\hat{\Omega}^*$ of Ω^* such that $\hat{\Omega}^* \xrightarrow{p} \Omega^*$, usually based on some HAC-type estimate, we can construct a t-test:

$$\mathcal{T} = \frac{|\bar{f}_2(\beta^*) - E[f_{t+2}(\beta^*)]|}{\sqrt{\hat{\Omega}^*/(P-1)}} = \frac{|\bar{f}_2(\beta^*)|}{\sqrt{\hat{\Omega}^*/(P-1)}} \xrightarrow{d} \mathcal{N}(0,1),$$

and we reject the null of equal forecasting performance at the $1-\alpha$ level when $\mathcal{T} > z_{\alpha/2}$.

The above example assumes that the parameters are known. But in the majority of cases, we have to estimate these parameters with one of the procedures described in Section (51.4.1). Define the sample counterpart of (51.4) as

$$e_{i,t+h} = y_{t+h} - x'_{i,t}\hat{\beta}_i, \quad i \in \{1,2\},$$

$$f_{t+h}(\hat{\beta}_t) = g(e_{1,t+h}) - g(e_{2,t+h}), \quad t = R, \dots, T-h,$$

$$\bar{f}_h(\hat{\beta}) = (P-h+1)^{-1} \sum_{t=R}^{T-h} f_{t+h}(\hat{\beta}_t). \tag{51.5}$$

Note the difference between $\bar{f}_h(\hat{\beta})$ and $\bar{f}_h(\beta^*)$ where the former is the out-of-sample mean of f_{t+h} evaluated at the estimate $\hat{\beta}$, and the latter is the out-of-sample mean evaluated at the true value β^*. Let F be the gradient evaluated at the true parameter:

$$F = \left.\frac{\partial E f_{t+h}(\beta)}{\partial \beta}\right|_{\beta=\beta^*}.$$

The following decomposition holds:

$$\begin{aligned} &\sqrt{P-h+1}\left(\bar{f}_t(\hat{\beta}) - E[f_{t+h}(\beta^*)]\right) \\ &\quad = \sqrt{P-h+1}\left(\bar{f}_h(\beta^*) - E[f_{t+h}(\beta^*)]\right) \\ &\qquad + F\sqrt{\frac{P-h+1}{R}}\,[O_p(1) \text{ terms}] + o_p(1). \end{aligned} \tag{51.6}$$

This tells us that $\bar{f}_t(\hat{\beta})$, which depends on the estimate $\hat{\beta}$, can be used to make inference about $E[f_{t+h}(\beta^*)]$. The first term in (51.6) represents the uncertainty of our forecast if β^* is assumed to be known. The second term can be seen as the additional noise due to estimation uncertainty about $\hat{\beta}$. We use the term "noise" in a "loose" way as this term in principle can reduce the overall variance. This happens when the correlation is negative and sufficiently large in absolute value.

There are three cases for which the estimation uncertainty is irrelevant; see the work of West (1996):

1. $F = 0$. In this case, the second term disappears. This means that the uncertainty about the unknown parameter does not affect the distribution. This happens when using the MSFE as the loss function, as shown in the following.

2. $(P - h + 1)/R \to 0$. In this case, the second term converges to 0 since we have either a large sample to estimate β^* (big R) so that $\hat{\beta} \xrightarrow{p} \beta^*$ or a small forecasting sample (small P), where the uncertainty surrounding $\hat{\beta}$ is negligible.
3. The variance of the second term is completely offset by the covariance between itself and the first term. This can happen in some specific circumstances: (i) The forecast errors are conditionally homoskedastic, (ii) $\hat{\beta}$ is estimated recursively, and (iii) the loss function is one of the following: MSFE, serial correlation, or no correlation between two different model forecasts.

When any of the three conditions apply, we have

$$\sqrt{P - h + 1}\left(\bar{f}_{t+h}(\hat{\beta}) - E[f_{t+h}(\beta^*)]\right) \xrightarrow{d} N(0, \Omega),$$

where

$$\Omega = \Omega^* = \sum_{i=-\infty}^{\infty} E[(f_{t+h} - Ef_{t+h})(f_{t+h-j} - Ef_{t+h})],$$

and we can proceed as in Example 51.4.

The most important case in which parameter uncertainty is of concern and needs to be accounted for is when the size of the estimation window R is small relative to the forecast sample period. This occurs often when using a rolling window scheme to estimate the parameters. On the other hand, parameter uncertainty is no concern, at least in large enough samples, when using the MSFE as the loss function and the predictors are uncorrelated with the prediction errors, in which case the conditions of Case 1 apply. To see this, we consider an example of Case 1 with the models in (51.2)–(51.3) and the null hypothesis:

$$H_0 : E[f_{t+h}(\beta^*)] = E[\epsilon^2_{1,t+h} - \epsilon^2_{2,t+h}] = 0.$$

Assume that f_{t+h} is covariance stationary. For simplicity, assume again we have $P + 1$ observations (since we are not estimating any parameter we would have in principle T observations). We have

$$f_{t+h}(\beta^*) = g(\epsilon_{1,t+h}) - g(\epsilon_{2,t+h}) = \epsilon_{1,t+h}^2 - \epsilon_{2,t+h}^2,$$

$$\bar{f}_h(\beta^*) = (P-h+1)^{-1}\sum_{t=R}^{T-2}\left(\epsilon_{1,t+h}^2 - \epsilon_{2,t+h}^2\right),$$

$$f_{t+h}(\hat{\beta}_t) = g(e_{1,t+h}) - g(e_{2,t+h}) = e_{1,t+h}^2 - e_{2,t+h}^2,$$

$$\bar{f}_h(\hat{\beta}) = (P-h+1)^{-1}\sum_{t=R}^{T-2}\left(e_{1,t+h}^2 - e_{2,t+h}^2\right).$$

Now, the gradient is given by

$$F = \left.\frac{\partial Ef(\epsilon_{1,t},\epsilon_{2,t})}{\partial\beta}\right|_{\beta=\beta^*} = (2E[x_{1,t}\epsilon_{1,t+h}], 2E[x_{2,t}\epsilon_{2,t+h}])' = 0,$$

where the last equality follows from the fact that the errors and the regressors are uncorrelated. This means that MSFE loss function implies having a situation in which the estimation uncertainty about the parameter is irrelevant because $F = 0$. Hence,

$$\begin{aligned}
&(P-h+1)^{-1/2}\left(\bar{f}_h(\hat{\beta}) - E[f_{t+h}(\beta)]\right)\\
&\quad = (P-h+1)^{-1/2}\left(\sum_{t=R-h}^{T}\left(e_{1,t+h}^2 - e_{2,t+h}^2\right) - E\left(\epsilon_{1,t+h}^2 - \epsilon_{2,t+h}^2\right)\right)\\
&\quad \xrightarrow{d} N(0,\Omega^*),
\end{aligned}$$

where

$$\Omega^* = \sum_{i=-\infty}^{\infty} E[(f_{t+h} - Ef_{t+h})(f_{t+h-j} - Ef_{t+h})]$$

is the long-run variance of $f_{t+h}(\beta)$. As before, given a consistent estimate $\hat{\Omega}^*$, we can test the null hypothesis using a t-test of the form

$$\mathrm{t} = \frac{\bar{f}_h(\hat{\beta})}{\sqrt{\hat{\Omega}^*/(P-h+1)}}.$$

51.4.4 Comparing $m+1$ non-nested models

Consider $m+1$ non-nested models to forecast h-steps ahead:

$$\begin{aligned} y_{t+h} &= x'_{1,t}\beta_1^* + \epsilon_{1,t+h}, \\ &\vdots \\ y_{t+h} &= x'_{m+1,t}\beta_{m+1}^* + \epsilon_{m+1,t+h}, \end{aligned} \tag{51.7}$$

with $x_{i,t}$ a $l_i \times 1$ vector, $x_{i,t} \neq x_{j,t}, \forall i \neq j = 1, \ldots, m$. Define $f_{t+h}(\beta)$, with $\beta = (\beta_1, \ldots, \beta_{m+1})$, to be the forecast function for the horizon h at time t, which is now a vector $m \times 1$.

Example 51.5. Suppose we choose the MAFE $g(\epsilon_{i,t+h}) = |\epsilon_{i,t+h}|$ as a measure of forecast accuracy. The forecast function at time t for horizon h is defined as

$$f_{t+h}(\beta) = \begin{bmatrix} g(\epsilon_{1,t+h}) - g(\epsilon_{2,t+h}) \\ g(\epsilon_{1,t+h}) - g(\epsilon_{3,t+h}) \\ \cdots \\ g(\epsilon_{1,t+h}) - g(\epsilon_{m+1,t+h}) \end{bmatrix} = \begin{bmatrix} |\epsilon_{1,t+h}| - |\epsilon_{2,t+h}| \\ |\epsilon_{1,t+h}| - |\epsilon_{3,t+h}| \\ \cdots \\ |\epsilon_{1,t+h}| - |\epsilon_{m+1,t+h}| \end{bmatrix}$$

which is an $m \times 1$ vector. Assume the expected value of the forecast function, $E(f_{t+h}(\beta))$, to be differentiable in a neighborhood around β^*. Suppose we have an estimator of the form

$$\hat{\beta} = \beta^* + B(t)H(t) \xrightarrow{d} N(\beta^*, V_{\beta^*}),$$

with

$$V_{\beta^*} = BS_{hh}B',$$

where we have the following:

- $B(t) \xrightarrow{p} B$ with B a $k \times m$ matrix of rank k.
- $H(t)$ a $m \times 1$ matrix that depends on the type of estimator (recursive/rolling/fixed) used; note that $H(t)$ in principle can be $q \times 1$ with $q > k$ if we have an overidentified model, as in GMM. Let $h_{s+h}(\beta^*)$ be the orthogonality condition which satisfies $Eh_{s+h}(\beta^*) = 0$, then for the various forecasting schemes,

we have (a) for recursive, $H(t) = t^{-1}\sum_{s=1}^{t-h} h_{s+h}(\beta^*)$, (b) for rolling, $H(t) = R^{-1}\sum_{s=t-R+1}^{t-h} h_{s+h}(\beta^*)$, and (c) for fixed, $H(t) = R^{-1}\sum_{s=1}^{R-h} h_{s+h}(\beta^*)$.

- $S_{hh} = \lim_{T\to\infty} \mathrm{Var}(T^{-1/2}\sum_{s=1}^{T-h} h_{t+h}(\beta^*)) = \sum_{j=-\infty}^{\infty} Eh_{t+h}(\beta^*) h_{t+h-j}(\beta^*)'$, a $k \times k$ matrix.

To understand the notation, we consider the following example.

Example 51.6. Consider the models in (51.7). For each model, $i = 1, \ldots, m+1$,

$$B_i = \left(plim_{T\to\infty} \sum_{t=1}^{T} x_{i,t}x_{i,t}'\right)^{-1}$$

so that the matrix B is

$$B = \begin{bmatrix} B_1 & & 0 \\ & \ddots & \\ 0 & & B_m \end{bmatrix}.$$

The orthogonality condition is

$$h_{i,t+h}(\beta_i^*) = x_{i,t}'\epsilon_{i,t+h}$$

so that the vector h_{t+h} is

$$\begin{aligned} h_{t+h}(\beta^*) &= (h_{1,t+h}(\beta_1^*), \ldots, h_{m,t+h}(\beta_m^*))' \\ &= (x_{1,t}'\epsilon_{1,t+h}, \ldots, x_{m,t}'\epsilon_{m,t+h})'. \end{aligned}$$

To proceed, we also impose the following assumptions:

- Both the estimation sample and the forecast samples are large, i.e., $R, P \to \infty$ and their ratio satisfies $\lim_{P,R\to\infty} = P/R = \pi \in [0, \infty)$.
- The gradient $F = [\partial f_{t+h}(\beta)/\partial\beta]_{\beta=\beta^*}$ is finite.

Define the out of sample average of $f_{t+h}(\beta)$ as

$$\bar{f}_h(\hat{\beta}) = (P - h + 1)^{-1} \sum_{t=R-h}^{T} f_{t+h}(\hat{\beta}_t).$$

Then, the following expansion holds:

$$\begin{aligned}
&\sqrt{P-h+1}\left(\bar{f}_h(\hat{\beta}) - E(f_{t+h}(\beta^*))\right)\\
&= \sqrt{P-h+1}\left(\bar{f}_h(\beta^*) - Ef_{t+h}(\beta^*)\right)\\
&+ F\sqrt{\frac{P-h+1}{R}}\left[B\sqrt{R}\bar{H}\right] + o_p(1). \qquad (51.8)
\end{aligned}$$

As noted before, this tells us that $\bar{f}_t(\hat{\beta})$, which depends on the estimate $\hat{\beta}$, can be used to make inference about $E[f_{t+h}(\beta^*)]$. The first term represents the uncertainty of our forecast when β^* is assumed to be known. The second term can be seen as the additional component due to estimation uncertainty of $\hat{\beta}$. West (1996) proved that, under some other technical conditions, the limiting distribution of (51.8) is normal with mean 0 and variance Ω, i.e.,

$$\sqrt{P-h+1}(\bar{f}_h(\hat{\beta}) - Ef_{t+h}(\beta^*)) \xrightarrow{d} \mathcal{N}(0,\Omega),$$

with

$$\Omega = \underbrace{V^*}_{(A)} + \underbrace{\lambda_{fh}(FBS'_{fh} + S_{fh}B'F')}_{(B)} + \underbrace{\lambda_{hh}FV_{\beta^*}F'}_{(C)}, \qquad (51.9)$$

where

$$\begin{aligned}
V^* &= \lim_{T\to\infty} \mathrm{Var}\left(T^{-1/2}\sum_{s=1}^{T-h} f_{t+h}(\beta^*)\right)\\
&= \sum_{j=-\infty}^{\infty} E[f_{t+h}(\beta^*) - Ef_{t+h}(\beta^*)][f_{t+h-j}(\beta^*) - Ef_{t+h}(\beta^*)]',
\end{aligned}$$

$$\begin{aligned}
S_{fh} &= \lim_{T\to\infty} \mathrm{Cov}\left(T^{-1/2}\sum_{s=1}^{T-h} f_{t+h}(\beta^*), T^{-1/2}\sum_{s=1}^{T-h} h_{t+h}(\beta^*)\right)\\
&= \sum_{j=-\infty}^{\infty} E[f_{t+h}(\beta^*) - Ef_{t+h}(\beta^*)]h_{t+h-j}(\beta^*)',
\end{aligned}$$

and λ_{fh} and λ_{hh} are defined as follows for the various forecasting schemes:

	λ_{fh}	λ_{jh}
Recursive	$1 - \ln(1+\pi)/\pi$	$2\,[1 - \ln(1+\pi)/\pi]$
Rolling, $\pi \leq 1$	$\pi/2$	$\pi - \pi^2/3$
Rolling, $\pi > 1$	$1 - (2\pi)^{-1}$	$1 - (3\pi)^{-1}$
Fixed	0	π

From (51.9), the variance depends on three terms:

(A) the long-run variance of $\sqrt{P-h+1}\left(\bar{f}_h(\beta^*) - Ef_{t+h}(\beta^*)\right)$, which captures the uncertainty that would be present even if β was assumed to be known;
(C) the long run variance of $F[(P-h+1)/R]^{1/2}[B\sqrt{R}\bar{H}]$, which is present because of the use of the estimate $\hat{\beta}$;
(B) the covariance between the two terms (A) and (B).

As before, $\Omega = V^*$ in three cases: (i) $F = 0$, (ii) $P/R \to 0$, and (iii) when the covariance (B) exactly offsets the variance (C). The conditions are roughly similar to the case of comparing only two models. Note, however, that for condition (i), each prediction error needs to be uncorrelated with the corresponding predictors, even if the competing models use different information sets so that one model's prediction error is correlated with another model's prediction.

A crucial requirement for the theory outlined above is the positive definiteness of Ω. When dealing with nested models, this condition is not satisfied, hence modifications are in order, which are discussed in the following section.

51.4.5 Nested models

When comparing nested models, the details are more challenging. To understand the difficulties, we first consider an example which shows that under the null of equal forecast accuracy the distribution derived in the previous section is degenerate.

Example 51.7. Consider two nested models

$$y_{t+h} = x'_{1,t}\beta_1^A + \epsilon_{1,t+h} = x'_t\beta^A + \epsilon_{1,t+h},$$
$$y_{t+h} = x'_{1,t}\beta_1^B + x'_{2,t}\beta_2^B + \epsilon_{2,t+h} = x'_t\beta^B + \epsilon_{2,t+h},$$

where $x'_t = (x_{1,t}, x_{2,t})$, $\beta^A = (\beta_1^A, 0)$, $\beta^B = (\beta_1^B, \beta_2^B)$. Suppose that we want to test $H_0 : \beta_2^B = 0$. Under the null hypothesis, the models are nested since $\beta^A = \beta^B = (\beta_1, 0)$ so that

$$\epsilon_{1,t+h} = \epsilon_{2,t+h}.$$

This means that we can have $f_{t+h}(\beta^*) = g(\epsilon_{1,t+h}) - g(\epsilon_{2,t+h}) = 0$. For example, for the following measures of forecast accuracy, we have

$$\text{MSFE} : f_{t+h}(\beta^*) = \epsilon_{1,t+h}^2 - \epsilon_{2,t+h}^2 = 0,$$
$$\text{MAFE} : f_{t+h}(\beta^*) = |\epsilon_{1,t+h}| - |\epsilon_{2,t+h}| = 0,$$
$$\text{Serial Correlation} : f_{t+h}(\beta^*) = \epsilon_{1,t+h}(\epsilon_{1,t+h} - \epsilon_{2,t+h}) = 0.$$

Note that $f_{t+h}(\beta^*) = 0$ implies

$$F = 0, \quad V^* = 0, \quad S_{fh} = 0$$

so that the asymptotic variance in equation (51.9) is $\Omega = 0$. The reason why we care about this problem is that when constructing a test of equal forecast accuracy, we end up always rejecting the null hypothesis, even when the null is true given that $\Omega = 0$.

The example above shows that for the most popular specifications of g, the distribution is degenerate. Chao *et al.* (2001) specified $g = e_{1,t+1}x_{2,t}$ and showed that the formulas in the previous section still apply. But, in general, new sets of results are needed. The major contributions to address these problems are the works of Clark and McCracken (2001), Clark and McCracken (2005a), Clark and McCracken (2005b), and McCracken (2007), which characterize the limiting distributions of a variety of statistics, including a modified MSFE. Before going into details, we need to modify the alternative hypothesis since we are in the case of nested models. Until now, we assumed a two-sided alternative hypothesis, but here, it cannot happen that the smaller model leads to strictly better predictions. The intuition is that when the null hypothesis does not hold, the larger model has better predictive performance, hence lower variance. For this reason, Ashley *et al.* (1980) claimed that the alternative hypothesis in a test of equal forecasting accuracy between two nested models should be one-sided.

Adjusted MSFE

We start by looking at how we can modify the MSFE to account for the features described above. Our treatment applies to cases for which the following conditions hold:

- The estimator must be either linear or nonlinear least squares.
- The forecasts should be based on a direct multi-step prediction; see Section 51.2.

The new proposed statistics are (recall that e_t stands for the estimated residuals)

$$\text{MSFE}(t) = \frac{\sum_{t=R}^{T-h}\left(e_{1,t+h}^2 - e_{2,t+h}^2\right)}{\sqrt{P-h+1}\sqrt{\hat{S}_{ee}}},$$

$$\text{MSFE}(F) = \frac{\sqrt{P-h+1}\sum_{t=R}^{T-h}\left(e_{1,t+h}^2 - e_{2,t+h}^2\right)}{\sum_{t=R}^{T-h} e_{2,t+h}^2},$$

where $\hat{S}_{ee}$ is the estimate of the long run variance of $(e_{1,t+h}^2 - e_{2,t+h}^2)$. Their limiting distributions are functions of Brownian motions and nuisance parameters. There are two cases in which the limiting distribution does not depend on nuisance parameters:

1. the forecast is a one-step ahead forecast, i.e., $h = 1$, and the errors are conditionally homoskedastic,
2. when there is a single additional regressor in the larger model, i.e., when the dimension of $x_{2,t}'$ in our example is one.

Under these two cases, McCracken (2007), Clark and McCracken (2005a), and Clark and McCracken (2001) tabulated the limiting distributions that depend on the sample split $\pi = \lim_{P,R\to\infty} P/R$ and on the number of additional regressors in the larger model. When not dealing with these two special cases, Clark and McCracken (2005a) developed two procedures to recover the limiting distributions: one based on simulations of the limiting distribution via some Monte Carlo algorithm and the other based on the bootstrap. We refer the reader to these original papers for additional details on the procedures, as well as the work of Clark and McCracken (2012) which developed a different bootstrap procedure that is easier to implement.

Other Statistics

McCracken (2007), Clark and McCracken (2005a), and Clark and McCracken (2001) proposed other statistics for which they established the asymptotic distribution. These are

$$\mathrm{ENC}(t) = \frac{\sum_{t=R}^{T-h} e_{1,t+h}\left(e_{1,t+h} - e_{2,t+h}\right)}{\sqrt{P-h+1}\sqrt{\hat{S}_{cc}}},$$

$$\mathrm{ENC}(F) = \frac{\sqrt{P-h+1}\sum_{t=R}^{T-h} e_{1,t+h}\left(e_{1,t+h} - e_{2,t+h}\right)}{\sum_{t=R}^{T-h} e_{2,t+h}^2},$$

where $\hat{S}_{cc}$ is the estimate of the long run variance of $[e_{1,t+h}(e_{1,t+h} - e_{2,t+h})]$. The notation ENC stands for encompassing, a situation in which a forecast incorporates all the information contained in the other forecasts; see the work of Chong and Hendry (1986). As before, their limiting distributions are functions of Brownian motions and nuisance parameters. Clark and West (2006) showed that, under specific circumstances, the limit distribution of ENC(t) is normal or approximately so. The reason is that one can view this test as a modification to adjust the MSFE test where one corrects the variance of the larger model by subtracting the noise due to the estimation of the additional irrelevant regressors.

51.4.6 Testing conditional predictive ability

As mentioned in Section 51.4.3, the testing procedures above were developed to compare the population-level predictive ability of two or more models which seek to answer the following question: "Suppose we have an infinite sample, which model provides a better forecast?" Giacomini and White (2006) insisted that a more appropriate approach involves two additional modifications: (a) We should compare forecasts in such a way that the finite sample properties of the estimators (on which the forecasts are based) are preserved asymptotically and (b) a proper test procedure should also accommodate conditional evaluation objectives, for instance, what is the best forecast of some variable conditional on being in a recession, or some asset return conditional on future negative returns.

The idea behind the first objective is that a more parsimonious, but possibly biased, model can have better finite-sample performance than the true fully specified model if the latter involves many parameters that are poorly estimated. This happens because the estimation uncertainty associated with the additional parameters in the larger model outweighs the bias of the misspecification in the smaller model. An alternative, rarely used in practice, is to specify a loss function that includes a penalty for larger models. Giacomini and White (2006) constructed a test that is valid for both nested and non-nested models that has as a null hypothesis equal predictive ability in finite samples. One difficulty in constructing this type of test is in the asymptotic approximation. Clearly, one cannot let the sample size of the window R go to infinity, otherwise the effect of the parameter estimation uncertainty vanishes. This rules out the possibility of using the rolling scheme. For this reason, Giacomini and White (2006) focused on models estimated using a fixed or recursive scheme with expanding window R as T increases.

Until now, the null hypothesis was specified using the unconditional expectation, e.g.,

$$H_0 : E[f_{t+h}(\beta^*)] = 0. \tag{51.10}$$

But now, given two h-step ahead forecasting models, the goal is to test the following null hypothesis:

$$H_0 : E[f_{t+h}(\hat{\beta})|\mathcal{I}_t] = 0, \tag{51.11}$$

where $\mathcal{I}_t$ is some set of events known at time t. The theory is general enough to accommodate both conditional and unconditional null hypotheses as the latter is a special case of the former. Note that in general the set of events contained in $\mathcal{I}_t$ should be selected by the researcher. It need not be the full information set available at time t. It can be some indicator functions pertaining to specific events, e.g., expansions or recessions.

As mentioned before, their test compares the finite sample performance and is valid only with the recursive or fixed scheme, regardless of the nested or non-nested nature of the models to be compared. This type of hypothesis can be common, for example, in comparing which model performs better in a boom or a recession. It can happen that two models have equal forecasting ability *on average*, but one can have better *conditional* performance during booms and the other during recessions. This is clearly an important question that decision-makers are constantly facing, so it motivates the development of tests of this type of conditional null hypothesis.

Note the difference between hypotheses (51.10) and (51.11): the former concerns the population-level conditional predictive ability, while the latter hypothesis tested in the work of Giacomini and White (2006) is for the finite sample conditional predictive ability. Define k_t a $q \times 1$ vector of instruments in the information set $\mathcal{I}_t$. For instance, k_t could be an indicator function about whether we are in a recession or not. We can now transform the conditional expectation in (51.11) into an unconditional one

$$H_0 : E[k_t f_{t+h}(\hat{\beta})] = 0.$$

Define

$$\bar{Z}_T^h = (P - h + 1)^{-1} \sum_{t=R}^{T-h} k_t f_{t+h}(\hat{\beta}),$$

and let $\hat{\Omega}_T^h$ be an estimator of the long run variance of $\bar{Z}_T^h$ which can be constructed using popular kernel functions, e.g., Andrews (1991b). Given the nature of the conditional null hypothesis, $k_t f_{t+h}(\hat{\beta})$ has an $MA(h-1)$ correlation structure. It is natural now to think about a Wald test of the from

$$T_T^h = (P - h + 1)^{-1} \bar{Z}_T^{h\prime} \hat{\Omega}_T^h \bar{Z}_T^h.$$

We then have

$$T_T^h \xrightarrow{d} \chi_q^2, \quad \text{as } P - h + 1 \to \infty.$$

While this is fine on a theoretical level, from a practical perspective, there is a serious problem. As shown by McCracken (2020b), it is very difficult to find a pair of forecasting models (let alone more than two), which satisfy (51.11). He was able to concoct a rather non-practically relevant example, but even then, though the test had the right size, it had little power; see also the work of McCracken (2019). Hence, from a practical perspective, these finite sample comparisons do not appear fruitful. In other words, as discussed in the work of Clark and McCracken (2013), the framework of testing for finite sample accuracy is not applicable to fixed window size R but with expanding windows (recursive or fixed schemes). In such cases, the distinction between population or finite sample forecast accuracy becomes irrelevant. The work nevertheless fostered greater attention about making inference when the estimation window R is small. It also extended prior results pertaining to testing for unconditional superior predictive performance to contexts in which a researcher wants to compare the relative performance conditional upon some events.

Still, for the null hypothesis involving the comparison of only two models,

$$H_0 : E[f_{t+h}(\hat{\beta})] = 0,$$

Giacomini and White (2006) proved that, when using the recursive or fixed estimation schemes (see the work of McCracken (2020a) for a clarification about the technical conditions required),

$$\sqrt{P-h+1}(\bar{f}_{t+h}(\hat{\beta}) - E[f_{t+h}(\hat{\beta})])/(S_{\hat{f}\hat{f}})^{1/2} \xrightarrow{d} N(0,1),$$

with

$$S_{\hat{f}\hat{f}} = \text{Var}\left[\sqrt{P-h+1}\left(\bar{f}_{t+h}(\hat{\beta}) - E[f_{t+h}(\hat{\beta})]\right)\right].$$

Clark and McCracken (2012) used a different approach to construct a test. They focused on the case in which the bias vanishes at the same rate as the convergence of the parameter estimates. They consider two nested models estimated by OLS where the additional parameter is weak given by

$$y_{t+h} = x'_{1,t}\beta_1^B + x'_{2,t}\frac{\beta_2^B}{\sqrt{R}} + \epsilon_{2,t+h}.$$

In this framework, when R increases, the parameter is estimated more precisely but also the bias of the smaller model goes to zero. Since this procedure allows for R diverging, we can also use the rolling estimator. Using this idea, they studied the limiting distribution which is a function of Brownian motions; we refer to the paper for more details. Calhoun (2014) let the dimension of the model increase with the sample size so that there is no more constraint about using the recursive estimator.

As described by Clark and McCracken (2013), a slight modification of the theory developed by West (1996) can accommodate the conditional null hypothesis in (51.11). Define k_t a $q \times 1$ vector of instruments in the information set $\mathcal{I}_t$. We can now transform the conditional expectation in (51.11) into an unconditional one:

$$H_0\colon E[k_t f_{t+h}(\beta^*)] = 0.$$

Hence, the null hypothesis states that the weighted unconditional expected predictive ability is the same. Define

$$\bar{Z}_T^h = (P - h + 1)^{-1} \sum_{t=R}^{T-h} k_t f_{t+h}(\hat{\beta}),$$

and let $\tilde{\Omega}_T^h$ be an estimator of the variance (51.9), i.e.,

$$\Omega = V^* + \lambda_{fh}(FBS'_{fh} + S_{fh}B'F') + \lambda_{hh}FV_{\beta^*}F'.$$

The nature of the conditional null hypothesis restricts $k_t f_{t+h}(\beta^*)$ to have an $MA(h-1)$ correlation structure. It is then possible to show that

$$\tilde{T}_T^h = (P - h + 1)^{-1} \bar{Z}_T^{h\prime} \tilde{\Omega}_T^h \bar{Z}_T^h \xrightarrow{d} \chi_q^2,$$

as $P - h + 1 \to \infty$. This approach has been extended along the line of White (2000) and Hansen (2005) by Li *et al.* (2022) to test the null hypothesis of conditional superior predictive ability. The difficulty here is in dealing with the fact that the original intended null hypothesis $E[f_{t+h}(\hat{\beta})|\mathcal{I}_t] = 0$ implies that $E[k_t f_{t+h}(\beta^*)] = 0$ should hold over all conditioning states k_t, not only a finite number of states, i.e., it is a functional testing problem as opposed to a point-wise testing one. This involves non-parametric methods. While this later work is of interest, often many practitioners have in mind specific conditioning states (e.g., expansions versus recessions), so it is not clear which approach is better. There is inevitably a loss in power incurred by adopting a general functional approach, which may be a deterrent to researchers having particular states in mind.

51.5 Testing for structural changes in forecasts

In this section, we discuss two types of tests. The first is to detect a change in the forecasting performance of a single forecasting method. These are often called "forecast breakdown" tests. The second is to determine the relative out-of-sample predictive ability between two competing models in the presence of possible breaks.

51.5.1 Forecast breakdown tests

It is useful to clarify the purpose of forecast breakdown tests. The aim is to assess retrospectively whether a given forecasting model provides forecasts which show evidence of changes (improvements or deterioration) with respect to some loss function. Since the losses can change because of changes in the variance of the shocks (e.g., good luck), detection of a forecast failure does not necessarily mean that a forecast model should be abandoned. Care must be exercised to assess the source of the changes. But if a model is shown to provide stable forecasts, it can more safely be applied in real time.

In practice, forecasts are made at the time of the last available data, using a fixed, recursive, or rolling window. Hence, there is a natural separation between the in-sample and out-of-sample periods simply dictated by the last data point. Such is not the case when trying to assess retrospectively whether a given model provides stable forecasts. There is then the need for a somewhat artificial separation between the in and out-of-sample periods at some date labeled m, say. This divides the sample of length T into an in-sample of length m and an out-of-sample of length $n = T - m - h + 1$. This separation date should be such that the model in the in-sample period is stable in some sense, e.g., yielding stable forecasts. This can, however, create problems because one needs a truncation point m to assess forecast failures, but the choice of this value is itself predicated on some knowledge of stability.

The forecast failure test of Giacomini and Rossi (2009) is a global and retrospective test which compares the in-sample average with the out-of-sample average of the sequence of forecast losses. Define at time $(t+h)$ a surprise loss given by the deviation between the time-$(t+h)$ out-of-sample loss and the average in-sample loss:

$$SL_{t+h}(\hat{\beta}_t) = L_{t+h}(\hat{\beta}_t) - \bar{L}_t(\hat{\beta}_t),$$

for $t = m, \ldots, T-h$, where $\bar{L}_t(\hat{\beta}_t)$ is the average in-sample loss computed according to the specific forecasting scheme, with $\hat{\beta}_t$ some estimator of the model parameters and m the in-sample size. One can then define the average of the out-of-sample surprise losses

$$\overline{SL}_n(\hat{\beta}_t) = n^{-1} \sum_{t=m}^{T-h} SL_{t+h}(\hat{\beta}_t),$$

where $n = T - m - h - 1$ denotes the time span of the out-of-sample window. Under the hypothesis of no forecast instability, $\overline{SL}_n$ should have zero mean, i.e., no systematic surprise losses in the out-of-sample window. Under the null hypothesis of no forecast failure, the test

$$t_{GR} = n^{1/2}\overline{SL}_n(\hat{\beta}_t)/\hat{\sigma}_{m,n}$$

follows asymptotically a standard normal distribution, where $\sigma^2_{m,n}$ is an estimate of the long-run variance of the out-out-sample loss differentials $SL_{(t+h)}(\hat{\beta}_t)$.

Perron and Yamamoto (2019b) adapted the classical structural change tests to the forecast failure context. First, they recommended that all tests should be carried with a fixed scheme to have the best power, which ensures the maximum difference between the fitted in- and out-of sample means of the losses. There are contamination issues under the rolling and recursive schemes that induce power losses.

With such a fixed scheme, the test of Giacomini and Rossi (2009) is simply a Wald test for a one-time change in the mean of the total (the in-sample plus out-of-sample) losses at a known break date m. To alleviate this problem, which leads to important losses in power when the break in forecasting performance is not exactly at m, one can follow the work of Rossi and Inoue (2012) and consider maximizing the test over all possible values of m within a prespecified range. This then corresponds to a sup-Wald test for a single change at some date constrained to be the separation point between the in and out-of-sample periods. The test is still not immune to non-monotonic power problems when multiple changes occur. To see why, consider the case with two breaks. Then, for any choice of m in the range $[m_0, m_1]$, at least one segment will be contaminated due to biased parameter estimates and the average loss will be reduced, thereby decreasing the power of the test. This problem can be especially severe when the range $[m_0, m_1]$ is large.

Perron and Yamamoto (2019b) proposed a double sup-Wald test which, for each $m \in [m_0, m_1]$, performed a sup-Wald test for a change in the mean of the out-of-sample losses, and took the maximum of such tests over the range $m \in [m_0, m_1]$:

$$\text{DSW} = \max_{m \in [m_0, m_1]} SW_{L^o(m)},$$

where $SW_{L^o(m)}$ is the sup-Wald test for a change in the mean of the out-of-sample loss series $L_t^o(\hat{\beta})$ for $t = m+h, \ldots, T$, defined by

$$SW_{L^o(m)} = \max_{T_b(m) \in [m+\epsilon T, m+(1-\epsilon)T]} [\text{SSR}_{L^o(m)} - \text{SSR}\,(T_b(m))_{L^o(m)}]/\hat{V}_{L^o(m)},$$

where $\text{SSR}_{L^o(m)}$ is the unrestricted sum of squares, $\text{SSR}\,(T_b(m))_{L^o(m)}$ is the sum of squared residuals assuming a one-time change at time $T_b(m)$, and $\hat{V}_{L^o(m)}$ is the long-run variance estimate of the out-of-sample loss series. The parameter ϵ is a small trimming value set at 0.1. Too small a value leads to size distortions and larger ones to power problems. The results are not sensitive to minor variations, e.g., $\epsilon = 0.05$ or 0.15. They provide the limit distribution. To construct it, (1) start with an out-of-sample method with an in-sample length m_0 small but large enough to estimate the model. Let $n \equiv T - m - h + 1$. (2) Compute the out-of-sample loss series $\{L_{t+h}^o\}_{t=m}^{T-h}$. (3) Consider a regression with only a constant: $L_{t+h}^o = \gamma + e_{t+h}$. Apply a sup-Wald test for the constancy of γ, with an HAC variance estimate if there is evidence of serial correlation in the losses. Store the value as $SW_{L^o(m)}$. (4) Update m to $m+1$ and repeat Steps 2–3 up to $m = m_1$. The range of m, $m_1 - m_0$, is some fraction of n, denoted by $\bar{\mu}$. (5) Take the maximum of the sequence of $\{SW_{L^o(m)}\}_{m=m_0}^{m_1}$.

The reason why the DSW test improves upon the test of Giacomini and Rossi (2009) (SGR) test is because it produces three segments instead of only two, which is beneficial with more than one break. Two are defined by m and the other by the date at which the Wald test is maximized in the range $[m + h + \epsilon n, m + h + (1 - \epsilon)n]$. Hence, three segments can be inserted within the total sample, which guarantees that the two segments with the largest difference can be separated by a break, thereby increasing power. With a single break, the mean of at least one segment is contaminated by the values of the means in the other segments, reducing power. The idea is akin to that of Qu (2007) who showed that when searching whether any part of a sample is stationary all one needs is a search with two breaks or three segments.

An alternative is to work directly with the total loss series $L(m)$ instead of only using the out-of-sample losses and consider a test similar to the UDmax test for multiple changes of Bai and Perron (1998). This can yield higher power given that more information is used. Perron and Yamamoto (2019b) considered two tests following this approach: the Total Loss sup-Wald test (TLSW) and the Total Loss UDmax test (TLUD). More precisely,

$$\text{TLSW} = \max_{m \in [m_0, m_1]} SW_{L(m)},$$

where $SW_{L(m)}$ is the sup-Wald test applied for a mean-change in the total loss series $L(m)$:

$$SW_{L(m)} = \max_{T_b(m) \in [h+\epsilon(T-2h+1), h+(1-\epsilon)(T-2h+1)]} [\text{SSR}_{L(m)} - \text{SSR}(T_b(m))_{L(m)}]/\hat{V}_{L(m)},$$

where $\text{SSR}_{L(m)}$ is the restricted SSR, $\text{SSR}(T_b(m))_{L(m)}$ is the SSR assuming a one-time change at time $T_b(m)$, and $\hat{V}_{L(m)}$ is the long-run variance estimate of the total loss series using the demeaned total loss series with the mean changing at date $T_b(m)$; ϵ is some small trimming parameter. Also,

$$\text{TLUD}(k) = \max_{m \in [m_0, m_1]} UD^k_{L(m)},$$

where

$$UD^k_{L(m)} = \max_{i=1,\ldots,k} \max_{\{T^i_b(m)\}^k_{i=1} \in \Lambda_\epsilon} [\mathrm{SSR}_{L(m)} - \mathrm{SSR}(\{T^i_b(m)\}^k_{i=1})_{L(m)}]/\hat{V}_{L(m)},$$

with

$$\Lambda_\epsilon = \Big\{(T^1_b(m), \ldots, T^k_b(m)) : \big|T^i_b(m) - T^{i-1}_b(m)\big| \geq h + \epsilon(T - 2h + 1), T^0_b(m) = 1, T^k_b(m) \leq h + (1 - \epsilon)(T - 2h + 1)\Big\},$$

and $\hat{V}_{L(m)}$ the long-run variance estimate of the total loss series using the demeaned total loss series with the mean changing at dates $T^1_b(m), \ldots, T^k_b(m)$. The value $k = 5$ is used, though other values are possible. To summarize the construction of the TL tests, (1) start with a value of the in-sample length, e.g., $m_0 = \lfloor 0.15T \rfloor$, (2) compute the total loss series $\{L_{t+h}\}^{T-2h+1}_{t=1}$, and (3) for the regression with only a constant, $L_{t+h} = \gamma + e_{t+h}$, apply the sup-Wald or UDmax test for the constancy of γ with a HAC variance estimate if there is evidence of serial correlation in the losses. Store the value as $SW_{L(m)}$ or $UD^k_{L(m)}$. (4) Update m to $m+1$ and repeat Steps 2–3. Take a choice of $m_1 > m_0$, say $m_1 = \lfloor 0.85T \rfloor$, and continue up to $m = m_1$. The choices of m_0 and m_1 do not affect the asymptotic critical values. (5) Take the maximum of the sequence of $\{SW_{L(m)}\}^{m_1}_{m=m_0}$ or $\{UD^k_{L(m)}\}^{m_1}_{m=m_0}$.

Using extensive simulations, they showed that with forecasting models potentially involving lagged dependent variables, the only tests having a monotonic power function are the double sup-Wald and total loss UDmax tests, constructed with a fixed forecasting window scheme. So, the recommended tests are the TLUD test followed by the DSW, both with a fixed forecasting scheme.

51.5.2 Forecast comparisons allowing for breaks

Next, we turn to testing for forecast comparisons in unstable environments. Here, the goal is to determine the relative out-of-sample predictive ability between two competing models in the presence of possible breaks. Giacomini and Rossi (2010) proposed two tests:

the fluctuation test and the one-time reversal test. The former tests whether the local relative forecasting performance equals zero at each point in time, whereas the latter tests the null hypothesis that the two models perform equally well at each point in time against the alternative that there is a break in the relative performance.

Here, we discuss the fluctuation test only. Suppose we compare two h-step ahead forecast models for the scalar y_k. The first model is characterized by a parameter θ and the second model by a parameter γ. The relative performance is evaluated by a sequence of out-of-sample loss differences for $t = m + h, \ldots, T$,

$$\Delta L_t(\hat{\theta}_{t-h,m}, \hat{\gamma}_{t-h,m}) = L^{(1)}(y_t, \hat{\theta}_{t-h,m}) - L^{(2)}(y_t, \hat{\gamma}_{t-h,m}).$$

The expressions for the estimators $\hat{\theta}_{t-h,m}$ and $\hat{\gamma}_{t-h,m}$ depend on the forecasting scheme. The fluctuation test is

$$\text{Fluct}^o_{t,m} = m^{-1/2}\hat{\sigma}^{-1} \sum_{k=t-m/2}^{t+m/2-1} \Delta L_t(\hat{\theta}_{k-h,m}, \hat{\gamma}_{k-h,m}),$$

for $t = m + h + m/2, \ldots, T - m/2 + 1$, where $\hat{\sigma}^2$ is an estimate of the long-run variance of the sequence of out-of-sample losses and m is the size of the window. The asymptotic null distribution is non-standard and critical values are computed by simulations. The test has good finite-sample properties under serially uncorrelated losses when scaled by an estimate of the variance instead of the long-run variance. However, Martins and Perron (2016) showed that the test suffers from non-monotonic power when constructed with the long-run variance estimate, as it should be, whether or not the sequence of loss differences exhibits serial correlation. They propose using simple structural change tests such as the sup-Wald test of Andrews (1993b) and the UDmax test of Bai and Perron (1998). These are preferred since they have the highest monotonic power even with a long-run variance constructed with a constrained small bandwidth.

Related work and surveys that relate to the issue of testing for structural changes in forecasting and/or forecasting allowing for possible in and out-of-sample changes include, among others, the works of Clements and Hendry (1998a,b, 2006), Banerjee *et al.* (2008), Rossi (2013), Giacomini (2015), and Giacomini and Rossi (2015).

51.6 Forecast combinations

Model combination is a valid alternative to model selection when dealing with multiple models. The idea is very much like in financial matters. Picking the stock that has performed well over the past is no guarantee that it will perform well in the future. What is recommended most often is to use a diversified portfolio of assets. Exactly the same principle is expected to hold with respect to forecasting. Instead of trying to select the best forecasting model based on past information, one should consider all models and produce a global forecast that aggregates all the individuals ones by weighting them in some appropriate fashion. Also, some models may forecast well (badly) for some periods and perform badly (well) for others. Another reason is that various forecasts may be affected differently by structural breaks. Also, forecasting models may all be subject to some type of misspecification bias of unknown form. In a sense, forecasting models can be viewed as local approximations, so that none dominates at all times. The forecast resulting from a combination using different models may be viewed as more robust, a reasoning similar to the asset diversification argument. Another argument is that, as discussed in Section 51.1, the various forecasts may be based on different loss functions. For instance, suppose you have a symmetric loss function but the forecasts you have are, for whatever reasons, constructed by individuals having asymmetric loss functions. Aggregation may then yield a forecast with properties closer to your goal.

But herein lies the problem, namely how to weight the various forecasts. This is the problem addressed by the literature dealing with model or forecast combinations. An excellent review of this literature is contained in the work of Timmermann (2006). Many of the arguments advanced to justify forecast combinations can be used to cast doubt on it because the same problems can impact the estimation of the weights, e.g., structural breaks. In the end, it is likely that forecast combinations with simple weighting schemes would be preferred.

In this section, we review the basic principles underlying this approach focusing mostly on the MSFE criterion, when choosing a particular loss function. We first look at the work of Bates and Granger (1969), which shows the benefit of forecast combination and proposed five methods to obtain a combination of forecasts that adapts to the change in forecast accuracy of the underlying model over time. We refer to these as adaptive forecast combination. Then, we discuss the work of Granger and Ramanathan (1984), which highlights that there is no reason for imposing that the weights of the models sum to one, advocating for unrestricted combination with a constant term. We then introduce the Mallows model averaging criterion by Hansen (2007) extended to the forecasting context by Hansen (2008). We also discuss extensions to the context in which the regressors are integrated or near-integrated.

51.6.1 Adaptive forecast combinations

The early work by Bates and Granger (1969) showed the benefit of forecast combination over using a single original forecast. When we have two or more forecasts, usually neither of them is optimal so even a rough simple average can improve the forecast accuracy. The intuition is that each original forecast can contain independent information that, combined together in a new forecast, provides a better approximation. The different information contained in competing forecasts may come from different information sets, e.g., two non-nested models, or from different assumptions about the form of the relationship between the variables. Bates and Granger (1969) used the mean-squared forecast error (MSFE) as a measure of forecast accuracy. After acknowledging that even a simple average of unbiased forecasts can lead in many cases to a lower mean-square error, they asked which is the optimal way to combine these forecasts to produce a forecast combination with the lowest mean-square error. Before looking at the details, it is useful to start with a simple illustrative example.

Example 51.8. Consider two unbiased forecasts, $f_{2,t}$ and $f_{1,t}$, with constant variance of the errors σ_1^2 and σ_2^2 for all t. The correlation between the two forecasts is denoted by ρ. If we take a linear combination with $k \in [0, 1]$ of the two forecasts, we obtain

$$f_{c,t}(k) = kf_{1,t} + (1 - k)f_{2,t}.$$

The variance of the forecast error of is

$$\sigma_c^2(k) = k^2\sigma_1^2 + (1 - k)^2\sigma_2^2 + 2\rho k(1 - k)\sigma_1^2\sigma_2^2.$$

The optimal value of k, denoted k^*, is chosen to minimize the variance of the combined forecast:

$$k^* = \arg\min_{k\in[0,1]} \sigma_c^2(k) = \frac{\sigma_2^2 - \rho\sigma_1\sigma_2}{\sigma_1^2 - \sigma_2^2 - 2\rho\sigma_1\sigma_2}.$$

Clearly, this procedure can be generalized to allow more than two forecasts. In this example, we assume that the forecasts are unbiased and that their performance is constant over time. Note that we use the subscript c to denote "combination".

In Exercise 51.1, you are asked to show that $\sigma_c^2(k^*) \leq \sigma_1^2$ and $\sigma_c^2(k^*) \leq \sigma_2^2$. In other words, the optimal combination is weakly better than each of the two original forecasts.

The method to determine the optimal weight k described in Example 51.8 is not applicable in practice. We usually do not know the performance of each forecast nor if such performance is constant over time, as we assumed in the example. For this reason, Bates and Granger (1969) proposed five methods to determine k^* which depend only on the past known errors $e_{i,1}, \ldots, e_{i,T-1}$ for $i = 1, 2$. Since the value may depend upon the forecast period, we denote such optimal value by k_T^*:

1. $k_T^* = E_2/(E_1 + E_2)$ with $E_i = \sum_{t=T-v}^{T-1} e_{i,t}^2$. Note that we need to specify the integer v.
2. $k_T^* = xk_{T-1} + (1-x)E_2/(E_1 + E_2)$ for $i = 1, 2$. Note that we need to specify the integer v and the scalar $x \in [0, 1]$.
3. $k_T^* = S_2/(S_1 + S_2)$ with $S_i = \sum_{t=1}^{T-1} w^t e_{i,t}$ for $i = 1, 2$. Note that we need to specify the scalar w. When $w > 1$, we give more weight to recent observations.
4. $k_T^* = (S_2 - C)/(S_1 + S_2 - 2C)$ with $C = \sum_{t=1}^{T-1} w^t e_{1,t} e_{2,t}$ being the weighted covariance. Note that we need to specify the scalar w.
5. $k_T^* = xk_{T-1}^* + (1-x)|e_{2,t-1}|/(|e_{1,t-1}| + |e_{2,t-1}|)$ with $C = \sum_{t=1}^{T-1} w^t e_{1,t} e_{2,t}$. Note that we need to specify the scalar w and the value $x \in [0, 1]$.

Overall, these methods work better than the individual forecasts; in the majority of cases, the combined forecast leads to a considerably lower variance of errors. With regard to the choice of the parameters x, w, and v, they recognize that (i) the optimal value of x is sometimes negative (which is not ideal in theory), (ii) a large value of w performs better than a small one, and (iii) there is no clear pattern for the choice of v. In conclusion, the key takeaways from the work of Bates and Granger (1969) are as follows: (1) A forecast combination can be better than each of the individual forecasts and (2) the weights of each forecast may vary over time as a consequence of the change in performance of the underlying forecasts.

51.6.2 Unconstrained forecasts with a constant

Granger and Ramanathan (1984) pointed out that combining two unbiased forecasts, with a constant performance, by taking a weighted average, e.g.,

$$f_{c,t}(k) = kf_{1,t} + (1 - k)f_{2,t},$$

with $k \in [0, 1]$, is not optimal. The reason is that we are implicitly imposing that the sum of the weights is 1. This results in an additional constraint in the variance-minimization problem which yields a weakly higher mean-square error. The assumption of weights summing to 1 is commonly used as it guarantees the unbiasedness of the combined forecast. However, Granger and Ramanathan (1984) proposed to abandon this common practice in favor of an unrestricted combination which includes a constant term:

$$f_{c,t} = k_0 + k_1 f_{1,t} + k_2 f_{2,t}. \tag{51.12}$$

The intuition is that the unrestricted combination weakly reduces the MSFE and the constant term guarantees that the resulting combination is unbiased.

51.6.3 General framework: Multiple forecast combinations

To understand more formally why this procedure is preferable compared to a constrained forecast, let us consider the more general case where we have K forecasts $f_{k,t}$ $(k = 1, \ldots, K)$ for the variable x_t for $t = 1, \ldots, T$. Let us define the $T \times K$ matrix $F = (f_1, , \ldots, f_K)$, where each column contains the one-step-ahead forecasts for model $k \in \{1, \ldots, K\}$ for each point in time; define $x = (x_1, \ldots, x_T)'$, the time series vector of the variable to be forecasted, and $k = (k_1, \ldots, k_K)'$ the vector of weights. Note the change in notation. Here, k is a vector. Consider the unrestricted combination (uc) of the forecasts

$$\begin{aligned} f_{uc,t} &= k_1 f_{1,t} + \cdots + k_K f_{K,t} \\ &= (f_{1,t}, \ldots, f_{K,t})k, \end{aligned}$$

or in matrix form,

$$f_{uc} = Fk.$$

If we choose k such that the sum of squared errors is minimized, i.e.,

$$\hat{k} = \arg\min_k (x - Fk)'(x - Fk),$$

then the attained minimum sum of squared errors is

$$\text{MSFE}_{uc} = (x - F\hat{k})'(x - F\hat{k}).$$

Consider the forecast error $e = x - F\hat{k}$. Let $\mathbf{1}$ be a vector of ones. In Exercise 51.2, you are asked to prove that the following conditions are sufficient for the unbiasedness of the combined forecast: (1) Each forecast has zero mean error, $\mathbf{1}'x = \mathbf{1}'f_k$. (2) The weights sum to one, $\mathbf{1}'\hat{k} = 1$. This exercise shows that there is no guarantee that the combined unconstrained forecast is unbiased; imposing the two conditions is sufficient to have unbiasedness. If we have unbiased forecasts, we can impose that the resulting combination is unbiased as well by assuming that the weights sum to one, as is usually done in practice. We refer to this constrained combination as cc, defined by

$$\begin{aligned} f_{cc,t} &= k_1 f_{1,t} + \cdots + k_{K-1} f_{K-1,t} + (1 - k_1 - \cdots - k_{K-1}) f_{K,t} \\ &= (f_{1,t}, \ldots, f_{K,t})\bar{k}, \end{aligned}$$

where $\bar{k} = (k_1, \ldots, k_{K-1}, 1 - k_1 - \cdots - k_{K-1})$. In matrix form,

$$f_{cc} = F\bar{k}.$$

We choose $\bar{k}$ that minimizes the sum of squared errors, i.e.,

$$\begin{aligned}\bar{k} &= \arg\min_k (x - Fk)'(x - Fk), \quad \text{s.t. } \mathbf{1}'k = 1, \\ &= \arg\min_k (x - Fk)'(x - Fk) + 2\lambda(\mathbf{1}'k - 1).\end{aligned}$$

Then, one can show that the attained minimum sum of squared errors is

$$\text{MSFE}_{cc} = \text{MSFE}_{uc} + \lambda^2[\mathbf{1}'(F'F)^{-1}\mathbf{1}].$$

Clearly, we see that $\text{MSFE}_{cc} \geq \text{MSFE}_{uc}$. This means that the mean squared error of the forecast when we impose the constraint is larger than the mean square error of the forecast where the optimal k is unconstrained. For this reason, Granger and Ramanathan (1984) recommend the unconstrained combination with a constant over the constrained combination. We can generalize equation (51.12) to

$$\begin{aligned}f_{ucc,t} &= k_0 + k_1 f_{1,t} + \cdots + k_K f_{K,t} \\ &= k_0 + (f_{1,t}, \ldots, f_{K,t})k,\end{aligned}$$

where $k = (k_1, \ldots, k_K)$. In matrix form,

$$f_{ucc} = k_0\mathbf{1} + Fk.$$

If we choose k such that it minimizes the sum of squared errors, i.e.,

$$\bar{k} = \arg\min_k (x - k_0\mathbf{1} - Fk)'(x - k_0\mathbf{1} - Fk),$$

then one can show that the attained minimum sum of squared errors is

$$\text{MSFE}_{ucc} = \text{MSFE}_{uc} - \frac{(\mathbf{1}'\hat{e}_{uc})^2}{T - \mathbf{1}'F(F'F)^{-1}F'\mathbf{1}},$$

where $\hat{e}_{uc}$ are the estimated errors from the unconstrained forecast. We can finally claim that, see Exercise 51.3,

$$\text{MSFE}_{cc} \geq \text{MSFE}_{uc} \geq \text{MSFE}_{ucc}. \qquad (51.13)$$

51.6.4 Various remarks

In the context of trying to mitigate the effect of structural breaks, the evidence is mixed. In some applications related to output growth, Stock and Watson (2004) argued that combined forecasts tend to be more stable than the individual forecasts. However, many of the combination methods that attempt to tailor the specification of the weights to account for time variations have not been successful, in general. This issue was investigated by Aiolfi and Timmermann (2006) who concluded that when the weights have to be estimated, the instabilities create biases such that the performance of the forecast combination may be lower than that of the best performing model. More importantly, they highlight examples for which forecast combinations are the optimal thing to do in the absence of breaks but are inferior when breaks occur. This is mostly due to the fact that with structural breaks, the combination weights should be changing over time and properly accounting for such changes is difficult.

The previous remark relates to a more general point of importance. In theory, when dealing with population values of the various parameters, choosing proper weights does indeed lead to forecast combinations having a superior performance. However, in practice, the weights have to be estimated. This usually introduces bias and parameter estimation errors. Then, sub-optimal methods, such as equal weighting of all forecasts, tend to deliver better forecasts than the combination weights delivered according to large sample theory.

In a sense, the very exercise of constructing forecast combinations can be viewed as an admission of guilt, namely that we did not work hard enough to construct the proper forecasting model. However, this line of argument is incorrect as one can construct examples where one forecast dominates another, yet in population, some combination of the two yields a superior forecast; see Section 51.6.1. One can also construct examples in which two forecasts yield identical losses, yet it is not optimal to combine them, mostly because of the estimation errors in the combination weights.

Instead of averaging, one can try to seek whether one forecast encompasses the others, labeled forecast encompassing and advocated by Chong and Hendry (1986). Consider two forecasts for y_{t+h}, namely $\hat{y}^{(1)}_{t+h}$ and $\hat{y}^{(2)}_{t+h}$, and estimate the following regression:

$$y_{t+h} = \beta_0 + \beta_1 \hat{y}^{(1)}_{t+h} + \beta_2 \hat{y}^{(2)}_{t+h} + u_{t+h}.$$

Then, forecast (1) encompasses forecast (2) when $(\beta_0, \beta_1, \beta_2) = (0, 1, 0)$ and, conversely, the second encompasses the first when $(\beta_0, \beta_1, \beta_2) = (0, 0, 1)$. If neither holds, then both forecasts contain additional relevant information over the other. When considering multiple models, a relevant question is to establish which models can be viewed as "reliable" and which are to be treated as "unreliable". Hence, the aim is to construct a model confidence set which contains all models whose forecasts are good or "not bad enough" to be considered as potential contenders. This is covered in Section 51.7.

Various methods have been advocated to allow the weights to be time varying. We discussed some proposed by Bates and Granger (1969) in Section (51.6.1). For a more complete survey, see the work of Timmermann (2006).

A class of methods advocated to construct the weights relies on shrinkage methods. The main idea is to downweight estimated coefficients with large variance. So, if the error is large and positive, we would like to pull the estimate downward and vice versa for large negative errors. Diebold and Pauly (1990) advocated shrinking towards equal weights, which can be justified using some Bayesian arguments. Stock and Watson (2004) proposed shrinkage toward the average of the forecasts. But a problem with such methods involves the rate at which one shrinks toward a particular target. There is no optimal rule.

51.6.5 Mallows model averaging

We now introduce a popular way to select the weights analyzed by Hansen (2008) who extended his prior work Hansen (2007) dealing with model selection obtained by minimizing the Mallows criterion to the forecasting context. The Mallows criterion was first introduced by Mallows (2000) for model selection following much earlier unpublished work, namely the works of Mallows (1964b) and Mallows (1964a). The analysis was subsequently extended by Li (1987) and Andrews (1991a) who demonstrated the asymptotic optimality of this selection method for the homoskedastic and heteroskedastic cases, respectively. In the context of model averaging, Hansen (2007) suggested the Mallows model averaging estimator. We see that this criterion is asymptotically equivalent to the mean squared error so that the resulting estimator, which minimizes it, is asymptotically optimal. Hansen (2008) expanded the analysis to forecast combination proving that the Mallows criterion is also asymptotically equivalent to the mean square forecast error. Accordingly, a detour about model selection using the Mallows criterion is in order.

The results of Hansen (2007) pertain only to a random sample of data, which are not of much concern with issues of forecasting, given that time-series data are most often serially correlated. Hence, we provide a brief overview of the main results to set the framework and define the relevant estimators.

Consider a random sample $(y_t, x_t), t = 1, \ldots, T$ with $x_t = (x_{1,t}, x_{2,t}, \ldots)$. The data-generating process is the linear regression with countably infinite regressors and homoskedastic errors:

$$y_t = \mu_t + \epsilon_t, \tag{51.14}$$

$$\mu_t = \textstyle\sum_{j=1}^{\infty} a_j x_{j,t} = a' x_t, \tag{51.15}$$

$$E(\epsilon_t | x_t) = 0,$$

$$E(\epsilon_t^2 | x_t) = \sigma^2, \tag{51.16}$$

with $a = (a_1, a_2, \ldots)'$, $E(\mu_t^2) < \infty$, and (51.15) converging in mean square. Consider the finite approximation

$$\begin{aligned} y_t &= \sum_{j=1}^{k_m} a_j x_{j,t} + \epsilon_{(m),t} \\ &= a'_{(m)} x_{(m),t} + \epsilon_{(m),t}, \end{aligned}$$

where $x_{(m),t} = (x_{1,t}, \ldots, x_{k_m,t})'$, $a_{(m),t} = (a_{1,t}, \ldots, a_{k_m,t})'$ and $\epsilon_{(m),t} = \sum_{j=k_m+1}^{\infty} a_j x_{j,t} + \epsilon_t$. In matrix notation,

$$y = X_{(m)} a_{(m)} + \epsilon_{(m)},$$

where $X_{(m)} = (x_1, , \ldots, x_{k_m})$ and $\epsilon_{(m)} = (\epsilon_{(m),1}, \ldots, \epsilon_{(m),T})$. Suppose we have a sequence of approximating models $m = 1, 2, \ldots$, where the

mth model uses the first k_m elements of x_t. Note that we are implicitly assuming that the models are nested since $x_{(m),t}$ contains the first k_m elements of x_t and not a random subset of any k_m elements. The more general results where the models are not necessarily nested is developed by Wan *et al.* (2010) as discussed later. Consider the first M models, where M should be such that $X'_{(m)}X_{(m)}$ is invertible for all $m = 1, \ldots, M$. The least square estimate of $a(m)$ is

$$\hat{a}_{(m)} = (X'_{(m)}X_{(m)})^{-1}X'_{(m)}y, \quad m = 1, \ldots, M.$$

The estimator of μ for $m = 1, \ldots, M$ is

$$\begin{aligned}\hat{\mu}_{(m)} &= X_{(m)}\hat{a}_{(m)} \\ &= X_{(m)}(X'_{(m)}X_{(m)})^{-1}X'_{(m)}y \\ &= P_{(m)}y,\end{aligned}$$

and the vector of residuals is

$$e_{(m)} = y - \hat{\mu}_{(m)}.$$

Let us now build the forecast combinations. The sequence of forecasts for period $T+1$ has the following form:

$$\hat{f}_{(m),T+1} = x'_{(m),T+1}\hat{a}_{(m)}, \quad m = 1, \ldots, M.$$

We now assign a weight $w_{(m)}$ to model $m = 1, \ldots, M$. Define the vector of weights $w = (w_{(1)}, \ldots, w_{(M)})$ and the vector of corresponding forecasts $\hat{f}_t = (\hat{f}_{(1),t}, \ldots, \hat{f}_{(M),t})'$. The forecast combination is

$$\begin{aligned}\hat{f}_{T+1}(w) &= w'\hat{f}_{T+1} \\ &= \sum_{m=1}^{M} w_{(m)}\hat{f}_{(m),T+1} \\ &= \sum_{m=1}^{M} w_{(m)}x'_{(m),T+1}\hat{a}_{(m)}.\end{aligned}$$

We now slightly change the notation. Define $\hat{a}_{(m)} = (a_1, a_2, \ldots, a_{k_m}, 0, 0, \ldots)'$ as an infinite-dimensional vector where the entries are 0 beyond the mth element. Then,

$$\hat{f}_{T+1}(w) = x'_{T+1} \sum_{m=1}^{M} w_{(m)} \hat{a}_{(m)}$$
$$= x'_{T+1} \hat{a}(w),$$

where $\hat{a}(w) = \sum_{m=1}^{M} w_{(m)} \hat{a}_{(m)}$. Turning to the choice of the vector of weights w, we already covered some methods proposed by Bates and Granger (1969) and Granger and Ramanathan (1984). In the following, we review the proposal by Hansen (2008) to select the weights w using the Mallows model averaging criterion of Hansen (2007). The Mallows criterion is

$$C_T(w) = \left(y - X_{(M)} \hat{a}(w)\right)' \left(y - X_{(M)} \hat{a}(w)\right) + 2\sigma^2 \sum_{m=1}^{M} w_{(m)} k_m,$$

where σ^2 is unknown. The Mallows model averaging weights minimize the penalized sum of square residuals, under the non-negativity and sum-to-one constraints:

$$\hat{w} = \arg\min_{w \in \mathcal{H}} C_T(w), \quad \mathcal{H} = \left\{ w \in [0,1]^M : \sum_{m=1}^{M} w_{(m)} = 1 \right\}.$$

Define the $T \times M$ matrix $e = \left(e_{(1)}, \ldots, e_{(M)}\right)$, and the $M \times 1$ vector $K = (k_1, \ldots, k_M)'$. Then, we can write

$$C_T(w) = w'e'ew + 2w'K\sigma^2,$$

which is linear quadratic in w. The analytical solution to the minimization problem is not available. However, given that the objective function is linear quadratic in w, it is straightforward to solve numerically. Hansen (2007) advocated the use of the Mallows criterion based on the following two results:

1. *Approximate unbiasedness*: The Mallows criterion yields an unbiased estimate of the in-sample mean squared error up to some constant.

2. *Efficiency*: When the weights are restricted to a discrete set, those obtained by minimizing the Mallows criterion asymptotically minimizes the in-sample mean squared error.

Wan *et al.* (2010) noted that the modeling assumption of strictly nested models and the assumption that the weights are chosen over a discrete set are too restrictive. They proved a more general result that allows the sequence of models indexed by m to be non-nested. Remember that the setup by Hansen (2007) requires that each approximating model m uses the first k_m regressors of x_t. Here, instead the model, m can include any combination of k_m regressors of x_t, thus allowing for a wider set of models to be considered. Second, their result does not restrict the weights to the discrete set $\mathcal{H}^*$, allowing choosing them over a continuous set. They argued that their results provide further support for the use of the Mallows model averaging estimator. Liu and Okui (2013) extended the Mallows model averaging estimator for the case of heteroskedastic errors.

The results stated above apply only for *i.i.d.* data. Hansen (2008) extended the above Mallows model averaging estimator to forecasts. He showed that the Mallows criterion is unbiased for the mean squared forecast error (MSFE) for strictly stationary observations. However, the proof of efficiency does not extend to stationary-dependent data. Since the in-sample mean squared error is approximately equal to the out-of-sample mean squared error for stationary data, the Mallows criterion is also approximately unbiased for the mean squared forecast error. Whether it is efficient remains an open question.

51.6.6 Some extensions

Other criteria that have been used for model averaging and model selection are the accumulated prediction error (APE) and cross-validation (CV). Kejriwal *et al.* (2022) and Kejriwal and Yu (2021) extended the analysis to forecasting regressions involving potentially integrated or near-integrated regressors. In the context of model selection, it amounts to decision rules about whether to use the forecast from the model that assumes stationarity or the one that imposes a unit root. This decision rule can be based on a pre-test for a unit root or the relative value of either of the criteria discussed above

(Mallows, APE, and CV). In the case of the Mallows criterion, the penalty function is slightly different when considering models with integrated regressors. For model averaging, the forecasts are linear combinations of the two forecasts (assuming stationarity or not) with weights that are a function of the criterion used. These can be done as well for multi-step ahead forecasts and for autoregressive forecasting models with an unknown number of lags selected via some information criterion. In such cases, the exact forms of the rules changes slightly, but the rules remain qualitatively the same.

51.6.7 Summary

A summary of the evidence with respect to forecast combinations is the following, which we paraphrase from p. 181 of Timmermann (2006): (1) Simple combination schemes are difficult to beat due to the importance of parameter estimation errors in the combination weights. (2) Forecasts based on models with the best in-sample performance often lead to poor out-of-sample performance. (3) With a large number of forecasts, deleting the worst performers and combining those with similar performance can lead to combinations with substantial improvements in forecasting. (4) Shrinkage to simple forecasting combination weights often improves forecasting performance. (5) Some adaptive or time-varying adjustment can lead to improved forecasts.

51.7 The model confidence set

Hansen *et al.* (2011) considered the case in which one has multiple forecasts from different models and wished to establish which models can be viewed as "reliable" and which are to be treated as "unreliable". Hence, the aim is to construct a model confidence set which contains all models whose forecasts are good or "not bad enough" to be considered as potential contenders.

Consider a set $\mathcal{M}^0$ that contains a finite number of objects indexed by $i = 1, \ldots, m_0$. These objects are evaluated in terms of a loss function L (e.g., the mean squared forecast errors or the mean absolute forecast errors) over the sample $t = 1, \ldots, T$, where the loss associated with period t is denoted $L_{i,t}$. Define the relative performance $d_{i,j,t}$ for all $i, j \in \mathcal{M}^0$, which is usually the difference in the loss functions. Then, the set of superior objects are

$$\mathcal{M}^* \equiv \{i \in \mathcal{M}^0 : E[d_{i,j,t}] \leq 0, \text{ for all } j \in \mathcal{M}^0\}.$$

The objective is to determine $\mathcal{M}^*$ and this is done via a sequence of significance tests where the significantly inferior objects of $\mathcal{M}^0$ are eliminated. The null hypothesis may be stated as

$$H_{0,\mathcal{M}}: E[d_{i,j,t}] = 0, \quad \text{for all } i, j \in \mathcal{M} \subset \mathcal{M}^0,$$

which is tested against the alternative $E[d_{i,j,t}] \neq 0$, for some $i, j \in \mathcal{M}$. The test is based on an algorithm, which consists of an equivalence tests, $\delta_{\mathcal{M}}$, and an elimination rule, $e_{\mathcal{M}}$. The equivalence test is used to test $H_{0,\mathcal{M}}$ and it takes values $\delta_{\mathcal{M}} = \{1, 0\}$ corresponding to rejecting or not $H_{0,\mathcal{M}}$, respectively. The elimination rule $e_{\mathcal{M}}$ determines the object of $\mathcal{M}$ that is to be removed in the event that $H_{0,\mathcal{M}}$ is rejected. The algorithm may therefore be described by three steps:

1. Initially set $\mathcal{M} = \boldsymbol{\mathcal{M}}^0$.
2. Test $H_{0,\mathcal{M}}$ using $\delta_{\mathcal{M}}$ at a given significance level α.
3. If $\delta_{\mathcal{M}} = 0$, define $\hat{\mathcal{M}}^*_{1-\alpha} = \mathcal{M}$; otherwise, use $e_{\mathcal{M}}$ to eliminate an object from $\mathcal{M}$ and repeat the procedure from Step 1.

The set $\hat{\mathcal{M}}^*_{1-\alpha}$ consists of the surviving objects, and this is referred to as the model confidence set (MCS).

51.7.1 MCS *p*-values

To facilitate the interpretation of the p-values, consider the sequence of random sets

$$\mathcal{M}^0 = \mathcal{M}_1 \supset \mathcal{M}_2 \supset \cdots \supset \mathcal{M}_{m_0},$$

where

$$\mathcal{M}_i = \{e_{\mathcal{M}_i}, \ldots, e_{\mathcal{M}_{m_0}}\}$$

so that $e_{\mathcal{M}_1}$ is the first element to be eliminated in the event that $H_{0,\mathcal{M}_1}$ is rejected, $e_{\mathcal{M}_2}$ is the second element, and so on. Then, let $\mathcal{P}_{H_{0,\mathcal{M}_i}}$ denote the p-value associated with the null hypothesis $H_{0,\mathcal{M}_i}$, with the convention that $\mathcal{P}_{H_{0,\mathcal{M}_0}} = 1$. The MCS p-value for model $e_{\mathcal{M}_j} \subset \mathcal{M}^0$ is defined in this setup by $\hat{p} = \max_{i \leq j} \mathcal{P}_{H_{0,\mathcal{M}_j}}$.

The interpretation of the MCS p-values is analogous to that of standard p-values. The MCS may thus be interpreted as containing the best random subset of models, $\mathcal{M}^*$, with some probability.

51.7.2 Equivalence test and elimination rule

Several equivalence tests and elimination rules have been suggested, see the work of Hansen *et al.* (2011). A commonly used equivalence test is the "range statistic":

$$T_{R,\mathcal{M}} = \max_{i,j \in \mathcal{M}} |t_{ij}|,$$

where t_{ij} is a t-statistic constructed as

$$t_{ij} = \frac{\bar{d}_{ij}}{\sqrt{V(\bar{d}_{ij})}} \quad \text{for } i, j \in \mathcal{M},$$

with

$$\bar{d}_{ij} = T^{-1} \sum_{t=1}^{T} d_{ijt},$$

i.e., the average relative loss between the ith and jth models and $V(\bar{d}_{ij})$ is its variance. The elimination rule is then given by

$$e_{R,\mathcal{M}} = \arg\max_{i \in \mathcal{M}} \sup_{j \in \mathcal{M}} t_{ij}.$$

The variance and the p-values is constructed using simulation methods. For a package in R, see the work of Bernardi and Catania (2018).

51.8 Forecasting with large datasets

It is possible to consider a very large number of possible variables as candidates for constructing a predictive regression. Suppose that we have K such variables with K large, possibly much larger than T. While the use of information criteria is well suited when K is small relative to T, other approaches need to be adopted with K large. There are two main avenues that can deliver useful forecasting models. The first is to try to select a small subset of variables that are deemed most relevant to predict the variable of interest. This is sometimes called "dimension reduction" and usually involves using methods such as the Lasso; see Chapter 33. The second approach is to try to find a way to aggregate all the relevant information from all variables, sometimes called "regularization". This usually involves using factor models and principal components. These are discussed in this section. Useful surveys include the works of Stock and Watson (2006) and Ng (2013). For an interesting review and application of the methods to forecasting inflation, see the work of Medeiros *et al.* (2021).

51.8.1 Variable selection

When the number of K candidate predictor variables x_t becomes large, the use of information criteria rapidly becomes unmanageable as the dimension K increases. For instance, if there is no natural ordering (as in pure autoregressive models), the number of permutations is roughly 2^K. Also, if $K = T$, a perfect fit can be achieved in-sample, which leads to a useless method. A main concern here with many possible predictors is to avoid issues of overfitting. It is most often the case that an overfitted model, which predicts well in-sample, can provide very poor forecasts. Sometimes, methods that prevent such overfitting are called "regularization" methods. One way to avoid the overfitting problem is to downweigh the less relevant predictors. This is usually referred to as "shrinkage". Stock and Watson (2012b) argued that shrinkage methods can be used as a unifying framework for various forecasting methods. Ridge regressions were covered in Section 33.1.1. They can help alleviate issues of multi-collinearity across the regressors but still leave non-zero estimates for most coefficients.

An alternative way to proceed is to assume that the true model is "sparse", in the sense that only a relatively small subset of the variables have an effect on the forecast. Then, one can adopt a Lasso-type method to estimate the model; see Section 33.1.2. In a sense, Lasso performs shrinkage and variable selection at the same time, though the shrinkage is of an extreme form, namely to zero for most variables. Although much of the literature on Lasso pertains to data collected from a random sample, it has been shown to be effective in time series contexts as well. Of course, adaptive Lasso can be used as well.

These fall into a class called “shrinkage methods”. We already covered ridge regression, Lasso, and adaptive Lasso. Another one that falls into this category is the so-called “Elastic Net”. It is a generalization of the Lasso and ridge framework and includes both as a special case. It adopts a penalty factor given by

$$(1-\alpha)\lambda\sum_{j=1}^{K}|\beta_j| + \alpha\lambda\sum_{j=1}^{K}\beta_j^2,$$

for some selected values of α and λ.

51.8.2 Principal components and factor models

While the use of Lasso and its variants is akin to model selection, the use of factor models is more like model averaging. We discussed principal components in Chapter 31 and factor models in Section 42.4. Here, we briefly review how these methods can be applied in the context of forecasting with many predictors, when the intent is to summarize all the relevant information in the data into a few components. The particular structure of the factor model to be used depends obviously on the context. To illustrate, consider the structure

$$y_t = \alpha W_t + \Gamma(L) f_t + e_t, \tag{51.17}$$

where f_t is a vector of r_f unobserved common factors, with r_f determined using one of the methods discussed in Section 42.4; e.g., that suggested by Bai and Ng (2002), $\Gamma(L)$ is a polynomial of order p_f in the lag operator L, W_t is a vector of covariates, and e_t is some *i.i.d.* random error term. Often, W_t contains lags of the dependent variables, though it can include any variable that the researcher deems relevant for forecasting. Then using estimates of the parameters and the factors, the forecast h periods ahead is given by

$$\hat{y}_{T+h|T} = \alpha\hat{W}_{T+h|T} + \Gamma(L)\hat{f}_{T+h|T},$$

where $\hat{z}_{T+h|T}$ (for z being y, W or f) being the best forecast of z_{T+h} given information available at time T. Note first that if W_t includes lagged values of y_t, then one could use the direct or iterated method as discussed in Section 51.2. Of importance is to have an estimate of the factors $\hat{f}_t$ so that their forecasts can be constructed. These are usually obtained from estimating the factor model for the potential predictors using a model of the form

$$x_{it} = W_X\Psi + \lambda_{it} f_t + e_{it},$$

for $i = 1, \dots, N$ and $t = 1, \dots, T$, using principal component methods applied to a large panel, i.e., with r_f much smaller than N. The estimates $\hat{f}_t$ are sometimes referred to as diffusion indices. The presence of the term $W_X\Psi$ allows using lagged values of y_t. These could overlap with W_t in the prediction equation (51.17). Methods to estimate such models are discussed in Section 42.4. Of course, any of the structures discussed in that section could be used as a factor model for forecasting purposes.

The main idea behind the use of factor models in prediction is the belief that most of the variation in a large set of potential predictors x_{it} can be summarized via a small number of factors. Although, principal component analysis differs from factor models, the differences get smaller as N increases. Hence, dynamic principal component analysis can be used to construct consistent estimates of the factors in dynamic factor models. Of interest is that the issue pertaining to the non-identifiability of the factors (up to some rotation) is of no consequence when dealing with linear forecasting. All we care about is some linear combination of the factors that allows forecasts with minimal mean squared errors.

Some extensions of the factor model approach have been proposed. One is labeled as "Target Factors", suggested by Bai and Ng (2008a). The idea is that many candidate predictors may be irrelevant, thereby causing noisy factors and poor forecasts. Let w_t be a set of control variables, typically lagged values of the variable to be forecasted. Then, the procedure amounts to the following:

(a) For $i = 1, \dots, K$, regress y_{t+h} on w_t and $x_{i,t}$ and construct the t-statistic pertaining to the coefficient on $x_{i,t}$.

(b) Keep only the candidate regressors $x_{i,t}$ with significant t-statistics and estimate the factors using the selected variables.
(c) The forecasts are then obtained from a predictive regression of y_{t+h} on w_t and f_{t-j} ($j = 1, \ldots, p$) with p often selected using an information criterion.

An alternative is "Factor Boosting"; see the work of Bai and Ng (2008a) which attempts to take into account the fact that some factors deemed irrelevant using the previous method can still be useful to improve forecasts.

51.8.3 Averaging in the context of large datasets

In the context of very large datasets, several methods using computer intensive methods have been suggested as alternatives to factor models to average the information in a large set of predictors. Here, we briefly review some of them. For an application to inflation, see the work of Medeiros *et al.* (2021).

(1) **Bagging:** This refers to a bootstrap aggregation procedure and was proposed by Breiman (1996). The basic insight is to average the forecasts when the models are estimated over different bootstrap sub-samples. The intuition is that some models may perform well in some periods, while others can perform better in others periods and vice versa. So, the steps are as follows: (a) For each bootstrap sample, run an OLS regression with all candidate predictors and keep those with a large enough t-statistic; i.e., above some pre-specified threshold in absolute value. Estimate a new regression with the variables selected and use the estimated model for the actual sample to produce a forecast. (b) Repeat these steps B times (say 500 or other values) and compute the final forecast as the average over the B forecasts. One problem here is that the number of predictor variables may be larger than the number of observations so that the first step is infeasible. This can be solved by randomly dividing the predictors used into some smaller groups and applying step (a) for each group.
(2) **Jackknife Model Averaging:** This method is based on the jackknife method discussed in Section 9.3. It was advocated as

a method for model averaging useful in the forecasting context by Hansen and Racine (2012) and Zhang *et al.* (2013). Suppose we have M models, indexed by $m = 1, \ldots, M$. Associated with each model is a forecast $\hat{y}_{t+h}^{(m)}$. We wish to set the final forecast as

$$\hat{y}_{t+h} = \sum_{m=1}^{M} \omega_m \hat{y}_{t+h}^{(m)},$$

subject to the constraints that $0 \leq \omega_m \leq 1$ and $\sum_{m=1}^{M} \omega_m = 1$. Suppose that x_t is the vector of covariates. Then, for each observation (y_{t+h}, x_t), estimate all candidate models leaving this observation out of the estimation. Note that if x_t contains p lags of y_t, then one should also leave out p observations before and after (y_{t+h}, x_t). Then, compute the forecasts from each model. The weights are chosen so as to minimize the cross-validation MSFE subject to the constraints.

(3) **Random Forests:** The random forest procedure was suggested by Breiman (2001). It can be viewed as an adaptively weighted nearest neighbors method; see the work of Lin and Jeon (2006). Random forest is a substantial modification of bagging (bootstrap aggregation); see the work of Hastie *et al.* (2009). Bagging methods aim to reduce the variance by averaging many noisy but approximately unbiased models. Random forest methods can capture complex interaction structures in the data and have relatively low bias. The exact details are, however, much more complex and we refer the readers to the original papers referenced.

51.8.4 Variable selection versus averaging

As argued by Ng (2013) and Chernozhukov (2017), and illustrated via the methodologies described above, the issue of forecasting in the context of large datasets can be broadly divided in two categories. The first assumes some kind of sparse modelling, meaning that there is some true model with a few variables that forecasts best, though these variables are unknown up to the fact that they belong to a potentially large set of variables available. A clear example is the Lasso procedure. The second avenue assumes that all variables could be potentially valuable in providing improved forecasts, even though their individual contribution may be small. This is labeled as "dense-modeling" approach. Here, factor models are the leading example in this class. An issue of interest is then whether economic predictive problems are best addressed using a dense or sparse approach. Tackling such a problem is important but the literature on this subject is quite sparse. Hence, our coverage is obviously limited and indicative of some advances made.

Giannone *et al.* (2021) provided an interesting framework to address this issue. They adopt a Bayesian framework with so-called hyper-parameters, namely parameters that influence the structure or parameterization of the model. The main prior is that some parameters can be zero with some probability q, say. This then determines the degree of sparsity since it dictates whether a variable should enter the model or not. When a parameter is non-zero, it is a draw form some normal distribution whose variance depends on some parameter γ^2 so that larger values of γ^2 imply higher prior variance and less shrinkage when a predictor is included. So, the model allows three features: (a) the possibility of sparsity, i.e., zero coefficients; (b) it shrinks the non-zero coefficient toward zero to reduce estimation uncertainty and avoid overfitting; (c) the degree of sparsity and shrinkage are treated separately via the parameters q and γ^2. In their applications, they consider a variety of contexts covering time series, cross-sections, and panel data. They argue that, in general, the data favor larger values of q, i.e., using a dense approach. They also find that the estimates of q and γ^2 are negatively correlated. This implies that a higher probability of including a variable is associated with a lower prior variance on the non-zero coefficients. The implication is that larger models are preferable because they involve a high degree of shrinkage without overfitting. Also, the data are not informative about the identity of the predictors to include. Hence, they argue for methods targeted to dense models as opposed to sparse ones. Of course, Giannone *et al.* (2021) recognized that the results may not be reliable if their parametric assumption about the non-zero coefficients is not a good approximation. So, while the results are of considerable interest, they are most likely not the final verdict on this issue. This should remain an active research topic.

51.9 Exercises

Exercise 51.1. Prove that $\sigma_c^2(k^*) \leq \sigma_1^2$ and $\sigma_c^2(k^*) \leq \sigma_2^2$. In other words, the optimal combination is weakly better than each of the two original forecasts.

Exercise 51.2. Consider the forecast error $e = x - F\hat{k}$. Prove that the following conditions are sufficient for the unbiasedness of the combined forecast: (1) Each forecast has zero mean error, $1'x = 1'f_k$. (2) The weights sum to one, $1'\hat{k} = 1$.

Exercise 51.3. Prove equation (51.13), i.e.,

$$\text{MSFE}_{cc} \geq \text{MSFE}_{uc} \geq \text{MSFE}_{ucc}.$$

forecasting + [illegible] (51.[illegible])

51.3 Exercises

Exercise 51.1. Prove that $\hat{\sigma}^2(K^*) \le \sigma_1^2$ and $\hat{\sigma}^2(K^*) \le \sigma_2^2$. In other words, the optimal combination is weakly better than each of the two original forecasts.

Exercise 51.2. Consider the [illegible] error [illegible] e_t [illegible]. Prove that the following conditions are sufficient for the unbiasedness of the combined forecast: (1) Each forecast has zero mean error, [illegible]. (2) The weights sum to one: $\sum K = 1$.

Exercise 51.3. Prove equation (51.13), [illegible]

$$FE_{ew} \le MFE_{[illegible]} \le MSFE_{[illegible]}$$

Chapter 52

Numerical Methods

In this chapter, various Monte Carlo methods useful for estimation are reviewed. We start with the basic examples of how simulation-based computational methods work and then cover two popular Monte Carlo Markov Chain (MCMC) methods: the Gibbs sampler and the Metropolis–Hastings algorithms. We then see how these methods can be used to solve some econometric challenges. We do this by presenting a practical example where we highlight some potential issues which computational methods can help solve. Useful references for this chapter include the works of Feller (1968), Gelman *et al.* (1995), Chib (2001), Geweke and Keane (2001), Gill (2015), Johansen and Evers (2007), and Robert and Casella (2013). Throughout this chapter, we adopt the following notation. Let x be a random vector of dimension K distributed according to $p(x)$. Also, $x^{(i)} = (x_1^{(i)}, \ldots, x_K^{(i)})$ is a realization of the random vector and $h(x)$ is a function of x. We let N be the sample size.

Before describing these methods, we need to understand why they became so popular. One of the main challenges we face is to evaluate multidimensional integrals of the form

$$E_p[h(X)] = \int h(x)p(x)dx.$$

Monte Carlo methods are some of the main tools used to approximate such integrals. They provide a viable way to generate samples from the distribution $p(x)$. In this way, one can approximate the integral with the sample analog, $N^{-1}\sum_{i=1}^{N} h(x^{(i)})$, provided a sufficiently large sample is available:

- Monte Carlo methods are especially useful in Bayesian inference. Computing the posterior distribution requires applying Bayes' rule:

$$p(\theta|X) = \frac{p(X|\theta)p(\theta)}{\int_{\Theta} p(X|\theta)p(\theta)d\theta}. \tag{52.1}$$

  The main challenge is computing the integral in the denominator. From a theoretical viewpoint, the so-called conjugate priors of the model allow obtaining an analytical expression for the posterior distribution. In other words, for some choice of the likelihood function and the prior distribution, the posterior distribution has a closed form. However, in many applications, conjugate priors do not exist or are not good enough to represent our beliefs. In these cases, Monte Carlo methods are useful alternatives to compute numerically the integral of the denominator of (52.1) and obtain the posterior mean or distribution. A useful reference for this case is the work of Kruschke (2014).
- Monte Carlo methods are extensively used in a variety of contexts in economics. For example, the estimation of the discrete choice model requires integrating over many alternatives. Monte Carlo methods are widely used to accomplish this task. For brevity, we do not cover this application but the reader can refer to the work of Geweke and Keane (2001).
- Monte Carlo methods are widely used to estimate dynamic stochastic general equilibrium models. These often involve dynamic nonlinear state-space models for which sequential Monte Carlo methods are useful. Such models are also often used in financial applications.
- In Section 52.4.1, we present a random-level shift model and discuss various Monte Carlo methods that can be applied to estimate a rather complex problem.

From the above examples, Monte Carlo methods are useful and sometimes the only available tool to sample from a multi-dimensional distribution. The main idea underlying these methods is to express a quantity of interest θ as the expected value of a random variable X distributed according to some density function $p(x)$. By simulating the random variable a large number of times, we can use the sample average of the simulated values which can serve as an estimate of the quantity of interest. The theoretical justification relies simply on the standard law of large numbers. An advantage of Monte Carlo methods is that in theory one can increase arbitrarily the number of simulated values to reach any desired level of precision as the convergence rate is independent of the dimensionality of the integral provided the dimension is in some sense small relative to the sample size, i.e., if d is the dimension and T the sample size, then we need $d/T \to 0$.

We start with the simplest setting where we can directly sample from the distribution $p(x)$ of the random variable. Then, when independent samples from $p(x)$ are difficult to obtain directly, as in the majority of the cases, one can rely on the so-called MCMC algorithms. The idea is to generate a Markov process such that the resulting sequence has the same ergodic distribution as the target $p(x)$, where ergodicity refers to stochastic processes for which a sufficiently large collection of random samples can represent the average statistical properties of the entire process. Before covering the MCMC algorithms, it is convenient to review some basic computational algorithms. We start by discussing the inversion method which allows us to sample from a large set of univariate distributions starting from a sample of uniform draws between 0 and 1, provided that the inverse of the cumulative distribution exists. We then review the composition method that explains how to sample from the marginal distributions to obtain a sample from the joint distribution. We then cover two other, more broadly applicable, methods that are suitable when the inverse does not exist. One is the rejection sampling method whose basis is to sample candidate values from an instrumental distribution and reject some of them based on a rejection rule. The other is the importance sampling method, which instead reweights the candidate values from the instrumental distribution and uses them as a sample. While these methods are rarely applied alone, we see that the MCMC algorithms build on these to generate more advanced algorithms.

52.1 The basic elements of simulation methods

We start by presenting the basic ingredients underlying most simulation algorithms. Suppose first we are interested in approximating the expectation $E_p[h(x)]$.

Algorithm 52.1 (MC). For a given sample size N, the Monte Carlo algorithm consists of two steps:

1. **Sampling Step:** Sample N times from $p(x)$ and store the realizations $(x^{(1)}, \ldots, x^{(N)})$.
2. **Approximation Step:** Compute $\hat{\mu} = N^{-1} \sum_{i=1}^{N} h(x^{(i)})$ and use it as the approximation for $E_p[h(x)]$.

The main differences between the MC algorithms we cover concern the sampling step, while the approximation step is in general common across the majority of methods. For this reason, we report only the sampling step if no significant differences are present in the approximation step.

Before describing the inversion method, it is necessary to understand how we can simulate random numbers. Pseudo-random number generators have been developed to produce deterministic sequences of numbers given an initial starting point called the seed. Given a seed, the deterministically associated sequence resembles a realization of a random variable distributed uniformly on $[0, 1]$. The prefix pseudo indicates that the generated sequences are not random but can be used as if they were random. It is outside the scope of this chapter to review the details about how to generate uniform pseudo-random variables on [0, 1]. This literature is huge and has evolved considerably over time. For econometric applications, it is generally safe to perceive methods coded in standard packages or coding languages as being reliable. A useful reference is the work of Devroye (2006).

52.1.1 Inversion method

We saw that with the pseudo-random number generators, we can sample from a uniform on $[0, 1]$. The inversion method enables us, under some assumptions, to obtain a random sample from another distribution $f(x)$.

Theorem 52.1 (CDF Inversion Method). *Let* $u \sim U[0,1]$ *a uniform distribution on [0,1] and* F *be a cumulative distribution function (CDF). If* F *is continuous, then* $F^{-1}(U)$ *has CDF* F*.*

Algorithm 52.2 (Inversion Sampling). Repeat for $i = 1, \dots, N$:

- Draw $u^{(i)} \sim U[0,1]$.
- Compute $x^{(i)} = F^{-1}(u^{(i)})$.

Then, the resulting sequence $(x^{(1)}, \dots, x^{(N)})$ is a random sample from $F(x)$.

To illustrate this method, suppose that we want to simulate a sample of *i.i.d.* random variables having an exponential distribution $x \sim Exp(\lambda)$, whose support is $[0,\infty]$. Then, $F = F_\lambda(x) = 1 - \exp(-\lambda x)$ and it is continuous in x. Given that its inverse is $F_\lambda^{-1}(u) = -\log(1-u)/\lambda$, we can generate a random sample $(x^{(1)}, \dots, x^{(N)})$ from $x \sim Exp(\lambda)$ in the following way. Repeat for $i = 1, \dots, N$:

- Draw $u^{(i)} \sim U[0,1]$.
- Compute $x^{(i)} = -\log(1-u^{(i)})/\lambda$.

Then, the resulting $(x^{(1)}, \dots, x^{(N)})$ is a sample from $Exp(\lambda)$.

From this simple example, we see how we can use pseudo-random generators to sample from distributions other than the uniform. The CDF inversion method is very efficient but can be restrictive in scope: It can be applied only to distributions for which a CDF exists, whose inverse can be computed, and does not apply to random vectors or discrete random variables. Also, one needs to compute the inverse of the target CDF F^{-1}, which may be difficult in some cases.

52.1.2 Composition method

Here, instead of generating a sequence for a single random variable, we are interested in a random vector. We start with a simple bivariate case, where the object of interest is the sampling distribution of the pair (x_1, x_2). A popular sampling method is the composition method.

The idea is to rely on the following identity:

$$p(x_1, x_2) = p(x_2|x_1)p(x_1).$$

Whenever the conditional and the marginal distributions on the right-hand side are known, we can sample from them to obtain a sample from the joint distribution. We see later that this method is the basis of the Gibbs sampler. The algorithm is the following.

Algorithm 52.3 (Composition Sampling). Repeat for $i = 1, \ldots, N$:

- Draw $x_1^{(i)}$ from $p(x_1)$.
- Draw $x_2^{(i)}$ from $p(x_2|x_1)$.
- Let $x^{(i)} = (x_1^{(i)}, x_2^{(i)})$.

Then, the resulting sequence $(x^{(1)}, \ldots, x^{(N)})$ is a sample from $p(x_1, x_2)$.

As an example, suppose that a bivariate vector is generated by

$$(x_1, x_2) \sim N\begin{pmatrix} \sigma^2 & \rho\sigma^2 \\ \rho\sigma^2 & \sigma^2 \end{pmatrix}.$$

Then, $p(x_1) \sim N(0, \sigma^2)$ and $p(x_2|x_1) \sim N(\rho x_1, (1-\rho^2)\sigma^2)$. For an application, see Example (52.3) which is a combination of the composition and the rejection methods, the latter being discussed in the following.

52.1.3 Rejection sampling

Given the limitations of the inversion method, we need to deal with a more general method where we cannot rely on the inversion of a function. We review the rejection and importance sampling methods. They are based on the idea of sampling from an instrumental distribution $g(x)$ and either rejecting some values or reweighting the values, respectively. We start by presenting the rejection sampling.

Algorithm 52.4 (Rejection Sampling). Given two distributions p and f such that p is bounded by $c \times f$, with $c > 0$, we can sample from p using the following algorithm. Repeat for $i = 1, \ldots, N$:

- Sample $x^{(i)}$ from $f(x)$.
- Sample $u^{(i)}$ from $U(0, 1)$.
- Accept $x^{(i)}$ if $u^{(i)} \leq p(x^{(i)})/(c \times f(x^{(i)}))$, reject otherwise.

The resulting accepted sequence $(x^{(1)}, \ldots, x^{(N)})$ is a sample from $p(x)$.

To get the intuition of this method, we review simple versions where the function $p(x)$ has finite support.

Example 52.1. A simple example is when $f \sim U[0, 1]$ and $p \sim U[0, 1/2]$, so that $p \leq cf$ for any $c > 1/2$. Then, $p \leq 2f$. Then we draw some $u^{(i)}$ from $U(0, 1)$ and accept if $u^{(i)} \leq p(u^{(i)})/(c \times f(u^{(i)}))$.

Example 52.2. Consider the following function:

$$p(x) = \begin{cases} 2x, & \text{if } 0 \leq x \leq 1/2, \\ 3/4 - x/2, & \text{if } 1/2 \leq x \leq 3/2. \end{cases}$$

Note that $p(x)$ is bounded by a uniform distribution on $[0, 1]$ scaled by some factor $c \geq 1$. Now, we can think of $p(x)$ as the marginal distribution of a bivariate uniform distribution $f(x, u) = \{(x, u) : 0 \leq u \leq p(x)\}$:

$$p(x) = \int_0^{3/2} 1_{0 \leq u \leq p(x)} du = \int_0^{3/2} f(u, x) du.$$

Then, if we draw from the uniform distribution $f(x, u)$, we can recover draws from $p(x)$ by accepting those points (x^i, u^i) that lie below the curve $u = p(x)$; see Figure 52.1. The fact that we draw from a uniform distribution makes all data points in the light-shaded rectangle randomly distributed. Accordingly, those points that lie in the dark-shaded area will also be randomly distribution and have the desired support dictated by the distribution $p(x)$. The factor c can be anything large enough. Visually, from the graph, we could draw from a rectangle of any size, as long as its region includes the support of the distribution of interest. The randomly drawn sample from $c \times f(u, x)$ will still include valid random draws from $p(x)$.

For the case of an unbounded function, the idea is similar. We want to draw random points (x^i, u^i) in the two-dimensional space from the region below the curve $c \times f(x)$. Then, we accept those

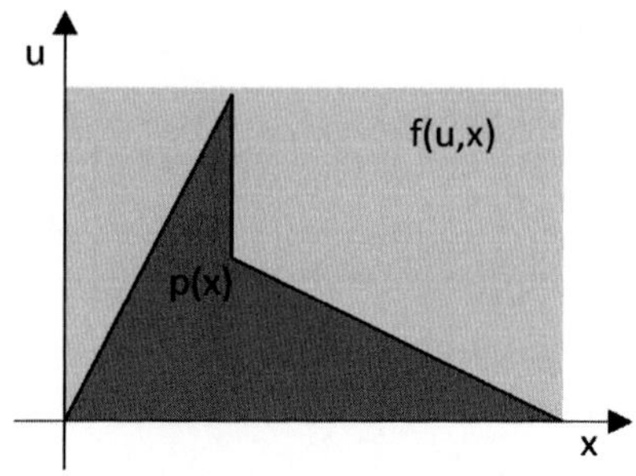

Figure 52.1. Example of the rejection sampling method.

points that lay below the curve $p(x)$. In other words, we can sample x^i from $f(x)$ and accept x^i with probability $p(x^i)/(c \times f(x^i))$.

The method, however, can fail. Suppose that $f \sim N(0,1)$ and $p \sim \exp(1)$. Then, p/f is not bounded. We need the tails of p to be thinner than the tails of f, which is not satisfied here.

Example 52.3 (Conditional Sampling). Suppose we want to sample from the conditional distribution $p(x_2|x_1 = x^*)$ for a particular value x^*. Assume that we know the distributions $p(x_1|x_2)$ and $p(x_2)$. This is a common setting in Bayesian methods where x_2 is some parameter θ and x_1 is the random data. Then, $p(\theta|x_1 = x^*)$ is the posterior distribution, $p(x_1|\theta)$ is the likelihood function, and $p(\theta)$ is the prior. We can apply the rejection sampling algorithm, and the composition method jointly as follows. Repeat for $i = 1, \ldots, N$:

- Sample $x_2^{(i)}$ from $p(x_2)$.
- Sample $x_1^{(i)}$ from $p(x_1|x_2)$.
- Accept $x_2^{(i)}$ if $x_1^{(i)} = x^*$.

Then, the resulting sequence $(x_2^{(1)}, \ldots, x_2^{(N)})$ is a sample from $p(x_2|x_1 = x^*)$.

Many approximate Bayesian computation relies on this approach. The limitation of this algorithm is that in many cases the third step is almost always rejected making it computationally intensive to obtain a large sample from the target distribution. It all depends on the nature of the sampling distribution, in particular, whether we have discrete versus continuous random variables. Here, the method is tailored especially for discrete random variables whose possible values are not "too" large.

52.1.4 Importance sampling

As we mentioned before, this method consists of sampling candidate values having a distribution $p(x)$ from a different distribution $f(x)$ and reweighting the observation using a factor $w(x)$. It is assumed that the support of the distribution p is contained in the support of the distribution f. To understand how importance sampling works, suppose we want to compute the integral

$$E_p[h(x)] = \int h(x)p(x)dx = \int h(x)\frac{p(x)}{f(x)}f(x)dx.$$

This suggests that we can generate a random sample from $f(x)$ and apply the weight $w(x) = p(x)/f(x)$ so that the resulting sample is as if it was drawn from our target distribution $p(x)$. Given that it requires reweighting the observation, this method also requires specifying a new approximation step.

Algorithm 52.5 (Importance Sampling). Given two distribution functions p and f, under some technical conditions, we can sample from p using the following algorithm. (a) Sampling step. Repeat for $i = 1, \ldots, N$:

- Sample $x^{(i)}$ from $f(x)$.
- Compute $w^{(i)} = p(x^{(i)})/f(x^{(i)})$.
- Store the values $(x^{(i)}, w^{(i)})$.

(b) Approximation step: For a given value of the normalization constant $\tilde{N}$ (see the following for a list of possible values), compute

$$\hat{\mu}(\tilde{N}) = \tilde{N}^{-1}\sum_{i=1}^{N} w^{(i)}h(x^{(i)})$$

and use it as an approximation for $E_p[h(x)]$. Note that the variance depends on $\text{Var}_f(p(x^{(i)})/f(x^{(i)}))$, which can be large in some applications. This can affect whether the limiting distribution is a useful approximation. Here, in the case of a random sample of data, the "effective sample size"

$$ESS = \left(\sum_{i=1}^{N} w^{(i)}\right)^2 \Big/ \sum_{i=1}^{N} (w^{(i)2}) \in [0, N]$$

can provide a useful idea about whether the estimate is reasonably accurate. For time series data, similar measures have been proposed based on the long-run variance.

We can specify the normalization constant $\tilde{N}$ in multiple ways; for example, we can use N, or $\sum_{i=1}^{N} w(x^i)$. While the use of the former constant induces a bias in the estimator, the latter, which uses the sum of all the weights as a normalization, yields an unbiased estimator. These estimators have different properties. For a more detailed treatment, see the work of Johansen and Evers (2007).

52.2 Markov Chain Monte Carlo

The Markov Chain Monte Carlo (MCMC) is one of the most popular simulation methods to draw samples from a distribution $p(x)$. As discussed above for the algorithm "Inversion Sampling", the simple Monte Carlo algorithm implies that the output is a random sample with independent values from the distribution $p(x)$. This, in many situations, is not what is needed or it may not be feasible. MCMC circumvents the issue of independent samples by generating specific dependent samples from a Markov chain such that, under some conditions, these samples are distributed according to $p(x)$. Before covering these methods, we need to introduce the concepts of a Markov chain and the convergence and ergodic theorems. Readers familiar with these concepts can skip to Section 52.2.2.

In a general context related to econometric problems, Chernozhukov and Hong (2003) proposed Laplace-type estimators, which include means and quantiles of quasi-posterior distributions defined as transformations of general (non-likelihood-based) statistical criterion functions, such as those in GMM, nonlinear IV, empirical likelihood, and minimum distance methods. The approach generates an alternative to classical extremum estimation and also falls outside the parametric Bayesian approach. These are computed using

MCMC methods, which help circumvent the computational curse of dimensionality.

52.2.1 The basics of a Markov chain

Here, we present a brief introduction of the concepts of Markov Chains and ergodicity. For a more formal treatment, the reader is referred to the work of Feller (1968). The Markov chain is a stochastic process for which the current realization depends on the past only via the previous realization. We adopt the following notation: We use x to indicate a random variable and use the subscript x_k to indicate the kth entry if x is a vector. Whenever we have more than one random variable, we use the superscript x^i for random variable i, $x^{(i)}$ for a realization of x^i, and $\{x^i,\ i \geq 0\}$ or $\{x^i\}$ for a sequence.

Definition 52.1 (Markov Chain). A discrete-time stochastic process $\{x^i,\ i \geq 0\}$, is a Markov chain if it satisfies the Markov property, namely if

$$p(x^i|x^{i-1}, x^{i-2}, \ldots, x^1) = p(x^i|x^{i-1}).$$

In other words, this means that the current realization is conditionally independent of the past given the previous realization. Note that independent observations are a special case of Markov chains, though a degenerate one. We can now define the associated transition probability which describes the evolution from one state to another. For simplicity, we assume the transition probability to be time invariant and we consider only Markov chains with a discrete state space so that the transition probability can be represented as a matrix with entries $p_{t,j} = P(x^i = t|x^{i-1} = j)$ for every t, j in the discrete state space.

Under some technical conditions, there exists a limiting or invariant distribution $g(x)$ associated with the Markov chain such that if we sample from $g(x)$ and we apply the transition probabilities, we obtain a new sample that is also distributed as $g(x)$. The idea is then to specify the transition probabilities in a way such that the associated limiting distribution is our target distribution $p(x)$. It remains to see how we can obtain a sample from $g(x)$. For this purpose, we now state a simple version of the so-called convergence theorem.

Theorem 52.2 (Convergence Theorem). *Given a Markov chain $\{x^i\}$, then under some regularity conditions, the distribution of x^i converges to some limit distribution $g(x)$.*

This theorem suggests that for any initial starting point, as long as we iterate over the transition probabilities an adequate number of times, then x^i is approximately distributed as $g(x)$. This shows why the Markov chain is useful for the purpose of sampling from $g(x)$. Note that to obtain a sample all that is needed is a Markov chain specified in a way such that the limiting distribution is equal to $g(x)$. In many applications, this is much simpler than sampling directly from $g(x)$. Given this result, one can already construct an algorithm, although inefficient, to sample from the target distribution $p(x)$ as follows. Iterate the Markov chain starting from any initial point $x^{(1)}$ until convergence and use the last realization as a draw from $p(x)$. By repeating this process S times, we can obtain a sample from $p(x)$. However, one can immediately realize that if the convergence is slow the algorithm is even slower as we need to repeat the process S times. Every time we discard all the realizations $x^{(1)}, \ldots, x^{(N-1)}$ and retain only $x^{(N)}$. Fortunately, the ergodic theorem, stated below, tells us that under some regularity conditions, we can use the entire sequence $x^{(1)}, \ldots, x^{(N)}$ as a sample form $p(x)$. This means that we just need one iteration of this algorithm.

Theorem 52.3 (Ergodic Theorem). *Given a Markov chain $\{x^i\}$ with $g(x)$ as a limiting distribution, then under some regularity conditions, for any function $h(x)$, the empirical average converges in probability to the expected value as $S \to \infty$, i.e.,*

$$S^{-1} \sum_{t=1}^{S} h(x^i) \xrightarrow{p} E_g[h(x)].$$

In practice, since this holds only in the limit, it is recommended to discard the first observations from the sequence as they usually are bad approximations and it is likely that they lay on the extremes of the distribution $g(x)$.

52.2.2 MCMC

We start by giving a general formulation of an MCMC algorithm. Suppose we are interested in computing the expectation $E_p[h(x)]$, where x has distribution $p(x)$.

Algorithm 52.6 (MCMC). Choose the sample size parameter N to be sufficiently large and how many initial observations b to exclude. Given a starting value $x^{(0)}$, and a Markov chain $\{x^i\}$ with $p(x)$ as the associated limiting distribution, the MCMC algorithm consists of two steps:

1. **Simulation Step:** Simulate the Markov chain $N + b$ times starting with $x^{(1-b)} = x^{(0)}$. Store the last N resulting realizations $(x^{(1)}, \ldots, x^{(N)})$ for the next step (the first b are discarded as they are simply used to initialize the process).
2. **Approximation Step:** Compute $\hat{\mu} = N^{-1} \sum_{i=1}^{N} h(x^{(i)})$ and use it as an approximation for $E_p[h(x)]$.

We can immediately note the main difference between the simple Monte Carlo and the MCMC algorithms. The former samples directly from the distribution of interest, while the latter simulates a Markov chain. As before, since the main difference between the MCMC algorithms is in the simulation step, we will report only the simulation step whenever the approximation does change. Moreover, to make the exposition simpler, in what follows, we present the algorithms by setting $b = 0$ but in practice one should set b to an adequately large value. We now cover two popular MCMC algorithms which are the Gibbs sampler and the Metropolis–Hastings algorithms.

52.2.3 Gibbs sampler

Within the class of MCMC algorithms, the Gibbs sampler is arguably one of the most popular. It is named after the physicist Josiah Willard Gibbs, who died in 1903, but the algorithm was described by Geman and Geman (1984). For a useful introduction, see the work of Casella and George (1992). This algorithm can be seen as an extension of the composition method described in Section 52.1.2 to the MCMC setting.

Algorithm 52.7 (Gibbs Sampler). Consider a distribution $p(x)$, where x is a K dimensional vector $x = (x_1, \ldots, x_K)$. Given a vector of initial values $x^{(0)} = (x_1^{(0)}, \ldots, x_K^{(0)})$, repeat for $i = 0, \ldots, N-1$:

1. Sample $x_1^{(i+1)}$ from $p(x_1|x_2^{(i)}, \ldots, x_K^{(i)})$, i.e.,
   $p(x_1|x_2 = x_2^{(i)}, \ldots, x_K = x_K^{(i)})$;
2. Sample $x_2^{(i+1)}$ from $p(x_2|x_1^{(i+1)}, x_3^{(i)}, \ldots, x_K^{(i)})$;
   ...
3. Sample $x_t^{(i+1)}$ ... from $p(x_t|x_1^{(i+1)}, \ldots, x_{t-1}^{(i+1)}, x_{t+1}^{(i+1)}, \ldots, x_K^{(i+1)})$;
   ...
4. Sample $x_K^{(i+1)}$ from $p(x_K|x_1^{(i+1)}, x_2^{(i)}, \ldots, x_{K-1}^{(i)})$;
5. Assign $x^{(i+1)} = (x_1^{(i+1)}, \ldots, x_K^{(i+1)})$.

Then, the resulting sequence of realizations $(x^{(1)}, \ldots, x^{(N)})$ is the output of the simulation step.

The advantage of the Gibbs sampler is that we do not need to sample directly from $p(x) = p(x_1, x_2, \ldots, x_K)$ but we just need to repeatedly sample from the univariate marginal $p(x_j|x_1, \ldots, x_{j-1}, x_{j+1}, \ldots, x_K)$ which simplifies the calculations in many applications. Also, it has a geometric rate of convergence, which is very fast; see the work of Roberts and Polson (1994). The following is an example from the finance literature.

Example 52.4 (Geometric Brownian Motion). Assume a stock price S_t follows the following stochastic differential equation:

$$d \log S(t) = \mu dt + \sigma dW(t),$$

where μ and σ are the parameters of interest and W_t is a standard Brownian motion. The discrete-time version is given by

$$y_t := \log(S_t/S_{t-1}) = \mu + \sigma \epsilon_t, \quad \epsilon_t \sim \mathcal{N}(0, 1).$$

We specify the following independent priors for the parameters: a normal prior for μ and an inverse Gamma for σ^2. Given a sample

$y_1, \ldots, y_T$, we have

$$\begin{aligned}\mu &\sim \mathcal{N}(\mu_0, \sigma_0^2),\\ \sigma^2 &\sim \mathcal{IG}(\alpha, \beta),\\ y_1, \ldots, y_T|\mu, \sigma^2 &\sim \mathcal{N}(\mu, \sigma^2).\end{aligned}$$

The posterior distribution is

$$p(\mu, \sigma^2|y_1, \ldots, y_T) \propto p(y_1, \ldots, y_T|\mu, \sigma^2) \times p(\mu)p(\sigma^2).$$

Sampling directly from the posterior distribution is hard; however, using the Gibbs sampler we can still draw realizations from the posterior by sampling from the conditional distributions. These conditional distributions have a known form because they are the conjugate of the normal model for the mean and the variance once we treat them separately

$$\mu|y_1, \ldots, y_T, \sigma^2 \sim \mathcal{N} \quad \text{and} \quad \sigma^2|y_1, \ldots, y_T, \mu \sim \mathcal{IG}.$$

Given an initial value $\sigma^{2,(0)}$, the Gibbs sampler algorithm is the following. Repeat for $i = 1, \ldots, N$:

1. Sample $\mu^{(i)}$ from $p(\mu|\sigma^{2,(i-1)}, y_1, \ldots, y_T)$;
2. Sample $\sigma^{2,(i)}$ from $p(\sigma^2|\mu^{(i)}, y_1, \ldots, y_T)$.

Then, the resulting sequence of realizations $((\mu^{(1)}, \sigma^{2,(1)}), \ldots, (\mu^{(N)}, \sigma^{2,(N)}))$ is the output of the simulation step.

The Gibbs sampler can be applied to more complex models as the following example shows.

Example 52.5 (Normal Multivariate Model). Given a sample $y_1, \ldots, y_T$, a vector with means $\mu^{(0)} = (\mu_1^{(0)}, \ldots, \mu_K^{(0)})$, and variance–covariance matrix $\Sigma^{(0)}$, the normal multivariate model with normal and inverse Wishart ($\mathcal{IW}$) priors is the following:

$$\begin{aligned}\mu &\sim \mathcal{N}(\mu_0, \Sigma_0),\\ \Sigma &\sim \mathcal{IW}(\alpha, \beta),\\ y_1, \ldots, y_T|\mu, \Sigma &\sim \mathcal{N}(\mu, \Sigma).\end{aligned}$$

The Gibbs sampler for this model is, starting from some initial value $\Sigma^{(0)}$, and for $i = 1, \ldots, N$, as follows:

1. Sample $\mu^{(i)}$ from $p(\mu|\Sigma^{(i-1)}, y_1, \ldots, y_T)$ using the fact that

$$\mu|\Sigma, y_1, \ldots, y_T \sim \mathcal{N}((\Sigma_0^{-1} + T\Sigma^{-1})^{-1}(\Sigma_0^{-1}\mu_0 + T\Sigma^{-1}\bar{y}), (\Sigma_0^{-1} + T\Sigma^{-1})^{-1}); \tag{52.2}$$

2. Sample $\Sigma^{(i)}$ from $p(\Sigma|\mu^{(i)}, y_1, \ldots, y_T)$ using the fact that

$$\Sigma|\mu, y_1, \ldots, y_T \sim \mathcal{IW}(\alpha + T, \beta + S_\mu). \tag{52.3}$$

where S_μ is the residuals sum of squares matrix for $(y_1, \ldots, y_T)$ with population mean μ. Then, the resulting sequence of realizations $((\mu^{(1)}, \Sigma^{(1)}), \ldots, (\mu^{(N)}, \Sigma^{(N)}))$ is the output of the simulation step.

See Exercise 52.4 for the derivations of (52.2) and (52.3). For a more extensive Bayesian treatment, the reader is referred to the works of Bolstad (2009) and Robert and Casella (2013).

52.2.4 Metropolis–Hastings method

The Metropolis–Hastings algorithm is a version of the Markov chain Monte Carlo (MCMC) method to obtain a sequence of random samples from a probability distribution $p(x)$ for which direct sampling is difficult. In some sense, it includes the idea of the rejection and importance sampling covered before in the MCMC framework. If we are not able to obtain a Markov chain that is $p(x)$-invariant, we can still, under some conditions, sample from this Markov chain and reweight/reject the observations to obtain a sample from the $p(x)$ distribution. The starting point of this method is the work by Metropolis *et al.* (1953), which was generalized in its modern form by Hastings (1970). Again, see the work of Robert and Casella (2013) for a comprehensive treatment and also the work of Chib and Greenberg (1995).

Algorithm 52.8 (Metropolis–Hastings). Consider the Markov chain $\{x^i\}$ and the associated invariant distribution $p(x)$. Assume that the transition probabilities are $P(x^i|x^{i-1})$ and $P(x^{(i-1)}|\tilde{x}^{(i)})$ and we start from some initial value $x^{(0)}$. The algorithm is the following. Repeat for $i = 1, \dots, N$:

1. Sample $\tilde{x}^{(i)}$ from $P(x^i|x^{(i-1)})$;
2. Calculate the ratio

$$r = \frac{p(\tilde{x}^{(i)})P(x^{(i-1)}|\tilde{x}^{(i)})}{p(x^{(i-1)})P(\tilde{x}^{(i)}|x^{(i-1)})} = \frac{p(\tilde{x}^{(i)})/P(\tilde{x}^{(i)}|x^{(i-1)})}{p(x^{(i-1)})/P(x^{(i-1)}|\tilde{x}^{(i)})};$$

- if $r \geq 1$ set $x^{(i)} = \tilde{x}^{(i)}$;
- if $r < 1$ set

$$x^{(i)} = \begin{cases} \tilde{x}^{(i)}, & \text{with probability } r, \\ x^{(i-1)}, & \text{with probability } 1 - r. \end{cases}$$

The algorithm initiates by sampling a candidate value from the proposal distribution. Similar to the previously discussed rejection and reweighting sample algorithms, the objective is to either accept or reweight the observation in a way that the resulting sequence mimics being drawn from $p(x)$. This is achieved by calculating the ratio r, which indicates the likelihood of the new sample compared to the previous one. If the new sample is more probable, it is accepted outright; otherwise, it is accepted with a probability of r. In essence, the algorithm usually moves the transitions to states with a higher likelihood under $p(x)$, but in certain instances, it may shift to states with lower probabilities of occurring. This guarantees that the entire state space is being visited by the algorithm but it concentrates more on high-density regions.

In practical applications, the effectiveness of the MH algorithm heavily depends on the choice of the proposal distribution as the algorithm produces a correlated sample. It is then essential to specify the proposal distribution in a manner that minimizes this correlation. Opting for an overly broad proposal distribution may result in low correlation, as consecutive samples are likely to be widely spaced in the parameter space. However, a drawback of this approach is that the acceptance probability becomes low. Conversely, a highly concentrated proposal distribution leads to highly correlated samples. Finding the optimal trade-off is a delicate task. It is then useful to monitor the autocorrelation and the acceptance rate.

A large number of variations on the Metropolis–Hastings algorithms have been proposed. One common choice is the independence

Metropolis–Hastings sampler in which $P(x^i|x^{i-1})$ does not depend on x. Then,

$$r = \frac{p(\tilde{x}^{(i)})P(x^{(i-1)})}{p(x^{(i-1)})P(\tilde{x}^{(i)})} = \frac{p(\tilde{x}^{(i)})/P(\tilde{x}^{(i)})}{p(x^{(i-1)})/P(x^{(i-1)})}.$$

When the number of parameters is large, a useful variant is the Metropolis-adjusted Langevin Algorithm originally proposed by Besag (1994) and further analyzed by Roberts and Tweedie (1996) and Roberts and Rosenthal (1998). The latter is, however, not commonly used in economics. A variant that has received considerable attention and is widely used is the random walk Metropolis–Hastings sampler in which $\tilde{x}^{(i)} = x^{(i-1)} + \varepsilon_i$, where ε_i is a random perturbation of the current state of the chain. It was first applied in the work of Metropolis *et al.* (1953). Its appeal lies in the fact that it implies symmetric transition probabilities provided the distribution of ε_i, say $g(\varepsilon_i)$, is symmetric since $P(\tilde{x}^{(i)}|x^{(i-1)}) = g(\varepsilon_i)$ and $P(x^{(i-1)}|\tilde{x}^{(i)}) = g(-\varepsilon_i)$. The details are as follows:

Algorithm 52.9 (Random-Walk Metropolis). Consider the Markov chain $\{x^i\}$ and the associated invariant distribution $p(x)$. Assume that we start from some initial value $x^{(0)}$. A good choice to speed up convergence is to choose the value x that maximizes $p(x)$. The algorithm is the following. Repeat for $i = 1, \ldots, N$:

1. Set $x^{(i)} = x^{(i-1)} + \varepsilon_i$, where ε_i is a random perturbation of the current state of the chain, which is symmetrically distributed around 0. It can be normally distributed or have some finite support.
2. Compute $\alpha = \min\{p(x^{(i)})/p(x^{(i-1)}), 1\}$.
3. Simulate μ from a $U[0,1]$ distribution.
4. If $\mu < \alpha$, accept the change and set $x^{(i)} = x^{(i-1)} + \varepsilon_i$; otherwise, make no change and set $x^{(i)} = x^{(i-1)}$.

This algorithm works well unless the variance of ε_i is very small or very large, in which case the sample is highly correlated. A further variant that calibrates the choice of the variance is the so-called adaptive Metropolis–Hastings method; see, e.g., the work of Haario *et al.* (2001).

52.3 EM algorithms

In this section, we describe the EM (Expectation Maximization) and the MCEM (Monte Carlo Expectation Maximization) algorithms. They are used to find the maximum likelihood estimator of the parameters of a function when there are missing values in the data. They both consist in two steps. Given an initial guess of the maximizer, the expectation step integrates the complete data log-likelihood function with respect to the missing data. Then, the maximization step maximizes the resulting function to obtain a revised guess for the maximizer. When the integral in the expectation step is intractable, one can rely on the MCEM algorithm which uses Monte Carlo integration to compute the expectation.

Suppose the complete dataset is $Z = (Y, X)$, in which Y is observed but X is unobserved, and Θ is the parameter vector. For the joint density

$$p(z|\Theta) = p(y, x|\Theta) = p(y|\Theta)p(x|y, \Theta),$$

we define the complete-data likelihood function by $L(\Theta|Y, X) = p(Y, X|\Theta)$. The original likelihood $L(\Theta|Y)$ is the incomplete-data likelihood. Since X is unobserved and may be generated from an underlying distribution, e.g., the transition equation in a state space model, $L(\Theta|Y, X)$ is indeed a random variable.

52.3.1 EM algorithm

The EM algorithm was initially proposed by Dempster *et al.* (1977) and consists of the following two steps. Given an initial input value for the parameters $\Theta^{(0)}$, repeat the following iterative computation until $\Theta^{(k)}$ converges:

- E-step: Compute the expectation of $\log L(\Theta|Y, X)$ with respect to X, conditional on Y and $\Theta^{(k-1)}$, defined by

$$\begin{aligned} Q(\Theta, \Theta^{(k-1)}) &= E[\log L(\Theta|Y, X)|Y, \Theta^{(k-1)}] \\ &= \int \log[p(Y, x|\Theta)p(x|Y, \Theta^{(k-1)})]dx. \end{aligned}$$

- M-step: Maximise the expectation

$$\Theta^{(k)} = \arg\max_{\Theta} Q(\Theta, \Theta^{(k-1)}).$$

The rate of convergence has been studied by many researchers; e.g., Dempster *et al.* (1977), Wu (1983), and Xu and Jordan (1996).

52.3.2 MCEM algorithm

The MCEM algorithm was initially proposed by Olsson *et al.* (2008) and Wei and Tanner (1990) and has been developed to overcome situations when the integral in the expectation step is intractable. The difference between the MCEM and the basic EM algorithms is that when evaluating $Q(\Theta, \Theta^{(k-1)})$, the MCEM uses a Monte Carlo-based sample average to approximate the expectation. The expectation step then becomes as follows:

- E-step: Compute the expectation of $\log L(\Theta|Y, X)$ with respect to X, conditional on Y and $\Theta^{(k-1)}$, approximated by

$$Q^*(\Theta, \Theta^{(k-1)}) = M^{-1} \sum_{i=1}^{M} \log(p(Y, x^{(i)}|\Theta)),$$

where $\{x^{(i)}\}_{i=1}^{M}$ are random samples from $p(x|Y, \Theta^{(k-1)})$.

52.4 Applications in econometrics

In this section, we discuss an application of the MCMC algorithms in a particular econometrics setting. To understand the challenges that the MCMC algorithms can help solve, we start with a concrete example of a random level shift model in Subsection 52.4.1. This example provides the steps needed for the following topics: (a) extensions of the Kalman filter to non-Gaussian distributions, (b) the particle filter to obtain samples from some joint density, (c) the Monte Carlo Expectation Maximization (MCEM) method to evaluate the likelihood function in the presence of some latent variables, and (d) methods to obtain in-sample or out-of-sample (i.e., for forecasts) confidence bands. It is a more complete description of the forecasting method discussed in Section 51.3.4. We present this model for no particular reason other than it is well know to us and involves a wide variety of the tools discussed in this chapter.

52.4.1 Example: Random level shift model

The model adopted follows the treatment in the work of Xu and Perron (2023), which extended the work of McCulloch and Tsay (1993), though the latter used a Bayesian method of estimation. Note that we use the same notation as in their paper. It is a forecasting model specified by

$$y_t = X_t\beta_t + e_t, \tag{52.4}$$

where y_t is a scalar variable to be forecasted, X_t is a k-vector of covariates, and, in the base case, $e_t \sim i.i.d.\ N(0, \sigma_e^2)$. It is assumed that some or all of the parameters are time-varying and exhibit structural changes at some unknown time. The specification adopted for the time-variation in the parameters is the following:

$$\beta_t = \beta_{t-1} + K_t^\beta \eta_t,$$

where

$$K_t^\beta = \text{diag}(K_{1,t}^\beta, \ldots, K_{k,t}^\beta),$$

and

$$\eta_t = (\eta_{1,t}, \ldots, \eta_{k,t})' \sim i.i.d.\ N(0, \Sigma).$$

Of importance is the presence of latent variables such that $K_{j,t}^\beta \sim Ber(p^{(j)})$, which are independent across j, where $\text{Ber}(p^{(j)})$ denotes a Bernoulli random variable that takes value 1 with probability $p^{(j)}$, and 0 with probability $1 - p^{(j)}$. Hence, each parameter evolves according to a Random Level Shift (RLS) process such that the shifts are dictated by the outcomes of the Bernoulli random variables $K_{j,t}^\beta$. When $K_{j,t}^\beta = 1$, a shift $\eta_{j,t}$ occurs drawn from a $N(0, \sigma_{\eta,j}^2)$ distribution, otherwise, when $K_{j,t}^\beta = 0$, the parameter does not change. The shifts can be rare (small values of $p^{(j)}$) or frequent (larger values of $p^{(j)}$).

This specification is ideally suited to model changes in the parameters occurring at unknown dates. Many specifications are possible depending on the assumptions imposed on K_t^β and Σ. First, when $K_{1,t}^\beta = \cdots = K_{k,t}^\beta$, we can interpret the model as one in which all parameters are subject to change at the same times, akin to the pure structural change model of Bai and Perron (1998). A partial structural model can be obtained by setting $p^{(j)} = 0$ for the parameters not allowed to change, or equivalently by setting the corresponding rows and columns of Σ to 0. The case with $K_{1,t}^\beta = \cdots = K_{k,t}^\beta$ is arguably the most interesting for a variety of applications. However, it is also possible not to impose equality for the different $K_{j,t}^\beta$. This allows the timing of the changes in the different parameters to be governed by different independent latent processes. This may be desirable in some cases. For instance, it is reasonable to expect changes in the constant to be related to low-frequency variations of the random level shift type, while changes in the coefficients associated with random regressors to be related to business-cycle-type variations. In such cases, it would therefore be more convenient to allow the timing of the changes to be different for the constant and the other parameters. Of course, many different specifications are possible.

The assumption that the latent Bernoulli processes $K_{j,t}^\beta$ are independent across j imply that for the jth parameter β_j ($j = 1, \ldots, k$), we have

$$\beta_{j,t} = \beta_{j,t-1} + K_{j,t}^\beta \eta_{j,t}, \tag{52.5}$$

where $\eta_{j,t} \sim N(0, \sigma_{\eta,j}^2)$ and $K_{j,t}^\beta \sim \text{Ber}(p^{(j)})$. In some cases, it may also be of interest to allow for changes in the variance of the errors. The specification for the distribution is then $e_t = \sigma_{\epsilon,t}\epsilon_t$ with

$$\ln \sigma_{\epsilon,t}^2 = \phi \ln \sigma_{\epsilon,t-1}^2 + K_t^\sigma v_{\epsilon,t}, \tag{52.6}$$

where $\epsilon_t \sim N(0,1)$, $K_t^\sigma \sim \text{Ber}(p^\sigma)$, and $v_{\epsilon,t} \sim N(0, \sigma_v^2)$. For the sake of simplicity, we do not cover this extension. This is done without loss of generality given our intent to illustrate various procedures.

Two features that are likely to improve the fit and the forecasting performance is to allow for changes in the probability of shifts and explicitly model a mean-reverting mechanism for the level shift component. Xu and Perron (2023) specified the jump probability to be

$$p_t^{(j)} = f(\gamma, w_t),$$

where γ is an m-vector of parameters, w_t are m covariates that allow better predictions of the probability of shifts, and f is a function that ensures $p_t \in [0, 1]$. Note that w_t needs to be in the information set at time t in order for the model to be useful for forecasting. They adopted a linear specification with the standard normal cumulative distribution function $\Phi(\cdot)$ so that $K_{j,t}^{\beta} \sim \text{Ber}(p_t^{(j)})$ with $p_t^{(j)} = \Phi(r_0 + r_1' w_t)$, where r_0 is a scalar and r_1 and m-vector of parameters.

The second step involves adding a mean reverting mechanism to the level shift model. The motivation for doing so is that we often observe evidence that parameters do not jump arbitrarily and that large upward movements tend to be followed by a decrease. This feature can be beneficial to improve the forecasting performance if explicitly modeled. The specification adopted is the following:

$$\eta_{j,t} \sim N(\mu_{\eta,j,t}, \sigma_{\eta,j}^2),$$

$$\mu_{\eta,j,t} = \rho(\beta_{j,t-1} - \beta_j^{(t-1)}),$$

where $\beta_{j,t-1}$ is the filtered estimate of the parameter subject to change at time $t-1$ and $\bar{\beta}_j^{(t-1)}$ is the mean of all the filtered estimates of the jump component from the beginning of the sample up to time $t-1$. This implies a mean-reverting mechanism provided $\rho < 0$. The magnitude of ρ then dictates the speed of reversion. Similar specifications can be made to p^{σ} and $v_{\epsilon,t}$ for the changes in the variance of the errors.

Conditional on K_t^{β}, the system is a linear and Gaussian state space model and $p(\beta_t | K_t^{\beta}, Y; \Theta)$, where $Y = (y_1, \ldots, y_T)$ and Θ is the vector of parameters, can be evaluated by the Kalman filter. The measurement equation is (52.4) and the transition equation is (52.5).

Remark 52.1. When $p^{(j)} = 0$ for all j, the model reduces to the classic regression model with time invariant parameters. When $p^{(j)} = 1$ for all j, it becomes the standard time varying parameter model; e.g., Rosenberg (1973), Chow (1984), Nicholls and Pagan (1985), and Harvey (2006).

At first sight, the model appears to be a standard state-space model for which we can apply the Kalman filter algorithm as discussed in Chapter 39. Actually, the model is much more complex and falls in the category of nonlinear non-Gaussian state space models for which standard Kalman filter-type algorithms cannot be used. The state-space representation is actually a linear dynamic mixture model in the sense that it is linear and Gaussian conditional on some latent random variables. Hence, we need to deal with the following issues:

1. How can we modify the Kalman filter algorithm to handle non-Gaussian distributions? Here, a sequential Monte Carlo method is discussed. It is referred to as the mixture Kalman filter since it uses a random mixture of Gaussian distributions to approximate a target distribution. We discuss the method of Chen and Liu (2000). A useful reference is the work of Chopin and Papaspiliopoulos (2020).
2. The EM (Expectation Maximization) algorithm is used to obtain the maximum likelihood estimates of the parameters. This allows treating the latent state variables as missing data and using a complete or data-augmented likelihood function which is easier to evaluate than the original likelihood. Since the missing information is random, the complete-data likelihood function is a random variable and we end up maximizing the expectation of the complete-data log-likelihood with respect to the missing data; see the works of Bilmes (1998) and also Giordani *et al.* (2007) for a treatment closer to this application.
3. The Monte Carlo EM algorithm, where the evaluation step is executed by Monte Carlo methods, as suggested by Wei and Tanner (1990).
4. Random samples from the conditional distribution of the missing data (state variables) can be obtained via a particle smoothing algorithm. We discuss the method of Godsill *et al.* (2004).

5. The forecasting procedure is then relatively simple and can be carried out in a straightforward fashion once the model has been estimated, but special care must be applied to generate in and out-of-sample confidence bands. For this purpose, we review the method suggested by Perron and Xu (2016).

52.4.2 Mixture Kalman filtering

In this section, we use the conventional notation x_t to denote the state variable, while $\lambda_t \equiv (K_t^{\beta})$ are the latent variables. Let $y^t = (y_1, \ldots, y_t)$, $\Lambda_t = (\lambda_1, \ldots, \lambda_t)$, and let λ^t be realizations of Λ_t. The filtering distribution of x_t can be written as

$$p(x_t|y^t) = \int p(x_t|y^t, \lambda^t)p(\lambda^t|y^t)d\lambda^t,$$

where $p(x_t|y^t, \lambda^t) \sim N\left(\mu_t(\lambda^t), \Sigma_t(\lambda^t)\right)$, for which $\left(\mu_t(\lambda^t), \Sigma_t(\lambda^t)\right)$ can be obtained by running the Kalman filter with a given trajectory λ^t. The main idea of the mixture Kalman filter is to use a weighted sample of the indicators

$$S_t = \{(\lambda^{t,(1)}, w_t^{(1)}), \ldots, (\lambda^{t,(M)}, w_t^{(M)})\}$$

to represent the distribution $p(\lambda^t|y^t)$, where $w_t^{(i)}$ are some weights to be defined below and $\lambda^{t,(i)}$ are simulated latent variables; e.g., in the basic model $\lambda^{t,(i)} \equiv (K_1^{\beta,(i)}, \ldots, K_t^{\beta,(i)})$ so that given a jump probability p, $\lambda^{t,(i)}$ can be generated as random draws from the Bernoulli distribution with probability p. One then uses a random mixture of Gaussian distributions

$$W_t^{-1} \sum_{i=1}^{M} w_t^{(i)} N\left(\mu_t(\lambda^{t,(i)}), \Sigma_t(\lambda^{t,(i)})\right),$$

where $W_t = \sum_{i=1}^{M} w_t^{(i)}$, to represent the target distribution $p(x_t|y^t)$.

Example 52.6. Consider the random level shift model. At $t = 0$, for $i = 1, \ldots, M$, given initial parameters $\Theta_0 = (r_0, r_1, \sigma_e, \sigma_\eta, \rho)$, draw $K_0^{(i)} \sim \text{Ber}(p_0)$, $\beta_0^{(i)}$, $P_0^{(i)} \sim f(\beta_0; \Theta_0)$ and set $w_0^{(i)} = 1/M$. For $t = 1, \ldots, T$ and $i = 1, \ldots, M$:

1. Construct the Kalman predictions:
$$\beta_{t|t-1}^{(i)} = \beta_{t-1|t-1}^{(i)} + K_{t-1}^{(i)} \mu_{\eta,t|t-1}^{(i)},$$
$$P_{t|t-1}^{(i)} = P_{t-1|t-1}^{(i)} + K_{t-1}^{(i)} \sigma_\eta^2,$$
where $\mu_{\eta,t|t-1}^{(i)} = \rho(\beta_{t-1|t-1}^{(i)} - \bar{\beta}^{t-1,(i)})$.
2. Compute an estimate of the forecast of y_t: $E[f(\beta_{t|t-1})] \approx \sum_{i=1}^{M} w_{t-1}^{(i)} f(\beta_{t|t-1}^{(i)})$.
3. Compute the importance weights $w_t^{(i)} \sim N(v_t^{(i)}, F_t^{(i)})$, where
$$v_t^{(i)} = y_t - X_t \beta_{t|t-1}^{(i)},$$
$$F_t^{(i)} = X_t P_{t-1|t-1}^{(i)} X_t' + \sigma_e^2,$$
and set the normalized importance weights as $\hat{w}_t^{(i)} = w_t^{(i)} / \sum_{j=1}^{M} w_t^{(j)}$.
4. Resample M samples $\{\beta_{t-1|t-1}^{(i)}, P_{t-1|t-1}^{(i)}, K_{t-1}^{(i)}\}_{i=1}^{M}$ with probabilities $\{\hat{w}_t^{(i)}\}_{i=1}^{M}$ and, for $i = 1, \ldots, M$, set $w_t^{(i)} = 1/M$.
5. Draw $K_t^{(i)} \sim \text{Ber}(p_t)$ and construct the following steps of the Kalman filter:
$$\beta_{t|t-1}^{(i)} = \beta_{t-1|t-1}^{(i)} + K_t^{(i)} \mu_{\eta,t|t-1}^{(i)},$$
$$P_{t|t-1}^{(i)} = P_{t-1|t-1}^{(i)} + K_t^{(i)} \sigma_\eta^2,$$
$$v_t^{(i)} = y_t - X_t \beta_{t|t-1}^{(i)},$$
$$F_t^{(i)} = X_t P_{t-1|t-1}^{(i)} X_t' + \sigma_e^2,$$
$$\beta_{t|t}^{(i)} = \beta_{t|t-1}^{(i)} + P_{t|t-1}^{(i)} X_t' F_t^{-1,(i)} v_t^{(i)},$$
$$P_{t|t}^{(i)} = P_{t|t-1}^{(i)} - P_{t|t-1}^{(i)} X_t' F_t^{-1,(i)} X_t P_{t|t-1}^{(i)}.$$
6. Compute an estimate of the filtered estimate: $E[f(\beta_t)] \approx \sum_{i=1}^{M} \hat{w}_{t-1}^{(i)} f(\beta_{t|t}^{(i)})$.

52.4.3 Particle smoothing

The particle smoothing algorithm is designed to obtain particle smothers $\{s_t^{(i)}\}_{i=1}^M$ with certain weights $\{w_t^{(i)}\}_{i=1}^M$ from $p(x_t|y^T)$. Godsill *et al.* (2004) provided a forward-filtering and backward-simulation smoothing procedure. It allows drawing random samples from the joint density $p(x_0, x_1, \ldots x_T|y^T)$, not only the individual marginal smoothing densities $p(x_t|y^T)$. The smoothing algorithm relies on a pre-filtering procedure and a previously obtained set of filters $\{w_t^{(i)}, x_t^{(i)}\}_{i=1}^M$ for each time period. The main ingredients behind the smoothing algorithm are the relations

$$p(x_1, \ldots, x_T|y^T) = p(x_T|y^T) \prod_{t=1}^{T-1} p(x_t|x_{t+1}, \ldots, x_T, y^T)$$

and

$$\begin{aligned} p(x_t|x_{t+1}, \ldots, x_T, y^T) &= p(x_t|x_{t+1}, y^t) \\ &= \frac{p(x_t|y^t)p(x_{t+1}|x_t)}{p(x_{t+1}|y^t)} \propto p(x_t|y^t)p(x_{t+1}|x_t). \end{aligned}$$

The first equality follows from the Markov property of the model and the second from Bayes' rule. Since random samples $\{x_t^{(i)}\}_{i=1}^M$ from $p(x_t|y^t)$ can be obtained from the mixture Kalman filtering algorithm, $p(x_t|x_{t+1}, \ldots, x_T, y^T)$ can be approximated as $\sum_{i=1}^M w_{t|t+1}^{(i)} \delta_{x_t^{(i)}}(x_t)$ with modified weights

$$w_{t|t+1}^{(i)} = \frac{w_t^{(i)} p(x_{t+1}|x_t^{(i)})}{\sum_{i=1}^M w_t^{(i)} p(x_{t+1}|x_t^{(i)})},$$

where $\delta_{x_t^{(i)}}(x_t)$ is the Dirac delta function. This procedure is performed in a reverse-time direction conditioning on future states. Given a random sample $\{s_{t+1}, \ldots, s_T\}$ drawn from $p(x_{t+1}, \ldots, x_T|y^T)$, we then take one step back and sample s_t from

$$p(x_t|s_{t+1}, \ldots, s_T, y^T).$$

Example 52.7. Particle smoothing algorithm for the random level shift model. Consider the weighted samplers obtained from the filtering algorithm $\{w_t^{(i)}, \beta_t^{(i)}, K_t^{\beta(i)}\}_{i=1}^M$ for $i = 1, \ldots, M$, and $t = 1, \ldots, T$. Let $\{s_{\beta,t}^{(j)}, s_{K_1,t}^{(j)}\}_{j=1}^M$ be a set of particle smoothers. First, set $s_{\beta,T}^{(j)} = \beta_T^{(i)}$ and $s_{K_1,T}^{(j)} = K_T^{\beta(i)}$ with probability $(1/M)$. Then, for $t = T-1, T-2, \ldots, 1$, compute

$$w_{t|t+1}^{(i)} \propto w_t^{(i)} p(s_{\beta,t+1}^{(j)}|\beta_t^{(i)})$$

$$\propto \{p_{t+1} \exp(-\frac{(s_{\beta,t+1}^{(j)} - \beta_t^{(i)} - \mu_\eta)^2}{2\sigma_\eta^2})\}^{s_{K_1,t+1}^{(j)}} \{1 - p_{t+1}\}^{1 - s_{K_1,t+1}^{(j)}},$$

for $i = 1, \ldots, M$, and let $s_{\beta,t}^{(j)} = \beta_t^{(i)}$ and $s_{K_1,t}^{(j)} = K_t^{\beta(i)}$ with probability $w_{t|t+1}^{(i)}$. Repeat the steps above decreasing from $t-1$ until 1 to obtain $\{s_{\beta,t}^{(j)}, s_{K_t^\beta,t+1}^{(j)}\}$ as approximations to $p(\beta_t, K_t^\beta|y^T)$, for $j = 1, \ldots, M$.

52.4.4 MCEM algorithm

Frequentist likelihood-based parameter estimation of conditionally linear and Gaussian state-space models using the mixture Kalman filters and smoothers is not straightforward. The gradient-based optimizer suffers from a discontinuity problem caused by the resampling. This problem occurs in a variety of contexts. A common approach is to use the Monte Carlo Expectation Maximization (MCEM) method discussed in Section 52.3.1. Recall that one needs $\{x^{(i)}\}_{i=1}^M$ as random samples from $p(x|Y, \Theta^{(k-1)})$. Given current parameter estimates, these are simply the particle smoothers $\{s_t^{(i)}\}_{i=1}^M$ obtained as described above.

Example 52.8. For the random level shift model, the steps needed are as follows: For the E-step, the complete likelihood of $\{\beta_1, \ldots, \beta_T, K_1^\beta, \ldots, K_T^\beta, y_1, \ldots, y_T\}$ is

$$f(\beta, K_1, Y) = \prod_{t=1}^T f(\beta_t|\beta_{t-1}, K_t^\beta) \prod_{t=1}^T f(K_t^\beta) \prod_{t=1}^T f(y_t|\beta_t, K_t^\beta)$$

$$= \left\{ \prod_{t=1}^T (2\pi\sigma_\eta^2)^{-1/2} \exp(-(\beta_t - \beta_{t-1} - \mu_{\eta t})^2/(2\sigma_\eta^2)) \right\}^{K_t^\beta}$$

$$\times \prod_{t=1}^{T} p_t^{K_t^\beta} (1-p_t)^{1-K_t^\beta} \prod_{t=1}^{T} (2\pi\sigma_e^2)^{-1/2}$$
$$\times \exp(-(y_t - X_t\beta_t)^2/(2\sigma_e^2)).$$

The log-likelihood function is

$$\begin{aligned}-2\log f(\beta, K^\beta, Y) = &\sum_{t=1}^{T} K_t^\beta [\log(\sigma_\eta^2) + (\beta_t - \beta_{t-1} - \mu_{\eta t})^2/\sigma_\eta^2] \\ &- 2\sum_{t=1}^{T} [K_t^\beta \log(p_t) + (1-K_t^\beta)\log(1-p_t)] \\ &+ \sum_{t=1}^{T} [\log(\sigma_e^2) + (y_t - X_t\beta_t)^2/\sigma_e^2].\end{aligned}$$

The expectation of the complete log-likelihood function with respect to the unknown state variables β, K^β given Y and the current parameter estimates $\Theta^{(k-1)}$ is the objective function to be maximized. For the Monte Carlo EM algorithm, the expectation is approximated by Monte Carlo sample averages with random samples drawn from $p(\beta_t, K_t^\beta | y^T)$ obtained using the particle smoothing algorithm. Then,

$$\begin{aligned}Q(\Theta, \Theta^{(k-1)}) &= E[-2\log f(\beta, K^\beta, Y)|Y, \Theta^{(k-1)}] \\ &= M^{-1} \sum_{i=1}^{M} \{ \sum_{t=1}^{T} K_t^{\beta(i)} [\log(\sigma_\eta^2) + (\beta_t^{(i)} - \beta_{t-1}^{(i)} - \mu_{\eta t})^2/\sigma_\eta^2] \\ &\quad - 2\sum_{t=1}^{T} [K_t^{\beta(i)} \log(p_t) + (1-K_t^{\beta(i)})\log(1-p_t)] \\ &\quad + \sum_{t=1}^{T} [\log(\sigma_e^2) + (y_t - X_t\beta_t^{(i)})^2/\sigma_e^2] \}.\end{aligned}$$

For the M-step, the objective function becomes the usual log-likelihood function of Θ. Hence, standard maximum likelihood estimates are obtained by solving the first order conditions.

Overall, the estimation procedure is summarized in the following steps: Let $\Theta^{(0)}$ be a vector of initial parameter values.

1. (Mixture Kalman filtering): Obtain mixture Kalman filters $\{x_t^{(i)}\}_{i=1}^M$ from
$$p(x_t|y^t, \Theta^{(k-1)}), \quad i = 1, \dots, M, \ \ t = 1, \dots, T.$$
2. (Particle smoothing): Obtain particle smoothers $\{s_t^{(i)}\}_{i=1}^M$ from $p(x_t|y^T, \Theta^{(k-1)})$, $i = 1, \dots, M$, $t = 1, \dots, T$.
3. (Estimation): Evaluate $Q(\Theta, \Theta^{(k-1)})$ using $\{s_t^{(i)}\}_{i=1}^M$ from the previous step and maximize it to obtain updated parameter estimates $\Theta^{(k)}$.
4. Repeat steps 1–3 with k updated to $k + 1$ until the parameter estimates converge.

In order to reduce the number of iterations of the estimation algorithm, we can use information from the data to provide better initial parameter values. Consider the simple model

$$\begin{aligned} y_t &= \beta_t + e_t, \\ \beta_t &= \beta_{t-1} + K_t^\beta \eta_t, \end{aligned}$$

where $\eta_t \sim N(0, \sigma_\eta^2)$, $e_t \sim N(0, \sigma_e^2)$, and $K_t^\beta \sim \text{Ber}(p)$. The initial parameter values are set to $p^{(0)}$, according to prior judgment about the frequency of the jumps. Then,

$$\begin{aligned} \sigma_\eta^{2(0)} &= |\text{Var}(y_t - y_{t-2}) - \text{Var}(y_t - y_{t-1})|, \\ \sigma_e^{2(0)} &= (\text{Var}(y_t - y_{t-1}) - p^{(0)}\sigma_\eta^{2(0)})/2. \end{aligned}$$

To construct the standard errors of the estimates, Louis (1982) provided a way of obtaining the information matrix when using the EM algorithm. It is given by

$$\begin{aligned} I = \sum_{t=1}^{T} E[B(\chi_t, \hat{\Theta})|\chi_t] &- \sum_{t=1}^{T} E[S(\chi_t, \hat{\Theta})S^T(\chi_t, \hat{\Theta})|\chi] \\ &- 2\sum_{t<k}^{T} E[S(\chi_t, \hat{\Theta})|\chi]E[S(\chi_k, \hat{\Theta})|\chi]', \end{aligned}$$

where $S(\chi_t, \hat{\Theta})$ and $B(\chi_t, \hat{\Theta})$ are the first and second-order derivatives, respectively, and χ refers to the complete dataset including observed data and unobserved state variables. Since simulations are used in the EM algorithm, this may cause discontinuities, in which case this method is unstable and cannot always provide a positive definite covariance matrix. Duan and Fulop (2011) proposed a stable estimator of the information matrix applicable to the EM algorithm. They estimate the variance using the smoothed individual scores. Define $a_t(\Theta) = E[\partial \log f(x_t|\chi_{t-1}, \Theta)/\partial\Theta|Y, \Theta]$, then the estimate of the information matrix is

$$\hat{I} = \Omega_0 + \sum_{j=1}^{l} w(l)(\Omega_j + \Omega_j'),$$

where $\Omega_j = \sum_{t-1}^{T-j} a_t(\hat{\Theta})a_{t+j}(\hat{\Theta})'$ and $w(j) = 1 - j/(l+1)$. This method is easy to compute and does not require evaluations of the second-order derivatives of the complete data log-likelihood.

52.4.5 Confidence bands

The material in this section is mostly from the work of Perron and Xu (2016). Cox (1981) classified time-varying parameter models into two categories: observation-driven and parameter-driven models. In observation-driven models, the parameter updating equation is a deterministic function that includes past parameters and observations. The parameters are perfectly predictable one-step-ahead given past information and the likelihood function is available in closed-form. See the work of Blasques *et al.* (2016) for a method to construct in and out-of-sample confidence bands in this case. On the other hand, in parameter-driven models, the parameters evolve as a stochastic process with idiosyncratic innovations. A closed-form expression of the likelihood function is usually not available for this type of model. The parameters are estimated via more involved simulation-based filtering algorithms. The example in this section falls into this category.

The updating equation (process) for the time-varying parameters in parameter-driven models can be written as

$$f_{t+1} = h(f_t, \eta_t; \psi),$$

where $\eta_t \sim g_\eta(\psi)$ is the idiosyncratic innovation and ψ is the static parameter. The time-varying parameter f_t follows a recurrence process with its own innovations. Therefore, the in-sample confidence band needs to incorporate both parameter uncertainty and innovation uncertainty. The parameter estimate $\hat{\psi}$ is constructed via Monte Carlo maximum likelihood estimation. Let the estimate of the asymptotic covariance matrix of $\hat{\psi}$ be defined by

$$\hat{\Sigma} = -\{\partial^2 \log \hat{L}(\hat{\psi})/\partial\psi\partial\psi'\}^{-1},$$

where $\hat{L}(\hat{\psi})$ is the Monte Carlo estimate of the likelihood function evaluated at $\hat{\psi}$. The estimate $\hat{\Sigma}$ can be computed numerically. The estimate $\hat{\psi}$ is subject to simulation errors, while $\hat{\Sigma}$ is a measure of the uncertainty that does not account for such simulation errors. However, as shown in the work of Durbin and Koopman (1997), the effect of the latter is quite small and can safely be ignored. Once an estimate of the asymptotic distribution of $\hat{\psi}$ is obtained, the in-sample confidence band for $\hat{f}_{t+1}$ can be constructed using simulation methods. The procedure can be described as follows:

1. Draw M parameter values $\hat{\psi}^i$ from the asymptotic distribution

$$\hat{\psi}^i \sim N(\hat{\psi}, T^{-1}\hat{\Sigma}).$$

   Note that if the limit distribution is not normal, one can simply use the one that applies.
2. Given $\hat{\psi}^i$ and for each time t, draw S sequences $\eta_t^1, \ldots, \eta_t^S$ from the estimated density $\eta_t^s \sim g_\eta(\hat{\psi}^i)$ for $s = 1, \ldots, S$ and $t = 1, \ldots, T$.
3. Given the observations $(\eta_t^1, \ldots, \eta_t^S)$, the filtered sequence $(\hat{f}_1^s, \ldots, \hat{f}_T^s)$ can be determined using the updating function

$$\hat{f}_{t+1}^s = h(\hat{f}_t^s, \eta_t^s; \hat{\psi}^i).$$

4. Repeat steps 2–3 for $i = 1, \ldots, M$ to obtain $M \times S$ filtered paths of $\hat{f}_t^{i,s}$.

5. Calculate the appropriate percentiles for each t over the $M \times S$ draws of $\hat{f}_t^{i,s}$ to obtain the in-sample confidence band of $\hat{f}_t$.

The procedure to construct the out-of-sample forecast band for $\hat{f}_{T+n}$ is actually the same as described above. We simply need to obtain $M \times S$ extrapolated paths of $\hat{f}_{T+n}^{i,s}$ to compute the percentiles.

52.5 Exercises

Exercise 52.1. Write the rejection sampling algorithm for the case described in Example 52.2 when trying to sample from $\mathbb{B}(a, b)$, a Beta distribution with parameters a and b.

Exercise 52.2. Write the rejection sampling algorithm for sampling from a standard normal distribution given a Cauchy proposal distribution. What is the lowest value of M that can be set? Is it possible to do otherwise?

Exercise 52.3. Write the likelihood function $p(Y_1, \ldots, Y_T|\mu, \sigma^2)$ and the conditional posteriors $p(\mu|y_1, \ldots, y_T, \sigma^2)$ and $p(\sigma^2|y_1, \ldots, y_T, \mu)$ corresponding to Example 52.4.

Exercise 52.4. Given a sample $y_1, \ldots, y_T$, a vector with means $\mu^{(0)} = (\mu_1^{(0)}, \ldots, \mu_K^{(0)})$ and a covariance matrix $\Sigma^{(0)}$, the normal multivariate model with normal and inverse Wishart ($\mathcal{IW}$) priors is the following:

$$\begin{aligned} \mu &\sim \mathcal{N}(\mu_0, \Sigma_0), \\ \Sigma &\sim \mathcal{IW}(\alpha, \beta), \\ Y_1, \ldots, Y_T|\mu, \Sigma &\sim \mathcal{N}(\mu, \Sigma). \end{aligned}$$

What are $p(\mu|\Sigma, y_1, \ldots, y_T)$ and $p(\Sigma|\mu, y_1, \ldots, y_T)$?

References

Abadir, K. M. (1993). "The limiting distribution of the autocorrelation coefficient under a unit root." *The Annals of Statistics*, 21, 1058–1070.

Acemoglu, D., Johnson, S., and Robinson, J. A. (2005). "Institutions as a fundamental cause of long-run growth." *Handbook of Economic Growth, Vol. 1*, P. Aghion and S. N. Durlauf, eds., Vol. 1, Elsevier, 385–472.

Ahn, D.-H., Dittmar, R. F., and Gallant, A. R. (2002). "Quadratic term structure models: Theory and evidence." *Review of Financial Studies*, 15, 243–288.

Ahn, S. C. and Horenstein, A. R. (2013). "Eigenvalue ratio test for the number of factors." *Econometrica*, 81, 1203–1227.

Ahn, S. C. and Schmidt, P. (1995). "Efficient estimation of models for dynamic panel data." *Journal of Econometrics*, 68, 5–27.

Ahn, S. K. and Reinsel, G. C. (1990). "Estimation for partially nonstationary multivariate autoregressive models." *Journal of the American Statistical Association*, 85, 813–823.

Aiolfi, M. and Timmermann, A. (2006). "Persistence in forecasting performance and conditional combination strategies." *Journal of Econometrics*, 135, 31–53.

Akaike, H. (1974). "A new look at the statistical model identification." *IEEE Transactions on Automatic Control*, 19, 716–723.

Amengual, D. and Watson, M. W. (2007). "Consistent estimation of the number of dynamic factors in a large N and T panel." *Journal of Business & Economic Statistics*, 25, 91–96.

Amisano, G. and Giannini, C. (1997). *Topics in Structural VAR Econometrics*. Springer, New York, NY.

Amsler, C. and Lee, J. (1995). "An LM test for a unit root in the presence of a structural change." *Econometric Theory*, 11, 359–368.

An, S. and Schorfheide, F. (2007). "Bayesian analysis of DSGE models." *Econometric Reviews*, 26, 113–172.

Andersen, T. G. and Varneskov, R. T. (2021). "Consistent inference for predictive regressions in persistent economic systems." *Journal of Econometrics*, 224, 215–244.

Anderson, T. W. (1958). *An Introduction to Multivariate Statistical Analysis*. Wiley, New York, NY.

Anderson, T. W. (1971). *The Statistical Analysis of Time Series*. Wiley, New York, NY.

Anderson, T. W. and Darling, D. A. (1952). "Asymptotic theory of certain "goodness of fit" criteria based on stochastic processes." *The Annals of Mathematical Statistics*, 23, 193–212.

Anderson, T. W. and Hsiao, C. (1982). "Formulation and estimation of dynamic models using panel data." *Journal of Econometrics*, 18, 47–82.

Ando, T. and Bai, J. (2015). "Asset pricing with a general multifactor structure." *Journal of Financial Econometrics*, 13, 556–604.

Ando, T. and Bai, J. (2016). "Panel data models with grouped factor structure under unknown group membership." *Journal of Applied Econometrics*, 31, 163–191.

Andrews, D. W. K. (1991a). "Asymptotic optimality of generalized CL, cross-validation, and generalized cross-validation in regression with heteroskedastic errors." *Journal of Econometrics*, 47, 359–377.

Andrews, D. W. K. (1991b). "Heteroskedasticity and autocorrelation consistent covariance matrix estimation." *Econometrica*, 59, 817–858.

Andrews, D. W. K. (1993a). "Exactly median-unbiased estimation of first order autoregressive/unit root models." *Econometrica*, 61, 139–165.

Andrews, D. W. K. (1993b). "Tests for parameter instability and structural change with unknown change point." *Econometrica*, 61, 821–856.

Andrews, D. W. K., Lee, I., and Ploberger, W. (1996). "Optimal changepoint tests for normal linear regression." *Journal of Econometrics*, 70, 9–38.

Andrews, D. W. K. and Monahan, J. C. (1992). "An improved heteroskedasticity and autocorrelation consistent covariance matrix estimator." *Econometrica*, 60, 953–966.

Andrews, D. W. K. and Ploberger, W. (1994). "Optimal tests when a nuisance parameter is present only under the alternative." *Econometrica*, 62, 1383–1414.

Andrews, D. W. K. and Sun, Y. (2004). "Adaptive local polynomial Whittle estimation of long-range dependence." *Econometrica*, 72, 569–614.

Ang, A. and Timmermann, A. (2012). "Regime changes and financial markets." *Annual Review of Financial Economics*, 4, 313–337.

Angeletos, G. M., Collard, F., and Dellas, H. (2020). "Business-cycle anatomy." *American Economic Review*, 110, 3030–3070.

Anselin, L. (1988). *Spatial Econometrics: Methods and Models.* Springer Science & Business Media, Berlin, Germany.

Antoch, J., Hušková, M., and Prášková, Z. (1997). "Effect of dependence on statistics for determination of change." *Journal of Statistical Planning and Inference*, 60, 291–310.

Antolin-Diaz, J. and Rubio-Ramirez, J. F. (2018). "Narrative sign restrictions for SVARs." *American Economic Review*, 108, 2802–2829.

Arbia, G. (2006). *Spatial Econometrics: Statistical Foundations and Applications to Regional Convergence.* Springer Science & Business Media.

Arellano, M. and Bond, S. (1991). "Some tests of specification for panel data: Monte Carlo evidence and an application to employment equations." *The Review of Economic Studies*, 58, 277–297.

Arellano, M. and Bover, O. (1995). "Another look at the instrumental variable estimation of error-components models." *Journal of Econometrics*, 68, 29–51.

Arias, J. E., Rubio-Ramirez, J. F., and Waggoner, D. F. (2018). "Inference based on structural vector autoregressions identified with sign and zero restrictions: Theory and applications." *Econometrica*, 86, 685–720.

Arnold, L. (2013). *Stochastic Differential Equations: Theory and Applications.* Dover Publications, Mineola, NY.

Arteche, J. (2004). "Gaussian semiparametric estimation in long memory in stochastic volatility and signal plus noise models." *Journal of Econometrics*, 119, 131–154.

Arteche, J. (2006). "Semiparametric estimation in perturbed long memory series." *Computational Statistics & Data Analysis*, 51, 2118–2141.

Ashley, R., Granger, C. W. J., and Schmalensee, R. (1980). "Advertising and aggregate consumption: An analysis of causality." *Econometrica*, 48, 1149–1167.

Aue, A., Cheung, R. C., Lee, T. C., and Zhong, M. (2014). "Segmented model selection in quantile regression using the minimum description length principle." *Journal of the American Statistical Association*, 109, 1241–1256.

Bachelier, L. (1900). "Theory of Speculation", Doctoral Thesis, Coot-ner. Reprinted as Random Character of Stock Market Prices, Massachusetts Institute of Technology (1964), 17–78. In The History of Actuarial Science Vol VII, 15–78, 1996. Routledge.

Bai, J. (1997a). "Estimating multiple breaks one at a time." *Econometric Theory*, 13, 315–352.

Bai, J. (1997b). "Estimation of a change point in multiple regression models." *Review of Economics and Statistics*, 79, 551–563.

Bai, J. (1999). "Likelihood ratio tests for multiple structural changes." *Journal of Econometrics*, 91, 299–323.

Bai, J. (2000). "Vector autoregressive models with structural changes in regression coefficients and in variance-covariance matrices." *Annals of Economics and Finance*, 1, 303–339.

Bai, J. (2009a). "Likelihood approach to small T dynamic panel with interactive effects." *Econometrica*, 77, 1229–1279.

Bai, J. (2009b). "Panel data models with interactive fixed effects." *Econometrica*, 77(4), 1229–1279.

Bai, J. (2010). "Common breaks in means and variances for panel data." *Journal of Econometrics*, 157, 78–92.

Bai, J. (2013). "Panel data models and factor analysis." *Advances in Economics and Econometrics: Tenth World Congress*, D. Acemoglu, M. Arellano, and E. Dekel, eds., Vol. 3 of *Econometric Society Monographs*, Cambridge University Press, 437–484.

Bai, J., Duan, J., and Han, X. (2024). "The likelihood ratio test for structural changes in factor models." *Journal of Econometrics*, 238, 105631.

Bai, J. and Han, X. (2016). "Structural changes in high dimensional factor models." *Frontiers of Economics in China*, 11, 9–39.

Bai, J., Han, X., and Shi, Y. (2017). "Estimation and inference of structural changes in high dimensional factor models." *Unpublished Manuscript, Department of Economics, Columbia University.*

Bai, J. and Li, K. (2014). "Theory and methods of panel data models with interactive effects." *The Annals of Statistics*, 42, 142–170.

Bai, J., Lumsdaine, R. L., and Stock, J. H. (1998). "Testing for and dating common breaks in multivariate time series." *The Review of Economic Studies*, 65, 395–432.

Bai, J. and Ng, S. (2002). "Determining the number of factors in approximate factor models." *Econometrica*, 70, 191–221.

Bai, J. and Ng, S. (2004). "A PANIC attack on unit roots and cointegration." *Econometrica*, 72, 1127–1177.

Bai, J. and Ng, S. (2007). "Determining the number of primitive shocks in factor models." *Journal of Business & Economic Statistics*, 25, 52–60.

Bai, J. and Ng, S. (2008a). "Forecasting economic time series using targeted predictors." *Journal of Econometrics*, 146, 304–317.

Bai, J. and Ng, S. (2008b). "Large dimensional factor analysis." *Foundations and Trends in Econometrics*, 3, 89–163.

Bai, J. and Perron, P. (1998). "Estimating and testing linear models with multiple structural changes." *Econometrica*, 66, 47–78.

Bai, J. and Perron, P. (2003a). "Computation and analysis of multiple structural change models." *Journal of Applied Econometrics*, 18, 1–22.

Bai, J. and Perron, P. (2003b). "Critical values for multiple structural change tests." *The Econometrics Journal*, 6, 72–78.

Bai, J. and Perron, P. (2006). "Multiple structural change models: A simulation analysis." *Econometric Theory and Practice: Frontiers of Analysis and Applied Research*, D. Corbai, S. N. Durlauf, and B. Hansen, eds., Cambridge University Press, New York, NY, 212–237.

Bai, J. and Wang, P. (2016). "Econometric analysis of large factor models." *Annual Review of Economics*, 8, 53–80.

Bai, L. and Wu, W. (2024). "Difference-based covariance matrix estimation in time series nonparametric regression with application to specification tests." *Biometrika*, 111, 1277–1292.

Baillie, R. T. (1996). "Long memory processes and fractional integration in econometrics." *Journal of Econometrics*, 73, 5–59.

Bakshi, G., Cao, C., and Chen, Z. (1997). "Empirical performance of alternative option pricing models." *The Journal of Finance*, 52, 2003–2049.

Bala, V. and Goyal, S. (2001). "Conformism and diversity under social learning." *Economic Theory*, 17, 101–120.

Baltagi, B. H., Feng, Q., and Kao, C. (2016). "Estimation of heterogeneous panels with structural breaks." *Journal of Econometrics*, 191, 176–195.

Baltagi, B. H. and Griffin, J. M. (1997). "Pooled estimators vs. their heterogeneous counterparts in the context of dynamic demand for gasoline." *Journal of Econometrics*, 77, 303–327.

Baltagi, B. H., Kao, C., and Wang, F. (2015). "Change point estimation in large heterogeneous panels." *Unpublished Manuscript*, Syracuse University.

Baltagi, B. H., Kao, C., and Wang, F. (2017). "Identification and estimation of a large factor model with structural instability." *Journal of Econometrics*, 197, 87–100.

Baltagi, B. H., Kao, C., and Wang, F. (2021). "Estimating and testing high dimensional factor models with multiple structural changes." *Journal of Econometrics*, 220, 349–365.

Baltagi, B. H. and Levin, D. (1986). "Estimating dynamic demand for cigarettes using panel data: The effects of bootlegging, taxation and advertising reconsidered." *The Review of Economics and Statistics*, 148–155.

Baltagi, B. H. and Liu, L. (2011). "Instrumental variable estimation of a spatial autoregressive panel model with random effects." *Economics Letters*, 111, 135–137.

Bańbura, M., Giannone, D., Modugno, M. and Reichlin, L. (2013). Nowcasting and the real-time data flow. In *Handbook of Economic Forecasting*, vol. 2, G. Elliot and A. Timmerman (eds). Elsevier, 195–237.

Banerjee, A., Lumsdaine, R. L., and Stock, J. H. (1992). "Recursive and sequential tests of the unit-root and trend-break hypotheses: Theory and international evidence." *Journal of Business & Economic Statistics*, 10, 271–287.

Banerjee, A., Marcellino, M., and Masten, I. (2008). "Forecasting macroeconomic variables using diffusion indexes in short samples with structural change." *CEPR Discussion Paper*, DP6706, 149–194.

Barsky, R. B. (1987). "The Fisher hypothesis and the forecastability and persistence of inflation." *Journal of Monetary Economics*, 19, 3–24.

Bartlett, M. S. (1950). "Periodogram analysis and continuous spectra." *Biometrika*, 37, 1–16.

Bates, D. S. (1996). "Jumps and stochastic volatility: Exchange rate processes implicit in Deutsche Mark options." *The Review of Financial Studies*, 9, 69–107.

Bates, J. M. and Granger, C. W. J. (1969). "The combination of forecasts." *Journal of the Operational Research Society*, 20, 451–468.

Baumeister, C. and Hamilton, J. D. (2015). "Sign restrictions, structural vector autoregressions, and useful prior information." *Econometrica*, 83, 1963–1999.

Baumeister, C. and Hamilton, J. D. (2018). "Inference in structural vector autoregressions when the identifying assumptions are not fully believed: Re-evaluating the role of monetary policy in economic fluctuations." *Journal of Monetary Economics*, 100, 48–65.

Baumeister, C. and Hamilton, J. D. (2019). "Structural interpretation of vector autoregressions with incomplete identification: Revisiting the role of oil supply and demand shocks." *American Economic Review*, 109, 1873–1910.

Baumeister, C. and Hamilton, J. D. (2024). "Advances in using vector autoregressions to estimate structural magnitudes." *Econometric Theory*, 40, 472–510.

Baxter, M. and King, R. G. (1999). "Measuring business cycles: Approximate band-pass filters for economic time series." *Review of Economics and Statistics*, 81, 575–593.

Beaudry, P., Galizia, D., and Portier, F. (2020). "Putting the cycle back into business cycle analysis." *American Economic Review*, 110, 1–47.

Bellman, R. and Roth, R. (1969). "Curve fitting by segmented straight lines." *Journal of the American Statistical Association*, 64, 1079–1084.

Beran, J. (1994). *Statistics for Long-Memory Processes*. CRC Press, Boca Raton, FL.

Bergstrom, A. (1976). *Statistical Inference in Continuous Time Economic Models.* North-Holland Amsterdam, Netherlands.

Berk, K. N. (1974). "Consistent autoregressive spectral estimates." *The Annals of Statistics*, 2, 489–502.

Bernanke, B. S. (1986). "Alternative explanations of the money-income correlation." *Carnegie-Rochester Conference Series on Public Policy*, 25, 49–99.

Bernanke, B. S., Boivin, J., and Eliasz, P. (2005). "Measuring the effects of monetary policy: A factor-augmented vector autoregressive (FAVAR) approach." *The Quarterly Journal of Economics*, 120, 387–422.

Bernardi, M. and Catania, L. (2018). "The model confidence set package for R." *International Journal of Computational Economics and Econometrics*, 8, 144–158.

Besag, J. (1994). "Comments on "Representations of knowledge in complex systems" by U. Grenander and M. Miller." *Journal of the Royal Statistical Society, Series B*, 56, 591–592.

Bester, C. A. and Hansen, C. B. (2016). "Grouped effects estimators in fixed effects models." *Journal of Econometrics*, 190, 197–208.

Beveridge, S. and Nelson, C. R. (1981). "A new approach to decomposition of economic time series into permanent and transitory components with particular attention to measurement of the business cycle." *Journal of Monetary Economics*, 7, 151–174.

Beyer, A. and Farmer, R. E. (2004). "On the indeterminacy of New-Keynesian economics." *Available at SSRN 526986.*

Bhattacharya, R. N., Gupta, V. K., and Waymire, E. (1983). "The Hurst effect under trends." *Journal of Applied Probability*, 20, 649–662.

Bianchi, F., Ludvigson, S. C., and Ma, S. (2022). "Belief distortions and macroeconomic fluctuations." *American Economic Review*, 112, 2269–2315.

Bierens, H. (1994). *Topics in Advanced Econometrics: Estimation, Testing, and Specification of Cross-Section and Time Series Models.* Cambridge University Press, Cambridge, UK.

Billingsley, P. (1999). *Convergence of Probability Measures.* Wiley, New York, NY.

Bilmes, J. A. (1998). "A gentle tutorial of the EM algorithm and its application to parameter estimation for Gaussian mixture and hidden Markov models." *International Computer Science Institute*, 4, 126.

Binder, M. and Pesaran, M. H. (1998). "Decision making in the presence of heterogeneous information and social interactions." *International Economic Review*, 39, 1027–1052.

Black, F. (1976). "Studies of stock market volatility changes." *Proceedings of the American Statistical Association, Business and Economic Statistics Section*, 177–181.

Black, F. and Scholes, M. (1973). "The pricing of options and corporate liabilities." *Journal of Political Economy*, 81, 637–654.

Blanchard, O. J. (1981). "What is left of the multiplier accelerator?" *American Economic Review, Papers and Proceedings*, 71, 132–143.

Blanchard, O. J. (1989). "A traditional interpretation of macroeconomic fluctuations." *American Economic Review*, 79, 1146–1164.

Blanchard, O. J., Diamond, P., Hall, R. E., and Murphy, K. (1990). "The cyclical behavior of the gross flows of U.S. workers." *Brookings Papers on Economic Activity*, 2, 85–155.

Blanchard, O. J. and Quah, D. (1989). "The dynamic effects of aggregate demand and supply disturbances." *American Economic Review*, 79, 655–673.

Blanchard, O. J. and Watson, M. W. (1986). "Are business cycles all alike?" *The American Business Cycle: Continuity and Change*, R. J. Gordon, ed., University of Chicago Press, Chicago, IL, 123–156.

Blasques, F., Koopman, S. J., Lasak, K., and Lucas, A. (2016). "In-sample confidence bands and out-of-sample forecast bands for time-varying parameters in observation driven models." *International Journal of Forecasting*, 32, 875–887.

Bleakley, K. and Vert, J.-P. (2011). "The group fused Lasso for multiple change-point detection." *arXiv:1106.4199*.

Blough, S. R. (1992). "The relationship between power and level for generic unit root tests in finite samples." *Journal of Applied Econometrics*, 7, 295–308.

Blundell, R. and Bond, S. (1998). "Initial conditions and moment restrictions in dynamic panel data models." *Journal of Econometrics*, 87, 115–143.

Blundell, R., Bond, S., Devereux, M., and Schiantarelli, F. (1992). "Investment and Tobin's Q: Evidence from company panel data." *Journal of Econometrics*, 51, 233–257.

Bobkoski, M. (1983). "Hypothesis testing in nonstationary time series." Ph.D. thesis, The University of Wisconsin-Madison, Madison, WI.

Bok, B., Caratelli, D., Giannone, D., Sbordone, A. M., and Tambalotti, A. (2018). "Macroeconomic nowcasting and forecasting with big data." *Annual Review of Economics*, 10, 615–643.

Boldea, O., Cornea-Madeira, A., and Hall, A. R. (2019). "Bootstrapping structural change tests." *Journal of Econometrics*, 213, 359–397.

Boldea, O., Hall, A. R., and Han, S. (2012). "Asymptotic distribution theory for break point estimators in models estimated via 2SLS." *Econometric Reviews*, 31, 1–33.

Bollerslev, T. (1986). "Generalized autoregressive conditional heteroskedasticity." *Journal of Econometrics*, 31, 307–327.

Bollerslev, T. (2010). "Glossary to ARCH (GARCH)." *Volatility and Time Series Econometrics: Essays in Honour of Robert F. Engle*, T. Bollerslev, J. R. Russell, and M. W. Watson, eds., Oxford University Press, UK, 137–163.

Bollerslev, T., Chou, R. Y., and Kroner, K. F. (1992). "ARCH modeling in finance: A review of the theory and empirical evidence." *Journal of Econometrics*, 52, 5–59.

Bollerslev, T., Engle, R. F., and Nelson, D. B. (1994). "ARCH models." *Handbook of Econometrics, Vol. 4*, R. Engle and D. McFadden, eds., Elsevier, Amsterdam, Netherlands, 2959–3038.

Bolstad, W. M. (2009). *Understanding Computational Bayesian Statistics*. Wiley, New York, NY.

Bonhomme, S. and Manresa, E. (2015). "Grouped patterns of heterogeneity in panel data." *Econometrica*, 83, 1147–1184.

Boot, T. and Pick, A. (2020). "Does modeling a structural break improve forecast accuracy?" *Journal of Econometrics*, 215, 35–59.

Box, G. E. and Jenkins, G. (1970). *Time Series Analysis: Forecasting and Control*. Holden-Day, San Francisco, CA.

Box, G. E., Jenkins, G. M., Reinsel, G. C. and Ljung, G. M. (2015). *Time Series Analysis: Forecasting and Control*. Wiley, New York, NY.

Box, G. E. and Pierce, D. A. (1970). "Distribution of residual autocorrelations in autoregressive-integrated moving average time series models." *Journal of the American Statistical Association*, 65, 1509–1526.

Box, G. E. and Tiao, G. C. (1975). "Intervention analysis with applications to economic and environmental problems." *Journal of the American Statistical Association*, 70, 70–79.

Breiman, L. (1996). "Bagging predictors." *Machine Learning*, 24, 123–140.

Breiman, L. (2001). "Random forests." *Machine Learning*, 45, 5–32.

Breitung, J. (2002). "Nonparametric tests for unit roots and cointegration." *Journal of Econometrics*, 108, 343–363.

Breitung, J. and Choi, I. (2013). "Factor models." *Handbook of Research Methods and Applications in Empirical Macroeconomics*, N. Hashimzade and M. A. Thornton, eds., Edward Elgar Publishing, UK, 249–265.

Breitung, J. and Pigorsch, U. (2013). "A canonical correlation approach for selecting the number of dynamic factors." *Oxford Bulletin of Economics and Statistics*, 75, 23–36.

Brillinger, D. R. (2001). *Time Series: Data Analysis and Theory*. Society for Industrial and Applied Mathematics, Philadelphia, PA.

Brock, W. A. and Durlauf, S. N. (2001). "Discrete choice with social interactions." *The Review of Economic Studies*, 68, 235–260.

Brockwell, P. J. and Davis, R. A. (1991). *Time Series: Theory and Methods.* Springer, New York, NY.

Brockwell, P. J.; Davis, R. A. (2009). *Time Series: Theory and Methods (2nd edition).* Springer, New York, NY.

Brown, R. L., Durbin, J., and Evans, J. M. (1975). "Techniques for testing the constancy of regression relationships over time." *Journal of the Royal Statistical Society*, 37, 149–192.

Browning, M. and Carro, J. M. (2014). "Dynamic binary outcome models with maximal heterogeneity." *Journal of Econometrics*, 178, 805–823.

Burdekin, R. C. and Siklos, P. L. (1999). "Exchange rate regimes and shifts in inflation persistence: Does nothing else matter?" *Journal of Money, Credit, and Banking*, 31, 235–247.

Burns, A. F. and Mitchell, W. C. (1946). *Measuring Business Cycles.* NBER, Cambridge, MA.

Burridge, P. and Wallis, K. F. (1984). "Unobserved-components models for seasonal adjustment filters." *Journal of Business & Economic Statistics*, 2, 350–359.

Busetti, F. and Taylor, A. M. R. (2005). "Tests of stationarity against a change in persistence." *Journal of Econometrics*, 123, 33–66.

Calhoun, G. (2014). "Out-of-sample comparisons of overfit models." *Working Paper 11002, Department of Economics, Iowa State University.*

Camacho, M. (2013). "Mixed-frequency VAR models with Markov-switching dynamics." *Economics Letters*, 121, 369–373.

Camacho, M., Perez-Quiros, G., and Poncela, P. (2013). "Short-term forecasting for empirical economists: A survey of the recently proposed algorithms." *Foundations and Trends in Econometrics*, 6, 101–161.

Campbell, J. Y. and Mankiw, N. G. (1987). "Permanent and transitory components in macroeconomic fluctuations." *American Economic Review*, 77, 111–117.

Campbell, J. Y. and Perron, P. (1991). "Pitfalls and opportunities: What macroeconomists should know about unit roots." *NBER Macroeconomics Annual*, Vol. 6, O. Blanchard and S. Fisher, eds., MIT Press, Cambridge, MA, 141–201.

Canova, F. and de Nicolo, G. (2002). "Monetary disturbances matter for business fluctuations in the G-7." *Journal of Monetary Economics*, 49, 1131–1159.

Carrion-i Silvestre, J. L. and Gadea, M. D. (2023). "Testing for multiple level shifts with an integrated or stationary noise component." *Journal of Applied Econometrics*, 38, 801–819.

Carrion-i Silvestre, J. L., Kim, D., and Perron, P. (2009). "GLS-based unit root tests with multiple structural breaks under both the null and the alternative hypotheses." *Econometric Theory*, 25, 1754–1792.

Carrion-i Silvestre, J. L. and Sansó, A. (2006). "Joint hypothesis specification for unit root tests with a structural break." *The Econometrics Journal*, 9, 196–224.

Carrion-i-Silvestre, J. L., Sansó-i Rosselló, A., and Ortuño, M. A. (1999). "Response surfaces estimates for the Dickey-Fuller unit root test with structural breaks." *Economics Letters*, 63, 279–283.

Casella, G. and George, E. I. (1992). "Explaining the Gibbs sampler." *The American Statistician*, 46, 167–174.

Casini, A., Deng, T., and Perron, P. (2024). "Theory of low frequency contamination from nonstationarity and misspecification: Consequences for HAR inference." *Econometric Theory* (forthcoming).

Casini, A. and Perron, P. (2019). "Structural breaks in time series." *Oxford Research Encyclopedia of Economics and Finance*, J. H. Hamilton, A. Dixit, S. Edwards, and K. Judd, eds., Oxford University Press, UK.

Casini, A. and Perron, P. (2024). "Continuous record asymptotics for change-point models." *Journal of Time Series Analysis* (forthcoming).

Cavanagh, C. L. (1986). "Roots local to unity." *Unpublished Manuscript.* Harvard Institute of Economic Research.

Chamberlain, G. (1983). "Funds, factors, and diversification in arbitrage pricing models." *Econometrica*, 51, 1305–1323.

Chan, K. W. (2022). "Optimal difference-based variance estimators in time series: A general framework." *The Annals of Statistics*, 50, 1376–1400.

Chan, N. H. (1988). "The parameter inference for nearly nonstationary time series." *Journal of the American Statistical Association*, 83, 857–862.

Chan, N. H. and Wei, C.-Z. (1987). "Asymptotic inference for nearly nonstationary AR(1) processes." *The Annals of Statistics*, 15, 1050–1063.

Chan, N. H. and Wei, C. Z. (1988). "Limiting distributions of least squares estimates of unstable autoregressive processes." *The Annals of Statistics*, 16, 367–401.

Chan, N. H., Yau, C. Y., and Zhang, R.-M. (2014). "Group Lasso for structural break time series." *Journal of the American Statistical Association*, 109, 590–599.

Chang, S. Y. and Perron, P. (2018). "A comparison of alternative methods to construct confidence intervals for the estimate of a break date in linear regression models." *Econometric Reviews*, 37, 577–601.

Chang, Y. and Park, J. Y. (2002). "On the asymptotics of ADF tests for unit roots." *Econometric Reviews*, 21, 431–447.

Chao, J., Corradi, V., and Swanson, N. R. (2001). "Out-of-sample tests for Granger causality." *Macroeconomic Dynamics*, 5, 598–620.

Chauvet, M. (1998). "An econometric characterization of business cycle dynamics with factor structure and regime switching." *International Economic Review*, 39, 969–996.

Chauvet, M. and Hamilton, J. D. (2006). "Dating business cycle turning points." *Contributions to Economic Analysis*, C. Milas, P. Rothman, and D. van Dijk, eds., Elsevier, Amsterdam, Netherlands, 1–54.

Chen, L., Dolado, J. J., and Gonzalo, J. (2014). "Detecting big structural breaks in large factor models." *Journal of Econometrics*, 180, 30–48.

Chen, L., Dolado, J. J., and Gonzalo, J. (2021). "Quantile factor models." *Econometrica*, 89, 875–910.

Chen, R. and Liu, J. S. (2000). "Mixture Kalman filters." *Journal of the Royal Statistical Society Series B*, 62, 493–508.

Cheng, C. H. and Chan, K. W. (2024). "A general framework for constructing locally self-normalized multiple-change-point tests." *Journal of Business & Economic Statistics*, 42, 719–731.

Cheng, X., Liao, Z., and Schorfheide, F. (2016). "Shrinkage estimation of high-dimensional factor models with structural instabilities." *The Review of Economic Studies*, 83, 1511–1543.

Chernoff, H. and Zacks, S. (1964). "Estimating the current mean of a normal distribution which is subjected to changes in time." *The Annals of Mathematical Statistics*, 35, 999–1018.

Chernozhukov, V., Hansen, C. and Liao, Y. (2017). "A lava attack on the recovery of sums of dense and sparse signals." *The Annals of Statistics*, 45, 39–76.

Chernozhukov, V. and Hong, H. (2003). "An MCMC approach to classical estimation." *Journal of Econometrics*, 115, 293–346.

Chib, S. (2001). "Markov chain Monte Carlo methods: Computation and inference." *Handbook of Econometrics, Vol. 5*, J. Heckman and E. Leamer, eds., Elsevier, 3569–3649.

Chib, S. and Greenberg, E. (1995). "Understanding the Metropolis-Hastings algorithm." *The American Statistician*, 49, 327–335.

Choi, I. (2015). *Almost All about Unit Roots: Foundations, Developments, and Applications.* Cambridge University Press, Cambridge, UK.

Chong, T. T. L. (1995). "Partial parameter consistency in a misspecified structural change model." *Economics Letters*, 49, 351–357.

Chong, T. T. L. (2001). "Structural change in AR(1) models." *Econometric Theory*, 17, 87–155.

Chong, Y. Y. and Hendry, D. F. (1986). "Econometric evaluation of linear macro-economic models." *The Review of Economic Studies*, 53, 671–690.

Chopin, N. and Papaspiliopoulos, O. (2020). *An Introduction to Sequential Monte Carlo.* Springer: Berlin.

Chow, G. (1984). "Random and changing coefficient models." *Handbook of Econometrics, Vol. 2*, Z. Griliches and D. Intriligator, eds., North Holland Elsevier, Amsterdam, Netherlands, 1213–1245.

Christiano, L. J. (1992). "Searching for a break in GNP." *Journal of Business & Economic Statistics*, 10, 237–250.

Christiano, L. J., Eichenbaum, M., and Vigfusson, R. (2003). "What happens after a technology shock?" National Bureau of Economic Research, Working Paper 9819.

Christiano, L. J. and Fitzgerald, T. J. (2003). "The band pass filter." *International Economic Review*, 44, 435–465.

Christoffersen, P. F. and Diebold, F. X. (1997). "Optimal prediction under asymmetric loss." *Econometric Theory*, 13, 808–817.

Christoffersen, P. F. and Diebold, F. X. (2006). "Financial asset returns, direction-of-change forecasting, and volatility dynamics." *Management Science*, 52, 1273–1287.

Chudik, A. and Pesaran, M. H. (2013). "Large panel data models with cross-sectional dependence: A survey." *CAFE Research Paper 13.15.*

Chudik, A. and Pesaran, M. H. (2015). "Common correlated effects estimation of heterogeneous dynamic panel data models with weakly exogenous regressors." *Journal of Econometrics*, 188, 393–420.

Chun, S. and Perron, P. (2013). "Comparisons of robust tests for shifts in trend with an application to trend deviations of real exchange rates in the long run." *Applied Economics*, 45, 3512–3528.

Ciuperca, G. (2014). "Model selection by Lasso methods in a change-point model." *Statistical Papers*, 55, 349–374.

Clarida, R., Gali, J., and Gertler, M. (2000). "Monetary policy rules and macroeconomic stability: Evidence and some theory." *The Quarterly Journal of Economics*, 115, 147–180.

Clark, T. E. and McCracken, M. W. (2013). "Advances in forecast evaluation." *Handbook of Economic Forecasting, Vol. 2B*, G. Elliott and A. Timmermann, eds., North-Holland Elsevier, 1107–1201.

Clark, T. E. and McCracken, M. W. (2001). "Tests of equal forecast accuracy and encompassing for nested models." *Journal of Econometrics*, 105, 85–110.

Clark, T. E. and McCracken, M. W. (2005a). "Evaluating direct multistep forecasts." *Econometric Reviews*, 24, 369–404.

Clark, T. E. and McCracken, M. W. (2005b). "The power of tests of predictive ability in the presence of structural breaks." *Journal of Econometrics*, 124, 1–31.

Clark, T. E. and McCracken, M. W. (2012). "Reality checks and comparisons of nested predictive models." *Journal of Business & Economic Statistics*, 30, 53–66.

Clark, T. E. and West, K. D. (2006). "Using out-of-sample mean squared prediction errors to test the martingale difference hypothesis." *Journal of Econometrics*, 135, 155–186.

Clemente, J., Montañés, A., and Reyes, M. (1998). "Testing for a unit root in variables with a double change in the mean." *Economics Letters*, 59, 175–182.

Clements, M. P. and Hendry, D. F. (1998a). "Forecasting economic processes." *International Journal of Forecasting*, 14, 111–131.

Clements, M. P. and Hendry, D. F. (1998b). *Forecasting Economic Time Series*. Cambridge University Press, Cambridge, UK.

Clements, M. P. and Hendry, D. F. (2006). "Forecasting with breaks." *Handbook of Economic Forecasting*, 1, G. Elliott, C. W. J. Granger and A. Timmerman (eds.), 605–657.

Cliff, A. and Ord, J. (1973). *Spatial Autocorrelation*. Monographs in Spatial and Environmental Systems analysis. Pion, U.K.

Cliff, A. D. and Ord, J. K. (1981). *Spatial Processes: Models & Applications*. Pion, UK.

Coakley, J., Fuertes, A.-M., Smith, R., *et al.* (2002). "A principal components approach to cross-section dependence in panels." *10th International Conference on Panel Data, Berlin, July 5-6, 2002*, Number B5-3, International Conferences on Panel Data.

Cochrane, J. H. (1991). "A critique of the application of unit root tests." *Journal of Economic Dynamics and Control*, 15, 275–284.

Cogley, T. and Nason, J. M. (1995). "Effects of the Hodrick-Prescott filter on trend and difference stationary time series implications for business cycle research." *Journal of Economic Dynamics and Control*, 19, 253–278.

Cogley, T. and Sargent, T. J. (2005). "Drifts and volatilities: Monetary policies and outcomes in the post WWII U.S." *Review of Economic Dynamics*, 8, 262–302.

Cooley, J. W. and Tukey, J. W. (1965). "An algorithm for the machine calculation of complex Fourier series." *Mathematics of Computation*, 19, 297–301.

Cornea-Madeira, A. (2017). "The explicit formula for the Hodrick-Prescott filter in a finite sample." *The Review of Economics and Statistics*, 99, 314–318.

Cox, D. R. (1981). "Statistical analysis of time series: Some recent developments." *Scandinavian Journal of Statistics*, 8, 93–115.

Crainiceanu, C. M. and Vogelsang, T. J. (2007). "Nonmonotonic power for tests of a mean shift in a time series." *Journal of Statistical Computation and Simulation*, 77, 457–476.

Creal, D., Koopman, S. J., and Lucas, A. (2013). "Generalized autoregressive score models with applications." *Journal of Applied Econometrics*, 28, 777–795.

Csörgö, M. and Horváth, L. (1997). *Limit Theorems in Change-point Analysis.* Wiley, New York, NY.

Dagum, E. B. (1983). "Spectral properties of the concurrent and forecasting seasonal linear filters of the X-11-ARIMA method." *Canadian Journal of Statistics*, 11, 73–90.

Dahlhaus, R. (1989). "Efficient parameter estimation for self-similar processes." *The Annals of Statistics*, 17, 1749–1766.

Danielsson, J. (1994). "Stochastic volatility in asset prices estimation with simulated maximum likelihood." *Journal of Econometrics*, 64, 375–400.

Datta, G. S. and Ghosh, M. (1996). "On the invariance of noninformative priors." *The Annals of Statistics*, 24, 141–159.

Davidson, J. (1994). *Stochastic Limit Theory: An Introduction for Econometricians.* Oxford University Press, UK.

Davidson, J. (2006). "Asymptotic methods and functional central limit theorems." *Palgrave Handbook of Econometrics, Vol. 1: Econometric Theory* K. Patterson and T. C. Mills, eds., Palgrave Macmillan, London, UK, 159–211.

Davidson, J. and Hashimzade, N. (2009). "Type I and type II Brownian motions: A reconsideration." *Computational Statistics and Data Analysis*, 53, 2089–2106.

Davidson, J. E. H., Hendry, D. F., Srba, F., and Yeo, S. (1978). "Econometric modelling of the aggregate time series relationship between consumers expenditure and income in the United Kingdom." *Economic Journal*, 88, 661–692.

Davies, R. B. (1977). "Hypothesis testing when a nuisance parameter is present only under the alternative." *Biometrika*, 64, 247–254.

Davies, R. B. (1987). "Hypothesis testing when a nuisance parameter is present only under the alternative." *Biometrika*, 74, 33–43.

Davig, T. (2004). "Regime-switching debt and taxation." *Journal of Monetary Economics*, 51, 837–859.

Davis, S. J. and Haltiwanger, J. (1999). "On the driving forces behind cyclical movements in employment and job reallocation." *American Economic Review*, 89, 1234–1258.

De Long, J. B., Summers, L. H., Mankiw, N. G., and Romer, C. D. (1988). "How does macroeconomic policy affect output?" *Brookings Papers on Economic Activity*, 19, 433–494.

De Wachter, S. and Tzavalis, E. (2012). "Detection of structural breaks in linear dynamic panel data models." *Computational Statistics & Data Analysis*, 56, 3020–3034.

Deaton, A. S. (1987). "Life cycle models of consumption: Is the evidence consistent with facts?" *Advances in Econometrics*, 2, 121–148.

Deb, P. and Trivedi, P. K. (2013). "Finite mixture for panels with fixed effects." *Journal of Econometric Methods*, 2, 35–51.

DeJong, D. N., Nankervis, J. C., Savin, N., and Whiteman, C. H. (1992). "The power problems of unit root test in time series with autoregressive errors." *Journal of Econometrics*, 53, 323–343.

Del Moral, P. (1996). "Non linear filtering: Interacting particle solution." *Markov Processes and Related Fields*, 2, 555–580.

Del Moral, P. (1998). "Measure valued processes and interacting particle systems. application to non linear filtering problems." *The Annals of Applied Probability*, 8, 438–495.

Del Moral, P. and Guionnet, A. (1999a). "Central limit theorem for nonlinear filtering and interacting particle systems." *The Annals of Applied Probability*, 9, 275–297.

Del Moral, P. and Guionnet, A. (1999b). "On the stability of measure valued processes with applications to filtering." *Comptes Rendus de l'Académie des Sciences-Series I-Mathematics*, 329, 429–434.

Del Moral, P. and Guionnet, A. (2001). "On the stability of interacting processes with applications to filtering and genetic algorithms." *Annales de l'Institut Henri Poincaré (B) Probability and Statistics*, 37, 155–194.

Demetrescu, M. and Hassler, U. (2016). "(When) do long autoregressions account for neglected changes in parameters?" *Econometric Theory*, 32, 1317–1348.

Demetrescu, M. and Salish, N. (2024). "(Structural) VAR models with ignored changes in mean and volatility." *International Journal of Forecasting*, 40, 840–854.

Dempster, A. P., Laird, N. M., and Rubin, D. B. (1977). "Maximum-likelihood from incomplete data via the EM algorithm." *Journal of the Royal Statistical Society. Series B*, 39, 1–38.

Deng, A. and Perron, P. (2006). "A comparison of alternative asymptotic frameworks to analyse a structural change in a linear time trend." *The Econometrics Journal*, 9, 423–447.

Deng, A. and Perron, P. (2008). "A non-local perspective on the power properties of the CUSUM and CUSUM of squares tests for structural change." *Journal of Econometrics*, 142, 212–240.

Deo, R. S. and Hurvich, C. M. (2001). "On the log-periodogram regression estimator of the memory parameter in long memory stochastic volatility model." *Econometric Theory*, 17, 686–710.

Deshayes, J. and Picard, D. (1984a). "Lois asymptotiques des tests et estimateurs de rupture dans un modèle statistique classique." *Annales de l'Institut Henri Poincaré (B) Probability and Statistics*, 20, 309–327.

Deshayes, J. and Picard, D. (1984b). "Principe d'invariance sur le processus de vraisemblance." *Annales de l'Institut Henri Poincaré (B) Probability and Statistics*, 20, 1–20.

Deshayes, J. and Picard, D. (1986). "Off-line statistical analysis of change-point models using non parametric and likelihood methods." *Detection of Abrupt Changes in Signals and Dynamical Systems*, M. Basseville and A. Benveniste, eds., Springer-Verlag, New York, NY, 103–168.

Devroye, L. (2006). "Nonuniform random variate generation." *Handbooks in Operations Research and Management Science*, Vol. 13, 83–121.

Dickey, D. A. and Fuller, W. A. (1979). "Distribution of the estimators for autoregressive time series with a unit root." *Journal of the American Statistical Association*, 47, 427–431.

Dickey, D. A. and Fuller, W. A. (1981). "Likelihood ratio statistics for autoregressive time series with a unit root." *Econometrica*, 49, 1057–1072.

Diebold, F. X. and Inoue, A. (2001). "Long memory and regime switching." *Journal of Econometrics*, 105, 131–159.

Diebold, F. X. and Mariano, R. S. (1995). "Comparing predictive accuracy." *Journal of Business & Economic Statistics*, 13, 253–263.

Diebold, F. X. and Pauly, P. (1990). "The use of prior information in forecast combination." *International Journal of Forecasting*, 6, 503–508.

Diebold, F. X. and Rudebusch, G. D. (1996). "Measuring business cycles: A modern perspective." *The Review of Economics and Statistics*, 78, 67–77.

Ding, Z., Engle, R. F., and Granger, C. W. J. (1993). "A long memory property of stock market returns and a new model." *Journal of Empirical Finance*, 1, 83–106.

Doan, T., Litterman, R., and Sims, C. (1984). "Forecasting and conditional projection using realistic prior distributions." *Econometric Reviews*, 3, 1–100.

Dolado, J. J. and Lütkepohl, H. (1996). "Making Wald tests work for cointegrated VAR systems." *Econometric Reviews*, 15, 369–386.

Doucet, A., De Freitas, N., Murphy, K., and Russell, S. (2013). "Rao-Blackwellised particle filtering for dynamic Bayesian networks." *arXiv:1301.3853*.

Duan, J., Bai, J., and Han, X. (2023). "Quasi-maximum likelihood estimation of break point in high-dimensional factor models." *Journal of Econometrics*, 233, 209–236.

Duan, J.-C. and Fulop, A. (2011). "A stable estimator of the information matrix under EM for dependent data." *Statistics and Computing*, 21, 83–91.

Duffy, J. A. and Kasparis, I. (2021). "Estimation and inference in the presence of fractional d=1/2 and weakly nonstationary processes." *The Annals of Statistics*, 49, 1195–1217.

Dufour, J.-M. (1997). "Some impossibility theorems in econometrics with applications to structural and dynamic models." *Econometrica*, 65, 1365–1387.

Durbin, J. and Koopman, S. J. (1997). "Monte Carlo maximum likelihood estimation for non-Gaussian state space models." *Biometrika*, 84, 669–684.

Efron, B. and Tibshirani, R. J. (1994). *An Introduction to the Bootstrap.* CRC Press, Boca Raton, FL.

Elhorst, J. P. (2014). *Spatial Econometrics: From Cross-Sectional Data to Spatial Panels*, Vol. 479. Springer Berlin Heidelberg, Germany.

Elliott, G., Komunjer, I., and Timmermann, A. (2005). "Estimation and testing of forecast rationality under flexible loss." *Review of Economic Studies*, 72, 1107–1125.

Elliott, G. and Müller, U. K. (2006). "Efficient tests for general persistent time variation in regression coefficients." *The Review of Economic Studies*, 73, 907–940.

Elliott, G. and Müller, U. K. (2007). "Confidence sets for the date of a single break in linear time series regressions." *Journal of Econometrics*, 141, 1196–1218.

Elliott, G., Rothenberg, T. J., and Stock, J. H. (1996). "Efficient tests for an autoregressive unit root." *Econometrica*, 64, 813–836.

Elliott, G. and Timmermann, A. (2008). "Economic forecasting." *Journal of Economic Literature*, 46, 3–56.

Engle, R. F. (1974). "Band spectrum regression." *International Economic Review*, 15, 1–11.

Engle, R. F. (1980). "Exact maximum likelihood methods for dynamic regressions and band spectrum regressions." *International Economic Review*, 21, 391–407.

Engle, R. F. (1982). "Autoregressive conditional heteroscedasticity with estimates of the variance of United Kingdom inflation." *Econometrica*, 50, 987–1007.

Engle, R. F. and Granger, C. W. J. (1984). "Applications of spectral analysis in econometrics." *Handbook of Statistics, Vol. 3*, D. Brillinger and P. Krishnaiah, eds., Elsevier, Amsterdam, Netherlands, 93–109.

Engle, R. F. and Granger, C. W. J. (1987). "Co-integration and error correction: Representation, estimation, and testing." *Econometrica*, 55, 251–276.

Engle, R. F., Hendry, D. F., and Richard, J.-F. (1983). "Exogeneity." *Econometrica*, 51, 277–304.

Engle, R. F., Lilien, D. M., and Robins, R. P. (1987). "Estimating time varying risk premia in the term structure: The ARCH-M model." *Econometrica*, 55, 391–407.

Engle, R. F. and Watson, M. W. (1987). "The Kalman filter: Applications to forecasting and rational-expectations." *Advances in Economic Theory: Fifth World Congress*, T. F. Bewley, ed., Cambridge University Press, New York, NY, 245–284.

Eo, Y. and Morley, J. (2015). "Likelihood-ratio-based confidence sets for the timing of structural breaks." *Quantitative Economics*, 6, 463–497.

Estrada, F. and Perron, P. (2019). "Breaks, trends and the attribution of climate change: A time-series analysis." *Economía*, 42, 1–31.

Estrada, F., Perron, P., and Martínez-López, B. (2013). "Statistically derived contributions of diverse human influences to 20th-century temperature changes." *Nature Geoscience*, 6, 1050–1055.

Estrada, F., Perron, P., and Yamamoto, Y. (2024). "On the persistence of near-surface temperature dynamics in a warming world." *Annals of the New York Academy of Sciences*, 1531, 69–83.

Evans, G. B. A. and Savin, N. E. (1981a). "The calculation of the limiting distribution of the least squares estimator of the parameter in a random walk model." *The Annals of Statistics*, 9, 1114–1118.

Evans, G. B. A. and Savin, N. E. (1981b). "Testing for unit roots: 1." *Econometrica*, 49, 753–779.

Evans, G. B. A. and Savin, N. E. (1984). "Testing for unit roots: 2." *Econometrica*, 52, 1241–1269.

Faust, J. (1998). "The robustness of identified VAR conclusions about money." *Carnegie-Rochester Conference Series on Public Policy*, 49, 207–244.

Feller, W. (1968). *An Introduction to Probability Theory and its Applications.* John Wiley and Sons.

Fernández-Val, I. and Weidner, M. (2018). "Fixed effects estimation of large T panel data models." *Annual Review of Economics*, 10, 109–138.

Fernández-Villaverde, J., Guerrón-Quintana, P., Rubio-Ramirez, J. F., and Uribe, M. (2011). "Risk matters: The real effects of volatility shocks." *American Economic Review*, 101, 2530–2561.

Fernández-Villaverde, J. and Rubio-Ramìrez, J. F. (2007). "Estimating macroeconomic models: A likelihood approach." *The Review of Economic Studies*, 74, 1059–1087.

Fernández-Villaverde, J., Rubio-Ramírez, J. F., Sargent, T. J., and Watson, M. W. (2007). "ABCs (and Ds) of understanding VARs." *American Economic Review*, 97, 1021–1026.

Fernández-Villaverde, J., Rubio-Ramìrez, J. F., and Schorfheide, F. (2016). "Solution and estimation methods for DSGE models." *Handbook of*

Macroeconomics, Vol. 2, J. B. Taylor and H. Uhlig, eds., North Holland Elsevier, Amsterdam, Netherlands, 527–724.

Fisher, W. D. (1958). "On grouping for maximum homogeneity." *Journal of the American Statistical Association*, 53, 789–798.

Flury, T. and Shepard, N. (2011). "Bayesian inference based only on a simulated likelihood." *Econometric Theory*, 27, 933–956.

Fox, R. and Taqqu, M. S. (1986). "Large-sample properties of parameter estimates for strongly dependent stationary Gaussian time series." *The Annals of Statistics*, 14, 517–532.

Frederiksen, P. S., Nielsen, F. S., and Nielsen, M. Ø. (2012). "Local polynomial Whittle estimation of perturbed fractional processes." *Journal of Econometrics*, 167, 426–447.

Fridman, M. and Harris, L. (1998). "A maximum likelihood approach for non-Gaussian stochastic volatility models." *Journal of Business & Economic Statistics*, 16, 284–291.

Fruhwirth-Schnatter, S. (2001). "Fully Bayesian analysis of switching Gaussian state space models." *Annals of the Institute of Statistical Mathematics*, 53, 31–49.

Fry, R. and Pagan, A. R. (2011). "Sign restrictions in structural vector autoregressions: A critical review." *Journal of Economic Literature*, 49, 938–960.

Fu, Y.-X. and Curnow, R. (1990). "Maximum likelihood estimation of multiple change points." *Biometrika*, 77, 563–573.

Fuller, W. A. (1996). *Introduction to Statistical Time Series.* Wiley, New York, NY.

Garcia, R. and Perron, P. (1996). "An analysis of the real interest rate under regime shifts." *The Review of Economics and Statistics*, 78, 111–125.

Gardner, L. (1969). "On detecting changes in the mean of normal variates." *The Annals of Mathematical Statistics*, 40, 116–126.

Gelman, A., Carlin, J. B., Stern, H. S., and Rubin, D. B. (1995). *Bayesian Data Analysis.* Chapman and Hall/CRC, New York, NY.

Geman, S. and Geman, D. (1984). "Stochastic relaxation, Gibbs distributions, and the Bayesian restoration of images." *IEEE Transactions on Pattern Analysis and Machine Intelligence*, 6, 721–741.

Genovese, C. R. and Wasserman, L. (2000). "Rates of convergence for the Gaussian mixture sieve." *The Annals of Statistics*, 28, 1105–1127.

Geweke, J. (1982). "Measurement of linear dependence and feedback between multiple time series." *Journal of the American Statistical Association*, 77, 304–313.

Geweke, J. and Keane, M. (2001). "Computationally intensive methods for integration in econometrics." *Handbook of Econometrics, Vol. 5*, J. J. Heckmann and E. Leamer, eds., Elsevier, 3463–3568.

Geweke, J. and Porter-Hudak, S. (1983). "The estimation and application of long memory time series models." *Journal of Time Series Analysis*, 4, 221–238.

Ghosal, S. (2001). "Convergence rates for density estimation with Bernstein polynomials." *The Annals of Statistics*, 29, 164–1280.

Ghosal, S. and van der Vaart, A. (2007). "Convergence rates of posterior distributions for non-iid observations." *The Annals of Statistics*, 35, 192–233.

Ghysels, E. (1984). "The economics of seasonality: The case of the money supply." Ph.D. thesis, Northwestern University, Chicago, IL.

Ghysels, E. and Perron, P. (1993). "The effect of seasonal adjustment filters on tests for a unit root." *Journal of Econometrics*, 55, 57–98.

Ghysels, E., Sinko, A., and Valkanov, R. (2007). "MIDAS regressions: Further results and new directions." *Econometric Reviews*, 26, 53–90.

Giacomini, R. (2015). "Economic theory and forecasting: Lessons from the literature." *The Econometrics Journal*, 2, 22–41.

Giacomini, R., Kitagawa, T., and Read, M. (2022). "Narrative restrictions and proxies." *Journal of Business & Economic Statistics*, 40, 1415–1425.

Giacomini, R. and Rossi, B. (2009). "Detecting and predicting forecast breakdowns." *The Review of Economic Studies*, 76, 669–705.

Giacomini, R. and Rossi, B. (2010). "Forecast comparisons in unstable environments." *Journal of Applied Econometrics*, 25, 595–620.

Giacomini, R. and Rossi, B. (2015). "Forecasting in nonstationary environments: What works and what does not in reduced-form and structural models." *Annual Reviews of Economics*, 7, 207–229.

Giacomini, R. and White, H. (2006). "Tests of conditional predictive ability." *Econometrica*, 74, 1545–1578.

Giannini, C. (1991). *Topics in Structural VAR Econometrics.* Springer, New York, NY.

Giannone, D., Lenza, M., and Primiceri, G. E. (2021). "Economic predictions with big data: The illusion of sparsity." *Econometrica*, 89, 2409–2437.

Gill, J. (2015). *Bayesian Methods: A Social and Behavioral Sciences Approach, 3rd ed.* Chapman and Hall/CRC, New York, NY.

Giordani, P., Kohn, R., and van Dijk, D. (2007). "A unified approach to nonlinearity, structural change, and outliers." *Journal of Econometrics*, 137, 112–133.

Glosten, L. R., Jagannathan, R. and Runkle, D. E. (1993). "On the relation between the expected value and the volatility of the nominal excess return on stocks." *The Journal of Finance*, 48, 1779–1801.

Godsill, S. J., Doucet, A., and West, M. (2004). "Monte Carlo smoothing for nonlinear time series." *Journal of the American Statistical Association*, 99, 156–168.

Gordon, N. J., Salmond, D. J., and Smith, A. F. M. (1993). "Novel approach to nonlinear/non-Gaussian Bayesian state estimation." *Radar and Signal Processing, IEE Proceedings F*, 140, 107–113.

Gouriéroux, C. and Jasiak, J. (2001). "Memory and infrequent breaks." *Economics Letters*, 70, 29–41.

Gouriéroux, C. and Monfort, A. (1997). *Time Series and Dynamic Models.* Cambridge University Press, Cambridge, UK.

Granger, C. W. J. (1966). "The typical spectral shape of an economic variable." *Econometrica*, 34, 150–161.

Granger, C. W. J. (1969). "Investigating causal relations by econometric models and cross-spectral methods." *Econometrica*, 37, 424–438.

Granger, C. W. J. (1981). "Some properties of time series data and their use in econometric model specification." *Journal of Econometrics*, 16, 121–130.

Granger, C. W. J. (1983). "Co-integrated variables and error-correcting models." *Discussion Paper 83-13, Department of Economics, University of California at San Diego.*

Granger, C. W. J. (1986). "Developments in the study of cointegrated economic variables." *Oxford Bulletin of Economics and Statistics*, 48, 213–228.

Granger, C. W. J. and Hyung, N. (2004). "Occasional structural breaks and long memory with an application to the SP 500 absolute stock returns." *Journal of Empirical Finance*, 11, 399–421.

Granger, C. W. J. and Joyeux, R. (1980). "An introduction to long memory time series models and fractional differencing." *Journal of Time Series Analysis*, 1, 15–29.

Granger, C. W. J. and Newbold, P. (1974). "Spurious regressions in econometrics." *Journal of Econometics*, 2, 111–120.

Granger, C. W. J. and Newbold, P. (1986). *Forecasting Economic Time Series.* Academic Press, New York, NY.

Granger, C. W. J. and Ramanathan, R. (1984). "Improved methods of combining forecasts." *Journal of Forecasting*, 3, 197–204.

Granziera, E., Moon, H. R., and Schorfheide, F. (2018). "Inference for VARs identified with sign restrictions." *Quantitative Economics*, 9, 1087–1121.

Gu, J. and Volgushev, S. (2019). "Panel data quantile regression with grouped fixed effects." *Journal of Econometrics*, 213, 68–91.

Gurland, J. (1948). "Inversion formulae for the distribution of ratios." *The Annals of Mathematical Statistics*, 2, 228–237.

Guthery, S. B. (1974). "Partition regression." *Journal of the American Statistical Association*, 69, 945–947.

Haario, H., Saksman, E., and Tamminen, J. (2001). "An adaptive Metropolis algorithm." *Bernoulli*, 7, 223–242.

Hahn, J. and Kuersteiner, G. (2011). "Bias reduction for dynamic nonlinear panel models with fixed effects." *Econometric Theory*, 27, 1152–1191.

Hahn, J. and Moon, H. R. (2010). "Panel data models with finite number of multiple equilibria." *Econometric Theory*, 26, 863–881.

Hahn, J. and Newey, W. (2004). "Jackknife and analytical bias reduction for nonlinear panel models." *Econometrica*, 72, 1295–1319.

Hájek, J. and Rényi, A. (1955). "Generalization of an inequality of Kolmogorov." *Acta Mathematica Academiae Scientiarum Hungarica*, 6, 281–283.

Hakkio, C. S. and Rush, M. (1991). "Is the budget deficit too large?" *Economic Inquiry*, 29, 429–445.

Haldrup, N. and Jansson, M. (2006). "Improving size and power in unit root testing." *Palgrave Handbook of Econometrics, Vol. 1*, K. Patterson and T. C. Mills, eds., Palgrave Macmillan, UK, 252–277.

Hall, A. R., Han, S., and Boldea, O. (2012). "Inference regarding multiple structural changes in linear models with endogenous regressors." *Journal of Econometrics*, 170, 281–302.

Hall, R. E. (1978). "Stochastic implications of the life cycle-permanent income hypothesis: Theory and evidence." *Journal of Political Economy*, 86, 971–987.

Hallin, M. and Liška, R. (2007). "Determining the number of factors in the general dynamic factor model." *Journal of the American Statistical Association*, 102, 603–617.

Hamilton, J. D. (1988). "Rational-expectations econometric analysis of changes in regime: An investigation of the term structure of interest rates." *Journal of Economic Dynamics and Control*, 12, 385–423.

Hamilton, J. D. (1989). "A new approach to the economic analysis of nonstationary time series and the business cycle." *Econometrica*, 57, 357–384.

Hamilton, J. D. (1994). *Time Series Analysis*. Princeton University Press, Princeton, NJ.

Hamilton, J. D. (2005). "What's real about the business cycle?" *Federal Reserve Bank of St. Louis Review*, 87, 435–52.

Hamilton, J. D. (2010). "Regime switching models." *Macroeconometrics and Time Series Analysis*, S. N. Durlauf and L. E. Blume, eds., The New Palgrave Economics Collection, Springer, Amsterdam, Netherlands, 202–209.

Hamilton, J. D. (2016). "Macroeconomic regimes and regime shifts." *Handbook of Macroeconomics, Vol. 2*, J. B. Taylor and H. Uhlig, eds., Elsevier, Amsterdam, Netherlands, 163–201.

Hamilton, J. D. (2018). "Why you should never use the Hodrick-Prescott filter." *Review of Economics and Statistics*, 100, 831–843.

Han, X. and Inoue, A. (2015). "Tests for parameter instability in dynamic factor models." *Econometric Theory*, 31, 1117–1152.

Hannan, E. J. (1971). "Non-linear time series regression." *Journal of Applied Probability*, 8, 767–780.

Hannan, E. J. and Deistler, M. (2012). *The Statistical Theory of Linear Systems*. Wiley, New York, NY.

Hansen, B. E. (1992a). "Efficient estimation and testing of cointegrating vectors in the presence of deterministic trends." *Journal of Econometrics*, 53, 87–121.

Hansen, B. E. (1992b). "Tests for parameter instability in regressions with I(1) processes." *Journal of Business & Economic Statistics*, 10, 521–535.

Hansen, B. E. (1995). "Rethinking the univariate approach to unit root testing: Using covariates to increase power." *Econometric Theory*, 11, 1148–1171.

Hansen, B. E. (1996). "Inference when a nuisance parameter is not identified under the null hypothesis." *Econometrica*, 64, 413–430.

Hansen, B. E. (2000). "Testing for structural change in conditional models." *Journal of Econometrics*, 97, 93–115.

Hansen, B. E. (2007). "Least squares model averaging." *Econometrica*, 75, 1175–1189.

Hansen, B. E. (2008). "Least-squares forecast averaging." *Journal of Econometrics*, 146, 342–350.

Hansen, B. E. and Racine, J. S. (2012). "Jackknife model averaging." *Journal of Econometrics*, 167, 38–46.

Hansen, H. and Johansen, S. (1999). "Some tests for parameter constancy in cointegrated VAR-models." *The Econometrics Journal*, 2, 306–333.

Hansen, L. P. and Sargent, T. J. (1990). "Recursive linear models of dynamic economies." National Bureau of Economic Research, Working Paper 3479.

Hansen, L. P. and Sargent, T. J. (1991). "Exact linear rational expectations models: Specification and estimation." *Rational Expectations Econometrics*, L. P. Hansen and T. Sargent, eds., Westview Press, Nashville, TN, 45–76.

Hansen, P. R. (2005). "A test for superior predictive ability." *Journal of Business & Economic Statistics*, 23, 365–380.

Hansen, P. R. and Lunde, A. (2005). "A forecast comparison of volatility models: Does anything beat a GARCH(1,1)?" *Journal of Applied Econometrics*, 20, 873–889.

Hansen, P. R., Lunde, A., and Nason, J. M. (2011). "The model confidence set." *Econometrica*, 79, 453–497.

Hao, K. (1996). "Testing for structural change in cointegrated regression models: Some comparisons and generalizations." *Econometric Reviews*, 15, 401–429.

Harchaoui, Z. and Lévy-Leduc, C. (2010). "Multiple change-point estimation with a total variation penalty." *Journal of the American Statistical Association*, 105, 1480–1493.

Harris, D., Harvey, D. I., Leybourne, S. J., and Taylor, A. M. R. (2009). "Testing for a unit root in the presence of a possible break in trend." *Econometric Theory*, 25, 1545–1588.

Harvey, A. C. (1975). Discussion of the Paper by Brown, Durbin and Evans. *The Journal of the Royal Statistical Society Series B*, 37, 179–180.

Harvey, A. (1981). *Time Series Models.* Wiley, New York, NY.

Harvey, A. and De Rossi, G. (2006). "Signal extraction." *Palgrave Handbook of Econometrics, Vol. 1*, K. Patterson and T. C. Mills, eds., Palgrave Macmillan, UK, 970–1000.

Harvey, A. C. (1987). "Applications of the Kalman filter in econometrics." *Advances in Econometrics, Vol. 1*, T. F. Bewley, ed., Cambridge University Press, New York, NY, 285–313.

Harvey, A. C. (1990). *Forecasting, Structural Time Series Models and the Kalman Filter.* Cambridge University Press, Cambridge, UK.

Harvey, A. C. (2006). "Forecasting with unobserved components time series models." *Handbook of Economic Forecasting*, G. Elliott, C. W. J. Granger, and A. Timmermann, eds., Elsevier Science, Amsterdam, Netherlands, 327–408.

Harvey, D. I., Leybourne, S. J., and Newbold, P. (2001). "Innovational outlier unit root tests with an endogenously determined break in level." *Oxford Bulletin of Economics and Statistics*, 63, 559–575.

Harvey, D. I., Leybourne, S. J., and Taylor, A. M. R. (2006). "Modified tests for a change in persistence." *Journal of Econometrics*, 134, 441–469.

Harvey, D. I., Leybourne, S. J., and Taylor, A. M. R. (2007). "A simple, robust and powerful test of the trend hypothesis." *Journal of Econometrics*, 141, 1302–1330.

Harvey, D. I., Leybourne, S. J., and Taylor, A. M. R. (2009a). "Simple, robust, and powerful tests of the breaking trend hypothesis." *Econometric Theory*, 25, 995–1029.

Harvey, D. I., Leybourne, S. J., and Taylor, A. M. R. (2009b). "Unit root testing in practice: Dealing with uncertainty over the trend and initial condition." *Econometric Theory*, 25, 587–636.

Harvey, D. I., Leybourne, S. J., and Taylor, A. M. R. (2013). "Testing for unit roots in the possible presence of multiple trend breaks using minimum Dickey-Fuller statistics." *Journal of Econometrics*, 177, 265–284.

Hastie, T., Tibshirani, R., and Friedman, J. (2009). *The Elements of Statistical Learning: Data Mining, Inference, and Prediction.* Springer, New York, NY.

Hastings, W. K. (1970). "Monte Carlo sampling methods using Markov chains and their applications." *Biometrika*, 57, 97–109.

Hatanaka, M. and Yamada, K. (1999). "A unit root test in the presence of structural changes in I(1) and I(0) models." *Cointegration, Causality and Forecasting: A Festschrift in Honour of Clive W.J. Granger*, R. F. Engle and H. White, eds., Oxford University Press, UK, 256–282.

Hausman, J. A. and Taylor, W. E. (1981). "Panel data and unobservable individual effects." *Econometrica*, 49, 1377–1398.

Hawkins, D. (1987). "A test for a change point in a parametric model based on a maximal Wald-type statistic." *Sankhyā: The Indian Journal of Statistics*, 49, 368–376.

Hawkins, D. M. (1976). "Point estimation of the parameters of piecewise regression models." *Journal of the Royal Statistical Society: Series C*, 25, 51–57.

Hawkins, D. M. (1977). "Testing a sequence of observations for a shift in location." *Journal of the American Statistical Association*, 72, 180–186.

Hayashi, F. and Sims, C. (1983). "Nearly efficient estimation of time series models with predetermined, but not exogenous, instruments." *Econometrica*, 51, 783–798.

Hecq, A. and Urbain, J.-P. (1993). "Misspecification tests, unit roots and level shifts." *Economics Letters*, 43, 129–135.

Heideman, M., Johnson, D., and Burrus, C. (1985). "Gauss and the history of the fast Fourier transform." *Archive for History of Exact Sciences*, 34, 265–277.

Hendry, D. F. (1980). "Econometrics-alchemy or science?" *Economica*, 47, 387–406.

Hendry, D. F. (1986). "Econometric modelling with cointegrated economic variables." *Oxford Bulletin of Economics and Statistics*, 48, 201–212.

Hendry, D. F., Pagan, A. R., and Sargan, J. D. (1984). "Dynamic specification." *Handbook of Econometrics, Vol. 2*, Z. Griliches and M. D. Intriligator, eds., Elsevier, Amsterdam, Netherlands, 1023–1100.

Hendry, D. F. and Richard, J.-F. (1982). "On the formulation of empirical models in dynamic econometrics." *Journal of Econometrics*, 20, 3–33.

Heston, S. L. (1993). "A closed-form solution for options with stochastic volatility with applications to bond and currency options." *The Review of Financial Studies*, 6, 327–343.

Hidalgo, J. and Seo, M. H. (2013). "Testing for structural stability in the whole sample." *Journal of Econometrics*, 175, 84–93.

Hirano, K. and Wright, J. H. (2022). "Analyzing cross-validation for forecasting with structural instability." *Journal of Econometrics*, 226, 139–154.

Hodrick, R. J. and Prescott, E. C. (1981). "Postwar U.S. business cycles: An empirical investigation." *Discussion Paper, No. 451, Northwestern University, Kellogg School of Management, Center for Mathematical Studies in Economics and Management Science*, Evanston, IL.

Hodrick, R. J. and Prescott, E. C. (1997). "Postwar U.S. business cycles: An empirical investigation." *Journal of Money, Credit, and Banking*, 29, 1–16.

Holtz-Eakin, D., Newey, W. K., and Rosen, H. S. (1988). "Estimating vector autoregressions with panel data." *Econometrica*, 56, 1371–1395.

Hood, W. C. and Koopmans, T. C. (1953). *Studies in Econometric Methods, Cowles Commission for Research in Economics, Monograph No. 14*. Wiley, New York, NY.

Horváth, L. (1995). "Detecting changes in linear regressions." *Statistics: A Journal of Theoretical and Applied Statistics*, 26, 189–208.

Hosking, J. R. M. (1981). "Fractional differencing." *Biometrika*, 68, 165–176.

Hou, J. and Perron, P. (2014). "Modified local Whittle estimator for long memory processes in the presence of low frequency (and other) contaminations." *Journal of Econometrics*, 182, 309–328.

Hsiao, C. and Tahmiscioglu, A. K. (1997). "A panel analysis of liquidity constraints and firm investment." *Journal of the American Statistical Association*, 92, 455–465.

Hualde, J. and Nielsen, M. Ø. (2023). "Fractional integration and cointegration." *Oxford Encyclopedia of Economics and Finance*.

Hurst, H. E. (1951). "Long-term storage capacity of reservoirs." *Transactions of the American Society of Civil Engineers*, 116, 770–799.

Hurvich, C. M., Deo, R., and Brodsky, J. (1998). "The mean squared error of Geweke and Porter-Hudak's estimator of the memory parameter of a long-memory time series." *Journal of Time Series Analysis*, 19, 19–46.

Hurvich, C. M., Moulines, E., and Soulier, P. (2005). "Estimating long memory in volatility." *Econometrica*, 73, 1283–1328.

Hurvich, C. M. and Ray, B. K. (2003). "The local Whittle estimator of long-memory stochastic volatility." *Journal of Financial Econometrics*, 1, 445–470.

Iacone, F. (2010). "Local Whittle estimation of the memory parameter in presence of deterministic components." *Journal of Time Series Analysis*, 31, 37–49.

Iacone, F., Leybourne, S. J., and Taylor, A. M. R. (2013a). "On the behavior of fixed-b trend break tests under fractional integration." *Econometric Theory*, 29, 393–418.

Iacone, F., Leybourne, S. J., and Taylor, A. M. R. (2013b). "Testing for a break in trend when the order of integration is unknown." *Journal of Econometrics*, 176, 30–45.

Im, K. S., Pesaran, M. H., and Shin, Y. (2003). "Testing for unit roots in heterogeneous panels." *Journal of Econometrics*, 115, 53–74.

Im, K. S., Pesaran, M. H., and Shin, Y. (2023). "Reflections on "Testing for unit roots in heterogeneous panels"." *Journal of Econometrics*, 234, 111–114.

Imhof, J.-P. (1961). "Computing the distribution of quadratic forms in normal variables." *Biometrika*, 48, 419–426.

Inoue, A., Jin, L., and Rossi, B. (2017). "Rolling window selection for out-of-sample forecasting with time-varying parameters." *Journal of Econometrics*, 196, 55–67.

Itô, K. (1944). "Stochastic integral." *Proceedings of the Imperial Academy*, 20, 519–524.

Jacquier, E., Polson, N. G., and Rossi, P. E. (2004). "Bayesian analysis of stochastic volatility models with fat-tails and correlated errors." *Journal of Econometrics*, 122, 185–212.

Jacquier, E. Polson, N. G. and Rossi, P. E. (1994). "Bayesian analysis of stochastic volatility models." *Journal of Business & Economic Statistics*, 12, 371–417.

James, B., James, K. L., and Siegmund, D. (1987). "Tests for a change-point." *Biometrika*, 74, 71–83.

Jandhyala, V. and MacNeill, I. (1989). "Residual partial sum limit process for regression models with applications to detecting parameter changes at unknown times." *Stochastic Processes and their Applications*, 33, 309–323.

Jandhyala, V. and MacNeill, I. (1992). "On testing for the constancy of regression coefficients under random walk and change-point alternatives." *Econometric Theory*, 8, 501–517.

Jandhyala, V. and Minogue, C. (1993). "Distributions of Bayes-type change-point statistics under polynomial regression." *Journal of Statistical Planning and Inference*, 37, 271–290.

Jazwinski, A. H. (1970). *Stochastic Processes and Filtering Theory.* Academic Press, New York, NY.

Jeganathan, P. (1991). "On the asymptotic behavior of least-squares estimators in AR time series with roots near the unit circle." *Econometric Theory*, 7, 269–306.

Johansen, A. M. and Evers, L. (2007). "Monte Carlo methods: Lecture notes." *Department of Mathematics*, University of Bristol.

Johansen, S. (1988). "Statistical analysis of cointegration vectors." *Journal of Economic Dynamics and Control*, 12, 231–254.

Johansen, S. (1991). "Estimation and hypothesis testing of cointegration vectors in Gaussian vector autoregressive models." *Econometrica*, 59, 1551–1580.

Johansen, S. (1994). "The role of the constant and linear terms in cointegration analysis of nonstationary variables." *Econometric Reviews*, 13, 205–229.

Johansen, S. (1995). *Likelihood-Based Inference in Cointegrated Vector Autoregressive Models.* Oxford University Press, Oxford, UK.

Johansen, S. (2006). "Cointegration: An overview." *Palgrave Handbook of Econometrics, Vol. 1*, K. Patterson and T. C. Mills, eds., Palgrave Macmillan, London, UK, 540–577.

Johansen, S. and Juselius, K. (1990). "Maximum likelihood estimation and inference on cointegration with applications to the demand for money." *Oxford Bulletin of Economics and Statistics*, 52, 169–210.

Johansen, S. and Juselius, K. (1992). "Testing structural hypotheses in a multivariate cointegration analysis of the PPP and the UIP for UK." *Journal of Econometrics*, 53, 211–244.

Jordà, Ò. (2005). "Estimation and inference of impulse responses by local projections." *American Economic Review*, 95, 161–182.

Juglar, C. (1889). *Des Crises Commerciales et de leur Retour Periodique en France, en Angleterre et aux Etats-Unis. 2nd ed.* Guillaumin et Cie, Paris, France.

Julier, S. J. and Uhlmann, J. K. (1997). "New extension of the Kalman filter to nonlinear systems." *Signal Processing, Sensor Fusion, and Target Recognition VI*, Bellingham WA, SPIE, 182–193.

Kalman, R. E. (1960). "A new approach to linear filtering and prediction problems." *Journal of Basic Engineering*, 82, 35–45.

Kalman, R. E. (1963). "Lyapunov functions for the problem of Lur'e in automatic control." *Proceedings of the National Academy of Sciences of the United States of America*, 49, 201–205.

Kalman, R. E. and Bertram, J. F. (1960). "Control system analysis and design via the second method of Lyapunov." *Journal of Basic Engineering*, 88, 371–394.

Kander, Z. and Zacks, S. (1966). "Test procedures for possible changes in parameters of statistical distributions occurring at unknown time points." *The Annals of Mathematical Statistics*, 37, 1196–1210.

Kapetanios, G. (2005). "Unit-root testing against the alternative hypothesis of up to m structural breaks." *Journal of Time Series Analysis*, 26, 123–133.

Kapetanios, G. (2010). "A testing procedure for determining the number of factors in approximate factor models with large datasets." *Journal of Business & Economic Statistics*, 28, 397–409.

Kasahara, H. and Shimotsu, K. (2009). "Nonparametric identification of finite mixture models of dynamic discrete choices." *Econometrica*, 77, 135–175.

Keane, M. P. and Runkle, D. E. (1992). "On the estimation of panel-data models with serial correlation when instruments are not strictly exogenous." *Journal of Business & Economic Statistics*, 10, 1–9.

Keating, J. W. (1990). "Identifying VAR models under rational expectations." *Journal of Monetary Economics*, 25, 453–476.

Kejriwal, M., Nguyen, L., and Yu, X. (2022). "Multistep forecast averaging with stochastic and deterministic trends." *Econometrics*, 11, 28., 1–43.

Kejriwal, M. and Perron, P. (2008a). "Data dependent rules for selection of the numbers of leads and lags in the dynamic OLS cointegrating regression." *Econometric Theory*, 24, 1425–1441.

Kejriwal, M. and Perron, P. (2008b). "The limit distribution of the estimates in cointegrated regression models with multiple structural changes." *Journal of Econometrics*, 146, 59–73.

Kejriwal, M. and Perron, P. (2010a). "A sequential procedure to determine the numbers of breaks in trend with an integrated or stationary noise component." *Journal of Time Series Analysis*, 31, 305–328.

Kejriwal, M. and Perron, P. (2010b). "Testing for multiple structural changes in cointegrated regression models." *Journal of Business & Economic Statistics*, 28, 503–522.

Kejriwal, M. and Perron, P. (2012). "A note on estimating a structural change in persistence." *Economics Letters*, 117, 932–935.

Kejriwal, M., Perron, P., and Zhou, J. (2013). "Wald tests for detecting multiple structural changes in persistence." *Econometric Theory*, 29, 289–323.

Kejriwal, M. and Yu, X. (2021). "Generalized forecast averaging in autoregressions with a near unit root." *The Econometrics Journal*, 24, 83–102.

Kejriwal, M., Yu, X., and Perron, P. (2020). "Bootstrap procedures for detecting multiple persistence shifts in heteroskedastic time series." *Journal of Time Series Analysis*, 41, 676–690.

Kelejian, H. H. and Prucha, I. R. (1998). "A generalized spatial two-stage least squares procedure for estimating a spatial autoregressive model with autoregressive disturbances." *The Journal of Real Estate Finance and Economics*, 17, 99–121.

Kelejian, H. H. and Prucha, I. R. (2010). "Specification and estimation of spatial autoregressive models with autoregressive and heteroskedastic disturbances." *Journal of Econometrics*, 157, 53–67.

Kilian, L. (1998). "Small-sample confidence intervals for impulse response functions." *Review of Economics and Statistics*, 80, 218–230.

Kilian, L. and Lütkepohl, H. (2017). *Structural Vector Autoregressive Analysis.* Cambridge University Press, Cambridge, UK.

Kim, C.-J. and Nelson, C. R. (1998). "Business cycle turning points, a new coincident index, and tests of duration dependence based on a dynamic factor model with regime switching." *The Review of Economics and Statistics*, 80, 188–201.

Kim, C.-J. and Nelson, C. R. (1999). *State-Space Models with Regime Switching: Classical and Gibbs-Sampling Approaches with Applications.* The MIT Press, Cambridge, MA.

Kim, D. (2011). "Estimating a common deterministic time trend break in large panels with cross sectional dependence." *Journal of Econometrics*, 164, 310–330.

Kim, D. (2014). "Common breaks in time trends for large panel data with a factor structure." *The Econometrics Journal*, 17, 301–337.

Kim, D., Oka, T., Estrada, F., and Perron, P. (2020). "Inference related to common breaks in a multivariate system with joined segmented trends with applications to global and hemispheric temperatures." *Journal of Econometrics*, 214, 130–152.

Kim, D. and Perron, P. (2009a). "Assessing the relative power of structural break tests using a framework based on the approximate Bahadur slope." *Journal of Econometrics*, 149, 26–51.

Kim, D. and Perron, P. (2009b). "Unit root tests allowing for a break in the trend function at an unknown time under both the null and alternative hypotheses." *Journal of Econometrics*, 148, 1–13.

Kim, H.-J. and Siegmund, D. (1989). "The likelihood ratio test for a change-point in simple linear regression." *Biometrika*, 76, 409–423.

Kim, J.-Y. (2000). "Detection of change in persistence of a linear time series." *Journal of Econometrics*, 95, 97–116.

Kim, S., Shepherd, N., and Chib, S. (1998). "Stochastic volatility: Likelihood inference and comparison with ARCH models." *The Review of Economic Studies*, 65, 361–393.

King, M. L. and Shively, T. S. (1993). "Locally optimal testing when a nuisance parameter is present only under the alternative." *Review of Economics and Statistics*, 75, 1–7.

King, R. G., Plosser, C. I., Stock, J. H., and Watson, M. W. (1991). "Stochastic trends and economic fluctuations." *American Economic Review*, 81, 819–840.

King, R. G. and Watson, M. W. (1994). "The post-war U.S. Phillips curve: A revisionist econometric history." *Carnegie-Rochester Conference Series on Public Policy*, 41, 157–219.

Kitagawa, G. (1996). "Monte Carlo filter and smoother for non-Gaussian nonlinear state space models." *Journal of Computational and Graphical Statistics*, 5, 1–25.

Kitchin, J. (1923). "Cycles and trends in economic factors." *The Review of Economics and Statistics*, 5, 10–16.

Koenker, R. (2005). *Quantile Regression.* Cambridge University Press, Cambridge, UK.

Koenker, R. and Bassett, G. (1978). "Regression quantiles." *Econometrica*, 46, 33–50.

Kondratieff, N. D. (1935). "The long waves in economic life (translated by W. F. Stolper)." *The Review of Economics and Statistics*, 17, 105–115.

Koo, B. and Seo, M. H. (2015). "Structural-break models under misspecification: Implications for forecasting." *Journal of Econometrics*, 188, 166–181.

Koop, G. and Potter, S. M. (2007). "Estimation and forecasting in models with multiple breaks." *Review of Economic Studies*, 74, 763–789.

Krämer, W., Ploberger, W., and Alt, R. (1988). "Testing for structural change in dynamic models." *Econometrica*, 56, 1355–1369.

Kruschke, J. (2014). *Doing Bayesian Data Analysis: A Tutorial with R, JAGS, and Stan, 2nd ed.* Elsevier, Amsterdam, Netherlands.

Kulperger, R. (1987a). "On the residuals of autoregressive processes and polynomial regression." *Stochastic Processes and their Applications*, 21, 107–118.

Kulperger, R. (1987b). "Some remarks on regression with autoregressive errors and their residual processes." *Journal of Applied Probability*, 24, 668–678.

Kunitomo, N. and Sato, S. (1995). "Tables of limiting distributions useful for testing unit roots and co-integration with multiple structural breaks." *Unpublished Manuscript*, Department of Economics, University of Tokyo.

Kunsch, H. (1987). "Statistical aspects of self-similar processes." *Proceedings of the First World Congress of the Bernoulli Society, Vol. 1*, Y. Prohorov and V. Sazarov, eds., VNU Science Press, Utrecht, Netherlands, 67–74.

Kuo, B. S. (1998). "Test for partial parameter instability in regressions with I(1) processes." *Journal of Econometrics*, 86, 337–368.

Kurozumi, E. (2015). "Testing for multiple structural changes with non-homogeneous regressors." *Journal of Time Series Econometrics*, 7, 1–35.

Kurozumi, E. (2017). "Monitoring parameter constancy with endogenous regressors." *Journal of Time Series Analysis*, 38, 791–805.

Kurozumi, E. and Arai, Y. (2007). "Efficient estimation and inference in cointegrating regressions with structural change." *Journal of Time Series Analysis*, 28, 545–575.

Kurozumi, E. and Yamamoto, Y. (2015). "Confidence sets for the break date based on optimal tests." *The Econometrics Journal*, 18, 412–435.

Kuznets, S. (1930). *Secular Movement in Production and Prices: Their Nature and their Bearing upon Cyclical Fluctuations.* Houghton Mifflin and Company, Boston, MA.

Kuznets, S. (1946). *National Product Since 1869.* NBER, Cambridge, MA.

Kuznets, S. (1958). "Long swings in the growth of population and in related economic variables." *Proceedings of the American Philosophical Society*, 102, 25–52.

Kwiatkowski, D., Phillips, P. C. B., Schmidt, P., and Shin, Y. (1992). "Testing the null hypothesis of stationarity against the alternative of a unit root." *Journal of Econometrics*, 54, 159–178.

Lanne, M. and Lütkepohl, H. (2002). "Unit root tests for time series with level shifts: A comparison of different proposals." *Economics Letters*, 75, 109–114.

Lanne, M., Lütkepohl, H., and Saikkonen, P. (2002). "Comparison of unit root tests for time series with level shifts." *Journal of Time Series Analysis*, 23, 667–685.

Laroque, G. (1977). "Analyse d'une méthode de désaisonnalisation: Le programme X-11, du U.S. Bureau of Census, version trimestrielle." *Annales de l'INSEE*, 105–127.

Lee, J. (2000). "On the end-point issue in unit root tests in the presence of a structural break." *Economics Letters*, 68, 7–11.

Lee, J., Huang, C. J., and Shin, Y. (1997). "On stationary tests in the presence of structural breaks." *Economics Letters*, 55, 165–172.

Lee, J. and Strazicich, M. C. (2001). "Break point estimation and spurious rejections with endogenous unit root tests." *Oxford Bulletin of Economics and Statistics*, 63, 535–558.

Lee, L.-f. and Yu, J. (2015). "Spatial panel data models." *The Oxford Handbook of Panel Data*, B. H. Baltagi, ed., Oxford University Press, Oxford, UK, 363–401.

Lee, T.-H., Parsaeian, S., and Ullah, A. (2022). "Forecasting under structural breaks using improved weighted estimation." *Oxford Bulletin of Economics and Statistics*, 84, 1485–1501.

Lewis, R. and Reinsel, G. C. (1985). "Prediction of multivariate time series by autoregressive model fitting." *Journal of Multivariate Analysis*, 16, 393–411.

Leybourne, S. J., Mills, T. C., and Newbold, P. (1998). "Spurious rejections by Dickey-Fuller tests in the presence of a break under the null." *Journal of Econometrics*, 87, 191–203.

Leybourne, S. J. and Newbold, P. (2000). "Behaviour of the standard and symmetric Dickey-Fuller-type tests when there is a break under the null hypothesis." *The Econometrics Journal*, 3, 1–15.

Leybourne, S. J. and Taylor, A. M. R. (2004). "On tests for changes in persistence." *Economics Letters*, 84, 107–115.

Li, D., Qian, J., and Su, L. (2016). "Panel data models with interactive fixed effects and multiple structural breaks." *Journal of the American Statistical Association*, 111, 1804–1819.

Li, J. and Barron, A. (1999). "Mixture density estimation." *Advances in Neural Information Processing Systems*, 12, 279–285.

Li, J., Liao, Z., and Quaedvlieg, R. (2022). "Conditional superior predictive ability." *The Review of Economic Studies*, 89, 843–875.

Li, K.-C. (1987). "Asymptotic optimality for Cp, CL, cross-validation and generalized cross-validation: Discrete index set." *The Annals of Statistics*, 15, 958–975.

Li, Y. and Perron, P. (2017). "Inference on locally ordered breaks in multiple regressions." *Econometric Reviews*, 36, 289–353.

Lin, C.-C. and Ng, S. (2012). "Estimation of panel data models with parameter heterogeneity when group membership is unknown." *Journal of Econometric Methods*, 1, 42–55.

Lin, Y. and Jeon, Y. (2006). "Random forests and adaptive nearest neighbors." *Journal of the American Statistical Association*, 101, 578–590.

Lippi, M. and Reichlin, L. (1993). "The dynamic effects of aggregate demand and supply disturbances: Comment." *American Economic Review*, 83, 644–652.

Litterman, R. B. and Weiss, L. (1985). "Money, real interest rates, and output: A reinterpretation of postwar U.S. data." *Econometrica*, 53, 129–156.

Liu, J., Wu, S., and Zidek, J. V. (1997). "On segmented multivariate regression." *Statistica Sinica*, 7, 497–525.

Liu, Q. and Okui, R. (2013). "Heteroscedasticity-robust Cp model averaging." *The Econometrics Journal*, 16, 463–472.

Ljung, G. M. and Box, G. E. (1978). "On a measure of lack of fit in time series models." *Biometrika*, 65, 297–303.

Lo, A. W. (1991). "Long-term memory in stock market prices." *Econometrica*, 59, 649–662.

Lobato, I. N. and Savin, N. E. (1998). "Real and spurious long-memory properties of stock-market data." *Journal of Business & Economic Statistics*, 16, 261–268.

Lopes, H. F. and Tsay, R. S. (2011). "Particle filters and Bayesian inference in financial econometrics." *Journal of Forecasting*, 30, 168–209.

Louis, T. A. (1982). "Finding the observed information matrix when using the EM algorithm." *Journal of the Royal Statistical Society: Series B*, 44, 226–233.

Lu, Y. K. and Perron, P. (2010). "Modeling and forecasting stock return volatility using a random level shift model." *Journal of Empirical Finance*, 17, 138–156.

Lubik, T. A. and Schorfheide, F. (2004). "Testing for indeterminacy: An application to U.S. monetary policy." *American Economic Review*, 94, 190–217.

Lucas, R. E. (1976). "Econometric policy evaluation: A critique." *Carnegie-Rochester Conference Series on Public Policy*, K. Brunner and A. Meltzer, eds., North-Holland, Amsterdam, Netherlands, 19–46.

Lucas, R. E. and Sargent, T. J. (1979). "After Keynesian macroeconomics." *Quarterly Review*, 3, 1–16.

Ludvigson, S. C., Ma, S., and Ng, S. (2020). "Shock restricted structural vector-autoregressions." National Bureau of Economic Research, Working Paper 23225.

Ludvigson, S. C., Ma, S., and Ng, S. (2021). "Uncertainty and business cycles: Exogenous impulse or endogenous response?" *American Economic Journal: Macroeconomics*, 13, 369–410.

Lumsdaine, R. L. and Papell, D. H. (1997). "Multiple trend breaks and the unit-root hypothesis." *Review of Economics and Statistics*, 79, 212–218.

Lusompa, A. (2023). "Local projections, autocorrelation, and efficiency." *Quantitative Economics*, 14, 1199–1220.

Lütkepohl, H. (2006). "Vector autoregressive models." *Palgrave Handbook of Econometrics, Vol. 1, Econometric Theory*, K. Patterson and T. C. Mills, eds., Palgrave Macmillan, London, UK, 477–510.

Macaulay, F. R. (1931). *The Smoothing of Time Series.* NBER Books, New York, NY.

MacNeill, I. B. (1974). "Tests for change of parameter at unknown times and distributions of some related functionals on Brownian motion." *The Annals of Statistics*, 2, 950–962.

MacNeill, I. B. (1978). "Properties of sequences of partial sums of polynomial regression residuals with applications to tests for change of regression at unknown times." *The Annals of Statistics*, 6, 422–433.

Maddala, G. S. and Hu, W. (1996). "The pooling problem." *The Econometrics of Panel Data: a Handbook of the Theory with Applications*, L. Mátyás and P. Sevestre, eds., Dordrecht: Springer Netherlands,, 307–322.

Magnusson, L. M. and Mavroeidis, S. (2014). "Identification using stability restrictions." *Econometrica*, 82, 1799–1851.

Maheu, J. M. and Gordon, S. (2008). "Learning, forecasting and structural breaks." *Journal of Applied Econometrics*, 23, 553–583.

Maheu, J. M. and McCurdy, T. H. (2009). "How useful are historical data for forecasting the long-run equity return distribution?" *Journal of Business & Economic Statistics*, 27, 95–112.

Malinvaud, E. (1980). *Statistical Methods of Econometrics.* North-Holland Amsterdam, Netherlands.

Mallows, C. L. (1964a). "Choosing a subset regression." *Unpublished Paper Presented at the Annual Meeting of the American Statistical Association, Los Angeles, August 15-19.*

Mallows, C. L. (1964b). "Choosing variables in a linear regression: A graphical aid." *In Central Regional Meeting of the Institute of Mathematical Statistics*, Manhattan, KS.

Mallows, C. L. (2000). "Some comments on Cp." *Technometrics*, 42, 87–94.

Mandelbrot, B. B. and Taqqu, M. S. (1979). *Robust R/S Analysis of Long Run Serial Correlation.* IBM Thomas J. Watson Research Division, Yorktown Heights, NY.

Mankiw, N. G., Miron, J. A., and Weil, D. N. (1987). "The adjustment of expectations to a change in regime: A study of the founding of the Federal Reserve." *American Economic Review*, 77, 358–372.

Marcellino, M., Stock, J. H., and Watson, M. W. (2006). "A comparison of direct and iterated multistep AR methods for forecasting macroeconomic time series." *Journal of Econometrics*, 135, 499–526.

Marinucci, D. and Robinson, P. M. (1999). "Alternative forms of fractional Brownian motion." *Journal of Statistical Planning and Inference*, 80, 111–122.

Marriott, J. and Newbold, P. (2000). "The strength of evidence for unit autoregressive roots and structural breaks: A Bayesian perspective." *Journal of Econometrics*, 98, 1–25.

Martins, L. F. and Perron, P. (2016). "Improved tests for forecast comparisons in the presence of instabilities." *Journal of Time Series Analysis*, 37, 650–659.

Masson, P. R. (2000). *Exchange Rate Regime Transitions.* Report number 2000-2134. International Monetary Fund, Research Department, Washington, DC.

Mavroeidis, S. (2021). "Identification at the zero lower bound." *Econometrica*, 89, 2855–2885.

Maybeck, P. S. (1982). *Stochastic Models, Estimation and Control.* Academic Press, New York, NY.

McCloskey, A. and Hill, J. B. (2017). "Parameter estimation robust to low-frequency contamination." *Journal of Business & Economic Statistics*, 35, 598–610.

McCloskey, A. and Perron, P. (2013). "Memory parameter estimation in the presence of level shifts and deterministic trends." *Econometric Theory*, 29, 1196–1237.

McCracken, M. W. (2007). "Asymptotics for out of sample tests of Granger causality." *Journal of Econometrics*, 140, 719–752.

McCracken, M. W. (2019). "Tests of conditional predictive ability: Some simulation evidence." *Report No. 2019-11*, Federal Reserve Bank of St. Louis.

McCracken, M. W. (2020a). "Diverging tests of equal predictive ability." *Econometrica*, 88, 1753–1754.

McCracken, M. W. (2020b). "Tests of conditional predictive ability: Existence, size, and power." *Report No. 2020-50*, Federal Reserve Bank of St. Louis.

McCulloch, R. E. and Tsay, R. S. (1993). "Bayesian inference and prediction for mean and variance shifts in autoregressive time series." *Journal of the American Statistical Association*, 88, 968–978.

McLeish, D. (1975a). "Invariance principles for dependent variables." *Probability Theory and Related Fields*, 32, 165–178.

McLeish, D. (1975b). "A maximal inequality and dependent strong laws." *The Annals of Probability*, 3, 829–839.

McLeish, D. (1977). "On the invariance principle for nonstationary mixingales." *The Annals of Probability*, 5, 616–621.

Medeiros, M. C., Vasconcelos, G. F., Veiga, A., and Zilberman, E. (2021). "Forecasting inflation in a data-rich environment: The benefits of machine learning methods." *Journal of Business & Economic Statistics*, 39, 98–119.

Meitz, M. and Saikkonen, P. (2021). "Testing for observation-dependent regime switching in mixture autoregressive models." *Journal of Econometrics*, 222, 601–624.

Mertens, K. and Ravn, M. O. (2013). "The dynamic effects of personal and corporate income tax changes in the United States." *American Economic Review*, 103, 1212–1247.

Metropolis, N., Rosenbluth, A. W., Rosenbluth, M. N., Teller, A. H., and Teller, E. (1953). "Equation of state calculations by fast computing machines." *Journal of Chemical Physics*, 21, 1087–1092.

Mikosch, T. and Stărică, C. (2004). "Nonstationarities in financial time series, the long-range dependence, and the IGARCH effects." *Review of Economics and Statistics*, 86, 378–390.

Mincer, J. A. and Zarnowitz, V. (1969). "The evaluation of economic forecasts." *Economic Forecasts and Expectations: Analysis of Forecasting Behavior and Performance*, J. Mincer, ed., National Bureau of Economic Research, 14–20.

Monfort, A., Renne, J.-P., and Roussellet, G. (2015). "A quadratic Kalman filter." *Journal of Econometrics*, 43-56, 187.

Montañés, A. (1997). "Level shifts, unit roots and misspecification of the breaking date." *Economics Letters*, 54, 7–13.

Montañés, A. and Olloqui, I. (1999). "Misspecification of the breaking date in segmented trend variables: Effect on the unit root tests." *Economics Letters*, 65, 301–307.

Montañés, A., Olloqui, I., and Calvo, E. (2005). "Selection of the break in the Perron-type tests." *Journal of Econometrics*, 129, 41–64.

Montañés, A. and Reyes, M. (1998). "Effect of a shift in the trend function on Dickey-Fuller unit root tests." *Econometric Theory*, 14, 355–363.

Montañés, A. and Reyes, M. (1999). "The asymptotic behaviour of the Dickey–Fuller tests under the crash hypothesis." *Statistics & Probability Letters*, 42, 81–89.

Montañés, A. and Reyes, M. (2000). "Structural breaks, unit roots and methods for removing the autocorrelation pattern." *Statistics & Probability Letters*, 48, 401–409.

Montiel Olea, J.L. and Plagborg-Møller, M. (2021). "Local projection inference is simpler and more robust than you think." *Econometrica*, 89, 1789–1823.

Moon, H. R. and Schorfheide, F. (2012). "Bayesian and frequentist inference in partially identified models." *Econometrica*, 80, 755–782.

Moon, H. R. and Weidner, M. (2015). "Linear regression for panel with unknown number of factors as interactive fixed effects." *Econometrica*, 83, 1543–1579.

Morley, J. C., Nelson, C. R., and Zivot, E. (2003). "Why are the Beveridge-Nelson and unobserved-components decompositions of GDP so different?" *Review of Economics and Statistics*, 85, 235–243.

Müller, C., Lütkepohl, H., and Saikkonen, P. (2001). "Unit root tests for time series with a structural break when the break point is known." *Thirteenth International Symposium in Economic Theory and Econometrics*, C. Hsiao, K. Morimune, and J. Powell, eds., Cambridge University Press, UK, 327–348.

Müller, U. K. and Elliott, G. (2003). "Tests for unit roots and the initial condition." *Econometrica*, 71, 1269–1286.

Mundlak, Y. (1978). "On the pooling of time series and cross section data." *Econometrica*, 46, 69–85.

Nabeya, S. and Perron, P. (1994). "Local asymptotic distribution related to the AR(1) model with dependent errors." *Journal of Econometrics*, 62, 229–264.

Nabeya, S. and Perron, P. (1995). "Approximations to some exact distributions in the first order autoregressive model with dependent errors." *Econometric Reviews*, 14, 421–457.

Nabeya, S. and Sørensen, B. E. (1994). "Asymptotic distributions of the least-squares estimators and test statistics in the near unit root model with non-zero initial value and local drift and trend." *Econometric Theory*, 10, 937–966.

Nabeya, S. and Tanaka, K. (1988). "Asymptotic theory of a test for the constancy of regression coefficients against the random walk alternative." *The Annals of Statistics*, 16, 218–235.

Nabeya, S. and Tanaka, K. (1990). "A general approach to the limiting distribution for estimators in time series regression with nonstable autoregressive errors." *Econometrica*, 58, 145–163.

Nadler, J. and Robbins, N. B. (1971). "Some characteristics of Page's two-sided procedure for detecting a change in a location parameter." *The Annals of Mathematical Statistics*, 42, 538–551.

Nankervis, J. C. and Savin, N. E. (1985). "Testing the autoregressive parameter with the t statistic." *Journal of Econometrics*, 27, 143–161.

Nelson, C. R. and Plosser, C. R. (1982). "Trends and random walks in macroeconmic time series: Some evidence and implications." *Journal of Monetary Economics*, 10, 139–162.

Nelson, D. B. (1991). "Conditional heteroskedasticity in asset returns: A new approach." *Econometrica*, 59, 347–370.

Neyman, J. and Pearson, E. S. (1933). "On the problem of the most efficient tests of statistical hypotheses." *Philosophical Transactions of the Royal Society of London. Series A*, 231, 289–337.

Ng, S. (2013). "Variable selection in predictive regressions." *Handbook of Economic Forecasting, Vol, 2B*, G. Elliott and A. Timmermann, eds., North-Holland Elsevier, 753–789.

Ng, S. and Perron, P. (1995). "Unit root tests in ARMA models with data-dependent methods for the selection of the truncation lag." *Journal of the American Statistical Association*, 90, 268–281.

Ng, S. and Perron, P. (1996). "The exact error in estimating the spectral density at the origin." *Journal of Time Series Analysis*, 17, 379–408.

Ng, S. and Perron, P. (1997). "Estimation and inference in nearly unbalanced nearly cointegrated systems." *Journal of Econometrics*, 79, 53–81.

Ng, S. and Perron, P. (2001). "Lag length selection and the construction of unit root tests with good size and power." *Econometrica*, 69, 1519–1554.

Ng, S. and Perron, P. (2005). "A note on the selection of time series models." *Oxford Bulletin of Economics and Statistics*, 67, 115–134.

Nicholls, D. F. and Pagan, A. R. (1985). "Varying coefficient regression." *Handbook of Statistics 5*, E. J. Hannan, P. R. Krishnaiah, and M. M. Rao, eds., North Holland Elsevier, Amsterdam, 413–450.

Nickell, S. (1981). "Biases in dynamic models with fixed effects." *Econometrica*, 49, 1417–1426.

Nunes, L. C., Newbold, P., and Kuan, C.-M. (1996). "Spurious numbers of breaks." *Economics Letters*, 50, 175–178.

Nunes, L. C., Newbold, P., and Kuan, C.-M. (1997). "Testing for unit roots with breaks: Evidence on the Great Crash and the unit root hypothesis reconsidered." *Oxford Bulletin of Economics and Statistics*, 59, 435–448.

Nyblom, J. (1989). "Testing for the constancy of parameters over time." *Journal of the American Statistical Association*, 84, 223–230.

Nyblom, J. and Harvey, A. (2000). "Tests of common stochastic trends." *Econometric Theory*, 16, 176–199.

Nyblom, J. and Mäkeläinen, T. (1983). "Comparisons of tests for the presence of random walk coefficients in a simple linear model." *Journal of the American Statistical Association*, 78, 856–864.

Oh, H. K. and Zivot, E. (2006). "The Clark model with correlated components." *Unpublished Manuscript, University of Washington.*

Ohanissian, A., Russell, J. R., and Tsay, R. S. (2008). "True or spurious long memory? A new test." *Journal of Business & Economic Statistics*, 26, 161–175.

Ohara, H. I. (1999). "A unit root test with multiple trend breaks: A theory and an application to U.S. and Japanese macroeconomic time-series." *The Japanese Economic Review*, 50, 266–290.

Oka, T. and Perron, P. (2018). "Testing for common breaks in a multiple equations system." *Journal of Econometrics*, 204, 66–85.

Oka, T. and Qu, Z. (2011). "Estimating structural changes in regression quantiles." *Journal of Econometrics*, 162, 248–267.

Oksendal, B. (1985). *Stochastic Differential Equations: An Introduction with Applications*. Springer, New York, NY.

Okui, R. and Wang, W. (2021). "Heterogeneous structural breaks in panel data models." *Journal of Econometrics*, 220, 447–473.

Olsson, J., Cappé, O., Douc, R., and Moulines, É. (2008). "Sequential Monte Carlo smoothing with application to parameter estimation in nonlinear state space models." *Bernoulli*, 14, 155–179.

Onatski, A. (2010). "Determining the number of factors from empirical distribution of eigenvalues." *The Review of Economics and Statistics*, 92, 1004–1016.

Onatski, A. and Wang, C. (2021). "Spurious factor analysis." *Econometrica*, 89, 591–614.

Orphanides, A. (2001). "Monetary policy rules based on real-time data." *American Economic Review*, 91, 964–985.

Ouliaris, S., Park, J. Y., and Phillips, P. C. B. (1989). "Testing for a unit root in the presence of a maintained trend." *Advances in Econometrics and Modelling*, B. Raj, ed., Springer, Amsterdam, Netherlands, 7–28.

Page, E. (1955). "A test for a change in a parameter occurring at an unknown point." *Biometrika*, 42, 523–527.

Page, E. (1957). "On problems in which a change in a parameter occurs at an unknown point." *Biometrika*, 44, 248–252.

Pantula, S. G. (1991). "Asymptotic distributions of the unit root tests when the process is nearly stationary." *Journal of Business & Economic Statistics*, 9, 63–72.

Patterson, K. (2010). *A Primer for Unit Root Testing.* Palgrave Macmillan, UK.

Pearson, K. (1905). "The problem of the random walk." *Nature*, 72, 294–294.

Percival, D. B. (1993). "Three curious properties of the sample variance and autocovariance for stationary processes with unknown mean." *The American Statistician*, 47, 274–276.

Perron, P. (1988). "Trends and random walks in macroeconomic time series: Further evidence from a new approach." *Journal of Economic Dynamics and Control*, 12, 297–332.

Perron, P. (1989a). "The calculation of the limiting distribution of the least-squares estimator in a near-integrated model." *Econometric Theory*, 5, 241–255.

Perron, P. (1989b). "The Great Crash, the oil price shock, and the unit root hypothesis." *Econometrica*, 57, 1361–1401.

Perron, P. (1989c). "Testing the random walk: A simulation experiment of power when the sampling interval is varied." *Advances in Econometrics and Modeling*, B. Raj, ed., Kluwer Academic Publisher, Amsterdam, Netherlands, 47–68.

Perron, P. (1990a). "Testing for a unit root in a time series with a changing mean." *Journal of Business & Economic Statistics*, 57, 153–162.

Perron, P. (1990b). "Tests of joint hypotheses for time series regression with a unit root." *Advances in Econometrics: Cointegration, Spurious Regression and Unit Roots*, T. Fomby and C. Rhodes, eds., JAI Press, Greenwich, CT, 135–159.

Perron, P. (1991a). "A continuous time approximation to the stationary first-order autoregressive model." *Econometric Theory*, 7, 236–252.

Perron, P. (1991b). "A continuous time approximation to the unstable first-order autoregressive process. The case without an intercept." *Econometrica*, 59, 211–236.

Perron, P. (1991c). "Test consistency with varying sampling frequency." *Econometric Theory*, 7, 341–368.

Perron, P. (1991d). "A test for changes in a polynomial trend function for a dynamic time series." *Unpublished Manuscript, Centre de Recherche et Développement en Économique, Université de Montréal.*

Perron, P. (1994a). "Non-stationarities and non-linearities in Canadian inflation." *In Economic Behaviour and Policy Choice Under Price Stability, Bank of Canada, Ottawa*, 235–291.

Perron, P. (1994b). "Trend, unit root and structural change in macroeconomic time series." *Cointegration for the Applied Economist*, B. Rao, ed., Palgrave Macmillan, London, UK, 113–146.

Perron, P. (1996). "The adequacy of asymptotic approximations in the near-integrated autoregressive model with dependent errors." *Journal of Econometrics*, 70, 317–350.

Perron, P. (1997a). "Further evidence on breaking trend functions in macroeconomic variables." *Journal of Econometrics*, 80, 355–385.

Perron, P. (1997b). "L'estimation de modeles avec changements structurels multiples." *L'Actualité Économique*, 73, 457–505.

Perron, P. (2006). "Dealing with structural breaks." *Palgrave Handbook of Econometrics, Vol. 1, Econometric Theory*, K. Patterson and T. C. Mills, eds., Palgrave Macmillan, London, UK, 278–352.

Perron, P. (2019). "A test for changes in a polynomial trend function for a dynamic time series." *Time Series Econometrics: Vol. 2: Structural Change*, P. Perron, ed., World Scientific, Singapore, 1–65.

Perron, P. and Campbell, J. Y. (1993). "A note on Johansen's cointegration procedure." *Empirical Economics*, 18, 777–789.

Perron, P. and González-Coya, E. (2024). "Feasible GLS for time series regression." *Unpublished Manuscript*, Department of Economics, Boston University.

Perron, P. and Mallet, S. (2000). "A look at the quality of the approximation of the functional central limit theorem." *Economics Letters*, 68, 225–234.

Perron, P. and Ng, S. (1996). "Useful modifications to some unit root tests with dependent errors and their local asymptotic properties." *The Review of Economic Studies*, 63, 435–463.

Perron, P. and Ng, S. (1998). "An autoregressive spectral density estimator at frequency zero for nonstationarity tests." *Econometric Theory*, 14, 560–603.

Perron, P. and Qu, Z. (2006). "Estimating restricted structural change models." *Journal of Econometrics*, 134, 373–399.

Perron, P. and Qu, Z. (2007). "A simple modification to improve the finite sample properties of Ng and Perron's unit root tests." *Economics Letters*, 94, 12–19.

Perron, P. and Qu, Z. (2010). "Long-memory and level shifts in the volatility of stock market return indices." *Journal of Business & Economic Statistics*, 28, 275–290.

Perron, P. and Rodríguez, G. (2003). "GLS detrending, efficient unit root tests and structural change." *Journal of Econometrics*, 115, 1–27.

Perron, P. and Rodríguez, G. (2016). "Residuals-based tests for cointegration with generalized least-squares detrended data." *The Econometrics Journal*, 19, 84–111.

Perron, P. and Varneskov, R. T. (2017). "Combining long memory and level shifts in modelling and forecasting the volatility of asset returns." *Quantitative Finance*, 18, 371–393.

Perron, P. and Vodounou, C. (2001). "Asymptotic approximations in the near-integrated model with a non-zero initial condition." *The Econometrics Journal*, 4, 143–169.

Perron, P. and Vogelsang, T. J. (1992a). "Nonstationarity and level shifts with an application to purchasing power parity." *Journal of Business & Economic Statistics*, 8, 301–320.

Perron, P. and Vogelsang, T. J. (1992b). "Testing for a unit root in a time series with a changing mean: Corrections and extensions." *Journal of Business & Economic Statistics*, 10, 467–470.

Perron, P. and Vogelsang, T. J. (1993a). "The Great Crash, the oil price shock and the unit root hypothesis: Erratum." *Econometrica*, 61, 248–249.

Perron, P. and Vogelsang, T. J. (1993b). "A note on the asymptotic distributions of unit root tests in the additive outlier model with breaks." *Brazilian Review of Econometrics*, 13, 181–201.

Perron, P. and Wada, T. (2009). "Let's take a break: Trends and cycles in U.S. real GDP." *Journal of Monetary Economics*, 56, 749–765.

Perron, P. and Xu, J. (2016). "Comments on "In-sample confidence bands and out-of-sample forecast bands for time-varying parameters in observation driven models"." *International Journal of Forecasting*, 32, 891–892.

Perron, P. and Yabu, T. (2009a). "Estimating deterministic trends with an integrated or stationary noise component." *Journal of Econometrics*, 151, 56–69.

Perron, P. and Yabu, T. (2009b). "Testing for shifts in trend with an integrated or stationary noise component." *Journal of Business & Economic Statistics*, 27, 369–396.

Perron, P. and Yamamoto, Y. (2014). "A note on estimating and testing for multiple structural changes in models with endogenous regressors via 2SLS." *Econometric Theory*, 30, 491–507.

Perron, P. and Yamamoto, Y. (2015). "Using OLS to estimate and test for structural changes in models with endogenous regressors." *Journal of Applied Econometrics*, 30, 119–144.

Perron, P. and Yamamoto, Y. (2016). "On the usefulness or lack thereof of optimality criteria for structural change tests." *Econometric Reviews*, 35, 782–844.

Perron, P. and Yamamoto, Y. (2019a). "Pitfalls of two-step testing for changes in the error variance and coefficients of a linear regression model." *Econometrics*, 7, 1–22.

Perron, P. and Yamamoto, Y. (2019b). "Testing for changes in forecasting performance." *Journal of Business & Economic Statistics*, 39, 148–165.

Perron, P., Yamamoto, Y., and Zhou, J. (2020). "Testing jointly for structural changes in the error variance and coefficients of a linear regression model." *Quantitative Economics*, 11, 1019–1057.

Perron, P. and Zhu, X. (2005). "Structural breaks with deterministic and stochastic trends." *Journal of Econometrics*, 129, 65–119.

Pesaran, M. H. (2006). "Estimation and inference in large heterogeneous panels with a multifactor error structure." *Econometrica*, 74, 967–1012.

Pesaran, M. H. (2007). "A simple panel unit root test in the presence of cross section dependence." *Journal of Applied Econometrics*, 22, 265–312.

Pesaran, M. H. (2012). "On the interpretation of panel unit root tests." *Economics Letters*, 116, 545–546.

Pesaran, M. H., Pettenuzzo, D., and Timmermann, A. (2006). "Forecasting time series subject to multiple structural breaks." *The Review of Economic Studies*, 73, 1057–1084.

Pesaran, M. H. and Pick, A. (2011). "Forecast combination across estimation windows." *Journal of Business & Economic Statistics*, 29, 307–318.

Pesaran, M. H., Pick, A., and Pranovich, M. (2013). "Optimal forecasts in the presence of structural breaks." *Journal of Econometrics*, 177, 134–152.

Pesaran, M. H., Shin, Y., and Smith, R. J. (2001). "Bounds testing approaches to the analysis of level relationships." *Journal of Applied Econometrics*, 16, 289–326.

Pesaran, M. H., Shin, Y., and Smith, R. P. (1999). "Pooled mean group estimation of dynamic heterogeneous panels." *Journal of the American Statistical Association*, 94, 621–634.

Pesaran, M. H. and Smith, R. (1995). "Estimating long-run relationships from dynamic heterogeneous panels." *Journal of Econometrics*, 68, 79–113.

Pesaran, M. H. and Timmermann, A. (2002). "Market timing and return prediction under model instability." *Journal of Empirical Finance*, 9, 495–510.

Pesaran, M. H. and Timmermann, A. (2007). "Selection of estimation window in the presence of breaks." *Journal of Econometrics*, 137, 134–161.

Petropoulos, F. *et al.* (2022). "Forecasting: Theory and practice." *International Journal of Forecasting*, 38, 705–871.

Phillips, P. C. B. (1986). "Understanding spurious regressions in econometrics." *Journal of Econometrics*, 33, 311–340.

Phillips, P. C. B. (1987). "Time series regression with a unit root." *Econometrica*, 55, 277–301.

Phillips, P. C. B. (1988). "Regression theory for near-integrated time series." *Econometrica*, 56, 1021–1043.

Phillips, P. C. B. (1991). "Optimal inference in cointegrated systems." *Econometrica*, 59, 283–206.

Phillips, P. C. B. (2007). "Unit root log periodogram regression." *Journal of Econometrics*, 138, 104–124.

Phillips, P. C. B. and Durlauf, S. N. (1986). "Multiple time series regression with integrated processes." *The Review of Economic Studies*, 53, 473–495.

Phillips, P. C. B. and Hansen, B. E. (1990). "Statistical inference in instrumental variables regression with I(1) processes." *The Review of Economic Studies*, 57, 99–125.

Phillips, P. C. B. and Jin, S. (2021). "Business cycles, trend elimination, and the HP filter." *International Economic Review*, 62, 469–520.

Phillips, P. C. B. and Loretan, M. (1991). "Estimating long-run economic equilibria." *The Review of Economic Studies*, 58, 407–436.

Phillips, P. C. B. and Ouliaris, S. (1990). "Asymptotic properties of residual based tests for cointegration." *Econometrica*, 58, 165–193.

Phillips, P. C. B. and Perron, P. (1988). "Testing for a unit root in time series regression." *Biometrika*, 75, 335–346.

Phillips, P. C. B. and Shi, Z. (2021). "Boosting: Why you can use the HP filter." *International Economic Review*, 62, 521–570.

Phillips, P. C. B. and Solo, V. (1992). "Asymptotics for linear processes." *The Annals of Statistics*, 20, 971–1001.

Phillips, P. C. B. and Sul, D. (2003). "Dynamic panel estimation and homogeneity testing under cross section dependence." *The Econometrics Journal*, 6, 217–259.

Phillips, P. C. B. and Sul, D. (2007a). "Bias in dynamic panel estimation with fixed effects, incidental trends and cross section dependence." *Journal of Econometrics*, 137, 162–188.

Phillips, P. C. B. and Sul, D. (2007b). "Transition modeling and econometric convergence tests." *Econometrica*, 75, 1771–1855.

Picard, D. (1985). "Testing and estimating change-points in time series." *Advances in Applied Probability*, 17, 841–867.

Pipiras, V. and Taqqu, M. S. (2017). *Long-Range Dependence and Self-Similarity*. Cambridge University Press, Cambridge, UK.

Pitarakis, J.-Y. (2004). "Least squares estimation and tests of breaks in mean and variance under misspecification." *Econometrics Journal*, 7, 32–54.

Pitt, M. K. and Shephard, N. (1999). "Filtering via simulation: Auxiliary particle filters." *Journal of the American Statistical Association*, 94, 590–599.

Plagborg-Møller, M. and Wolf, C. K. (2021). "Local projections and VARs estimate the same impulse responses." *Econometrica*, 89, 955–980.

Plagborg-Møller, M. and Wolf, C. K. (2022). "Instrumental variable identification of dynamic variance decompositions." *Journal of Political Economy*, 130, 2164–2202.

Ploberger, W. and Krämer, W. (1990). "The local power of the CUSUM and CUSUM of squares tests." *Econometric Theory*, 6, 335–347.

Ploberger, W. and Krämer, W. (1992). "The CUSUM test with OLS residuals." *Econometrica*, 60, 271–285.

Ploberger, W., Krämer, W., and Kontrus, K. (1989). "A new test for structural stability in the linear regression model." *Journal of Econometrics*, 40, 307–318.

Pötscher, B. M. (2002). "Lower risk bounds and properties of confidence sets for ill-posed estimation problems with applications to spectral density and persistence estimation, unit roots, and estimation of long memory parameters." *Econometrica*, 70, 1035–1065.

Priestley, M. (1981). *Spectral Analysis and Time Series.* Academic Press, New York, NY.

Qian, J. and Su, L. (2016). "Shrinkage estimation of common breaks in panel data models via adaptive group fused Lasso." *Journal of Econometrics*, 191, 86–109.

Qin, A. and Qu, Z. (2021). "Modeling regime switching in high-dimensional data with applications to U.S. business cycles." *Unpublished Manuscript*, Department of Economics, Boston University.

Qu, Z. (2007). "Searching for cointegration in a dynamic system." *The Econometrics Journal*, 10, 580–604.

Qu, Z. (2008). "Testing for structural change in regression quantiles." *Journal of Econometrics*, 146, 170–184.

Qu, Z. (2011). "A test against spurious long memory." *Journal of Business & Economic Statistics*, 29, 423–438.

Qu, Z. and Perron, P. (2007a). "Estimating and testing structural changes in multivariate regressions." *Econometrica*, 75, 459–502.

Qu, Z. and Perron, P. (2007b). "A modified information criterion for cointegration tests based on a VAR approximation." *Econometric Theory*, 23, 638–685.

Qu, Z. and Perron, P. (2013). "A stochastic volatility model with random level shifts and its applications to S&P 500 and NASDAQ return indices." *The Econometrics Journal*, 16, 309–339.

Qu, Z. and Zhuo, F. (2020). "Likelihood ratio-based tests for Markov regime switching." *The Review of Economic Studies*, 88, 937–968.

Quah, D. (1987). "What do we learn from unit roots in macroeconomic time series?" National Bureau of Economic Research, Working Paper 2450.

Quah, D. (1990). "Permanent and transitory movements in labor income: An explanation for "excess smoothness" in consumption." *Journal of Political Economy*, 98, 449–475.

Quandt, R. E. (1958). "The estimation of the parameters of a linear regression system obeying two separate regimes." *Journal of the American Statistical Association*, 53, 873–880.

Quandt, R. E. (1960). "Tests of the hypothesis that a linear regression system obeys two separate regimes." *Journal of the American Statistical Association*, 55, 324–330.

Quintos, C. E. (1998). "Stability tests in error correction models." *Journal of Econometrics*, 82, 289–315.

Ramey, V. A. (2016). "Macroeconomic shocks and their propagation." *Handbook of Macroeconomics 2*, J. B. Taylor and H. Uhlig, eds., North Holland, Netherlands, 71–162.

Rao, M. M. (1978). "Asymptotic distribution of an estimator of the boundary parameter of an unstable process." *The Annals of Statistics*, 6, 185–190.

Ravn, M. O. and Uhlig, H. (2002). "On adjusting the Hodrick-Prescott filter for the frequency of observations." *Review of Economics and Statistics*, 84, 371–376.

Rigobon, R. (2003). "Identification through heteroskedasticity." *Review of Economics and Statistics*, 85, 777–792.

Rivera-Batiz, L. A. and Romer, P. M. (1991). "Economic integration and endogenous growth." *The Quarterly Journal of Economics*, 106, 531–555.

Robert, C. P. and Casella, G. (2013). *Monte Carlo Statistical Methods*. Springer, New York, NY.

Roberts, G. O. and Polson, N. G. (1994). "On the geometric convergence of the Gibbs sampler." *Journal of the Royal Statistical Society: Series B*, 56, 377–384.

Roberts, G. O. and Rosenthal, J. S. (1998). "Optimal scaling of discrete approximations to Langevin diffusions." *Journal of the Royal Statistical Society, Series B*, 60, 255–268.

Roberts, G. O. and Tweedie, R. L. (1996). "Exponential convergence of Langevin distributions and their discrete approximations." *Bernoulli*, 2, 341–363.

Robinson, P. M. (1994). "Time series with strong dependence." *Advances in Econometrics, 6th World Congress*, C. Sims, ed., Cambridge University Press, Cambridge, UK, 47–95.

Robinson, P. M. (1995a). "Gaussian semiparametric estimation of long range dependence." *The Annals of Statistics*, 23, 1630–1661.

Robinson, P. M. (1995b). "Log-periodogram regression of time series with long range dependence." *The Annals of Statistics*, 23, 1048–1072.

Robinson, P. M. (2005). "The distance between rival nonstationary fractional processes." *Journal of Econometrics*, 128, 283–300.

Rojas, C. R. and Wahlberg, B. (2014). "On change point detection using the fused Lasso method." *arXiv:1401.5408.*

Romer, C. D. and Romer, D. H. (2023). "Presidential address: Does monetary policy matter? The narrative approach after 35 years." *American Economic Review*, 113, 1395–1423.

Rosenberg, B. (1973). "Random coefficient models: The analysis of a cross-section of time series by stochastically convergent parameter regression." *Annals of Economic and Social Measurement*, 2, 399–428.

Rossi, B. (2013). "Advances in forecasting under instability." *Handbook of Economic Forecasting, Vol. 2*, G. Elliot and A. Timmermann, eds., Elsevier, Amsterdam, Netherlands, 1203–1324.

Rossi, B. and Inoue, A. (2012). "Out-of-sample forecast tests robust to the window size choice." *Journal of Business & Economic Statistics*, 30, 432–453.

Roy, A. and Fuller, W. A. (2001). "Estimation for autoregressive time series with a root near 1." *Journal of Business & Economic Statistics*, 19, 482–493.

Rozanov, Y. A. (1967). *Stationary Random Processes.* Holden-Day, San Francisco, CA.

Rubio-Ramirez, J. F., Waggoner, D. F., and Zha, T. A. (2010). "Structural vector autoregressions: Theory of identification and algorithms for inference." *The Review of Economic Studies*, 77, 665–696.

Runkle, D. E. (1987). "Vector autoregressions and reality." *Journal of Business & Economic Statistics*, 5, 437–442.

Said, S. E. and Dickey, D. A. (1984). "Testing for unit roots in autoregressive-moving average models of unknown order." *Biometrika*, 71, 599–607.

Saikkonen, P. (1991). "Asymptotically efficient estimation of cointegration regressions." *Econometric Theory*, 7, 1–21.

Saikkonen, P. and Lütkepohl, H. (2001). "Testing for unit roots in time series with level shifts." *Advances in Statistical Analysis*, 1, 1–25.

Saikkonen, P. and Lütkepohl, H. (2002). "Testing for a unit root in a time series with a level shift at unknown time." *Econometric Theory*, 18, 313–348.

Salmon, M. (1982). "Error correction mechanisms." *The Economic Journal*, 92, 615–625.

Samuelson, P. A. (1939). "Interactions between the multiplier analysis and the principle of acceleration." *The Review of Economics and Statistics*, 21, 75–78.

Sandmann, G. and Koopman, S. (1998). "Estimation of stochastic volatility models via Monte Carlo maximum likelihood." *Journal of Econometrics*, 87, 271–301.

Sarafidis, V. and Robertson, D. (2009). "On the impact of error cross-sectional dependence in short dynamic panel estimation." *The Econometrics Journal*, 12, 62–81.

Sarafidis, V. and Weber, N. (2015). "A partially heterogeneous framework for analyzing panel data." *Oxford Bulletin of Economics and Statistics*, 77, 274–296.

Sargan, J. D. (1964). "Wages and prices in the United Kingdom: A study in econometric methodology." *Econometric Analysis for National Economic Planning*, 16, 25–54.

Sargent, T. J. (1979). *Macroeconomic Theory.* Academic Press, New York, NY.

Sargent, T. J. (1987). *Dynamic Macroeconomic Theory.* Harvard University Press, Cambridge, MA.

Sayginsoy, Ö. and Vogelsang, T. J. (2011). "Testing for a shift in trend at an unknown date: A fixed-b analysis of heteroskedasticity autocorrelation robust OLS-based tests." *Econometric Theory*, 27, 992–1025.

Schwarz, G. (1978). "Estimating the dimension of a model." *The Annals of Statistics*, 6, 461–464.

Schwert, G. W. (1989a). "Tests for unit roots: A Monte Carlo investigation." *Journal of Business & Economic Statistics*, 7, 147–159.

Schwert, G. W. (1989b). "Why does stock market volatility change over time?" *The Journal of Finance*, 44, 1115–1153.

Sen, P. K. (1982). "Invariance principles for recursive residuals." *The Annals of Statistics*, 10, 307–312.

Seo, B. (1998). "Tests for structural change in cointegrated systems." *Econometric Theory*, 14, 222–259.

Shao, X. (2015). "Self-normalization for time series: A review of recent developments." *Journal of the American Statistical Association*, 110, 1797–1817.

Shao, X. and Zhang, X. (2010). "Testing for change points in time series." *Journal of the American Statistical Association*, 105, 1228–1240.

Shapiro, M. D. and Watson, M. W. (1988). "Sources of business cycle fluctuations." *NBER Macroeconomics Annual*, 3, M. Eichenbaum, E. Hurst and V. Ramey (eds), 111–148.

Shibata, R. (1980). "Asymptotically efficient selection of the order of the model for estimating parameters of a linear process." *The Annals of Statistics*, 8, 147–164.

Shiller, R. J. and Perron, P. (1985). "Testing the random walk hypothesis: Power versus frequency of observation." *Economics Letters*, 18, 381–386.

Shiskin, J., Musgrave, J. C., and Young, A. H. (1967). *The X-11 Variant of the Census Method 11 Seasonal Adjustment Program.* U.S. Government Printing Office, Washington, DC.

Siegmund, D. (1988). "Confidence sets in change-point problems." *International Statistical Review*, 56, 31–48.

Silverman, B. W. (1986). *Density Estimation for Statistics and Data Analysis.* CRC Press, Boca Raton, FL.

Sims, C. A. (1972). "Money, income, and causality." *American Economic Review*, 62, 540–552.

Sims, C. A. (1980a). "Comparison of interwar and postwar business cycles: Monetarism reconsidered." *American Economic Review: Papers and Proceedings*, 70, 250–257.

Sims, C. A. (1980b). "Macroeconomics and reality." *Econometrica*, 48, 1–48.

Sims, C. A. (1986). "Are forecasting models usable for policy analysis?" *Quarterly Review*, 10, 2–16.

Sims, C. A. (2002). "Solving linear rational expectations models." *Computational Economics*, 20, 1–21.

Sims, C. A., Stock, J. H., and Watson, M. W. (1990). "Inference in linear time series models with some unit roots." *Econometrica*, 58, 113–144.

Sims, C. A. and Zha, T. (1998). "Bayesian methods for dynamic multivariate models." *International Economic Review*, 39, 949–968.

Smets, F. and Wouters, R. (2007). "Shocks and frictions in U.S. business cycles: A Bayesian DSGE approach." *American Economic Review*, 97, 586–606.

Song, M. (2013). "Asymptotic theory for dynamic heterogeneous panels with cross-sectional dependence and its applications." *Unpublished Manuscript.*

Sørensen, B. E. (1992). "Continuous record asymptotics in systems of stochastic differential equations." *Econometric Theory*, 8, 28–51.

Stărică, C. and Granger, C. W. J. (2005). "Nonstationarities in stock returns." *Review of Economics and Statistics*, 87, 503–522.

Stock, J. H. (1987). "Asymptotic properties of least squares estimators of cointegrating vectors." *Econometrica*, 55, 1035–1056.

Stock, J. H. (1991). "Confidence intervals for the largest autoregressive root in U.S. macroeconomic time series." *Journal of Monetary Economics*, 28, 435–459.

Stock, J. H. (1994). "Unit roots, structural breaks and trends." *Handbook of Econometrics, Vol. 4*, R. Engle and D. L. McFadden, eds., Elsevier, Amsterdam, Netherlands, 2739–2841.

Stock, J. H. (1999). "A class of tests for integration and cointegration." *Cointegration, Causality and Forecasting: A Festschrift in Honour of Clive W.J. Granger*, R. Engle and H. White, eds., Oxford University Press, UK, 135–167.

Stock, J. H. (2008). *What's New in Econometrics: Time Series, Lecture 7 slides.* NBER Summer Institute.

Stock, J. H. and Watson, M. W. (1988). "Variable trends in economic time series." *Journal of Economic Perspectives*, 2, 147–174.

Stock, J. H. and Watson, M. W. (1991). "A probability model of the coincident economic indicators." *The Leading Economic Indicators: New Approaches and Forecasting Records*, K. Lahiri and G. H. Moore, eds, Cambridge University Presss, Cambridge, MA., 63–90.

Stock, J. H. and Watson, M. W. (1993). "A simple estimator of cointegrating vectors in higher order integrated systems." *Econometrica*, 61, 783–820.

Stock, J. H. and Watson, M. W. (1996). "Evidence on structural instability in macroeconomic time series relations." *Journal of Business & Economic Statistics*, 14, 11–30.

Stock, J. H. and Watson, M. W. (1999). "Business cycle fluctuations in U.S. macroeconomic time series." *Handbook of Macroeconomics, Vol. 1*, J. B. Taylor and M. Woodford, eds., North Holland Elsevier, Amsterdam, Netherlands, 3–64.

Stock, J. H. and Watson, M. W. (2002). "Forecasting using principal components from a large number of predictors." *Journal of the American Statistical Association*, 97, 1167–1179.

Stock, J. H. and Watson, M. W. (2004). "Combination forecasts of output growth in a seven-country data set." *Journal of Forecasting*, 23, 405–430.

Stock, J. H. and Watson, M. W. (2005). "Implications of dynamic factor models for VAR analysis." National Bureau of Economic Research, Working Paper 11467.

Stock, J. H. and Watson, M. W. (2006). "Forecasting with many predictors." *Handbook of Economic Forecasting, Vol. 1*, G. Elliott, C. W. J. Granger, and A. Timmermann, eds., North-Holland Elsevier, 515–554.

Stock, J. H. and Watson, M. W. (2007). "Why has U.S. inflation become harder to forecast?" *Journal of Money, Credit and Banking*, 39, 3–33.

Stock, J. H. and Watson, M. W. (2012a). "Disentangling the channels of the 2007-2009 recession." *Brookings Papers on Economic Activity*, 1, 81–135.

Stock, J. H. and Watson, M. W. (2012b). "Generalized shrinkage methods for forecasting using many predictors." *Journal of Business & Economic Statistics*, 30, 481–493.

Stock, J. H. and Watson, M. W. (2016). "Dynamic factor models, factor-augmented vector autoregressions, and structural vector autoregressions in macroeconomics." *Handbook of Macroeconomics, Vol. 2*, J. B. Taylor and H. Uhlig, eds., North Holland Elsevier, Amsterdam, Netherlands, 415–525.

Stock, J. H. and Watson, M. W. (2018). "Identification and estimation of dynamic causal effects in macroeconomics using external instruments." *The Economic Journal*, 128, 917–948.

Stratonovich, R. (1966). "A new representation for stochastic integrals and equations." *SIAM Journal on Control*, 4, 362–371.

Su, L., Shi, Z., and Phillips, P. C. B. (2016). "Identifying latent structures in panel data." *Econometrica*, 84, 2215–2264.

Sun, Y. (2005). "Estimation and inference in panel structure models." *Available at SSRN 794884*.

Sun, Y., Hong, Y., Lee, T.-H., Wang, S., and Zhang, X. (2021). "Time-varying model averaging." *Journal of Econometrics*, 222, 974–992.

Swamy, P. A. (1970). "Efficient inference in a random coefficient regression model." *Econometrica*, 38, 311–323.

Tanaka, K. (1990). "The Fredholm approach to asymptotic inference on nonstationary and noninvertible time series models." *Econometric Theory*, 6, 411–432.

Tanaka, K. (1993). "An alternative approach to the asymptotic theory of spurious regression, cointegration, and near cointegration." *Econometric Theory*, 9, 36–61.

Tanaka, K. (1999). "The nonstationary fractional unit root." *Econometric Theory*, 15, 549–582.

Tang, S. and MacNeill, I. (1993). "The effect of serial correlation on tests for parameter change at unknown time." *The Annals of Statistics*, 21, 552–575.

Taylor, J. B. (1993). "Discretion versus policy rules in practice." *Carnegie-Rochester Conference Series on Public Policy*, 39, 195–214.

Taylor, S. J. (1986). *Modeling Financial Time Series*. Wiley, Chichester, UK.

Taylor, S. J. (2011). *Asset Price Dynamics, Volatility, and Prediction.* Princeton University Press, Princeton, NJ.

Tian, J. and Anderson, H. M. (2014). "Forecast combinations under structural break uncertainty." *International Journal of Forecasting*, 30, 161–175.

Tibshirani, R. (1996). "Regression shrinkage and selection via the Lasso." *Journal of the Royal Statistical Society: Series B*, 58, 267–288.

Timmermann, A. (2006). "Forecast combinations." *Handbook of Economic Forecasting, Vol. 1*, G. Elliott, C. W. J. Granger, and A. Timmermann, eds., North-Holland Elsevier, 135–196.

Toda, H. Y. and Phillips, P. C. B. (1993). "Vector autoregressions and causality." *Econometrica*, 61, 1367–1393.

Toda, H. Y. and Yamamoto, T. (1995). "Statistical inference in vector autoregressions with possibly integrated processes." *Journal of Econometrics*, 66, 225–250.

Uhlig, H. (2000). "Should we be afraid of Friedman's rule?" *Journal of the Japanese and International Economies*, 14, 261–303.

Uhlig, H. (2005). "What are the effects of monetary policy on output? Results from an agnostic identification procedure." *Journal of Monetary Economics*, 52, 381–419.

Van Der Merwe, R., Doucet, A., De Freitas, N., and Wan, E. (2000). "The unscented particle filter." *Advances in Neural Information Processing Systems*, 13, 584–590.

van der Merwe, R. and Wan, E. A. (2001). "The square-root unscented Kalman filter for state and parameter-estimation." *IEEE International Conference on Acoustics, Speech, and Signal Processing, Vol. 6*, IEEE, Salt Lake City, UT, 3461–3464.

Velasco, C. (2000). "Non-Gaussian log-periodogram regression." *Econometric Theory*, 16, 44–79.

Vogelsang, T. J. (1997). "Wald-type tests for detecting breaks in the trend function of a dynamic time series." *Econometric Theory*, 13, 818–849.

Vogelsang, T. J. (1998). "Testing for a shift in mean without having to estimate serial-correlation parameters." *Journal of Business & Economic Statistics*, 16, 73–80.

Vogelsang, T. J. (1999). "Sources of nonmonotonic power when testing for a shift in mean of a dynamic time series." *Journal of Econometrics*, 88, 283–299.

Vogelsang, T. J. (2001). "Testing for a shift in trend when serial correlation is of unknown form." *Unpublished Manuscript*, Department of Economics, Cornell University.

Vogelsang, T. J. and Perron, P. (1998). "Additional tests for a unit root allowing for a break in the trend function at an unknown time." *International Economic Review*, 39, 1073–1100.

Walker, G. T. (1931). "On periodicity in series of related terms." *Proceedings of the Royal Society of London. Series A, Containing Papers of a Mathematical and Physical Character*, 131, 518–532.

Wallis, K. F. (1974). "Seasonal adjustment and relations between variables." *Journal of the American Statistical Association*, 69, 18–31.

Wan, A. T., Zhang, X., and Zou, G. (2010). "Least squares model averaging by Mallows criterion." *Journal of Econometrics*, 156, 277–283.

Wan, E.A. van der Merwe, R. and Nelson, A. T. (2000). "Dual estimation and the unscented transformation." *Advances in Neural Information Processing Systems*, S. Solla, T. Leen and K. Müller, eds., MIT Press, Cambridge, MA, 666–672.

Wang, J. and Zivot, E. (2000). "A Bayesian time series model of multiple structural changes in level, trend, and variance." *Journal of Business & Economic Statistics*, 18, 374–386.

Wang, R., Zhu, C., Volgushev, S., and Shao, X. (2022). "Inference for change points in high-dimensional data via selfnormalization." *The Annals of Statistics*, 50, 781–806.

Wansbeek, T. and Kapteyn, A. (1982). "A simple way to obtain the spectral decomposition of variance components models for balanced data." *Communications in Statistics-Theory and Methods*, 11, 2105–2112.

Watson, M. W. (1986). "Univariate detrending methods with stochastic trends." *Journal of Monetary Economics*, 18, 49–75.

Watson, M. W. (1989). "Recursive solution methods for dynamic linear rational expectations models." *Journal of Econometrics*, 41, 65–89.

Watson, M. W. (1994). "Vector autoregressions and cointegration." *Handbook of Econometrics, Vol. 4*, R. F. Engle and D. L. McFadden, eds., Elsevier, Amsterdam, Netherlands, 2843–2915.

Wei, G. C. G. and Tanner, M. A. (1990). "A Monte Carlo implementation of the EM algorithm and the poor man's data augmentation algorithms." *Journal of the American Statistical Association*, 85, 699–704.

West, K. D. (1996). "Asymptotic inference about predictive ability." *Econometrica*, 64, 1067–1084.

West, K. D. (2006). "Forecast evaluation." *Handbook of Economic Forecasting*, Vol. 1, G. Elliott, C. W. J. Granger, and A. Timmermann, eds., Elsevier, 99–134.

White, H. (2000). "A reality check for data snooping." *Econometrica*, 68, 1097–1126.

White, H. (2001). *Asymptotic Theory for Econometricians.* Academic Press, New York, NY.

White, J. S. (1958). "The limiting distribution of the serial correlation coefficient in the explosive case." *The Annals of Mathematical Statistics*, 29, 1188–1197.

White, J. S. (1959). "The limiting distribution of the serial correlation coefficient in the explosive case II." *The Annals of Mathematical Statistics*, 30, 831–834.

Whittle, P. (1954). "On stationary processes in the plane." *Biometrika*, 434–449.

Wold, H. (1938). A study in the analysis of stationary time series. Doctoral dissertation, Almqvist & Wiksell.

Wold, H. (1954). "Causality and econometrics." *Econometrica*, 22, 162–177.

Wolf, C. K. (2020). "SVAR (mis) identification and the real effects of monetary policy shocks." *American Economic Journal: Macroeconomics*, 12, 1–32.

Worsley, K. (1986). "Confidence regions and tests for a change-point in a sequence of exponential family random variables." *Biometrika*, 73, 91–104.

Wu, C. J. (1983). "On the convergence properties of the EM algorithm." *The Annals of Statistics*, 11, 95–103.

Xu, J. and Perron, P. (2014). "Forecasting return volatility: Level shifts with varying jump probability and mean reversion." *International Journal of Forecasting*, 30, 449–463.

Xu, J. and Perron, P. (2023). "Forecasting in the presence of in and out of sample breaks." *Empirical Economics*, 64, 3001–3035.

Xu, L. and Jordan, M. I. (1996). "On convergence properties of the EM algorithm for Gaussian mixtures." *Neural Computation*, 8, 129–151.

Yamamoto, Y. (2018). "A modified confidence set for the structural break date in linear regression models." *Econometric Reviews*, 37, 974–999.

Yamamoto, Y. and Hara, N. (2022). "Identifying factor-augmented vector autoregression models via changes in shock variances." *Journal of Applied Econometrics*, 37, 722–745.

Yamamoto, Y. and Perron, P. (2013). "Estimating and testing multiple structural changes in linear models using band spectral regressions." *The Econometrics Journal*, 16, 400–429.

Yang, J. (2017). "Consistency of trend break point estimator with underspecified break numbers." *Econometrics*, 5, 1–19.

Yang, S.-C. S. (2005). "Quantifying tax effects under policy foresight." *Journal of Monetary Economics*, 52, 1557–1568.

Yao, Y.-C. (1987). "Approximating the distribution of the maximum likelihood estimate of the change-point in a sequence of independent random variables." *The Annals of Statistics*, 15, 1321–1328.

Yao, Y.-C. (1988). "Estimating the numbers of change-points via Schwarz criterion." *Statistics & Probability Letters*, 6, 181–189.

Yu, P. (2015). "Consistency of the least squares estimator in threshold regression with endogeneity." *Economics Letters*, 131, 41–46.

Yu, P. and Phillips, P. C. B. (2018). "Threshold regression with endogeneity." *Journal of Econometrics*, 203, 50–68.

Yuan, M. and Lin, Y. (2006). "Model selection and estimation in regression with grouped variables." *Journal of the Royal Statistical Society: Series B*, 68, 49–67.

Yule, G. U. (1927). "On a method of investigating periodicities in disturbed series, with special reference to Wolfer's sunspot numbers." *Philosophical Transactions of the Royal Society of London*, 226, 267–298.

Zellner, A. (1986). "Bayesian estimation and prediction using asymmetric loss functions." *Journal of the American Statistical Association*, 81, 446–451.

Zhang, T. and Lavitas, L. (2018). "Unsupervised self-normalized change-point testing for time series." *Journal of the American Statistical Association*, 113, 637–648.

Zhang, X., Wan, A. T., and Zou, G. (2013). "Model averaging by jackknife criterion in models with dependent data." *Journal of Econometrics*, 174, 82–94.

Zhao, Z., Jiang, F., and Shao, X. (2022). "Segmenting time series via self-normalisation." *Journal of the Royal Statistical Society Series B*, 84, 1699–1725.

Ziliak, J. P. (1997). "Efficient estimation with panel data when instruments are predetermined: An empirical comparison of moment-condition estimators." *Journal of Business & Economic Statistics*, 15, 419–431.

Zivot, E. and Andrews, D. W. K. (1992). "Further evidence on the Great Crash, the oil-price shock, and the unit-root hypothesis." *Journal of Business & Economic Statistics*, 10, 251–270.

Zivot, E. and Phillips, P. C. B. (1994). "A Bayesian analysis of trend determination in economic time series." *Econometric Reviews*, 13, 291–336.